AGING: THE UNIVERSAL HUMAN EXPERIENCE

George L. Maddox, Ph.D., Professor of Medical Sociology, is Chairman of the University Council on Aging and Human Development at Duke University and Director of Duke's WHO/PAHO Collaborating Research Center on Aging. His current research focuses on age-related changes in capacity to function independently and expenditures for health care in late adulthood. Currently Secretary General of the International Association of Gerontology, he is past president of the Gerontological Society of America and a founding member of the National Advisory Council of the National Institute on Aging. In 1983, Dr. Maddox received the Sandoz International Prize for Longitudinal Research in Aging, and in 1985 both the Distinguished Contribution in Aging Award of the American Sociological Association and the Kleemeir Research Award of the Gerontological Society of America. Dr. Maddox has published a number of scientific papers on social aspects of adult development and aging, and co-edited *Inflation and the Economic Well-being of the Elderly* (1984); *The Nature and Extent of Alcohol Problems Among the Elderly* (1985); *The Duke Longitudinal Studies of Aging, 1955-1980* (1985); and the *Annual Review of Gerontology and Geriatrics* (1985); and *The Encyclopedia of Aging* (1987).

Ewald W. Busse, M.D., is President of the North Carolina Institute of Medicine, Dean Emeritus, and Professor Emeritus of Psychiatry at Duke University Medical Center. He was Chairman of the Department of Psychiatry from 1953 to 1974 and the founding Director (1957-1970) of the Center for the Study of Aging, where he was the Principal Investigator for the Longitudinal Studies of Aging. Dr. Busse has served as President of the American Psychiatric Association, the American Geriatrics Society, the Gerontological Society of America, The Southern Council of Deans, and, in 1983, the International Association of Gerontology. A director of the American Board of Psychiatry and Neurology for eight years, Dr. Busse was also a member of the Institute of Medicine of the Academy of Sciences. He has received numerous research and professional awards including the Edward B. Allen Award (1967), the Strecker Award (1967), The Kleemeier Award (1968), The Menninger Award (1971), the Modern Medicine Award (1972), the Freeman Award (1978), The Thewlis Award (1979), the Brookdale Award (1982), and the Sandoz Award (1983). Dr. Busse earned his B.A. degree at Westminster College which also awarded him the Sc.D. degree in 1960. He received his M.D. from Washington University in St. Louis in 1942.

AGING

THE UNIVERSAL
HUMAN EXPERIENCE

SELECTED PAPERS FROM THE SYMPOSIA OF THE
XIIITH CONGRESS
OF THE INTERNATIONAL ASSOCIATION
OF GERONTOLOGY

George L. Maddox, Ph.D
E. W. Busse, M.D.

EDITORS

SPRINGER PUBLISHING COMPANY
New York

128154

Copyright © 1987 by Springer Publishing Company, Inc.

Springer Publishing Company, Inc.
536 Broadway
New York, NY 10012

87 88 89 90 91 / 5 4 3 2 1

LIBRARY OF CONGRESS
Library of Congress Cataloging-in-Publication Data

International Congress of Gerontology (13th : 1985 : New York, N.Y.)
    Aging, the universal human experience : papers presented at the XIIIth Congress of the International Association of Gerontology / George L. Maddox, E.W. Busse, editors.
        p.   cm.
    Congress held July 12-17, 1985 in New York, N.Y.
    Includes bibliographies and index.
    ISBN 0-8261-5490-5
    1. Aging—Congresses.   2. Geriatrics—Congresses.   3. Gerontology—Congresses.   I. Maddox, George L.   II. Busse, Ewald W., 1917-   .   III. Title.
    [DNLM: 1. Aging—congresses.   2. Geriatrics—congresses.   W3 IN384 13th 1985a / WT 100 1613 1985a]
    QP86.I58 1985   362.6—dc19   87-26624
                               CIP

Printed in the United States of America

Contents

B. New Medical Technologies in Diagnosis and Treatment

PART V. PSYCHOLOGICAL AND BEHAVIORAL RESEARCH

PART VI. BASIC AND SOCIAL SCIENTIFIC RESEARCH
A. Health Care Organization and Financing

B. Housing and Living Environments

C. Policy, Planning, and Practice

PART VII. ETHICAL ISSUES IN AGING SOCIETIES: THE CASE OF GERIATRICS

Preface

The XIIIth Congress of the International Association of Gerontology (IAG) in New York, July 12-17, 1985, illustrated particularly well that aging is a universal human experience. Over 3,000 research scientists, teachers, and practitioners in gerontology and geriatrics from 52 countries participated in a broad range of plenary sessions, symposia, roundtables, paper and poster sessions, and audiovisual presentations. There were 39 scientific exhibits; 33 corporations, foundations, and governmental agencies contributed financially.

The American Geriatric Society, the Canadian Gerontological Society, and the Gerontological Society of America were co-hosts for the Congress and were joined in sponsorship by 14 national and international organizations.

The nonprofit organization responsible for organizing the Congress was Gerontology International, Inc. This organization's officers and Board of Trustees were E.W. Busse, President, who also presided as President of the Congress; George L. Maddox, Secretary/Treasurer; and Corinne Houpt, Juanita Kreps, and Bernice Neugarten, Trustees. Mr. Steven Zaleznick, Counsel for the American Association of Retired Persons, served as Counsel to the Board. The Secretariat of the Congress was provided by contract with the Gerontological Society of America. Persons principally responsible for the Secretariat were Gwynne Anderson, John Cornman, Pam Dawson, Jeanne Francese, and Carol Schutz.

The committees responsible for planning and implementing the Congress are acknowledged in detail elsewhere in this volume. They are to be praised for the quantity of their work and praised even more for its quality. Congress participants were generous in their praise for the scientific content of the program which includes state-of-the-art presentations on basic and applied research in biology, biomedicine, psychology, and the social sciences; on gerontological and geriatric training; and on policy and practice issues. The chapters of this volume must speak for themselves. But the editors are particularly pleased with the breadth and variety of presentations on aging from scholars and scientists around the world.

Participants also volunteered praise for the attention given in this Congress to the issues of particular interest to developing countries. Over 150 persons from 35 countries participated actively in this special program organized by Gary Andrews (Australia) and his committee. Special attention was directed to developing countries initially at the XIIth Congress of IAG in Hamburg, Germany, in 1981. Resources of the United Nations Trust Fund for Aging, the National Institute on Aging (U.S.), and the Congress were combined to partially support many participants from developing countries.

The chapters in this volume reporting highlights of the Congress were drawn primarily from papers presented in symposia and invited roundtables. The parts of this volume reflect the multidisciplinary organization of gerontology and geriatrics that includes biology, clinical medicine, psychological and behavioral science, and the social sciences, policy and practice. Additionally, within these disciplinary areas several distinctive sets of papers appear on special topics such as multidisciplinary functional assessment; housing for elderly persons; advances in applications of medical technology in diagnosis and treatment; and ethical issues in the terminal years of life.

Two sets of related papers presented in symposia at the Congress will appear as separate volumes. *Epidemiology and Aging: An International Perspective*, edited by George Maddox and Jacob Brody, and *The Role of Hospitals in Geriatric Care*, edited by Carl Eisdorfer and George Maddox, will follow shortly after this volume. Both volumes will be published by Springer Publishing Company.

The organizers of the Congress, and the editors of this volume particularly, are grateful to the authors whose papers appear in this volume. They submitted excellent manuscripts in English in a timely fashion from all corners of the world, which is a considerable accomplishment.

We have already expressed our indebtedness officially to many people who made the Congress possible. But there are several persons who warrant special note such as Bill Connelly and Craig Burrell, both of Sandoz, Inc., and Bernice Neugarten and Gunhild Hagestad who provided key leadership of the North American Regional Committee, which served as the lead regional committee in planning the Congress.

Finally, we thank Betty P. Ray and Evelyn G. Maddox for their editorial assistance in the final preparation of the manuscript.

E.W. Busse, M.D.
George L. Maddox, Ph.D.

Program Committees
XIIIth International
Congress
of Gerontology

CONGRESS PROGRAM COMMITTEE

E.W. Busse (Chairman, U.S.), G.L. Maddox (Secretary, U.S.), G.R. Andrews (Australia), M. Bergener (Germany), M. Murakami (Japan), B.L. Neugarten (U.S.), H. Orimo (Japan), R. Schmitz-Scherzer (Germany), H. Thomae (Germany), A. Viidik (Denmark), S. Bravo Williams (Mexico).

NORTH AMERICAN REGIONAL PROGRAM
SUB-COMMITTEE

B.L. Neugarten (Chairman, U.S.), G.O. Hagestad (Secretary, U.S.), R. Bayne (Canada), V.J. Cristofalo (U.S.), B. Havens (Canada), T. Hickey (U.S.), I. Rossman (U.S.), G.F. Streib (U.S.)

AUDIOVISUAL PROGRAM

J. Davis and R. Davis (Co-Chairs).

DEVELOPING COUNTRIES PROGRAM

G.R. Andrews (Chairman, Australia), R. Schmitz-Scherzer (Co-Chair, Germany), E. Anzola Perez (PAHO), N. Van Ham Apt (Ghana), J. Gonzalez Aragon (Mexico), W. Beattie, Jr. (U.S.), S. Bergman (Israel), P.C.Y. Chen (Phillipines), J. Flesch (France), S. Greengross (U.K.), M. Ibrahim (Bangladesh), M.S. Kanungo (India), D. Macfadyen (WHO), J. McDonald (U.S.), T. Shuman (UN), A.R. Sidky (Egypt), G.F. Streib (U.S.), K. Tout (U.K.).

LOCAL ARRANGEMENTS

Msgr. C.J. Fahey (Chairman), L. Hiddemen Barondess, M. Cantor, M. Chamberlain, W. Connelly, P. FitzGerald, R.E. Hall, A. Hudis, M. Hudis, J. Janover, G. Landau, J. Sainer, J. Sugarman; Subcommittee: W. Gould, A. Monk, J. Puryear.

Contributors

Joseph M. Anderson, Ph.D.
ICF Incorporated
Washington, D.C.

Gary R. Andrews, M.D.
Professor, Department of Primary Care & Community Medicine
Flinders University of South Australia
Bedford Park, Australia

H. Arai
MRC Group
AFRC Institute of Animal Physiology
Babraham, Cambridge, United Kingdom

Ruben Ardila
National University of Columbia
Columbia

Pamela Babb, R.N.
Mexico City, Mexico

Lars Bäckman, Ph.D.
Department of Psychology
University of Umea
Umea, Sweden

Thomas A. Ban, M.D.
Professor of Psychiatry
Vanderbilt University School of Medicine
Nashville, Tennessee

M.J. Bendall, MB, MRCP
Department of Health Care of the Elderly
University of Nottingham Medical School
Queen's Medical Centre
Nottingham, United Kingdom

Dr. P. Bendall
Department of Health Care of the Elderly
University of Nottingham Medical School
Queen's Medical Centre
Nottingham, United Kingdom

Edit Beregi, C.M.Sc., D.M.Sc.
Gerontology Center
Budapest, Hungary

Stig Berg, Ph.D.
Institute of Gerontology
Jönköping, Sweden

Hans Berglind
Professor, School of Social Work
Stockholm University
Stockholm, Sweden

A.L. Bersier, M.D.
University of Geneva Geriatric Institutions
Geneva, Switzerland

Paul Berthaux
Professeur de Gérontologie
Faculté de Médecine Pitié - Salpetrière
Paris, France

Laurence G. Branch, Ph.D.
Chief, Health Services Section
Boston University School of Public Health
Boston, Massachusetts

Sally A. Brown
Department of Neurology
University of Rochester Medical Center
Rochester, New York

L. Butturini
Department of Patologia Medica
University of Parma
Parma, Italy

Scott T. Cain, Ph.D.
Assistant Medical Research Professor, Department of Psychiatry
Duke University Medical Center
Durham, North Carolina

Arthur L. Caplan, Ph.D.
Associate Director
The Hastings Center
Hastings-on-Hudson, New York

William S. Cartwright, Ph.D.
Chief, Demography and Economics Office
Epidemiology, Demography, and Biometry Program
National Institute on Aging, NIH
Bethesda, Maryland

Esther Contreras de Lehr, Ph.D.
Mexico City, Mexico

Richard Coppedge, M.D.
Adult Development & Aging Program
Arizona State University
Tempe, Arizona

Paul T. Costa, Ph.D.
Gerontology Research Center
National Institute on Aging
Baltimore, Maryland

Vincent J. Cristofalo, Ph.D.
Professor, The Wistar Institute of Anatomy and
*   Biology,*
Professor of Biochemistry, University of Pennsylvania
Director, The Center for the Study of Aging
Philadelphia, Pennsylvania

D. Dawbarn
MRC Group
AFRC Institute of Animal Physiology
Babraham, Cambridge, United Kingdom

Guy De Backer, M.D.
Cardiac Rehabilitation Center
Akademisch Ziekenhuis
Gent, Belgium

D.J.H. Deeg, M. Math.
Research Associate
Department of Public Health
Erasmus University
Rotterdam, The Netherlands

W.J. Dekoninck, M.D.
Geriatric Unit of Montigny and Cyclotron Research
Center of Liege University
Liege, Belgium

J.C. Depresseux
Geriatric Unit of Montigny and Cyclotron Research
Center of Liege University
Liege, Belgium

Antoon De Schryver, M.D.
Cardiac Rehabilitation Center
Akademisch Ziekenhuis
Gent, Belgium

Nancy Neveloff Dubler, LL.B.
Department of Epidemiology and Social Medicine
Montefiore Medical Center and Albert Einstein
*   College of Medicine*
Bronx, New York

Elisa Dulcey-Ruiz
Center for Gerontological Psychology
Bogota, Columbia

P.C. Emson
MRC Group
AFRC Institute of Animal Physiology
Babraham, Cambridge, United Kingdom

K. Farkas
Division of Restorative and Geriatric Medicine
Dept. of Medicine at Cleveland Metropolitan Gen-
*   eral/Highland View Hospital*
Case Western Reserve University
Cleveland, Ohio

Gerda G. Fillenbaum, Ph.D.
Associate Medical Research Professor
Center for the Study of Aging and Human Develop-
*   ment*
Duke University
Durham, North Carolina

Albert A. Fisk, M.D.
The Department of Medicine and the Geriatric
*   Institute*
University of Wisconsin Medical School
Milwaukee, Wisconsin

Jeffrey S. Freed, M.D., FACS, FACG
Assistant Clinical Professor
Mount Sinai School of Medicine
New York, New York

J. Dermot Frengley, M.D.
Division of Restorative and Geriatric Medicine
Department of Medicine at Cleveland Metropolitan
*   General/Highland View Hospital*
Case Western Reserve University
Cleveland, Ohio

Xavier Gaullier
Director of Research, Centre National de la Recherche
*   Scientifique*
Paris, France

Barry J. Gurland, M.D.
Director, Center for Geriatrics & Gerontology
Columbia University
New York, New York

Gloria M. Gutman, Ph.D.
Director, Gerontology Research Centre and Associate
*   Professor*
Faculty of Interdisciplinary Studies
Simon Fraser University
Burnaby, British Columbia, Canada

Paul A.H. Haber
Regional Coordinator for Aging
Veterans Administration
Palo Alto, California

Jack Habib, Ph.D.
Director, JDC-Brookdale Institute of Gerontology
and The Hebrew University
Jerusalem, Israel

Betty Havens
Manitoba Department of Health
Winnipeg, Manitoba, Canada

James V. Haxby
Laboratory of Neurosciences
National Institutes of Health
Bethesda, Maryland

Tamako Hayashi, M.E.
Tokyo Metropolitan Institute of Gerontology
Tokyo, Japan

Leonard Hayflick, Ph.D.
Director, Center for Gerontological Studies
University of Florida
Gainesville, Florida

Haim Hazan
Department of Sociology & Anthropology
Tel-Aviv University
Tal-Aviv. Israel

Marsel A. Heisel, M.A., Ed.D.
School of Social Work
Rutgers University
New Brunswick, New Jersey

H. Hermanova
Regional Office for Europe
World Health Organization
Copenhagen, Denmark

Th. Hovaguimian, M.D.
University of Geneva Geriatric Institutions
Geneva, Switzerland

Sandra C. Howell, Ph.D.
Associate Professor
Department of Architecture
Massachusetts Institute of Technology
Cambridge, Massachusetts

O. Juge, M.D.
Department of Neurology
University Hospital of Geneva
Geneva, Switzerland

William B. Kannel, M.D.
Professor of Medicine and Chief, Section of Preven-
tive Medicine and Epidemiology
Evans Memorial Department of Clinical Research
and Department of Medicine
University Hospital
Boston University School of Medicine
Boston, Massachusetts

Robert Kastenbaum, Ph.D.
Adult Development & Aging Program
Arizona State University
Tempe, Arizona

Leonie A. Kellaher
Centre for Environmental & Social Studies in Ageing
Polytechnic of North London
London, England

Robert D. Kennedy, M.B., Ch.B.
Division of Geriatrics, Department of Medicine
Montefiore Medical Center
Bronx, New York

Willem H.C. Kerkhoff,
Director, Institut voor Sociale en Bedrijfpsychologie
University of Amsterdam
Amsterdam, Netherlands

Paul V. Knight, MBCHB, MRCP
Lecturer
University Department of Geraitric Medicine
Glasgow, Scotland

Laurie L. Koek
Department of Neurology
University of Rochester Medical Center
Rochester, New York

M. Leponcin Lafitte, Ph.D.
Institut National de Recherche sur la Prevention du
Vieillissement Cerebral
Hopital Bicetre
Le kremlin Bicetre, France

Dan Lane
Doctoral Candidate, Division of Management Science
Faculty of Commerce and Business Administration
The University of British Columbia
Vancouver, British Columbia, Canada

E. Lefton, M.D.
Division of Restorative and Geriatric Medicine
Dept. of Medicine at Cleveland Metropolitan Gen-
eral/Highland View Hospital
Case Western Reserve University
Cleveland, Ohio

David M. Macfadyen, MSc, FRCPE,
FFCM
Manager, Global Programme for Health of the
Elderly
World Health Organization
Copenhagen, Denmark

Ian R. Mackay, M.D.
Clinical Research Unit of the Walter and Eliza Hall
Institute of Medical Research
The Royal Melbourne Hospital
Victoria, Australia

Daisaku Maeda
Director, Department of Sociology
Tokyo Metropolitan Institute of Gerontology
Tokyo, Japan

Kenneth G. Manton, Ph.D.
Research Professor
Center for Demographic Studies
Duke University
Durham, North Carolina

Robert R. McCrae
Gerontology Research Center
National Institute on Aging, NIH
Baltimore, Maryland

Darlene Schroedl McKenzie, R.N.,
Ph.D.
The Oregon Health Sciences University Community
Health Care Systems Department
Portland, Oregon

Thomas H. McNeill, Ph.D.
Departments of Neurology and of Oncology in the
Cancer Center
University of Rochester Medical Center
Rochester, New York

P. Migeon
Institut National de Recherche sur la Prevention du
Vieillissement Cerebral
Hopital Bicetre
Le kremlin Bicetre, France

L. Mion, M.S.N.
Division of Restorative and Geriatric Medicine
Dept. of Medicine at Cleveland Metropolitan Gen-
eral/Highland View Hospital
Case Western Reserve University
Cleveland, Ohio

Vincent Mor, Ph.D.
Director, Center for Health Care Research
Brown University
Providence, Rhode Island

George C. Myers, Ph.D.
Professor of Sociology and Director, Center for
Demographic Studies
Duke University
Durham, North Carolina

Charles B. Nemeroff, M.D., Ph.D.
Associate Professor, Department of Psychiatry
Duke University Medical Center
Durham, North Carolina

Bernice L. Neugarten, Ph.D.
Professor, School of Education
Northwestern University
Evanston, Illinois

Paul Paillat
Head, Department of Social Demography
National Institute for Population Studies
Paris, France

Mrs. Dögg Pálsdóttir
Chief of Division, Matters of Elderly
Ministry of Health
Reykjavik, Iceland

Thomas M. Pamilla, CSW
Executive Director
Heights and Hill Community Council
Brooklyn, New York

Fitzhugh C. Pannill, III, M.D.
The Department of Medicine and the Geriatrics
Institute
University of Wisconsin Medical School
Milwaukee, Wisconsin

Mario Passeri, M.D.
Department of Patologia Medica
University of Parma
Parma, Italy

Sheila M. Peace, Ph.D.
Research Associate, Centre for Environmental &
Social Studies in Ageing
Polytechnic of North London
London, England

Harvey Peskin, Ph.D.
Department of Psychology
San Francisco State University
San Francisco, California

Jose Rafols, Ph.D.
Department of Anatomy
Wayne State University
Detroit, Michigan

G. Rancurel, M.D.
Hopital de la Salpetriere
Paris, France

J.R. Rapin, Ph.D.
Institut National de Recherche sur la Prevention du
Vieillissement Cerebral
Hopital Bicetre
Le Kremlin Bicetre, France

Stanley I. Rapoport, M.D.
Laboratory of Neurosciences
National Institute on Aging, NIH
Bethesda, Maryland

C. Raynaud, M.D.
Hopital d'Orsay
Orsay, France

Mark A. Reiner, M.D., FACS, FACG
Assistant Clinical Professor
Mount Sinai School of Medicine
New York, New York

Matilda White Riley, D.Sc.
Associate Director, Behavioral Sciences Research
National Institute on Aging
National Institutes of Health
Bethesda, Maryland

Pauline K. Robinson
Emeritus Research Professor
University of Southern California
Balboa Island, California

M.N. Rossor, M.D.
National Hospital
Queen Square
London, England

Bernardo Samper, M.D.
Columbia

J. Sanches, M.D.
Department of Radio Diagnostics
University Hospital of Geneva
Geneva, Switzerland

C. Sebban, M.D.
Laboratoire de Biologie du Vieillissement
C.H.U. Ritie-Salpetriere
Paris, France

Nathan W. Shock, Ph.D.
Chief, Gerontology Research Center
National Institute on Aging,
Baltimore, Maryland

Tarek, Shuman, Ph.D.
Chief, Aging Unit, United Nations
Programme for Developing Countries
Vienna, Austria

Annette Stark, Ph.D.
Director, Division of Health Services Research and
 Development and Associate Professor, Department
 of Health Care and Epidemiology
The University of British Columbia
Vancouver, British Columbia, Canada

Leroy O. Stone, Ph.D.
Statistics Canada
Ottawa, Ontario, Canada

Gerald A. Straka
Professor of Education
Bremen University
Bremen, Federal Republic of Germany

Myron R. Szewczuk, Ph.D.
Department of Microbiology and Immunology
Queen's University
Kingston, Ontario, Canada

R.C. Taylor, M.D.
MRC Medical Sociology Unit
Glasgow, Scotland

John Toner, Ed.D.
Center for Geriatrics & Gerontology
Faculty of Medicine
Columbia University
New York, New York

Dean Uyeno, Ph.D.
Associate Professor, Faculty of Commerce and
 Business Administration
The University of British Columbia
Vancouver, British Columbia, Canada

N.P. van der Schaft-Kleywegt
Medical Student
Erasmus University
Rotterdam, Netherlands

M.P. van Tol
Medical Student
Erasmus University
Rotterdam, Netherlands

R.J. van Zonneveld, M.D., Ph.D.
Associate Professor, Social Gerontology, Department
 of Environmental Health and Tropical Health,
 Agric. University
Wageningen, Netherlands

Pantel S. Vokonas, M.D.
Director, Normative Aging Study
Veterans Administration Outpatient Clinic
Associate Professor of Medicine, Section of Preventive
 Medicine and Epidemiology
Evans Memorial Department of Clinical Research
 and Department of Medicine
University Hospital
Boston, Massachusetts

Anthony M. Warnes, Ph.D.
Reader in Geography and Gerontology
Age Concern, Institute of Gerontology
King's College
London, England

Marcella Bakur Weiner, Ed.D.
Adj. Professor, Fordham University
Graduate School of Social Services at Lincoln Center
New York, New York

James B. Wyngaarden, M.D.
Director, National Institute of Health
Bethesda, Maryland

PART I
Plenary Presentations

CHAPTER 1

Aging as a Priority in Research

James B. Wyngaarden

The National Institute on Aging (NIA) was created in May 1974. Passage of the Research on Aging Act that established the Institute was the culmination of a 20-year effort to gain governmental recognition and support for basic research on aging. At the forefront of the effort were organizations such as the Gerontological Society and mass membership organizations such as the American Association of Retired Persons, National Retired Teachers Association, and the National Council of Senior Citizens. The Research on Aging Act represented one of the first instances where scientific and senior interests worked closely toward a common goal. This collaboration resulted in a highly effective campaign both in Washington, D.C. and at the grass roots level. A number of key individuals played a decisive role in securing passage of the Act. Any list of such individuals beyond the Congressional sponsors and proponents of the legislation would of necessity include Mrs. Florence Mahoney, the first person to organize support on Capitol Hill for a separate aging institute, and your current president, Dr. Busse, as well as two other past presidents of the Gerontological Society, Drs. Eisdorfer and Sinex. Their vision, drive, and determination set the pace for later constructive effort.

The legislative charter of the NIA designated the Institute as the chief Federal agency responsible for promotion, coordination, and support of basic research and training relevant to the aging process and the diseases or problems of the elderly. The mandate of NIA is unique among the NIH institutes in a number of ways. For instance, it is charged by Congress to conduct research not only in the biological and biomedical sciences but also in the behavioral and social sciences.

The Institute came into being in the mid-1970s at a time when the total NIH research budget had reached a plateau. In spite of the timing, however, the Institute's funding for basic research has increased more than eightfold, from $7.6 million in 1976 to the 1985 level of $72.3 million.

Permit me to point out a few facts for those of you not entirely familiar with the structure and mechanisms of the National Institutes of Health (NIH). The agency is made up of 11 Institutes, the National Library of Medicine, and several specialized divisions. Most of the institutes were created to concentrate their efforts around specified disease families or organ systems; for example, the National Cancer Institute or the National Heart, Lung, and Blood Institute. We operate a large research program within the NIH, with more than 2,000 scientists actively engaged in our extensive laboratories and in our 500-plus bed Clinical Center and Ambulatory Care Research Facility. Of special significance to research on aging is an off-campus Gerontological Research Center in Baltimore.

Our in-house research program is large, but it represents significantly less than a fifth of our total research and research training activity. Eighty percent of the total NIH budget of over $5 billion this year is expended through grants and contracts awarded to more than 1,200 academic institutions, hospitals, and laboratories in the United States as well as in other countries.

Over half of our entire budget goes to support research projects proposed by individual investigators. This mechanism is considered to be our most effective means for encouraging creativity. The response of the scientific community is such that even though our budget is substantial, we can fund only about a third of the meritorious applications, and consequently must make difficult choices among excellent proposals. The quantity and the subjects of investigator-initiated research proposals provide an index of how the research community perceives scientific opportunity in various fields and disciplines.

That is why we feel it to be encouraging and significant that grant applications in the field of gerontology have more than tripled in number since 1976. Nearly 700 applications have been received by the NIA in the current year. Another example of increased interest in aging research is the number of trainees being supported under research training programs. Currently, 221 individuals are in the NIA training programs as compared with 151 in 1976. This roughly 50% increase happened while the total number of trainees supported by NIH *decreased* by about 7%.

During this decade, knowledge of the disease states common to the elderly and about the changes that occur with aging has improved significantly. Many important scientific questions, however, remain to challenge us. Continued research is needed to understand the mechanisms of aging and to understand the nature of age-associated diseases and disorders such as Alzheimer's disease and osteoarthritis. This research is vital to assure rational and cost-effective plans for providing health care to our present and future elderly.

Research on Alzheimer's disease, the most common form of dementia among the aged, continues to be a high priority for the NIA as scientists and grantees attempt to identify what causes the disease and how it can be prevented or treated. An aggressive attack by the NIA on this devastating disease associated with old age has given hope that treatments may one day be available for those who suffer from this form of mental impairment. The establishment during 1984 of five centers for Alzheimer research provides a major step toward intensifying research on this important question. In our intramural Laboratory of Neurosciences based in the Clinical Center in Bethesda, the course of Alzheimer's disease and other dementias is being examined in patient volunteers with a variety of clinical test instruments including positron emission tomography (PET).

A workshop on molecular genetics, held in September 1984, urged increased attention to using molecular genetic techniques to study aging. This should provide insight into the mechanisms of aging and may permit a better understanding of age-related diseases. In the last few years, powerful new techniques have emerged in molecular biology. In order to provide leadership in this field in our intramural program and to aid established laboratories in extending their research capabilities through the use of these new techniques, NIA is establishing an intramural Laboratory of Molecular Genetics. Research will be directed at examining changes that occur with aging in gene function and structure.

The NIA's Baltimore Longitudinal Study of Aging has done much to improve our understanding of the aging process. This study, conducted by NIA's Gerontology Research Center, is in its 26th year of study for males and 6th year of study for females, and currently includes about 900 active participants. Among the significant results from this study during the past year is the finding that in persons who are free of any evidence of heart disease, there is no significant decline in maximum heart capacity with age. While there is a slower heart rate response to exercise stress, the older heart compensates by having a larger effective volume maintaining the same heart output.

A number of disorders and diseases that afflict older people and result in disability and institutionalization have received too little research attention from the medical community. These include the major types of functional disabilities such as incontinence, falls, and hip fractures. Through NIA's teaching nursing home program, support for clinical research in geriatrics is increasing dramatically. This NIA program has provided the example for private organizations to initiate programs involving a nursing home and medical school that examine basic clinical problems. While seven of these programs have been funded, 10 times that number of medical and nursing schools have begun collaboration with long-term care facilities.

Yesterday, I was privileged to address the American Foundation for Aging Research. I told them of a general concern within the biomedical research community over what appears to be a continuing decline in the number of physicians devoting significant portions of their careers to research. Over the past dozen years, there has been essentially no increase in the overall number of research grants awarded by the NIH to M.D.'s at a time when the number of such awards to Ph.D.'s has doubled. This situation is caused in part by a decline in the number of proposals submitted by M.D.'s. Furthermore, competition is much more intense now than it was a decade or so ago. When looking at success rates, one finds that since about 1970, new M.D. applicants have not competed as well as Ph.D.'s.

Science has become increasingly complex, the methods more sophisticated, and the training period so long that even after 2 or 3 years of fellowship training, the physician remains less well trained than the Ph.D. scientist who has been in research training since the baccalaureate degree. Success for an M.D. investigator is increasingly dependent upon substantial training in the information concepts and the methodologies of complex modern science. I repeated to the foundation group yesterday an observation whose validity is self-evident: To be a first-rate scientist and a well-qualified physician is a demanding calling.

Scientists committed to careers in gerontology and geriatrics with high competencies in various biomedical, behavioral, and social sciences are critical to advancing research in aging. The wide range of disciplines of importance in aging challenge both M.D.'s and Ph.D.'s. The need for clinically trained investigators in all areas of biomedical research is an international problem. I commend this challenge to the attention of this International Congress and its constituent organizations. For these challenges are universal in scope—there is a worldwide need for more knowledge about aging and for the development of a knowledge base that will distinguish between normal aging and disease states that may or may not be associated with aging.

More must be known about the health, social, and environmental factors that promote the independence, well-being, and effective functioning among the elderly worldwide so that reliable data can be used to determine present and future needs for the growing populations of older persons. An epidemiological approach, possible only through international collaboration, can provide an understanding of the determinants of ill health among the elderly and provide the bases for scientifically sound health policies.

Various NIA programs are developing complementary studies to understand trends and cross-national variables in patterns of morbidity and cause-specific mortality, especially as they affect persons over 85, the fastest growing segment of the developed world. Scientists from other countries supported by the NIA and U.S. investigators working with European scientists are studying Alzheimer's disease. The NIA promotes international collaboration in geriatrics and gerontology through exchanges among individual investigators, development of studies related to program objectives, and cooperation with nongovernment and multilateral organizations. Its role as a collaborating center of the World Health Organization has been extended under a renewed agreement based upon research on health of the elderly.

Occasionally, one hears an optimistic statement regarding the disease-specific institutes of the NIH—that their basic purpose is to be so successful they put themselves out of business. An example of such success would be to find a fully effective means for preventing a disease so that the need for further research on the target disorder would be minimized. Whatever the real merit of this statement, it definitely is not applicable to the NIA. It takes no prophet to foresee the increased demand for persons with knowledge and skills in both geriatrics and gerontology to help care for the growing elderly population. Enormous benefits can be realized from research that leads to more effective methods of disease and disability prevention and care for the aging and the aged.

By continuing to support and conduct research aimed at improving the quality of life for the elderly, we will be promoting changes that will improve the quality of life and sense of well-being of all ages. The aging research of today will undoubtedly help bring about the changes that will benefit all mankind in the future.

CHAPTER 2

Social and Behavioral Issues in Gerontology

Matilda White Riley

Two issues regarding social and behavioral sciences and aging are: How we can use scientific research (a) to optimize the strengths and potential strengths of older people, and (b) to optimize the opportunities for old people to perform rewarding roles in society. In discussing these two issues emphasis is on the *possible*, since we can build confidently on two decades of research in the social sciences. The theme is that we can begin now to use this knowledge base for identifying and optimizing the abilities of old people to function productively, and for finding useful roles for them in every society throughout the world. Indeed we must bring science to bear on these issues if our worldwide goal is to slow the aging process; to sustain well-being, vigor, and productivity into the middle and later years; and to postpone dependency and disability until the last years of the life course.

To be sure, we are currently surrounded by many dismal forebodings about aging, as the numbers of older people multiply everywhere, and lives—especially women's lives—are lengthened to an extent unprecedented in all history. Yet social research clearly demonstrates that the majority of older people still function effectively. And many of the problems that do exist arise from failures to address the two issues before us: from failures to recognize or to foster older people and from failures in the economy, the polity, the health care system, and other social institutions to adapt to the mounting numbers of the old. In short, we must find scientifically sound ways to treat as a resource, not as a burden, as many old people as possible for as long as possible.

STRENGTHS OF OLDER PEOPLE

As to the first issue, then, how can we optimize the strengths of older people? Before we can optimize these strengths, however, we must ensure that they are recognized. Unfortunately, these strengths are now grossly underestimated. We start here under the handicap of ageism. Stereotypes of the complete immutability of age-related declines, though false, still persist. Even today, medical textbooks continue to preach the doctrine—which is only now being set straight— that deterioration due to aging is universal and inevitable. Doctors in industrialized countries still spend less time with older than with younger patients; and older people themselves attribute their aches and pains to old age, overlooking possible symptoms of disease. Thus popular views and professional practice lag behind scientific knowledge about the aging process.

Of course, we in this great Congress recognize that many of these negative stereotypes arose from faulty interpretation of the scientific evidence. As we ourselves have learned, it is simply not true that, *because of aging*, all older people are destined to be ill, impoverished, cut off from society, sexually incapacitated, despondent, or unable to reason or to remember. The first task before us, then, is to communicate to others what we already know—that aging is more than a biological process. People do not grow old in laboratories. They grow old in families or tribes, in communal villages or kibbutzim, in congested cities or wide-open fields, under conditions of wealth or poverty, in preliterate or technologized cultures—in environments that influence the way they grow old. We know all this. But we must make clear to others that, depending on the social context, different individuals grow old in widely varied ways. And that, as society changes, cohorts of older people today are growing old in ways that differ markedly from their predecessors in the past or their successors in the future.

To be crystal clear, social science has formulated a general principle here: the principle of *mutability* of the aging process. That is, aging is *not* an entirely immutable or biologically fixed process; it changes with social structure and social change. Declines with aging, even biological declines, are not universal or inevitable; for aging is a whole set of processes in which biological aging continually interacts with social and psychological aging. And the important corollary to this principle of mutability is the *potential for intervention* and deliberate modification of the aging process. Hence my emphasis on the scientifically possible.

Once this principle of mutability becomes recognized, massive evidence is accumulated that begins to specify *how* the principle and its corollary, intervention, can be implemented. It is not enough just to talk about life-style or well-being. Social science is needed to tell us exactly *which* life-styles will have *which* effects on well-being. Recent studies in Israel, West Germany, Scandinavia, Japan, Poland, the United States, and elsewhere are producing highly useful findings. For example:

- Among older workers, intellectual functioning improves with aging if the work situation is challenging and demands self-direction.
- Very old people whose performance on intelligence tests has deteriorated can be brought back to their performance levels of 20 years earlier, if the social environment affords incentives and opportunities for practicing and learning new strategies.
- Even slowed reaction time, long attributed to irreversible aging losses in central nervous system functioning, can be speeded up if the social situation provides training, consistent feedback, and encouragement.
- In nursing homes, changing the environment to increase the sense of independence in aged patients can result in greater activity and even lowered mortality.
- And the remarkable capacities for self-care by older people themselves are evidenced in research reports from such disparate sources as the feldshers in the Soviet Union, the barefoot doctors in China, and the district nurses in Sweden and the United Kingdom.

All such research findings and many more, as they are tested, replicated, and examined under world conditions, can be used as clues to understanding the potential strengths and functioning of people who are growing old today, and they can be used as guides to policy and practice.

The lives of older people of the future—those not yet old—are still more prone to modification. There are evidences from the many countries represented in this Congress that future older people will differ from their predecessors in education, work history, diet, exercise, standard of living, medical care, and experience with chronic versus acute diseases. A highly critical question, as mortality is postponed, is how healthy the older people of the future will be. Studies in the United States are providing a few indications that more recent cohorts are increasingly aware of their own future health and the importance of primary prevention of chronic disease. And there are examples from many countries of growing interest in health promotion: gymnastic programs for seniors in Switzerland, traditional shadow boxing in China, concern with nutrition in Scandinavian "study circles," universities for "health and longevity" in the Soviet Union. The key to optimizing the strengths of older people of the future is to begin promotion of health early, while people are still young.

On the first issue, then, it is now time to make use of the scientific evidence. Longevity means postponement of death, but it does not mean inevitable deterioration for everyone, or even necessarily for most old people.

OPPORTUNITIES IN SOCIETY

The second issue: How can we optimize the opportunities in society for the many long-lived people? What do we know, and what can we do, about the kinds of places in society where older people's strengths can be sustained, enhanced, esteemed, and rewarded? Here again scientific guidance is essential.

The sheer numbers of older people are already pressing for changes in social structures throughout the world: in work settings, in educational organizations, in families, in communities, and in health and welfare institutions. Social structures, like aging processes, are mutable too. Our conceptions of work, the organization of work, and of retirement are changing in helpful ways. We are beginning to think of education as a lifelong process. Intergenerational relationships are being sustained even as families adapt to new conditions. And older adults are increasingly active in community affairs.

As a final example, in *care of the frail elderly*, research is showing *how* self-care by older people themselves and informal care by families and neighbors can operate most effectively. Here the optimum models come from the less well–developed countries. Thus, on the second issue, research is specifying, slowly and gradually, how new places are being made for long-lived people.

This article concludes by responding to the two major issues it posed: (a) We have been grossly underestimating the strengths of older people and failing to develop their potentials, and (b) only now are we beginning to understand how increasingly long-lived people can perform productive and rewarding roles in ever-changing societies. The need for comparative research and communication across disciplines, across countries, and across languages has never been greater or more relevant. (For example, the just published *International Glossary of Social Gerontology* in Spanish, French, German, and English, with a Russian supplement, is a new and valuable tool for research, now available from the International Federation on Aging.)

The social and behavioral sciences have taken the lead in this remarkable enterprise of understanding what is possible for older people, through the two principles of mutability of aging and social adaptability. It is my own belief that the possible is already close at hand: that, while extending the scientific knowledge base, we can also put it to work. Each one of us in each country and in each discipline has something to contribute to make the possible a reality.

CHAPTER 3

Emerging Issues in the Economics of Aging

Jack Habib

The reference to economics as the dismal science would seem appropriate in light of recent developments such as the following:

1. In many countries there is a sense of crisis in the ability to sustain public systems of support for the elderly.

2. The extraordinary levels of unemployment in the decade of the 70s have been accompanied in many developed countries by dramatic declines, ranging from 20% to 50%, in the labor force participation of males aged 60 to 64 and by more recent attempts in several countries to induce those 55 to 60 to leave the labor force. Thus, opportunities for older workers are in sharp decline despite the warnings and pleas of many gerontologists (UNESCO, 1985).

3. Poverty among the elderly in developed countries is still common and is increasing, and the shopping bag ladies and the homeless have become more and more common on the streets and in the transportation systems of some of our major cities.

4. As government retreats, there is a call for the expansion of family responsibility. Yet most gerontologists predict that the decline in the ratio of potential caretakers to elderly, the possible extension of the length of the period of disability and the rise in female labor force participation will create a crisis in the ability even to maintain present levels of family support.

5. As reported by the World Bank, the developing world has been particularly affected by the recession of the 80s, and obviously, the elderly in those countries have been affected as well. The overall rate of growth in per capita income between 1980 and 1985 was half that of the developed world, and most regions experienced declines in living standards with Africa, the scene of cataclysmic economic collapse and mass starvation, the hardest hit (IBRD, 1984).

It is important to note that our economic difficulties may have been generated in part or aggravated by the new economic theories that have become dominant in policy circles, and may or may not be justified in the longer run. Thus, while economists have been part of the search for solutions, in the final analysis it may turn out that they have been part of the problem.

The role of the gerontologist is to help sort out which aspects of these trends may be attributed to the process of population aging and which may be associated with more short-run economic conditions. In the area of public expenditures, major new projects such as the European Economic Community (EEC) study of the consequences of changes in the age structure are now bearing fruit (UNESCO, 1985). This study points to a ratio of about 3 to 1 between per capita public expenditures on the elderly and on children, replicating the earlier findings in the U.S. (Clark & Spengler, 1980; Sheppard & Rix, 1977). However, when these ratios are applied to the age structure changes expected up to the year 2000, the implied increase in public sector expenditures is small. The relative economic status of the elderly in a cross-cultural framework is also being intensively studied and important progress has been made in understanding the status of subgroups such as women, the very old, and minorities (Adult & Tamir, 1985; Hedstrom & Ringen, 1985).

While the data base has indeed been expanding rapidly, we have not, as economists, been equally careful to contribute useful information to the public debate. We seem to be continually surprised by that which should have been expected. Is it not to be expected that as a group's share in the population rises, its share of public expenditures will also rise? Is it not to be expected that as pension systems mature their cost will increase in relation to gross national product (GNP) or public budgets? Can we nationalize an industry and then complain that the public sector has to pay the wage bill? In an aging society the taxes required to finance pensions will increase, but they need to be viewed in relation to the reduction in taxes required to finance public expenditures on children as their population share declines. Very seldom does the discussion on Social Security make these links.

The unbalanced critique of expenditures on the elderly may have also engendered an unbalanced response on the part of elderly advocacy groups who fear that giving an inch may mean the amputation of an arm or a leg. It is difficult, for example, to justify a position that the elderly be exempt from whatever declines in living standards are being experienced by the broader society.

While we must continue to study the problem of allocating existing resources, I believe that as economists and gerontologists, we need to shift our attention to mechanisms for mitigating some of the pressures both to reduce expenditures and to force older adults out of the labor force.

LONG-RUN ADJUSTMENTS

The aging process involves the nexus of four independently significant yet interrelated changes: changes in (a) fertility, (b) life-expectancy, (c) women's labor force participation, and (d) the age structure. Societal institutions and particularly the organization of production have not yet caught up with these changes, thereby creating inherent contradictions and a state of disequilibrium that will have to eventually yield to a new set of norms and productive relations. As economists and gerontologists we can help facilitate and ease the process of adjustment.

There are two thrusts that deserve greater emphasis: The first is the need for a renewed interest in fertility in the developed world. Below-replacement fertility rates can have severe consequences for dependency ratios. Indeed, the dependency ratio is expected to increase considerably in Europe after the year 2000. In addressing the factors that affect fertility, a major question is how to accommodate a concern with equality of opportunity for women and high fertility rates. That some progress along these lines may have been made is reflected in the fact that the highest rates of increase in labor force participation for women in the last decade have been among women with young children. However, ultimately there are two underlying factors that may prove critical: At home will men accept more household responsibility and at work will both men and women adjust to the demands made by the world of work and to the needs of the two-earner couple with two or three children.

Whether fertility patterns change or not, and no matter how the age structure develops, there remains the imperative of accommodating the new human life cycle. We need to proceed much more vigorously with the exploration of schemes to redistribute nonmarket activity over the life cycle rather than bunching it all at the end, realizing that benefits may accrue to all age groups. Correspondingly, we will be able to expand employment opportunities in the last quarter of life. While such a redistribution enhances the need for investments in maintaining lifetime productivity, it also creates the opportunities to do so.

The measures needed to maintain the productivity of workers in an extended work life include investment in the updating of knowledge, and the promotion of career shifts and job adaptations that reflect the comparative advantages of older workers and that counteract the wear and tear of working at the same thing for longer and longer periods.

In addition, we may have to readjust attitudes with respect to the prerogatives associated with seniority. Rigidities in the ability to reassign or dismiss workers that are no longer suitable to particular jobs contribute to demands for mandatory retirement for all elderly workers. Moreover, if one takes the Israeli kibbutz as an example of a framework in which opportunities for continuing participation are maintained late into life, one finds that the intergenerational support for that policy is in part based on the willingness of the elderly to relinquish their claim to specific positions—to step aside, and not uncommonly, to assume what outsiders at least would view as lower status roles. The destigmatization of downward job mobility in the later years may be a further contribution to providing employment over the extended life cycle.

Opinion seems to be divided as to whether we will face a labor shortage or surplus in the years ahead. The outlook appears to vary regionally, with labor shortages already an issue in the Soviet Union and some other Eastern Block countries (UNESCO, 1985). Yet, even under conditions of surplus, the adjustments we have described remain important and increased labor force participation in the later years can be used to economically support opportunities for periods of retraining and leisure over the life cycle.

The emphasis here on market roles should not be construed as denying the importance of the role of the elderly in the informal support system or what economists refer to as home production. In contrast to the clear implications of an aging population for growth in public-expenditure needs, the total need for informal support may not increase. The greater care needs of the elderly may be offset by the decrease in the care needs of children. Moreover, the total supply of informal support may increase. While there are fewer supporters per elderly parent, there is more elderly parent-time per adult child or grandparent-time per grandchild. As more recent studies have suggested, the elderly as a group are net providers rather than recipients of care from their families. Moreover, in an aging society the age structure of children shifts toward the teenage group. This may further reduce informal support needs for children, and children in this age group may be an important potential informal resource. A fuller understanding of the resource needs and potential of an aging society requires a broad view of the balance of informal caring and exchange (Habib, 1985).

THE DEVELOPING COUNTRIES

The rapid aging of the developing countries has been emphasized and will be a continuous concern. There are, however, two contrasting interpretations of this process. One interpretation would emphasize that the elderly continue to share in the fate of the general population through their employment in the rural economy and through extended family ties. Thus, the need is for general economic and particularly rural development rather than for special programs of assistance. The second interpretation would emphasize incipient processes of family breakdown as particularly influenced by the urban migration of the young with the elderly often left behind (International Center for Social Gerontology, 1984).

There is certainly little question of the bitter fate of the elderly in famine-stricken countries. It seems appropriate to better document that fate and the consequences for the aging adult population of physical deprivation and family disruption. However, aside from these tragic examples, the alleged disruption of family caring patterns needs to be subject to the same kind of critical and empirical scrutiny that has served to challenge the myth of family disruption in the developed world.

There is also a clear need for intensified research on the economic implications of population aging in developing regions. In this context, the question is raised as to the nature of the age-related productivity curve when given levels of life expectancy are achieved at much lower levels of per capita income than was the case in developed economies.

The policy discussion on this issue has been marked by the same ambivalence. At what point and to what extent should state systems designed to supplement the role of the family be introduced? There is no simple answer. A frequent recommendation has been to adopt policies of support for the family to maintain or strengthen its role. The rapid diffusion of cash allowances to families caring for older persons even in developing countries reflects this thrust. Yet such programs could prove to be very inefficient ways of addressing the need, if most of the support goes to families who would anyway have provided the care. Thus, an important agenda item shared by the developed and the developing world is the evaluation of cash incentives to families and the clarification of how they relate to other community service programs. A research project on the economic and social consequences of aging populations in developing regions has been initiated by the United Nations Population Division (United Nations, 1984).

A STRATEGY FOR ADDRESSING THESE ISSUES

It will not be possible to address the kind of questions that we have posed without a radical shift in research strategies, changes in our educational programs and a reorientation of the practice and policy agendas. There are several directions to be considered. Much can be learned from existing cross-cultural variations in the organization of the labor market and in cultural norms, as well as from some of the innovative programs adopted in specific contexts that can help us to understand the feasibility of the adjustments that are required. Exposés of these successes are needed. Beyond these natural experiments, there is a need for a new era of social experimentation, similar if not greater in magnitude to that conducted by economists over the last 15 years in the area of income maintenance programs or with respect to health and social service systems for the elderly. The third component of an overall strategy is an accelerated program of research into life-enhancing technological advances that will mitigate the effects of impairment, extend the capacity for learning in the older years, adapt jobs to the skills and interests of older workers, and the like. Economists have much to contribute in the design of public policies that will promote such technological advances.

Rather than accepting the inevitability of reduced social welfare expenditures and reduced labor force opportunities for the elderly, an enhanced commitment to the broad-based structural changes that will enable us to accommodate the new human life cycle, the new demands of women, and the new age structure of society is needed. The lot of the elderly in the developing countries is closely linked with the policies adopted in the developed world. A developed world that has lost its sense of optimism and control over its future will be ill-prepared and ill-disposed to contribute its share to the struggle for subsistence that is still the preoccupation of much of the world's elderly.

While there is room for optimism, it must be backed up by a lot of hard work. Conventional approaches to generating, supporting, and even conducting research may not be adequate to ensure the sustained development of this kind of agenda and thus, new mechanisms will be required.

REFERENCES

Ahdut L., & Tamir, Y. (1985). Inequality and economic status among the elderly. In *Luxembourg income study* (Working paper series). Luxembourg.

Clark, R.L., Spengler, J.J. (1980). *The economics of individual and population aging.* New York: Cambridge University Press.

Habib, Jack. (1985). The economy and the aged. In R. Binstock & E. Shanas (Eds.), *Handbook of aging and the social sciences.* (2nd ed., pp. 479-502). New York: Van Nostrand Reinhold.

Hedstrom, P., & Ringen, S. (1985). Age and income in contemporary society: A comparative study. In *Luxembourg income study* (Working paper series). Luxembourg.

International Bank for Reconstruction and Development (IBRD)/The World Bank. (1984). *World development report, 1984.* New York: Oxford University Press.

International Center for Social Gerontology. (1984, December). *Recommendations adopted by the African conference of gerontology.* Dakar.

Sheppard, H.L. & Rix, S.E. (1977). *The graying of working America.* New York: Free Press.

United Nations. Department of International Economic and Social Affairs. (1984). *Bulletin on aging Vol. IX. No. 3.* Vienna: Centre for Social Development and Humanitarian Affairs.

United Nations Economic and Social Council (UNESCO). (1985, February). *Economic implications of the aging of population in the ECE region: A preliminary overview.* Economic Commission for Europe, Senior Economic Advisors to ECE Governments.

CHAPTER 4

Pillars of Society: Supporting Health of the Elderly

David M. Macfadyen

Four years ago, there was no representation from the World Health Organization (WHO) on the platform at the IAG Congress in Hamburg. Today, all six regional program managers from Africa, the Americas, Europe, east Mediterranean, Southeast Asia and the western Pacific are participating in the Congress, in addition to the WHO. Here is proof that aging is, indeed, a universal human experience.

Perhaps in 1981 we had only a little to offer to the medical, biological, and social constituencies that the IAG represents. But this is certainly not the situation in 1985. Let me try to analyse the process by which the WHO has achieved a higher profile in the international scene on aging. Hopefully, this is a process beneficial to IAG, especially as it looks forward to its next congress in Mexico—the first-ever congress in the "South."

Is WHO's increasing commitment to aging impacting on the well-being of elders around the world? A personal concern with evaluating the impact of WHO's expanding national, regional and international activities is explained by my having to exercise all efforts of persuasiveness to obtain resources for the elderly within an organization that has zero budget growth. Even the noneconomist can understand how within a limited budget one pays Peter by robbing Paul. Paul in this case is a group of lean, categorical programs serving the least and lesser developing countries, all of them with overwhelming health and social problems.

Against this background, the resources for WHO country programs will increase in 1986/1987 by three-quarters and for regional programs by half. And the presence here of all six of WHO's regional program managers underscores the universality of WHO's commitment. These regional managers are ready to describe WHO's program of collaboration with the countries of their region. One point that highlights the significance of the IAG decision to convene the next congress in Mexico is that the WHO region of the Americas now matches Europe in terms of its 1986/1987 program and budget.

Surely money is not everything. However, I adhere to two complementary beliefs about money. The first belief is in my Scottish genes: All money, personal or public, must be spent prudently. The second belief is simply old-fashioned (an adjective chosen carefully): You have to spend money to improve the well-being of people. However, the simple point to be made with the WHO budget figures is to illustrate the organization's commitment in terms of geographical coverage and in terms of support to efforts in countries.

The increasing international profile of WHO in the field of aging stems, primarily, from the fact that we know where we are going. Our guide, or road map, comes from clearly defined policies established by WHO's World Health Assembly. These policies are expressed in terms of specific resolutions to which all member states plus the Director-General and Secretariat are committed. The most recent resolution directs us to go beyond traditional medical concerns and involve the health sector in the larger context of improving the quality of life for aging people. This is the first-ever resolution built on the twin pillars of health maintenance and alternatives to institutional care.

A second reason for the increasing international profile of WHO is that the program is not just an advocacy program; it is also a technological one. If one pillar of our policy is indeed health maintenance, then it follows that we have to use technology to learn what it is that keeps us healthy as we age. The appropriate technology for assessing this, unequivocally in human populations, is the epidemiological method for investigating health and disease. And, since 1982, there has been an explicit policy—symbolized in the name of the program "Health of the Elderly"—that the WHO program should be an epidemiological program rather than a geriatric program or a disability program.

At WHO's first international meeting on aging, held in Mexico City, Professor James Birren promoted the use of the verb "to elder" in order to differentiate the social processes of aging from the biological or senescing processes. This focused international attention on the nature of the societal contexts in which mankind ages. The dynamic character of societies, especially in the developing world, is thought to be generating new patterns of "eldering." Thus the developing programs in the newer aging countries have a large social component; the main public efforts of these programs emphasize preserving values and life-styles that aim to support traditional patterns of eldering.

These global epidemiological and regional sociological approaches are bringing us increasingly in touch with professional constituencies outside the confines of gerontology and geriatrics. Indeed, the awareness of the process of aging in other disciplines has been an explicit intention of the program. It may have been obvious to others, but it was a late realization for me that the pillar of health maintenance in old age is hollow. We know remarkably little about what to do to stay healthy as we age. If there is to be a preventive medicine of old age, then there needs to be a broader base of scientific knowledge. And to establish this base we have to mobilize the intellectual talent of the world's biologists, neuroscientists, nutritionists, immunologists, and related disciplines. I am delighted that this Congress has captured some of these constituent professions and that the IAG continues to offer a respected international forum for them to present their exciting work.

There is also at these IAG meetings an opportunity to internationalize scientific endeavors. In the vanguard of international collaborative research are the social scientists. Dr. Margaret Dieck has identified, for the United Nations, some 44 cross-country studies of the elderly.[1] This profusion, contrasted with perhaps only a single collaborative endeavor in the basic sciences, indicates that social scientists are in fact social. However, I hold this up as an example in order to get across my oft-repeated message that all stand to gain by going beyond national boundaries, by breaking away from the confines of "aging Americans," "aging Austrians," "aging Australians," and "aging Argentinians," and by extending one's scientific perspective to the aging of mankind as a universal experience.

Let me return to the profile of WHO with other constituencies, especially in relation to that second pillar of the program—alternatives to institutional care. The profession in closest day-to-day contact with elders is the nursing profession. This profession is undergoing important transitions. One of these is toward community nursing and health teamwork.

In relation to maintaining the health of the elderly, these transitions are described in a forthcoming WHO monograph entitled "AGING: Implications for Nursing," the text of which was reviewed and revised

---

[1]Cross-national Research and International Comparative Research in Gerontology—A Preliminary Inventory, Berlin (West), May 1984.

at the recent Quadrennial Congress of the International Council of Nurses in Tel Aviv. This pattern of getting aging issues into the international arena is being extended to other disciplines, such as the world's epidemiologists, immunologists, nutritionists, schools of public health and physical therapists. And we would seize any opportunity offered by other disciplines represented at the congress to join efforts within their international congresses.

It is a happy coincidence that the IAG has chosen the United States this year to celebrate the universality of aging, since it is exactly 40 years ago since the birth, in this country, of the United Nations. When the United Nations convened its World Assembly on Aging in Vienna in 1982, some of the aspirations of 40 years back re-emerged. It was clearly apparent that aging is an international issue that is nonpolarizing; aging is the universal experience of West and East and of North and South. Indeed, here is one field in which the South feels it may provide guidance to the North. Several delegations at the UN World Assembly on Aging in Vienna in 1982, notably that of France and of some small countries, saw the potential for international cooperation in aging as a means to constructive collaboration and dialogue, at best to improve the human condition, at least to improve human relations. And these countries struggled to achieve a follow up from Vienna that would institutionalize universal efforts on behalf of an aging universe.

In concluding with this historical perspective, my aim is to reopen the appeal for a mechanism to provide solidarity among the elders of the world. I especially hope that this appeal will achieve resonance in our host country, since the United States fulfills all the conditions necessary to play a leadership role. You have an enviable accumulation of intellectual capital in your seats of learning and research institutes; you have an effective mechanism of national solidarity among retired persons; your elders adhere aggressively to attitudes that are health-oriented; you are a continental nation with a geography that models the world's; you are a multiethnic country.

In the international world in which I live there is an unchallenged ethic of solidarity among all people of the world. This internationalism is derived from the mixed motives of altruism and enlightened self-interest that are captured in the poem of John Donne, with which I conclude:

> Any man's death diminishes me
> For I am involved in mankind
> And therefore never send to know
> For whom the bell tolls
> It tolls for thee.

CHAPTER 5

The International Plan of Action in Aging

Tarek Shuman

It is heartening and inspiring that such a distinguished and widely representative group from developing countries has gathered to examine the issues of aging from the developing countries' point of view. The International Congress follows a period of intense United Nations (UN) activity on aging issues. In 1982, the UN convened the historic World Assembly on Aging, with representatives from 124 nations in all world regions. The rationale of the World Assembly was to spur forward-looking policies to anticipate and respond, in time, to the far-reaching socio-economic and humanitarian implications of this demographic change. The strategies for the future drawn up at the World Assembly were distilled in the Vienna International Plan of Action on Aging. This action program, the first comprehensive international instrument in the field of aging, was adopted unanimously by all Member States of the United Nations in 1982.

Subsequently in this chapter, I will summarize international reflections on the Plan of Action and present a brief assessment of progress achieved in implementing the recommendations contained in the Plan as reflected in the first review and appraisal undertaken by the UN in 1984.

The 1982 World Assembly on Aging was conceived as a springboard

The author would like to thank the President of the IAG and Dr. Gary Andrews for inviting the UN to address this important forum.

for responding to the economic, social, cultural, and humanitarian implications of the aging of populations and the tremendous increases in numbers of older persons anticipated worldwide in coming decades. This projected demographic change is associated with current and projected fertility decline, a concomitant slowing of population growth, a decrease in the size of the youngest age groups, and marked increases in the number of the elderly in the population. Trends toward the aging of the population are projected to become increasingly significant in developing as well as developed countries; by 2025 nearly 14% of the world's population is projected to be in the 60-plus age group, 11% of the population of the developing regions, and 23% of the population of the developed regions. At the same time, as the large birth cohorts of recent years progress through the life cycle to old age, absolute numbers of the elderly are projected to jump from an estimated 370 million in 1980 to more than one billion in 2025, with over 70% living in developing regions. Additional useful information about population aging worldwide is found in the 1985 publication of the Department of International Economic and Social Affairs of the United Nations, *The World Aging Situation: Strategies and Policies.*

Three years have now passed since the Plan of Action was so strongly endorsed. One may ask, with justification, whether it has had a tangible impact, whether it has spurred decision makers at the national, regional, and international levels to anticipate the social and economic implications of the aging of their population structures, whether it has led to the allocation of sufficient resources to meet the individual needs of growing numbers of the elderly.

It was to answer these questions that the United Nations recently conducted the First Review and Appraisal of the Implementation of the Vienna International Plan of Action on Aging. As a part of the Review and Appraisal, over 100 UN Member States, concerned regional and international organizations, and nongovernmental organizations (NGOs) assessed their progress to date in carrying out the Plan's recommendations. The results of the Review and Appraisal exercise show clearly that there has been progress since 1982. National and international awareness of the impact of aging trends on development has increased. The contribution that the elderly themselves can make to development is more widely understood. And the role of forward planning in responding to the needs of future generations is increasingly recognized. This awareness is apparent even among governments of countries whose population structures are still very young. Given the speed with which their populations will begin to age in the next few decades, and the enormous increases projected in numbers of their elderly, this improved understanding is a vital prerequisite for effective policy making.

This gathering goes beyond examining aging in developing countries. We are, indeed, in a process of exchanging experience, knowledge, and technologies between and among ourselves and with the scientific community of the developed world.

The Vienna International Plan of Action calls for a coordinated approach to policies and research permitting countries to learn from one another's experience to the greatest degree possible. Member States at the World Assembly on Aging stressed that countries should establish or improve existing information exchange facilities since the exchange of skills, knowledge, and experience among countries would be a particularly fertile form of international cooperation. They strongly recommended that the rich opportunities for mutual learning and cooperation in training and research should be vigorously explored.

Realizing, however, that data collection, surveys, and exchange of information are complex activities, the United Nations is giving priority consideration to the questions of standardizing definitions, terms, and research methodologies. This has been identified as a key means for facilitating communication, exchange of information, and comparison of research findings.

We have undertaken a number of activities to this end including the convening of an Expert Group Meeting last March. This was the first step toward the ultimate end of facilitating this exchange among all countries of the world.

An important and indispensable element in the process of implementing the plan of action is NGOs. They have played a vital role in mobilizing resources to meet the needs of the elderly and in stimulating their participation in community life. During the 1980s, the activities of NGOs in the aging field have clearly continued their momentum; as urged in the International Plan of Action they have thus contributed fully to the cooperative effort of governments and intergovernmental organizations to accomplish the Plan's objectives.

This meeting itself is an excellent example of the NGO commitment to promote international understanding in the field of aging. We will continue to rely heavily on NGOs in all facets of our work. We know the NGOs are invaluable in heightening government awareness of aging issues, in campaigning for new policies and programs and for making the recommendations of the Plan of Action reality. We are counting on your cooperation and are confident of your continuing support.

CHAPTER 6

Aging in the Developing World

Gary R. Andrews

The organization of a special series of activities to meet the needs of participants from developing countries within this congress was a new venture for the International Association of Gerontology (IAG). Many colleagues—too many to name individually here—were involved in planning and implementing the special activities that attracted over 150 individuals representing 35 countries of the world. A report on this special program following the Congress will document in detail sources of support to the program and the support of the Congress to selected participants.

BACKGROUND

In January 1984 a proposal was submitted to the United Nations (UN) Trust Fund for Aging seeking support for "a workshop on the uses of scientific information in planning, implementing, and disseminating humanitarian and developmental programs for older adults." The Trust Fund subsequently awarded a grant to support some Congress participants from less developed nations. The UN funds were supplemented by other Congress funds.

The workshop was seen as a logical follow-up on the activities associated with the XIIth Congress of the International Association of Gerontology, which took place in Hamburg, West Germany, in July 1981. At that Congress a precongress workshop brought together scientists and decision makers from more and less developed countries to formulate recommendations. A plenary session of the IAG Congress discussed relevant issues and recommendations to be considered in the Assembly from the perspectives of four regions of the world (Asia/Pacific, Europe, Latin America, North America). Following the XIIth Congress the IAG produced and distributed a volume, *New Perspectives on Old Age: A Message to Decision Makers* (Thomae & Maddox, 1982) outlining the actual and potential uses of scientific information by decision makers responsible for the welfare of aging adults.

These activities were in preparation for the 1982 World Assembly on Aging during which the Vienna Plan of Action on Aging was drafted. The Plan of Action was subsequently adopted by the General Assembly of the United Nations at its 38th Session.

The XIIIth Congress of the International Association of Gerontology held in New York in July 1985 thus provided an excellent opportunity to express key recommendations of the Vienna Plan of Action relating to exchange of knowledge, skills and experience, and research and international cooperation especially between developed and developing countries of the world. In addition, the opportunity was thus presented to review progress made since the 1982 World Assembly and to propose future directions to ensure continuing international cooperation and exchange.

The Developing Countries Program within the XIIIth Congress was the direct outcome of these considerations. No better opportunity could be foreseen to realize the above objectives.

OBJECTIVES

Broad objectives were established for the Program for Developing Country participants at the outset. They were:

1. To provide a forum for examining the issues associated with aging in the less developed regions of the world.

2. To bring together scientists and decision makers from both the more and less developed nations of the world.

3. To provide a means of critically interpreting and reviewing the Congress in terms of the needs and perspectives of the developing regions.

4. To explore avenues for fruitful exchange at every level between more and less developed countries, specifically in relation to educational, research, and practical aspects of gerontology and geriatrics.

5. To review progress made toward the objectives of the Vienna Plan of Action, which was developed by the UN World Assembly on Aging in 1982.

6. To point to future directions for training, program development, and research, especially in those spheres where there is real potential for international cooperation and exchange.

In addition an objective expressed specifically in the submission to the United Nations for support was, ". . . to maintain a vital continuing exchange between IAG and UN/CSDHA and enhance a continuing network of relationships among scientists and decision makers throughout the world."

A SPECIAL PROGRAM

The special program for Congress participants from less developed countries ranged widely over timely topics such as

- Overviews of programs on aging in the UN and the WHO.
- Background information on population aging from demographers and epidemiologists.
- Discussion of the distinctive role of nongovernmental (private) organizations nationally and internationally.
- Presentation of special topics (e.g., on dementia) and of a related special seminar on the applicability of first-world models of aging and responses to aging in third-world nations.

It is now clear that while the relative members and proportion of aged people in most developing countries is still small, during the next few decades this sector of the population will grow very rapidly in both absolute and proportional terms. The aging population will, as a consequence, present a major challenge to health care policy makers and providers in developing countries.

The scale of population aging in the developing world generally is astounding (Figure 6-1). The total aged population in developing countries is already as numerically large as the total aged population of the rest of the world and is also growing at a significantly greater rate. By the year 2000 the aged population in the developing world is expected to have increased by 100 million, compared with an increase of 35 million in the developed world (see Table 6-1).

The International Association of Gerontology is in a unique position to encourage and foster exchange among the international community of scientists with interests in gerontology and geriatric medicine. Building on the success of this first venture in the exchange of scientific information, the Association will continue to facilitate communication, especially among scientists from the developed and developing countries of the world in the area of aging; will continue to work with the

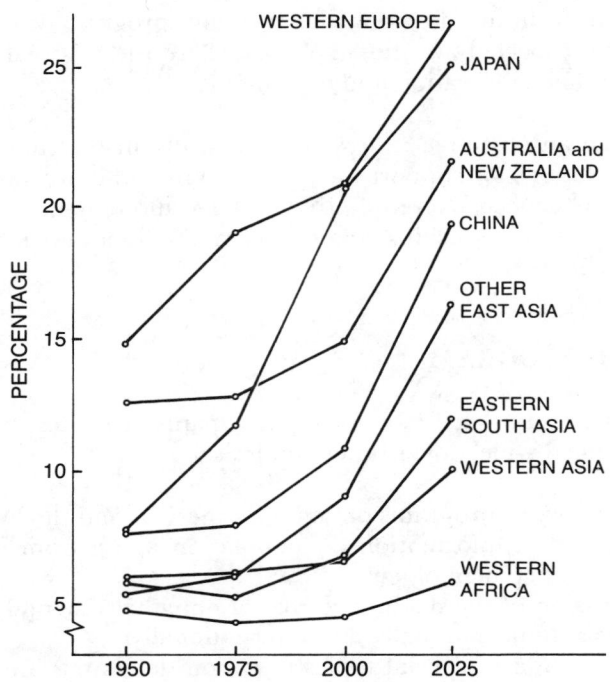

FIGURE 6-1. Proportion of the total population that is 60 years and over, by selected subregions, for 1950, 1975, 2000, 2025.

Source: United Nations World Assembly on Aging, 1982. "Introductory Document: Demographic Considerations." A/Cont. 113/4.

World Health Organization (WHO) and the United Nations in implementing the objectives of the Vienna Plan of Action adopted by the UN at its 38th Assembly; and finally, will plan to give particular emphasis to the special needs of participants from less developed countries at future international congresses through all the means available.

TABLE 6-1. World Population Projections

Year	Total population (millions)	Population 65 + years	Percentage 65 + years
Developing countries			
1980	3284	129	3.9
2000	4297	229	4.7
Developed countries			
1980	1131	129	11.4
2000	1272	167	15.2

Source: UN Age and Sex Composition by Population by Country, 1960–2000. New York, 1979.

It is clear that the rapid socioeconomic changes occurring in developing countries will have a significant effect upon the life-style and well-being of these large numbers of elderly people. Most of these countries are experiencing rapid development, urbanization, industrialization, and technological and social change. Patterns of family structure are changing and traditional values are being challenged. Because of these influences the aged are likely to become increasingly dependent in some degree upon governmental health, medical, and welfare services.

Planners and policy makers in countries throughout the developing world will be faced with a complex task. They will be aware of the demographic changes produced by the combined effects of improved life expectancy, reduced fertility, and migration, which result in the aging of the population as a whole. They will be conscious of the pressures on the traditional joint family structure and traditional cultural pattern under which the younger generation was duty bound to care for the older. They will be conscious of the fact that in the future more and more aged persons will need assistance and support outside of family structures. While old age is not at all necessarily a time of ill health, disability, and misery, a variety of chronic disorders occur much more frequently among the aged than among younger people.

From anecdotal evidence, planners and policy makers will be aware of the increasing impact of the aged upon already overstretched health and welfare services. It would be less than satisfactory to depend upon the information available from the developed countries to provide the basic data essential for the underpinning of rational planning and policy formulation with respect to aging. The necessary basic data will not, however, be immediately available to them.

The lack of a sound data base to support planning and policy is all too evident in developed country situations where heavy emphasis on institutional care, overlapping of programs, gaps in service provisions, and a general approach characterized as "ad hoc incrementalism" has prevailed in policy development and planning. Developing countries are now in a sound position to take careful stock of their current situation. Given present demographic patterns and trends it will be some time before the aging of their populations emerges as a critical issue in comparison with other social and health problems. Thus the opportunity presents for the development of a comprehensive data base and for the identification of key areas of knowledge where further in-depth research will be important for policy and program planning purposes.

DISSEMINATING AND USING INFORMATION

An objective expressed specifically in the submission to the UN for support was, ''. . . to maintain a vital continuing exchange between IAG and UN/CSDHA and enhance a continuing network of relationships among scientists and decision makers throughout the world.'' A broadly based committee was established to undertake planning for the special program. An extensive range of topics was developed which reviewed for participants WHO's global and regional activities and UN programs on aging; the role of the elderly in promoting economic, social, and cultural development; the contribution of voluntary organizations, demographic issues, and epidemiologic aspects of aging; the family and aging; the impact of dementia; alternative mechanisms for contributing money and expertise to programs for older people in developing countries; and the International Federation on Aging (IFA) skills exchange program. How research findings might relate to public policy issues and programs in aging societies is summarized in Table 6-2.

Building on the success of this program, the association will continue to facilitate communication among scientists from the developed and developing countries of the world in the area of aging; will continue to work with the World Health Organization and the United Nations in implementing the objectives of the Vienna Plan of Action adopted by the UN at its 38th Assembly; and finally, will plan to give particular emphasis to the special needs of participants from less developed countries at future international congresses through all the means available.

CONCLUSIONS AND FUTURE DIRECTIONS

It was clear from the response to the Program for Developing Country participants and from the presented papers and discussion that the issues associated with the aging of populations are increasingly important in the developing countries of the world.

While in recent years there has been a rapid increase in research activity on the health and welfare of the aging, not surprisingly, the vast amount of that work has been carried out in the developed world.

It is now recognized that the greatest impact of aging in the future will fall upon the less developed countries of the world where the greatest increase in numbers of the aged in the population in absolute terms will occur in the coming decades. The Vienna Plan of Action, which resulted from the World Assembly on Aging held in July and August 1982 in Vienna, specifically referred to the need for basic research and especially for programs of cooperation and exchange of skills and knowledge between countries.

TABLE 6-2. Relationship of Population-Based Data to Policy and Program Development

Population data	Issue	Policy	Program
Mental status	Prevalence of dementia and depression	Promotion of mental health of the aging	Counseling and community mental health care
Economic resources	Poverty	Minimum income	Financial supplementation or assistance
Health status	Relationship of health and aging	Health care of the aging	Provision of primary health care
Utilization of health services	Relationship of utilization and aging	Health care planning for the aged	Provision of comprehensive health services
Lifestyle	Relationship of lifestyle and health	Prevention	Health education and promotion
Disabilities	Relationship of disability and aging	Minimization of handicap	Provision of aids and community assistance
Activities of daily living			
Transport	Mobility and aging	Access	Provision of transport
Housing	Housing problems and aging	Housing	Alternative accommodation provisions
Social resources and family support	Family and community roles and aging	Family and community responsibility	Family support services

REFERENCES

Thomae, H., & Maddox, G.L. (Eds.). (1982). *New perspectives on old age: A message to decision makers.* New York: Springer Publishing Co.

CHAPTER 7

The International Association of Gerontology: Its Origins and Development

Nathan W. Shock

At the request of the President of the International Association of Gerontology (IAG), the origins and history of the IAG will be described by one who was present at the first meeting, has participated in all 12 of the congresses that have met over the past 35 years (1950–1985), and served as president of the Association (1969–1972).

Although aging and the life span of humans have been favorite subjects for discussion and speculation since biblical times, it was not until the end of the 1930s that aging became a topic of concern to serious scientists. A key event in providing scientific basis for the study of aging (i.e., gerontology) was in the publication, in 1942, of *Problems of Aging* (Cowdry, 1942). This book of 936 pages with chapters written by eminent scientists from many disciplines brought together for the first time the scientific data on aging. Aging became visible as a legitimate subject for scientific study.

It was during this period (1940–1950) that Dr. V. Korenchevsky, a Russian physician and pathologist who had migrated to England in 1920 when the Soviets came into power, saw the importance of aging and gerontology as an area for future research. He also recognized the advantages to be gained from close association among scientists from various countries. He was able to challenge the interest of Lord Nuffield, a British philanthropist who provided funds that permitted Dr. Korenchevsky to travel to a number of countries in Europe and to come to the United States to discuss the possibility of forming an international association of gerontological societies.

The first meeting, held in Liège in July 1950 under the sponsorship of Professor L. Brull (Professor of Medicine at the University of Liège), consisted of 96 representatives from 16 gerontological societies representing 13 different countries (Proceedings, 1950). The formation of these societies was stimulated largely by previous visits from Dr. Korenchevsky. In addition to reading reports of clinical research, which were for the most part concerned with the diseases of older people, the group turned their attention to drawing up a set of rules for the formation of an International Association of Gerontological Societies.

The aims of the International Association were (a) to represent the associated gerontological societies and national or international groups in all matters of foreign or international affairs and (b) to facilitate biological, medical, and social gerontological research in the associated gerontological societies by all possible means, in particular by facilitating the cooperation among willing members of these societies.

It is important to note that, from its very inception, the IAG was conceived as an association among gerontological societies that were concerned with research and training in gerontology and geriatrics. Organizations that were concerned primarily with the delivery of social and medical services to older people were not regarded as appropriate for membership in the IAG.

The second requirement for admission to the IAG was a membership of at least 10 investigators (later revised to 50) representing the scientific disciplines of biology, medicine, and sociology/psychology. In addition to a multidisciplinary approach, member organizations were also required to be national in scope.

The IAG is governed by a council with representatives from each member society based on the number of members enrolled. Congresses are held every 3 or 4 years for the purpose of exchanging research results and ideas among members.

The first four congresses under the presidencies of Dr. L. Brull (Liège, 1950), Dr. E. Cowdry (St. Louis, 1951), Dr. J. Sheldon (London, 1954), and Dr. J. Geill (Copenhagen, 1957) set the tone and direction of the IAG as primarily a biomedical organization whose primary goal was to foster research to increase the understanding of the mechanisms and causes of aging and to improve the background and training of those concerned with the care of elderly people.

Although social gerontological research was one of the three sections of the IAG at its original formation, it was not until the Vth Congress in San Francisco in 1960 that the distinction between sociology and social work became an issue. Mr. L. Kuplan and Mr. C. Tibbitts, delegates from the United States, felt strongly that there should be a fourth division of the IAG concerned with the delivery of both medical and social services to older people. However, when proposals to establish a fourth section (Social Welfare) of the IAG were brought before the council of the IAG they were consistently voted down. European delegates were firm in their conviction that a fourth section of the IAG was unnecessary.

In 1970 Dr. R. Van Zonneveld, Chairman of the European Social Research Committee, wrote to the President of the IAG. He stated, "there exists in Europe, besides the Biology and Clinical Medicine Committees only one committee more; the one and only Social Research Committee (of the IAG). There does *not* and will *not* exist in Europe a so-called Applied Social Research Committee. The European Social Research Committee encompasses 'applied social research' as well. Psychology and social sciences are of course from the beginning (1954) included."

The program for each Congress is determined by Research Committees representing (1) biology, (2) medicine, and (3) sociology for each region of the Association (Europe, North America, Latin America, Asia-Oceania). Programs for International Congresses since the Vth, held in 1960, have included a fourth section concerned with social welfare. Revisions of the constitution and by-laws introduced in 1985 placed responsibility for the planning of future Congresses in the hands of a program committee consisting of the President of the IAG, the Past President, the President-elect, the Secretary and the Treasurer and the chairpersons of the four currently recognized regional communities of the Association.

Over the following 35 years, 13 Congresses have been convened. Table 7-1 lists historical information from the Congresses.

The primary accomplishment of the IAG has been to establish gerontology as a visible scientific discipline dedicated to the study of aging, with roots in biology, medicine, and social science. The number of countries represented in the IAG has increased from the original 16 to some 42 member societies. Furthermore, attendance at each Congress has grown from the original 96 participants in 1950 to as many as 3,000 registered delegates for some of the more recent Congresses. Members of the IAG Council report that in those countries that have served as host for an international congress, interest in the program of the local gerontological society has increased remarkably. Thus, there is no question that the IAG has played a primary role in increasing the interest in research on gerontology and geriatrics that has taken place in recent years.

Congresses have served as a forum for reporting important advances in the fields of gerontology and geriatrics. For example, in 1960, at the Vth Congress in San Francisco, Dr. A. Aslan first reported to a worldwide assembly of scientists the results of her experiments on the

TABLE 7-1. Historical Data on First 13 Congresses of the IAG

Congress	Place/date	President
I	Liège (July 1950)	Dr. L. Brull
II	St. Louis, MO (1951)	Dr. E.V. Cowdry
III	London (1954)	Dr. Sheldon
IV	Merano & Venice (1957)	Dr. Greppi
V	San Francisco, CA (1960)	Dr. L. Kuplan
VI	Copenhagen (1963)	Dr. T. Geill
VII	Vienna (1966)	Dr. W. Doberauer
VIII	Washington, DC (1969)	Dr. N.W. Shock
IX	Kiev (1972)	Dr. D. Chebotarev
X	Jerusalem (1975)	Dr. D. Danon
XI	Tokyo (1978)	Dr. M. Murakami
XII	Hamburg (1981)	Dr. H. Thomae
XIII	New York (1985)	Dr. E.W. Busse

administration of procaine to lengthen life span in rats and to prevent and alleviate the effects of old age in human subjects. It was at this Congress that the "error hypothesis" of cellular aging, conceived by Dr. Medvedev of the U.S.S.R., was first announced to an international audience (even though Dr. Medvedev was unable to attend the Congress in person).

Seminars and round table discussions held at international congresses have served as a medium to improve the design of experiments on the biological basis of aging and to emphasize the idea that aging is a normal process and not a disease in itself. This has led to discussions about appropriate criteria for the selection of healthy human subjects for the study of aging and to the recognition of the importance of making serial observations on the same subject as he ages in order to characterize the processes of aging.

Contacts between individual investigators established at the time of international congresses led to a number of collaborative studies in which patterns of work and retirement in different countries and different societies were compared. The IAG, through its research committees, served as the vehicle for the scheduling of regional conferences in Europe and in South America on biology and clinical medicine. Similar conferences were scheduled by the Social Science Research Committee of the IAG. These conferences took place in the years between the international congresses, and gave European and South American investigators an opportunity to maintain their scientific contacts.

The expanding recognition of the importance of research in gerontology led to the formation of additional regional divisions of the IAG, namely, the Latin American Region (1969) and the Asia-Oceania Region, which held its first meeting in Melbourne, Australia, in December 1980. The Asia-Oceania Region, consisting of Australia, New Zealand, Japan, and Hong Kong, now has its own Executive and Research Committees as does the Latin American Region consisting of Argentina, Uruguay, Brazil, Colombia, Venezuela, and Mexico.

The IAG has also introduced a new approach to the reporting of Congresses. Rather than publishing many short abstracts of individual papers, summaries of groups of papers concerned with a specific topic have been prepared and published in the final proceedings of each Congress. This method of reporting offers a more systematic presentation of the current status of research.

In recent years (Tokyo, 1978; Hamburg, 1981) the IAG has become more and more involved in policy issues relating to the delivery of medical and social services to the elderly. In 1982, Dr. Thomae and Dr. Maddox, on authorization of the Governing Body of the IAG, edited a volume entitled *New Perspectives on Old Age: A Message to Decision Makers,* which included a policy statement for the aged for transmittal to the World Assembly on Aging of the UN which met in Vienna in 1982. The first section of the report consists of 12 recommendations for action. The second part of the report summarizes current research that supports the recommendations. The recommendations for action deal with methods for delivering services to the elderly, social security programs, housing for the elderly, expanded health care delivery systems, long-term medical care, training of personnel to deliver social services to the elderly, development of services for elderly in rural areas, and maintaining a resource center on aging under aegis of the UN. Although these are goals worthy of support, the document needs greater emphasis on the support of basic research in biology, medicine, and sociology to determine the underlying mechanisms of aging, which is a primary goal of the IAG.

As an international organization the IAG must recognize the disparities among countries with respect to social goals, resources, and facilities available to deal with the problems of the aged. Policy decisions about action programs for the aged may be based more on political considerations than on scientific evidence. In my opinion, the IAG should avoid playing the role of advocate for programs for older people—especially those designed for individual countries. If the IAG joins the ranks of other advocacy organizations it is my fear that it will lose its credibility as an organization that bases its recommendations and decisions on scientific data and hard facts. To me, the role of the IAG should be limited to assembling and analyzing data about various types of programs and offering considered judgments about their relative efficacy.

With the increasing number of older people in the population, the social, economic, and medical problems of the aged will become more and more visible. The pressures to do something about these problems will mount. However, it should be remembered that the ultimate solution of the problems of gerontology can be achieved only by basic research in biology, medicine, psychology, and sociology. Members of the IAG must continue to do what they can do best, namely, extend the frontiers of knowledge about all aspects of aging.

In the future, the IAG should, in my view, place more emphasis on basic research and less emphasis on advocacy for action programs for the elderly, since many other organizations such as the AARP, NCOA, NCSC, and the Old People's Welfare Association are able to fulfill the advocacy function. No organization is better equipped than the IAG to speak for knowledge and research on a worldwide basis. This is the area in which the IAG can make its greatest contribution, particularly if its voice remains firm and untainted by the controversies of advocacy positions that are often influenced by political considerations. The IAG should examine and emphasize its original goals, namely, the support of research and training in gerontology—the science of aging.

REFERENCES

Brull, L. (Ed.) (1950). *Proceedings of the First International Gerontological Congress,* Liège, July 10–12, 1950. *Revue Medicale de Liège, 5,* 593–732.

Cowdry, E.V. (Ed.) (1942). *Problems of Aging. Biological and medical aspects* (2nd ed.). Baltimore, MD: Williams & Wilkins.

Thomae, H., & Maddox, G.L. (Eds.) (1982). *New perspectives on old age: A message to decision makers.* New York: Springer Publishing Co.

CHAPTER 8

The XIIIth Congress of the IAG: A Postscript

Bernice L. Neugarten

More than 3,000 persons from 52 countries attended the XIIIth International Congress of Gerontology in New York City in July, 1985. This, despite the unfavorable rate of currency exchange for persons coming from countries outside the United States and the fact that the single language of the Congress was English. Altogether there were some 2,000 individual presentations, organized into symposia, round tables, and sessions of submitted papers. The presentations covered the latest research in biological sciences, social sciences, clinical medicine, and social planning and practice in the delivery of services to older people. A large number of sessions were interdisciplinary in character, in keeping with the desire of the Program Committee of the IAG to increase communication across the disciplines that constitute the broad field of gerontology.

The Program Committee of the host countries—in this instance, United States and Canada—must, for obvious reasons, take the lead in organizing and scheduling the program. As Chairman of the North American Committee I had wide correspondence with gerontologists in many parts of the world. I draw upon this correspondence in commenting that as the IAG has grown in size and as the programs of successive congresses have become diversified both in form and content, a certain tension has become apparent with regard to appropriate program balance. Some would prefer congresses small in size and focused almost entirely on the reporting of research. Others would pay equal attention to research, to the translation of knowledge into practice, and to issues of social policy. Such differences of opinion may be inevitable as scientific and professional organizations increase in size. In my own view, such tensions are constructive and indicate a vitality that bodes well for the future of gerontology. The program of the XIIIth Congress reflected the second perspective; presentations covered a very wide range of issues. Across the diversity of topics, the presentations and discussions were for the most part at a high level of sophistication.

In pursuing the theme of the Congress, "Aging: The Universal Human Experience," the Program Committee gave special attention to the challenges facing the developing countries of the world. This was not the first time the IAG has given attention to those issues, as evidenced particularly in the congress in Hamburg in 1981. On the present occasion, a Special Program Planning Committee, chaired by Dr. Gary Andrews of Australia, and supported in part by the UN Trust Fund on Aging, created a special program for participants from developing countries. Sessions were devoted to the initiatives taken by the UN and the WHO, to demographic and epidemiological trends, to organizational and financial strategies in the delivery of health and social services, and to the roles of older people as contributors as well as beneficiaries of social and economic development. These sessions were well attended, with over 150 persons from 35 countries participating.

In these and other sessions of the Congress, it was recognized that just as the developing countries of the world can benefit from the knowledge about aging that has accumulated in the developed countries, so also the latter countries have much to learn from the former with regard to the enhancement of life for older people. Futhermore, first-world models for meeting the changing needs of an aging society may not be directly applicable to third-world countries. It is to be hoped that what we learn from each other can be translated for the benefit of all countries and for the benefit of all people, the old and the not-yet old.

The Program Committee undertook another organizational innovation by enabling a group of junior scholars in gerontology to attend the Congress. With the approval of the U.S. government agencies that provided travel funds (the National Institute on Aging, the Administration on Aging, and the National Institute of Mental Health), 40 predoctoral and postdoctoral students were selected. Each university in the U.S. that offers a graduate program in gerontology was asked to name its most promising students: in particular, its most promising foreign students. From that pool of nominees, members of the North American Committee selected a group who represented the wide range of disciplines in both biological and social sciences. Unfortunately, because of U.S. government rules regarding eligibility for travel funds, we were unable to include students residing in countries other than the U.S. The junior scholars wore special badges and were given other types of special attention. Their reports received during and after the Congress were enthusiastic. We hope similar arrangements can be made in future congresses to encourage the participation of students, and thus to help them adopt an international perspective in pursuing their studies in gerontology.

PART II
Biology and Biomedicine
A. Basic and Clinical Research

CHAPTER 9

Basic Biological Research in Aging: An Overview

Vincent J. Cristofalo
Leonard Hayflick

This overview of biogerontological research provides a brief summary of basic issues in research on the biology of aging and relates illustrative presentations of biological research at the 1985 Congress to those issues. Topics covered include molecular genetics, cellular mechanisms, immunology, endocrinology, neuroendocrinology, free radical mechanisms, altered pharmacological and neurotransmitter responsiveness, and nutritional deprivation.

Although biogerontological research probably had its beginnings among the alchemists of the middle ages, the modern era of research really can be considered to have begun some time in the late 1940s or perhaps the 1950s. For most of this period research dealt primarily with age-associated and age-correlated changes. It has been a period of description and phenomenology. However, in recent years the development of new techniques in the biological sciences has allowed gerontologists to ask questions that were not possible to ask before. Modern biogerontology deals now with why and how senescence works rather than merely with a description of what happens.

The XIIIth International Congress of Gerontology brought together scientists from throughout the world and provided a focus for these modern approaches and new technologies. The material presented deals, for the most part, with penetrating research on mechanisms at the molecular, cellular, and organismic level. We will describe the salient features of this work which focuses on molecular genetics;

cellular aspects of altered immune response; cellular mechanisms; neuroendocrinology; nutritional deprivation; altered endocrine neurotransmitter responsiveness.

MOLECULAR GENETICS

Background

The fundamental approach of genetics is to study biological functions through the analysis of variant and mutant organisms. The classical approach has evolved to studies at the cellular and molecular levels. Especially at the molecular level, advances during the last 10 years or so have been very rapid. The goal of this research is the clarification of the mechanisms regulating aging. One cannot address the question of molecular biology without including recent studies on cytogenetics and somatic cell genetics.

Somatic cell genetics have relied mainly on cell fusion techniques to study the mechanism of aging. Studies by a number of workers have shown that senescence is dominant in fusions between young and senescent diploid cells. Thus senescent cells are able to quench the ability of young cells to synthesize DNA in heterokaryons between young and old cells. In contrast, heterokaryons between senescent human diploid cells and HeLa cells which have an indefinite life span result in the dominance of the HeLa phenotype (i.e., DNA replication). However, when hybrids are formed between these two cell types, there is an initial phase of proliferation followed by a senescence phase. Thus senescence is dominant overall. Other studies suggest that senescence may be controlled by a factor that inhibits DNA synthesis.

Related to these studies is a controversial and as yet unresolved finding that the ability of cells to repair their DNA declines as they age. The ability does not seem to decline significantly although there may be a correlation between species longevity and DNA repair capacity. In any case, this area of research remains to be clarified. Similarly, reports of erroneously synthesized proteins have not been verified. Aberrant proteins in old cells and tissues are probably the result of posttranslational modifications. Other studies indicate that the fidelity of DNA polymerase-α remains constant over the replicative life span of cells in culture.

Current Research

Studies in recent years indicate that development and aging may involve similar molecular genetic mechanisms. Recent studies by Dawid (1985) have shown that in *Xenopus*, at the gastrula stage, most mRNAs are still derived from the egg. However, the need for new RNA synthesis implies that novel mRNAs are synthesized at this stage. A cDNA library of those new mRNA that are present in the gastrula but not in the egg has been prepared. Investigators have found that most of these new mRNAs are expressed for only a short time. These early mRNAs do not appear to require cell–cell interaction for their expression. This cell–cell interaction as a regulator of gene expression may occur at a later development stage. This approach to developmental control has obvious relevance to the study of "gene switching" as a basis for the process of senescence.

Courtois, Counis, Jeanny, Laurent, and Muel, et al. (1985) have used a similar approach to study crystallin expression in the lens. The process is under sequential activation/inactivation of crystallins by differential gene expression. These workers prepared cDNA to follow the process. They also found that the coordination of gene expression in the lens may be dependent on a specific growth factor found in the retina.

An approach to the mechanism of differential gene expression has been the study of methylation of the bases in DNA as "modifiers" of gene expression. Huang, Butcher, and Morgan (1985) have studied changes in methylation in tissues of mice at different ages. Livers of old mice appear to contain DNA that are less methylated than young mouse DNA.

CELLULAR ASPECTS OF ALTERED IMMUNE RESPONSE IN AGING

Background

One of the hallmarks of age changes is the decline in response by the immune system to the challenge of new antigens and an increase in reactions against self-antigens (autoimmunity). There is probably no other constellation of physiological decrements of aging that contributes more to increased vulnerability to death than do these losses. Thus, knowledge of this system commands the attention of many biogerontologists.

Probably the greatest age-related decline in the immune system occurs in thymus-dependent cellular immunity. A decline of comparable magnitude may also occur in immune surveillance. Both result in the appearance of aberrant cells in older individuals that contribute to greater susceptibility to microbial diseases and to cancer. The latter, contrary to prevailing opinion, does not increase linearly with age but, in humans, peaks at about age 60.

Humoral immunity, or the production of antibodies, also is impaired with age. Regulatory, or self-antibodies, which help to remove damaged cells from circulation and to transport molecules, decline in function. Autoantibodies, or those that are "mistakenly" directed toward ones' own normal cells, may result in one of several autoimmune diseases.

Many investigators in this field believe that the declining immune system is so central to the aging process that it may, in fact, be the root cause of most, if not all, age changes. Regardless of the truth of this belief, it is clear that the declining immune system is responsible for a substantial share of the infirmities associated with aging. A better understanding of this system will certainly contribute to treating the deficiencies that it produces and, perhaps, even restore normal function.

Immune system function apparently declines with age in all mammalian species that have been studied. The thymus begins to involute at puberty and immunity that is dependent on this organ declines with passing years to reach eventually a nadir of 5% to 25% of peak value. Some believe that diminution of the immune response, which more or less parallels thymus involution, may be one of the chronometers that determines the rate of aging.

Immune reactions that depend on thymic function include graft rejection, antibody production, ability to distinguish self from nonself antigens and, perhaps, the ability to recognize and destroy aberrant cancer cells or those infected with viruses. Studies in mice reveal that immune function correlates well with life span. In mice, maintenance of the integrity of the major histocompatibility gene complex, which is the major gene system that regulates T-cell immunity, correlates well with maximum life span.

B-cells, which are components of the immune system that produce antibodies essential for the maintenance of health, decrease both in quality and quantity with advancing age. Three important changes occur: (a) the number of functioning antibody cells decreases, (b) the ability of T-cells to be recruited to particular sites in the body declines, and (c) surface receptors change in conformation.

Age-related changes have also been found to occur in the relations that exist between T-cells and B-cells. Suppressor cells, which are a subset of T-cells, suppress that class of immune cells that reacts with foreign antigens. Others suppress B- and T-cells, which react against self-antigens. The former type suppressor cells increase with age and the latter immune cells decline. This increases the expression of autoimmune phenomena with consequent injury to several organ systems. With advancing age, antibodies are found to increase against DNA, thyroid, brain, gastric tissue, and other cells.

Dietary restriction, which significantly extends longevity, inhibits decline in the immune system and prevents autoantibody formation. Other means of "rejuvenating" the immune system have been found.

These include bone marrow and thymic grafts, thymic hormone administration, and T-cell stimulating chemicals.

All four major cell types involved in immune phenomena are the subject of considerable attention. These are stem cells, T-cells, B-cells, and macrophages. Qualitative changes appear to occur in all of these cells as their host ages. Changes occur in cyclic nucleotides; enzymes of the purine salvage pathway and DNA repair all show age-related alterations in mammalian lymphocytes. Age-related decrements in tolerance induction occur in both T-cells and B-cells. Immunoregulation also declines as does the behavior of natural killer cells.

The collection of genes known as the major histocompatibility complex regulates T-cell-dependent immunity and other aspects of aging as well. Some diseases associated with aging appear to be influenced by alleles at the major histocompatibility locus.

The interplay of decline in immune system function and similar decrements found to occur in the neuroendocrine system apparently conspire to produce pathology in the central nervous system. Brain reactive autoantibodies have been found. Hypothalamic lesions may also affect the immune system. Investigations are underway to determine the immune effects of neurotransmitters and the significance of receptors for hormones on lymphocytes.

In recent years cellular communication in the immune system mediated in particular by lymphokines and idiotype interactions as they impact on age changes has received much attention.

Current Research

Several aspects of these topics were addressed at the 1985 International Association of Gerontology Congress. Walford, for example, reported that the major histocompatibility complex influences a number of fundamental immune processes associated with aging. Many T-cell-mediated responses were found to respond to exogenous lymphokines such as interleukin-2 and thymosin (Doria, Adorini, and Frasca, 1985). Gene activation in senescent human lymphocytes was reported by Gamble, Schwab, and Wekster (1985) to occur and the beneficial effects of anti-idiotype antibodies were found to downregulate cross-reactivity toward self-antigens in aging. Also studied were the idiotypic repertoires expressed by systemic and mucosal immune cells of aged animals.

Most cellular immune responses that are age-associated, such as mixed lymphocyte reactions and cellular cytotoxicity, are regulated by the major histocompatibility complex. Antigen presentation may be a key factor in the decline of cellular cytotoxicity with age. The major histocompatibility complex in addition to its effect on immune function may influence free radical scavengers, DNA, and levels of mixed function oxidases. It may even represent the major genetic "umbrella" under which a number of the fundamental processes of aging are affected. Goidl and Martin (1985), and also Szewczuk (1985) discussed these issues.

CELLULAR MECHANISMS OF AGING

Background

The body of an organism is entirely made up of cells, most of which have specialized functions. The overall rationale of cell biogerontology is that the functional capacity of the organism is related to the functional capacity of the individual cells of that organism. It is virtually impossible to delineate a clear difference between cell biology and molecular biology. Much of the background discussion of molecular biology is also relevant here. In fact, much of molecular biological research is dependent on the techniques of cell biology.

In recent years techniques have been developed for the growth of various cell types in culture, including fibroblasts, keratinocytes, glial cells, lymphocytes, vascular endothelial cells, and smooth muscle cells. In many cases serum-free media are available for these cell types. The finite proliferative life span of these cells provides a model for cell senescence. Cell cultures prepared from the various tissues mentioned above undergo a period of vigorous proliferation followed by a period of declining proliferative activity during which the cells acquire characteristics reminiscent of senesecent cells, and finally, the cells lose the capacity for proliferation and eventually the culture dies. Salient observations are that the replicative life span of these cultures is directly related to the maximum life span of the donor species and inversely related to the age of the donor. Thus, aging in vivo is expressed in culture just as most other biological properties of cells. Whether the aging process in culture is a parallel of cell aging in the body still remains to be clarified. However, by any definition of aging these cells age. That is, they lose functional capacity (e.g., DNA synthesis), they accumulate aging pigment, and show a spectrum of morphologic and physiologic changes that are similar to changes in vivo. This may provide a useful model that can be studied under controlled environmental conditions. Over the last 15 or so years a number of workers have investigated whether the aging process in culture is related to replications or to calendar time. It seems clear now that aging is related to replications and independent of calendar time. One can extrapolate the significance of this observation to indicate that aging really proceeds based on a sequential set of various molecular events such as replications.

Current Research

Numerous growth factors and hormones have been identified that have highly specific effects on the various cell types and their rate of aging. These specific factors, along with viruses such as SV40, present powerful probes to understanding the mechanism of regulation of the aging process.

In recent reports, Bayreuther, Hommel, Kontermann, Mollenhauer, and Rodermann (1985) have presented detailed studies of the senescence of rat fibroblasts. They have identified a sequence of cell lineage changes: from stem cell to noncommitted progenitor cells to committed progenitor cell. The cells then proceed to the mutatic fibroblast, the postmutatic fibroblast, the terminally differentiated fibroblast, and finally, the degenerating fibroblast.

Smith and Pereira-Smith (1985) have extended the work mentioned previously on somatic cell hybrids between cells with finite and indefinite proliferative capacities. They have identified three complementation subgroups. By fusion of these subgroups they have obtained evidence that cellular immortality results from recessive changes in normal cell growth control and that at least three different classes of changes can result in immortalization.

In a more biochemical approach, Remacle, Houben, Somville, Mbemba, and Houbion (1985) have reexamined thermolabile enzymes. Thermolability is used as an index of "errors" in protein structure. They found that in all thermolabile enzymes studied the thermolability was associated with a change in the molecular association of the enzyme subunits. Thus the appearance of thermolabile protein species is not an indication of mis-synthesis.

Phillips, Brooks, and Cristofalo (1985) have studied the EGF receptor and its metabolism. They have found that receptor number does not change during aging. However, immunoprecipitated receptors from old cells have lost the ability to carry out tyrosine antiphosphorylation. Intact membranes, on the other hand, retain this ability suggesting that the loss in phosphorylating ability is a marker of a more subtle change in protein lability or tertiary structure.

Azzarone, Icard-Liepkalns, Gabbiani, and Macieira-Coelho (1985) have pointed out that senescence in vitro is characterized by cell enlargement, changes in cell adhesion, and reduced contractile ability. At the molecular level the action of senescent cells is less vulnerable to depolymerization. There was also an increase in the vimentin content of old cells.

Daniel, Silberstein, and Strickland (1985) reported research on mammary epithelial cells in vivo. These cells proliferate in mammary epithelial fat pads, but have a limited proliferative capacity analogous to fibroblasts and other cell types in vitro. When these senescent cells were treated with cholera toxin, a cyclic AMP stimulatory agent, there was a temporary reversal of the senescent phenotype. This finding and others also suggest that cell aging is not a general deterioration of the cell, but rather the result of a "switching system" change.

NEUROENDOCRINOLOGY OF MAMMALIAN AGING

Background

The neuroendocrine system, together with the immune system, probably represents the source of many of the decrements that contribute to age changes in mammals. The neuroendocrine system, for example, incurs decrements with age that result in the loss of visual and auditory acuity, impairment of homeostatic mechanisms, and loss of endocrine and autonomic functions. Circadian rhythmicity alters, thus changing both quantity and quality of sleep. Changes in memory storage and retrieval occur, as do alterations in peripheral and central nervous system function. Changes may be as subtle as a slowing of neuromuscular reflex time and mild tremor to such serious pathology as progressive dementia or cerebrovascular accidents.

Together, the central and peripheral nervous systems govern an animal's adjustment to its environment. In humans it makes possible knowledge of self and transmission of culture. Thus the aging nervous system is central to human and animal existence. Extreme examples of neurobiological pathology can be found in the memory and learning losses that are characteristic of senile dementia—a condition found in about half of patients admitted to nursing homes. Alzheimer's disease accounts for about 60% of all such cases while multi-infarct dementia constitutes 10% and a combination of both adds an additional 10%. The causes of Alzheimer's disease are unknown and no effective treatment is currently available. There is no animal model of the disease.

This common disorder interferes with the function of specific brain cells, producing intellectual disability or senile dementia in 15% of all humans over the age of 65. The 1¹/₂ million Americans affected incur medical costs of $20 billion annually. Alzheimer's disease may be the fourth most common cause of death in the United States. One family in three will have one of their parents succumb to the disease if they live long enough. There is some evidence for a genetic predisposition to the development of Alzheimer's disease but the responsible genes have eluded detection.

Two major goals of neurobiologists are to understand the biology of senile dementia of the Alzheimer's type and the normal decrements in mental capacity that might be associated with aging. A primary objective in Alzheimer's disease is to determine whether the pathognomonic lesions of neurofibrillary tangles and neuritic plagues are related and whether their induction is endogenous or exogenous.

Multidisciplinary longitudinal studies have begun to reveal a few aspects of the epidemiology, natural history, and putative genetic and environmental factors that make Alzheimer's disease the most common and devastating form of dementia. For example, a loss of choline acetyltransferase activity in the brains of dying Alzheimer's disease patients has been found. Increased amounts of specific trace elements, especially aluminum, also have been found. The chemistry of the bihelical filaments in affected neurons highlight some of the advancements. Large amounts of amyloid have been found to be present in the blood vessels of Alzheimer's patients. A prevailing problem is the difficulty that clinicians have in diagnosing the disease.

Depression, which is especially common in older humans, has received greater attention in recent years in view of the general belief that the condition has a biological basis. Several kinds of changes in neurotransmitter metabolism have been identified in depressed states.

Several studies have provoked interest in the possibility of a slow-virus etiology of Alzheimer's disease and, perhaps, other dementias. The evidence includes suggestive entities seen in neurons by electron microscopy, electron analysis of degenerating cells, and microchemical assays of enzymes that control neurotransmitter metabolism.

Our understanding of Parkinson's disease has benefitted substantially from the recent discovery that a by-product of the illegal synthesis of cocaine can produce the clinical manifestations of the disease. The chemical has the unique property of destroying the substantia nigra which, apparently, produces the symptoms of Parkinsonism.

One type of depression has been found to have a likely hereditary predisposition. The dexamethasone suppression test (DST) appears to serve well as a diagnostic test of the depressive state and the response of a pituitary stimulating hormone appears to be a useful marker for the condition. Several antidepressive drugs now under development may provide the clinician with a means of effective treatment.

One barrier to research in neuroendocrinology is the common misconception that pathological changes in the central nervous system and their manifestations as senile dementia, depression, or memory loss is a part of the normal aging process. Although progress in overcoming this barrier has been made, much more educating remains to be done.

Current Research

Several aspects of the neurobiology of mammalian aging were discussed at the 1985 International Association of Gerontology Congress. The regulation of neuroreceptors was given specific attention and it was found that D_1 dopaminergic sites in the striatum tended to increase with age whereas D_2 and serotonergic S_2 sites in the cortex decreased. It was concluded that decreases with age in D_2 and S_2 loci are general markers for neurochemical aging in mammals. Finch and Morgan (1985) hypothesized that the increase of D_1 sites with age in the human striatum reflects a super sensitivity-type response to loss of nigrostriatal input.

Based on the well-established association with advancing age of biochemical changes in neurotransmitter and neuropeptide systems of the basal ganglia, dendritic profiles of striatum neurons have been studied in the mouse. McNeill, Koek, Brown, and Haycock (1985) found that the total dendritic length of medium spiny neurons as well as the total number of dendritic segments remained unchanged with age. However, there is an age-related reduction in the linear density of dendritic spines on terminal segments of medium spiny neurons. Thus, the loss of dendritic spines of medium spiny neurons may provide a morphological basis for the reduction in dopaminergic postsynaptic binding sites in the striatum as well as for some of the motor deficits associated with old age. Aging has also been found by Trabbuch, Govoni, Battaini, and Pasinetti (1985) to be associated with an impaired ability of neurons to synthesize, store, and release neurotransmitters which may be correlated with a change in their ability to handle calcium ions.

Although the transplantation of brains is usually relegated to science fiction, the transplantation of small amounts of brain tissue into functioning animal brains has revealed exciting possibilities. Many investigators have reported the recovery of impaired brain function by transplantation to intact brains of selected neural tissue. For example, in aged female rats, the function of the gonads declines and ovaries begin to atrophy. Morphological changes in these organs were studied following transplantation of the medial basal hypothalamus from newborn rats. The tissue was transplanted into the third ventricle of the aged female rats. All of the grafts survived in the host brain for 3 weeks after transplantation. The ovaries of five out of the eight rats studied grew follicles of various sizes and a normal corpora lutea. The mean ovarian weight of experimental animals was significantly greater than that of controls. The results, Kobayashi, Matsumoto, Murakami, Arai, and Osanai (1985) suggest, indicate that brain grafts may restore ovarian function in aged females. Establishment of the functional connections between the grafts and the host brain was also examined.

AGING AND NUTRITIONAL DEPRIVATION

Background

One of the most reproducible findings in gerontology is the striking increase in the maximum and average life span of rats and mice reared under conditions of caloric restriction, usually 60% of ad libitum feeding. The mechanism for this effect is not understood. However, it is the only way known to extend the life span of homeotherms and, as such, may be the most powerful research probe available for understanding the mechanism of aging.

Current Research

Walford and Weindruch (1985) reported at the Congress that, under carefully controlled conditions, life span prolongation occurs whether restriction occurs at weaning or in adulthood. Caloric restriction in either case is accompanied by an overall decrease and shift in peak tumor incidence. Age changes in immune function are delayed. Changes in the lens proteins are delayed as well. These authors suggest that oxidative phosphorylation may be more efficient in restricted animals.

Everitt and Wyndham (1985) reported investigation of the possibility that food restriction may operate through the pituitary-endocrine system. Rats were divided into several groups including ad libitum fed, hypophysectomized-restricted, hypophysectomized nonrestricted, and control restricted. The rate of aging was monitored by following a series of biomarkers such as basement membrane thickening, creatinine clearance, and others. The authors found that for most of the parameters hypophysectomy had a greater antiaging effect than did food restriction.

Merry and Holehan (1985), also examined neuroendocrine aspects of dietary restrictions. Their experiments suggest that the effect of dietary restriction may be due to modification of hypothalamic–pituitary control of cyclicity of hormone release.

Olson (1985) reviewed his criticism of the extrapolation and application of the animal studies to man. He suggests that the differences between the experimental animals and man are so great as to make extrapolation unwarranted and perhaps misleading.

ALTERED ENDOCRINE STATUS

Background

Perhaps the hallmark of aging is reduced homeostatic capability. Thus the vulnerability of the individual to a changing environment increases with age. The endocrine system assumes a central role in the maintenance of homeostasis and has long been postulated as a key element in the declining ability to maintain homeostasis. Changes in endocrine function could be at the level of the target tissue responsivity or on the endocrine tissues themselves or both. There is a vast literature on endocrine aging.

Reports at the 1985 Congress addressed possible mechanisms for each of four diverse examples of age-associated change. In one report, Roth (1985a) showed that endocrine changes include changes at the receptor and postreceptor levels. Estrogen stimulation of various enzyme activities, energy and nucleic acid metabolism deteriorate in the senescent nucleus. Interestingly, receptors from senescent uteri are less efficient at binding to nuclei. This results in a decrease in RNA polymerase II and thus transcription.

In a second report Ito, Nakao, Morita, and Murota (1985) examined the migration of smooth muscle cells from the media to the intima of blood vessels in response to endothelial injury. One of the metabolites of arachidonic acid stimulates smooth muscle cell migration. Migration was higher in older rat vessels and may be related to calcium metabolic differences.

In a third approach Adelman (1985) examined glucose stimulated secretion of insulin. Both in vivo and in vitro secretion is impaired in older animals. The basis for the impairment appears to be increased heterogeneity of somatostatin and an increase in the species of this molecule which are inhibitory to insulin secretion.

In the fourth study Trabucchi and Govoni (1985) examined the age-related changes in endogenous opiates in various central and peripheral nervous tissues and reported a decrease of Met-enkephalin in some tissues and, in contrast, increase in both Met-enkephalin and β-endorphin in the pituitary of old rats. The authors noted that the specificity of the changes raises questions about the mechanisms regulating endogenous opiates.

THE ROLE OF FREE RADICAL MECHANISMS IN AGING

Background

It has been recognized for almost 100 years that for warm-blooded animals larger organisms have lower metabolic rates. This is related to the fact that surface-to-volume ratio changes. As animals get larger there is less surface/volume for heat dissipation. Survival requires a lower metabolic rate and thus a lower rate of heat production. It is also recognized that, in a general way, larger animals have longer maximal life spans. Various workers have theorized that there is some mechanistic relevance to the inverse relationship between metabolic rate and life span. One approach focuses on free radical damage as a mechanism of age-related changes because free radical production is related to metabolic rate.

Various studies have suggested that free radical mechanisms are implicated in the etiology of age-related disease (e.g., emphysema, cancer, arthritis, atherogenesis, and senile dementia of the Alzheimer type). Specific free radical-mediated processes could include peroxidation of lipids, DNA strand scission, and oxidative modification of key metabolic enzymes. A general observation has been that of a positive correlation between free radical damage and aging.

Current Research

Yagi reported at the 1985 Congress on studies of serum lipid peroxides in atherogenesis. He reported that lipid peroxides exert their effect through membrane damage as they migrate from the site of synthesis causing damage first to the blood vessel itself. Injected linoleic acid and hydroperoxide, for example, provoked endothelial cell injury in the thoracic aorta. Aggregated platelets adhered to the injury sites. Since serum lipid peroxide levels increase with age they are a likely candidate for the age-associated increase in atherogenesis.

Ames (1985) reported research on DNA damage and its relationship to aging and age-associated diseases. He points out that 80% of chemical carcinogens tested are mutagens. There are many sources of mutagens in the environment and many of these exert their effects by generating oxygen radicals. Antimutagens such as vitamins A, E, and C protect us from these environmental mutagens. Pryor (1985) has also made similar arguments using emphysema, cancer, and arthritis as examples.

Harman (1985), the originator and primary proponent of the free radical theory of aging, reported that lipofuscin pigment accumulates. in the central nervous system in parallel with oxidative enzyme activity. This is probably also true for neuromelanin, and these substances serve as measures of random free radical reactions. Harman also suggested that the excessive loss of cell function in senile dementia of the Alzheimer's type may produce a decreased capacity to inhibit random free radical reactions and to repair such damage. He also emphasizes the importance of dietary antioxidants in preventing these changes.

ALTERED PHARMACOLOGICAL AND NEUROTRANSMITTER RESPONSIVENESS WITH AGE

Background

Only within the last few years has significant attention been paid to the rational use of prescription drugs by the elderly. Attention has been focused on this question currently because of the realization that although most drugs are used by the elderly, clinical trials designed for drug licensing rarely include older patients. Reasons for current interest in this area also derive from several profound statistical considerations such as the following:

1. About 80% of people over the age of 65 suffer from at least one major disease and about 15% of those over 65 are disabled.

2. The rate of acute hospitalization for the elderly is three times greater than that of the general population and the duration of stay is twice as great.

3. About 85% of ambulatory and 95% of institutionalized elderly receive prescription medication. It has been estimated that about 25% may be unneeded or contraindicated.

4. Most elderly receive multiple drugs. Those with two major diagnoses average 11 different medications. Institutionalized patients receive between 5 and 12 prescription drugs.

5. Many of the drugs prescribed for older patients are potent and may lead to serious side effects.

6. Twenty-two percent of all prescriptions are written for the elderly and about 20% of the average older person's income is spent on drugs.

Once these facts became well known, it was apparent that the biomedical research community needed to give more attention to drug therapy for the elderly. The primary goal of studies in this field is to determine the effects of age on the patterns of drug response. All aspects of drug absorption, transport, metabolism, target organ sensitivity, and excretion now command attention. Special notice is being given to problems of adverse side effects of drugs and drug-to-drug interactions.

The increased vulnerability for adverse drug reactions among the elderly has not been fully explained. Several studies have suggested that elderly persons may have an increased sensitivity of cell receptors to the presence of foreign chemicals. Studies in which this phenomenon has been observed include central depressive drugs of the benzodiazepine type, anticoagulants, and β-adrenergic agonists and antagonists.

Improved methods have been developed for the quantification of drugs in body fluids. Age-related decline in kidneys has been shown to adversely affect the clearance rates of several important drugs. There is also evidence that drugs metabolized by oxidative transformation in the liver have reduced clearance in old age. There is also the suggestion that the effects of life-style influence drug metabolism. These include dietary habits, smoking, alcohol, and coffee consumption.

Current Research

Several current drug surveillance studies are yielding significant information on drug use by the elderly in several settings. Particular attention is being paid to isolating age as a research variable from confounding factors such as disease effects, nutritional deficiencies, psychosocial variables, and environmental influences. A search is underway for methods to validate the assumption that increased sensitivity of cell receptors to drugs occurs with age and this accounts for the increase in adverse drug reactions seen in older people.

At the 1985 International Association of Gerontology Congress, Castelden reported on measurements of central nervous system responses to drugs in older persons. An increased sensitivity to drugs acting on the central nervous system with aging was found to occur. This response is unexplainable on pharmacokinetic grounds. The elderly are more sensitive to benzodiazepines, such as diazepam, nitrazepam, flurazepam, and midazolam. Older patients with central nervous system disease due to neurotransmitter imbalance react differently to drugs than do controls.

Another study by O'Malley (1985) reported that α-adrenoceptors mediate several important biochemical and physiological functions. Although changes in responsiveness to drugs acting on α-adrenoceptors in vascular tissues has been demonstrated, there is no definitive evidence that these changes are specific to α-mediated constriction. Thus, unlike β-adrenoceptor effects, where there is a clear age-related decrease in responsiveness, the situation with α-receptors is less clear.

Other studies reported at the Congress focused on the fact that regulation of many physiological functions by hormones or neurotransmitters is altered during aging. The molecular changes responsible for impairment of these processes occur at the receptor and postreceptor levels. Two systems representative of these actions during aging are the α-adrenergic-stimulated parotid and dopamine-stimulated striatum of the rat. Roth (1985b) reported that dopaminergic-stimulated motor function, adenylate cyclase and regulation of neurotransmitter release also decreases with age. These functional losses appear to be partially based on loss of dopamine receptors, apparently as the result of a decreased biosynthetic rate in the aged corpus striatum. This decrement might be delayed by dietary restriction and reversed by prolactin administration.

Beta-receptor sensitivity is reduced, Wood (1985) reported, in both the vasculature and the heart in older subjects. Circulating leukocytes provide a readily accessible tissue for study of β-reception in man. The ability of isoproterenol to stimulate adenylate cyclase is reduced in lymphocytes in older patients. There appears to be no reduction in β-reception density in the elderly. It has been found that the proportion of receptors binding agonist with high affinity was decreased in the elderly who had higher catecholamine levels than young controls. This might explain the decreased β-responsiveness in the elderly.

There is considerable evidence that the autonomic nervous system control of cardiac function is altered with age and that this, together with failure of the effector organ to adjust to altered neural input, leads to the breakdown of homeostatic mechanisms regulating the heart.

Studies in rats reported by Goldberg, Kreider, and Roberts (1985) show that changes occur both prejunctionally and postjunctionally, which are consistent with this hypothesis. Adrenergic terminal axon degeneration increases in the aging heart. The cardiac content of norepinephrine decreases with age. Neuronal uptake of norepinephrine also increases with age since the capacity of cocaine to potentiate the cardiac effect of norepinephrine increases.

REFERENCES

Adelman, R.C. (1985, July). Regulation of insulin secretion by somatostatin. Abstracts of papers presented at the XIIIth International Congress of Gerontology (p. 33). New York.

Ames, B.N. (1985, July). Oxygen radicals and DNA damage as related to aging and cancer. Abstracts of papers presented at the XIIIth International Congress of Gerontology (p. 34). New York.

Azzarone, B., Icard-Liepkalns, C., Gabbiani, G. and Macieira-Coehlo, A. (1985, July). Relationship between functional changes and genome reorganization during cell senescence. Abstracts of papers presented at the XIIIth International Congress of Gerontology (p. 29). New York.

Bayreuther, K., Hommel, R., Kontermann, Mollenhauer, J. & Rodermann, H.P. (1985, July). Cellular aging of the fibroblasts is a terminal differentiation process. Abstracts of papers presented at the XIIIth International Congress of Gerontology (p. 28). New York.

Castleden, C.M. (1985, July). Changes in response to centrally acting drugs in elderly man. Abstracts of papers presented at the XIIIth International Congress of Gerontology (p. 35). New York.

Courtois, Y., Counis, M.F., Jeanny, J.C., Laurent, M., Meul, A.S., Simonneau, L., & Treton, J. (1985, July) Genomic integrity and crystallin expression as a function of development and aging in the lens. Abstracts of papers presented at the XIIIth International Congress of Gerontology (p. 25). New York.

Daniel, C.W., Silberstein, G.B., & Strickland, P. (1985, July). Reinitiation of growth and morphogenesi's in senescent mouse mammary epithelium. Abstracts of papers presented at the XIIIth International Congress of Gerontology (p. 29). New York.

Dawid, I.B. (1985, July). Gene expression in early embryonic development: An approach to biological aging. Abstracts of papers presented at the XIIIth International Congress of Gerontology (p. 25). New York.

Doria, G., Adorini, L., & Frasca, D. (1985, July). Reconstitution of T-cell functions in aged mice by immunoregulatory molecules. Abstracts of papers presented at the XIIIth International Congress of Gerontology (p. 26). New York.

Everitt, A.V., & Wyndham, J.R., (1985, July). Modulation of aging by food restriction: Physiological considerations. Abstracts of papers presented at the XIIIth

International Congress of Gerontology (p. 31). New York.

Finch, C., & Morgan, D. (1985, July). Dopaminergic and serotonergic receptor regulation during aging. Abstracts of papers presented at the XIIIth International Congress of Gerontology (p. 30). New York.

Gamble, D.A., Schwab, R., & Weksler, M.E. (1985, July). The kinetics of gene activation in senescent human lymphocytes. Abstracts of papers presented at the XIIIth International Congress of Gerontology (p. 26). New York.

Goidl, E.A., & Martin, S.J. (1985, July). Autoimmunity and the immune network in aging. Abstracts of papers presented at the XIIIth International Congress of Gerontology (p. 27). New York.

Goldberg, P.B., Kreider, M.S., & Roberts, J. (1985, July). Effects of age on the adrenergic cardiac neuroeffector junction. Abstracts of paper presented at the XIIIth International Congress of Gerontology (p. 36). New York.

Harmon, D. (1985, July). Free radical reactions in senile dementia of the Alzheimer's type. Abstracts of papers presented at the XIIIth International Congress of Gerontology (p. 35). New York.

Huang, R.C., Butcher, H., & Morgan, R. (1985, July). Undermethylation of mouse genes during development. Abstracts of papers presented at the XIIIth International Congress of Gerontology (p. 25). New York.

Ito, H., Nakao, J., Morita, I., & Murota, S. (1985, July). Age-related changes in biochemical action of arachidonic acid metabolites. Abstracts of papers presented at the XIIIth International Congress of Gerontology (p. 33). New York.

Kobayashi, S., Matsumoto, A., Murakami, S., Arai, Y., & Osanai, M. (1985, July). Transplantation of newborn neural tissue into aged rat brain: Effect on ovarian function. Abstracts of papers presented at the XIIIth International Congress of Gerontology (p. 30). New York.

McNeill, T. H., Koek, L. L., Brown, S. A., & Haycock, J. (1985, July). Aging and the basal ganglia. Abstracts of papers presented at the XIIIth International Congress of Gerontology (p. 30). New York.

Merry, B.J., & Holehan, A. M. (1985, July). Action of life-prolonging food restriction on the endocrine system and on protein biosynthesis. Abstracts of papers presented at the XIIIth International Congress of Gerontology (p. 31). New York.

Olson, R.E. (1985, July). Concerns in application of findings on rodents to the human situation. Abstracts of papers presented at the XIIIth International Congress of Gerontology (p. 32). New York.

O'Malley, K. (1985, July). Alpha-andrenoceptor function in aging man. Abstracts of papers presented at the XIIIth International Congress of Gerontology (p. 35). New York.

Phillips, P.D., Brooks, K.M., & Cristofalo, V.J. (1985, July). Growth factor responsiveness and receptor regulation in young and senescent WI-38 Cells. Abstracts of papers presented at the XIIIth International Congress of Gerontology (p. 29). New York.

Pryor, W.A. (1985, July). Free radicals and mammalian aging. Abstracts of papers presented at the XIIIth International Congress of Gerontology (p. 34). New York.

Remacle, J., Houben, A., Somville, M., Mbemba, F., Houbion, A., & Raes, M. (1985, July). Abstracts of papers presented at the XIIIth International Congress of Gerontology (p. 28). New York.

Roth, G.S. (1985, July). Aging and the mechanisms of hormone action. Abstracts of papers presented at the XIIIth International Congress of Gerontology (p. 32). New York.

Roth, G.S. (1985, July). Effect of aging on alpha-adrenergic and dopaminergic action. Abstracts of papers presented at the XIIIth International Congress of Gerontology (p. 35). New York.

Smith, J.R., & Pereira-Smith, O. (1985, July). Somatic cell genetic studies of in vitro aging. Abstracts of papers presented at the XIIIth International Congress of Gerontology (p. 28). New York.

Szewczuk, M.R. (1985, July). Aging and compartmentalization of the mucosal immune system. Abstracts of papers presented at the XIIIth International Congress of Gerontology (p. 27). New York.

Trabucchi, M., & Govoni, S. (1985, July). Regulation of endogenous opiate system during aging. Abstracts of papers presented at the XIIIth International Congress of Gerontology (p. 33). New York.

Trabucchi, M., Govoni, S., Battaini, F., & Pasinetti, G. (1985, July). Calcium channel regulation in the brain of aged rats. Abstracts of papers presented at the XIIIth International Congress of Gerontology (p. 30). New York.

Walford, R.L. (1985, July). Regulation of immune and nonimmune aging processes by the major histocompatibility complex. Abstracts of papers presented at the XIIIth International Congress of Gerontology (p. 26). New York.

Walford, R.L., & Weindruch, R. (1985, July). Life extension by food restriction: Disease and immune considerations. Abstracts of papers presented at the XIIIth International Congress of Gerontology (p. 31). New York.

Wood, A.J.J. (1985). Effects of aging on beta-receptors. Abstracts of papers presented at the XIIIth International Congress of Gerontology (p. 36). New York.

Yagi, K. (1985). Role of serum lipid peroxides in atherogenesis. Abstracts of papers presented at the XIIIth International Congress of Gerontology (pp. 33–34). New York.

SUGGESTED READINGS

Cristofalo, V.J. (Ed.). (1985). *Handbook of cell biology.* New York: CRC Press.

Finch, C. E., & Schneider, E. L. (Eds.) (1985). *Handbook of the biology of aging.* (2nd Ed.) New York: Van Nostrand Reinhold.

Gaitz, C., & Samorajski, R. (Eds.). (1985). *Aging 2000: Our health care destiny: Vol. 1. Biomedical issues.* New York: Springer-Verlag.

Jarvik, L.F., Greenblatt, D.J., & Harman, D. (Eds.). (1981). *Clinical pharmacology and the aging patient.* New York: Raven Press.

Lamy, P.P. (1980). *Prescribing for the elderly.* Littleton, MA: PSG Publishing.

Morin, R.J., & Bing, R.J. (Eds.). (1985). *Frontiers in medicine: Implications for the future.* New York: Human Sciences Press.

Platt, D. (Ed.). (1986) *Drugs and aging.* Berlin: Springer-Verlag.

Rothstein, M. (Ed.). (1985). *Review of biological research in aging,* (Vol. 2). New York: Alan R. Liss.

Shock, N.W. (Ed.). (1984). *Normal human aging: The Baltimore longitudinal study of aging.* Washington, D.C.: Department of Health and Human Services.

Walford, R.L., Weindruch, R.H., Gottesman, S.R.S., et al. (1981). The immuno-pathology of aging. In C. Eisdorfer, B. Stan, & V.J. Cristofalo (Eds.), *Annual review of gerontology and geriatrics.* New York: Springer Publishing Co.

CHAPTER 10

Neuropeptides and Neurotransmitters in Alzheimer's Disease

Scott T. Cain
Charles B. Nemeroff

In the past decade, much research has been focused on delineating the neurochemical and neuropathological alterations that are responsible for the clinical symptomatology of Alzheimer's disease. The degeneration of the cholinergic pathway from the basal forebrain to the neocortex has received considerable attention (for review, see Coyle, Price, & DeLong, 1983). Decreased activity of both the enzyme that synthesizes acetylcholine, choline acetyltransferase (CAT), and the enzyme that degrades acetylcholine, acetylcholinesterase (AChE), have been found in postmortem cortical tissue from Alzheimer's patients. There is, however, increasing evidence of destruction of a number of other neurotransmitter and neuropeptide systems in Alzheimer's disease. Included among these are possible degeneration of the noradrenergic and serotonergic pathways originating in the locus ceruleus and raphe nucleus, respectively. In addition, there is significant degeneration of neurons containing both somatostatin and corticotropin-releasing factors in Alzheimer's disease. Clearly, more work must be conducted before the neurochemical pathology of Alzheimer's disease is fully understood.

Supported by NIMH MH-40524, MH-39415, MH-40159, MH-15177-09 and NIA AG-05128. Charles B. Nemeroff is the recipient of a Nanaline H. Duke fellowship from Duke University Medical Center. We are grateful to Molly McMullen for preparation of the manuscript.

Senile dementia of the Alzheimer's type (SDAT) is a debilitating, irreversible disorder characterized by progressive mental impairment. The initial deficit is loss of memory for recent events, but eventually, the patient's cognitive dysfunction is so profound that even the ability for self-care is lost.

The primary histopathological trademarks of SDAT in the brain are neuronal (senile) plaques and neurofibrillary tangles (Terry & Katzman, 1983). These are primarily localized in the cortex and hippocampus and their presence correlates with the degree of cognitive disruption. In addition, a limited group of subcortical structures (e.g., hypothalamus, amygdala, striatum) contain neurofibrillary tangles (McDuff & Sumi, 1985). The involvement of these structures and the neural pathways emanating from them may underly certain of the observed clinical symptomatology.

Currently, there is no effective therapy to ameliorate the cognitive deterioration and personality changes characteristic of SDAT. The focus of this chapter is on the biochemical changes reported to occur in specific neurotransmitter and neuropeptide systems in SDAT. Other excellent reviews on the biochemical basis of Alzheimer's disease are available (DeKosky & Bass, 1985; Hardy, Adolfsson, Alafuzoff, Bucht, & Marcusson, et al., 1985). The goals of research in this area are twofold. Most immediately, specific pharmacological agents may be developed to alleviate some or all of the symptoms of SDAT and/or to retard the progression of the disease. This line of research also promises to provide insights into the etiology and pathogenesis of SDAT.

ACETYLCHOLINE

There is little question that in SDAT there is a degeneration of the cholinergic pathway which originates in the nucleus basalis of Meynert (NbM) and projects to the neocortex. The NbM is located in the substantia innominata of the basal forebrain (Rossor, Mountjoy, Roth, & Reynolds, 1985). Virtually every research group that has studied the NbM in SDAT has verified that there is a loss, primarily of the large cells which comprise the primary cholinergic innervation to the cortex (Rossor, Svendsen, Hunt, Mountjoy & Roth, et al., 1982; Whitehouse, Price, Clark, Coyle, & DeLong, 1981; Whitehouse, Hedreen, White, & Price, 1982). It has recently been suggested that rather than a loss of cholinergic cells, the large cells shrink in diameter as a result of retrograde degeneration following cerebrocortical damage (Pearson, Sofroniew, Cuello, Powell, & Eckenstein, et al., 1983). Of course, whether the initial damage is at the cortical or NbM levels, it is evident that the NbM-cortical pathway degenerates in SDAT.

In addition to the histological and histochemical studies described above, biochemical indices of cholinergic neuronal integrity in neocortex are consistent with a marked reduction of cholinergic neuronal integrity in SDAT. Until recently, because of technical considerations, it was difficult to measure acetylcholine (ACh) concentrations directly. Thus, the acetylcholine synthetic enzyme, choline acetyltransferase (CAT), and the acetylcholine-degrading enzyme acetylcholinesterase (AChE) have been used as markers of the integrity of cholinergic neurons. The former is known to be a more specific marker of cholinergic neurons. Choline acetyltransferase activity is markedly decreased in the cortex and hippocampus of postmortem SDAT tissue (Bowen, Smith, White, & Davison, 1976; Davies, 1979). There is a significant negative correlation between measures of cortical cholinergic integrity and measures of neuropathology (e.g., plaques, tangles) in SDAT (Mountjoy, Rossor, Iversen, & Roth, 1984). There is also a positive correlation between cholinergic deterioration and tests of mental ability in Alzheimer's disease (Perry, Tomlinson, Blessed, Bergman, & Gibson et al., 1978). In aged monkeys, CAT is present in the neurites of some senile plaques, indicating a cholinergic innervation of these plaques (Kitt, Price, Struble, Cork, & Wainer et al., 1984).

Acetylcholinesterase has been measured largely in cerebrospinal fluid (CSF) in the hope that it would prove to be a useful diagnostic tool. Although decreases in CSF acetylcholinesterase content have been observed in some studies (Soininen, Pitkanen, Halonen, & Riekkinen, 1984b; Tune, Gucker, Folstein, Oshida, & Coyle, 1985), the finding is by no means universal (Davies, 1979). Moreover, although the mean AChE activity in the SDAT group is significantly lower than in the controls, considerable overlap between the two groups occurs. The diagnostic utility of CSF acetylcholinesterase content is thus questionable. However, AChE activity is present in the senile plaques of aged primates, providing further evidence for a cholinergic involvement in the pathology of SDAT (Struble, Cork, Whitehouse, & Price, 1982; Struble, Hedreen, Cork, & Price, 1984a).

Attempts to demonstrate changes in the number or affinity of ACh receptors in SDAT have mostly been unsuccessful (e.g., Davies and Verth, 1978). Decreases in muscarinic binding in SDAT have been reported by Reisine, Yamamura, Bird, Spokes, and Enna (1978) and Rinne, Laakso, Mölsä, Paljärvi, and Portin, et al. (1985). The latter research group localized the decreased binding to the hippocampus, amygdala, and nucleus accumbens, but not to the frontal cortex or striatum. Recently, M_2, but not M_1, muscarinic receptors in cerebral cortex have been reported to be lost in SDAT (Mash, Flynn, & Potter, 1985). As the M_2 receptors are hypothesized to be presynaptically located, the accumulated findings have lent credence to the hypothesis that the primary degeneration is within the cholinergic neuron rather than in neurons postsynaptic to the ACh neuron. Consistent with this hypothesis are the findings that demonstrate a reduction in choline uptake in hippocampal and cortical synaptosomes prepared from post-mortem Alzheimer's tissue (Rylett, Boll, & Colhoun, 1983) and those that show a decrease in acetylcholine synthesis and release in temporal cortex biopsy tissue from patients with SDAT (Simms, Bowen, Allen, Smith & Neary et al., 1983).

Given the nature of the cholinergic deterioration in SDAT and the voluminous evidence supporting a role for ACh in a variety of learning and memory tasks (Davis & Roitblat, 1984; Squire & Davis, 1981), it is not surprising that much effort has been expended upon studying whether pharmacological stimulation of ACh neurotransmission would ameliorate the symptoms of SDAT. Two main strategies have been employed. In the first, ACh precursors such as choline chloride or lecithin are administered for a period of 2 to 8 weeks and then the patients are tested on various memory and cognitive tasks. With only a few exceptions, the results have proven disappointing, as little or no improvement has been seen (Bartus, Dean, Beer, & Lippa, 1982; Levy, Little, Chuaqui, & Reith, 1985; Sitaram, 1984). Aside from the question of whether these ACh precursors reliably increase ACh levels in brain, the negative findings are expected if there are only a small number of nondegenerated ACh neurons to metabolize the precursor.

The second major strategy to potentiate cholinergic neurotransmission is by administration of an AChE inhibitor such as physostigmine. Modest gains in performance in memory and cognition tests have been reported (Johns, Haroutunian, Greenwald, Mohs, Davis, et al., 1985; Mohs, Davis, Mathe, Rosen, Johns, et al., 1985). However, the optimal effective dose varies widely and the improvements are generally transient.

There are two findings from the literature reporting research on animals which bear further investigation in relation to SDAT. In aged rodents, the conduction velocity in the cholinergic pathway from the NbM to the cerebral cortex is significantly decreased (Aston-Jones, Rogers, Shaver, Dinan & Moss, 1985). Such a mechanism, along with the cholinergic neuron degeneration in SDAT, may jointly lead to the marked functional deficits. Also, in aged rodents, there is evidence for a decrease in sensitivity of the muscarinic receptor (Lippa, Loullis, Rotrosen, Cordasco, & Critchett et al., 1985). Combined with presynaptic cholinergic degeneration in SDAT, a decrease in receptor sensitivity could exacerbate the functional loss.

MONOAMINES

The majority of evidence supports a decrement in norepinephrine

(NE) function in Alzheimer's disease. This is primarily reflected in two sets of experimental findings. First, numerous reports have demonstrated that, in SDAT, cell loss is observed in the locus ceruleus, one of the major groups of NE perikarya in the central nervous system (Bondareff, Mountjoy, & Roth, 1981, 1982; Mann, Yates, & Marcyniuk, 1984). In addition, the magnitude of the locus ceruleus cell loss is greater in patients who develop Alzheimer's disease at a younger age, formerly referred to as presenile dementia. Second, NE concentrations are decreased in a variety of postmortem brain regions in SDAT (Adolfsson, Gottfries, Roos, & Winblad, 1979; Arai, Kosaka, & Iizuka, 1984a; Gottfries, Adolfsson, Aquilonius, Carlsson & Eckerman et al., 1983; Yates, Simpson, Gordon, Maloney, & Allison et al., 1983b). It is noteworthy, however, that although NE concentrations have been reported to be decreased in the cerebral cortex, the largest NE deficit is found in the hypothalamus. This is in contrast to the marked deficits in acetylcholine, somatostatin, and corticotropin-releasing factor (described elsewhere in this chapter) which occur primarily in neocortical and hippocampal areas. A significant correlation between clinical symptoms in SDAT and the reduction in hypothalamic NE has been reported. No consistent changes in adrenergic receptors (both a and β) have been found in Alzheimer's tissue (Cross, Crow, Johnson, Perry, & Perry, et al., 1984b). Unfortunately, the few attempts to evaluate adrenergic receptors have been restricted to hippocampal and cortical areas. In view of the reductions in hypothalamic NE in Alzheimer's disease, it will be of importance to determine if there are alterations of NE binding in this brain region. In one study, NE uptake was found to be reduced in temporal cortex biopsy tissue from patients with presumed SDAT (Benton, Bowen, Allen, Haan, & Davison et al., 1982). Using data obtained in preclinical research (both rodents and primates), some investigators have suggested that age-related cognitive dysfunction is related to degeneration of NE pathways (Arnsten, Goldman-Rakic, 1985; Zornetzer, 1984). Degeneration of NE neurons in patients with SDAT may, therefore, contribute to the cognitive dysfunction observed in this disorder.

The evidence for a dopaminergic involvement in SDAT is, at best, minimal. On the positive side, a number of research groups have found either reductions in dopamine (DA) or the DA metabolite, homovanillic acid (HVA), in Alzheimer's tissue. The most consistent reduction in DA has been found in the basal ganglia (caudate and putamen) (Arai et al., 1984a; Gottfries et al., 1983; Pearce, Palmer, Bowen, Wilcock, & Esiri et al., 1984; Sparks & Slevin, 1985). Concentrations of HVA have been found to be reduced most consistently in CSF (Bareggi, Franceshi, Bonini, Lecca, & Smirne, 1982; Palmer, Sims, Bowen, Neary, & Palo et al., 1984). However, a discordant note has been sounded in the case of both the DA and HVA reductions. In each instance, reports have appeared in which DA in the caudate (Yates et al., 1983b) or HVA in the CSF was unchanged in Alzheimer's (Kay, Milstein, Kaufman, Rapoport, & Culter, 1984). In contrast to ACh and NE, there is no evidence of cell loss in the midbrain regions of origin of the DA pathways in SDAT. One confounding variable in these studies is the reduction in DA concentration in the striatum that occurs in normal individuals as they age (Hornykiewicz, 1985). Due to the variable nature of the DA findings in SDAT, little effort has been expended upon study of DA receptors, though in one recent report Cross, Crow, Ferrier, Johnson, & Markakis (1984a) cited a significant reduction in D_2, but not D_1, DA receptors in the putamen of SDAT patients. This is in contrast to an earlier study which found reduced [^{3}H]-spiroperidol binding in caudate, but not putamen of patients with SDAT (Reisine et al.,1978). There is insufficient data on epinephrine-containing neurons in SDAT to draw any conclusions about their integrity in this disease at the present time.

Similar to the NE and ACh pathways, there is evidence for Alzheimer's disease-associated degeneration of serotonergic (5HT) systems. Both serotonergic cell loss (Yamamoto & Hirano, 1985) and the presence of neurofibrillary tangles (Ishii, 1966; Yamamoto & Hirano, 1985) have been found in the nucleus raphe dorsalis in SDAT. Not surprisingly, reductions in the concentrations of both 5-HT and its primary metabolite 5-hydroxyindoleacetic acid (5-HIAA) have also been observed. Serotonin concentrations are reduced in the hippocampus, hypothalamus, cingulate cortex and caudate (Gottfries et al., 1983; Winblad, Adolfsson, Carlsson, & Gottfries, 1982). Reductions in the concentration of 5-HIAA have been reported in the CSF of SDAT patients (Palmer et al., 1984), as well as in the aforementioned brain regions (Arai et al., 1984a; Cross, Crow, Johnson, Joseph, & Perry et al., 1983); although Volicer, Direnfeld, Freedman, Albert, and Langlais et al. (1985) found no decrease in cerebrospinal 5-HIAA in SDAT patients. Uptake of 5-HT is reduced in SDAT in temporal cortex biopsy tissue (Benton et al., 1982). Radiolabeled imipramine binding, which is believed to be intimately associated with 5-HT uptake sites, is also reduced in temporal cortex (Bowen, Allen, Benton, Goodhardt, & Haan et al., 1983). The number of both S_1 and S_2 5-HT receptors is decreased in SDAT, at least in both hippocampal and cortical tissue (Cross et al., 1984b; Reynolds, Arnold, Rossor, Iversen, & Mountjoy et al., 1984).

NEUROPEPTIDES

In conjunction with the rapid expansion of research concerning identification of novel neuropeptides, much interest has focused on the potential disruption of peptidergic pathways in neuropsychiatric disorders. The predominant research strategy has been to measure the concentration of specific peptides in either postmortem tissue samples or CSF using radioimmunoassay procedures.

Although a variety of peptides have been assayed in postmortem samples from Alzheimer's patients, consistent alterations in only two peptides (somatostatin and corticotropin-releasing factor) have been found. The most widely replicated finding is a reduction in the concentration of somatostatin (or somatotropin-releasing inhibiting factor, SRIF) in several cerebral cortical areas and hippocampus.

In a series of pioneering studies, Davies and colleagues (Davies, Katzman, & Terry, 1980; Davies & Terry, 1981) found markedly decreased SRIF concentrations in the hippocampus, midfrontal cortex, inferior parietal cortex, occipital cortex, superior temporal gyrus, midtemporal gyrus and inferior temporal gyrus. Ferrier, Cross, Johnson, Roberts, & Crow et al. (1983) also observed a reduction in SRIF concentration in frontal, temporal and parietal cortex as well as in the septum of Alzheimer's patients. However, no decrease in hippocampal SRIF was found. Both our group (Nemeroff, Bissette, Busby, Youngblood, & Rossor et al., 1983), and Rossor and his colleages (Rossor, Emson, Mountjoy, Roth & Iversen, 1980) have observed reduced SRIF concentrations in postmortem brain samples from patients with Alzheimer's disease, though the reductions were somewhat more limited than those reported previously. We found SRIF reductions in frontal cortex, temporal cortex, and hypothalamus but not in parietal cortex, amygdala, caudate nucleus, nucleus accumbens, or posterior hippocampus. In the studies by Rossor and colleagues, decreased concentrations of SRIF were measured only in temporal cortex. Arai, Moroji, & Kosaka (1984b) reported that the concentration of SRIF was reduced in the hippocampus, orbital cortex, and putamen. In most studies, Alzheimer's-related reductions in SRIF concentration have not been found in subcortical structures. Both Davies' group and Rossor's group have noted that the reductions in SRIF concentrations are most prominent in patients with early onset of the disease. Preliminary results have also indicated that a number of the layer III and V frontal cortical SRIF cells are shrunken in size in Alzheimer's tissue (Joynt & McNeil, 1984). In addition, SRIF immunoreactivity has been observed in both the neuritic plaques of primates (Struble, Kitt, Walker, Cork & Price, 1984b) as well as in the 30% to 50% of cortical plaques in postmortem brain tissue from Alzheimer's disease patients (Armstrong, LeRoy, Shields & Terry, 1985; Morrison, Rogers, Scherr, Benoit, & Bloom, 1985). Finally, it is interesting that SRIF receptor binding has been reported to be diminished in SDAT, in spite of the reduction in SRIF itself—evidence of lack of receptor upregulation (Beal, Mazurek, Tran, Chattha, & Bird et al., 1985).

The CSF studies are largely consistent with the postmortem studies in that SRIF concentrations are reduced in the CSF of SDAT patients (Bissette, Walléus, Widerlöv, Karlsson, & Eklund et al., 1984; Serby, Richardson, Twente, Siekiersski, & Corwin et al., 1984; Soininen, Jolkkonen, Reinikainen, Halonen, & Riekkinen, 1984a). In addition, in a recent preliminary study in collaboration with Widerlöv and his colleagues, we found that intensive environmental (psychosocial) stimulation of Alzheimer's disease patients results in an increase in CSF concentrations of SRIF (Karlsson, Widerlöv, Malin, Nyth, & Brine et al., 1985). The use of the diminution of cerebrospinal SRIF as a diagnostic marker for SDAT is of questionable value due to the non-specificity of reductions in cerebrospinal SRIF. The peptide is also diminished in major depression, Parkinson's disease with dementia, and multiple sclerosis (Bissette et al., 1984; Serby et al., 1984; Sorensen, Hammer, Vorstrup, & Gjerris, 1983). Beta-endorphin and ACTH have also been reported to be reduced in the CSF of Alzheimer's patients (Kaiya, Tanaka, Takeuchi, Morita & Adachi et al., 1983), while both increases (Tsuji, Takahashi, & Akatawa, 1981) and decreases (Sorensen et al., 1983) in the CSF concentration of arginine-vasopressin have been found.

Our group has recently discovered that corticotropin-releasing factor (CRF) concentrations in the frontal cortex (Brodmann's area 10) and temporal cortex (Brodmann's area 38) are reduced by 50% in SDAT; a 70% decrease in the CRF concentration was observed in the caudate nucleus of Alzheimer's patients as well (Bissette, Reynolds, Kitts, Widerlöv, & Nemeroff, 1985). These findings have now been confirmed and extended by DeSouza, Whitehouse, Kuhar, Price, & Vale (1986); they have not only shown a reduction in CRF concentrations in SDAT, but also have shown a marked increase in the number of CRF receptors.

The majority of remaining studies that have evaluated the integrity of peptide-containing neurons in Alzheimer's disease have proved negative. Neuropeptides that have been studied in some detail are: thyrotropin-releasing hormone (TRH) (Biggins, Perry, McDermott, Smith, & Berry, 1983; Nemeroff et al., 1983; Yates, Harmar, Rosie, Sherward, & Sanchez de Levy et al., 1983a), vasoactive-intestinal peptide (VIP), cholecystokinin (CCK), substance P, and neurotensin (NT). Arai et al. (1984b) reported that VIP concentrations were reduced in insular and cingular cortices in Alzheimer's. A number of others, however, have been unable to replicate this finding (Ferrier et al., 1983; Rossor, Emson, Iversen, Mountjoy, & Roth et al., 1984). Contradictory findings have also been obtained with substance P. One group found a slight decrease in cortical substance P (Crystal & Davies, 1982), but this has not been verified (Ferrier et al., 1983). Cortical CCK (Ferrier et al., 1983; Sanders, Zahedi-Asi, & Marr, 1982) and NT (Nemeroff et al., 1983; Rossor et al., 1984) are consistently unchanged in Alzheimer's disease. We did, however, observe a 30% decrease in the NT concentration in the amygdala of Alzheimer's disease patients. Recent reports indicate that enkephalin and VIP-immunoreactive hippocampal pyramidal cells contain neurofibrillary tangles in both Alzheimer's disease tissue and aged brain (Kulmala, 1985), and that neuropeptide Y-like immunoreactivity is present in 10% to 20% of hippocampal neuritic plaques from SDAT tissue (Dawbarn & Emson, 1985).

In summary, it must be noted that study of neuropeptides in Alzheimer's disease is still in a formative stage. It is not surprising that the anatomical loci where SRIF has been found to be depleted vary slightly across laboratories. Given the variability in patient populations and the clinical course of the disease, it is, in fact, quite remarkable that such consistent and selective reductions in SRIF have been found in frontal and temporal cortices. Clearly, much work remains to be done to determine if any relationship exists between the SRIF deficits and the clinical symptoms of SDAT. Recently, in collaboration with Walsh (Walsh, Emerich, Winokur, Banki, & Bissette et al., 1985), we have shown that depletion of SRIF induced by cysteamine is associated with deficits in passive avoidance learning. To date, the few studies that have attempted neuropeptide replacement therapy for Alzheimer's disease have been disappointing. An SRIF analog (Cutler, Haxby, Narano, May, & Burg, 1985), ACTH fragment (Ferris, 1983), vasopressin (Ferris, 1983; Tinklenburg, Pigache, Pfefferbaum, & Berger, 1982), and the opiate receptor blocker naltrexone (Hyman, Eslinger, & Damasio, 1985), have been tried with equally unspectacular results. Problems of limited entry of neuropeptides into brain after parenteral administration and rapid degradation in vivo must be overcome.

AMINO ACIDS

Although Alzheimer's disease-associated changes in concentration or receptor binding of the putative amino acid neurotransmitters, γ-aminobutyric acid (GABA) and glutamic acid, are not particularly striking, a few differences from control samples have been reported.

Reductions in GABA concentrations in the CSF of SDAT patients have been documented (Zimmer, Teelken, Trieling, Weber, & Weihmayer et al., 1984). Cortical concentrations of GABA (Mountjoy et al., 1984) and activity of the GABA synthesizing enzyme, glutamic acid decarboxylase (GAD) (Perry et al., 1978), have been reported to be reduced slightly in Alzheimer's disease. These deficits, however, do not correlate well with estimates of neuron counts, senile plaques, or neurofibrillary tangles. In addition, others have been able to find no change in the cortical GABA concentration in SDAT (Perry, Atack, Hardy, Dodd, & Edwardson et al., 1984). With the exception of Reisine et al. (1978), who found decreased GABA binding in the frontal cortex and caudate nucleus, no changes in GABA receptor binding have been reported in Alzheimer's disease brain tissue.

Pearce et al. (1984) reported that (^{3}H)-glutamate binding is increased in the caudate nucleus of SDAT patients. However, Greenamyre, Penney, Young, D'Amato, & Hicks, et al. (1985) could find no such alterations in glutamate binding in the caudate, putamen, or nucleus basalis of Meynert in SDAT but did, however, observe a decrease in cortical glutamate binding. These studies must be replicated and the discrepancies resolved before their significance can be evaluated.

In a recent study utilizing cortical biopsy tissue, by Bowen and his co-workers (Smith, Bowen, Sims, Neury, & Davison, 1983), neither GABA nor glutamate release was different in Alzheimer's disease tissue compared with controls.

BRAIN METABOLISM

Positron emission tomography (PET) has been used to evaluate glucose utilization in the brains of patients suffering from Alzheimer's disease. The rationale for this type of study is that glucose utilization can be used as a marker for quantifying synaptic activity within particular brain regions, and by extension, perhaps identifying deficits of specific neurotransmitter systems. As PET scans can be obtained at various stages throughout the course of the disease, it has been suggested that they may ultimately be used both as a diagnostic tool and for demonstrating the physiological progression of the disease. The ability to observe in vivo changes in brain metabolism obviates the many problems associated with examination of postmortem tissue from patients in the advanced stages of Alzheimer's disease.

To date, studies of glucose utilization in SDAT patients have found a decrease which averages approximately 30% (Chase, Foster, Fedio, Brooks, & Mansi et al., 1984; Foster, Chase, Mansi, Brooks, & Fedio et al., 1984; Friedland, Budinger, Koss, & Ober, 1985). This impairment is localized in the parietal and temporal cortices, and is positively correlated with decline in intellectual function. The focal nature of these hypometabolic changes is somewhat in contrast to the diffuse reductions in neocortical cholinergic markers found in postmortem tissue. Consistent with the decrease in other glucose utilization and cholinergic metabolism are the reports of attenuated activity of the integral metabolic enzyme pyruvate dehydrogenase (PDH) in the parietal, temporal and frontal cortices of Alzheimer's disease patients (Perry, Perry, Tomlinson, Blessed, & Gibson, 1980; Sorbi, Bird, & Blass, 1983). It has been speculated that there is a nonmitochondrial subpopulation of PDH in cholinergic neurons that mediates the synthesis of acetyl CoA or acetylcholine synthesis (LeFresne, Beaujovan, & Glowinski, 1978). Interestingly, the enzymatic activity of brain PDH is altered by aversive training in rodents (Morgan & Routtenberg, 1981). The activities of a number of other glycolytic enzymes are also reduced in the temporal lobe of Alzheimer's patients (Meier-Ruje, Iwangoff, & Reichlmeier, 1984).

CONCLUSIONS

In this review, the major changes in neurotransmitter/neuropeptide systems that have been found in tissue and CSF samples from patients with SDAT have been described. The weight of the accumulated evidence is in favor of Alzheimer's disease-related neuronal degeneration in multiple neurotransmitter and neuropeptide systems. The most clearly characterized and most consistently found changes are those of the cholinergic and somatotropin-releasing inhibitory factor (SRIF) systems. In both cases, the anatomical, cortical, and hippocampal localization of the deficits correspond quite well with the presence of neuronal plaques. Less well-defined, but still fairly consistent deficits are found in specific noradrenergic and serotonergic pathways. These have, in common with the cholinergic deficits, neuronal loss in the brain areas containing the cell bodies of origin for each compound: nucleus basilis of Meynert for ACh, locus ceruleus for NE, and nucleus raphe dorsalis for 5-HT. An intriguing recent development is the marked deficit of CRF in SDAT. This particular finding is extremely exciting because of the apparent compensatory increase in CRF receptors, which appears to be contrasted with the absence of such change in receptors for SRIF, ACh, and NE. It will be worthwhile to pursue this finding in greater detail. An integral part of the Joseph and Kathleen Bryan Alzheimer Disease Research Center at Duke University is the rapid autopsy studies—studies of Alzheimer's disease brain tissue and controls obtained 30 min after death, which allow for dynamic studies of neurotransmitter function (e.g., choline uptake).

Research into the clinical relevance of these neurotransmitter deficits has clearly been hampered by the lack of a suitable animal model. Researchers have been limited to cataloging biochemical changes guided largely by studying neurotransmitters known to be present in brain areas altered in the disease process. Recently, attempts have been made to simulate the cholinergic losses by purportedly selective lesions of the NbM in rodents (de Belleroche, Gardiner, & Hamilton, 1985), analogous to simulating Parkinson's disease by a 6-hydroxydopamine-induced lesion of the nigrostriatal DA pathway. Unfortunately, this strategy is not likely to be as productive in studying SDAT, because in this disorder there is more generalized neuronal degradation, and because these lesioning methods destroy cells other than cholinergic neurons, rendering the model's validity questionable. Moreover, it would be quite surprising if the cholinergic, somatostatinergic and noradrenergic lesions are not all involved in the cognitive and memory deficits which characterize SDAT. As noted earlier, the reliance on postmortem tissue is also limiting. By definition, the postmortem findings are almost exclusively limited to the advanced forms of the disease, and are confounded by the accompanying factors such as drug treatment, diet, or agonal factors. Ultimately, the etiologic and pathogenetic importance of the reported neurotransmitter and neuropeptide changes must be validated by their diagnostic and therapeutic utility. Examples of this might include CSF concentration changes of a particular transmitter or metabolite as a predictive indicator, or clinical improvement by manipulation of one or more neurotransmitter systems. In the past decade, much progress has been made. The use of modern techniques derived from molecular biology and molecular genetics will undoubtedly result in diagnostic and treatment breakthroughs.

REFERENCES

Adolfsson, R., Gottfries, C.G., Roos, B.E., & Winblad, B. (1979). Changes in brain catecholamines in patients with dementia of Alzheimer type. *British Journal of Psychiatry, 135,* 216–223.

Arai, H., Kosaka, K., & Iizuka, R. (1984a) Changes of biogenic amines and their metabolites in postmortem brains from patients with Alzheimer-type dementia. *Journal of Neurochemistry, 43,* 388–393.

Arai, H., Moroji, T., & Kosaka, K. (1984b) Somatostatin and vasoactive intestinal polypeptide in post-mortem brains from patients with Alzheimer-type dementia. *Neuroscience Letter, 52,* 73–78.

Armstrong, D.M., LeRoy, S., Shields, D., & Terry, R.D. (1985). Somatostatin-like immunoreactivity within neuritic plaques. *Brain Research, 338,* 71–79.

Arnsten, A.F.T., & Goldman-Rakic, P.S. (1985). α_2-Adrenergic mechanisms in prefrontal cortex associated with cognitive decline in aged nonhuman primates. *Science, 230,* 1273–1276.

Aston-Jones, G., Rogers, J., Shaver, R.D., Dinan, T.G., & Moss, D.E. (1985). Age-impaired impulse flow from nucleus basalis to cortex. *Nature, 318,* 462–464.

Bareggi, S., Franceshi, M., Bonini, L., Lecca, K., & Smirne, S. (1982). Decreased CSF concentration of homovanillic acid and GABA in Alzheimer's disease. *Archives of Neurology, 39,* 709–712.

Bartus, R.T., Dean, R.L., III, Beer, B., & Lippa, A.S. (1982). The cholinergic hypothesis of geriatric memory dysfunction. *Science, 217,* 408–417.

Beal, M.F., Mazurek, M.F., Tran, V.T., Chattha, G., Bird, E.D., & Martin, J.B. (1985). Reduced numbers of somatostatin receptors in the cerebral cortex in Alzheimer's disease. *Science, 229,* 289–291.

Benton, J.S., Bowen, D.M., Allen, S.J., Haan, E.A., Davison, A.N., Neary, D., Murphy, R.P., & Snowden, J.S. (1982). Alzheimer's disease as a disorder of the isodendritic core. *Lancet, i,* 456.

Biggins, J., Perry, E.K., McDermott, J.R., Smith, I.A., Berry, R.H., & Edwardson, J.A (1983). Post-mortem levels of thyrotropin-releasing hormone and neurotensin in the amygdala in Alzheimer's disease, schizophrenia and depression. *Journal for Neurological Sciences, 58,* 117–122.

Bissette, G., Reynolds, G.P., Kilts, C.D., Widerlöv, E., & Nemeroff, C.B. (1985). Corticotropin-releasing factor-like immunoreactivity in senile dementia of the Alzheimer type. *Journal of American Medical Association, 254,* 3067–3069.

Bissette, G., Walléus, A., Widerlöv, E., Karlsson, I., Eklund, K., Loosen, P.T. & Nemeroff, C.B. (1984). Reductions of cerebrospinal fluid concentrations of somatostatin-like immunoreactivity in dementia, major depression and schizophrenics. *Society of Neuroscience Abstracts, 10,* 1093.

Bondareff, W., Mountjoy, C.Q., & Roth, M. (1981). Selective loss of neurones of origin of adrenergic projections to cerebral cortex (nucleus locus coeruleus) in senile dementia. *Lancet, i,* 783–784.

Bondareff, W., Mountjoy, C.Q., & Roth, M. (1982). Loss of neurons of origin of adrenergic projection to cerebral cortex (nucleus locus coeruleus) in senile dementia. *Neurology, 32,* 164–168.

Bowen, D.M., Allen, S.J., Benton, .S., Goodhardt, M.J., Haan, E.A., Palmer, A.N., Sims, N.R., Smith, C.C.T., Spillane, J.A., Esiri, M.M., Neary, D., Snowdon, J.S., Wilcock, C.J., & Davison, A.N. (1983). Biochemical assessment of serotonergic and cholinergic dysfunction and cerebral atrophy in Alzheimer's disease. *Journal of Neurochemistry, 41,* 266–272.

Bowen, D.M., Smith, C.B., White,P., & Davison, A.N. (1976). Neurotransmitter-related enzymes and indices of hypoxia in senile dementia and other abiotrophies. *Brain, 99,* 459–496.

Chase, T.N., Foster, N.L., Fedio, P., Brooks, R., Mansi, L., & DiChiro, G. (1984). Regional cortical dysfunction in Alzheimer's disease as determined by positron emission tomography. *Annals of Neurology, 15* (suppl.), S170–S174.

Coyle, J.T., Price, D.L., & DeLong, M.R. (1983). Alzheimer's disease: A disorder of cortical cholinergic innervation. *Science, 219,* 1184–1190.

Cross, A.J., Crow, T.J.,Ferrier, I.N., Johnson, J.A., & Markakis, D. (1984a). Striatal dopamine receptors in Alzheimer-type dementia. *Neuroscience Letter, 52,* 1–6.

Cross, A.J., Crow, T.J., Johnson, J.A., Joseph, M.H., Perry, E.K., Perry, R.H., Blessed, G., & Tomlinson, B.E. (1983). Monoamine metabolism in senile dementia of Alzheimer type. *Journal of Neurological Sciences, 60,* 383–392.

Cross, A.J., Crow, T. J., Johnson, J.A., Perry, E.K., Perry, R.H., Blessed, G., & Tomlinson, B.E. (1984b). Studies on neurotransmitter receptor systems in neocortex and hippocampus in senile dementia of the Alzheimer type. *Journal of the Neurological Sciences, 64,* 109–117.

Crystal, H.A., & Davies, P. (1982). Cortical substance P-like immunoreactivity in cases of Alzheimer's disease and senile dementia of the Alzheimer type. *Jounal of Neurochemistry, 38,* 1781–1784.

Cutler, N.R., Haxby, J.V., Narano, P.K., May, C., & Burg, C. (1985). Evaluation of an analogue of somatostatin (L363,586) in Alzheimer's disease. *New England Journal of Medicine, 312,* 725.

Davies, P. (1979). Neurotransmitter-related enzymes in senile dementia of the Alzheimer type. *Brain Research, 171,* 319–327.

Davies, P., Katzman, R., & Terry, R.D. (1980). Reduced somatostatin-like immuno-reactivity in cerebral cortex from cases of Alzheimer's disease and Alzheimer senile dementia. *Nature, 288,* 279–280.

Davies, P., & Terry, R.D. (1981). Cortical somatostatin-like immunoreactivity in cases of Alzheimer's disease and senile dementia of the Alzheimer type. *Neurobiology of Aging, 2,* 9–14.

Davies, P., & Verth, A.H. (1978). Regional distribution of muscarinic acetylcholine receptors in normal and Alzheimer type dementia brains. *Brain Research, 138,* 385–392.

Davis, H.P., & Roitblat, H.L. (1984). Cholinergic pharmacology, behavior, and age-related memory decline. In L.R. Squire & N. Butters (Eds.), *Neuropsychology of memory.* New York: The Guilford Press.

Dawbarn, D., & Emson, P.C. (1985). Neuropeptide Y-like immunoreactivity in neuritic plaques of Alzheimer's disease. *Biochemical and Biophysical Research Communications, 126,* 289–294.

de Belleroche, T., Gardiner, I.M., & Hamilton, M. (1985). Biochemical changes following lesion of the substantia innominata of the rat: a model for Alzheimer's disease. *Interdisciplinary Topics in Gerontology, 19,* 213–221.

DeKosky, S.T., & Bass, N.H. (1985). Biochemistry of senile dementia. In A. Lajtha (Ed.), *Handbook of neurochemistry, Vol. 10.* New York: Plenum Press.

DeSouza, E.B., Whitehouse, P.J., Kuhar, M.J., Price,D.L. & Vale, W.W. (1986). Reciprocal changes in corticotropin-releasing factor (CRF)-like immunoreactivity and CRF receptors in cerebral cortex of Alzheimer's disease. *Nature, 319,* 593–595.

Ferrier, I.N., Cross, A.J., Johnson, J.A., Roberts, G.W., Crow, T.J., Corsellis, J.A.N., Lee, Y.C., O'Shaughnessy, D., Adrian, T.E., McGregor, G.P., Baracese-Hamilton, A.J. & Bloom, J.R. (1983). Neuropeptides in Alzheimer's type dementia. *Journal of Neurological Sciences, 62,* 159–170.

Ferris, S.H. (1983). Neuropeptides in the treatment of Alzheimer's disease. In B. Reisberg (Ed.), *Alzheimer's disease: The standard reference.* New York: Macmillan.

Foster, N.L., Chase, T.N., Mansi, L., Brooks, R., Fedio, P., Patronas, N.J. & DiChiro, G. (1984). Cortical abnormalities in Alzheimer's disease. *Annals of Neurology, 16,* 649–654.

Friedland, R.P., Budinger, T.F., Koss, E. & Ober, B.A. (1985). Alzheimer's disease: Anterior-posterior and lateral hemispheric alterations in cortical glucose utilization. *Neuroscience Letter, 53,* 235–240.

Gottfries, C-G., Adolfsson, R., Aquilonius, S-M., Carlsson, A., Eckernas, S-A., Nordberg, A., Oreland, L., Svennerholm, L., Wiberg, A. & Winblad, B. (1983). Biochemical changes in dementia disorders of Alzheimer type (AD/SDAT). *Neurobiology of Aging, 4,* 261–271.

Greenamyre, J.T., Penney, J.B., Young, A.B., D'Amato, C.J., Hicks, S.P. & Shoulson, I. (1985). Alterations in L-glutamate binding in Alzheimer's and Huntington's diseases. *Science, 227,* 1496–1498.

Hardy, J., Adolfsson, R., Alafuzoff, I., Bucht, G., Marcusson, J., Nyberg, P., Perdahl, E., Wester, P. & Winblad, B. (1985). Transmitter deficits in Alzheimer's disease. *Neurochemistry International, 7,* 545–563.

Hornykiewicz, O. (1985). Brain dopamine and aging. *Interdisciplinary Topics in Gerontology, 19,* 143–155.

Hyman, B.T., Eslinger, P.J. & Damasio, A.R. (1985). Effect of naltrexone on senile dementia of the Alzheimer type. *Journal of Neurosurgery and Psychiatry, 48,* 1169–1171.

Ishii, T. (1966). Distribution of Alzheimer's neurofibrillary changes in the brain stem and the hypothalamus of senile dementia. *Acta Neuropathologica, 6,* 181–187.

Johns. C.A., Haroutunian, V., Greenwald, B.S., Mohs, R.C., Davis, B.M., Kanof,

P., Horvath, T.B. & Davis, K.L. (1985). Development of cholinergic drugs for the treatment of Alzheimer's disease. *Drug Development Research, 5,* 77–96.

Joynt, R.J. & McNeil, T.H. (1984). Neuropeptides in aging and dementia. *Peptides, 5* (Suppl.), 269-274.

Kaiya, H., Tanaka, T., Takeuchi, K., Morita, K., Adachi, S., Shirakawa, H., Veki, H. & Namba, M. (1983). Decreased level of β-endorphin-like immunoreactivity in cerebrospinal fluid of patients with senile dementia of Alzheimer type. *Life Sciences, 33,* 1039-1043.

Karlsson, I., Widerlöv, E., Malin, E., Nyth, A.L., Brine, G., Rybo, E., Rehfeld, J., Bissette, G., & Nemeroff, C.B. (1985). Changes of CSF neuropeptides after environmental stimulation in dementia. *Nordic Psychiatric Journal, 39* (Suppl), 75–81.

Kay, A.D., Milstein, S., Kaufman, S., Rapoport, S.I. & Culter, N.R. (1984). 5-HIAA and HVA in the CSF of patients with Alzheimer's disease. *Neurology, 34* (Suppl), 161.

Kitt, C.A., Price, D.L., Struble, R.G., Cork, L.C., Wainer, B.H., Becker, M.W. & Mobley, W.C. (1984). Evidence for cholinergic neurites in senile plaques. *Science, 226,* 1443-1445.

Kulmala, H.K. (1985). Some enkephalin- or VIP-immunoreactive hippocampal pyramidal cells contain neurofibrillary tangles in the brains of aged humans and persons with Alzheimer's disease. *Neurochemical Pathology, 3,* 41–51.

LeFresne, P., Beaujovan, J.C. & Glowinski, J. (1978). Origin of the acetyl moiety of acetylcholine in rat striatal synaptosomes: A specific pyruvate dehydrogenase involved in ACh synthesis. *Biochimie, 60,* 479–487.

Levy, R.,Little, A., Chuaqui, P. & Reith, M. (1985). The effects of long-term administration of lecithin on the course of Alzheimer senile dementia. *Interdisciplinary Topics in Gerontology, 20,* 153–166.

Lippa, A.S., Loullis, C.C., Rotrosen, J., Cordasco, D.M., Critchett, D.J. & Joseph, J.A. (1985). Conformational changes in muscarinic receptors may produce diminished cholinergic neurotransmission and memory deficits in aged rats. *Neurobiology of Aging, 6,* 317-323.

Mann, D.M.A., Yates, P.O. & Marcyniuk, B. (1984). Alzheimer's presenile dementia, senile dementia of Alzheimer type and Down's syndrome in middle age from an age-related continuum of pathological changes. *Neuropathology and Applied Neurobiology, 10.* 185-207.

Mash, D.C., Flynn, D.D. & Potter, L.T. (1985). Loss of M_2 muscarine receptors in the cerebral cortex in Alzheimer's disease and experimental cholinegic denervation. *Science, 228,* 1115-1117.

McDuff, T. & Sumi, S.M. (1985). Subcortical degeneration in Alzheimer's disease. *Neurology, 35,* 123-126.

Meier-Ruje, W., Iwangoff, P. & Reichlmeier, K. (1984). Neurochemical enzyme changes in Alzheimer's and Pick's disease. *Archives of Gerontology and Geriatrics, 3,* 161-165.

Mohs, R.C., Davis, B.M., Mathé, A.A., Rosen, W.G., Johns, C.A., Greenwald, B.S., Horvath, T.B. & Davis, K.L. (1985). Intravenous and oral physostigmine in Alzheimer's disease. *Interdisciplinary Topics in Gerontology, 20,* 140-152.

Morgan, D.G. & Routtenberg, A. (1981). Brain pyruvate dehydrogenase: Phosphorylation and enzyme activity altered by a training experience.*Science, 214,* 470-471.

Morrison, J.H., Rogers, J., Scherr, S., Benoit, R. & Bloom, F. (1985). Somatostatin immunoreactivity in neuritic plaques of Alzheimer's patients. *Nature, 314,* 90-92.

Mountjoy, C.Q., Rossor, M.N., Iversen, L.L. & Roth, M. (1984). Correlation of cortical cholinergic and GABA deficits with quantitative neuropathological findings in senile dementia. *Brain, 107,* 517-518.

Nemeroff, C.B., Bissette, G., Busby, W.H., Jr., Youngblood, W.W., Rossor, M.N., Roth, M. & Kizer, J.S. (1983). Regional brain concentrations of neurotensin, thyrotropin-releasing hormone and somatostatin in Alzheimer's disease. *Society of Neuroscience Abstracts, 9,* 1052.

Palmer, A.M., Sims, N.S., Bowen, D.M., Neary, D., Palo, J., Wikstrom, J. & Davison, A.N. (1984). Monoamine metabolite concentrations in lumbar cerebrospinal fluid of patients with histology verified Alzheimer's dementia. *Journal of Neurology, Neurosurgery, and Psychiatry, 47,* 481–484.

Pearce, B.R., Palmer, A.M., Bowe, D.M., Wilcock, G.K., Esiri, M.M. & Davison, A.N. (1984). Neurotransmitter dysfunction and atrophy of the caudate nucleus in Alzheimer's disease. *Neurochemical Pathology, 2,* 221–232.

Pearson, R.C.A., Sofroniew, M.V., Cuello, A.C., Powell, T.P.S., Eckenstein, F., Esiri, M.M. & Wilcock, G.K. (1983). Persistence of cholinergic neurons in the basal nucleus in a brain with senile dementia of the Alzheimer's type demonstrated by immunohistochemical staining for choline acetyltransferase. *Brain Research, 289,* 375–379.

Perry, E.K., Atack, J.R., Perry, R.H.,Hardy, J.A., Dodd, P.R., Edwardson, J.A., Blessed, G., Tomlinson, B.E. & Fairbairn, A.F. (1984). Intralaminar neurochemical distributions in human midtemporal cortex: Comparison between Alzheimer's disease and the normal. *Journal of Neurochemistry, 42,* 1402–1410.

Perry, E.K., Perry, R.H., Tomlinson, B.E., Blessed, G. & Gibson, P.H. (1980). Coenzyme A-acetylating enzymes in Alzheimer's disease: Possible cholinergic "compartment" of pyruvate dehydrogenase. *Neuroscience Letter, 18,* 105–110.

Perry, E.K., Tomlinson, B.E., Blessed, G. Bergman, K., Gibson, P.H. & Perry, R.H. (1978). Correlation of cholinergic abnormalities with senile plaques and mental test scores in senile dementia. *British Medical Journal, 2,* 1457–1459.

Reisine, T.D., Yamamura, H.I., Bird, E.D., Spokes, E. & Enna, S. (1978). Pre- and post-synaptic neurochemical alterations in Alzheimer's disease. *Brain Research, 159,* 477–481.

Reynolds, G.P., Arnold, L., Rossor, M.N., Iversen, L.L., Mountjoy, C.Q. & Roth, M. (1984). Reduced binding of [³H]ketanserin to cortical 5HT2 receptors in senile dementia of the Alzheimer type. *Neuroscience Letter, 44,* 47–51.

Rinne, U.K., Laakso, K., Mölsä, P., Paljärvi, L.,Portin, R., Rinne, J.K., Rinne, J.O., & Säkö, E. (1985). Dementia and brain receptor changes in Parkinson's disease and in senile dementia of the Alzheimer type. In C.G. Gottfries (Ed.), *Normal aging, Alzheimer's disease and senile dementia: Aspects on etiology, pathogenesis, diagnosis and treatment.* Bruxelles: Éditions de l'Université de Bruxelles.

Rossor, M.N., Emson, P.C., Iversen, L.L., Mountjoy, C.Q. & Roth, M. (1984). Patterns of neuropeptide deficits in Alzheimer's disease. In R.J. Wurtman, S.H. Corkin & J.H. Growden (Eds.), *Alzheimer's disease: Advances in basic research and therapies.* Brain Sciences and Metabolites in Charitable Trust.

Rossor, M.N., Emson, P.C., Mountjoy, C.Q., Roth, M. & Iversen, L.L. (1980). Reduced amounts of immunoreactive somatostatin in the temporal cortex in senile dementia of Alzheimer type. *Neuroscience Letter, 20,* 373–377.

Rossor, M.N., Mountjoy, C.Q., Roth, M. & Reynolds, G.P. (1985). Ascending systems in Alzheimer's disease. *Interdisciplinary Topics Gerontology, 19,* 198–212.

Rossor, M.N., Svendsen, C., Hunt, S.P., Mountoy, C.Q., Roth, M. & Iversen, L.L. (1982). The substantia innominata in Alzheimer's disease: An histochemical and biochemical study of cholinergic marker enzymes. *Neuroscience Letter, 28,* 217–222.

Rylett, R.T., Ball, M.J. & Calhoun, E.H. (1983). Evidence for high affinity choline transport in synaptosomes prepared from hippocampus and neocortex of patient with Alzheimer's disease. *Brain Research, 289,* 169–175.

Sanders, D.J., Zahedi-Asi, S. & Marr, A.P. (1982). Glucagon and CCK in human brain: Control and patients with senile dementia of the Alzheimer type. *Brain Research, 55,* 465–471.

Serby, M., Richardson, S.B., Twente, S., Siekierski, J., Corwin, J. & Rotrosen, J. (1984). CSF somatostatin in Alzheimer's disease. *Neurobiology of Aging, 5,* 187–189.

Sims, N.R., Bowen, O.M., Allen, S.J., Smith, C.C.T., Neary, D., Thomas, D.J. & Davison, A.N. (1983). Presynaptic cholinergic dysfunction in patients with dementia. *Joural of Neurochemistry, 40,* 503–509.

Sitaram, N. (1984). Cholinergic hypothesis of human memory: Review of basic and clinical studies. *Drug Development Research, 4,* 481–488.

Smith, C.C.T., Bowe, D.M., Sims, N.R., Neary, D. & Davison, A.N. (1983). Amino acid release from biopsy specimens of temporal neocortex from patients with Alzheimer's disease. *Brain Research, 264,* 138–141.

Soininen, H.S., Jolkkonen, J.T., Reinikainen, K.J., Halonen, T.O. & Riekkinen, P.J. (1984a). Reduced cholinesterase activity and somatostatin-like immunoreactivity in the cerebrospinal fluid of patients with dementia of the Alzheimer type. *Joural of Neurological Sciences, 63,* 167–172.

Soininen, H., Pitkanen, A., Halonen, T. & Riekkinen, P.J. (1984b). Dopamine-beta-hydroxylase and acetylcholinesterase activities of cerebrospinal fluid in Alzheimer's disease. *Acta Neurologica Scandinavica, 69,* 29–34.

Sorbi, S., Bird, E.D. & Blass, J.P. (1983). Decreased pyruvate dehydrogenase complex activity in Huntington and Alzheimer brain. *Annals of Neurology, 13,* 72–78.

Sorensen, P.S., Hammer, M., Vorstrup, S. & Gjerris, F. (1983). CSF and plasma vasopressin concentrations in dementia. *Journal of Neurology, Neurosurgery, and Psychiatry, 46,* 911–916.

Sparks, D.L. & Slevin, J.T. (1985). Determination of tyrosine, tryptophan, and their metabolic derivatives by liquid chromatography-electrochemical detection: Application to post-mortem samples from patients with Parkinson's and Alzheimer's disease. *Life Science, 36,* 449–457.

Squire, L.R. & Davis, H.P. (1981). The pharmacology of human memory: A neurobiological perspective. *Annual Review of Pharmacology and Toxicology, 21,* 323–356.

Struble, R.G., Cork, L.C., Whitehouse, P.J. & Price, D.L. (1982). Cholinergic innervation in neuritic plaques. *Science, 216,* 413–415.

Struble, R.G., Hedreen, J.C., Cork, L.C. & Price, D.L. (1984a). Acetylcholinesterase activity in senile plaques of aged macaques. *Neurobiology of Aging, 5,* 191–198.

Struble, R.G., Kitt, C.A., Walker, L.L., Cork, L.C. & Price, D.L. (1984b). Somatostatinergic neurites in senile plaques of aged non-humans primates. *Brain Research, 324,* 394–396.

Terry, R.D. & Katzman, R. (1983). Senile dementia of the Alzheimer type. *Neurology, 14,* 497–506.

Tinklenburg, J.R., Pigache, R., Pfefferbaum, A. & Berger, P.A. (1982). Vasopressin peptides and dementia. In S.C. Corkin, K.L. Davis, J.H. Growden, E. Usdin & R.J. Wurtman (Eds.), *Alzheimer's disease: A report of progress.* New York: Raven Press.

Tsuji, M., Takahashi, S. & Akazawa, S. (1981). CSF vasopressin and cyclic nucleotide concentrations in senile dementia. *Psychoneuroendocrinology, 6,* 171–176.

Tune, L., Gucker, S., Folstein, M., Oshida, L. & Coyle, J.T. (1985). Cerebrospinal fluid acetylcholinesterase activity in senile dementia of the Alzheimer type. *Annals of Neurology, 17,* 46–48.

Volicer, L., Direnfeld, L.K., Freedman, M., Albert, M.L.,Langlais, P.J. & Bird, E.D. (1985). Serotonin and 5-hydroxyindoleacetic acid in CSF. *Archives of Neurology, 42,* 127–129.

Walsh, T.J., Emerich, D.F., Winokur, A., Banki, C., Bissette, G. & Nemeroff, C.B. (1985). Intrahippocampal injection of cysteamine depletes somatostatin and produces cognitive impairment in the rat. *Soc. Neurosci. Abst.,* 11, 621.

Whitehouse, P.J., Hedreen, J.C., White, L.L. & Price, D.L. (1982). Alzheimer's disease and senile dementia—loss of neurons in the basal forebrain. *Science, 215,* 1237–1239.

Whitehouse, P.J., Price, D.L., Clark, A.W., Coyle, J.T. & Delong, M.K. (1981). Alzheimer's disease: Evidence for selective loss of cholinergic neurons in the nucleus basalis. *Annals of Neurology, 10,* 122–126.

Winblad, B., Adolfsson, R., Carlsson, A., & Gottfries, C.G. (1982). Biogenic amines in brains of patients with Alzheimer's disease. In S. Corkin (Ed.), *Alzheimer's disease: A report of progress.* New York: Raven Press.

Yamamoto, T. & Hirano, A. (1985). Nucleus raphe dorsalis in Alzheimer's disease: Neurofibrillary tangles and loss of large neurons. *Annals of Neurology, 17,* 573–577.

Yates, C.M., Harmar, A.J., Rosie, R. Sherward, J., Sanchez de Levy, G., Simpson, J., Maloney, A.F.J., Gordon, A. & Fink, G. (1983a). Thyrotropin-releasing hormone and substance P immunoreactivity in post-mortem brain from cases of Alzheimer-type dementia and Down's syndrome. *Brain Research, 258,* 45–52.

Yates, C.M., Simpson, J., Gordon, A., Maloney, A.F.J., Allison, Y., Ritchie, I.M. & Urquhart, A. (1983b). Catecholamines and cholinergic enzymes in pre-senile and senile Alzheimer-type dementia and Down's syndrome. *Brain Research, 280,* 119–126.

Zimmer, R., Teelken, A.W., Trieling, W.B., Weber, W., Weihmayr, T. & Lauter, H. (1984). γ-aminobutyric acid and homovanillic acid concentration in the CSF of patients with senile dementia of Alzheimer's type. *Achives of Neurology, 41,* 602–604.

Zornetzer, S.F. (1984). Brain substrates of senescent memory decline. In L.R. Squire & N. Butters (Eds.), *Neuropsychology of memory.* New York: The Guilford Press.

CHAPTER 11

Cellular Aspects of Altered Immune Response in Aging

Myron R. Szewczuk
Ian R. Mackay

Aging is one of the principal unresolved enigmas remaining in cellular biology. A systematic review of cellular aspects of altered immune response in aging is presented. The findings of several studies addressed some aspects of altered immune response during the aging process, including: (a) the role played by the major histocompatibility gene complex, (b) reconstitution of many murine T-cell-mediated responses with exogenous interleukin-2 or thymosin, (c) gene activation in senescent human lymphocytes, (d) the effects of anti-idiotypic antibodies in aging, and (e) the idiotypic repertoire expressed by systemic and mucosal immune cells of aged animals. Cellular aspects of altered immune response in aging animals and humans are analyzed and the potential for future progress in this area assessed.

In the last few years we have seen enormous growth in our understanding of cell–cell communications and the important role of lymphokines and idiotypic interactions in influencing the immune response. These cellular aspects and the role of lymphokines and

Myron Szewczuk is a career scientist in the Ontario, Canada, Ministry of Health, MA7347 and his work is supported in part by a grant-in-aid of research from the Medical Research Council of Canada, MA7347. The work of Ian Mackay is supported by the National Health and Medical Research Council of Australia.

idiotypes in the altered immune response of aging animals and humans are now beginning to receive attention.

Over 50 years ago the first descriptions of age-related changes in the immune system were published by Friedberger, Bock, and Furstenheim (1929), and Thomsen and Kettel (1929), who described that serum antibodies to blood group antigens and xenogeneic erythrocytes declined with age. Since then a significant portion of research on aging has focused on changes in the immune system for various reasons: (a) the thymus (controlling the maturation of T lymphocytes) is the first organ in mammals to undergo changes associated with senescence, (b) genes of the major histocompatibility complex (controlling immune reactivity) when transferred from a long-lived to a short-lived mouse strain, extend the lifespan of that short-lived mouse strain, (c) techniques amenable to the study of the molecular and cellular biological changes occurring with age are easily applied to the cells of the immune system, and (d) with age there is an increased incidence of diseases associated with an impaired immune system.

Aspects of the altered immune response during the aging process addressed in this chapter include (a) the role played by the major histocompatibility gene complex, MHC, influencing a number of the fundamental processes of aging, (b) reconstitution of many murine T-cell-mediated responses with exogenous interleukin-2 or thymosin, (c) gene activation in senescent human lymphocytes, (d) the beneficial effect of anti-idiotypic antibodies in down-regulating cross-reactivity toward self-antigens in aging, and (e) the idiotypic repertoire expressed by systemic and mucosal immune cells of aged animals.

AGING AND THE IMMUNE RESPONSE: AN OVERVIEW

A relationship exists between aging and a decline in B-cell function. Thymic (T)-dependent splenic B-cell responses are most affected by age as manifested by a depressed immune response to a variety of T-dependent antigens (Callard & Basten, 1978; Goidl, Innes, & Weksler, 1976; Weksler, Innes, & Goldstein, 1978). In addition, splenic B-cell responses in mice to T-independent antigens have been shown to decrease with age (Callard, Basten, & Waters, 1977). Explanations for this decline include decrease in T helper activity (Callard & Basten, 1978; Chin, Carey, & Woodruff, 1983; Goidl et al., 1976; Makinodan, Albright, Good, Peter, & Heidrick, 1976), increases in suppressor activity (Callard, Fazekas de St Groth, Basten & McKenzie, 1980; DeKruyff, Kim, Siskind & Weksler, 1980; Goidl et al., 1976; Makinodan et al., 1976; Segre & Segre, 1976; Singhal, Roder, & Duwe, 1978), or changes in the efficiency of cellular interactions required for the response (Doria, D'Agostaro & Garavini, 1980; Makinodan et al.,

1976). Intrinsic defects have also been suggested to account for some of this decline, as well as reducing the proliferative capacity of these cells (Callard et al., 1977; DeKruyff et al., 1980; Dupere & Kolodziej, 1983; Goidl et al., 1976; Goidl, Choy, Gibbans, Weksler, & Thorbecke et al., 1983; Liu, Segre, & Segre, 1982).

On the other hand, the number of B-cells in lymph nodes and spleen does not change appreciably with age (Makinodan & Adler, 1975). The total number of stem cells from mouse bone marrow remains quite constant with age (Chen, 1971) and such cells appear not to lose their lymphohematopoietic activity (Harrison & Doubleday, 1975). While these studies indicate that hematopoietic stem cells do not exhibit intrinsic defects with age, maturational and differentiational events affecting these cells may be important.

Reductions in various murine T-cell functions have been found to occur with age. These include decreases in cytotoxic T lymphocyte (CTL) function in mice (Miller & Stutman, 1981; Thoman & Weigle, 1982; Zharhary, Segev & Gershon, 1984), delayed type hypersensitivity (DTH) reactions in humans (Roberts-Thomson, Whittingham, Youngchaiyud, & Mackay, 1974), mixed leukocyte reactions (MLR) in mice (Thoman & Weigle, 1982), protective mediator T cells in *Listeria monocytogenes* infections in mice (Patel, 1981), and in helper T-cell activity in mice (Callard & Basten, 1978; Doria et al., 1980; Goidl et al., 1976; Liu et al., 1982; Thoman & Weigle, 1981). Conversely, suppressor T-cell activity has been found to increase with age in mice (Segre & Segre, 1976; Goidl et al., 1976; Makinodan et al., 1976; DeKruyff et al., 1980; Callard et al., 1980; Singhal et al., 1978; Callard & Basten, 1978; Liu et al., 1982). These findings in the mouse are in direct contrast to those found in humans where an increase in helper cell (Ceuppens & Goodwin, 1982) and a decrease in suppressor cell (Ceuppens & Goodwin, 1982) function have been reported.

Detection of B- and T-cell changes within the murine immune system with age has relied on mixing experiments with either whole spleen cell populations (DeKruyff et al., 1980; Goidl et al., 1976) or isolated B- and T-cell populations (Callard & Basten, 1978; Liu et al., 1982; Thoman & Weigle, 1981) from young and old syngeneic mice. These observations were made either in vitro (DeKruyff et al., 1980; Doria et al., 1980; Thoman & Weigle, 1981), or in vivo after adoptive cell transfers (Callard & Basten, 1978; Goidl et al., 1976; Szewczuk, 1982) or after growth of cells in diffusion chambers (Lie et al., 1982; Segre & Segre, 1976). Specific (Callard & Basten, 1978; DeKruyff et al., 1980; Goidl et al., 1976; Liu et al., 1982; Segre & Segre, 1976) or nonspecific (Klinman, 1981) suppressor cells for the most part were detected by treatment of cells with anti-Thy 1.2 or antilyt-2 antibody plus complement treatment, thereby enhancing the plaque forming cell response of "old" T and "young" B-cell mixtures.

AGING AND THE MAJOR HISTOCOMPATIBILITY GENE COMPLEX

The inclusion of various rodents in studies of aging offers many advantages for the researcher. Each species is functionally homogeneous in its genome and has a relatively short life span (2 to 3 years). These animals also maintain an immune system that is conveniently similar to that of humans. The availability of a large number of mouse strains differing at practically any gene locus allows for the evaluation of genetic influences (i.e., major histocompatibility complex H-2 for the mouse) on any identified immune deficiency. Most important, however, is the advantage of evaluating relatively "pure" aging events in genetically identical young and old mice.

Roy Walford has presented findings which indicate that the mean and maximum life spans differ significantly between different H-2 congenic mouse strains. He obtained similar findings with different F_1 hybrids wherein one parent was common, and the others represented different H-2 congenics. In addition, the proliferative response to mitogens varied between H-2 congenics, suggesting that genetic contributions to biomarker variability were important. Walford has suggested that a given immune parameter may mark "functional age" well in one mouse strain but poorly in another.

The influence of the MHC on immune responsiveness may account for the great heterogeneity among mouse strains when different immunogenic stimuli are used to investigate age-related changes. For example, old mice are found to produce lower levels of antibody in their serum, and depressed numbers of plaque-forming cells (PFC) in their spleen when immunized with a variety of antigens requiring variable degrees of T-cell participation (T-independent or T-dependent antigens) (Makinodan & Kay, 1980; Makinodan & Peterson, 1964; Wade & Szewczuk, 1984). Immunoglobulin G (IgG) responses are more severely affected, with antibody of only lower average affinity produced in their responses (Goidl et al., 1976; Szewczuk & Campbell, 1981b). The reduction of PFC responses to T-independent antigens at more advanced ages (versus T-dependent responses) has been taken as evidence for a greater aging effect on the T-cell, rather than the B-cell, compartment of old mice.

There is little agreement regarding the age-related changes that occur to the cell-mediated arm of the murine immune system, although reports generally described depressed (or unchanged, Stutman, 1974) graft-versus-host (GVH) and host-versus-graft (HVG) responses (Walters & Claman, 1975). The only study examining DTH responsiveness has revealed unaffected reactivity (Walters & Claman, 1975). More accepted, however, is the age-associated reduction in the activity of cytolytic T lymphocytes (CTL) against allogeneic (Menon,

Jaroslow, & Koesterer, 1974) or viral-infected (Effros & Walford, 1983) targets. Old mice also show an impairment of their ability to survive a tumor cell challenge (Goodman & Makiodan, 1975) or to respond following an inoculation of *Listeria monocyogenes* (Patel, 1981).

Further characterization of the lymphoid system of old mice has shown that the lymphocyte population in the spleen is not substantially changed in old mice. Numbers of B cells (Callard & Basten, 1977; Weiner, Moorhead, & Claman, 1976), T cells (Zharhary & Klinman, 1983), lyt-1[+] (Th) cells (Chang, Makinodan, Peterson, & Strehler, 1982) and lyt-2[+] (Ts/CTL) cells (Chang, Makinodan, Peterson, & Strehler, 1982) remain within the young-adult range throughout life. Similar studies in the rat have shown that total cell numbers and Thy-1[+] (immature) T cells decline in the spleen and cervical lymph nodes with age, while numbers of W3/13[+] (peripheral T) and W3/25[+](Th) cells are not changed in old animals.

Both the primary and secondary CTL responses to modified-self and allogeneic targets decline with age (Bruley-Rosset & Vergnon, 1984; Effros & Walford, 1983; Goodman & Makinodan, 1975; Nordin & Collins, 1983; Zharhary & Gershon, 1981; Zharhary, Segev, & Gershon, 1984). If limiting dilution analysis is performed with the responding cells, it is found that old mice have fewer spleen cells triggered by the antigen (Goodman & Makinodan, 1975; Zharhary et al., 1984). Diminished interleukin-2 (IL-2) levels are also found in these responses (Effros & Walford, 1983; Miller & Stutman, 1981), with exogenous IL-2 (in vivo or in vitro) able to restore levels of cytotoxicity (Bruley-Rosset & Vergnon, 1984; Effros & Walford, 1983; Miller & Stutman, 1981; Thoman & Weigle, 1982; Thoman & Weigle, 1985). Apart from helper cell defects, insufficient antigen presentation may also influence these responses (Effros & Walford, 1984; Urban & Schreiber, 1984). In a comprehensive study evaluating the primary CTL response of individual animals to both trinitral phenyl (TNP)-modified self and allogeneic targets, apart from changes in responding cell frequency, old mice display one of three possible unresponsiveness patterns: 20% were deficient in T-helper cells, 20% had augmented levels of suppression, while the remainder were not deficient in either of these activities (Zharhary et al., 1984). While this highlights the heterogeneity (presumably MHC-related) of the age-associated deficiencies in the CTL response to a single antigen, it provides little information on what might be the overall status of the CTL pool in old inbred animals or, of more relevance, of older members of outbred species.

When analysis of CTLs is performed under limiting dilution conditions, the frequency of precursor CTLs to some antigens increases with age whereas it decreases to others (Chang & Gorczynski, 1984). The comparison of all reactivity patterns from young and old mice revealed that the *CTL repertoire* was significantly different by old age (Chang & Gorczynski, 1984) with changes not only in the frequency, but also in the specificity of CTL (Flood, Urban, Kripke, & Schreiber, 1981; Zharhary & Gershon, 1981).

Heterogeneity apparently exists in the mechanisms affecting immune suppression not only between individual mice for a specific antigen, but also within individual mice for different antigens. The reduced CTL activity of old mice, therefore, results from the combined influences of an altered number of responsive cells (change in repertoire), a reduction in T-helper activity (and consequently IL-2 production), and augmented levels of suppression. It is noteworthy that most cellular immune responses, as described above, are regulated by the major histocompatibility gene complex.

Roy Walford also proposed that the MHC may influence nonimmune aging processes such as free radical scavengers, DNA repair, and levels of mixed function oxidases.

AGING AND THE ROLE FOR T-CELL FACTORS, INTERLEUKIN-2, AND THYMOSIN

The production of (IL-2), a lymphokine produced by helper T-cells, is reduced with age in mice after stimulation of such cells with concanavalin A (con A) (Chang et al., 1982; Thoman & Weigle, 1981; Thoman & Weigle, 1982), Fc fragments (Morgan & Weigle, 1982), antigen (Thoman & Weigle, 1982), PHA (Thoman & Weigle, 1981), or allogeneic cells (Thoman & Weigle, 1982). Active suppression was not responsible for this reduction but instead the reduction was the result of a defect in the lyt-1$^+$ helper T-cell (Chang et al, 1982; Morgan & Weigle, 1982; Thoman & Weigle, 1981; Thoman & Weigle, 1982) and/or in the synthesis of IL-1 by macrophages (Chang et al., 1982). The addition of exogenous IL-2 to cell cultures restored MLR (Thoman & Weigle, 1982), CTL activity (Thoman & Weigle, 1982), Con A (Chang et al., 1982) and PFC (Thoman & Weigle, 1981) responses to young-adult levels, while antigen-induced proliferative responses were not completely recovered by such treatment (Thoman & Weigle, 1982).

Thus, it appears that some of the age-related decline in the various immune parameters of old mice could be accounted for by a reduced production of IL-2 (or other lymphokine mediators) essential for an optimal immune response. Since exogenous IL-2 can recover some of this cell-mediated reactivity, a reduction in IL-2 receptors on T-cells does not seem likely in senescent animals. At present, the defect can not be unequivocally attributed to a primary reduction in IL-1 and IL-2 synthesis. The reduced endogenous production of these lymphokines could account, in part, for reductions in both antibody formation and the mitogenic proliferation of B- and T-cells. For an example, antibody production has been shown to be dependent upon the IL-2-induced proliferation of T-helper cells (Larsson, Gullberg, Bandeira, & Coutinho, 1984; Watson, 1979). The stimulation of T-cells by mitogens is also dependent upon proliferative IL-2 signals, since mitogens are thought simply to induce IL-2 receptor expression on these cells (reviewed in Larsson et al., 1984). The mitogenic stimulation of B-cells now is recognized to require the presence of IL-1 and a T-cell-derived B-cell growth factor. Recent work by Chang et al. (1982) has indicated that macrophages may play an important role via a decreased production in interleukin 1 (IL-1) in the reduced IL-2 production noted in aged mice. Further work is clearly required to define the precise role of defective lymphokine release in the aging process.

Doria's (1980) findings have demonstrated a reconstitution in vivo of T-cell functions in aged mice by thymosin α_1. It was inferred that the contribution of diminished helper T-cell maturation in the altered immune response in aged animals could be reversed by preinjecting old animals with various thymic extracts, thymopoietin pentapeptide, thymosin α_1 as reported by Weksler et al. (1978) and Frasca, Garavini, and Doria (1982) or interleukin-2 (IL-2) as reported by Thoman & Weigle (1985). Doria's proposal was that in aged animals, injection of thymosin-α_1 would enhance IL-2 production and mitotic responsiveness to IL-2 production by spleen cells; and thus, the effect of the thymic factor on helper activity would be mediated by changes in both IL-2 production and responsiveness to it.

GENE ACTIVATION IN SENESCENT HUMAN LYMPHOCYTES

The presentation of Weksler et al. (1978) was directed to the possibility that defects in gene activation (transcription) events might determine the well-established reduction in responses to mitogens of lymphocytes from old humans. When peripheral blood lymphocytes (PBL) from old humans are tested for their ability to proliferate in the presence of Con A, this activity invariably declines with advanced age (Gillis, Kozak, Durante, & Weksler, 1981; Inkeles, Innes, Kuntz, Kadish, & Weksler, 1977; Kennes, Brohee, & Neve, 1983; Kishimoto, Tomino, Inomata, Kotegawa, & Saito et al., 1978; Mark & Weksler, 1982). Age-associated changes in the response to another T-cell lectin, phytohemagglutinin (PHA), are not as uniform, but the proliferative responses are reduced in the majority of old individuals (Gillis et al., 1981; Hallgren, Buckley, Gilbersten, & Yunis, 1973; Gutowski, Innes & Weksler, 1984; Hefton, Darlington, Casazza, & Weksler, 1980; Inkeles et al., 1977;

Kennes et al., 1983; Kishimoto et al., 1978; Roberts-Thomson et al., 1974; Staiano-Coicco, Darzynkiewicz, Melamed, & Weksler, 1984). When these responses are examined in further detail under limiting dilution conditions, there is found to be a reduced number of mitogen-responsive cells in the blood of old individuals (Hefton et al., 1980; Inkeles et al., 1977). A T-helper cell (Th) deficiency may also be responsible as reduced levels of IL-2 are observed in cultures of "old" cells (Gillis et al., 1981; Kennes et al., 1983), and partial recovery of the response is possible by including exogenous IL-2 in the reaction mixtures (Kennes et al., 1983) or by preinjecting test subjects with the thymic hormone thymopoietin pentapeptide (Verhaegen, DeCock, Cree, & Goldstein, 1981).

Other indices of T-cell function, including proliferation of PBL to allogeneic cells (Weksler & Hutteroth, 1974) and to a lesser extent pokeweed mitogen (PWM) (Kennes et al., 1983; Kishimoto et al., 1978; Weksler & Hutteroth, 1974), are similarly depressed in cultures of lymphocytes from old individuals. In studies of antibody synthesis in cultures of (PWM)-stimulated PBL, for the most part, there is no reduction in total IgG synthesis in cultures of old cells (Ceuppens & Goodwin, 1982; Skias, Reder, Bania, & Antel, 1985). If isolated CDT4$^+$ (Th), CDT8$^+$ (Ts/CTL) and B cells from young and old individuals are mixed in various combinations and placed in culture with PWM, CDT4$^+$ cells from old donors induce unchanged or greater IgG synthesis in either young or old B cells than do OKT4$^+$ cells from young donors (Ceuppens & Godwin, 1982; Kishimoto et al., 1978; Skias et al., 1985). Using similar cultures, OKT8$^+$ cells from old individuals are less suppressive than the corresponding cells from young adults. Conclusions from this work were that old individuals had, respectively, higher and lower levels of Th and Ts function than did younger individuals. It may be argued that mixing of cells from genetically disparate individuals does not reveal the real regulatory function of these cell populations, but when allogeneic effects were controlled for, these results remained unchanged (Ceuppens & Goodwin, 1982; Skias et al., 1985). However, there is some reduction with age in B-cell sensitivity to T-cell factors (Ceuppens & Goodwin, 1982), enhancement in Th sensitivity to suppression (Skias et al., 1985), and enhanced rheumatoid factor production (Rodriguez, Ceuppens, & Goodwin, 1982) in these cultures.

In the few studies examining in vitro antibody production in the absence of PWM, old humans produce slightly reduced amounts of anti-influenza antibody (Ershler, Moore, & Socinski, 1985) and unchanged amounts of antitetanus toxoid antibody (Ershler, Moore, Hacker, Ninomiya, Naylor, & Goldstein, 1984a) as compared with young subjects. The addition of thymosin fraction 5 to these cultures enhanced the responses of old individuals to both antigens (Ershler et al., 1984a; Ershler, Moore, & Socinski, 1984b).

The decline in the proliferative response of PBL from old individuals to PHA has been attributed to a decrease in the number of cells responding to the stimulus and to a reduction in the levels of T-cell help or IL-2 activity in the cultures. When the proliferative ability of the cells that respond in these cultures is examined, cells from old individuals are maximally triggered by the same concentration of PHA that is required for optimal stimulation of cells from young adults. At each concentration of PHA, the proliferative kinetics of the responding cells are unchanged, with no alteration in (a) the time needed for the cells initially to respond and divide, and (b) the division process itself (cell cycle), including its total duration and the time spent in each cycle phase (Inkeles et al., 1977; Staiano-Coicco et al., 1984). Furthermore, the levels of the intracellular messengers, cyclic AMP and cyclic GMP, in unstimulated "old" PBL remain within the range determined for cells from young individuals (Mark & Weksler, 1982); and upon PHA stimulation, the cytoplasmic signal-generating system ("the second signal") is the same in cells from young or old individuals (Gutowski et al., 1984).

When any deficiencies were evident, they related to the inability of some cells within the total population to undergo second and third rounds of cell division (cell cycle arrest) (Staiano-Coicco et al., 1984; Tice, Shneider, Kram, & Thorne, 1979). It is unclear at present whether this is attributable to insufficient helper signals (Kennes et al., 1983), clonal exhaustion, or an artifact arising from the techniques used in these studies (Staiano-Coicco et al., 1984). Given the relatively minor contribution of this latter effect to the proliferative response of T cells (Staiano-Coicco et al., 1984), the depressed response of old individuals does not appear to result from overt changes in the intracellular machinery required for vigorous proliferation.

Accordingly, Weksler hypothesized that the proliferative defect and immune incompetence of senescent T cells may be at the gene activation (transcription) events.

AGING AND ANTI-IDIOTYPIC ANTIBODIES AGAINST SELF-ANTIGENS

If old mice are immunized with a T-dependent antigen (trinitrophenyl bovine gamma globulin, TNP-BGG) or a T-independent antigen (trinitrophenl lysyl-ficoll, TNP-ficoll) and examined for numbers of splenic PFC after a suitable period, the normally depressed response can be recovered to some degree by including low concentrations of the free hapten (TNP) in the assay mixture, revealing "hapten-augmentable" (HA) PFC (Goidl, Thorbecke, Weksler, & Siskind, 1980b;

Szewczuk & Campbell, 1980). The free TNP was thought to displace a regulatory antibody from the antigen receptor on the PFC from old mice, thus allowing their escape from its suppressive influences and permitting the subsequent expression of normal cell function. This antibody (anti-idiotypic antibody) was further found to be present in the serum of old mice in elevated amounts and to bind to an antigenic region (the idiotype) on the surface immunoglobulin of B cells (Goidl, Samarut, Schneider-Gadicke, Hochwald, & Thorbecke et al., 1984; Szewczuk, 1984; Szewczuk & Campbell, 1981a). Once displaced, it could be added to other immune cell suspensions similarly to inhibit their response (Goidl, Schrater, Siskind, & Thorbecke, 1979). Goidl, Thorbecke, Weksler, and Siskind (1980b), in presenting their work, exploited this finding to show that anti-idiotypic antibody in serum from old mice reversibly inhibited the response of immune spleen cells from young mice. The converse was also true: serum from young mice would selectively inhibit only the response of young mice without major effects on the PFC response of old mice. Evidently the cells responding to antigen in the old animal bear a new set of idiotypes or a different idiotypic repertoire. The interaction of idiotypes and anti-idiotypes (idiotypic regulation) is thought to be one of the mechanisms which regulate the immune response in young adult animals (Goidl, Schrater, Thorbecke, & Siskind, 1980a); however, its suppressive influences are more apparent in some mouse strains than others in old age (Szewczuk, 1984).

Autoantibodies of a nonregulatory nature are also found in the serum of old mice (Peterseon & Makinodan, 1972; Stutman, 1974). Antimouse red blood cell (RBC) antibodies have received the most attention (Naor, Bonavida & Walford, 1976; Peterson & Makinodan, 1972), although antibodies to nucleoprotein and thymocytes have also been found (Stutman, 1974). On the other hand, efforts to induce augmented autoantibody production in old mice through immunization with mouse RBC or xenogeneic thyroglobulin have been generally unsuccessful (Goidl, Michelis, Siskind, & Weksler, 1981; Meredith, Kristie, & Walford, 1979). The presence of autoantibodies in old mice does not correlate with overt autoimmune disease (Peterson & Makinodan, 1972; Stutman, 1974) and in many instances the modification of the target antigen is required to demonstrate such autoantibodies (Goidl et al., 1981; Naor et al., 1976; Peterson & Makinodan, 1972). The production of these antibodies however is shown to be regulated differently from responses to exogenous antigens, demonstrating their unique nature (Naor et al., 1976).

Goidl hypothesized that antiidiotypic antibodies produced in aged mice during the normal immune response may down-regulate idiotypic antibody arising after immunization, which cross-reacts with self-antigens. To test this hypothesis, plaque-forming cells obtained from aged mice during the course of the immune response to (TNP-ficoll) were tested for cross-reactivity to bromelin-treated autologous mouse erythrocytes (Br-MRBC). Goidl presented results to show that the anti-TNP PFC response of old mice was 40% cross-reactive to Br-MRBC. In comparison, the anti-TNP PFC response of young mice showed only a 10% to 20% cross-reactivity to Br-MRBC. Moreover when the anti-idiotypic antibody was eluted from the "old" immune splenocytes, the response against Br-MRBC in aged mice increased to 60% to 70% of the anti-TNP response. No increases were seen after the same treatment of immune splenocytes obtained from young animals. Goidl proposed that antiidiotypic antibody with cross-reactivity to self-antigens in aging may represent the accumulative effect of lifelong immune responses.

AGING AND IDIOTYPIC REPERTOIRE CHANGES BY SYSTEMIC AND MUCOSAL IMMUNE CELLS

It is now clearly evident that, for some antigens, the receptor/idiotype repertoire of B cells undergoes changes with age (Goidl et al., 1980b; Szewczuk, 1982). This repertoire change in systemic B cells from aged animals was not found in the stem cells of these animals (Goidl et al., 1983), implying that this change must develop after maturation and differentiation in the systemic environment. Other studies have demonstrated that the repertoire change may occur as a consequence of concomitant shifts in the receptor repertoire of T cells, through idiotype–antiidiotype interactions (Goidl et al., 1983; Gorczynski, Kennedy, & MacRae, 1983; Klinman, 1981).

Whereas most immunological research thus far has focused on the deleterious effects associated with aging on the immune response of tissues of the systemic immune system, blood, spleen, and peripheral lymph nodes, another important site to assess the nature of age-associated changes is the bone marrow (BM) in which production of precursor cells continues throughout life. The cellularity of this tissue doubles by old age, yet the ability to differentiate pluripotent stem cells into discrete foci in the spleen (colony-forming units, CFU-S) remains unchanged (Chen, 1971). If the bone marrow of old mice is forced repeatedly to regenerate within its supporting stroma (using multiple injections of hydroxyurea), no defect can be identified in its ability continually to repopulate the old animal (Ross, Anderson, & Micklem, 1982). If the bone marrow of old mice is shielded and the whole animal subjected to a dose of X-irradiation sufficient to deplete unshielded immune cells, the response to the antigen, TNP-ficoll, occurs without the augmented levels of anti-idiotypic antibody or hapten-augmentable PFC normally found in old mice (Kim, Goidl, Samarut, Weksler,

& Thorbecke et al., 1985). Consequently, the property of producing HA-PFC is not programmed in the stem cells from either young or old mice; rather, it is the radiation-sensitive cells within the systemic environment of old animals that induce stem cells to produce this regulatory auto-anti-idiotypic antibody, once they are outside the bone marrow of untreated old animals.

Szewczuk showed results that highlighted the importance of considering tissues other than those of the systemic immune system in studies of aging. For example, when the PFC response is measured in tissues of the mucosal immune system after immunization with a T-dependent antigen, no decrease is noted in old mice although reactivity is concomitantly depressed in the spleen of these animals (Szewczuk, Campbell & Jung, 1981). Further examination of this apparent paradox suggested that cells in the mesenteric (MLN) and mediastinal (BLN) lymph nodes do not respond to antigen with PFC of reduced average affinity (Szewczuk & Campbell, 1981b), or with a different repertoire of idiotypes (Szewczuk & Campbell, 1981a), as seen with cells in the systemic immune system of old mice. The difference in the idiotype repertoire on the mucosal cells of old animals from that expressed in the spleen was further shown by the finding that antibody in "old" immune serum could inhibit the PFC response of immune cells in the spleen, but not in the BLN or MLN of old mice (Wade & Szewczuk, 1985). In addition, the immune response does not decline with age when mucosal tissue is directly stimulated with a T-dependent antigen (Szewczuk et al., 1981; Wade & Szewczuk, 1985). Thus, by all the criteria examined, aging apparently affects cells differently in the mucosal and systemic immune systems.

Szewczuk also reported that aged C57BL/6J male mice, immunized with TNP-BGG, responded with higher PFC levels in the presence of low concentrations of TNPε-amino caproic acid (EACA). These HA-PFC are produced in the spleen of young animals during a normal immune response (Goidl et al., 1979, 1980a, 1984), but they increase in number by old age in response to both T-dependent antigens (Szewczuk, 1983) and T-independent antigens (Goidl et al., 1980b, 1983; Szewczuk, 1983). Since effector cell blockade by anti-idiotypic antibody has been shown to suppress antibody secretion (Thorbecke, Bhogal, & Siskind, 1984), it was proposed that this could be one additional mechanism for the diminished immune responsiveness of old animals (Goidl et al., 1980b; Szewczuk & Campbell, 1980).

When various aged C57BL/6J male mice were immunized intraperitoneally with TNP-BGG and their PFC responses examined in the spleen, MLN, and BLN 14 days later, the high numbers of IgM, IgG, and IgA HA-PFC in the spleen of old animals could not be identified in the mucosal-associated lymph nodes (Szewczuk & Campbell, 1981a). In this study, TNP-specific B cells were recognized, bound, and reversibly inhibited by anti-idiotypic antibody on their surface, whereas no such antibody could be demonstrated on the surface of mucosal lymphocytes of the same animals (Szewczuk & Campbell, 1981a). An analysis of this finding in nine mouse strains demonstrated that some strains (C57BL/6J, DBA/2J, and C3H/HeJ) that develop high levels of HA-PFC in their spleens by old age (Szewczuk, 1984) do not have HA-PFC in their MLN or BLN at any age (Szewczuk & Wade, 1985). In contrast, other strains (129/J, AKR/J, and C57L/J) that lose HA-PFC numbers with age, maintain high levels in their MLN and BLN over the age span examined. CBA/J and SJL/J mice, respectively, maintained high and low levels of HA-PFC in their spleens, MLN, and BLN at 2 months and at 7 to 11 months of age. NZB/BinJ mice produced low levels of HA-PFC in their spleens and high levels in their MLN and BLN at 2 and 6 months of age (Szewczuk & Wade, 1985). With the exception of the latter three mouse strains, the results indicate that mice produce comparable amounts of HA-PFC in their spleen and mucosal-associated lymph nodes when young, but as they age, splenic but not mucosal levels undergo a change. In the context of work performed by Goidl et al. (1980b) suggesting that the idiotype repertoire of B cells in mice changes with age in the spleen, these results indicate that at a young age the anti-TNP idiotype repertoire of cells within the mucosal-associated lymph nodes is similar to that in the spleen, but as the animal ages, any changes in the spleen are not mirrored in the mucosal tissues. The methods employed do not demonstrate any changes in the idiotype repertoire of PFC in the spleen and MLN of CBA/J or SJL/J mice over the age span. In contrast, the anti-TNP idiotype repertoire expressed in the spleen and MLN of NZB/BinJ mice are demonstrably different at both a young and old age (Szewczuk & Wade, 1985).

To evaluate the hypothesis that the anti-TNP idiotype repertoire in the spleen and MLN of C57BL/6J mice becomes nonoverlapping by old age, serum from young and old C57BL/6J mice previously immunized with TNP-BGG was tested for its ability to reversibly inhibit the PFC response of spleen and MLN cells from young and old mice. Since reversible suppression in this system is thought to be mediated by circulating anti-idiotypic antibody (Goidl et al., 1979, 1984; Szewczuk & Campbell, 1981a), it would be predicted that only PFC from the spleen (and not the MLN) of old mice would be inhibited in this protocol. In accord with previous findings (Szewczuk & Campbell, 1980), serum from old immune mice was more inhibitory than serum from young mice in the PFC cell responses of young and old mice. Similarly the greater inhibition of splenic PFC responses from old (versus young) mice by serum from old immune animals agrees with work performed by Goidl et al. (1980b), suggesting that the idiotype repertoire stimulated by TNP-ficoll undergoes a change with age.

Immune serum from old mice (a) inhibits PFC from the spleen of both young and old mice to a greater degree than serum from young immune animals, and (b) has little effect on PFC from the MLN of either young or old animals. The results, therefore, support the hypothesis that the idiotype repertoire produced in response to TNP-BGG is not the same on B cells in the spleen and MLN of old mice.

Szewczuk therefore concluded that in mouse strains, except for CBA/J, SJL/J and NZB/BinJ, the pattern of change in splenic HA-PFC responses with age is not seen in the mucosal-associated lymph nodes and HA-PFC responses in the mucosal tissues, and whether high or low, does not change with age. These findings support the hypothesis that the idiotypical repertoires expressed by systemic and mucosal immune B cells of aged mice are different and nonoverlapping.

CONCLUDING REMARKS

The focus of much of the past immunological aging research has been on the involuting thymus and its contribution to the depressed immune responses of aged animals and humans (Makinodan & Kay, 1980). However, this organ has now been shown to be fully capable of producing cells with an unchanged diversity even when involuted (Chang & Gorczynski, 1984; Gorczynski & Chang, 1984), and peripheral T cells within the old animal probably retain full cell function (Miller, 1984). Also there is clear evidence suggesting that cells within the bone marrow and mucosal sites remain relatively free of most age-associated immune functional alterations. If this is true, it follows that the stem cell, B-cell, and T-cell compartments must retain the ability to function normally in the aged animal. This therefore places into question the prevailing opinion that intrinsic lymphocyte defects account for approximately 90% of the immune deficits seen with age (Makinodan & Kay, 1980; Price & Makinodan, 1972a, 1972b), whereas, on the other hand, there is accumulating evidence for a major (micro)environmental role in the decline in immune function with age. In particular, there is solid evidence for a reduced frequency of responding cells in the spleen but not the bone marrow or thymus of old animals (Chang & Gorczynski, 1984; Gorczynski & Chang, 1984; Gorczynski, Kennedy & MacRae, 1983, 1984; Miller, 1984; Zharhary et al., 1984; Zharhary & Klinman, 1983), as well as evidence that shows restoration of T-cell function in aged mice with either thymic hormones (Ershler et al., 1984a, 1984b; Frasca et al., 1982; Pandolfi, Quinti, Montella, Voci, & Schipani et al., 1983; Thompson, Wekstein, Rhoades, Kirpatrick, & Brown et al., 1984; Weksler et al., 1978) or IL-2 (Chang et al., 1982; Miller & Stutman, 1982; Thoman & Weigle, 1981, 1982).

A strong indication from the present symposium was that the reduction in the immune potential of systemic lymphoid areas in old mice is more a function of the "aged environment," which (a) is defective in promoting the maturation, but not differentiation, of T-helper cells, and (b) influences regulatory mechanisms (idiotypic?) that change the frequency of responding cells in an immune response. The indication that the expressed idiotype repertoire is nonoverlapping in systemic and mucosal immune responses of aged mice lends strong evidence that the inductive signals responsible for the depressed immunity in systemic areas of aged mice are either not triggered or not effective in the mucosal immune system, which, therefore, does not express the aged environment of the systemic lymphoid areas.

There was emphasis in the symposium on the important role played by the major histocompatability (MHC) gene complex in influencing immune and nonimmune aging processes. Since the products of this gene complex dictate the capacity of animals to respond to any given antigenic stimulus, as well as being essential to certain effector functions, the MHC gene complex must make a major contribution to the changing idiotypic repertoire of the aging animal. Hence, further understanding of MHC effects on immune responses should provide some answers to questions on the diversity of cellular aspects of altered immune responses in aging.

REFERENCES

Bruley-Rosset, M. & Vergnon, I. (1984). Interleukin-1 synthesis and activity in aged mice. *Mechanisms of Aging and Developments, 24,* 247.

Callard, R.E., & Basten, A. (1977). Immune function in aged mice: I. T-cell responsiveness using phytohemagglutinin as a functional probe. *Cellular Immunology, 31,* 13.

Callard, R.E., & Basten, A. (1978). Immune function in aged mice: IV. Loss of T cell and B cell function in thymus-dependent antibody responses. *European Journal of Immunology, 8,* 552.

Callard, R.E., Basten, A., & Waters, L.K. (1977). Immune function in aged mice: II. B-cell function. *Cellular Immunology, 31,* 26.

Callard, R.E., Fazekas de St. Groth, B., Basten, A., & McKenzie, I.F.C. (1980). Immune function in aged mice: V. Role of suppressor cells. *Journal of Immunology, 124,* 52.

Ceuppens, J.L., & Goodwin, J.S. (1982). Regulation of immunoglobulin production in pokeweed mitogen-stimulated cultures of lymphocytes from young and old adults. *Journal of Immunology, 128,* 2429.

Chang, M-P., & Gorczynski, R.M. (1984). Peripheral (somatic) expansion of the murine cytotoxic T-lymphocyte repertoire: I. Analysis of diversity in recognition repertoire of alloreactive T cells derived from the thymus and spleen of adult or aged DBA/2J mice. *Journal of Immunology, 133,* 2375.

Chang, M-P., Makinodan, T., Peterson, W.J., & Strehler, B.L. (1982). Role of T cells and adherent cells in age-related decline in murine interleukin 2 production. *Journal of Immunology 129,* 2426.

Chen, M.G. (1971). Age-related changes in hematopoietic stem cell populations of a long-lived hybrid mouse. *Journal of Cellular Physiology, 78,* 225.

Chin, Y-H., Carey, G.D., & Woodruff, J.J. (1983). Lymphocyte recognition of lymph node high endothelium: V. Isolation of adhesion molecules from lysates of rat lymphocytes. *Journal of Immunology, 131,* 1368.

DeKruyff, R.H., Kim, Y.T., Siskind, G.W., & Weksler, M.E. (1980). Age-related changes in the in vitro immune response: Increased suppressor activity in immature and aged mice. *Journal of Immunlogy, 125,* 142.

Doria, G., D'Agostaro, G., & Garavini, M. (1980). Age-dependent changes of B-cell reactivity and T cell-T cell interaction in the *in vitro* antibody response. *Cellular Immunology, 53,* 195.

Dupere, S.L.F., & Kolodziej, B.J. (1983). Cellular and molecular aspects of thymus-dependent antibody production in aged C3H/HeBr mice. *Age, 6,* 11.

Effros, R.B., & Walford, R.L. (1983). The immune response of aged mice to influenza. Diminished T-cell proliferation, interleukin-2 production, and cytotoxicity. *Cellular Immunology, 81,* 298.

Effros, R.B., & Walford, R.L. (1984). The effect of age on the antigen-presenting mechanism in limiting dilution precursor cell frequency analysis. *Cellular Immunology, 88,* 531.

Ershler, W.B., Moore, A.L., Hacker, M.P., Ninomiya, J., Naylor, P., & Goldstein, A.L. (1984a). Specific antibody synthesis in vitro: II. Age-associated thymosin enhancement of antitetanus antibody synthesis. *Immunopharmacology, 8,* 69.

Ershler, W.B., Moore, A.L., & Socinski, M.A. (1984b). Influenza and aging, age-related changes and the effects of thymosin on the antibody response to influenza vaccine. *Journal of Clinical Immunology, 4,* 445.

Ershler, W.B., Moore, A.L., & Socinski, M.A. (1985). Specific antibody synthesis in vitro: III. Correlation of in vivo and in vitro antibody response to influenza immunization in young and old subjects. *Journal of Clinical Laboratory Immunology, 16,* 63.

Flood, P.M., Urban, J.L., Kripke, M.L., & Schreiber, H. (1981). Loss of tumor-specific and idiotype-specific immunity with age. *Journal of Experimental Medicine, 154,* 275.

Frasca, D., Garavini, M., & Doria, G. (1982). Recovery of T-cell functions in aged mice injected with synthetic thymosin- 1. *Cellular Immunology, 72,* 384.

Friedberger, E., Boch, G.L., & Furstenheim, A. (1929). Zur Normalantikorerkurve des Menschen durch die verschiedenen Lebensalter und ihre Bedeutung fur die Erklarung der Hautteste. *Zeitschrift Immunitaetsforsch Experimentelle Ther, 64,* 294.

Gillis, S., Kozak, R., Durante, M., & Weksler, M.E. (1981). Immunological studies of aging. Decreased production of and response to T-cell growth factor by lymphocytes from aged humans. *Journal of Clinical Investigation, 67,* 937.

Goidl, E.A., Choy, J.W., Gibbons, J.J., Weksler, M.E., Thorbecke, G.J., & Siskind, G.W. (1983). Production of auto-anti-idiotypic antibody during the normal immune response: VII. Analysis of the cellular basis for the increased auto-anti-idiotypic antibody production by aged mice. *Journal of Experimental Medicine, 157,* 1635.

Goidl, E.A., Innes, J.B., & Weksler, M.E. (1976). Immunological studies of aging: II. Loss of IgG and high avidity plaque-forming cells and increased suppressor cell activity in aging mice. *Journal of Experimental Medicine, 144,* 1037.

Goidl, E.A., Michelis, M.A., Siskind, G.W., & Weksler, M.E. (1981). Effect of age on the induction of autoantibodies. *Clinical and Experimental Immunology, 44,* 24.

Goidl, E.A., Samarut, C., Schneider-Gadicke, A., Hochwald, N.L., Thorbecke, G.J., & Siskind, G.W. (1984). Production of auto-anti-idiotypic antibody during the normal immune response: IX. Characteristics of the auto-anti-idiotype antibody and its production. *Cellular Immunology, 85,* 25.

Goidl, E.A., Schrater, A.F., Siskind, G.W., & Thorbecke, G.J. (1979). Production of auto-anti-idiotypic antibody during the normal immune response to TNP-ficoll: II. Hapten-reversible inhibition of anti-TNP plaque-forming cells by immune serum as an assay for auto-anti-idiotypic antibody. *Journal of Experimental Medicine, 150,* 154.

Goidl, E.A., Schrater, A.F., Thorbecke, G.J., & Siskind, G.W. (1980a). Production of auto-anti-idiotypic antibody during the normal immune response. IV. Studies of the primary and secondary responses to thymus-dependent and -independent antigens. *European Journal of Immunology, 10,* 810.

Goidl, E.A., Thorbecke, G.J., Weksler, M.E., & Siskind, G.W. (1980b), Production of auto-anti-idiotypic antibody during the normal immune response. Changes in the auto-anti-idiotypic antibody response and the idiotype repertoire associated with aging. *Proceedings of the National Academy of Sciences of the United States of America, 77,* 6788.

Goodman, S.A., & Madinodan, T. (1975). Effect of age on cell-mediated immunity in long-lived mice. *Clinical Experimental Immunology, 19,* 533.

Gorczynski, R.M., & Chang, M-P. (1984). Peripheral (somatic) expansion of the murine cytotoxic T lymphocyte repertoire: II. Comparison of diversity in recognition repertoire of alloreactive T cells in spleen and thymus of younger aged DBA/2J mice transplanted with bone marrow from young or aged donors. *Journal of Immunology, 133,* 2381.

Gorczynski, R.M., Kennedy, M., & MacRae, S. (1983). Alteration in lymphocyte recognition repertoire during aging: II. Changes in the expressed T-cell receptor repertoire in aged mice and the persistence of that change after transplantation to a new differentiative environment. *Cellular Immunology, 75,* 226.

Gorczynski, R.M., Kennedy, M., & MacRae, S. (1984). Altered lymphocyte recognition repertoire during aging: III. Changes in MHC restriction patterns in parental T lymphocytes and diminution in T suppressor function. *Immunology, 52,* 611.

Gutowski, J.K., Innes, J., & Weksler, M.E. (1984). Induction of DNA synthesis in isolated nuclei by cytoplasmic factors: II. Normal generation of cytoplasmic stimulatory factors by lymphocytes from aged humans with depressed proliferative responses. *Journal of Immunology, 132,* 559.

Hallgren, H.M., Buckley, C.E., III, Gilbertsen, V.A., & Yunis, E.J. (1973). Lymphocyte phytohemagglutinin responsiveness, immunoglobulins and autoantibodies in aging humans. *Journal of Immunology, 111,* 1101.

Harrison, D.E., & Doubleday, J.W. (1975). Normal function of immunologic stem cells from aged mice. *Journal of Immunology, 114,* 1314.

Hefton, J.M., Darlington, G.J., Casazza, B.A., & Weksler, M.E. (1980). Immunologic studies of aging: V. Impaired proliferation of PHA responsive human lymphocytes in culture. *Journal of Immunology, 125,* 1007.

Inkeles, B., Innes, J.B., Kuntz, M.M., Kadish, A.S., & Weksler, M.E. (1977). Immunological studies of aging: III. Cytokinetic basis for the impaired response of lymphocytes from aged humans to plant lectins. *Journal of Experimental Medicine, 145,* 1176.

Kennes, B., Brohee, D., & Neve, P. (1983). Lymphocyte activation in human aging: V. Acquisition of response to T-cell growth factor and production of growth factors by mitogen-stimulated lymphocytes. *Mechanisms of Aging and Development, 23,* 103.

Kim, Y.T., Goidl, E.A., Samarut, C., Weksler, M.E., Thorbecke, G.J., & Siskind, G.W. (1985). Bone marrow function: I. Peripheral T cells are responsible for the increased auto-antiidiotypic response of older mice. *Journal of Experimental Medicine, 161,* 1237.

Kishimoto, S., Tomino, S., Inomata, K., Kotegawa, S., Saito, T., Kuroki, M., Mitsuya, H., & Hisamitsa, S. (1978). Age-related changes in the subsets and functions of human T lymphocytes. *Journal of Immunology, 121,* 1773.

Klinman, N.R. (1981). Antibody-specific immunoregulation and the immunodeficiency of aging. *Journal of Experimental Medicine, 154,* 547.

Larsson, E-L., Gullberg, M., Bandeira, A., & Coutinho, A. (1984). Activation and growth requirements for cytotoxic and noncytotoxic T lymphocytes. *Cellular Immunology, 89,* 223.

Liu, J.J., Segre, M., & Segre, D. (1982). Changes in suppressor, helper, and B-cell functions in aging mice. *Cellular Immunology, 66,* 372.

Makinodan, T., & Adler, W.H. (1975). Effects of aging on the differentiation and proliferation potentials of cells of the immune system. *Federation Proceeding, 34,* 153.

Makinodan, T., Albright, J.W., Good, P.I., Peter, C.P., & Heidrick, M.L. (1976). Reduced humoral immune activity in long-lived old mice: An approach to elucidating its mechanisms. *Immunology, 31,* 903.

Makinodan, T., & Kay, M.M.B. (1980). Age influence on the immune system. *Advances in Immunology, 29,* 287.

Makinodan, T., & Peterson, W.J. (1964). Growth and senescence of the primary antibody-forming potential of the spleen. *Journal of Immunology, 93,* 886.

Mark, D.H., & Weksler, M.E. (1982). Immunologic studies of aging. VIII, No change in cyclic nucleotide concentration in T lymphocytes from old humans despite their depressed proliferative response. *Journal of Immunology, 129,* 2323.

Menon, M., Jaroslow, B.N., & Koesterer, R. (1974). The decline of cell-mediated immunity in aging mice. *Journal of Gerontology, 29,* 499.

Meredith, P.J., Kristie, J.A., & Walford, R.L. (1979). Aging increases expression of LPS-induced autoanibody-secreting B cells. *Journal of Immunology, 123,* 87.

Miller, RA. (1982). Age-associated decline in precursor frequency for different T-cell-mediated reactions, with preservation of helper or cytotoxic effect per precursor cell. *Journal of Immunology, 132,* 63.

Miller, R.A., & Stutman, O. (1987). Decline, in aging mice, of the anti-2,4,6-trinitrophenyl (TNP) cytotoxic T-cell response attributable to loss of lyt-2-, interleukin 2-producing helper cell function. *European Journal of Immunology, 11,* 751.

Miller, R.A., & Stutman, O. (1982). Limiting dilution analysis of IL-2 production: Studies of age, genotype, and regulatory interactions. *Lymphokine Research, 1,* 79.

Morgan, E.L., & Weigle, W.O. (1982). The immune response in aged C57BL/6 mice. II. Characterization and reversal of a defect in the ability of aged spleen cells to respond to the adjuvant properties of Fc fragments. *Journal of Immunology, 129,* 36.

Naor, D., Bonavida, B., & Walford, R.L. (1976). Autoimmunity and aging, The age-related response of mice of a long-lived strain to trinitrophenylated syngeneic mouse red blood cells. *Journal of Immunology, 117,* 2204.

Nordin, A.A., & Collins, G.D. (1983). Limiting dilution analysis of alloreactive cytotoxic precursor cells in aging mice. *Journal of Immunology, 131,* 2215.

Pandolfi, F., Quinti, L., Montella, F., Voci, M.C., Schipani, A., Urasia, G., & Aiuti, F. (1983). T-dependent immunity in aged humans: II. Clinical and immunological evaluation after three months of administering a thymic extract. *Thymus, 5,* 235.

Patel, P.J. (1981). Aging and antimicrobial immunity. Impaired production of mediator T cells as a basis for the decreased resistance of senescent mice to listeriosis. *Journal of Experimental Medicine, 154,* 821.

Peterson, W.J., & Makinodan, T. (1972). Autoimmunity in aged mice. Occurrence of autoagglutinating factors in the blood of aged mice with medium and long life spans. *Clinical Experimental Immunology, 12,* 273.

Price, G.B., & Makinodan, T. (1972a). Immunological deficiencies in senescence: I. Characterization of intrinsic deficiencies. *Journal of Immunology, 108,* 403.

Price, G.B., & Makinodan, T. (1972b). Immunological deficiencies in senescence: II.

Price, G.B., & Makinodan, T. (1972b). Immunological deficiencies in senescence: II. Characterization of extrinsic deficiencies. *Journal of Immunology, 108,* 413.

Roberts-Thomson, I.C., Whittingham, S., Youngchaiyud, U., & MacKay, I.R. (1974). Aging, immune response, and mortality. *Lancet, 2,* 368.

Rodriguez, M.A., Ceuppens, J.L., & Goodwin, J.S. (1982). Regulation of IgM rheumatoid factor production in lymphocyte cultures from young and old subjects. *Journal of Immunology, 128,* 2422.

Ross, E.A.M., Anderson, N., & Micklem, H.S. (1982). Serial depletion and regeneration of the murine hematopoietic system. Implications for hematopoietic organization and the study of cellular aging. *Journal of Experimental Medicine, 155,* 432.

Segre, D., & Segre, M. (1976). Increased suppressor T-cell activity in immunologically deficient old mice. *Journal of Immunology, 116,* 735.

Singhal, S.K., Roder, J.C., & Duwe, A.K. (1978). Suppressor cells in immunosenescence. *Federation Proceedings, 37,* 1245.

Skias, D., Reder, A.T., Bania, M.B., & Antel, J.P. (1985). Age-related changes in mechanisms accounting for low levels of polyclonally induced immunoglobulin secretion in humans. *Clinical Immunology and Immunopathology, 35,* 191.

Staiano-Coicco, L., Darzynkiewicz, Z., Melamed, M.R., & Weksler, M.E. (1984). Immunological studies of aging: IX. Impaired proliferation of T lymphocytes detected in elderly humans by flow cytometry. *Journal of Immunology, 132,* 1788.

Stutman, O. (1984). Cell-mediated immunity and aging. *Federation Proceedings, 33,* 2028.

Szewczuk, M.R. (1982). Synergistic cooperation between T and B lymphocytes from old mice in the production of auto-anti-idiotypic antibody regulation in adult irradiated hosts. *Canadian Journal of Aging, 1,* 3.

Szewczuk, M.R. (1983). Selective suppression by auto-anti-idiotypic antibody of B-cell idiotype repertoires generated after stimulation with the same hapten on T-dependent and T-independent carriers. *Cellular Immunology, 83,* 282.

Szewczuk, M.R. (1984). Strain differences in the development of auto-anti-idiotypic antibody regulation with age: Genetic linkage to the Igh-C locus. *Cellular Immunology, 84,* 393.

Szewczuk, M.R., & Campbell, R.J. (1980). Loss of immune competence with age may be due to auto-anti-idiotypic antibody regulation. *Nature, 286,* 164.

Szewczuk, M.R., & Campbell, R.J. (1981a). Lack of age-associated auto-anti-idiotypic antibody regulation in mucosal-associated lymph nodes. *European Journal of Immunology, 11,* 650.

Szewczuk, M.R., & Campbell, R.J. (1981b). Differential effect of aging on the heterogeneity of the immune response to a T-dependent antigen in systemic and mucosal-associated lymphoid tissues. *Journal of Immunology, 126,* 472.

Szewczuk, M.R., Campbell, R.J., & Jung, L.K. (1981). Lack of age-associated immune dysfunction in mucosal-associated lymph nodes. *Journal of Immunology, 126,* 2200.

Szewczuk, M.R., & Wade, A.W. (1985). Age-related strain differences in the development of auto-anti-idiotypic antibody regulation in the splenic and mucosal-associated lymphoid systems. *Gerontology, 31,* 251.

Thoman, M.L., & Weigle, W.O. (1981). Lymphokines and aging: Interleukin-2 production and activity in aged animals. *Journal of Immunology, 127,* 2102.

Thoman, M.L., & Weigle, W.O. (1982). Cell-mediated immunity in aged mice: An underlying lesion in IL-2 synthesis. *Journal of Immunology, 128,* 2358.

Thoman, M.L., & Weigle, W.O. (1983). Deficiency in suppressor T-cell activity in aged animals. Reconstitution of this activity by interleukin-2. *Journal of Experimental Medicine, 157,* 2184.

Thoman, M.L., & Weigle, W.O. (1985). Reconstitution of in vivo cell-mediated lympholysis responses in aged mice with interleukin-2. *Journal of Immunology, 134,* 949.

Thompson, J.S., Wekstein, D.R., Rhoades, J.L., Kirpatrick, C., Brown, S.A., Roszman, M., Straus, R., & Tietz, N. (1984). The immune status of healthy centenarians. *Journal of the American Geriatric Society, 32,* 274.

Thomsen, O., & Kettel, K. (1929). Die Starke der menschlichen Isoagglutinine und entsprechenden Blutkorperchennezeptoren in verschiedene Lebensaltern. *Z Immunitaetsforsch Exp Ther, 63,* 67.

Thorbecke, G.J., Bhogal, B.S., & Siskind, G.W. (1984). Possible mechanism for down-regulation of auto-antibody production by auto-anti-idiotype. *Immunology Today, 5,* 92.

Tice, R.R., Schneider, E.L., Kram, D., & Thorne, P. (1979). Cytokinetic analysis of the impaired proliferative response of peripheral lymphocytes from aged humans to phytohemagglutinin. *Journal of Experimental Medicine, 151,* 1029.

Urban, J.L., & Schreiber, H. (1984). Rescue of the tumor-specific immune response of aged mice in vitro. *Journal of Immunology, 133,* 527.

Verhaegen, H., DeCock, W., Cree, J., & Goldstein, G. (1981). Restoration of the impaired lymphocyte stimulation in old people by thymopoietin pentapeptide. *Journal of Clinical Laboratory Immunology, 6,* 103.

Wade, A.W., & Szewczuk, M.R. (1984). Aging, idiotype repertoire shifts, and compartmentalization of the mucosal-associated lymphoid system. *Advances in Immunology, 36,* 143.

Wade, A.W., & Szewczuk, M.R. (1985). Changes in the mucosal-associated B-cell response with age. In E.A. Goidl (Ed.). *Aging and the immune response.* New York: Marcel Dekker.

Walters, C.S., & Claman, H.N. (1985). Age-related changes in cell-mediated immunity in BALB/c mice. *Journal of Immunology, 115,* 1438.

Watson, J. (1979). Continuous proliferation of murine antigen-specific helper T lymphocytes in culture. *Journal of Experimental Medicine, 150,* 1510.

Weiner, H.L., Moorhead, J.W., & Claman, H.N. (1976). Anti-immunoglobulin stimulation of murine lymphocytes: I. Age dependency of the proliferative response. *Journal of Immunology, 116,* 1656.

Weksler, M.E., & Hutteroth, T.H. (1974). Impaired lymphocyte function in aged humans. *Journal of Clinical Investigation, 53,* 99.

Weksler, M.E., Innes, J.B., & Goldstein, G. (1978). Immunological studies of aging: IV. The contribution of thymic involution to the immune deficiencies of aging mice and reversal with thymopoietin. *Journal of Experimental Medicine, 148,* 996.

Zharhary, D., & Gershon, H. (1981). Allogeneic T-cytotoxic reactivity of senescent mice: Affinity for target cells and determination of cell number. *Cellular Immunology, 60,* 470.

Zharhary, D., & Klinman, N.R. (1983). Antigen responsiveness of the mature and generative B cell population of aged mice. *Journal of Experimental Medicine, 157,* 1300.

Zharhary, D., Segev, Y., & Gershon, H.E. (1984). T-cell cytotoxicity and aging: Differing causes of reduced response in individual mice. *Mechanics of Aging and Development, 25,* 129.

CHAPTER 12

The Basal Ganglia and Aging

*Thomas H. McNeill, Laurie L. Koek,
Sally A. Brown, Jose Rafols*

This study examined the dendritic arbors of medium spiny (MS) and large aspiny II (AS) neurons of the striatum to determine whether striatal target cells undergo compensatory dendritic growth or regression with advancing age. Data showed that while there was regression in the dendritic processes of some MS and AS neurons, dendrites of other neurons remain unchanged or enlarged. Overall, quantitative analysis of MS neurons from aged mice without significant motor impairment revealed no change in any of the dendritic parameters we examined. However, there was a positive correlation between the loss of motor function and decreased dendritic length in aged mice. In contrast, AS neurons showed a significant overall increase in total and terminal dendritic length with age. These data suggest that subpopulations of striatal neurons may be differentially affected with age and that the correlation of structure and function plays an important role in the analysis of aging cell populations.

Alterations in neurotransmitter systems of the basal ganglia have been postulated to contribute to a disruption of motor function and balance associated with advancing age (Hodkinson, 1980). Previous biochemical studies in rodent and human brain have reported age-related declines in a number of biologically active substances in the striatum

Thomas H. McNeill is the recipient of a Research Career Development Award from the National Institute on Aging (AGO0300). Studies supported by PHS grant AGO5445 and AGO3254.

and the substantia nigra (Finch, Randall, & Marshall, 1981) as well as decreases in the number of dopaminergic (Severson & Finch, 1980; Severson, Maccusson, Winbald, & Finch, 1982) and cholinergic binding sites (Strong, Hicks, Hsu, Bartus, & Enna, 1980) in the striatum. Morphological studies have reported age-correlated declines in the number of cells in both the striatum (Bugiani, 1978; Mensah, 1979) and the substantia nigra (McGeer, McGeer, & Suzuki, 1977) of rat and human brain. A previous report from our laboratory has also shown age-correlated morphological changes in A-9, but not all A-10 dopaminergic neurons of the midbrain in the C57BL/6N mouse (McNeill, Koek, & Haycock, 1984). Since it is known that both the medium spiny (MS) (Dimova, Vuillet, & Seite, 1980; Fox, Andrade, Hillman, & Schwin, 1971; Kemp & Powell, 1971; Rafols & Fox, 1979) and large aspiny II (AS) (DiFiglia, Pasik, & Pasik, 1976) neurons of the striatum are target populations for nigrostriatal dopamine fibers (Chang & Kitai, 1982; Freund, Powell, & Smith, 1984; Groves, 1980; Lehman & Langer, 1983; Wilson & Groves, 1980), we undertook a study to examine the question as to whether striatal medium spiny (MS) and large aspiny (AS) neurons undergo compensatory dendritic growth or regression with age in response to possible degeneration of neighboring and/or afferent projecting neurons.

Six age groups (3, 6, 10, 20, 25, and 30 months) of C57BL/6N mice were obtained through the National Institute on Aging. They were sacrificed by decapitation in random order and slides were prepared by the Golgi Cox method according to the procedure of Van der Loos (1956). Sections were cut in a coronal plane at 200 μm and slides were coded so that during data gathering, it would be unknown which slide came from which brain. A sample of 15 neurons (based on a predetermined 95% confidence interval) was randomly chosen at both a rostral and caudal level of the striatum from among all well-impregnated MS and AS neurons. Only cells with a soma in the center one third of the section and whose dendrites were unobscured by overlying glia, blood vessels, other neurons, or nonspecific deposits of stain were examined. Based on previous observations, terminal dendritic segments were required to be tapered at their tips and lack spines, indicating the complete impregnation of the dendrite. Profiles of the cell soma and dendrites were traced using a 40X objective lens and a camera lucida drawing tube and entered into an IBM microcomputer system using a digitizing tablet and Bioquant software. Analysis of dendritic parameters of MS and AS neurons included total and terminal segment lengths and number of segments using a computer-assisted processing system and DAN software (Moyer, Moyer, & Coleman, 1985). Motor performance of animals in all six groups was tested by recording coordination and balance using the rotorod and balance beam (Ingram, London, Reynolds, Waller, & Goldrick, 1981).

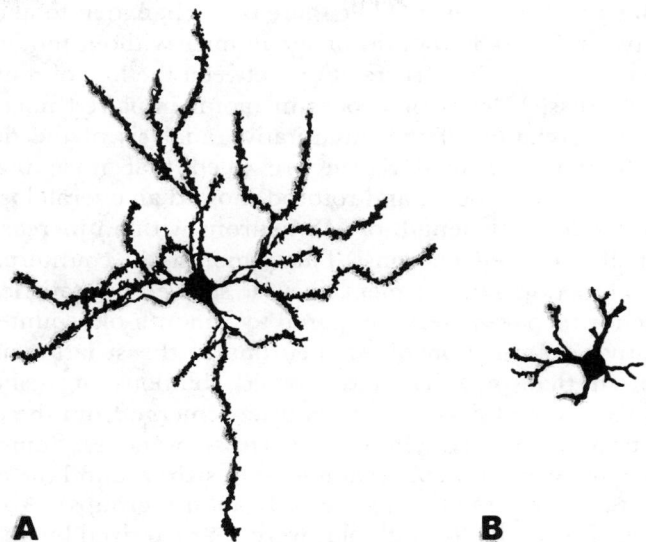

A   **B**

FIGURE 12-1. Camera lucida drawings of MS neurons of the striatum with a total dendritic length of (a) 600–1,200 μm, or (b) <600 μm. Although total dendritic length of MS neurons did not change with advancing age, the number of large-, medium-, and small-sized cells for each age group varied.

RESULTS

Qualitative examination of the striatum showed that MS neurons are characterized by round, ovoid, fusiform or triangular cell bodies. Four to eight dendritic trunks emerge from the cell body and gave rise to several or more branches that radiate in all directions. The dendritic trunks and the initial segments of the branches were spine free, however, the rest of the branches are covered with numerous spines of heterogeneous shapes and sizes. In general, MS neurons at caudal and ventral levels of the striatum had more robust dendritic arbors than MS neurons at more rostral and dorsal levels of the striatum. For all age groups examined, we identified three cell populations of MS neurons based on their total and terminal dendritic lengths (Figure 12-1). The first population was a group of cells with short dendrites with a total dendritic length of less than 600 μm. The second population represented a majority of the impregnated neurons of the striatum and had a total dendritic length ranging from 600 to 1,200 μm. The third population were neurons with total dendritic lengths longer than 1,200 μm. Our analysis of the six age groups based on the total or terminal dendritic length of all of the MS neurons drawn without significant motor impairment revealed no significant difference with advancing age (Figure 12-2). However, while there is no change in total dendritic length between 3 and 30 months of age in mice without motor impairment, there was a positive correlation between the loss of motor function and decreased dendritic arbors in motor-impaired mice (Figure 12-3). The correlation of the quantitative analysis of the dendrites' parameters and functional scoring revealed that mice that tested poorly on the balance beam and rotorod showed an overall loss of total and terminal dendritic length of MS neurons with an increased number of small shrunken neurons. Thirty-month-old counterparts that showed no functional impairment likewise showed no statistical difference in dendritic parameters compared to 3-month-old counterparts.

Qualitative examination of AS neurons of the striatum in young mice showed that they had large ovoid, bulbous or fusiform cell bodies. Two to nine thick or thin dendrites emerge from the cell body and may branch repeatedly into thin varicose branches. Some of these branches may bear a few spines and tend to swirl around the cell body. In contrast to young mice (3-, 6-, and 10-month groups), AS neurons in old mice (20-, and 30-month old) were characterized by an increase in total and terminal dendritic length as well as an increase in total number of dendritic segments. Since primary segments did not show a significant change in number, the increase in total dendritic length represented a net growth and branching of secondary and terminal dendrites.

DISCUSSION

Recent quantitative studies of the structural changes in the dendritic parameters of aged neurons have fostered a perception of aging as an integration of progressive and regressive cell changes that are brain-region, cell-type, and species specific (Buell & Coleman, 1981; Connor, Diamond, & Johnson, 1980; Flood, Buell, DeFiore, Horowitz, & Coleman, 1985; Hinds & McNelly, 1977; 1981). Our finding that total dendric length, terminal length, and segment number of MS neurons of the striatum remains relatively unchanged with age supports this view and adds another brain region to the growing list of structures that shows a significant degree of plasticity throughout life. The presence of three varying-size populations of MS dendrites within the striatum at each of the six age groups also supports the view that aging is a continuing process and made up of regressing and growing neurons (Buell & Coleman, 1979). The regressing population, characterized by shrinking dendritic branches, may be indicative of atrophic changes ultimately leading to cell death. In contrast, the surviving neurons show normal or expanded dendrites with age. Our data suggest that in normal aging without motor impairment there is a balance

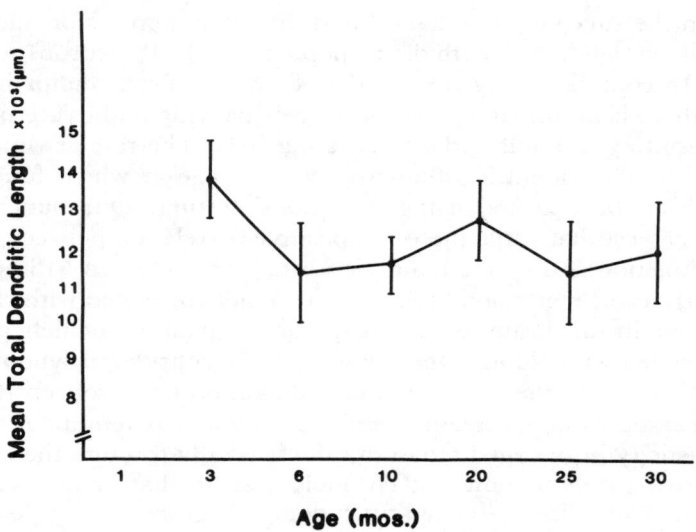

FIGURE 12-2. Age changes in total dendritic length of MS neurons at a caudal level of the striatum. Each data point represents the mean total dendritic length of 15 cells drawn from each of 5 mice ± sem.

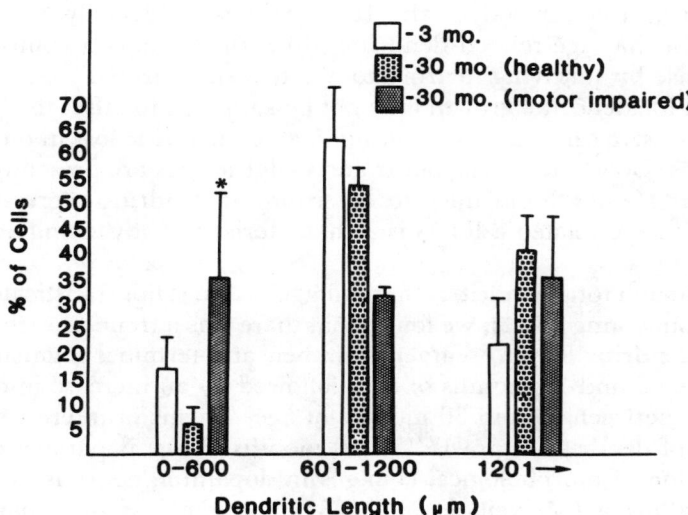

FIGURE 12-3. Frequency analysis of the number of large- ($>1,200$ μm), medium- (600-1,200 μm), and small-sized (<600 μm) neurons in motor-impaired and unimpaired 3- and 30–month-old mice. Thirty-month-old, motor-impaired mice showed a significant increase in the number of cells with short dendrites when compared with 30-month-old, nonimpaired mice, $p < .01$.

between the surviving population and the dying population such that the total net dendritic length of our population of MS neurons remains intact. In contrast, in aged mice that show significant motor impairment, there is an imbalance between the surviving and dying populations resulting in an abundance of dying cells. The rate at which this shift takes place identifies the chronological age at which functional deficits can be detected using behavioral testing. Our data in the mouse suggest that while there is a positive correlation between loss of motor function and regression of dendritic parameters in MS neurons of the striatum, regression of dendrites are not correlated with chronological age in this brain area. Thus, while striatal motor deficits may be associated with old age, they should not be considered synonymous with old age. On the contrary, our data support the concept that in normal aging without disease there is considerable potential for growth and plasticity in the aged striatum, and it is only through the correlation of structure, function, and chronological age that we may separate age-related and disease-related functional changes.

The question of whether dendritic regression in MS neurons of the striatum is inevitable in old, old mice (i.e., greater than 40 months) is not known at the present time. Previous studies have reported that in many brain regions where there is age-related neuronal loss there is concurrent dendritic growth of surviving neurons for most of the lifespan followed by dendritic regression in the oldest old (Cupp & Uemura, 1980; Flood et al., 1985; Hinds & McNelly, 1977). It is thought that age-related dendritic growth represents a compensatory response by surviving neurons to age-related neuronal loss. However, late in life dendritic growth may not be sufficient to offset the increases in regressive cell changes resulting in a net dendritic loss in these brain regions. Concurrent cell counts and Golgi studies are presently underway in 45-month-old mice to determine if dendritic regression as a result of age-related cell loss is a characteristic of advancing age in the striatum.

Although total dendritic length in aged mice is not statistically different from young adults, we found that there was a trend toward a loss of total dendritic length, segment number, and terminal segment length between 3 and 10 months of age, followed by an increase in dendritic length between 10 and 30 months of age. This is of interest since the onset of dendritic "growth" at 10 months of age is paralleled by the initiation of morphological changes in dopamine neurons of the substantia nigra (McNeill et al., 1984) and the loss of dopaminergic binding sites in the striatum (Severson & Finch, 1980). Previous anatomical and biochemical lesion studies have shown that the loss of dopaminergic inputs to striatal neurons have a significant effect on striatal function (Hirschhorn, Makman, & Sharpless, 1982; Hodge & Butcher, 1979; Sagar & Snodgrass, 1980; Ungerstedt, 1971) and recent data from our laboratory have reported that the loss of dopamine cells in the substantia nigra in Parkinson's disease results in transneuronal degeneration of MS neuron dendrites and are similar in appearance to the dendritic changes in our motor-impaired aged mice (McNeill, Brown, Lapham, Eskin, & Brumback et al., 1986). It may be suggested that while the biochemical and morphological changes that have been identified in dopaminergic neurons of the substantia nigra in normal aging are able to alter dopaminergic binding sites in the striatum, these changes are not of significant severity to irreparably alter the overall balance of growing and regressing dendrites of MS neurons in the aged brain.

The finding of a significant increase in dendritic branching and length of dendrites of large AS neurons but not MS cells is of interest based on the possible differences in their afferent inputs. Previous studies by Freund, Powell, and Smith (1984), have shown that while MS neurons of the striatum represent the principal target neuron for dopaminergic fibers of the substantia nigra, the dopaminergic synapse represents less than half of all the synaptic input to MS cells. They suggest that the principal role of the dopaminergic synapse on MS neurons is to modulate the afferent input of other neurotransmitter systems. In contrast, dopaminergic afferents to large AS cells are principally axodendritic and previous anatomical, pharmacological, and biochemical experiments strongly support the hypothesis of a direct dopaminergic-cholinergic interaction in extrapyramidal function (Leham & Langer, 1983). While the percentage of dopaminergic and other neurotransmitter-containing synapses on AS neurons of the striatum has not been determined, it may be suggested that the increase in total dendritic length of large AS neurons in the striatum represents a functionally relevant increase in dendritic material that has been integrated into the neuropil. Whether the increase in total dendritic length of large AS neurons may represent a compensatory growth in response to the death of neighboring striatal neurons or may be related to the loss of afferent neuronal input is not known. Studies directed at addressing this question are currently underway using anatomical and biochemical lesions of the various inputs to the striatum including the substantia nigra, thalamus, and cortex.

Since almost all dopaminergic synapses are found on dendritic spines of MS neurons, the finding that there is no overall regression in MS neurons with age does not necessarily lead to the conclusion that the functional integrity of the receptive fields of MS neurons remains uncompromised; the question of whether dendritic spine density remains the same throughout the aging process was not addressed. To this end, studies have been initiated to examine the linear density of dendritic spines on MS neurons of the striatum to determine if spine loss accompanies aging in the C57BL/6N mouse. Preliminary evidence using tissues from only three age groups (3, 10, and 30 months), indicates there is reduction in the linear density of dendritic spines on the terminal segments of MS neurons with age. These data suggest that the loss of dendritic spines on MS neurons of the striatum in the aged mouse may provide a morphological basis for the reduction of dopaminergic postsynaptic binding sites in the striatum as well as changes in motor function associated with old age. However, confirmation of dendritic spine loss in the aged mouse will necessitate a more complete study.

SUMMARY

These data support the view that the rate at which an organism ages is a summation of factors throughout life. While some cellular parameters seem to remain stable or even grow with age, others show significant regression. It is the summation of these changes that are expressed in the form of the morphological, neurochemical, and functional changes that are the subject of future neurogerontologic research. In addition, our data support the notion that the occurrence and severity of structural changes in the aged brain are not distributed homogenously and that many of the so-called "age-related" changes that were once generalized to the entire brain, brain region, or cell type, are species specific. Our data also reinforce the concept that the correlation of structure and function plays an important role in the analysis of an aging population since considerable bias may be introduced into data based on functionally impaired and unimpaired animals.

REFERENCES

Buell, S.J., Coleman, P.D. (1979). Dendritic growth in the aged human brain and failure of growth in senile dementia. *Science, 206,* 854–856.

Buell, S.J., Coleman, P.D. (1981). Quantitative evidence for selective dendritic growth in normal human aging but not in senile dementia. *Brain Research, 214,* 23–41.

Bugiani, O., Slavarani, S., Perdelli, F., Mancardi, G.L., Leonardi, A. (1978). Nerve cell loss with aging in the putamen. *European Neurology, 17,* 286–291.

Chang, H.T. & Kitai, S.T. (1982). Large neostriatal neurons in the rat: An electron microscope study of gold-toned, Golgi-stained cells. *Brain Research Bulletin, 8,* 631–643.

Connor, J.R., Diamond, M.C., & Johnson, R.E. (1980). Occipital cortical morphology of the rat: alterations with age and environment. *Experimental Neurology, 68,* 158–170.

Cupp, C.J. & Uemura, E. (1980). Age-related changes in prefrontal cortex of *Macaca mulatta:* quantitative analysis of dendritic branching patterns. *Exp. Neurol., 69,* 143–163.

DiFiglia, M., Pasik, P. & Pasik, T. (1976). A Golgi study of neuronal types in the neostriatum of monkeys. *Brain Research, 114,* 245–256.

Dimova, R., Vuilllet, J. & Seite, R. (1980). Study of the rat neostriatum using a combined Golgi-electron microscope technique and serial sections. *Neuroscience, 5,* 1581–1596.

Finch, C.E., Randall, P.E. & Marshall, J.F. (1981). Aging and basal gangliar functions. In: C. Eisdorfer, (Ed.) *Annual Review of Gerontology and Geriatrics,* (Vol. 2, pp. 48–86). New York: Springer Publishing Co.

Flood, D.G., Buell, S.J., DeFiore, C.H., Horwitz, G.J., & Coleman, P.D. (1985). Age-related dendritic growth in dentate gyrus of human brain is followed by regression in the "oldest old". *Brain Research, 345,* 366–368.

Fox, C.A., Andrade, A.N., Hillman, D.E. & Schwin, R.C. (1971). The spiny neurons in the primate striatum: A Golgi and electron microscopic study. *Journal for Hirnforschung, 13,* 181–201.

Freund, T.F., Powell, J.F. & Smith, A.D. (1984). Tyrosine hydroxylase-immunoreactive boutons in synaptic contact with identified striatonigral neurons, with particular reference to dendritic spines. *Neuroscience, 13,* 4, 1189–1215.

Groves, P.M. (1980). Synaptic endings and their postsynaptic targets in neostriatum: synaptic specializations revealed from analysis of serial sections. *Proceedings of the National Academy of Science,* U.S.A., 77, 6926–6929.

Hinds, J.W. & McNelly, N.A. (1977). Aging of the rat olfactory bulb: Growth and atrophy of constituent, layers and changes in size and number of mitral cells. *Journal of Comparative Neurology, 171,* 345–368.

Hinds, J.W. & McNelly, N.A. (1981). Aging in the rat olfactory system: Correlation of changes in the olfactory epithelium and olfactory bulb. *Journal of Comparative Neurology, 203,* 441–342.

Hirschhorn, I.D., Makman, M.H. & Sharpless, N.S. (1982). Dopamine receptor sensitivity following nigrostriatal lesion in the aged rat. *Brain Research, 234,* 357–368.

Hodge, G.K. & Butcher, L.L. (1979). Role of the pars compacta of the substantia nigra in circling behavior. *Pharmacology Biochemistry and Behavior, 10,* 695–702.

Hodkinson, H.M. (1980). *Common symptoms of disease in the elderly.* St. Louis, MO: Blackwell Scientific Publications.

Ingram, D.K., London, E.L., Reynolds, M.A., Waller, S.B., & Goodrick, C.G. (1981). Differential effects of age on motor performance in two mouse strains. *Neurobiology of Aging, 2,* 221–227.

Kemp, J.M., & Powell, T.P.S. (1971). The structure of the caudate nucleus of the cat: Light and electron microscopy. *Philosophical Transactions of the Royal Society of London. Series B., 262,* 383–401.

Lehman, J., & Langer, S.Z. (1983). The striatal cholinergic interneuron: Synaptic target of dopaminergic terminals? *Neuroscience, 10,* (4) 1105–1120.

McGeer, P.L., McGeer, E.G., & Suzuki, J.S. (1977). Aging and extrapyramidal function. *Archives of Neurology, 34,* 33–35.

McNeill, T.H., Koek, L.L., & Haycock, J.W. (1984). Age-correlated changes in dopaminergic nigrostriatal perikarya of the C57BL/6NNia mouse. *Mechanisms of Aging and Development, 24,* 293–230.

McNeill, T.H., Brown, S.A., Lapham, L.W., Eskin, T.A., Brumback, R.A., Shoulson, I., & Joynt, R.J. (1986). Dendritic regression of medium spiny neurons of the striatum in Parkinson's disease. *AAN Scientific Program.* New Orleans, LA, April 27–May 3.

Mensah, P.L. (1979). The effect of aging on neuron "cell islands" in the mouse neostriatum. *Society of Neuroscience, 5,* 250.

Moyer, A., Moyer, V., & Coleman, P.D. (1985). (SPON: V. Laties) An inexpensive

PC-based system for quantification of neuronal processes. *Society of Neuroscience, 11,* 261.18.

Rafols, J.A., & Fox, C.A. (1979). Fine structure of the primate striatum. *Applied Neurophysiology, 42,* 13–16.

Sagar, S.M., & Snodgrass, S.R. (1980). Effects of substantia nigra lesions on forebrain 2-deoxyglucose retention in the rat. *Brain Research, 185,* 335–348.

Severson, J.A. & Finch, C.E. (1980). Reduced dopaminergic binding during aging in the rodent striatum. *Brain Research, 192,* 147–162.

Severson, J.A., Maecusson, J., Winblad, B., & Finch, C.E. (1982). Age-correlated loss of dopaminergic binding sites in human basal ganglia. *Journal of Neurochemistry, 39,* 1623–1631.

Strong, R., Hicks, P., Hsu, L., Bartus, R.T., & Enna, S.J. (1980). Age-related alterations in the rodent brain cholinergic system and behavior. *Neurobiology of Aging, 1,* 59–63.

Ungerstedt, U. (1971). Postsynaptic supersensitivity after 6 hydroxy-dopamine-induced degeneration of the nigrostriatal dopamine system. *Acta Physiologica Scandinavica, 367,* (Suppl.) 69–93.

Van der Loos, H. (1956). Une combinaison de deux vieilles methodes histologiques pour le systeme nerveux central. *Monatsschrift für Psychiatrie und Neurologie, 132,* 330–334.

Wilson, C.J., & Groves, P.M. (1980). Fine structure and synaptic connections of the common spiny neuron of the rat neostriatum: A study employing intracellular injection of horseradish peroxidase. *Journal of Comparative Neurology, 194,* 599–615.

CHAPTER 13

Neuropeptides in Alzheimer-type Dementia

H. Arai, P.C. Emson,
M.N. Rossor, D. Dawbarn

Neurochemical research on postmortem brain specimens from Alzheimer-type dementia (ATD) patients has rapidly developed during the last 10 years following the original reports of cholinergic and monoaminergic deficits. More recently a number of peptides have been considered as potential neurotransmitter candidates and those neuropeptides have received attention in ATD brain research. The most prominent and uniform peptide deficit found in ATD brain is of somatostatin. A negative correlation between somatostatin content and tangle density or plaque counts seems to be a universal finding. As yet there is no consensus on other neuropeptides deficits, such as substance P, vasoactive intestinal polypeptide, cholecystokinin, and neuropeptide Y, in Alzheimer's dementia. Vasopressin, neurotensin, methioninenkephalin, thyrotropin-releasing hormone, and luteinizing-hormone-releasing-hormone have been reported to be unchanged in ATD brain. Combinations of radioimmunoassay, immunohistochemistry, and Northern analysis of mRNAs will be necessary to further understand the neuropeptide abnormalities in ATD brain.

Alzheimer's disease and senile dementia of Alzheimer-type (Alzheimer-type dementia, ATD) is rapidly emerging as a major medical problem, mostly because improved medical care prolongs the life span, creating an ever-growing section of the population at risk. Alzheimer-type dementia is characterized clinically by progressive dementia and pathologically by widespread presence of neuronal loss, senile plaques, and neurofibrillary tangles in the cerebral cortex and hippocampus.

Neurochemical research on postmortem material from ATD patients revealed little until the early 1970s when several groups reported that there was a striking loss of choline acetyltransferase (CAT) content from neocortex and allocortex with deficits particularly localized in "limbic" cortical areas and the hippocampus (Bowen, Smith, White, & Davison, 1975; Davies & Maloney, 1976; Perry et al., 1979; Perry, Candyr, & Perry, 1983). This cholinergic deficit has been confirmed and other deficits in monoamines (Adolfsson, Gottfries, Roos & Winblad, 1979; Arai, Kosaka, & Iizuka, 1984a; Cross, Crow, Johnson, Joseph, & Perry et al., 1983; Gottfries, Adolfsson, Aquilonius, Carlsson, & Eckernas, et al., 1983; Yates, Simpson, Gordon, Maloney, & Allison, et al., 1983b) or the neuropeptide somatostatin (Davies, Katzman, & Terry, 1980; Emson, Rossor, & Hunt, 1981) have also been reported.

The discovery of the enkephalins (Hughes, 1975) and the sequencing of substance P (Chang, Leeman, & Niall, 1971) and the first releasing factor thyrotropin-releasing hormone (TRH) (Boler, Enzmann, & Folkers et al., 1969; Burgus, Dunn, & Desiderio et al., 1969) led to a flood of research aimed at localizing, characterizing, and identifying central nervous system (CNS) peptides. There is now an ever-expanding list of neuropeptides, that is peptides with a localization in specific CNS neurons, which may be neurotransmitters or neurohormones. Human CNS studies have demonstrated that the human brain, like other mammalian brains, is equally full of neuropeptides and with few exceptions much of the organization of neuropeptide systems in lower mammals is retained in the human. Therefore, it is possible to use neuropeptides as markers of specific pathways, or neuronal cell types, and to use measurements of peptides as a means of assessing the integrity of peptide-containing cells or pathways. Neuropeptides have been studied in ATD from this aspect and the findings will be briefly reviewed in this paper.

POSTMORTEM STABILITY

Since it is usually difficult to obtain human brain tissue less than 4 to 6 hours after death, it has been important to establish if peptides remain intact postmortem and for how long this stability persists. In order to investigate the peptide stability we used an animal model to mimic the postmortem cooling curve of human brain (Emson, Arrequi, & Clement-Jones et al., 1980). We sampled the peptide content of the mouse brain at different times postmortem. A series of these studies revealed that methionine-enkephalin, substance P, cholecystokinin (CCK), vasoactive intestinal polypeptide (VIP), somatostatin (Emson, Rossor, & Hunt et al., 1981) and neurokinin $\alpha + \beta$ (see Table 13-1), for

TABLE 13-1. Postmortem Stability of Neurokinin α-like Immunoreactivity in Rat Brains (ng/g Tissue)

Postmortem period (hr)*	Neurokinin α-like immunoreactivity†
0	45.11 ± 2.41
4	50.33 ± 1.77
8	48.84 ± 1.53
12	49.10 ± 2.96
24	49.04 ± 2.58
48	50.18 ± 3.04
72	26.39 ± 4.86

* Rats were killed and left at room temperature for varying periods before removal of the brain.
† Valves were means ± SEM from four rats (eight hemispheres) at each time interval.
Source: Arai, H., and Emson, P.C. (1986). Regional distribution of neuropeptide K and other tachykinins (neurokinin A & neurokinin B and substance P) in rat central nervous system. *Brain Research, 399*, 240–249.

example, are surprisingly stable for up to 24 hours after death and suggested examination of human brain peptide content might be feasible. The reason for this stability is unknown but may lie in the packaging of neuropeptides in vesicles to avoid cytoplasmic peptidase activity.

Another important point is to establish the identity of the immunoreactivity as the authentic peptide rather than a "degraded" immunoreactive fragment. A combination of high pressure liquid chromatography (HPLC) or gel chromatography and sequence-directed radioimmunoassay (RIA) have demonstrated that the material detected in postmortem brain extracts is indistinguishable from the relevant authentic peptide (i.e., it separates at the position expected for the intact peptide) and is immunologically an intact peptide (i.e., it contains the appropriate amino acids to react with appropriate sequence-specific antiserum). These data are consistent with the assumption that the peptide detected contains the complete amino acid sequence.

ALZHEIMER-TYPE DEMENTIA

Of the many peptides measured in ATD postmortem brains somatostatin-like immunoreactivity (SRIF-1R) is the only one to show consistent alterations (Arai, Moroji, & Kosaka 1984b; Davies et al., 1980; Rossor et al., 1980a; Ferrier, Cross, Johnson, Roberts & Crow et al., 1983) (see Table 13-2). A low concentration of somatosatin-like immunoreactivity (SRIF-LI) was also reported in cerebrospinal fluid (Soininen, Jolkkonen, Reinikainen, Halonen & Reinikainen, 1984;

TABLE 13-2. Somatostatin-like Immunoreactivity in
ATD and Control Brain (pmol/g Tissue)

Region	Control $(n = 42)^*$	ATD $(n = 42)^*$
Frontal cortex	1.92 ± 0.03 (79.6)	1.77 ± 0.04† (61.2)
Temporal cortex	2.18 ± 0.03 (157.8)	1.81 ± 0.04** (62.8)

*Values are means ± SEM of logarithmically transformed data
with median values of untransformed data in parentheses.
†$p < 0.01$, **$p < 0.001$.

Wood et al., 1982). Somatostatin-like-LI shows a significant negative
correlation with tangle density and with plaque counts (Rossor, Emson, Iversen, & Mountjoy, 1984) for the overall control and ATD
group. Immunohisto-chemical studies also revealed that SRIF-like immunoreactive cell bodies contain neurofibrillary tangles (Roberts,
Crow & Polak, 1985) and that SRIF-like immunoreactive fibers exist
in senile plaques (Perry, Candy, & Perry, 1983). Positive correlations
between SRIF-LI concentration and decreased CHAT activity in the
frontal and temporal cortex of ATD brains (Davies & Perry, 1981)
suggests some correlation between them. However, there is no evidence that these two markers coexist in the ascending cholinergic
projection from basal forebrain (McKiney, Davies, & Coyle 1982). On
the other hand, there is a coexistence of acetylcholinesterase and SRIF-
LI within intrinsic cortical cholinergic neurons, although acetylcholinesterase is not a specific marker of cholinergic neurons (Delfs, Zhu, &
Dichter, 1984).

Although a deficit of substance P-like immunoreactivity was reported in cortical regions of ATD brain (Crystal & Davies, 1982), it
has not been confirmed in other studies (Ferrier et al., 1983; Yates,
Harmar, Rosie, Sherward, & Sanchez de Levy, et al., 1983a). Recently, it has been revealed that substance P is not the only tachykinin
in mammalian brain but other tachykinins [neurokinin-α and β (Kimura, Okada & Sugita et al., 1983) and neuropeptide K (Tatemoto,
Lundberg, & Jornvall et al., 1985)] are present in the mammalian
nervous system. Therefore, these peptides have to be examined separately in ATD brains. There are also controversial findings on VIP-
and CCK-LI in ATD brain. Neither VIP- or CCK-LI were found to
be significantly reduced in ATD (Ferrier et al, 1983; Rossor,
Frahrenkrug, & Emson et al., 1980b; Rossor, Rehfeld, & Emson et
al., 1981), although another study using postmortem brains from Japanese ATD patients (Arai et al., 1984b) found a decrease of VIP-LI in
the insular and angulate cortices, and Perry, Dockray, and Dimaline

TABLE 13-3. Neuropeptide Y-like Immunoreactivity in ATD and Control Brain (pmol/g Tissue)

Region	Control ($n = 20$)*	ATD ($n = 20$)*
Frontal cortex	1.27 ± 0.02 (18.3)	1.24 ± 0.02 (18.4)
Temporal cortex	1.08 ± 0.04 (10.3)	1.19 ± 0.03 (14.7)

*Values are means ± SEM of logarithmically transformed data with median values of untransformed data in parentheses. None of the differences are significant.

(1981) found a decrease of CCK-LI in the most severe ATD cases. These two peptides are of interest in ATD since they are found within intrinsic neurons, predominantly multipolar and bipolar; nonpyramidal cells in the cerebral cortex (Emson & Hunt, 1984) and VIP- and CCK-like immunoreactive fibers were found in senile plaques (Roberts et al., 1985). Moreover, 80% of the intrinsic cholinergic neurons in the cortex also contain VIP-LI (Eckenstein & Baughman, 1984). A morphometric study on cortex of ATD brain has revealed that the number of large neurons (pyramidal cells) is decreased while that of medium-sized cells is not changed when compared with control brains (Mountjoy, Roth, & Evans, 1983). These results, however, do not suggest that the numbers of interneurons (most of the medium-sized cortical cells) are unchanged in ATD brain, because both interneurons and glia cells could possibly be included in the same size group using this method; although the glia cells would be at the lower end of the histogram. Therefore, further study using other markers for interneurons will be necessary to investigate the extent of damage to these neurons in ATD. From the viewpoint of coexistence with somatostatin, neuropeptide Y (NPY) is of particular interest. Neuropeptide-like immunoreactive fibers can be seen in senile plaques (Dawbarn & Emson, 1985). However, NPY-LI in ATD brain was unchanged in cerebral cortex (Allen, Ferrier, & Roberts et al., 1984; Dawbarn, Rossor, & Mountjoy et al., 1985) (see Table 13-3), though Beal, Mazurek & Chattha et al. (1985) reported a decrease of NPY-LI. Vasopressin, neurotensin, methioin-enkephalin, TRH, and luteinizing-hormone-releasing-hormone are reported unchanged in ATD brain (Rossor et al., 1984).

As mentioned above, with exception of the somatostatin depletion on which everybody seems to be agreed, there are no uniform conclusions on peptide deficits in ATD brains. Even with somatostatin, the extent of its deficit or the region where the deficit was found differs between studies. This lack of uniformity may be accounted for by the

TABLE 13–4. α-MSH-like Immunoreactivity in
ATD and Control Brain (ng/g Tissue)

Region	Control*	ATD*
Caudate	0.30 ± 0.02	0.19 ± 0.02†
	$(n = 7)$	$(n = 5)$
Substantia nigra	4.34 ± 0.82	1.18 ± 0.23**
	$(n = 3)$	$(n = 3)$

*Values are means ± SEM.
†$p < 0.01$, **$p < 0.05$.

differences in a number of factors, which could affect the peptide content; for example, the age range of patients, clinical stage or severity of dementia, drug treatment, cause of death, brain region analyzed, specificity and sensitivity of antibody used in immunoassay for peptides, and method of extraction of peptide from brain tissue.

We have also carried out a preliminary study of the distribution of α-melanocyte-stimulating hormone (α-MSH)-LI in human brains (Arai et al., 1985). Although α-MSH-LI is distributed widely in rat brain (Swaab, Achterbury, & Boer et al., 1981) and α-MSH may be related to learning (Bohus & de Wied, 1981), this peptide has not been examined in ATD brain. Our recent study revealed the wide distribution of α-MSH in the extrahypophyseal regions of human brain (Arai, Moroji, & Kosaka et al., 1985). Interestingly, α-MSH-LI was significantly decreased in the caudate and substantia nigra of ATD brains (Table 13-4). At present, the number of ATD brains examined is relatively small and further study will be necessary to confirm this finding. However, an α-MSH-LI deficit in the nigrostriatal system could affect the activity of this dopaminergic system. Since the dopaminergic system in ATD brain seems to be relatively undamaged compared with the other monaminergic systems (Arai et al, 1984a; Cross et al., 1983; Yates et al., 1983b), this α-MSH abnormality may contribute to the extrapyramidal symptoms usually found in the ATD patients in the middle or later stages of the clinical course of the disease.

Finally, when neuropeptides are used as markers of neuronal integrity in ATD, what does the deficit of a neuropeptide mean? There are two major possibilities. First, and most usually, the neuropeptide deficit may reflect the loss of neurons that use the peptide as a neurotransmitter/neurohormone. Secondly, it could also reflect a higher turnover rate of the neuropeptide, which may be a secondary response of normal neurons to the primary pathological process. Immunohistochemistry is helpful for detecting specific neuronal loss (as in Huntington's chorea, for example). However, molecular biology procedures that involve measuring the specific mRNA content will also be helpful for the investigation of neuronal degeneration and for providing some assessment of the turnover rate of neuropeptides (as far as this is expressed in mRNA content). Although these types of studies have not yet been carried out to any extent, the available information on peptide changes in ATD would indicate selective neuronal damage. Combinations of radioimmunoassay, immunohistochemistry, and Northern analysis will hopefully answer these questions more clearly in the future. Such studies are also of interest from the viewpoint of the cholinergic hypothesis in which the damage of the basal forebrain region (nucleus basalis of Meynert) is considered as the primary and selective lesion in ATD, and studies of the content of nerve growth factor (NGF) (a possible trophic factor for cholinergic neurons) and NGF mRNA content are currently underway.

REFERENCES

Adolfsson, R., Gottfries, C.G., Roos, B.E., & Winblad, B. (1979). Changes in brain catecholamines in patients with dementia of Alzheimer type. *British Journal of Psychiatry, 135,* 216–223.

Allen, J.M., Ferrier, I.N., Roberts, G.W., et al. (1984). Elevation of neuropeptide Y (NPY) in substantia innominata in Alzheimer's type dementia. *Journal of the Neurological Sciences, 64,* 325–331.

Arai, H., Kosaka, K., & Iizuka, R. (1984a). Changes of biogenic amines and their metabolites in postmortem brains from patients with Alzheimer-type dementia. *Journal of Neurochemistry, 43,* 388–393.

Arai, H., Moroji, T., & Kosaka, K. (1984b). Somatostatin and vasoactive intestinal polypeptide in postmortem brains from patients with Alzheimer-type dementia. *Neuroscience Letter, 52,* 73–78.

Arai, H., Moroji, T., Kosaka, K., et al. (in press). Extrahypophysial distribution of α-melanocyte-stimulating hormone (α-MSH)-like immunoreactivity in postmortem brains from normal subjects and Alzheimer-type dementia patients. *Brain Research.*

Beal, M.F., Mazurek, M.F., Chattha, G., et al. (1985). Neuropeptide Y immunoreactivity is reduced in Alzheimer's disease cerebral cortex. *Abstracts of 15th Annual Meeting, Society for Neuroscience,* 1119.

Bohus, B. and de Wied, D. (1981). Actions of ACTH- and MSH-like peptides on learning performance and retention. In J.L. Martinez, Jr., R.A. Jensen, R.B. Messing et al. (Eds.), *Endogenous peptides and learning and memory processes.* New York: Academic Press.

Boler, J.P., Enzmann, F., Folkers, K., et al. (1969). The identity of chemical or hormonal properties of the thyrotropin-releasing hormone and pyroglutamylhystidy-prolineamide. *Biochemical and Biophysical Research Communications, 37,* 705–710.

Bowen, D.M., Smith, C.B., White, P., & Davison, A.N. (1977). Neurotransmitter-related enzymes and indices of hypoxia in senile dementia and other allotrophies. *Brain, 99,* 459–496.

Burgus, R., Dunn, T., Desiderio, D., et al. (1969). Structure male-culaire de facteur hypothalamique hypophysiotrope TRF d'origine ovine: Mise en evidence par

Spectrometric de messe de la sequence PCA-His-Pro-NHz. Compte Rendu Academie Sciences (Paris) *269,* 1870–1873.

Chang, M.M., Leeman, S.E., & Niall, H.D. Amino-acid sequence of substance P. *Nature New Biology, 232,* 86–87.

Cross, A.J., Crow, T.J., Johnson, J.A., Joseph, A.M., Perry, E.K., Perry, P.H. Blessed, G., & Tomlinson, B.E. (1983). Monoamine metabolism in senile dementia of Alzheimer type. *Journal of Neurological Sciences, 60,* 383–392.

Crystal, H.A., & Davies, P. (1982). Cortical substance P-like immunoreactivity in cases of Alzheimer's disease and senile dementia of the Alzheimer type. *Journal of Neurochemistry, 38,* 1781–1784.

Davies, P., Katzman, R., & Terry, R.D. (1980). Reduced somatostatin-like immunoreactivity in cerebral cortex from cases of Alzheimer's disease and Alzheimer senile dementia. *Nature, 288,* 279–280.

Davies, P., & Maloney, A.J. (1976). Selective loss of central cholinergic neurons in Alzheimer's disease. *Lancet, ii,* 1403.

Davies, P., & Terry, R.D. (1981). Cortical somatostatin-like immunoreactivity in cases of Alzheimer's disease and senile dementia of the Alzheimer type. *Neurobiology of Aging, 2,* 9–14.

Dawbarn, D., & Emson, P.C. (1985). Neuropeptide Y-like immunoreactivity in neuritic plaques of Alzheimer's disease. *Biochemical and Biophysical Research Communications, 126,* 289–293.

Dawbarn, D., Rossor, M.N., Mountjoy, C.Q., et al. (in press). Decreased somatostatin immunoreactivity but not neuropeptide Y immunoreactivity in cortex in senile dementia of Alzheimer type. *Peptides.*

Delfs, J.R., Zhu, C.H., & Dichter, M.A. (1984). Coexistence of acetylcholinesterase and somatostatin-immunoreactivity in neurons cultured from rat cerebrum. *Science, 223,* 61–63.

Eckenstein, F. and Baughman, R.W. (1984). Two types of cholinergic innervation in cortex, one co-localized with vasoactive intestinal polypeptide. *Nature, 309,* 153–155.

Emson, P.C., Arregui, A., Clement-Jones, V., et al. (1980). Regional distribution of methionine enkephalin and substance P-like immunoreactivity in normal human brain and in Huntington's disease. *Brain Research, 199,* 147–160.

Emson, P.C., & Hunt, S.P. (1984). Peptide containing neurons of the cerebral cortex. In E.G. Jones, A. Peters (Eds.). *Cerebral cortex.* New York: Plenum Press.

Emson, P.C., Rossor, M.N., Hunt, S.P., et al. (1981). Distribution and postmortem stability of substance P, metenkephalin, vasoactive intestinal polypeptide and cholecystokinin in normal human brain and in Huntington's disease. In F.C. Rosse (Ed.). *Metabolic disorders of the nervous system.* London: Pittman.

Ferrier, I.N., Cross, A.J., Johnson, J.A., Roberts, G.W., Crow, T.J., Corsellis, J.A.N., Lee, Y.C., O'Shaughnessy, D., Adrian, T.E., McGregor, G.P. (1983). Neuropeptides in Alzheimer type dementia. *Journal of the Neurological Sciences, 62,* 159–170.

Gottfries, G.C., Adolfsson, R., Aguilonius, S.M., Carlsson, A., Eckernas, S.-A., Nordberg, A., Oreland, L., Svennerholm, L., Wiberg, A., & Winblad, B. (1983). Biochemical changes in dementia disorders of Alzheimer type (AD/SDAT). *Neurobiology of Aging, 4,* 261–271.

Hughes, J. (1975). Isolation of an endogenous compound from the brain with pharmacological properties similar to morphine. *Brain Research, 88,* 295–306.

Kimura, S., Okada, M., Sugita, Y., et al. (1983). Novel neuropeptides, neurokinin α and β isolated from porcine spinal cord. *Proceedings of the Japanese Academy Series B., 59,* 101–104.

McKinney, M., Davies, P., & Coyle, J.T. (1982). Somatostatin is not co-localized in cholinergic neurons innervating the rat cerebral cortex-hippocampal formation. *Brain Research, 243,* 169–172.

Mountjoy, C.Q., Roth, M., & Evans, N.J.R. (1983). Cortical neuronal counts in normal elderly controls and demented patients. *Neurobiology of Aging, 4,* 1–11.

Perry, R.H., Candy, J.M., & Perry, E.K. (1983). Some observations and speculations concerning the cholinergic system and neuropeptides in Alzheimer's disease. In R. Katzman (Ed.). *Biological aspects of Alzheimer's disease.* (Banbury Report 15). Cold Spring Harbor, NY.

Perry, R.H., Dockray, G.J., & Dimaline, R. (1981). Neuropeptides in Alzheimer's disease, depression, and schizophrenia: A postmortem analysis of vasoactive intestinal polypeptide and cholecystokinin in cerebral cortex. *Journal of Neurological Sciences, 51,* 465–472.

Perry, E.K., Perry, R.H., & Blessed, G. (1979). Necropsy evidence of central cholinergic deficits in senile dementia. *Lancet, i,* 189.

Roberts, G.W., Crow, T.J., & Polak, J.M. (1985). Location of neuronal tangles in somatostatin neurones in Alzheimer's disease. *Nature, 314,* 92–94.

Rossor, M.N., Emson, P.C., Iversen, L.L., Mountjoy, C.Q. (1984). Patterns of neuropeptide deficits in Alzheimer's disease. In: R.J. Wurtman, S.H. Corkin, & J.H. Growdon (Eds.). *Advances in basic research and therapies.* Center for Brain Sciences and Metabolism Charitable Trust.

Rossor, M.N., Emson, P.C., Mountjoy, C.Q., Roth, M., & Iversen, L.L. (1980a). Reduced amounts of immunoreactive somatostatin in the temporal cortex in senile dementia of Alzheimer type. *Neuroscience Letter, 20,* 373–377.

Rossor, M.N., Fahrenkrug, J., Emson, P.C., et al. (1980b). Reduced cortical choline acetyltransferase activity in senile dementia of Alzheimer type is not accompanied by changes in vasoactive intestinal polypeptide. *Brain Research, 201,* 249–253.

Rossor, M.N., Rehfeld, J.F., Emson, P.C., et al. (1981). Normal cortical concentrations of cholecystokinin-like immunoreactivity with reduced choline acetyltransferase activity in senile dementia of the Alzheimer type. *Life Sciences, 29,* 405–410.

Soininen, H., Jolkkonen, J.T., Reinikainen, K.J., Halonen, T.O., & Reinikainen, P.J. (1984). Reduced cholinesterase activity and somatostatin-like immunoreactivity in the cerebrospinal fluid of patients with dementia of the Alzheimer type. *Journal of Neurological Sciences, 63,* 167–172.

Swaab, D.F., Achterberg, P.W., Boer, G.J., et al. (1981). The distribution of MSH and ACTH in the rat and human brain and its relation to pituitary stores. In J.L. Martinez, Jr., R.A. Jensen, & R.B. Messing, et al. (Eds.). *Endogenous peptides and learning and memory process,* New York: Academic Press.

Tatemoto, K., Lundberg, J.M., Jornvall, H., et al. (1985). Neuropeptide K: Isolation, structure, and biological activities of a novel brain tackykinin. *Biochemical and Biophysical Research Communications, 128,* 947–953.

Wood, P.L., Etienne, P., Lai, S., et al. (1982). Reduced lumbar CSF somatostatin levels in Alzheimer's disease. *Life Sciences, 31,* 2073–2079.

Yates, C.M., Harmar, A.J., Rosie, R., Sherward, J., Sanchez de Levey, G., Simpson, J., Moloney, A.F.J., Gordon, A. & Fink, G. (1983a). Thyrotropin-releasing hormone, luteinizing hormone-releasing hormone and substance P immunoreactivity in postmortem brain from cases of Alzheimer-type dementia and Down's syndrome. *Brain Research, 258,* 45–52.

Yates, C.M., Simpson, J., Gordon, A., Maloney, A.F.J., Alison, Y., Ritchie, I.M., & Urquhart, A. (1983b). Catecholamines and cholinergic enzymes in pre-senile and senile Alzheimer-type dementia and Down's syndrome. *Brain Research, 280,* 119–126.

CHAPTER 14

Bacteremia in the Elderly

M.J. Bendall
P. Bendall

Bacteremia occurs more frequently with increasing age. The reported study examined how frequently bacteremia occurred in frail elderly patients in a geriatric inpatient unit, the extent to which detection of bacteremia resulted in alteration of antimicrobial chemotherapy, and the outcome of bacteremia in this group of elderly patients. Bacteremia occurred in 1.7% of admissions, the commonest reason for blood culture (chest infection) producing the smallest proportion of significant isolates. Alteration of therapy on the basis of blood culture results did not lead to an obvious change in outcome. Of those with significant bacteremia, 38% died during the index illness, and 18% died in the following 3 months. Bacteremia in the frail elderly is probably a marker of overall debility and its detection may have little influence or outcome.

In discussing bacteremia in the elderly there are problems both in its definition and in assessing its extent and significance. In relation to the elderly some of the currently used definitions of bacteremia are not particularly useful. Powrie and Norman (1976) suggested that the term "bacteremia" should refer to the presence of bacteria in the blood without important sequelae, and that "septicemia" should refer to pathogens multiplying in the blood stream and producing signs of illness. Ispahani (1983) proposed a rather similar definition—namely that bacteremia is the presence of bacteria in the blood (i.e., a laboratory finding), and septicemia is bacteremia associated with clinical manifestations of infection (i.e., a clinical diagnosis). The term septicemia is also used by some clinicians to describe what others would call septicemic shock.

Blood cultures are undertaken in the presence, or, on suspicion, of clinical illness and hence, bacteria, if found, will inevitably be considered as significant. In the elderly, in whom the presentation of disease is often atypical, or even obscure, the use of the term septicemia, and its association with an implied clinical syndrome, may lead to failure to investigate elderly patients with nonspecific presentation of disease.

During the past 20 to 25 years there has been a steady increase in the incidence with which bacteremia has been diagnosed. Much of the increase is related to infection with gram-negative pathogens. Reported rates vary considerably and the differences are probably due to population variation and the diagnostic procedures used. The general increase in rate may reflect increased awareness of the condition and increased diagnostic pursuit rather than a true increase in incidence.

It is generally agreed that bacteremia becomes more common with advancing age, and that a considerable proportion of patients with the condition are over the age of 65 years. Information about how commonly bacteremia occurs in the elderly is limited. Some of it derives from studies in the United States, where the pattern of hospital referral and care of the elderly is rather different from that, for example, of the United Kingdom. Thus, McGowan, Barnes, and Finland (1975) found an increasing rate of bacteremia with increasing age among admissions to the Boston City Hospital in the later years of the Boston study. In 1972 the rate doubled from 21.1 cases per 1,000 admissions in those 40 to 49 years to 40.4 cases per 1,000 admissions in those 50 to 59 years. In patients over 70 years the rate was 50 per 1,000 admissions.

Comparing the rates of bacteremia against admissions tells us little about bacteremia in the population at large. In the United Kingdom the Hospital Inpatient Enquiry (HIPE) samples 10% of all hospital admissions in England and Wales, and provides diagnostic incidence rates per year measured against the population. Examination of HIPE data for 1979 to 1981 shows that the incidence of septicemia rises from between 0.1 and 0.2 cases per 10,000 of the population per year in the age group up to 50 years, to 2.1 cases per 10,000 of the population per year in those aged over 85 years. The incidence of infective endocarditis also rises with age from 0.1 to 0.2 cases per 10,000 of the population per year in those aged under 50 years to a peak of 0.6 cases per year per 10,000 of the population in those aged between 70 and 74 years. The incidence falls thereafter. This fall may represent underdiagnosis of infective endocarditis in very old age. On the other hand, there is good evidence that the peak incidence has moved from younger to older age groups, perhaps due to cohort effects relating to rheumatic heart disease.

The HIPE figures for septicemia almost certainly underestimate the frequency of bacteremia: Septicemic shock secondary to urinary tract infection is more likely to be reported as septicemia than, for example, bacteremia arising from pneumonia, cases of which are more likely to be reported as pneumonia. The HIPE figures also show that the mortality associated with septicemia and bacterial endocarditis rises rapidly with age, being 10% to 15% of all cases among those under 50 years and in excess of 50% among those over 75 years.

The Nottingham study arose for two reasons: First, patients classified clinically as suffering from septicemia, identified during a research project on trimethoprim resistance, had a very high mortality rate (60%). Second, although large numbers of blood cultures were being take from septicemic patients, very few cultures were positive.

The project aimed to answer three questions.

1. How common is bacteremia in geriatric in-patients?
2. How often does a positive blood culture alter the treatment being given?
3. What is the outcome in elderly patients with bacteremia?

METHODS

We retrospectively examined all blood cultures performed on patients admitted to our wards at the City Hospital in Nottingham during 1981 and 1982. Positive cultures were identified from laboratory records and a note was made of the total number of cultures performed and the reason the culture was requested. Patients identified as being bacteremic were examined for the nature of their disabilities, the circumstances in which blood cultures were performed, the treatment given, and the outcome. A number of septicemic patients from the trimethoprim study had died after the clinical episode had been successfully treated. In the current study, we therefore categorized death as having occurred either during the episode of bacteremia or after the episode but during the same admission within 3 months of the onset of bacteremia.

RESULTS

Where possible the results of the Nottingham study will be compared with those obtained in studies at Northwick Park Hospital, London (Denham & Goodwin, 1977) and Manor Park Hospital in Bristol (Windsor, 1983). During the Nottingham study there were 3,514 admissions, of which 626 (18%) were investigated by blood culture. This investigation rate was appreciably lower than that in the Northwick Park study (28%), but the proportion of the admissions found to be

TABLE 14-1. Indications for Blood Culture

Diagnostic group	Nottingham		Northwick Park	
	Patients	(% Total)	Patients	(% Total)
Chest infection	201	(32%)	95	(34%)
Pyrexia of unknown origin	128	(20%)	–	–
Possible septicemia	62	(10%)	–	–
Possible subacute bacterial endocarditis	59	(9%)	28	(10%)
Nonspecific malaise	–	–	32	(12%)
Recent confusion	–	–	90	(32%)
Septic focus (skin, joint)	28	(4%)	–	–
Urinary tract infection	29	(5%)	–	–
Diabetes-related	11	(2%)	–	–
Miscellaneous	108	(18%)	32	(12%)

bacteremic in the two studies (1.7% and 1.8%, respectively) were very comparable and perhaps slightly higher than that in the Bristol study (1.4%).

The frequency of stated indications for performing the blood cultures were rather different in the Nottingham and Northwick Park studies (Table 14-1). The presence of chest infection was the most frequently sited indication in both groups (32%), followed by recent onset of confusion (30%) and nonspecific malaise (11%) in the Northwick Park study and in the Nottingham study, followed by pyrexia of unknown origin (20%) and possible septicemia (10%). The attribution of pyrexia of unknown origin did not mean that the patients fulfilled the classic criteria of Petersdorf and Beeson (1961), the term being used in a much more imprecise sense.

The proportion of positive cultures in the different diagnostic groups varied considerably (Table 14-2), with the commonest indication (the presence of chest infection) producing one of the lowest isolation rates in both studies (6% of those cultured). In the Nottingham study the highest isolation rates were found in patients thought to be septicemic (16%), in the presence of an obvious septic focus (18%), and in the presence of urinary tract infection (21%).

The organisms isolated in the Nottingham and Bristol studies were very different from those in the Northwick Park study (Table 14-3). In the Nottingham and Bristol studies *Escherichia coli* was most frequently isolated (35% and 20% of all organisms respectively), whereas in the Northwick Park study *E. coli* was only isolated in 4% of positive cases and the most frequently isolated organism was *Pneumococcus* (26%). It seems unlikely that the low isolation rate of *E. coli* in the Northwick Park study arose as a result of different laboratory techniques. *E. coli* is generally regarded as an easy organism to isolate. The differences may

TABLE 14-2. Patients Bacteremic in Different Diagnostic Groups

Diagnostic group	Nottingham		Northwick Park	
	Number positive	% Total cultured	Number positive	% Total cultured
Chest infection	13	6%	6	6%
Pyrexia of unknown origin	10	8%	–	–
Possible septicemia	10	16%	–	–
Possible subacute bacterial endocarditis	6	10%	4	14%
Nonspecific malaise	–	–	5	16%
Recent confusion	–	–	1	1%
Septic focus	5	18%	–	–
Urinary tract infection	6	21%	–	–
Diabetes-related	3	27%	2	11
Miscellaneous	6	6%	1	3%

reflect differences in the type of patient being admitted or differences in bacterial populations.

Notes of 48 patients in whom organisms were isolated by blood culture were examined. In 3 patients the isolate was not considered to be significant. Four other patients were terminally ill and did not receive antimicrobial therapy. Forty-one patients received treatment and there were 24 of these in whom the blood culture result did not lead to an alteration in therapy. Of the remaining 17, one started treatment when the blood culture result was known, 4 patients had minor changes in therapy (for example, in pneumococcal infection a change from amoxicillin to penicillin), 2 patients were on inadequate therapy in view of the severity of their initial illness, and in only 10 patients did blood culture lead to a major alteration in therapy. Of these 10 patients, 4 died during the episode of bacteremia, 2 died

TABLE 14-3. Organisms Isloated for Study Populations

Organism	Nottingham		Northwick Park		Bristol	
	n	(% Total)	n	(% Total)	n	(% Total)
E. coli	21	(35%)	1	(4%)	11	(20%)
S. aureus	13	(22%)	6	(22%)	11	(20%)
Pneumococcus	9	(15%)	7	(26%)	6	(11%)
Proteus sp.	5	(8%)	3	(11%)	4	(7%)
S. viridans	6	(10%)	4	(14%)	4	(7%)
Pseudomonas	3	(5%)	2	(7%)	2	(3%)
Klebsiella	1	(2%)	2	(7%)	5	(9%)
β-hemolytic strep.	–		–		6	(11%)
Other	2	(3%)	2	(7%)	7	(12%)

subsequently and only 4 patients recovered and were alive 3 months later. These 4 represent 0.6% of those on whom blood cultures were originally performed.

In terms of the outcome there was not a significant difference between those whose therapy was altered on the basis of the blood culture result and those whose initial therapy was considered to be appropriate.

Seventeen (38%) of the 45 patients with significant bacteremia died during the index illness, and another 8 (18%) died within the next 3 months. Of these 8 who died subsequently, 6 did so within a month of the onset of the original bacteremia. Twenty patients survived, 17 returning to the community and 3 becoming long-term care patients.

Mortality was uninfluenced by whether the bacteremia was community-acquired or nosocomial in origin. Of the 17 patients who died during bacteremia, 9 died within the first 3 days of the illness, before meaningful blood culture results were available.

CONCLUSIONS

Three retrospective surveys have shown bacteremia to occur in between 1.4 and 1.8% of all admissions to geriatric units. In the Nottingham series the commonest reason for blood culture (chest infection) produced the smallest proportion of significant isolates. Alteration of therapy on the basis of blood culture did not lead to an obvious change in outcome. The fact that 50% of patients who died during the bacteremia did so before meaningful blood culture results were available, emphasizes the importance, if treatment is to be given, of ensuring that the initial antibiotic therapy be considered very carefully. Fried and Visti (1968), however, have indicated that in patients with other severe underlying illness appropriateness of initial antimicrobial therapy does not influence outcome. The patients in our series were largely frail elderly individuals with multiple chronic disabilities. It thus seems likely that bacteremia in such patients is a marker of their overall debility and that its detection may have little influence on outcome.

REFERENCES

Denham, M.J., & Goodwin, G.S. (1977). The value of blood cultures in geriatric practice. *Age and Aging, 6,* 85.

Freid, M.A., & Vosti, K.L. (1968). The importance of underlying disease in patients with gram-negative bacteremia. *Archives of Internal Medicine, 121,* 418.

Hospital Inpatient Enquiry. (1979). Department of Health and Social Security, Office of Population Censuses and Surveys. London: Her Majesty's Stationery Office.

Hospital Inpatient Enquiry. (1980). Department of Health and Social Security, Office of Population Censuses and Surveys. London: Her Majesty's Stationery Office.

Hospital Inpatient Enquiry. (1981). Department of Health and Social Security, Office of Population Censuses and Surveys. London: Her Majesty's Stationery Office.

Ispahani P. (1983). Bacteremia and endocarditis. In D. Greenwood (Ed.). *Antimicrobial chemotherapy.* London: Bailliere Tindall.

McGowan, J.E., Barnes M.W., & Finland, M. (1975). Bacteremia at Boston City Hospital: Ocurrence and mortality during 12 selected years (1935–1972). with special reference to hospital-acquired cases. *Journal of Infectious Diseases. 132,* 316.

Petersdorf. R.G., & Beeson, P.B. (1961). Fever of unexplained origin—Report on 100 cases. *Medicine, 40,* 1.

Powrie S., & Norman, J. (1976). Septicaemia. *British Journal of Anaesthesia, 48*41.

Windsor, A.C.M. (1983). Bacteremia in a geriatric unit. *Gerontology, 29,* 125.

CHAPTER 15

Pharmacological Perspectives in Therapy of Depression in the Elderly

Thomas A. Ban

The present status of pharmacotherapy in depressed psychogeriatric patients is reviewed with special emphasis on new approaches in treatment. Therapeutic implications of the increased incidence of delusional depression, elevated metabolic clearance of testosterone, increased type B MAO activity, depletion of norepinephrine (NE) and decreased responsivity to 5HT in the elderly are discussed and an attempt is made to shift emphasis from empirical to rational approaches to treatment.

There is no consensus regarding the prevalence of depression in the aged (Blazer, 1983). According to current estimates, the prevalence of depression among elderly persons in the community may be in the order of 13% (Gurland, Golden, & Dean, 1980), while in medical settings may exceed 30% (Cheah & Beard, 1980).

Depression is, at least in part, responsible for the high suicide rate in old age. This is best exemplified by the findings that those over age 65 account for 25% of all suicides while they constitute only 11% of the total population (Ban, 1980). In their epidemiologic study, Senbuehler and Goldstein (1977) found that attempted suicide rates rose progressively from 32 per 1,000 in the age group between 50 to 54, to 48 per 1,000 in the age group above 74.

TREATMENT: PRESENT STATUS

The different treatment approaches used in depression were reviewed
by Ban (1980), Salzman and van der Kolk (1984), and Gerner (1984).
Among the various treatment modalities cyclic or monoamine uptake
inhibitor (MAUI) antidepressants are the ones most extensively employed. While there is no conclusive evidence that any cyclic antidepressant is superior to another in overall therapeutic effects, there are
indications that some of the second generation antidepressants may
offer advantages insofar as side effects and/or the control of certain
specific symptomatology is concerned. Included among these sus-
btances are citalopram, fluoxetine, fluvoxamine, maprotiline, mian-
serin, nomifensine, and trazodone. Nevertheless, the fact remains that
"none of these compounds appear to offer substantial hope of a dramatic advance" (Crook, 1985).

TREATMENT: NEW APPROACHES

There are two major approaches that have opened new paths for
research in the pharmacotherapy of depression in the aged. One is
based on a better understanding of the phenomenological aspects of
depression in the elderly patient, while the other is based on a better
understanding of the biological changes in the aged with possible
relevance to depressive illness.

Phenomenological Aspects of Depression

Depressive subtypes in the elderly were described by Skodol and Spitzer (1983). Recently Meyers and Greenberg (1985) reported on the
high incidence of delusional depression in elderly patients. In 152
consecutively admitted *DSM-III*-diagnosed elderly major depressives,
delusional depression was seen in 67 (44%). Delusional patients were
significantly older at age of onset (63.4 ± 14.6 versus 60.6 ± 17.3; p
< .0001) but not at the age of their index admission (72.6 ± 6.8 versus
71 ± 6.5). Utilizing the median age of onset of 60 years as a cutoff,
only 17 of the 70 early onset patients (24%) were delusional compared
with 50 of the 82 late onset patients (61%). No evidence for an aging
effect was found; delusional early onset patients were not significantly
older at the time of their index admission than nondelusional early
onset patients. In both sexes there was a trend for an increase in the
prevalence of delusions with a later age of onset.

In the treatment of patients with delusional depression, cyclic antidepressants alone do not suffice. They have to be combined with a

neuroleptic. The finding that delusional depression occurs in such a high proportion of elderly depressed patients brings to attention the need for "transition compounds" that combine antidepressant with neuroleptic effects. Included among these compounds are carpipramine and chlorcarpipramine (i.e., drugs with a dibenzazepine (tricyclic) nucleus and a butyrophenone side chain) and amoxapine, a tricyclic dibenzoxazepine that hydroxylates into a dopamine receptor blocker with antipsychotic effects. It remains to be seen whether any of these substances will offer real advantages over electroconvulsive therapy (ECT) or drug combinations.

Biological Changes in Aged

It has been recognized that aging is associated with a lowering of plasma testosterone concentrations, increase in monoamine oxidase activity (MAO), and decrease in norepinephrine and serotonin levels at functionally active receptor sites.

Testosterone Concentrations. There is a normal production but an abnormally elevated metabolic clearance of testosterone in some elderly depressed men. To attain the normal testosterone/estradiol ratio it is necessary to increase the testosterone production by 70% or substitute for the relative testosterone deficiency by the administration of a synthetic exogenous hormone (Vogel, Klaiber, & Broverma, 1978). One possible substitute for the relative testosterone deficiency is mesterolone, a synthetic androgen. In a clinical neurophysiological study, mesterolone produced similar effects to CNS stimulants in low doses and to cyclic antidepressants in high doses (Itil, Herrmann, Blasucci, & Freedman, 1978).

In a double-blind, placebo-controlled clinical study, mesterolone (75 mg/day) was administered to 66 aging males for a period of 5 weeks. There was a tendency for improvement in activity and performance with decrease in somatic complaints in the mesterolone-treated group. However, no relationship between testosterone concentrations and therapeutic effects could be revealed (Kaiser, Nies, Maas, et al., 1978).

Findings with mesterolone have revived interest in fluoxymesterone, a synthetic methyltestosterone preparation. In a clinical study carried out approximately 25 years ago, this substance, in the dosage of 4 to 5 mg/day, increased perceptual alertness, interest in the environment, and motivation with a favorable effect on the recall of logical, meaningful material in patients with a "benign type" of senescent memory dysfunction (Kral & Wigdor, 1961).

Increase in MAO Activity. Monoamine oxidase (MAO) is the enzyme responsible for the intracellular deamination of monoamines in the brain. Taking into consideration the gradual increase in Type B MAO activity (the enzyme responsible for the deamination of benzy-lamine and B-phenethylamine) after age 35, with a peak in patients in their 70s (Robinson, Davies, & Nies et al., 1971), the possibility has been raised that MAOIs may be more effective than other types of antidepressants in geropsychiatric patients with depression (Fann, 1976). In favor of this contention were the findings that phenelzine was more effective than amitriptyline in aged patients (Robinson, 1981).

The present upsurge of interest in monoamine oxidase inhibitor (MAOIs) in geropsychiatric practice is related to the recognition that MAOI antidepressants are well tolerated and produce fewer and less severe side effects than cyclic antidepressants in elderly depressed pa-tients. Since there is no evidence for therapeutic superiority of any one MAOI over another, most clinicians are guided by their own prefer-ence for a particular MAOI (Salzman & van der Kolk, 1984).

One specific indication of treatment with MAOI antidepressants is depression in elderly patients with reversible cognitive dysfunction. In their study with 37 elderly depressed patents with "reversible" (23 patients) and "irreversible" (14 patients) dementias, Alexopoulos, Lieberman, Young, & Shamoian (1984) found that both patient groups had significantly high platelet MAO activity than patients of similar age with major depression but without cognitive impairment. After controlling depressive symptomatology, patients with major depression and a reversible dementia syndrome had similar platelet MAO activity as depressives with primary degenerative dementia. On the basis of these findings Alexopoulos, Young, & Shamoian et al. (1985) suggest that at least in some elderly patients a reversible dementia syndrome develops when pathophysiological changes of depression are added to an early asymptomatic dementia process. Considering that reversible cognitive dysfunction is usually indistinguishable clinically from irre-versible cognitive dysfunction, a trial with a MAO antidepressant is warranted in patients with a primary degenerative dementia syn-drome, and especially if the dementia syndrome is associated with platelet MAO activity in the high range. Furthermore, since the in-crease in MAO activity is restricted to the Type B enzyme, it is likely that deprenyl, a selective Type B enzyme inhibitor is more suitable in the treatment of these patients, than the nonspecific MAOIs.

Norepinephrine Deficiency. Depressive disorders that meet *DSM-III* criteria for either major depression or dysthymic disorder occur in approximately 20% to 25% in poststroke patients. Robinson, Lipsey and Price (1985) revealed a significant relationship between depression and the site of the lesion. In a study of right-handed patients with single ischemic lesions and no previous history of depressive disorder, 6 of 10 patients with left frontal lesions had symptoms of major depression while only 2 of 20 patients with other lesion locations manifested depressive symptoms. Among the patients with left frontal lesions there was a strong correlation between the proximity of the lesion on computed tomography (CT) scan to the frontal pole and severity of depression. The depression seen in these patients was attributed to the depletion of noreprinephrine (NE) because left anterior, but no right anterior lesions (induced experimentally in rats) were associated with a depletion of NE in the locus ceruleus.

In favor of the NE deficiency hypothesis of depression in poststroke patients are the results of a double-blind clinical study in which nortriptyline, a specific NE reuptake inhibitor, was found to be superior in its therapeutic effect to placebo in the treatment of poststroke depressions. However, because no specific serotonin uptake inhibitor was included in the comparison, findings of this clinical trial cannot provide conclusive evidence for the NE deficiency hypothesis of poststroke depression. Whether NE deficiency hypothesis of poststroke depression would be supported by further evidence or not, consideration should be given to the use of selective NE reuptake inhibitors in treatment.

Decreased Serotonin Responsivity. There is substantial evidence for a decreased responsivity to serotonin (5HT) in the elderly. In view of this another possible factor linked with old age depression is a relative deficiency of 5HT (Beregi, 1967).

Serotonin is produced from the amino acid tryptophan content of digested protein. The transport system responsible for carrying tryptophan from the blood to the brain has a lower affinity for tryptophan than for eight other neural amino acids. Therefore, increased amounts of trytophan enter the brain only if the relative concentration of tryptophan in relationship to other amino acids is increased. Recently, the possibility has been raised that cerebral 5HT levels might be influenced through diet. Whether by consistent dietary manipulation one could keep brain serotonin levels high and prevent depression in geropsychiatric patients remains to be seen.

In favor of the contention that 5HT deficiency plays a role in some types of depression are the findings that L-tryptophan decreases the reduction of time spent in rapid eye movement sleep associated with insomnia, a cardinal symptom of depression in the elderly (Hartman & Cravens, 1973). Piracetam, a nootropic agent, was found to enhance brain tryptophan levels in the mice (Giurgea, 1981). It remains to be seen whether it can enhance the antidepressant effects of tryptophan in the elderly.

REFERENCES

Alexopoulos, G.S., Lieberman, K.W., Young, R.C. & Shamoian, C.A. (1984, July). *Platelet monoamine activity in patients with depression and dementia.* Paper presented at the 14th Congress of the Collegium Internationale Neuro-Psychopharmacologicum, Florence.

Alexopoulos, G.S., Young, R.C., Shamoian, C.A. et al. (1985, May). *Depression with reversible dementia.* Paper presented at the 138th Annual Meeting of the American Psychiatric Association, Dallas.

Ban, T.A. (1980). *Psychopharmacology for the aged.* Basel: Karger.

Beregi, E. (1962). The biology of aging. In I. Tariska (Ed.), *Neuropsychiatric disorders in the aged.* Budapest: Medicina.

Blazer, D. (1983). The epidemiology of depression in late life. In L.D. Breslau and M.R. Haug (Eds.), *Depression and aging: Causes, care and consequences.* New York: Springer Publishing Co.

Cheah, K.C. & Beard, O.W. (1980). Psychiatric findings in the population of a geriatric evaluation unit: Implications. *Journal of the American Geriatric Society, 28,* 153–156.

Crook, T. (1985). Geriatric psychopharmacology: An overview of ailments and current therapies. *Drug Development Research, 5,* 5–24.

Fann, W.E. (1976). Pharmacotherapy of older depressed patients. *Journal of Gerontology, 31,* 304–310.

Gerner, R.H. (1984). Present status of drug therapy in depression in late life. *Clinical-Neuropharmacology, 7,* (Suppl. 1) 168–169.

Giurgea, C.E. (1981). *Fundamentals to a pharmacology of the mind.* Springfield: Charles C. Thomas.

Gurland, B.J., Golden G., & Dean, L. (1980). Depression and dementia in the elderly of New York City. In *Planning for the elderly in New York City.* New York: Community Council of Greater New York.

Hartman, E., & Cravens, J. (1973). The effect of long-term administration of psychotropic drugs on human sleep. *Psychopharmacologia, 33,* 153–245.

Itil, T.M., Herrmann, W.M., Blasucci, D., & Freedman, A. (1978). Male hormones in the treatment of depression. Effects of mesterolone. *Progress in Neuropsychopharmacology, 2,* 457–467.

Kaiser, E., Nies, N., Maas, G. et al. (1978). The measurement of the psychotropic effects of an androgen in aging males with psychovegetative symptomatology. A controlled double-blind study with mesterolone versus placebo. *Progress in Neuropsychopharmacology, 2,* 505–515.

Kral, V.A., & Wigdor, B.T. (1961). Further studies on androgen effect on senescent memory functions. *Canadian Psychiatric Association Journal, 6,* 345–352.

Meyers, B.S., & Greenberg, R.M. (1985, May). *Delusional depression in the elderly.* Paper presented at 138th Annual Meeting of the American Psychiatric Association, Dallas.

Robinson, D. (1981). Monoamine oxidase inhibitors and the elderly. In A. Raskin, D. Robinson & J. Levine (Eds.). *Age and the psychopharmacology of psychoactive drugs.* New York: Elsevier.

Robinson, D.S., Davies, J.M., Nies, A. et al. (1971). Relative relation of sex and aging to monoamine oxidase activity of human brain, plasma, and platelets. *Archives of General Psychiatry, 24,* 536–539.

Robinson, R.G., Lipsey, J.R. & Price, J.R. (1985, May). *Mood disorders in post stroke patients.* Paper presented at the 138th Annual Meeting of the American Psychiatric Association, Dallas.

Salzman, C. & van der Kolk, L. (1984). Treatment of depression. In C. Salzman (Ed.), *Clinical geriatric psychopharmacology.* New York: McGraw-Hill.

Senbuehler, J. & Goldstein, S. (1979). Attempted suicide among the aged. *Journal of the American Geriatric Society, 25,* 245–248.

Skodol, A.E., & Spitzer, R.L. (1983). Depression in the elderly: Clinical criteria. In L.D. Breslau & M.R. Haug (Eds.), *Depression and aging. Care and consequences.* New York: Springer Publishing Co.

Vogel, W., Klaiber,E.C., & Broverman, D.M. (1978). Roles of the gonadal steroid hormones in psychiatric depression in men and women. *Progress in Neuropsychopharmacology, 2,* 487–503.

CHAPTER 16

Cardiovascular Risk Factors in the Elderly: The Framingham Study

William B. Kannel
Pantel S. Vokonas

The contribution of established risk factors to the development of cardiovascular disease (CVD) in older subjects of the Framingham Study is systematically examined. Hypertension emerges as the dominant remediable risk factor for CVD in the elderly because of its high prevalence and sustained impact as age advances. Blood lipids are also important, particularly the LDL/HDL or total/HDL cholesterol ratios. Cigarette smoking is not significantly associated with overall CVD incidence but remains a significant factor for cardiovascular mortality. Glucose intolerance and diabetes mellitus make independent contributions to risk particularly in older women. Electrocardiographic evidence for left ventricular hypertrophy, probably the hallmark of a compromised coronary circulation, is also related to enhanced CVD risk. Obesity predisposes to CVD in the elderly, even when its atherogenic accompaniments are taken into account. Low vital capacity and high heart rate emerge as important risk factors for CVD in the aged. Exercise may exert a protective benefit even in older persons.

Although evidence from controlled clinical trials on the efficacy of correcting risk factors in the elderly is limited, the recent decline in cardiovascular mortality has also included the elderly, a trend that is most encouraging.

Cardiovascular heart disease (CVD) encompasses a broad spectrum of

---

The research reported here was supported in part by the National Institutes of Health (U.S.).

disease conditions of the heart and circulation that progress dramatically as age advances. In this context, CVD in all its clinical manifestations contributes heavily to disability and death throughout life but particularly in the elderly.

There is a common, but mistaken, notion that nearly all forms of CVD in the elderly represent age-related manifestations of long-standing atherosclerosis where modification of risk factors is unlikely to be of important benefit. Too often, this notion fosters a posture of either indifference or benign neglect on the part of physicians in pursuing preventive measures in older patients which is no longer tenable. Evidence is now emerging that preventive management, especially control of hypertension, may effectively forestall the development of coronary and cerebrovascular disease as well as congestive heart failure, even in the elderly. In addition, the recent decline in cardiovascular mortality observed in the United States and several other industrialized nations (Cooper, Stamler, Dyer, & Garside, 1978; Goldman & Cook, 1984; Walker, 1983) has also included the elderly, a trend that is most encouraging.

The Framingham cohort has now entered the geriatric age range providing a valuable opportunity to study the character of CVD in the elderly, change in risk factors with aging, and also whether or not risk factors for CVD established in the young and middle-aged also remain operative in older persons. This report on cardiovascular risk factors is based largely on 30 years of follow-up experience in the Framingham Study focusing on findings in participants who attained age 65 or older. Details regarding examination and laboratory procedures, response rates, and the criteria for disease outcomes in the Framingham Study have been previously described (Gordon & Kannel, 1970; Gordon & Shurtleff, 1977).

AGING AND CARDIOVASCULAR HEART DISEASE

Age-specific trends in CVD incidence for men and women in the Framingham Study are shown in Figure 16-1. Marked increments in the incidence of nearly all specific manifestations of CVD including coronary heart disease (CHD), cerebrovascular accident (CVA), congestive heart failure (CHF) and intermittent claudication (IC) are observed in subjects of both sexes as advanced age is attained. Coronary heart disease remains the most common form of CVD encountered throughout life, however, there appears to be no tendency for CHD to present as an increasing proportion of CVD events in the elderly. Cardiovascular disease accounts for 50% to 60% of all deaths in those 65 and older and nearly 30% of cardiovascular deaths are, in turn, due to CHD.

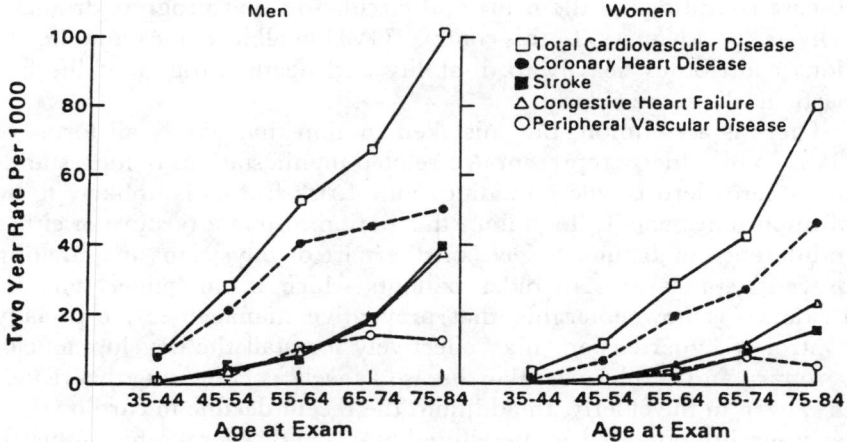

FIGURE 16-1. Biennial incident of specified manifestations of cardiovascular disease in the Framingham Study, 26-year follow-up.

Despite a prominent association with age, however, CVD should not be considered an inevitable concomitant of the aging process, as it involves the heart and circulation. Autopsy studies reveal that coronary arteries nearly free of atheroma and normal-sized hearts and valves are not uncommon, even among the very aged (Pomerance, 1976). Also, recent studies using noninvasive cardiac techniques demonstrate remarkable preservation of left ventricular function in older individuals screened to be free of CHD (Gerstenblith, 1977; Rodenheffer, 1984). Relatively minor but distinct changes in cardiac structure and performance attributable to aging in such individuals appear to be primarily adaptational in nature. Thus, the preponderance of clinically significant abnormalities of cardiac and circulatory function observed in the elderly should be considered the result of disease rather than expressions of normal senescence.

Risk Factors for Cardiovascular Heart Disease in the Elderly

Considerable uncertainty surrounds the issue of whether or not previously validated risk factors for CVD in young and middle-aged individuals also remain relevant in the elderly (Kannel & Gordon, 1978, 1980a). To be sure, prevalance is clearly substantial for the majority of factors suspected to contribute to CVD in this population (Table 16-1). Hypertension occurs frequently in the elderly of both sexes but is more prevalent in women. Hypercholesterolemia also occurs more commonly in older women, whereas obesity and glucose intolerance are somewhat more evenly distributed between the sexes. Cigarette smok-

TABLE 16–1. Percentage Prevalence [a] Cardiovascular Risk Factors in the Elderly Framingham Study, Exam 16

	Definite hypertension		Hypercholes-terolemia		Glucose intolerance		Obesity		Cigarette smoking	
Age	Men	Women	Men	Women	Men	Women	Men	Women	Men	Women
65-74	42.1	48.9	16.6	39.7	29.5	17.5	52.2	47.8	21.9	23.0
75-84	45.5	61.1	9.7	36.3	30.9	26.0	35.4	39.3	13.9	8.5
85-94	20.7	64.8	9.4	18.4	33.3	29.0	7.7	30.0	9.4	3.2

	ECG-LVH		Proteinuria		Tachycardia		High hematocrit	
Age	Men	Women	Men	Women	Men	Women	Men	Women
65-74	5.5	4.2	2.9	1.5	14.6	15.7	35.1	23.9
75-84	6.0	7.8	4.1	2.4	20.0	22.8	19.3	20.8
85-94	10.4	13.0	3.2	1.5	20.7	22.9	22.2	15.9

[a] Definitions for prevalence: Definite hypertension: BP > 160/95 mm Hg; hypercholesterolemia: serum cholesterol > 250 mg/dl; glucose intolerance: blood glucose > 120 mg/dl, glycosuria, or diabetes mellitus; obesity: relative weight > 120%; cigarette smoking: any (Exam 15); proteinuria: definite albumin in urine; tachycardia: heart rate > 84/min.; high hematocrit: men > 49%, women > 46%.

ing declines strikingly with advancing age irrespective of gender presumably reflecting the effects of both selective mortality and higher rates of discontinuation among the elderly.

Lest we create the impression that the rising incidence of CVD observed in the elderly occurs solely as a consequence of increasing levels of risk factors or accumulating more of them as people grow older, it is important to point out that incidence also rises steeply in older persons without identifiable risk factors (Kannel & Gordon, 1978, 1980). Chronologic age, therefore, represents the most dominant determinant of risk for CVD, particularly in the elderly. However, age as well as gender (which loses its strength in conferring risk predominantly for men as age advances) and certain hereditary factors are irremediable. Thus, attention is focused on those risk attributes that can potentially be modified. These may be broadly classified as either atherogenic personal traits (e.g., blood pressure, serum lipids, and glucose tolerance) or life-style influences (e.g., smoking and inactivity). Such risk factors can be considered either singly or in combination for their relative contribution to the development of disease in individuals of varying age.

Age-adjusted (bivariate) standardized regression coefficients for a number of risk factors classified by age group and sex are shown in Table 16-2. The magnitude and level of significance of standardized coefficients derived by regression analysis using a logistic model reflect

TABLE 16–2. Net Effect of Risk Factors on Cardiovascular Disease
Incidence—30-Year Follow-up, Framingham Study

	Bivariate standardized regression coefficients[a]			
Age:	35-64		65-94	
Risk factors	Men	Women	Men	Women
Systolic pressure	.406‡	.442‡	.463‡	.282‡
Diastolic pressure	.351‡	.368‡	.300‡	.122*
Serum cholesterol	.269‡	.249‡	.072§	.024§
Cigarettes	.289‡	.138†	.011§	.052§
Glucose intolerance	.148‡	.168‡	.162‡	.189‡
ECG-LVH	.199‡	.193‡	.231‡	.270‡
Vital capacity	-.188‡	-.360‡	-.145*	-.256‡
Relative weight	.145‡	.260‡	.141*	.081§
Heart rate	.230‡	.130†	.174†	.002§
Total of four categories	89	40		

[a]Age-adjusted coefficients.
*$p < .05$, †$p < .01$, ‡$p < .001$, §ns.

the strength of association between incidence of CVD and specific risk
factors when age, but not the concomitant influence of other risk
factors, is taken into account. It should be apparent from this analysis
that significant associations for the majority of previously validated
risk factors for CVD in younger individuals are maintained in the
older population but with some inconsistency with respect to gender.
Systolic blood pressure remains a strong risk factor in both age groups.
Serum total cholesterol, a potent predictor of CVD in younger individuals of both sexes, however, loses its strength in both older men and
women. Also, the influence of cigarette smoking as a factor for CVD
apparently wanes with advanced age. Glucose intolerance, ECG-LVH
and vital capacity remain important risk factors in the elderly. These
and other risk associations are commented on below.

Examination of CVD incidence corresponding to categorical levels
of specific risk factors (e.g., systolic and diastolic blood pressure, Table
16-3) reveals relationships with respect to age not readily discernible
from the above analysis. Absolute risk in older individuals is nearly
always higher at all categorical levels of a given risk factor even when
the risk factor is absent. Whether this effect reflects primarily the time-
dose product of action of specific risk factors or enhanced susceptibility
of vascular tissue to atherosclerotic disease as age advances remains
uncertain (Bierman, 1978). Cardiovascular disease incidence, nevertheless, tends to rise proportionately with increasing levels of risk
factors in both younger and older individuals indicating that trends in

TABLE 16–3. Incidence of Cardiovascular Disease by Levels of Systolic and Diastolic Pressure—30-Year Follow-up, Framingham Study

| Systolic pressure | Annual age-adjusted rate per 1,000 | | | | Diastolic pressure | | | | |
| | 35-64 | | 65-94 | | | 35-64 | | 65-94 | |
	Men	Women	Men	Women		Men	Women	Men	Women
74-119	10	4	20	14	20-74	12	6	32	25
120-139	12	6	26	23	75-84	12	6	32	23
140-159	21	11	39	25	85-94	19	10	41	33
160-179	31	13	61	27	95-104	25	13	70	23
180-300	40	23	86	48	105-160	39	22	94	44

relative risk are similar irrespective of age. These findings underscore the simple but often disputed concept that older individuals with risk factors develop substantially more CVD than those without them.

Cardiovascular Risk Profiles

It is now well established that the risk of CVD in young and middle-aged adults can be reliably estimated by combining a number of risk factors into a composite score based on a multiple logistic function (Gordon & Kannel, 1982; Kannel, McGee, & Gordon, 1976; Truett, Cornfield, & Kannel, 1967). Risk factors are assessed by standard office procedures (blood pressure, ECG, and smoking history) and routine laboratory studies (serum cholesterol and glucose levels). This type of composite index permits detection of individuals at relatively high risk either on the basis of marked elevation of a single factor or because of marginal abnormalities in several risk factors.

As indicated earlier, total serum cholesterol and cigarette smoking are less potent predictors of CVD in the elderly than in the young. Given these limitations, it is, therefore, of interest that inclusion of these factors along with age, systolic blood pressure, glucose intolerance, and ECG-LVH in a risk function continues to predict effectively several CVD outcomes in older Framingham subjects (Table 16-4). Although, as would be expected, considerably more impressive results are obtained in younger persons using this set of variables, the risk profile does permit identification of 1/10 of the population of older men and women in whom approximately 1/4 to 1/3 of CVD will arise. These findings underscore the importance of comprehensive evaluation of risk factors for CVD in the elderly as well as in younger patients. Substitution of LDL and HDL cholesterol for serum total cholesterol (vide infra) and the addition of other relevant factors in the elderly (e.g., vital capacity, relative weight, and heart rate) to the risk

TABLE 16–4. Efficiency of Cardiovascular Risk Profile by Age and Sex—30-Year Follow-up, Framingham Study

| | Percent of Specified Cardiovascular Events in Top Decile of Multivariate Risk[a] | | | | | | | |
| | CHD[b] | | CVA[b] | | CHF[b] | | IC[b] | |
Age	Men	Women	Men	Women	Men	Women	Men	Women
35-64	27.1	36.4	39.4	36.9	36.2	50.0	43.0	46.8
65-94	23.1	25.0	29.5	31.9	25.6	35.0	20.3	25.0

[a]Based on age, systolic blood pressure, serum cholesterol no. of cigarettes smoked, glucose tolerance, and ECG-LVH.
[b]CHD = Coronary heart disease, CVA = Cerebrovascular accident, CHF = Congestive heart failure, IC = Intermittent claudication.

profile would likely further increase the efficiency of risk prediction in the older population.

The major risk factors, even when taken together, do not entirely explain the variance in CVD incidence either within or between younger and older age groups, nor incidence between the sexes. It is quite possible that other major risk attributes exist among the elderly but are yet to be identified. It must be emphasized, however, that the factors that have already been delineated do identify high-risk subgroups of the elderly population who should be targeted for preventive management.

Preventive Management

The contribution of a number of specific risk factors to the development of CVD in the elderly and the rationale for applying preventive measures is discussed below.

Hypertension in the Elderly. Because elevated blood pressure represents the dominant remediable risk factor for CVD in the elderly, a more detailed examination of its contribution to enhanced risk is warranted. Blood pressure tends to rise with age, a phenomenon observed in nearly all Westernized populations surveyed. In well-characterized longitudinal data from the Framingham Study (Gordon & Shurtleff, 1977) reflecting change in pressure as individuals age, systolic blood pressure shows a nearly linear rise with advancing age in both sexes (Figure 16-2). Systolic blood pressure in women, while initially lower than that in men of younger ages, converges on that of men by age 60 but never exceeds them. Diastolic blood pressure in men rises considerably less strikingly with age and clearly declines after age 65. These trends are paralleled in women but levels consistently remain 5 to 10 mm Hg below those of men throughout life.

Increase in systolic blood pressure is due to progressive vascular stif-

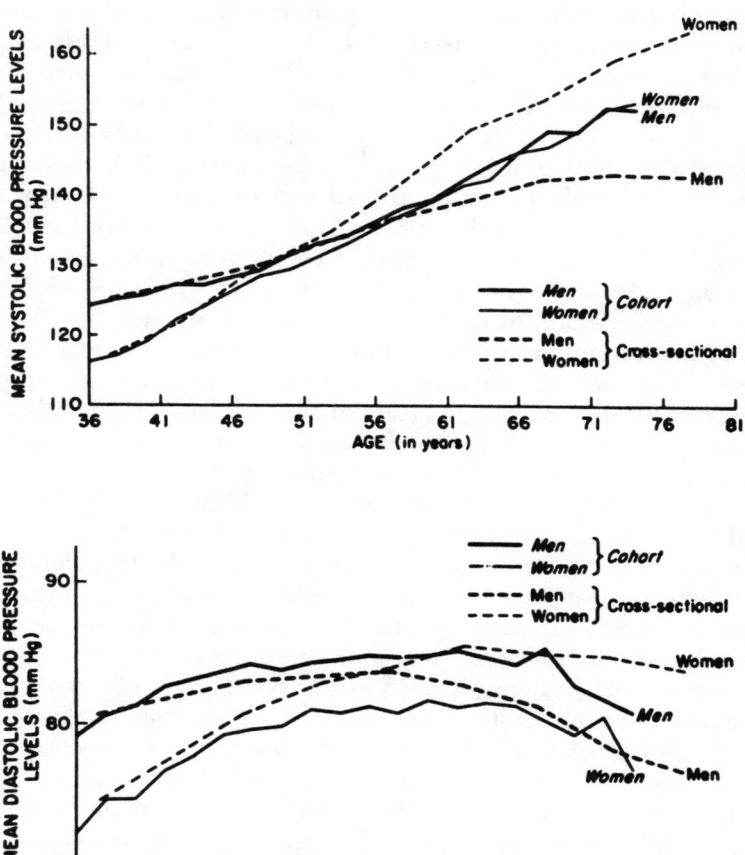

FIGURE 16-2. Average age trends in blood-pressure levels for men and women, based upon cross-sectional and cohort data on participants in the Framingham study. Data were obtained at biennial examinations No. 3 to 10.

Source: From "Evaluation of Cardiovascular Risk in the Elderly: The Framingham Study" by W.B. Kannel, & T. Gordon, 1978, *Bulletin of the New York Academy of Medicine, 54,* 579. Reproduced by permission.

fening attributable, in turn, to thickening of the arterial media and to changes in the nature and content of collagen and elastin that occur with advancing age (Milch, 1965). This process is dissimilar to that of atherosclerosis, which underlies the preponderance of CVD observed in older people. While age-related change in vascular rigidity serves to explain the rise in systolic blood pressure in most Westernized cultures, it is uncertain that this represents a uniform phenomenon of normal aging since in some isolated primitive populations, no rise in pressure is observed (Maddocks, 1976).

Despite its ubiquity in the elderly, elevated systolic blood pressure should not be construed as an innocuous concomitant of the aging process, since it clearly confers increased risk for CVD (Kannel & Gordon, 1978, 1980; Kannel, Wolf, McGee, Dawber, & McNamara et al., 1981). Although it may be argued that enhanced risk associated with elevated systolic blood pressure in the aged is derived not from pressure but from vascular rigidity of which systolic hypertension is only a sign (Dawber, Thomas, & McNamara, 1973; Koch-Weser, 1973), previous data from Framingham demonstrate that systolic blood pressure remains an independent contributor to cardiovascular risk even when arterial rigidity, as determined by pulse pressure recordings, is taken into account (Kannel et al., 1981a). Elevated diastolic blood pressure also occurs commonly in elderly and remains an important risk variable for CVD particularly in older men.

The above trends are well demonstrated in Table 16-3, which shows age-adjusted annual rates for CVD according to specified levels, respectively, of systolic and diastolic blood pressure. CVD incidence rises steeply with increasing systolic pressure for all age groups indicating that relative risk is similar irrespective of age and gender. Absolute risk in the elderly of both sexes, however, is approximately twice as great as that observed for younger persons at the same levels of systolic pressure. Similar risk associations are observed for diastolic pressure. For either systolic or diastolic blood pressure, absolute risk is always substantially higher for men than women irrespective of age. The results of regression analysis reflecting these relations by component of blood pressure are presented in Table 16-5. Significant risk associations for systolic blood pressure are consistently observed for all categories of subjects considered. For diastolic blood pressure, a significant association is retained in older men but appears to be lost in older women. These findings suggest a more consistent and reliable role for systolic blood pressure as a predictor of CVD in the elderly.

Risk gradients for incidence of CHD and CVA (stroke and transient ischemic attacks), which are similar in direction and magnitude to those suggested earlier are observed when individuals are classified according to hypertensive status instead of absolute level of blood pressure (Table 16-6). Treated hypertensives, although considered separately, show higher incidence rates for both coronary and cerebrovascular events, presumably reflecting more severe degrees of blood pressure elevation or hypertension of longer duration than untreated individuals (Shea, Cook, Kannel, & Goldman, 1985).

The risk of established diastolic hypertension, and hence the need to intervene therapeutically, is well-accepted among clinicians (Dyer, Stamler, Shekelle, Schoenberger, & Farinaro, 1977; Kaplan, 1983).

TABLE 16–5. Impact of Systolic Versus Diastolic Blood Pressure on Coronary and Cerebrovascular Disease Incidence— 30-Year Follow-up, Framingham Study

		Standardized multivariate regression coefficients[a]			
	Blood pressure	CHD		CVA	
Age	component	Men	Women	Men	Women
35-64	Systolic	.286*	.348*	.490*	.539*
	Diastolic	.286*	.293*	.524*	.535*
65-94	Systolic	.341*	.199*	.356*	.373*
	Diastolic	.248*	.037†	.129†	.289*

[a]Blood pressure adjusted for age, serum cholesterol, no. of cigarettes smoked, glucose tolerance, and ECG-LVH.
CHD = Coronary heart disease, CVA = Cerebrovascular accident.
*$p<.001$, †NS.

Indeed, evidence from controlled clinical trials already suggests that antihypertensive therapy may be effective in reducing the incidence of CHD, stroke and congestive heart failure, as well as mortality due to these conditions, even in older hypertensives (Amery et al, 1985; Hypertension Defection and Follow-up Program, 1979; Management Committee, 1981; Veterans Administration, 1972).

Isolated elevation of systolic blood pressure with normal or only slightly elevated diastolic pressure, however, is the most commonly encountered form of hypertension in the elderly (Rowe, 1983). Al-

TABLE 16–6. Risk of Coronary and Cerebrovascular Disease by Hypertensive Status According to Age and Sex— 30-Year Follow-up, Framingham Study

	Average annual age-adjusted rate per 1,000							
	Coronary Heart Disease				Stroke and TIA			
Hypertensive	35-64*		65-94*		35-64*		65-94*	
status[a]	Men	Women	Men	Women	Men	Women	Men	Women
Normal	8	3	13	11	1	1	6	5
Mild	15	7	27	13	2	1	9	7
Definite	20	10	37	18	6	3	17	12
Treated hypertension:	28	10	40	25	7	3	22	15

*All trends significant at $p<.001$ level
[a]Normal = < 140/90 mm Hg; mild = 140-160/90-95 mm Hg; definite = > 160/95 mm Hg.

though systolic blood pressure tends to rise with advancing age, in the majority of older individuals, this rise occurs within the clinically defined normal range (110 to 160 mm Hg). Thus, isolated elevation of systolic pressure in excess of 160 mm Hg defines a population of older individuals with substantially increased risk for cardiovascular morbidity and mortality (Curb, Borhani, Entwisle, Tung, & Kass et al., 1985; Kannel, Dawber, & McGee, 1980) who may potentially benefit from preventive therapeutic measures. That antihypertensive treatment will result in effective reduction of cardiovascular complications and accompanying mortality in this segment of the elderly population, at an acceptable cost of adverse drug effects, remains the subject of continuing debate. Early experience, however, is most encouraging (Gray, Weber, & Drayer, 1983; Schnaper, Furberg, & Kuller et al., 1983). The recently initiated multicenter Systolic Hypertension in the Elderly Program (SHEP) sponsored by the National Heart, Lung, and Blood Institute will hopefully provide definitive answers for these important questions.

Labile blood pressure elevations are widely considered by clinicians as less serious than fixed elevations. This is a common misconception because all blood pressures are labile and high pressures are more labile than low ones (Kannel, Sorlie, & Gordon, 1980). Lability of pressure is also considerably more pronounced in the elderly than in the young (Kannel & Gordon, 1980). Thus, it is patently unwise to judge the need for treatment in an older patient on the basis of the lowest blood pressure recorded if the average of several recordings is high. Recent information from Framingham (Harris, Cook, Kannel, Schatzkin & Goldman, 1985) also suggests that a single systolic blood pressure measurement at age 65 predicts risk for subsequent CVD almost as accurately as the average of systolic pressures prior to age 65 (Figure 16-3). A documented history of systolic blood pressures greater than 160 mm Hg before age 65 still represents some element of future cardiovascular risk even when recorded blood pressures are somewhat lower at age 65.

Blood Lipids. Data from Framingham and other studies (Castell, Doyle, Gordon, Hanes, & Hjortland, et al., 1977; Lipid Research Clinics, 1980) demonstrate that serum total cholesterol values in men tend not to rise significantly after about age 55 but instead progressively decline with advancing age. This is in substantial contrast to trends in women where total cholesterol levels continue to rise until age 70 before a decline is observed as age increases further.

As indicated earlier (Table 16-2), the significant risk association between CVD (especially CHD), and serum total cholesterol, which is exceedingly strong in younger subjects, disappears in older persons of both sexes. It is now well established, however, that when total choles-

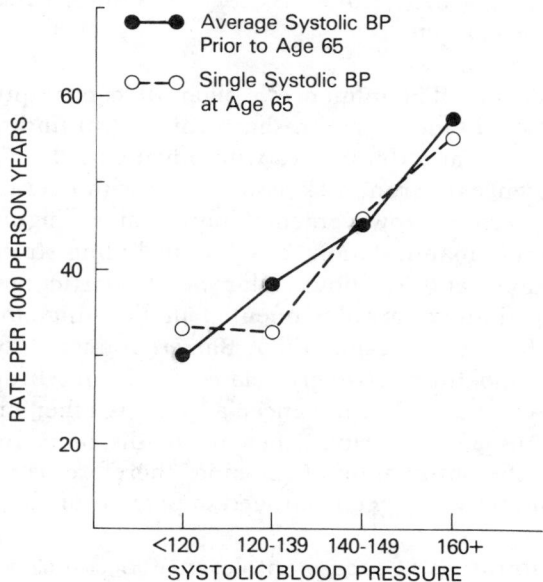

FIGURE 16-3. Systolic blood pressure and risk of cardiovascular disease after age 65.
Source: From "Blood Pressure Experience and Risk of Cardiovascular Risk in the Elderly" by T. Harris, E.F. Cook, W.B. Kannel, A. Schatkin, & L. Goldman, 1985, *Hypertension, 7,* 121. Reproduced by permission.

terol is partitioned into its lipoprotein subfractions, i.e., low density lipoprotein (LDL) and high density lipoprotein (HDL), the predictive relationship of cholesterol to CVD particularly in the elderly is fully restored (Gordon et al, 1977a; Kannel & Gordon, 1980; Kannel & Brand, 1985). These lipid components more accurately reflect the dynamic equilibrium of cholesterol movement both into and out of the tissues. In this context, LDL cholesterol appears to promote athero-genesis, while HDL is considered protective (Gordon, Castelli, Hjortland, Kannel & Dawber, 1977b). Whether diet and other preven-tive measures including drugs that decrease LDL while raising HDL cholesterol can exert an important impact on the development of CVD in the elderly, remains to be demonstrated. Some optimism, however, is justified (Hiermann, Velve Byre, Holme, & Leren 1981; Lipid Research Clinics, 1984).

There appears to be no convincing evidence that serum triglyceride represents an important risk factor for CVD in the elderly (Kannel & Gordon, 1980; Kannel & Brand, 1985). High triglyceride levels, how-ever, are often associated with obesity, glucose intolerance, and low

HDL values, all of which confer risk for CVD and, if possible, these factors should be corrected.

Cigarette Smoking. The influence of cigarette consumption as a risk factor for total CVD incidence, in sharp contrast to findings in younger persons, also clearly diminishes with advancing age (Table 16-2). Despite the absence of strong risk associations with overall CVD incidence in older persons, however, smoking remains a significant factor for several specific manifestations of CVD including stroke, intermittent claudication, and cardiovascular death particularly in older women. These findings are documented in Framingham as well as other studies (Kannel & Brand, 1985; Barret-Connor, 1984). In addition, cigarette smoking is strongly related to chronic bronchitis, pulmonary emphysema, and lung cancer as well as other malignancies. These conditions also contribute heavily to disability and death in older persons. Discontinuation of smoking, therefore, is a health measure that should be strongly encouraged in persons of all ages.

Glucose Intolerance. Glucose intolerance becomes progressively more prevalent as age advances (Andres, 1981; DeFronzo, 1981) (Table 16-1). Despite the prevalence of this finding as part of the normal aging process, it clearly makes an independent contribution to overall cardiovascular risk in both older men and women, even when the effect of other risk factors is accounted for in multivariate analysis (Kannel & McGee, 1979a).

Diabetes mellitus, per se, represents an extremely potent risk factor for both CVD events and cardiovascular death especially in older women (Kannel & McGee, 1979b; Kannel & Brand, 1985). Diabetes also emerges as an important risk factor in the development of congestive heart failure particularly in older women with insulin-dependent diabetes mellitus (Kannel, Hjortland, & Castelli, 1974). Presumably, a form of microvascular disease, which appears to be unique to diabetes as well as other mechanisms, serves to produce progressive damage to heart muscle ultimately resulting in compromised ventricular function and heart failure (Regan, Ahured, Haider, & Lyons 1978).

There is little evidence that control of hyperglycemia, either by oral hypoglycemic agents or insulin, effectively forstalls either the development or complications of CVD, especially mortality (Ingelfinger, 1977; Meinert, Knottervd, Prout, & Klimt, 1970; Siperstein, Foster, Knowles, Levial, & Madison et al., 1977; Winegrad & Green, 1978). Present evidence would, therefore, suggest that there is more to be gained in reducing the risk of CVD in diabetic persons by correction of associated risk factors than by attention confined to early detection and control of hyperglycemia.

ECG-LVH. Electrocardiographic evidence for left ventricular hypertrophy (ECG-LVH), an important concomitant of elevated blood pressure, shows striking associations with CVD incidence in older individuals of both sexes (Table 16-2). Indeed, judging from the magnitude of standardized regression coefficients, the net effect of ECG-LVH is considerably more potent in older than in younger subjects irrespective of gender. ECG-LVH remains a strong and independent predictor of several CVD outcomes including CHD, stroke, CHF, and cardiovascular mortality in both older men and women, even when the influence of blood pressure and other risk factors is taken into account (Kannel & Brand, 1985). Presumably, ECG-LVH also represents an important marker of early compromise of the underlying coronary circulation well before clinical manifestations of CHD occur (Campbell, Caird, & Jackson, 1974; Kannel, Gordon, Castelli, & Margolis, 1970).

Vital Capacity. Vital capacity is a simple and sensitive clinical technique to assess for compromise in either cardiac or pulmonary function (or both) in individuals of all ages. Vital capacity normally declines with advancing age, an effect that is strongly exacerbated by cigarette smoking and obesity (Ashley, Kannel, Sorlie, & Masson, 1975; Dontas, Jacobs, Corcondilas, Keys, & Hannan, 1984). Diminished vital capacity in older individuals is also correlated with loss of muscular strength as assessed by hand-grip (Kannel, Lew, Hubert, & Castelli, 1981), presumably reflecting overall muscular debility. For reasons not well understood, this test provides striking risk associations with overall CVD incidence including risk for cardiovascular death particularly in older women (Kannel, Hubert, & Lew, 1983; Kannel & Brand, 1985). Low vital capacity remains one of the strongest predictors of death from all causes in the elderly of either gender. Of interest, the striking inverse relation between vital capacity and cardiovascular events persists even when age is adjusted for and individuals with pulmonary disease or chest deformity as well as cigarette smokers are excluded from consideration. While there is little or no evidence that vital capacity can be greatly improved in the elderly by hygienic measures, it does identify individuals in urgent need of attention to modifiable risk factors. Measurement of this parameter, therefore, should become part of the standard risk assessment of all older patients.

Obesity. Body weight tends to progressively increase during the middle years often resulting in obesity as advanced age is encountered. Although, there is a tendency for body weight to decline as far-advanced age is attained, age-related loss of lean body mass results in a relatively greater degree of overall adiposity per unit of body weight (Borkan & Norris, 1977).

In the analysis of 30-year follow-up data, the strong risk association between relative weight and CVD particularly noted in younger women clearly abates in older women but is retained for older men, although at a lower level of statistical significance. This association holds even when risk factors that covary directly with body weight are taken into account (Ashley & Kannel, 1974; Hubert, Feinlieb, McNamara, & Castelli, 1983). These findings serve to underscore the importance of maintaining ideal body weight throughout life as a preventive measure to limit risk of CVD.

Heart Rate. The risk of CVD conferred by an elevated resting heart rate similar to the effect in younger persons is retained in older men, however, no such effect is observed in older women (Table 16-2). An explanation for this finding is not readily apparent. Conceivably, heart rate in men may be a more sensitive indicator of underlying cardiac dysfunction than in older women, or the net impact presumably of sympathetic influences on the heart in precipitating manifestations of CHD is greater in older men. High heart rates may also reflect physical deconditioning.

Physical Activity. There is limited evidence suggesting that vigorous physical activity will forestall CVD in the elderly (Morris, Chave, & Adam et al., 1973; Paffenbarger & Hyde, 1984). Previously reported data from Framingham indicated that overall mortality including cardiovascular death was inversely related to level of physical activity in men (Kannel & Sorlie, 1979). A benefit for exercise beyond age 50 was also suggested, however, the levels of exercise involved were quite modest. Although regular physical activity in the elderly is desirable and should be strongly encouraged for other reasons, it would be unwise to place undue emphasis on this approach in reducing risk for CVD.

PREVENTIVE IMPLICATIONS

Although it is quite logical to argue that preventive measures should be initiated early in life to reduce the ultimate burden of disease in both the young and the elderly, one should not conclude that instituting such measures in the aged is of little or no value. The risk of CVD in the elderly varies widely in relation to known risk factors, many of which are modifiable. Despite the paucity of direct evidence regarding the efficacy of correcting certain risk factors in older persons, a number of recommendations can be justified on the basis of available information. It is also important to keep in mind that because the incidence of CVD is relatively high in the elderly, the absolute impact of preventive measures short term may actually be greater in older than in young persons despite a lesser relative impact.

In this context, hypertension emerges as the dominant potentially remediable risk factor for CVD in the elderly. It is highly prevalent in the aged, easily detected, and can be corrected by the careful application of appropriate measures including drugs. As alluded to earlier, direct evidence from clinical trials already suggests the efficacy of antihypertensive measures in reducing the frequency of cardiovascular complications even in the elderly.

The emphasis here is not a quest for immortality but for a more meaningful quality of life for the aged. Too often, the sequelae of myocardial infarction or stroke rob older individuals of their vigor, mobility, and independence, ultimately making them dependent on others for maintenance of their care. Thus, appropriate preventive measures that forestall cardiovascular disease in the elderly could very well enhance the quality of the remaining years of life, if not its duration.

REFERENCES

Amery, A. et al. (1985). Mortality and morbidity results from the European Working Party on high blood pressure in the elderly trial. *Lancet, I,* 1349–1370.

Andres, R. (1981). Aging, diabetes, and obesity: Standards of normality. *Mt. Sinai Journal of Medicine, 48,* 489–495.

Ashley, F.W., & Kannel, W.B. (1974). Relation of weight change to changes in atherogenic traits: The Framingham Study. *Journal of Chronic Diseases, 27,* 103–114.

Ashley, F., Kannel, W.B., Sorlie, P., & Masson, R. (1975). Pulmonary function: Relation to aging, cigarette habit and mortality. The Framingham Study. *Annals of Internal Medicine, 82,* 739.

Barrett-Connor, E., Suarez, L., Khaw, K.T., Criqui, M.H., & Wingrad, D.L. (1984). Ischemic heart disease factors after age 50. *Journal of Chronic Diseases, 37,* 903–908.

Bierman, E.L. (1978). Atherosclerosis and aging. *Federation Proceedings, 37,* 2832.

Borkan, G.A., & Norris, A.H. (1977). Fat redistribution and the changing body dimensions of the adult male. *Human Biology, 49,* 495–514.

Campbell, A., Caird, F.I., & Jackson, T.R. (1974). Prevalence of abnormalities of electrocardiogram in old people. *British Heart Journal, 36,* 1005–1011.

Castelli, W.P., Doyle, J.R., Gordon, T., Hanes, C.G., Hjortland, M.C., Hulley, S.B., Kagan, A., & Zukel, W.J. (1977). HDL-cholesterol and other lipids in coronary heart disease: The Cooperative Lipoprotein Phenotyping Study. *Circulation, 62,* 707–714.

Cooper, R., Stamler, J., Dyer, A., & Garside, D. (1978). The decline in mortality from coronary heart disease. USA 1968-1975. *Journal of Chronic Diseases, 31,* 709.

Curb, J.D., Borhani, N.O., Entwisle, G., Tung, B., Kass, E., Schnaper, H., Williams, W., & Berman R., (1985). Isolated systolic hypertension in 14 communities. *American Journal of Epidemiology, 121,* 362–370.

Dawber, T.R., Thomas, H.E., Jr., & McNamara P.M. (1973). Characteristics of the dicrotic notch of the arterial pulse wave in coronary heart disease. *Angiology, 24,* 244–55.

DeFronzo, R.A. (1981). Glucose intolerance and aging. *Diabetes Care, 4,* 493.

Dontas, A.S., Jacobs, D.R., Corcondilas, A., Keys, A., & Hanna, P. Longitudinal versus cross-sectional vital capacity changes and affecting factors. *Journal of Gerontology, 39,* 430–438.

Dyer, A.R., Stamler, J., Shekelle, P., Schoenberger, J., & Farinaro, E., (1977). Hypertension in the elderly. *Medical Clinics of North America, 61,* 513–529.

Gerstenblith G., Fredericksen, J., Yin, F.C.P., Fortuin, N.J., Lakatta, E.G., & Weisfeldt, M.L., (1977). Echocardiographic assessment of a normal adult aging population. *Circulation, 56,* 273–278.

Goldman, L., & Cook E.F. (1984). The decline in ischemic heart disease mortality rates: An analysis of medical interventions and changes in lifestyle. *Annals of Internal Medicine, 101,* 825–836.

Gordon, T., Castelli, W.P., Hjortland, M.C. et al. (1977a). Predicting coronary heart disease in middle-aged and older persons. *JAMA 238,* 497–499.

Gordon, T., Castelli, W.P., Hjortland, M.C., Kannel, W.B., & Dawber, T.R. (1977b). High density lipoprotein as a protective factor against coronary heart disease: The Framingham Study. *American Journals of Medicine, 62,* 707–714.

Gordon, T., & Kannel, W.B. (1982). Multiple risk functions for predicting heart disease: The concept, accuracy, and application. *American Heart Journal, 103,* 1031–1039.

Gordon T., & Kannel, W.B. (1970). The Framingham Study 20 years later. In I.I. Kessler, & M.L. Levin (Eds.), *The community as an epidemiological laboratory: A casebook of community studies* (pp. 123–144). Baltimore: John Hopkins Press.

Gordon, T., & Shurtleff, D. (1977). Means at each examination and inter-examination variation of specified characteristics: Framingham Study, Exam 1 to Exam 10. In W.B. Kannel, T. Gordon (Eds.), *The Framingham Study: An epidemiological investigation of cardiovascular disease.* (U.S. DHEW No. 74-478), Washington, D.C: National Institutes of Health.

Gray, D.R., Weber, M.A., & Drayer, J.I.M. Effects of low-dose anti-hypertensive therapy in elderly patients with predominant systolic hypertension. *Journal of Gerontology, 38,* 302–306.

Harris, T., Cook, E.F., Kannel, W.B., Schatzkin, A., & Goldman, L. (1985). Blood pressure experience and risk of cardiovascular risk in the elderly. *Hypertension, 7,* 118–124.

Hjermann, I., Velve Byre, K., Holme, I., & Leren, P. (1981). Effect of diet and smoking intervention on the incidence of coronary heart disease: Report from the Oslo study group of a randomized trial in healthy men. *Lancet, 2;* 1303–1310.

Hubert, H.B., Feinleib, M., McNamara, P.M., & Castelli, W.P. (1983). Obesity as an independent risk factor for cardiovascular disease: A 26-year follow-up of participants in the Framingham Heart Study. *Circulation, 67,* 968–977.

Hypertension Detection and Follow-up Program Cooperative Group: Five-year findings of the Hypertension Detection and Follow-up Program: II. Mortality by race-sex and age. *JAMA* 242:2572–77.

Ingelfinger E.J. (1977). Debates on diabetes. *New England Journal of Medicine, 295,* 1128–1230.

Kannel, W.B., & Brand, F.N. (1985). Cardiovascular risk factors in the elderly. In *Principles of geriatric medicine* R. Andres, E.G., Bierman, W.R. Hazzard (Eds.), pp. 104–119. New York: McGraw-Hill.

Kannel, W.B., Dawber, T.R., & McGee, D.L. (1980). Perspectives on systolic hypertension: The Framingham study. *Circulation, 61,* 1179–1182.

Kannel, W.B., & Gordon, T. (1978). Evaluation of cardiovascular risk in the elderly:

The Framingham Study. *Bulletin of New York Academy of Medicine, 54,* 573–591.

Kannel, W.B., & Gordon, T. (1980). Cardiovascular risk factors in the aged: The Framingham Study. In J.S.G. Haynes, & M. Feinleib (Eds.), *Second Conference on the Epidemiology of Aging* (pp. 65–86) (DHHS, NIH publication no. 80-969) Washington, DC.

Kannel, W.B., Gordon, T., Castelli, W.R., & Margolis, J.R. (1970). Electrocardiographic left ventricular hypertrophy and risk of coronary heart disease. The Framingham Study. *Annals of Internal Medicine, 72,* 813–822.

Kannel, W.B., Hjortland, M., & Castelli, W.P., (1974). Role of diabetes in congestive heart failure: The Framingham Study. *American Journal of Cardiology, 34,* 29–34.

Kannel, W.B., Hubert, H., & Lew, E.A. (1983). Vital capacity as a predictor of cardiovascular disease: The Framingham Study. *American Heart Journal, 105,* 311–315.

Kannel, W.B., Lew, E.A., Hubert, H.B., & Castelli, W.P. (1981). The value of measuring vital capacity for prognostic purposes. *Transactions of the Association of Life Insurance Medical Directors of America, 64,* 66–81.

Kannel, W.B., & McGee, D.L. (1979a). Diabetes and glucose tolerance as risk factors for cardiovascular disease: The Framingham Study. *Diabetes Care, 2,* 120–126.

Kannel, W.B., & McGee, D.L. (1979b). Diabetes and cardiovascular disease. The Framingham Study. *JAMA, 241,* 2035–2038.

Kannel W.B., McGee D.L., & Gordon T. (1976). A general cardiovascular risk profile: The Framingham Study. *American Journal of Cardiology, 38,* 46–51.

Kannel, W.B., & Sorlie, P. (1979). Some health benefits of physical activity. The Framingham Study. *Archives of Internal Medicine, 139,* 857–861.

Kannel, W.B., Sorlie, P. & Gordon, T. (1980). Labile hypertension: A faulty concept? The Framingham Study. *Circulation, 61,* 1183–1187.

Kannel, W.B., Wolf, P.A., McGee, D.L., Dawber, T.R., McNamara, P., & Castelli, W.P. (1981). Systolic blood pressure, arterial rigidity, and risk of stroke: The Framingham Study. *JAMA 245,* 1225–1229.

Kaplan, N.M. (1983). Hypertension: Prevalance, risks and effect of therapy. *Annals of Internal Medicine, 98,* 705.

Koch-Weser, J. (1973). The therapeutic challenge of systolic hypertension. *New England Journal of Medicine, 289,* 481.

Lipid Research Clinics Coronary Primary Prevention Trial Results. I. Reduction in incidence of coronary heart disease. (1984). *JAMA, 251,* 351–364.

Maddocks, T. (1976). Possible absence of essential hypertension in two complete Pacific Island populations. *Lancet, 2,* 327–331.

Management Committee (Australian Therapeutic Trial in Mild Hypertension): Treatment of mild hypertension in the elderly. (1981). *Medical Journal of Australia, 2,* 398–402.

Meinert, C., Knatterud, G.L., Prout, T.E., & Klimt, C.R. (1970). A study of the effects of hypoglycemic agents on vascular complications in patients with adult-onset diabetes: II. Mortality results. *Diabetes* (Suppl.), *19,* 789–830.

Milch, R.A. (1965). Matrix properties of the aging arterial wall. *Monographs in Surgical Science, 2,* 261–341.

Morris, J.N., Chave, S.P., Adam, C. et al. (1973). Vigorous exercise in leisure time and the incidence of coronary heart disease. *Lancet, 1,* 333–339.

Paffenbarger, R.S., Jr., & Hyde, R.T. (1980). Exercise in the prevention of coronary heart disease. *Preventive Medicine, 13,* 3–22.

Pomerance, A. (1976). Pathology of the Myocardium and valves. In F.I. Caird, J.L.C. Dall, & J.R.D. Kennedy (Eds.), *Cardiology in old age* (pp. 11–55). New York and London: Plenum.

Regan, T.J., Ahured, S.S., Haider, B.B., & Lyons, M.M. (1978). The myocardium and its vasculature in diabetes mellitus. *Modern Concepts in Cardiovascular Disease,* *47,* 75–78.

Rodenheffer, R.J., Gerstenblith, G., Becker, L.C., Fleg, J.L., & Weisfeldt, M.L. (1984). Exercise cardiac output is maintained with advancing age in healthy human subjects: Cardiac dilatation and increased stroke volume compensate for a diminished heart rate. *Circulation, 69,* 203–313.

Rowe, J.W. (1983). Systolic hypertension in the elderly. *New England Journal of Medicine, 309,* 1246–1247.

Schnaper, H.W., Furberg, C.D., Kuller, L.H., et al. (1983). The response of isolated systolic hypertension to diuretic therapy. *CVD Epidemiology Newsletter, 33,* 30.

Shea, S., Cook, E.F., Kannel, W.B., & Goldman, L. (1985). Treatment of hypertension and its effect on cardiovascular risk factors: Data from the Framingham Heart Study. *Circulation, 71,* 22–30.

Siperstein, M.D., Foster, D.W., Knowles, H.C., Jr., Levial R., Madison, L.L., & Roth, J. (1977). Control of blood sugar and diabetic vascular disease. *New England Journal of Medicine, 296,* 1060–1063.

Truett, J., Cornfield, J., & Kannel, W. (1967). A multivariate analysis of the risk of coronary heart disease in Framingham. *Journal of Chronic Disease, 20,* 511–524.

U.S. Department of Health and Human Services PHS. (1980). *Lipid research clinics population studies data book.* Vol. I. *The prevalence study.* (NIH no. 80-1527). Washington, D.C.: Author.

Veterans Administration Cooperative Study Group on Antihypertensive Agents. (1972). Effects of treatment on morbidity in hypertension: III. Influence of age, diastolic pressure, and prior cardiovascular disease; further analysis of side effects. *Circulation, 45,* 991–1004.

Walker, W. (1983). Changing U.S. life-style and declining vascular mortality—a retrospective. *New England Journal of Medicine, 308,* 649–651.

Winegrad A.E., & Green, D.A. (1978). The complications of diabetes mellitus (Editorial). *New England Journal of Medicine, 298,* 1250–1252.

CHAPTER 17

Exercise Testing in Geriatric Postinfarct Patients

Antoon De Schryver
Guy De Backer

Exercise testing has now become widely used in postinfarct patients. The prognostic value of these tests has been well documented in younger and middle-aged patients. The purpose of this study was to determine if clinical and exercise variables collected during the first months after an infarct are useful indicators of late mortality in patients of 65 years and above, who had survived a myocardial infarction (MI); 68 male patients (mean age, 69.0 yr) were tested within 3 months (mean, 49 days) after MI. Mean follow-up period was 33.2 months. The study variables were (mean values): resting heart rate (HR) 74 bpm; systolic blood pressure (SBP), 133.4 mmHg; diastolic blood pressure (DBP), 80.8 mmHg; body mass index, 24.2 kg/m²; maximal HR during exercise, 130 bpm; maximal SBP, 179 mmHg; maximal O_2 consumption, 1,121 ml/min; maximal workload, 125 W. During follow-up 8 subjects died. Of the variables studied only maximal workload, HR at submaximal level, and resting HR were found to be significantly, different in the two groups. These results show that in exercise testing of postinfarct patients 65 and above, resting HR, maximal workload, and HR at submaximal level had prognostic significance.

Exercise testing has now become widely used in postinfarct patients as a part of rehabilitation programs. The prognostic value of these tests has been well documented in younger and middle-aged patients (De Busk et al., 1980, Rapaport & Remedios, 1933; Sivarajan, Bruce, Lindskog, Almes & Belanger et al., 1982). In view of the increase of the 65 plus population in Western societies, it is necessary to get information about the feasibility and the value of exercise tests in patients of that age. The aims of the present study were to examine:

1. The predictive value of exercise testing (i.e. to determine whether clinical and exercise variables, as collected during the first months after the infarction, are useful indicators of late mortality in patients of 65 years and above who have survived a myocardial infarction).
2. Age differences in exercise testing in postinfarction patients, specifically to compare the results with the data collected in younger patients studied and followed up under the same conditions (De Backer, Mercelis, Van Durme, Verheye, & Van Egmond, 1977).

METHODS

A symptom-limited exercise test was performed within 3 months after a myocardial infarction in all consecutive male patients, aged over 65 years who were seen in the cardiac rehabilitation center of the Akademisch Ziekenhuis of Gent between July 1, 1973 and December 31, 1983. The diagnosis of myocardial infarction was based on WHO-recommended criteria (WHO, 1969). Patients who showed one of the following symptoms where excluded beforehand:

1. Congestive heart failure [class 3 or 4 of New York Heart Association (NYHA)].
2. Pairs or runs of ventricular premature beats on the resting electrocardiogram (ECG).
3. Systolic blood pressure of more than 200 mm Hg or a diastolic blood pressure of more than 120 mm Hg.
4. Unstable angina.

The test procedure of the present study consisted of a routine physical examination, with blood pressure measurement in the supine position; a standard 12-lead resting ECG; measurements of height, weight, and vital capacity; and a symptom-limited maximal exercise test on a bicycle ergometer. Vital capacity was expressed as the difference between the observed value [adjusted for body temperature pressure saturated (BTPS)] and the expected value according to EC norms (Jouasset 1960). The exercise started at a work load of 50 W and was increased with steps of 25 W every 2 minutes. Three ECG leads (II, V4, V5) were monitored during and after exercise. Blood pressure was measured during the second minute of each step. Respiratory parameters including respiratory rate, oxygen consumption, and CO_2 production were continuously measured.

TABLE 17-1. Comparison of the Older and the Younger Post Infarction Patients in Various Characteristics

	Older >65 years (n = 68)		Younger <65 years (n = 302)		
	M	SD	M	SD	p
Age	69.0	3.4	51.9	7.3	<0.001
Resting HR/bpm	74.6	16.8	72.9	12.1	ns
SBP/mmHg	133.4	17.9	132.0	18.2	ns
DBP/mmHg	80.8	12.4	85.2	11.4	<0.01
BMI/KG/M^2	24.2	2.7	24.6	2.9	ns
Max hr/bpm	129.6	25.0	143.0	24.0	<0.001
Max VO$_2$/ml/min	1120.6	370.0	463.0	488.0	<0.001
Max SBP	178.8	26.9	174.0	29.0	ns
Maximal work load (W)	125	75	125	75	ns
Vital capacity (ml)	− 869	813	− 716	628	ns
Mean follow-up (M)	32	29	37	18	ns

ns = nonsignificant.

Criteria for interrupting the test were increasing angina, ST segment depression of more than 4 mm, drop in systolic blood pressure, excessive fatigue, second- or third-degree atrioventricular block, ventricular tachycardia, systolic blood pressure exceeding 250 mm Hg, or "maximal" oxygen consumption. Follow-up data with regard to total mortality were collected on a retrospective basis from the day of exercise to March 15, 1984. Vital status was known in all patients. The results obtained in these elderly patients where further compared with results observed in 302 male postinfarction patients aged 45-64 years and tested between 1970 and 1976 (De Backer et al., 1977). Both groups were compared by nonparametric statistical tests.

Patient Description

The characteristics of the older postinfarction population are compared with the younger population in Table 17-1 and summarized below:

1. By definition the two groups were different in age.
2. Resting heart rate was not significantly different, but the older patients tended toward higher resting heart rates.
3. Systolic blood pressure showed no difference between the two groups.
4. Diastolic blood pressure was significantly lower in older patients than in the younger group.

TABLE 17-2. Prospective Results in the Older Postinfarction Patients

Variable	Nonsurvivors ($n = 8$)		Survivors ($n = 60$)		
	M	SD	M	SD	p
Age (yr)	70.0	3.6	68.9	3.4	ns
Resting HR/bpm	86.5	16.8	73.1	16.5	<0.05
SBP	137.3	17.4	132.9	18.2	ns
BMI/kg/m^2	24.9	2.2	24.2	2.9	ns
HR/75W/bpm	130.7	20.7	112.5	20.1	<0.05
HR max/bpm	130	27	130	25	ns
SBP	177.5	29.4	178.3	24.5	ns
VO$_2$ max/ml/min	967.6	454.8	1147.8	358.7	ns
Vital capacity/ml	−969.4	008.7	−619.2	568.0	ns
Maximal work load (W)	100	75	150	125	<0.05

ns = nonsignificant.

5. Body mass index showed no difference between older and younger patients.
6. Maximal heart rate and maximal oxygen uptake were significantly lower in older patients, which is expected from physiology (Kennedy & Cavid, 1981; Astrand, 1969).
7. No significant differences were found in maximal systolic BP although the older group tended toward a somewhat higher maximal systolic blood pressure.
8. No difference was found in maximal work load between older and younger group.
9. No significant differences in vital capacity.
10. Mean follow-up was comparable in both groups.

During follow-up, 8 subjects died in the older group. Table 17-2 lists all characteristics that were analyzed as possible discriminators between the group of 8 who died and the group of 60 remaining subjects. For this analysis the Mann-Whitney test was used (Mann & Whitney, 1947). Those who died were not different in age; the resting heart rate, the heart rate at submaximal level, and the maximal work load turned out to be predictors of mortality. Systolic blood pressure at rest, maximal oxygen uptake, and vital capacity were not significantly different in those who died compared with survivors. Body mass index, maximal heart rate, and maximal systolic blood pressure during exercise were also comparable in survivors and nonsurvivors. When these variables were entered into a stepwise discriminant function, only resting heart rate was found to contribute significantly to mortality/survival.

The prognostic value of the exercise test in these older patients was compared with the results observed in a younger group. (De Backer et

TABLE 17-3. Prospective Results in the Younger Postinfarction Patients

Variable <65 years (n = 302)	Nonsurvivors (n = 16)		Survivors (n = 286)		p
	M	SD	M	SD	
Age/yr	50.4	6.9	52.2	7.4	ns
Resting HR/bpm	75.2	14.2	72.9	12.1	ns
SBP/mmHg	128.5	22.8	132.3	18.0	ns
HR/75W/bpm	116.4	20.0	116.2	17.3	ns
HR max/bpm	134.6	26.0	134.6	24.2	ns
Systolic blood pressure max/mmHg	160.1	31.5	174.4	29.4	ns
Maximal O$_2$ uptake/ml/mi	1056.0	277.5	1482.5	489.6	<0.001
Vital capacity (ml)	− 1072.1	675.9	− 704.8	6131	<0.02
Maximal work load (W)	125	75	150	125	<0.05

ns = nonsignificant.

al., 1977). Results are presented in Table 17-3.

Maximal work load, maximal O$_2$ consumption, and vital capacity were significantly different between prospective survivors and nonsurvivors. When both the younger and the older postinfarction patients are considered together, the only common predictive variable is maximal work load. In younger patients especially, maximal parameters were most predictive for death (i.e., maximal oxygen uptake and maximal work load). In older patients, besides maximal work load, only submaximal or resting parameters were predictive for death (i.e., resting heart rate and heart rate at submaximal level).

DISCUSSION

Results from exercise testing performed within 3 months after an acute MI have been analysed as prognostic indicators in middle-aged patients (De Backer et al., 1977). In this study especially, the maximal parameters were predictive for subsequent death. In older postinfarction patients not only was the amount of total work load predictive for mortality but also heart rate at submaximal level and heart rate at rest were predictive, the latter being the only parameter that was predictive of death in a stepwise discriminant function. An explanation could be that survivors took more β-blockers than did those who died. It turns out, however, that resting heart rate was *not* different in patients taking β-blockers compared with those who did not. On the other hand, only 1 out of the 8 subjects who died took β-blockers at the time of the exercise test compared with 16 of 60 who survived.

Another explanation, which is not in contradiction with the former, is that those who died had subclinical heart failure at the time of exercise testing. Forty percent of the nonsurvivors were taking digitalis compared with 20% of the survivors. The results show that in younger patients maximal exercise parameters are more predictive for late mortality, while in older patients submaximal and resting parameters are more important. However, in both groups maximal work load on the ergometer was significantly associated with late mortality. This is interesting since older people could be expected to have a reduced physical capacity of noncardiac origin.

REFERENCES

Astrand, I. (1969). Aerobic work capacity in men and women with special references to age. *Acta Physiologica Scandinavica, 49,* 1

DeBacker, G., Mercelis, L., Van Durme, J.P., Verheye, S., & Van Egmond, J. (1978). The prognostic significance of an exercise test performed within three months after acute myocardial infarction. In *Les épreuves d'effort.* Paris: Expansion scientifique.

De Busk, R.F., Davidson, D.M., Houston, N., Fitzgerald. J. (1980). Serial ambulatory electrocardiography and treadmill exercise testing after uncomplicated myocardial infarction. *American Journal of Cardiology, 45,* 547.

Jouasset, D. (1960). Normalisation des épreuves fonctionelles respiratoires dans la population de la communauté européenne du charbon et de l'acier. *Poumon et Coeur, 10,* 33.

Kenney, R.D., & Cavid, F.I. (1981). Physiology of aging of the heart. In R.J. Noble & D.A. Rothbaum (Eds.). *Geriatric cardiology.* Philadelphia: FA Davis.

Mann, H.B., & Whitney, D.R., (1947). On a test of whether one or two random variables is stochastically larger than the other. *Annals of Mathematics and Statistics, 18,* 50.

Rapapport E., & Remedios, P. (1983). The high-risk patient after recovery from myocardial infarction: Recognition and management. *Journal of the American College of Cardiology, 1* (2), 391.

Sami, M. Kraemer, H. De Busk, R.F. (1979). The prognostic significance of serial exercise testing after myocardial infarction. *Circulation, 60,* 1238-1243.

Sivarajan, E.S., Bruce, R.A., Lindskog, B.D., Almes, M.J., Belanger, L., & Green, B. (1982). Treadmill test responses to an early exercise program after myocardial infarction, a randomized study. *Circulation, 65,* 7

World Health Organization. *Working group in ischaemic heart disease registers, Copenhagen 1969.* Regional Office for Europe, Copenhagen: WHO.

CHAPTER 18

Osteoporosis and Aging

M. Passeri
L. Buttrini

Exercise and movement are of the utmost importance in the elderly; they contribute to maintaining and improving senile organic function, permit an active social life, and stimulate psychic activity with an improved global cerebral functioning. Physiological aging provokes a progressive loss of mass in the skeleton, which nevertheless is sufficient for its functions: metabolic (calcium storage and mineral exchange) and support. Frequently bone loss exceeds the normal standards (40% of females by age 60 have excessive trabecular bone loss) with the consequence that bone structure (compact and trabecular bone) grows thinner and is no longer able to resist mechanical stress; fractures take place and the syndrome of osteoporosis (postmenopausal, senile, or with secondary hyperparathyroidism) is manifested. Cumulative risk for fractures is very high (up to 50% in the aged 80-plus), particularly in females. It has been calculated that in the U.S.A. $3.4 billion were spent last year on fractures. In actual fact this figure concerns only pure fracture therapy, but it does not consider fracture consequence, which includes many organic problems (pneumonia, thrombosis, pressure sores, etc.) and the necessity of a period of immobility that often represents the onset of a period that will lead the elderly person to a definitive and complete dependence and lack of self-sufficiency.

Elderly people need more than anything else to have the possibility of maintaining themselves both physically and psychologically in order to manage their daily living activities and to participate in life. It is evident that, first, brain function and, secondly, physical fitness are fundamental to this purpose: these two aspects are strictly correlated, since physical activity is helped by the stimulations derived from con-

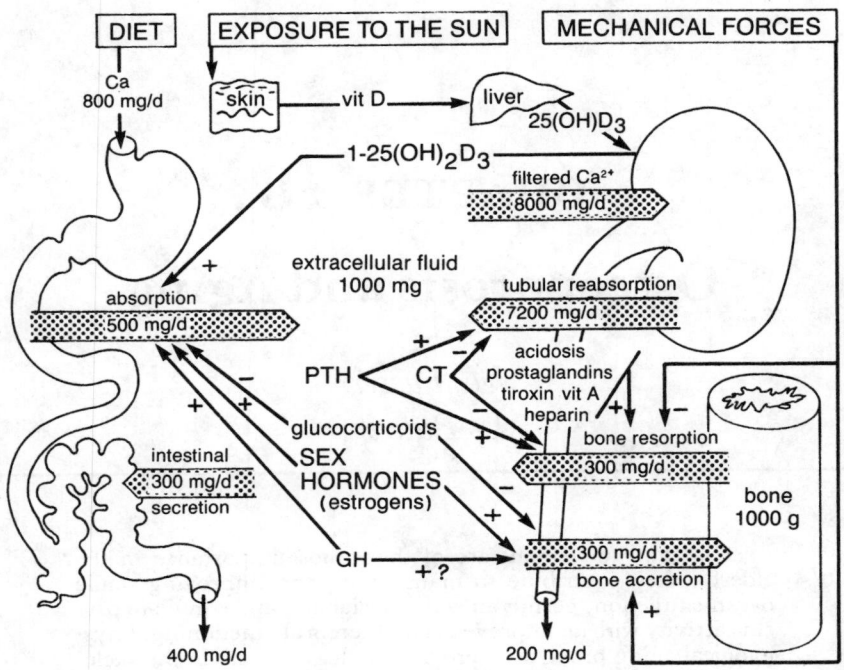

FIGURE 18-1. Main aspects of bone metabolism.

tacts with the environment and with other people (Peacock, Taylor, & Brown, 1981).

As is well known, movement is of the utmost importance, not only to maintain muscle function and circulation, but also to stimulate physical activity. In this context it is evident that bone function is basic, since the skeleton is the system devoted to the support of the body. Bone has another main function, a metabolic one, which is correlated with mineral homeostasis of the body and, in particular, with calcium-phosphorus balance (see Figure 18-1). This action is carried out through an irregularly distributed bone remodeling by the so-called bone remodeling units (BMUs), which act in compact bone, particularly in endosteal surfaces, and in cancellous skeletal structures (Frost, 1984).

The remodeling in BMUs begins with osteoclast activation, which destroys the bone's ability to dig a niche in the lamellar surface, and prevents transferring calcium from bone to interstitial fluids. Osteoblasts restore bone production and remain prisoners of the proteidic substance produced by them (ground matrix and collagen fibers) and

TABLE 18–1. Local Factors Controlling Bone Metabolism

Factor	Abbreviation
Osteoclast activating factor	OAF
Bone cells multiplication stimulating factor	BCMSA
Epidermal growth factor	EGF
Fibroblast growth factor	FGF

in which they subsequently provoke deposition of calcium salts (Bar & Hurwitz, 1979; Barlow & Hart, 1984; Recker, 1983).

In this functional remodeling great importance is attributed to some factors that may influence this process, or which are connected with it. In this regard we remember some local factors, indicated in Table 18-1 and some noncollagenous proteins, indicated in Table 18-2. It seems that among these a particular interest should be attributed to osteocalcin, a protein connected with the calcification process and probably synthesized by osteoblasts.

We cannot discuss in depth the possible role and importance of this protein: we can only affirm that, according to our (Price and Williamson, 1981) and other's (Malluche et al., 1983; Raisz & Kreau, 1983) results, osteocalcin represents a marker of bone turn-over; it is detectable in blood in different concentrations according to sex and age (Figures 18-2 and 18-3) (Heaney, 1984) and is related to the rate of bone remodeling.

Bone resorption produced by osteoclasts in BMU is incomplete, particularly in the proximity of the endosteal surface, so that with aging the reconstruction phase that follows osteoclast destruction is not sufficient to compensate for bone loss, resulting in a negative balance, characterized by trabecular thinning (up to disappearance) and cortical reduction at the endosteal site (Bar & Hurwitz, 1979; Barlow & Hart, 1984).

The entity of this phenomenon becomes more serious with age, probably due to senile impairment of bone cells and also to many other factors, which may influence bone metabolism and conditions (Nordin, 1984). White populations, and in particular females, are more

TABLE 18–2. Characteristics of K-Dependent GLA-Proteins

GLA-Proteins	—Having a small molecule (polypeptides) —Rich in γ-carboxyglutamic acid
Vitamin K-dependent	—Calcium-binder (calcificator? calification regulator? informer?)

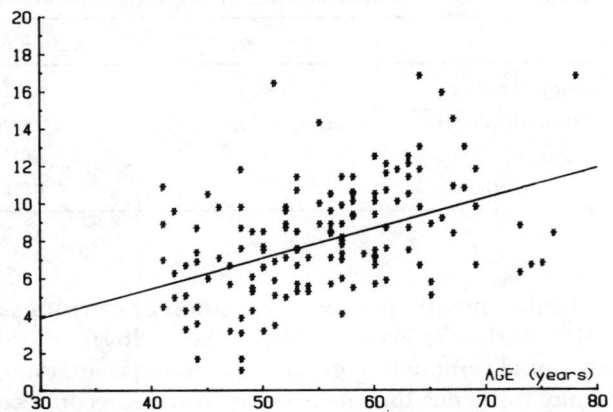

FIGURE 18–2. Correlation between osteocalcin levels and age (females).

prone to rapid bone loss, whereas blacks and orientals have the advantage of losing their bone mass more slowly with age (Heaney, 1984).

Regarding endogenous functions, it should be mentioned that adrenal steroids promote hyperfunction (Frost, 1983; Sawin et al., 1975; Sorensen, Lumholtz, Lund, Hjelmstrand & Mosekilde et al., 1982; Whitehead, Lane, & Townsend et al., 1981),which may cause defects in calcium absorption (Nordin, 1984) and in bone accretion. Another consideration is the senile tendency for acidosis, which hastens bone loss and which is frequently worsened by kidney and lung metabolic senile functional modifications. More important are sex hormone deficiencies (in particular estrogens), which is characteristic of old age

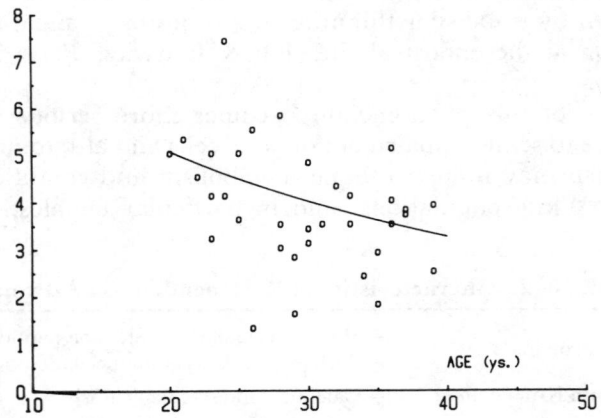

FIGURE 18–3. Correlation between osteocalcin levels and age (males).

(Grodin, Siiteri, & McDonald, 1973; Mazess, 1983; Papanicolau, Loraine, Dove, & Louden, 1969; Parfitt, 1983), reducing both vitamin D renal hydroxylation (Bar & Hurwitz, 1969; Navckis, Katzenellenbogen, & Nalbandov, 1979b; Nordin, 1984a; Pedrazzoni & Passeri, 1983; Spencer, Kramer, Osis, & Norris, 1976; Trufanov, 1981; West et al., 1961; Whedon et al., 1976) and perhaps calcitonin (CT) secretion (Takahashi et al., 1983; Thalassinos et al., 1982).

Other calcium-hormone senile modifications are represented by a tendency to increase PTH serum levels (Avioli, 1984; Lucanton, Lanza, Companari, & Amadio, 1983) and by a defective response of CT provocative stimuli (Butturini et al., 1985; Deftos, Weishman, & Williams et al., 1980).

In particular, the importance of calcium absorption capacity is to be considered. Calcium absorption capacity is reduced in the elderly, owing both to duodenal epithelial aging and to reduced renal α–hydroxylase activity, leading to an insufficient supply of 1-25-(OH) cholecalciferol and consequently to a scarce calcium absorption (Nordin, 1984).

Some exogenous factors are of importance. For example, diet: elderly people do not eat sufficient milk, cheese, and vegetables (which contain a noteworthy amount of calcium); hence, they are particularly deficient in calcium salt intake. This fact, plus the poor exposure to the sun's rays (elderly people prefer to be entirely dressed when they go outside) which reduces cutaneous vitamin D synthesis, make the above-mentioned defects of duodenal epithelial absorptive functions more important, with the consequence of negative calcium balance and compensatory bone deconstruction (Albanese, 1983; Heaney, Gallagher, Johnston, Neer, & Parfitt, et al.; Navickis, Katzenellenbogen, & Nalbandov, 1979a; Palummeri, Cervellin, Pedrazzonig, & Passeri, 1986; Passeri et al., 1984; Stevenson, 1982). This negative balance is worsened by another very frequent habit in the elderly—the reduction of movement and muscle stress. We know that mechanical forces are able to induce bone formation and are necessary for bone mass maintenance. It is sufficient to mention in this regard that bone loss occurs after a generalized palsy or in persons deprived of the force of gravity (Mack et al., 1967; Sommerville, Kitchin, & Mansfield, 1979; Whitehead, Lane, & Moesman, et al., 1984). On the other hand we have shown (Butterini et al., 1985) that mineralization of radius increases in weight-lifters after a training period.

For all of these reasons physiological aging is accompanied by bone mass loss; nevertheless, the skeleton lasts many years, exerting both metabolic and support functions; its strength and resistance are sufficient for the needs of the elderly individual.

Only when the subjects become extremely overaged, or when several of the above-mentioned factors exert their negative influence, possibly on the basis of a previously poor bone mass, does a physiological osteopenia give way to a pathological condition such as osteomalacia (when vitamin D deficiency prevails) or, more frequently, osteoporosis—a syndrome in which bone support function is partially or totally insufficient, resulting in bone pain, deformity, and finally in fractures.

So we may consider diffuse osteoporosis as a multifactorial illness that may assume peculiar aspects, according to the most important pathogenetic factors involved.

Postmenopausal osteoporosis is consequent to the end of ovarian function (Chestnut, 1984; Heaney, 1982; Nordin, 1984b). It is present in almost 40% of females over age 60 (Mundy, 1983) and particularly affects cancellous bone resulting in vertebral crushes (mostly in the lumbar region) and in Colles' wrist fractures.

Senile osteoporosis is also a multifactorial illness; it is the consequence of bone aging and of the general organic modifications of aging, particularly when a congenital predisposition is present. It occurs in both sexes, affecting both cancellous (e.g., femur, neck) and, more frequently, cortical compact bone (mainly appendicular) (Heaney, 1982; Mundy, 1983; Nordin, 1984b; Russel et al., 1983).

Another form of osteoporosis is related to impaired kidney function (with α–25-dihydroxycholecalciferol deficiency and secondary hyperparathyroidism). This condition occurs in less than 10% of the cases of senile osteoporosis.

In all cases, cumulative risk of fractures is very high, up to 50% in people over 80, particularly females. Appendicular bone fractures, vertebral crushes, bone deformities, and pain, all of which are the result of the failure of skeletal support, bring dramatic consequence to elderly people (Passeri, 1985). The associated personal, financial, medical, and social burdens are great.

One has to consider that functional impairment is accompanied by pain, particularly when a fracture occurs. In addition, time and money are necessary for surgery and rehabilitation. Nursing is necessary during the acute phase of fractures, when surgery or orthopedic devices are needed, and even more care is needed if a stable state characterized by difficulty of movement takes place.

As regards the financial aspects, it is not proper to calculate, as is commonly done, the damage of the decay of bone support function on the mere basis of the apparent cost (days spent in a hospital, medical and nursing care, and so on), since the real cost is much greater. In actual fact it is calculated that in the U.S. about $3.4 billion are spent each year on fracture treatment (in Italy the corresponding figure is $32 million), but the global financial and social cost is much higher. In fact, we also have to take into account that it is not always possible to obtain a complete recovery.

Ten percent of the persons who have femur fractures die from complications. Particularly after leg fractures, a number of people will remain invalid for the rest of their life, needing constant nursing and social assistance.

Persons experiencing vertebral crushes, of course, cannot recover, and there are important severe implications, such as radicular pain, ventilatory impairment due to the altered position of the thoracic cage (hiatal hernia, constipation, etc.) (AA.VV., 1985). Respiratory insufficiency is frequently caused or favored by these conditions; as are cardiac disturbances. Even more important, immobility sooner or later provokes thrombosis in leg and pelvic veins, often resulting in thromboembolism, which is sometimes lethal. Pressure sores and muscle atrophy often arise owing to long-lasting immobilization and confinement to bed.

But perhaps the most important consequence is the total impossibility of moving or having contact with the surroundings: the subjects, being obliged to lie in bed or to remain in the same room (maybe looking at the ceiling all day long) lack physical and mental stimulation, thus rapidly losing their mental awareness. In this situation the patient is moving toward a true hypokinetic syndrome, the worst condition for elderly people.

For all of these reasons it is of the utmost importance to clarify pathophysiological aspects of osteoporosis and to apply all means to arrive at an early diagnosis in order to correct, if possible, any risk factor with a timely therapy.

As it is well known, the diagnosis of osteoporosis may not be helped by the common laboratory findings; on the other hand, bone biopsy and histomorphometric examinations are invasive, complicated, and not easily repeatable. Nowadays we can perform such diagnosis with minimal patient discomfort, by means of the recently developed noninvasive techniques, which have a much greater precision than radiology and radiogrammetry, such as single- and dual-photon absorptiometry, quantitative computed tomography, and total body calcium evaluation (Dequeker & Johnston, 1982; Mundy, 1983).

Single- and dual-photon absorptiometry, in particular, offer a very practical and safe possibility of diagnosis and of follow-up of osteoporosis permitting the evaluation of bone loss with age and the determination of the efficacy, if any, of therapy.

There are several approaches to the treatment of osteoporosis: oestrogens, vitamin D, fluoride, calcitonin, diphosphonates, anabolic steroids, and more (Barlow & Hart, 1984; Chestnut, 1984; Eisinger, Laponche & Ouaniche, 1984; Geusens & Dequecker, 1984; Murray, 1984; Spencer, Kramer, Lesniak, DeBartolo, & Norris, 1984).

A very interesting approach to treating osteoporosis following the concepts of Rasmussen and Frost (Frost, 1981a; Frost, 1981b) has been proposed. According to this method, it is useful to attempt to increase the number of the so-called bone-remodeling units, which act upon bone turnover. The activation may be carried out through a 4- to 6-day period of therapy with a 1-34 fragment of PTH and phosphate, or with 1-25 vitamin D. Thereafter, osteoclast activity is suppressed with CT or diphosphonate for a period of 3 weeks. This modern strategy, with which we are presently experimenting, thus far seems to have some real efficacy in the treatment of osteoporosis (AA.VV., 1985 Papanicolau, Loraine, & Dove, 1969).

To conclude, then, the above-mentioned sequelae of osteoporosis surely make prevention an important priority. Doctors must always have in mind that osteoporosis is a progressive disease: they should be aware of the risk factors and which therapies (such as heparin, cortico-steroids, or antiepileptic drugs) may have adverse effects.

Unfortunately, there is not yet sufficient awareness of the impor-tance of this really serious social illness.

REFERENCES

AA.VV. (1985). Psicologia e Geriatria, a cura di M.A. Aveni Casucci, Edizioni Claire, Milano.

Albanese, A.A. (1983). Calcium nutrition throughout the life cycle. *Bibl. Nutrit. Dieta, 33,* 80:99.

Avioli, L.V., (1984). Calcium and osteoporosis. *Annual Review of Nutrition, 4,* 471–491.

Bar, A., & Hurwitz, S. (1979). The interaction between dietary calcium and gonadal hormones in their effect on plasma calcium, bone, 25-hydroxy-cholecalciferol-l-hydroxylase, and duodenal calcium-binding protein, measured by a radioimmu-noassay in chicks. *Endocrinology, 104,* 5, 1455–1460.

Barlow, D.H., & Hart, D.M. (1984). Prevention of postmenopausal bone mineral loss by implants of estradiol and testosterone. *Proceedings of the International Sympo-sium on Osteoporosis,* p. 673, Copenhagen.

Butturini, L., Benassi, G., et al. (in press). Effetto della pratica sportiva del solleva-mento pesi (powerlifters) sulla mineralizzazione ossea: studio longitudinale, *Me-dicina dello Sport.*

Butturini, L., Davoli, L., et al. (1985). Valutazione della riserva escretoria di Calci-tonina con un nuovo test di stimolo: differenze tra giovani ed anziani. *Atti del Congresso Nazionale di Gerontologia e Geriatria,* Perugia.

Chestnut, C.H., (1984). Treatment of postmenopausal osteoporosis. *Comprehensive Therapy, 10,* 41–47.

Deftos, L.J., Weisman, M.H., Williams, G.W., et al. (1980). Influence of age and sex on plasma calcitonin in human beings. *New England Journal of Medicine, 302* (24), 1351.

Dequeker, J., & Johnston, C.C.,Jr. (1982). *Non-invasive bone measurements: methodological problems.* Oxford/Washington D.C.: IRL Press.

Eisinger, J., Laponche, A.M., Ouaniche, J. (1984). Trabecular bone mass in post-menopausal osteoporosis: effect of various hormonal treatment. *Proceedings of the International Symposium on Osteoporosis* (p. 657), Copenhagen.

Frost, H.M. (1981a). Coherence treatment of osteoporosis. *Orthopedic Clinics of North America, 12,* 649–669.

Frost, H.M. (1981b). The ADFR concept revisited. *Calcified Tissue International, 36,* 349–353.

Frost, H.M. (1983). The skeletal intermediary organization. A review. *Journal of Metabolism and Bone Disease Related Research, 4,* 281–290.

Frost, H.M. (1984). Mathematical elements of lamellar bone remodeling. Springfield, IL: CC Thomas.

Geusens, P., & Dequecker, J. (1984). Effect of anabolic steroids, 1-alpha hydroxyvitamin D and intermittent calcium infusion on bone mineral content in osteoporosis. *Proceedings of the International Symposium on Osteoporosis* (p. 665), Copenhagen.

Gregerman, R.I., & Bierman, E. (1973). Aging and hormones. In: R.H. Williams (ed.), *Textbook of Endocrinology* (pp. 1059–1070).

Grodin, J.M., Siiteri, P.K., & McDonald, P.C. (1973). Source of estrogen production in postmenopausal women. *Journal of Endocrinology and Metabolism, 36,* 207.

Heaney, R.P. (1984). Risk factors in age-related bone loss and osteoporotic fracture. *Proceedings of the International Symposium on Osteoporosis* (p. 245), Copenhagen.

Heaney, R.P. (1982). Management of osteoporosis: nutritional considerations. *Clinical and Investigative Medicine, 5*(2-3), 185–187.

Heaney, R.P. (1982). Nutritional factors and estrogen in age-related bone loss. *Clinical and Investigative Medicine, 5*(2-3), 147–155.

Mack, P.B. et al. (1967). Bone demineralization of foot and hand in Gemini-Titan IV, V and VIII astronauts during orbital flight. *American Journal of Roentgenology, 100,* 503.

Malluche, H.H. et al. (1983). Bone protein: a marker for osteoblast activity, In: B. Frame, & J. Potts (Eds.), *Proceedings of the International Congress on Bone and Mineral Metabolism,* Detroit, MI.

Mazess, R.B. (1983). Problems in measurement of trabecular bone, In: B. Frame & J. Potts (Eds.), *Clinical disorders of bone and mineral metabolism, Excerpta Medica* (p. 30).

Mundy, J.R. (1983). The management of osteoporosis, *Comprehensive Therapy, 9*(9), 27–32.

Murray, T. (1984). Osteoporosis, the importance of nutrition for healthy bones, *Oral Health, 74*(11), 59–62.

Navickis, R.J., Katzenellenbogen, B.S., & Nalbandov, A.V. (1979). Effects of gonadal hormones on calcium-binding protein in chick duodenum. *American Journal of Physiology, 23*(5), 408–417.

Navickis, R.J., Katzenellenbogen, B.S., & Nalbandov, A.V. (1979). Effects of the sex steroid hormones and vitamin D_3 on calcium-binding proteins in the chick shell gland. *Biology of Reproduction, 21*(5), 1153–1162.

Nordin, B.E.C. (1984). Introduction to second session. *Proceedings of the International Symposium on Osteoporosis* (p. 243), Copenhagen.

Nordin, B.E.C. (1984). Calcium requirement and the menopause (Editorial). *Medical Journal of Australia, 141*(3), 144–146.

Palummeri, E., Cervellin, G., Pedrazzoni, M., & Passeri, M. (1986). Clinical trial of an ADFR regimen with calcitriol and calcitonin: biochemical observations. (Abstract). VI Workshop on Vitamin D, Merano.

Recker, R.R. (1983). Osteoporosis, *Boletin Asociacion Medica de Puerto Rico, 75*(9), 418–420.

Russel, R.G.G. et al. (1983). How useful is osteocalcin as an index of bone metabolism in man. In: B. Frame, J. Potts (Eds.), *Proceedings of the International Congress on Bone and Mineral Metabolism.* Detroit, MI.

Samuels, L.T. (1978). Effect of aging on the steroid metabolism, as reflected in plasma levels. In: E. Engl, G. Pincus (Eds.), *Hormone and the aging process* (p. 21). New York: Academic Press.

Sawin, C.F. et al. (1975). Instruments of personal exercise during long duration space flight. *Aviation Space and Environmental Medicine, 46,* 349.

Sommerville, I.F., Kitchin, Y., & Mansfield, M.D. (1979), Endocrine changes at the menopause. In: R.J. Beard (Ed.), *The Menopause,* (pp. 41). Lancaster, PA :MTP Press.

Sorensen, O.H., Lumholtz, B., Lund, B., Hjelmstrand, I.L., Mosekilde, L., Melsen, F., Bishop, J.E., & Norman, A.W. (1982). Acute effects of parathyroid hormone on vitamin D metabolism in patients with the bone loss of aging. *Journal of Clinical Endocrinology and Metabolism, 54*(6), 1258:1261.

Spencer, H., Kramer, L., Lesniak, M., De Bartolo, M., Norris, C., & Osis, D. (1984). Calcium requirements in humans. Report of original data and a review. *Clinical Orthopedics, 184,* 270–280.

Spencer, H., Kramer, L., Osis, D., & Norris, C. (1976). Effect of conventional and newer forms of treatment on calcium absorption in osteoporosis. *Israel Journal of Medical Science, 12*(7), 638–651.

Stevenson, J.C. (1982). Regulation of calcitonin and parathyroid hormone secretion by oestrogens. *Maturitas, 4*(1), 1-7.

Stevenson, J.C. (1984). Differenti effetti dell'eta e della anmenopausa sulla secrezione di calcitonina. In: A. Pecile (Ed.), *Abstract Congresso Internazionale Calcitonin '84* (p. 17). Milano.

CHAPTER 19

Surgery in the Aged: Special Considerations

Jeffrey S. Freed
Mark A. Reiner

Between July 1, 1979 and June 30, 1982 the co-authors performed 212 major general surgical procedures in patients over 65 years of age. Excluding patients with diffused carcinomatosis, the elective mortality rate was 0% and the emergency mortality rate 12%. These favorable results have led to certain conclusions. The geriatrician and the surgeon form a team to evaluate the effect of the patients' existing medical illnesses and the new surgical problem on the continuing health and independent function of the geriatric patient. Preoperatively, maximum correction of all preexisting medical problems is essential. The surgical procedure should be the one that accomplishes the goal of returning the patient to a healthy baseline state with the least physiologic disturbance. Postoperative attention to pulmonary toilet, and fluid and electrolyte balance is extremely important. Delay in definitive surgical treatment in emergencies is likely to lead to a poor result. Recognition of the lack of classic signs and symptoms and the frequency of change in mental status will focus the physician's attention on a potential intraabdominal problem. The geriatric surgical patient is unique requiring very specific perioperative care.

The diagnosis of surgically treatable intra-abdominal disease is often subtle in the geriatric age group with a dirth of clinical and laboratory findings. Delay in surgical intervention is a major factor resulting in the increased morbidity and mortality in this patient population. A knowledge of the disease entities affecting geriatric patients, coupled with a high index of suspicion should lead to early resuscitation, hemo-

TABLE 19-1. Surgical Procedures in the Geriatric Population (Reiner/
Freed Series)

	NUMBER	%
Total major general surgical procedures performed (65 years and older for the 3 year period 7/79-6/82)	212	100%
Total elective cases	120	57%
Total emergency cases	92	43%

dynamic stabilization, and definitive surgery. This, in turn, should result in decreased surgical complications and increased survival. We present such a series of 205 surgical patients over the age of 65 with special emphasis on preoperative evaluation, types of surgery, and age-related modifications of preoperative, intraoperative, and postoperative care.

METHODS AND MATERIALS

Between July 1, 1979 and June 30, 1982, 205 patients in the 65 and over age group underwent 212 major general surgical procedures performed by both authors in 95% of cases. All preoperative, intraoperative and postoperative care was delivered by at least one of the co-authors (Table 19-1).

The patients were all treated in a community hospital and more than 85% had been living either at home or in a senior citizen facility. The mean age of the entire group was 79 years. The age distribution of the different types of pathology is shown in Table 19-2, and the types of surgical procedures in Table 19-3. To be noted is the relatively high ratio of colonic/biliary surgical problems explained by the small number of elective biliary cases (usually the most common type of procedure in the geriatric age group).

Emergency surgery was defined as surgical intervention once a patient is hemodynamically stabilized, if possible, after necessary diagnostic tests, always *within 24 hours* of surgical evaluation.

RESULTS

Results are the most important criteria one uses when reviewing a clinical presentation; however, results are extremely confusing when

TABLE 19-2. Age Distribution and Pathology (212 Cases)

	65-69	70-79	80-89	90-104
Colon	12	22	23	6
Gastric	2	8	6	4
Biliary	11	13	9	3
Exp. lap	4	6	3	2
Appendectomy	1	3	1	0
Small bowel resection	2	3	0	1
Drainage abdominal abscess	0	1	3	0
Inguinal/femoral hernia	13	11	7	4
Incisional hernia	3	2	0	2
Hiatus hernia/esophagus	0	1	1	0
Double bypass	3	2	4	1
Misc. major abdominal	2	3	2	2
Totals	53	75	59	25

Mean age of series—79 years

perusing the geriatric surgical literature. To eliminate as much confusion as possible we have chosen to use the criteria established by Linn, Linn, & Wallen (1982). Mortality is described for each age bracket and similarly for emergency and elective operations. Where different statistical methods would yield different results, this is noted. Finally, and most importantly, mortality statistics include all patients dying from their surgical disease not just those who expire within 30 days of their surgical procedure. This has been done in order to allow more definite assessment of the risk of surgery in the aged.

Surgical mortality was specifically defined as a failure to discharge the patient to a nursing facility, rehabilitation unit, or home. The case mortality was 8.5% (Table 19-4). We have chosen a case mortality rate because no patient required a second operation on the same admission; second procedures in the same patient included relief of intestinal obstruction and colostomy closures on a later admission.

The elective mortality rate was 4% and the emergency mortality rate 14%. If patients with diffuse carcinomatosis are excluded, the elective rate is 0% and emergency rate 12% (Table 19-5).

TABLE 19-3. Types of Surgical Procedures

PROCEDURES	TOTAL	ELECTIVE	EMERGENCY
Colonic (All cases):	63	41	22
Colostomy	12	2	10
Resection	51	39	12
Gastric (All cases):	20	13	7
Resection or bypass for tumor	7	6	1
Plication	3	0	3
Definitive ulcer procedure	4	1	3
Gastrostomy	6	6	0
Biliary Tract (All cases):	36	10	26
Cholecystectomy	19	4	15
CBDE	10	4	6
Biliary bypass	7	2	5
Exploratory laparotomy/lysis of adhesions	15	9	6
Appendectomy	5	1	4
Small bowel resection/bypass	6	1	5
Drainage of abdominal abscess	4	0	4
Inguinal/femoral hernia	35	25	10
Incisional hernia	7	4	3
Hiatus hernia/esophagus	2	2	0
Double bypass	10	9	1
Misc major ABD	9	5	4
Total	212	120	92

DISCUSSION

Almost half a century ago, Barney Brooks (1937) noted, "without doubt (there is) a technic for handling sick old people which improves the chance of recovery." Even at that time it was already appreciated that geriatric patients required unique perioperative treatment. Today, our better understanding of the pathophysiology of aging is contributing to improved surgical results.

At extremes of life, clinical presentations of disease can be remark-

TABLE 19-4. Surgical Mortality Statistics[a]

	NUMBER	%
Total mortalities in this series	18/212	8.5%
Elective mortalities	5/120	4%
Emergency mortalities	13/92	14%

[a]Surgical mortality being defined as a failure of the patient to be discharged to a nursing facility, home, or transferred to a rehabilitation unit.

ably different than described in standard texts, rendering diagnosis and treatment more difficult. In the aged, multiple preexisting chronic medical conditions are not uncommon. This requires reorientation of diagnostic evaluation to uncover an often obscure intra-abdominal surgical problem. The more acutely ill the elderly patient, the more urgent and usually difficult the diagnosis becomes. Associated with aging itself is an unrelenting decline in respiratory reserve, renal function, and homeostatic mechanisms (e.g., temperature regulation, blood pressure control, and serum osmolatity) (Hodgkinson, 1980).

The enemy of the geriatric surgical patient is the chronic deterioration present with advancing age. Theories regarding the nature of the process are numerous. Orgell (1980) theorized that aging results from an accumulation of intracellular genetic errors or deleterious free radicals. A fixed environmentally determined number of cell duplications prior to death is the theory advocated by Hayflick (1965). Walford (1970) has suggested that aging is a generalized, mild, prolonged type of autoimmunity. None of these theories have been proven, but all attempt to explain the negative effect of age on the cell and its resultant

TABLE 19-5. Adjusted Surgical Mortality Statistics[a]

	NUMBER	%
Total adjusted mortality statistics	11/205	5%
Adjusted elective mortalities	0/115	0
Adjusted emergency mortalities	11/90	12%

[a]Obtained by the elimination of ALL patients found to have diffuse carcinomatosis on exploration, and who were not aggressively treated in the postoperative period.

deleterious effect on the aging organism (man), especially in a stress situation like intra-abdominal surgery.

At present there are almost 25 million Americans over the age of 65. It has been projected that by 2030 there will be 55 million in this category. The fastest growing segment is the group 75 to 84 years old. This group will increase 50% by the year 2000. When considering surgical problems in the aged, one must take social as well as medical factors into account. Rapidly returning these patients to their environment must be considered the major goal of any surgical intervention measured against the risks of any procedure proposed.

According to Hruza (1972), renal blood flow, vital capacity of the lungs, and the ability to return blood pH to normal after acidification all are severely impaired in the geriatric age group. Freed, Kaynan, & Szuchmacher, 1978, described an inability to maintain blood pressure because of impaired peripheral sympathetic tone in this population of patients. Therefore, whether it is an elective or emergent situation, specific attention must be paid to these systems (renal, pulmonary, homeostatic). Also, the main link between these systems must always be considered—the heart.

In patients with potential or actual dysfunction (i.e., heart failure, previous myocardial infarct, essential hypertension, abnormal cardiogram) preoperative insertion of a flow-directed balloon catheter as described by Swan, Ganz, Forrester, Marcer, & Diamond et al. (1970) is indicated. Not only can right and left ventricular pressures be determined but cardiac output (CO) can be measured. The CO can be maximized by judicious fluid loading. Maximization of intravascular volume also accomplishes increasing the renal blood flow and peripheral vascular bed filling. If it is found that even minimal fluid loading or increase in cardiac rate causes a fall in CO, the patient is considered a poor candidate for elective surgery, and the intended elective procedure is abandoned if the cardiac status cannot be improved.

Pulmonary function tests identify any potential ventilation or perfusion deficit, allowing preoperative improvement by good respiratory therapy or drugs (i.e., bronchodilators). It must be emphasized that these invasive and noninvasive procedures are only used when clinically indicated, being well aware that they all have risks and complications especially injurious to the geriatric patient if used indiscriminantly (Horst, Oberd, Vij, & Bivens, 1984).

Intraoperatively, certain dicta are followed. With two attending surgeons at most operations, the procedures were rapidly performed. Most laparotomies for general surgical problems were completed in under 2 hours. Although Djokovic and Hedly-Whyte (1979) had no increased mortality with increased time of surgery, we agree with Steen, Tinker, & Tanhaus (1978) that cardiac stress is definitely increased as operative time is extended. Choice of surgical procedure always should be considered carefully in the compromised geriatric surgical patient. Reiss, Deutsch, and Eleashiv (1983) have advocated definitive procedures as sometimes safer and more cost effective than lesser procedures. We, however, agree with Williams (1975) that relatively minimal procedures, such as limited colon resection for carcinoma of the colon or suture ligation of a bleeding duodenal ulcer with vagotomy and pyloroplasty rather than gastrectomy, are preferred. According to Howells (1976), the aged form a special population and judgment on an individual basis may be more satisfactory than considering the aged as a group when deciding on a surgical procedure.

Other technical points include: (a) the use of transverse incisions (Bluestone, Freed, & Szuchmacher, 1978), (b) the use of gastrostomies in preference to nasogastric tubes when gastric decompression is absolutely necessary, (c) infected or grossly contaminated wounds left to heal by delayed prior closure, and (d) judicious use of protective enterstomies when indicated. These techniques are aimed at decreasing pulmonary complications (a and b) and preventing septic complications (c and d), the two most preventable reasons for morbidity in surgery.

Geriatric patients with emergency surgical conditions pose special problems. We have defined our subset of emergency surgery as follows: surgical intervention once a patient is hemodynamically stabilized, if possible, and after necessary diagnostic tests are formed, *always* within 24 hours of surgical evaluation. All concepts mentioned for elective surgical procedures hold for emergent problems. However, because of the decreased reserve of these patients, rapid diagnosis and treatment are necessary to avoid progression of disease to irreversible organ failure. Adding to this problem is the lack of classical signs and symptoms of acute emergencies in this group. We have retrospectively analyzed nine signs and symptoms found in intra-abdominal emergencies according to standard surgical texts (Table 19-6). As the figures indicate in the infected intra-abdominal emergencies, tachycardia, abdominal pain, and tenderness were usually present. However, typical findings such as leukocytosis with left shift, peritoneal signs, and temperature greater than 37.8 °C were absent in a large proportion of cases. One sign found to correlate extremely well with significant intra-abdominal pathology was a change in mental status (Freed & Reiner, 1985). A change in mental status was defined as any noticeable decompensation of orientation as observed by a physician, family member, or acquaintance with immediate knowledge of the patient's baseline mental status. Although no specific sign or symptom was diagnostic of an intra-abdominal emergency, a combination of abdominal pain and tenderness associated with a change in mental status was uniformly indicative of intra-abdominal pathology (Table 19-7).

The most common indication for surgery in the elderly is calculous

TABLE 19-6. Standard Clinical Symptoms and Signs

- Tenderness
- Pain
- Tachycardia
- Leukocytosis—being defined as >10,000 cells per cmm
- ≥10% bands (shift to the left)
- Fever of >37.8°C
- Peritoneal signs
- Ileus or obstruction on abdominal x-rays
- Change in mental status—all patients in series evaluated by family, referring physician or/and one of the co-authors. There had to be an obvious mental status change in order to be placed in this category.

disease of the gallbladder (Morrow, Thompson, & Wilson 1978). It has been documented that in the geriatric age group cholelithiasis exists in approximately 20% of patients (Ratner & Rosenberg, 1975). Almost all patients who are asymptomatic will never require surgical therapy (McSherry, Ferstenberg, Calhoun, Cahman & Virshup,

TABLE 19-7. Clinical Symptoms and Signs of all Intraabdominal Infected Cases (67)

Tenderness	94%
Pain	90%
Tachycardia	80%
≥10% bands	78%
Ileus/obstructed pattern on abdominal x-rays	68%
Leukocytes (≥10,000)	58%
Peritoneal signs	55%
Fever >37.8°C	42%
Change in mental status	32%

1985). However, in the symptomatic group (biliary colic, acute chole-cystitis, choledocholithiasis), a significant percentage will come to emergency surgery. Although the elective mortality for cholecystec-tomy in this age group is 6.7% (Arnold, 1970), emergency interven-tion carries a mortality as high as 27% (Gagic & Frey, 1975). Of these, as many as 23% will have associated choledocholithiasis (Ibach, Hume, & Erb, 1968). In biliary tract disease a decision for surgical versus nonsurgical therapy rests with the geriatric team; evaluation of the nature of the patient's symptoms and associated medical problems will determine whether the elective intervention is indicated in view of the fact that an emergency surgical procedure will almost quadruple the mortality. When deciding the appropriate therapy for any geriatric patient with a potential surgical condition, the factors mentioned with regard to biliary tract disease must be kept in mind and *aggressive analysis* completed prior to a final decision.

Age itself is no longer a consideration in surgery. On occasion, because of debility or preexisting medical conditions, palliation rather than cure is the only option. Advancing age should definitely not be a factor when aggressive treatment of benign diseases that threaten life is necessary. If extension of life is equivalent to prolongation of suffering it is to be condemned. However, preservation of life including relief of pain and maintenance of health and vitality is completely indicated.

REFERENCES

Arnold, D.J. (1970). 28, 621 cholecystectomies in Ohio: Results of a survey in Ohio hospitals by the gallbladder survey committee, Ohio Chapter, American College of Surgeons. *American Journal of Surgery, 119,* 714-719.

Bluestone, J., Freed, J.S., & Szuchmacher, P.H. (1978). The interneural incision for biliary tract operations. *Surgery, Gynecology, and Obstetrics, 147,* 21-24.

Brooks, B. (1937). Surgery in patients of advanced age. *Annals of Surgery, 105,* 481-495.

Djokovic, J.L., & Hedley-Whyte, J. (1979). Prediction of outcome of surgery and anesthesia in patients over 80. *JAMA, 242,* 2301-2306.

Freed, J.S., Kaynan, A., & Szuchmacher, P.H. (1978). Dopamine and the aged. *Journal of the American Geriatric Society, 26,* 524-525.

Freed, J.S., & Reiner, M.A. (1984). Intra-abdominal infections in the elderly. *Journal of the American Geriatric Society, 32,* 408.

Gagic, N., & Frey, C.F. (1975). The results of cholecystostomy for the treatment of acute cholecystitis. *Surgery, Gynecology and Obstetrics, 140,* 255-257.

Hayflick, L. (1965). The limited in vitro lifetime of human diploid cell straw. *Experimental Cell Research, 37,* 614-639.

Hodgkinson, H.M. (1980). *Common symptoms of disease in the elderly, (2nd ed.).* London: Blackwell Scientific Publication.

Horst, H.M., Oberd, F.N., Vij, D., & Bivens, B.A. (1984). The risks of pulmonary arterial catheterization. *Annals of Surgery, 159,* 229-232.

Howells, J.G. (Ed.). (1976). *Modern perspectives in the psychiatric aspects of surgery.* New York: Brunner Mazel.

Hruza, F. (1972). Aging of cells and molecules. In G. Holle (Ed.). *Handbuch der allgemeinen pathologie, altern* (Vol 6, part IV). New York: Springer-Verlag.

Ibach, J.R. Jr., Hume, H.A., & Erb, W.H. (1968). Cholecystectomy in the aged. *Surgery, Gynecology and Obstetrics, 126,* 523–528.

Linn, B.S., Linn, M.W., & Wallen, N. (1982). Evaluation of results of surgical procedures in the elderly. *Annals of Surgery, 195,* 90–97.

McSherry, C.K., Ferstenberg, H., Calhoun, W.F., Cahman, E., & Virshup, M. (1985). The natural history of diagnosed gallstone disease in symptomatic and asymptomatic patients. *Annals of Surgery, 202,* 59–63.

Morrow, J.D., Thompson, J., & Wilson, S.E. (1978). Acute cholecystitis in the elderly. *Archives of Surgery, 113,* 1149–1152.

Orgell, L. (1980). Theories of aging. In G. Lesnoff-Caravaglia (Ed.) *Health care of the elderly.* New York: Human Sciences Press.

Ratner, J.T., & Rosenberg, G.M. (1975). Management of gallstones in the aged. *Journal of the American Geriatric Society, 11,* 422–425.

Reiss, R., Deutsch, A.A., & Eleashiv, A. (1983). Decision-making in abdominal surgery in the geriatric patient. *World Journal of Surgery, 7,* 522–526.

Steen, P.A., Tinker J.H., & Tanhaus, M. (1978). Myocardial reinfarction after anesthesia and surgery. *JAMA, 239,* 2566–2570.

Swan, H.J.C., Ganz, W., Forrester, J., Marcers, H., Diamond, G., & Chonette, D. (1970). Catheterization of the heart in man with use of a flow-directed balloon-tipped catheter. *New England Journal of Medicine, 283,* 447–456.

Walford, R.L. (1970). *Immunologic theory of aging.* Baltimore: Williams and Wilkins.

Williams, R.G. (1975). Management of gastrointestinal problems in the aged. In L. Greenfield (Ed.). *Surgery of the aged.* Philadelphia: Saunders.

PART II
Biology and Biomedicine
B. New Medical Technologies in Diagnosis and Treatment

CHAPTER 20

Introduction to New Medical Technologies

Paul Berthaux

One person cannot, at this point, discuss adequately all the important methods of noninvasive exploration used in the research on diagnosis and effective treatment among the aged. This is particularly true in geriatrics because it is among the elderly that methods of diagnosis such as the puncturing of arteries and catheterization bring about an indisputable risk. Further, complex problems in diagnosis are frequent in geriatrics, such as in the detection of mental deterioration, the valuation of cardiovascular pathology, and more generally, consideration of pathology for which the exploratory methods are particularly important for clinicians.

We can sum up at least partially the techniques that have contributed significantly to improvement of diagnosis in the last decade; techniques such as computed tomography (CT) or echography have played an undisputable role in the evaluation of intracerebral lesions. On the other hand, progress continues in other areas, thanks, for example, to the injection of radiocontrast substances, notably in clinical research studies. In the same area of technology, one must mention the use of pacemakers involved in solving the problems of heart rhythm and the many uses of echotomography, which are presently well established. It is most important here that we compare alternative techniques that have been suggested for the study of the same organs and which have as their objective the diagnosis of lesions.

In the examination of the central nervous system, for example, we have at our disposal several techniques that are continuously improving and which allow for the valuation of cerebral blood flow of the brain's morphology and often the brain's metabolic activities. The brain is the topic of great importance in discussions between technological specialists of medical imaging and those who are essentially geriatric physicians having a specific interest in the biology of aging, diagnostic problems of cerebral deficiencies, and the not very well understood area of "dementia" of the aged.

Several general comments about the uses of medical technology in geriatrics should be emphasized:

1. In France and in other developed countries, the aged often do not have access to new medical technology. I am not speaking only of the newest research technologies but also of technologies in use for several years and that, in principle, we all know how to use such as CT. This, in part, is explained by economic problems that face the majority of countries and the consequent limited application of costly medical technology. The average cost of using a particular technique does not always have a tendency to decrease; but, on the contrary, cost often increases progressively following the improvement of techniques. These improvements, which are the main elements of medical progress which one cannot deny, drive up cost. The result is often reduced accessibility of technology to a majority of the aged.

Nonetheless, we argue that the probability of timely diagnosis has been increased by recent technological progress in medicine, and in many cases this progress has facilitated diagnosis (for example, of dementia). Correct diagnosis has helped avoid unnecessary admission to a specialized institution, which has the potential of avoiding substantial cost to families and to society. Inappropriate admission is often the result of lack of timely diagnosis of a curable illness.

The relevance of the economics of health is best understood when we recognize that proper diagnosis can reduce the risk of dementia, of bedridden individuals, and of institutionalization.

2. We benefit from bringing together internationally renowned specialists who have been involved in developing advanced diagnostic techniques and also clinical specialists of geriatric medicine who search in common for useful applications of diagnostic techniques in clinical practice.

3. Now, as always, when these techniques are developed, one must distinguish between techniques that should be considered primarily as research procedures aimed at better understanding of the aging brain and those that can be considered primarily as tools for diagnosis and treatment of the aged. This distinction is clearly arbitrary because we understand that the new techniques must at least initially be the sub-

ject of precise experimental study that measures their worth for diagnosis or treatment.

4. It is clearly impossible to consider all new techniques. We have had to make choices. In every way, the notion of *new* techniques is strictly relative. For example, the use of a computer to complement a diagnostic procedure gives a new interest to established, widely used techniques. Electroencephalography (EEG) is a case in point. Progressive improvment in known techniques is also illustrated by nuclear magnetic resonance (NMR).

CHAPTER 21

Newer Noninvasive Cardiac Investigation in the Elderly

Paul V. Knight

Advances in cardiovascular pharmacology and cardiac surgery (Cory-Pearce, 1984), have improved the therapeutic possibilities for the elderly patient with cardiac disease. Newer noninvasive procedures that assist in accurate diagnosis of primary cardiac pathologies are described. These procedures are increasingly important to guide and monitor these powerful new treatments. Invasive cardiac investigation is considered unethical by many and is certainly impractical for routine serial measurements. Noninvasive procedures for investigating the heart and heart functioning are described here. Attention will focus on procedures useful in evaluating valvular heart disease, the ventricular wall, and cardiac rhythm.

VALVULAR HEART DISEASE

Echocardiography

Echocardiography gives both M-mode and 2D (real time) tracings, recorded on videotape or light-sensitive paper. Although the machinery was previously bulky and traveled poorly, it is now very compact and maneuverable. The main use in valvular disease is showing the presence and severity of stenosis of the aortic and mitral valves. St. John Sutton, St. John Sutton, Oldershaw, Sachetti, & Paneth et al. (1979) have shown that preoperative screening with echocardiography alone is just as efficient, in diagnostic terms and patient survival, as more conventional cardiac catheterization in a mainly elderly population. Mitral regurgitation when secondary to structural lesions such as mitral valve prolapse (MVP) or flail mitral valve displays a distinctive echocardiographic appearance. It is probable that idopathic MVP is an overdiagnosed condition in the elderly (Knight & Ballantyne, 1984). Solitary mitral regurgitation resultant from calcification of the valve ring or fibrosis residual from rheumatic heart disease may only really be inferred from an increased left atrial diameter and hyperkinetic left ventricular wall (Mintz, Katler, Segal, & Parry, 1979). Aortic regurgitation may result in gross diastolic fluttering of the mitral valve leaflets, which is often difficult to discern (D'Cruz, Cohen, Prabhu, Ayabe, & Glick, 1976), thus making the diagnosis by echocardiography more uncertain than that of mitral regurgitation.

In developed countries infective endocarditis is a disease of the elderly (Schnurr, Ball, Geddes, Gray, & McGhie, 1977), which may often be missed on purely clinical examination. Echocardiography facilitates the visualization of vegetations that are > 3 mm.

Left atrial, ventricular, and aortic root diameters tend to be increased in the elderly (Manyari, Patterson, Johnson, Melendez, Boughner, et al., 1982). Our own experience (Knight, Martin, & Ballantyne, unpublished data) suggests that good quality echocardiographs can be produced in approximately 90% of the elderly. The aortic and mitral valve structures can usually be visualized by echocardiography in the differentiation of significant from insignificant systolic murmurs in the elderly with other findings of cardiac disease. Reproducibility of the technique is good, and in our experience there is little dispute over structural lesions. However, emphysematous lungs and calcified costal cartilages may obscure the small echocardiographic window.

Doppler Echocardiography

This technique also employs ultrasound, utilizing the frequency shift of a beam of ultrasound placed parallel to blood flow when it is scattered back to the receiver. Using the formula $\Delta F = V \cos \theta$ where $\cos \theta$ is close to 1; the change in sound frequency is proportional to the blood flow. The technique in its continuous wave form, has been used extensively in the diagnosis of peripheral vascular disease. More recently pulsed-wave doppler has been employed in conjunction with M-mode echocardiography; the latter gives important anatomical and spatial resolution to study the heart. In this form it can give guidance on the global function of the heart (Pearlman, 1982), but perhaps more usefully on the presence or absence of valvular regurgitation and pressure gradients.

VENTRICULAR WALL MOTION, STRUCTURE AND FUNCTION

Echocardiography

Cavity dimensions within the heart can be most easily assessed by echocardiography. This circumvents the problems of chest x-ray interpretation of the cardiac silhouette (Cowan, 1965). Ejection fraction and cardiac output may be calculated from these dimensions with the help of various mathematical models. However, when only M-mode recordings are used this method is beset by the problems of regional wall abnormalities. Computer digitilization of 2-D recordings would help, and presently, this is being studied.

Ischemic, congestive, and hypertrophic cardiomyopathy may all be easily observed with echocardiography. The latter is more common in the elderly than generally realized (Whiting, Powell, Dinsmore, & Saunders, 1971). It is often confused with ischemic heart disease and therapy for the two conditions are contradictory. The rarities of tumor and pericardial effusion may also be visualized.

Nuclear and Impedance Cardiography

Thallium scanning is most useful for the diagnosis of the ischemic myocardium and may be used as a preoperative investigation for coronary artery bypass surgery. First-pass nuclear scans using ^{99m}Te and a gamma camera, allow spatial resolution of the chambers and are quick and easy to perform. Differentiation between atria and ventricles may give rise to some inter-observer error (Caird and Knight, unpublished data). Simultaneously, impedance cardiography, which measures the change in thoracic impedance with the heart cycle, may be performed using an isotope time marker; ejection fraction and cardiac output can be calculated for single beats. First-pasts scans and impedance cardiography are not suitable for the estimation of left ventricular function during exercise. Although equilibrium nuclear scans may be used in this fashion, Williams and Caird (1985) have shown that the correlation between impedance and first-pass scans is strong except in gross valvular regurgitation, chronic obstructive airways disease, atrial fibrillation, and right bundle-branch block. The first three all effect the measurement of the transthoracic impedance, whereas no satisfactory explanation is yet at hand for the discordance in patients with right bundle-branch block. Measurements of ejection fraction in the elderly have shown that this indication of left ventricular function only decreases with advancing age during exercise in the presence of an increased heart rate (particularly atrial fibillation), left ventricular hypertrophy and intrinsic myocardial disease (Strandell, 1982).

CARDIAC RHYTHM

There have been several studies of Holter or continuous ECG monitoring in the "normal" elderly (Glasser, Clark, & Applebaum, 1979; Clee, Smith, McNeill, & Wright, 1979; Camm, Evans, Ward, & Martin, 1980; Abdon, Johnsson, & Lessem, 1981; Fleg & Kennedy, 1982; Rai, 1982). The definition of normalcy and population size has been variable, making comparisons difficult. Surprisingly, they all show remarkably consistent results.

In the elderly the mean heart rate is 72 beats/min but greater in females than males. Significant bradycardia (i.e., < 30 beats/min), sinus pauses, or true heart block is very uncommon and therefore highly significant in a symptomatic patient. Ventricular ectopy is common (62%), as are complex ventricular arrhythmias (29%), but ventricular tachycardia is rare, occuring in only 2.9%. The incidence of atrial fibrillation, where recorded, was approximately 11%.

The presence of these arrhythmias was independent of discernible coronary artery disease or hypertension; tea and coffee consumption was irrelevant (Clee et al., 1979; Camm et al., 1980; Fleg & Kennedy, 1982). Fleg and Kennedy (1982) showed a slightly increased prevalence of arrhythmias in smokers. The prognostic significance of the arrhythmia is dependent on the presence of latent coronary artery or intrinsic myocardial disease.

Unfortunately, it has proven difficult in the elderly to definitely establish a direct correlation between symptoms such as dizziness, seizures, syncope, and falls and transient cardiac arrhythmias (Rai, 1982; De Bono, Warlow, & Hyman, 1982), often because of the frequent failure of the patient ⸱to complete logs and diaries or use event markers. Even when this is done meticulously an arrhythmia may not always produce symptoms, usually due to the complex interplay between various aspects of multiple pathology (e.g., carotid stenosis, patient position, and central nervous system atherosclerosis).

In practice, treatment of a predominant and persistent arrhythmia in a symptomatic patient will alleviate the majority of problems.

REFERENCES

Abdon, N.J., Johnsson, B.W., & Lessem, J. (1981). Predictive use of routine 24-hour electrocardiography in suspected Adams-Stokes syndrome. Comparison with cardiac rhythm during symptoms. *British Heart Journal, 47,* 533–558.

Camm, A.J., Evans, K.E., Ward, D.E., & Martin, A. (1980). The rhythm of the heart in acute elderly subjects. *American Heart Journal, 99,* 598–603.

Clee, M.D., Sith, N., McNeill, G.P., & Wright, G.S. (1979). Dysrhythmias in apparently healthy elderly subjects. *Age & Aging, 8,* 173–176.

Cory-Pearce, R. Surgical management. (1984). In A. Martin & A.J. Camm (Eds.). *Heart disease in the elderly.* New York: Wiley.

Cowan, N.R. (1965). The frontal cardiac silhouette in older people. *British Heart Journal, 27,* 231–235.

D'Cruz, I., Cohen, C., Prabhu, R., Ayabe, T., & Glick, G. (1977). Flutter of left ventricular structures in patients with aortic regurgitation, with special reference to patients with associated mitral stenosis. *American Heart Journal, 9,* 684.

De Bono, D.P., Warlow, C.P., & Hyman, N.M. (1982). Cardiac rhythm abnormalities in patients presenting with transient non-focal neurological symptoms: A diagnostic grey area? *British Medical Journal, 284,* 1437–1439.

Fleg, J.L., & Kennedy, H.L. (1982). Cardiac arrhythmias in a healthy elderly population. Detection by 24-hour ambulatory electro-cardiography. *Chest, 81,* 302–307.

Glasser, S.P., Clark, P.I., & Applebaum, H.J. (1979). Occurrence of frequent complex arrhythmias detected by ambulatory monitoring. Findings in an apparently healthy asymptomatic elderly population. *Chest, 75,* 565–568.

Knight, P.V., & Ballantyne, D. (1984). Idiopathic mitral valve prolapse in the elderly: A common event? *Journal of Clinical and Experimental Gerontology, 6,* 78–82.

Manyari, D., Patterson, C., Johnson, D., Melendez, L., Boughner, D., Kostuk, W., & Cape, R., (1982). An echocardiographic study on resting left ventricular function in healthy elderly subjects. *Journal of Clinical and Experimental Gerontology, 4,* 403–420.

Mintz, G.S., Kotler, M.N., Segal, B.L., & Parry, W. (1979). Two-dimensional echocardiographic evaluation of patients with mitral insufficiency. *American Journal of Cardiology, 4,* 670–678.

Pearlman, A.S. (1982). Evaluation of ventricular function using Doppler echocardiography. *American Journal of Cardiology, 49,* 1324–1330.

Rai, G.S. (1982). Cardiac arrhythmias in the elderly. *Age & Aging, 11,* 113–115.

St. John Sutton, M.G., St. John Sutton, M., Oldershaw, P.L. Sachetti, R., Paneth, M., Lenox, S.C., Gibson, R.V., & Gibson, D.G. (1981). Valve replacement without preoperative cardiac catheterization. *New England Journal of Medicine, 305,* 1233–1238.

Schnurr, L.P., Ball, A.P., Geddes, A.M., Gray, J., & McGhie, D. (1977). Bacterial endocarditis in England in the 1970's: A review of 70 patients. *Quarterly Journal of Medicine, 46,* 499.

Strandell, T. (1982). Cardiac output. In D. Platt (Ed.). *Geriatrics I.* New York: Springer-Verlag.

Whiting, R.B., Powell, W., Dinsmore, R.E., & Saunders, C.A. (1971). Idiopathic hypertrophic subaortic stenosis in the elderly. *New England Journal of Medicine, 285,* 196–200.

Williams. B.O., & Caird, F.I. (1985). Accuracy of the impedance cardiogram in the measurement of cardiac output in the elderly. *Age & Aging, 14,* 277–281.

CHAPTER 22

Quantified EEG for the Study of the Aging Brain

C. Sebban

A new device, allowing the computation of real-time fast Fourier transform, was developed in our laboratory in association with the Alvar Electronic, Inc. Its use in diagnosis of cerebral diseases was made by a cartographic representation of the power spectra computed simultaneously on 16 derivations. Gliomas and cerebrovascular diseases are easily diagnosed. Moreover, in Alzheimer's disease and senile dementia of the Alzheimer type (SDAT) characteristic pictures assist in the diagnosis and evaluation of the disease. In pharamacological research in young and old rats, we showed with this device net differences with age in the effects of drugs acting on noradrenergic and dopaminergic central receptors. Significant effects of Hydergine® and Duxil® were also observed.

A decrease of the dominant electroencephalogram (EEG) frequency and the increased occurence of Θ waves in the temporal areas are well-known observations in the human aging brain. However, use of the EEG for the study and quantitative evaluation of the aging brain was limited before spectral analysis of this signal could be easily performed. In the Charles Foix hospital at IVRY (France), in association with Alvar Electronic, Inc., we have developed an apparatus allowing a real-time Fourier transformation on 16 EEG signals. This low-cost apparatus could be used by a physician alone without the technical assistance of a computer engineer. Thus, at the end of the recording procedure, power spectra for the 16 leads, or their cartographic representation, could be immediately obtained. An example of the relation

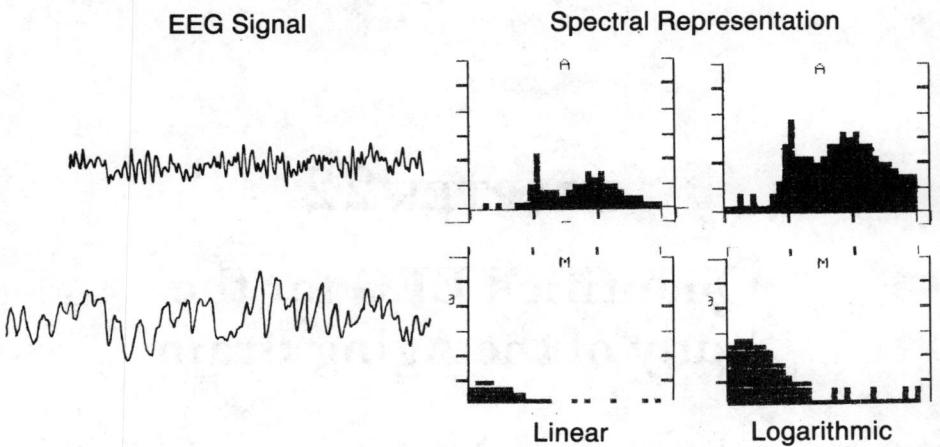

FIGURE 22-1. Correspondence between EEG records and their power spectra.

between EEG records and their power spectra is shown on Figure 22-1. The fast activities seen on the first record (top), explain the high power observed for the high frequencies on the spectrum. On the contrary, the second record (bottom) contains essentially slow waves and is associated with a clearly different power spectrum.

Using this analysis in 40 aged subjects with various degrees of impaired intellectual function, we have observed a good correlation between:

1. The Θ power and the degree of mental impairment that was assessed by the backward visual masking test (Figure 22-2).
2. The Δ power and the degree of mental impairment (Figure 22-3).
3. The attenuation of the α-blocking reaction with opening of the eyes and the degree of mental impairment (Figure 22-4).

Recently, a colored cartographic representation was developed in our laboratory in association with Alvar Electronic, S.A. in France and its subsidiary Alvar Inc. in Chicago (Illinois). From a practical point of view it is important to note that one cartograph is obtained in less than 4 seconds after the recording procedure is completed. For the aging brain two main results can be stressed: First, this technique allows us to diagnose pathological processes frequently observed in aged subjects. For example, glioma are generally associated with a decrease of total power above the lesion, while areas around the tumor show an increased power for all the EEG bands. Figure 22-5 shows the total power cartography for an enormous left hemispheric glioma. In

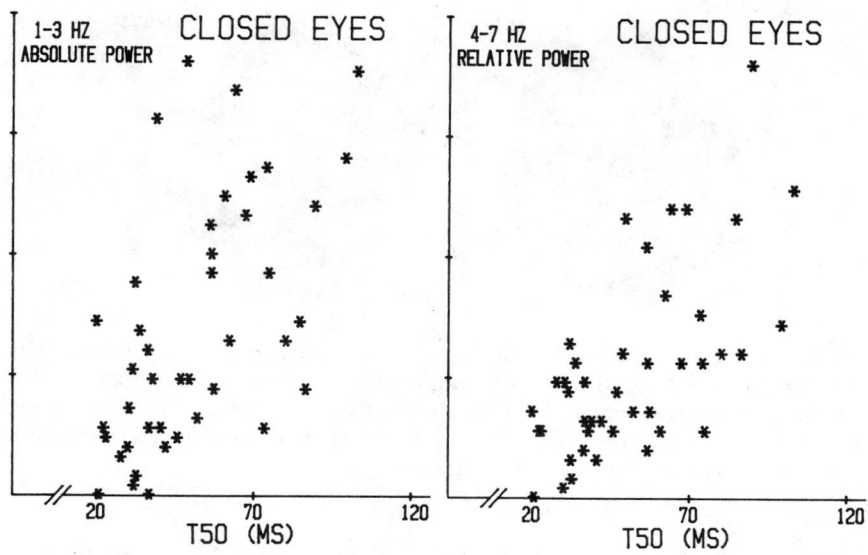

FIGURE 22-2. Correlation between the Θ power and the minimum inter-stimulus interval (ISIm) of the backward visual masking test in 40 aged subjects.

FIGURE 22-3. Correlation between the Δ power and the ISIm in 40 aged subjects.

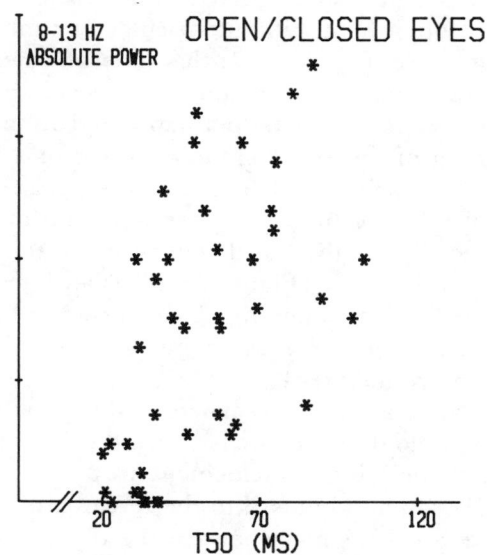

FIGURE 22-4. Correlation between the α blocking reaction with opening of the eyes and the ISIm in 40 aged subjects. As this reaction decreases, the power ratio of the eyes open/eyes closed situations increases.

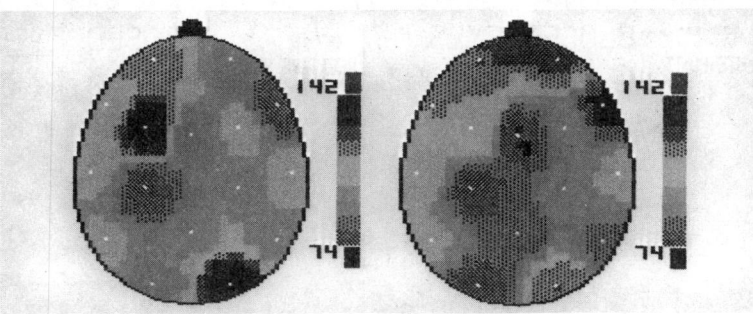

FIGURE 22-5. Total power cartography in a left hemispheric glioma. This glioma was parieto-occipital including the corpus callosum with compression of the third and lateral ventricals. A clear decrease of the total power was observed on the cortical projection of the tumor. This picture was enhanced in the eyes-open situation. *Left:* eyes closed; *right:* eyes open.

cortical ischemic disease there is always above the lesion a decrease in α and β power and an increased power for the Δ and Θ bands. Such an ischemic disease for the posterior territory of the middle cerebral artery is shown in Figure 22-6. Different pictures are observed for hemorrhagic disease and for ischemic lesions deep in the brain.

The second important result is that characteristic pictures are observed in mental impairment without vascular or tumoral pathology. These pictures are first (Figure 22-7) the anterior extension of the α power without attenuation with opening of the eyes. By comparison, Figure 22-8 shows the net occipital dominance and an important attenuation with opening of the eyes for the α power in a young healthy subject. Second and less frequently (Figure 22-9) an aberrant α topography is observed. This picture correlates well with gross ventricular enlargement especially in the third ventricle. A third picture frequently observed in dementia (Figure 22-10) is an important increase of the slow-wave power with opening of the eyes. Most frequently this increase is observed on posterior areas, but in some patients it clearly predominates in prefrontal areas.

All of these pictures are not associated in the same patient. Thus, EEG cartography could discriminate between the different pathophysiological processes underlying senile dementia.

Quantified EEG can also be used in the research of aging brain. In Paris (France) we are studying what are the differences in EEG responses to drugs between rats aged 9 and 22 months. The spectral action of a drug was described by dividing the power spectrum observed after drug administration by the power spectrum observed in the same rats after saline administration.

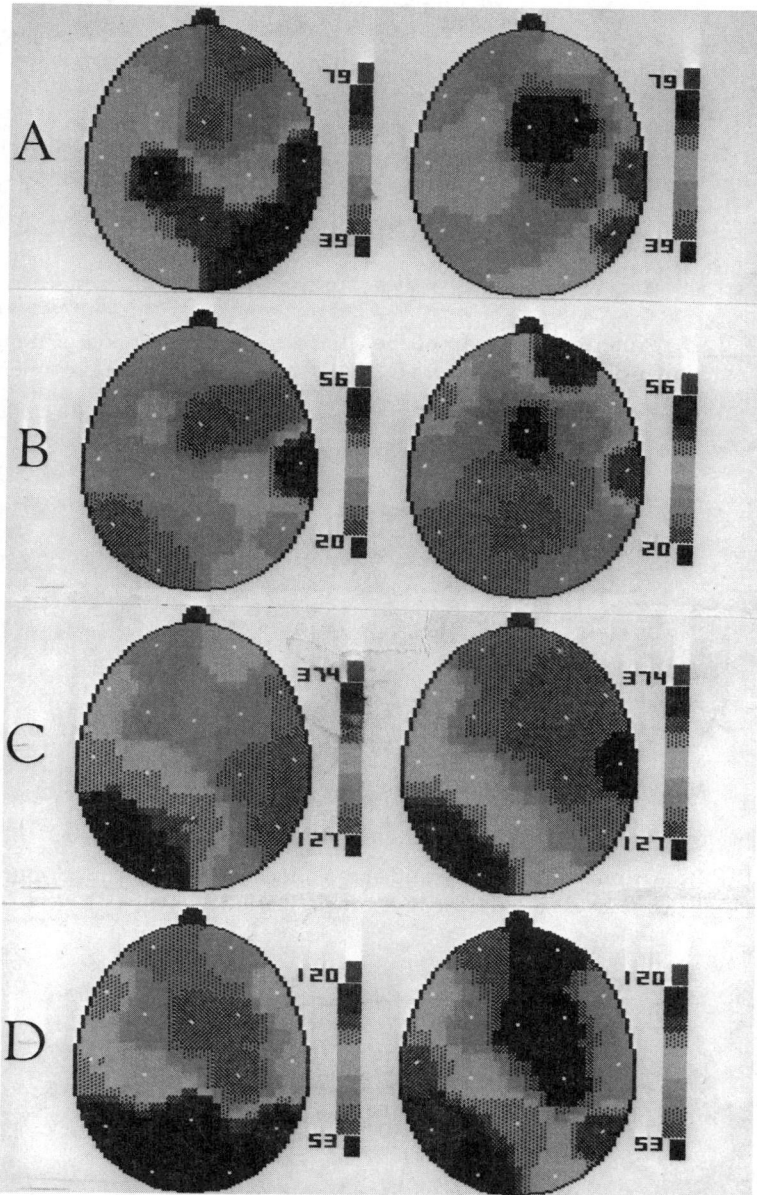

FIGURE 22-6. Cartographies in ischemic disease. Posterior territory of the left middle cerebral artery. From the top to the bottom, cartography of the α, β, Δ, and Θ bands. **A**: 8–13.5 Hz (α); **B**: 14–20 Hz (β); **C**: 0–3.5 Hz (Δ); **D**: 4–7.5 Hz (Θ).

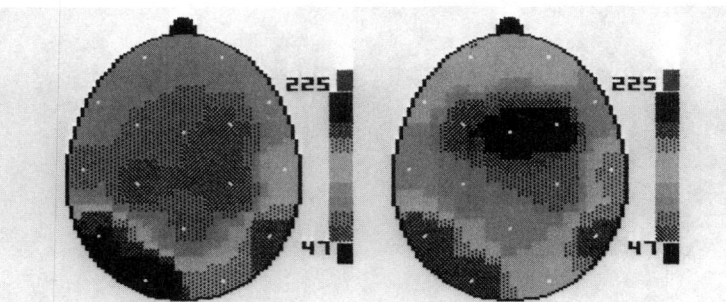

FIGURE 22-7. Anterior extension of the α power and attenuation of the β blocking reaction in an old patient with SDAT. *Left:* eyes closed; *right:* eyes open. 8–13.5 Hz (α).

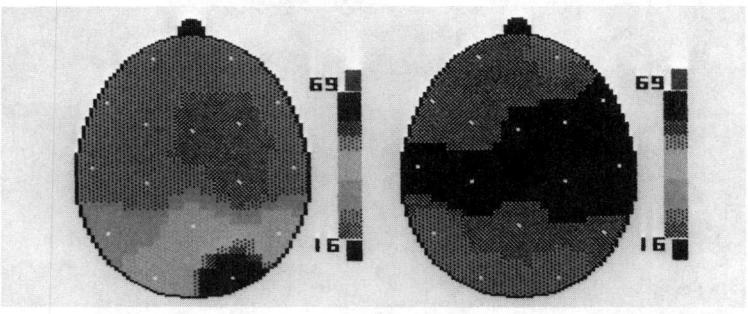

FIGURE 22-8. Alpha cartography and the α blocking reaction in a young healthy subject. *Left:* eyes closed; *right:* eyes open. 8–13.5 Hz (α).

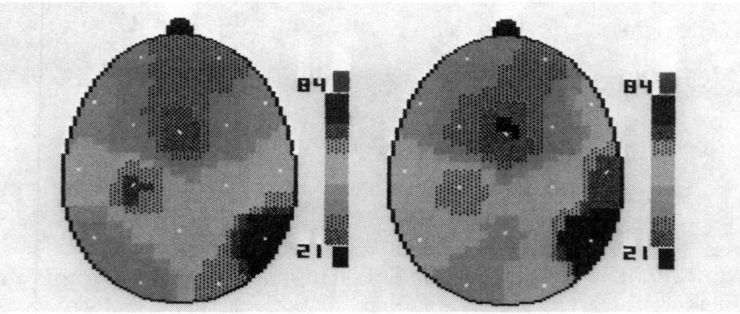

FIGURE 22-9. Aberrant α distribution in an old patient with SDAT. *Left:* eyes closed; *right:* eyes open. 8–13.5 Hz (α).

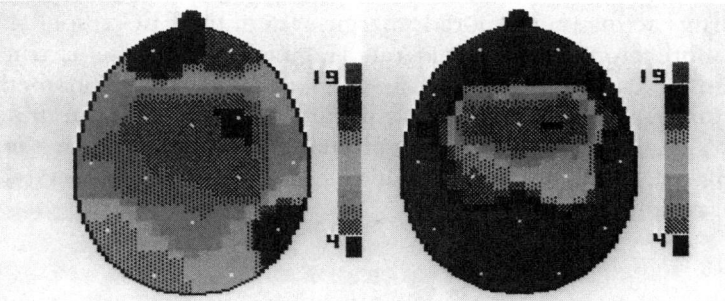

FIGURE 22-10. Delta cartography in Alzheimer's disease. *Left:* eyes closed; *right:* eyes open. 0–3 Hz (Δ).

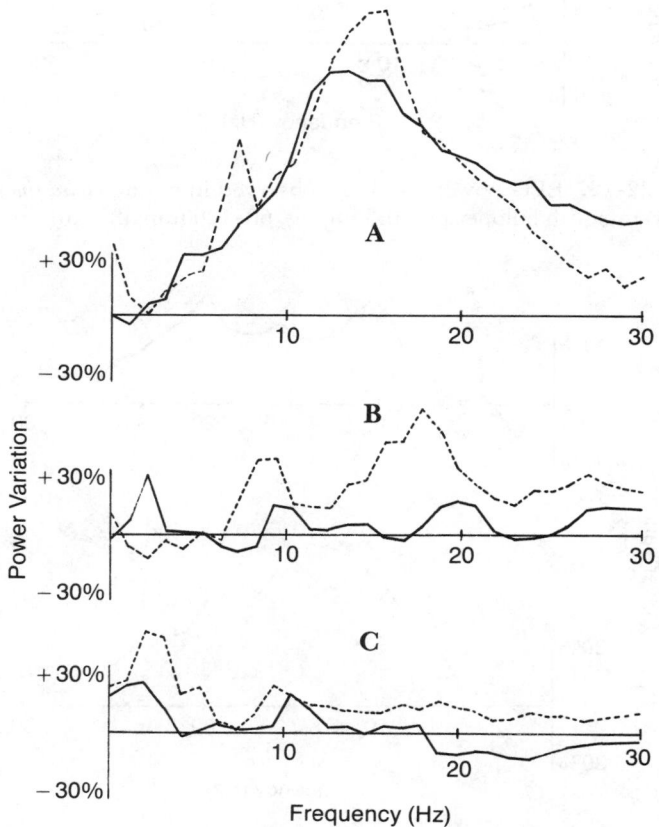

FIGURE 22-11. EEG power variations observed in young (*solid line*) and old (*dashed line*) rats with drugs acting on adrenergic receptors 60–120 min after injection. **A**: clonidine; **B**: raubasine; **C**: methoxamine.

For drugs acting on the noradrenergic system the EEG response was always more pronounced in old rats (Figure 22-11). This is true for clonidine an α_2 agonist, Raubasine (an α antagonist) and methoxamine (an α agonist). On the contrary, drugs acting on the dopaminergic system induced spectral changes less marked in the old rats. Figure 22-12 shows that this is true for haloperidol (a dopaminergic antagonist).

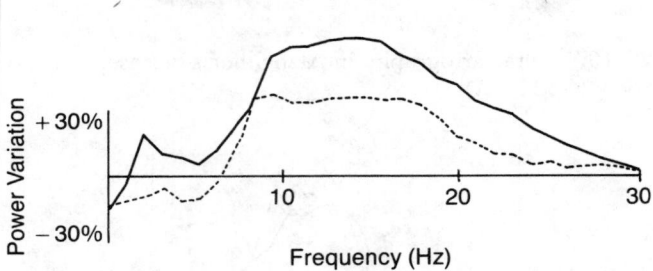

FIGURE 22-12. EEG power variatons observed in young (*solid line*) and old (*dashed line*) rats with haloperidol (0.5 mg/kg, 60–120 min after injection).

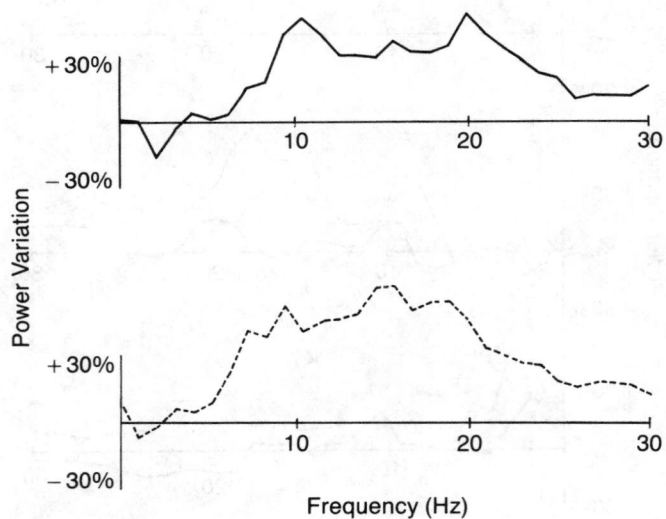

FIGURE 22-13. EEG power variations observed in young (*top*) and old (*bottom*) rats with Duxil® (10 mg/kg, 0–60 min after injection).

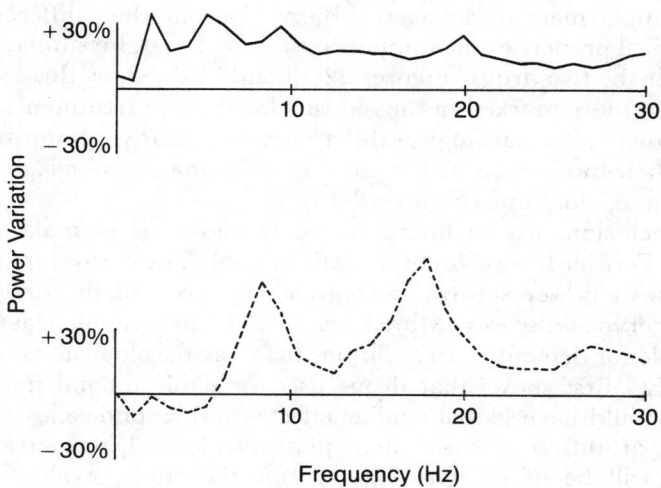

FIGURE 22-14. EEG power variations observed in young (*top*) and old (*bottom*) rats with Hydergine® (0.5 mg/kg, 0–60 min after injection).

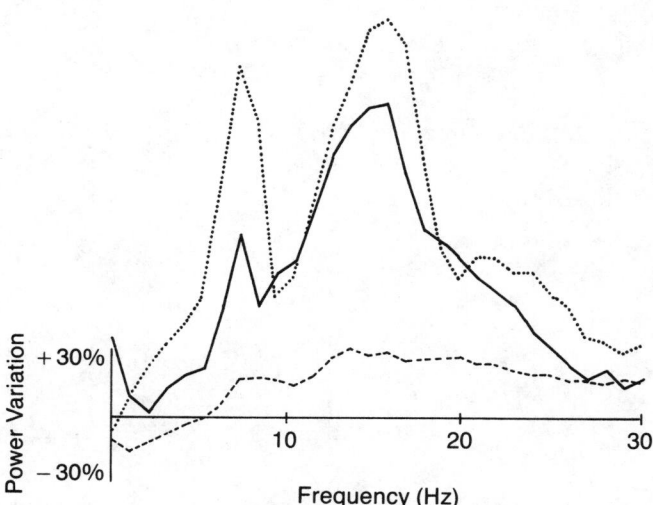

FIGURE 22-15. Alteration of the EEG power variations observed with clonidine (*solid line*) in old rats by simultaneous administration of Duxil® (*dotted line*) or Hydergine® (*dashed line*).

Duxil® and Hydergine® are two drugs used for the treatment of mental impairment in the aged subjects. Despite their different pharmacological properties, it is important to observe quite similar spectral effects for the two drugs. Figures 22-13 and 22-14 show this fact; EEG effects are more marked in the old rats for the two treatments. Nevertheless, their pharmacological differences are clearly demonstrated by testing their interaction with a more specific pharmacological reactive; for example, clonidine (Figure 22-15).

In conclusion, use of microprocessors allows us to make fast and low-cost Fourier transform of the EEG signal. The cartographic representation of power spectra is of great efficiency of the diagnosis of central nervous diseases. Moreover, a EEG cartographic classification is possible for dementia. In addition, the pharmacological use of quantified EEG first shows that drugs used in senile mental impairment therapy could have global similar effects, and second, allows demonstration of differences in their pharmacological properties. This method will be of primary interest for the study, evaluation, and therapeutic research on the aging brain.

CHAPTER 23

Regional Cerebral Flow and Metabolic Studies in Diagnosis and Treatment of Abnormal Brain Aging

W.J. Dekoninck
J.C. Depresseux

Positron emission tomography (PET) combined with the use of short-lived radiopharmaceuticals—notably water and molecular oxygen labeled with 15-oxygen and 2-fluoro-deoxy-glucose labeled with 18-fluor—makes possible the concomitant evaluation of local CBF, $CMRO_2$, and CMR. The availability of new positron emitting radiopharmaceuticals progressively allows the in vivo investigation of other parameters, particularly amino acid incorporation, ligand and neurotransmitter distribution, acid-base balance, and localization of water content. Although published results of CBF and metabolism in normal aging are somewhat controversial, it becomes gradually clear that aging per se is not accompanied by any significant alteration in CBF nor $CMRO_2$, while CMRgl decreases with age. Dementias are characterized by a reduction in CBF, $CMRO_2$, and CMRgl in correlation with the degree of mental deterioration and mainly located in frontal and temporal areas. Distinction between different types of dementing processes can be done in studying the regional PET patterns. These measurements contribute to reflect and quantify the cerebral metabolic and functional impairment in abnormal aging. They also allow us to map cerebral structures that are either biochemically altered or functionally involved in different types of dementia. Finally, such a cerebral approach gives the possibility to objectify flow and metabolic aspects of therapeutic strategies.

The last 20 years have brought a new insight in the evaluation of normal and abnormal brain aging, with the possibility of measurement of global and, more recently, local cerebral blood flow (CBF) and cerebral metabolic rates (CMR) in man. The combination of nitrous oxide with the measurement of arteriovenous differences allowed pioneering research on global CBF and metabolic data particularly oxygen consumption (CMRO$_2$)and glucose uptake (CMRgl). (Freyham, Woodford & Kety, 1951; Kety, 1956; Lassen, Feinberg, & Lane, 1960; Lassen, Munch, & Tottey, 1957). However, such an approach was soon limited by its invasiveness and its poor sensitivity to detect focal alterations.

The use of inert radioactive gases, such as [133] Xenon (Obrist, Chivian, Cronquist, & Ingvar, 1970), and the use of first-capillary-transit-trapped radioactive tracers, such as I[123]isopropyliodoamphetamine (Le Poncin-Lafitte, Askienazy, Raynaud, & Rapin, 1985), gave a better and safer opportunity to study regional CBF in normal brain aging and in different sorts of abnormal brain aging.

Besides, use of inert gases has also contributed to assessing the ability of psychomotor stimuli to activate primary and associative cerebral structures in healthy and diseased aging brain (Ingvar, Risberg & Schwartz, 1975). The possibility of measuring local cerebral flow and metabolism together was lacking in man until PET appeared a few years ago.

Positron emission tomography is a noninvasive scanning method that can provide a cross-sectional image of brain radioactivity. The process resembles x-ray CT, but unlike studies that can only show static qualities such as anatomic structure or cerebrovascular membrane permeability, PET can illustrate dynamic actions such as blood flow, metabolism, and other physiologic cerebral functions depending on the labeled compound chosen as a tracer (Ter-Pogossian, Raichle & Ficke, 1981). Two methods frequently employed in PET studies are the oxygen-15 inhalation technique (Lammertsma et al., 1981), and the F[18] deoxyglucose intravenous method (Phelps et al., 1979). The availability of new positron emitting radiopharmaceuticals has progressively allowed the in vivo investigation of other parameters, particularly amino acid incorporation, neurotransmitter distribution, acid-base balance, and water distribution.

CIRCULATORY AND METABOLIC PROFILES OF CEREBRAL AGING

Normal Aging

Although initially published observations on cerebral circulation and metabolism in normal aging could appear somewhat controversial, it becomes gradually clear that aging per se is characterized by no significant alteration (Sokoloff, 1966) or by mild decreases in CBF and

TABLE 23-1. Mean Results with Oxygen-15 in Temporal/Insular Region and the Centrum Semiovale

	rCBF ml/100g/'	rOEF	rCMRO$_2$ ml/100g/'
Gray matter			
Normal (14)	50 ± 8.7	0.53 ± 0.07	4.69 ± 0.64
Demented (22)	35.6 ± 9*	0.54 ± 0.08	3.31 ± 0.47*
% Change	− 30	+ 20	− 29
White matter			
Normal (14)	21.5 ± 2.6	0.49 ± 0.07	1.81 ± 0.21
Demented (22)	15.4 ± 4.9*	0.51 ± 0.1	1.33 ± 0.32*
% Change	− 28	+ 4	− 27

*p <0.001; rOEF = (A-V) O_2/AO_2
Source: From "Regional Cerebral Oxygen Supply and Utilization in Dementia" by R.S.J. Frackowiak et al., 1981, *Journal of Cerebral Blood Flow and Metabolism*, Vol. 1, Suppl. 1, 5453–5454.

CMRO$_2$ (Kety, 1956; Lassen et al, 1960). Glucose uptake was observed to decline with age in normal subjects (Sokoloff, 1966) in a range that was, however, not proven to be significant in comparison with young normal controls using a PET approach (Reivich, Alavi, Ferris, Christman, & Fowler et al., 1983).

Changes in local CMRgl have been observed (Metter, Riege, Kuhl, & Phelps, 1983) with differences in regional metabolic relationships between young and old normal subjects: evidence of a reduced functional cortical system in elderly assimilated to an attentional system. Decreased CBF with normal CMRO$_2$, as observed in asymptomatic elderly people, has been attributed to clinically subliminal cerebral vascular disease (Sokoloff, 1966).

Abnormal Aging

As shown in Tables 23-1 and 23-2, using PET oxygen-15 technique, dementias were univocally characterized by a decrease in average CBF, CMRO$_2$, and CMRgl when compared with normal subjects of the same age with a similar degree of mental impairment (Chase, Foster, Fedio, Di Chiro, & Brocke et al., 1983; Frackowiak, Pozzilli, Legg, DuBoulay & Marshall et al., 1981; Lassen et al., 1957; Obrist et al., 1970). No global or focal disturbances of the oxygen extraction coefficient (OEF) were observed in dementia of whatever origin, suggesting that chronic ischemia does not play any pathogenic role and that CBF measurements generally reflect oxygen utilization (Frackowiak et al., 1981).

Senile dementia is associated with CBF reduction occurring primarily in gray matter and, most pronounced in frontal and temporal areas

TABLE 23–2. Mean Gray Matter Results with PET Oxygen-15 by Severity and Dementia Type Compared with Normals (Same Age) in Temporal/Insular Region and Centrum Semiovale

Patients	rCBF	rOEF	rCMRO$_2$
Mild dementia (11)	40.2 ± 9.9 (−21%)*	0.51 ± 0.06 (−4%)	3.6 ± 0.35 (−23%)†
Severe dementia (11)	31.1 ± 5 (−39%)[+]	0.57 ± 0.08 (+8%)	3.02 ± 0.4 (−36%)†
Degenerative (13)	35. ± 6.9 (−31%)*	0.54 ± 0.06 (+2%)	3.32 ± 0.43 (−29%)*
Vascular (9)	36.5 ± 11.8 (−28%)[+]	0.53 ± 0.11 (0)	3.29 ± 0.56 (−30%)*

* % Change from normal, $p < 0.01$; †% change from normal, $p < 0.001$
Source: From "Regional Cerebral Oxygen Supply and Utilization in Dementia" by R.S.J. Frackowiak et al., 1981, *Journal of Cerebral Blood Flow and Metabolism*, Vol. 1, Suppl. 1, 5453–5454.

(Ingvar & Gustafson, 1970; Lavy, Melamed, Bentin, Cooper, & Rinot, 1978; Obrist et al., 1970).

Determination of local CMRgl with PET deoxyglucose technique showed a significant decrease in CMRgl from normal young to senile demented patients and most pronounced in frontal regions (Alavi et al., 1980; Ferris et al., 1980; Reivich et al., 1983).

Senile dementia of the Alzheimer type (SDAT) was found to be associated with reduction of CBF and metabolism most pronounced in frontal and parietal associative cortical areas and to a lesser extent, in subcortical structures (Benson, 1982; Chase et al., 1983).

Patients having multi-infarct dementia (MID) have shown the maximum of metabolic defects in the cortex, caudate, thalamus, white matter, and cerebellum without any changes in oxygen extraction, supporting the hypothesis that chronic ischemia is not a major mechamism in vascular dementia (Frackowiak et al., 1981).

Pick's dementia is associated with hypometabolism in frontal and prefrontal areas even in the absence of any x-ray-detected abnormalities. For Huntington's disease-demented patients, there is PET-observed hypometabolism in the caudate region with well-preserved cortical metabolism. The relative retention of cortical metabolic activity was also observed in dementia associated with normal pressure hydrocephalus (NPH) and with Wilson's disease.

The metabolic pattern of early Jakob-Creutzfeldt disease is characterized by mottled areas of hypermetabolism and hypometabolism in both cortical and subcortical regions (Benson, 1982). Table 23-3 gives a summary of the main local CMRgl defects obtained in different types of abnormal brain aging using PET deoxyglucose technique.

TABLE 23–3. Main Local CMRgl Defects Observed with PET in Brain Aging

| | Defects | |
| | Cortical | Subcortical |
Diagnosis	region	region
Normal aging	± Normal	± Normal
Unipolar depression	± Normal	± Normal
Alzheimer's disease	Temporal, parietal, External occipital	
SDAT	Association cortex	Basal ganglia, thalamus
MID	Diffuse	White matter, caudate, thalamus, cerebellum
Pick's disease	Frontal temporal	—
NPH	Minor	—

CONCLUSION

One consistent problem disturbing both clinical and research approaches to abnormal brain aging is the establishment of diagnosis during the patient's life. That many widely different disorders can underly dementia is well established, but it is also apparent that the features distinguishing the varieties of dementia in vivo are not all clear.

Recent technical advances (nuclear magnetic resonance, PET) have improved the capacity to obtain an in vivo correct diagnosis, but the widespread cerebral abnormalities of many causes of dementia lead to poor definition until the disease is well advanced. Although the PET method is complicated to carry out because it requires that a cyclotron be near the hospital and that there be a specialized full-time staff to attend the machinery, we think that this technique is, at least presently and in senile cases, necessary for clinical research to obtain a better understanding of brain pathophysiological processes occurring during life. Indeed, these PET measurements give us many possibilities:

- To reflect and quantify the cerebral, metabolic, and functional deterioration in abnormal aging.
- To characterize asymptomatic cerebral alterations in preclinical cases.

- To map the cerebral structures that are either biochemically altered or functionally involved in different types of dementia.
- To document the mechanisms involved in normal and abnormal aging, particularly mismatches between metabolism and flow and uncoupling between oxygen consumption and glucose uptake.
- To investigate reduced or improved ability of brain structures to be activated by psychomotor stimulation.
- To objectify circulatory and metabolic aspects of treatment, opening new therapeutic strategies in the puzzling field of dementia.

REFERENCES

Alavi, A., Ferris, F., Wolf, A., Reivich, M., Farkas, T., Dann, R., Christman, D., Mac Gregor, R., & Fowler, J. (1980). Determination of cerebral metabolism in senile dementia using F-18-deoxyglucose and positron emission tomography. *Journal of Nuclear Medicine, 21,* 121.

Benson, D.F. (1982). The use of positron emission scanning techniques in the diagnosis of Alzheimer's disease. In S. Corkin, K.L. Davis, J.H. Growdon, E. Usdin, & R.J. Wurtman (Eds.). *Aging: Vol. 19. Alzheimer's disease: A Report of Progress in Research,* New York: Raven Press.

Chase, T.N., Foster, N.L., Fedio, P., Di Chiro, G., Brocke, R., & Patronas, N.G. (1983). Alzheimer's disease: Local cerebral metabolism studies using the 18-F-fluorodeoxyglucose positron emission tomography technique. In S. Algeri, S. Gershon, D. Samuel, & G. Toffano (Eds.). *Aging: Vol 22. Aging of the brain.* New York: Raven Press.

Ferris, S.H., De Leon, M.O., Wolf, A.P., Farkas, T., Christman, D.R., Reisberg, B., Fowler, J.S., Mac Gregor, R., Goldman, A., George, A.E., & Rampal, S. (1980). Positron emission tomography in the study of aging and senile dementia. *Neurobiology of Aging, 1,* 127-131.

Frackowiak, R.S.J., Pozzilli, C., Legg, N.O., Du Boulay, G.H., Marshall, J., Jenzi, G.L., & Jones, T. (1981). Regional cerebral oxygen supply and utilization in dementia: a clinical and physiological study with oxygen-15 and positron tomography. *Brain, 104,* 753-778.

Frackowiak, R.S.J., Pozzilli, C., Legg, N., Du Buolay, G.H., Marshall, J., Lenzi, G.L., & Jones, T. (1981). A prospective study of regional cerebral blood flow and oxygen utilization in dementia using positron emission tomography and oxygen-15. In M.E. Raichle, R. Grubb, Jr., M.M. Ter-Pogossian (Eds.), *Journal of Cerebral Blood Flow and Metabolism, Vol. 1 (suppl. 1), 5453-5454.*

Freyham, F.A., Woodford, R.B., & Kety, S.S. (1951). Cerebral blood flow and metabolism in psychoses of senility. *Journal of Nervous and Mental Disease, 113,* 449-456.

Ingvar, D.H., & Gustafson, L. (1970). Regional cerebral blood flow in organic dementia with early onset. *Acta Neurologica Scandinavica, 43,* 42-73.

Ingvar, D.H., Risberg, J., & Schwartz, M.S. (1975). Evidence of subnormal function of association cortex in presenile dementia. *Neurology, 10,* 964-974.

Kety, S.S. (1956). Human cerebral blood flow and oxygen consumption as related to aging. *Research Publications—Association for Research in Nervous and Mental Disease, 35,* 31-45.

Lassen, N.A., Munch, O., & Tottey, E.R. (1957). Mental function and cerebral oxygen consumption in organic dementia. *Archives of Neurology and Psychiatry, 77,* 126–133.

Lassen, N.A., Feinberg, I., & Lane, M.H. (1960). Bilateral studies of cerebral oxygen uptake in young and aged normal subjects and in patients with organic dementia. *Journal of Clinical Investigation, 39,* 491–500.

Lavy, S., Melamed, E., Bentin, S., Cooper, G., & Rinot, T. (1978). Bihemispheric decreases of regional blood flow in dementia: Correlation with age-matched normal controls. *Annals of Neurology, 4,* 445–450.

Le Poncin-Lafitte, M., Askienazy, S., Raynaud, C., & Rapin, J.R. (1985). Local cerebral blood flow and cognitive functions in old age: Experimental and clinical studies. *Circulation et Métabolisme du Cerveau, 1,* (suppl. 1),6016–6087.

Metter, E.J., Riege, W.H., Kuhl, D.E., & Phelps, P.E. (1983). Differences in regional glucose metabolic intercorrelations with aging. In A. Bes, E.T. Mac Kenzie, & J. Seylaz (Eds.). *Journal of Cerebral Blood Flow and Metabolism (Vol. 3, Suppl. 1.)* New York:Raven Press.

Obrist, W.D., Chivian, E., Cronquvist, S., & Ingvar, D.H. (1970). Regional cerebral blood flow in senile and presenile dementia. *Neurology, 20,* 315–322.

Phelps, M.E., Huang, S.C., Hoffman, E.D., Selin, C., Sokoloff, L., & Huhl, D.E. (1979). Tomographic measurement of local cerebral glucose metabolic rate in humans with (F-18) 2-fluoro-2-deoxy-D-glucose; Validation of method. *Annals of Neurology, 6,* 371–388.

Reivich, M., Alavi, A., Ferris, S., Christman, D., Fowler, J., Mac Gregor, R., Farkas T., Greenberg, J., Dann, D., & Wolf, A. Assessment of regional glucose metabolism in aging brain and dementia with positron emission tomography. In A. Agnoli, G. Crepaldi, O.F. Spano, & M. Trabucchi (Eds.). *Aging brain and ergot alkaloids.* New York:Raven Press.

Sokoloff L. (1966). Cerebral circulatory and metabolic changes associated with aging. *Research publications—Association for Research in Nervous and Mental Disease, 41,* 237–254.

Ter-Pogossian, M.M., Raichle, M.E., & Fiche, D.C. (1981). Dynamic positron emission tomography of the brain. In M.E. Raichle, R.L. Grubb Jr, & M.M. Ter-Pogossian (Eds.). *Journal of Cerebral Blood Flow and Metabolism (Vol. 1, Suppl. 1).* New York:Raven Press.

CHAPTER 24

Variability of Cerebral Blood Flow Defects in Alzheimer's Disease: SPECT Studies at Rest and During Memorization

*M. Leponcin Lafitte, G. Rancurel, C. Raynaud,
P. Migeon, J. R. Rapin*

Fifteen cases of diffuse progressive mental deterioration, in patients between 55 and 75 years of age, without focal lesion on CT scan, were studied. The regional cerebral blood flow (rCBF) studies, at rest with ^{133}Xe, showed a marked general flow decrease involving frontal and/or temporal and parieto-occipital structures. The distribution of the cerebral blood flow studies with the isopropyliodoamphetamine during two memorizing tasks (fifteen words of Rey and Proteus maze) showed several subtypes or stages related to different psychometric or clinical syndromes. It can be possible to correlate a parietal and probably an associative visual-occipital defect with a nonspecific auditivo–verbal memory. A subcortical defect can be related with a specific auditivo–verbal defect without disturbances of visuospatial memory.

Alzheimer's disease in the early stages is primarily a gradual deterioration of the highest behavioral and cognitive functions. A major concern of neurophysiology is to define those cognitive changes that occur during the course of the disease and to separate the disorders in memory, language, visual perception, and praxis disturbances. Previous studies in patients with senile dementia of the Alzheimer type showed global and focal blood flow deficits (Prohovnik, Mayeux, & Sackheim et al., 1985) especially in occipito-parieto-temporal regions

(Lassen & Ingvar, 1980) and asymmetries in regional cerebral glucose metabolism (Netter, Riege, & Kuhl et al., 1985).

These different changes in cerebral hemodynamics and metabolism may be important for understanding of the functional state of brain affected by Alzheimer's disease, as Rapoport, Horwitz, & Duara (1985) have already shown in the case of healthy elderly patients.

The aim of this approach is to have sufficiently detailed information about memory abilities in order to prove that the type of brain blood flow defect is related to the cognitive deficit. Thus, rCBF is measured in Alzheimer's disease when the patient is at rest during a memory stimulation.

METHODS

Fifteen right-handed patients (8 men, 7 women, mean ± age SEM, 61 ± 3 years) with clinically diagnosed Alzheimer's disease were studied. The CT scan revealed general cerebral atrophy, and in 30% of the patients, a ventricular dilatation; the regional blood flow was diminished in the patients at rest studied by the clearance of ^{133}xenon in the brain (Derouene, Rancurel, Le Poncin-Lafitte et al., 1985). All patients had gradually progressive deterioration of intellectual functions; especially a disturbance of cognition and a defect of auditivo-verbal memory and/or visuospatial memory as Gainotti, Caltagirone, & Masullo et al. (1980) have already shown. Notwithstanding this, all patients were alert and cooperative to participation in an extensive psychometric test battery with no clinical or laboratory evidence of cerebrovascular disease, depression, or other neurological illness.

To evaluate the auditivo-verbal memory, we used the test of fifteen words of Rey. These words are listened to five times, and the patients have to recall a maximum number of these words. To evaluate the visuo-spatial memory, we used a Porteus maze in which the patients must draw the course from departure to arrival within 3 minutes. To establish a correlation between the performances of memory and the cerebral blood flow changes, single-photon emission tomography (Tomomatic 64. Medimatic-Copenhagen) studies were carried out under unstimulated conditions (closed eyes in a quiet environment) at rest or during memorizing tests.

In a first step, the list of fifteen words is listened to five times and the patient recalls a maximum number of these words; the patient also draws a course in a Porteus maze. They are then asked to memorize a maximum number of words and the right course of the maze. In a second step, during the silent recall of auditivo-verbal and visuospatial memory, 5 mCi ^{123}I-isopropyliodo amphetamine (IMP) is injected rapidly through a brachial intravenous catheter. The image of regional blood flow is obtained 10 minutes after the administration of ^{123}I-isopropyliodoamphetamine (initial uptake). Thus, the image of regional blood flow is strictly obtained during the memorizing task. In a third step, the answers to the memory tests are asked to check the memory efficiency.

RESULTS

The 15 patients can be separated into three groups in function of blood flow imaging and memory test results.

For the first type (CBF at rest) the xenon image showed an almost symmetrical decrease in parieto-temporal regions. During the memory test, the rCBF was measured with IMP and it was possible to observe an identical temporo parietal defect, probably associated with an associative visual occipital defect. Images obtained during the tests were asymmetrical (Figure 24-1A). In these patients the predominant symptoms were partial amnesia of recent memory and visuospatial agnosia. These patients only learned 6 words (6 ± 2) and did not find the right course in the maze with a specific perseverance of certain types of error (Figure 24-1B).

For the second type (at rest) the xenon images showed a decrease of rCBF in bilateral temporoparietal areas associated with a subcortical hypoperfusion (Figure 24-2A). This subcortical decrease corresponded, in part, to a ventricular dilatation observed on the CT scan. With IMP images, during memorizing tests the asymmetric subcortical defect was evident and could not simply be related to the ventricle dilatation, which is symmetrical. These patients only learned 3 words and they often added other extra-list words. Moreover they did not find the right course in the maze and like the first type, we observed repetitions in their errors (Figure 24-2B).

For the third type (subcortical defect) we observed an IMP hypofixation on the left anterior area (Figure 24-3A). The CT scan images were normal without ventricular dilatation. These patients learned 8 words, and like the second type, extra-list words were given as answers. The results in spatiotemporal tests were correct (Figure 24-3B).

DISCUSSION

The abnormal rCBF findings in Alzheimer patients suggest decreased neuronal activity in the posterior associative cortex related to complex visual and auditory processing. Moreover, in Alzheimer's disease there is variability of rCBF defects (Derouesne et al., 1985), which sometimes includes clear asymmetrics as is suggested by ^{18}F-fluoro-

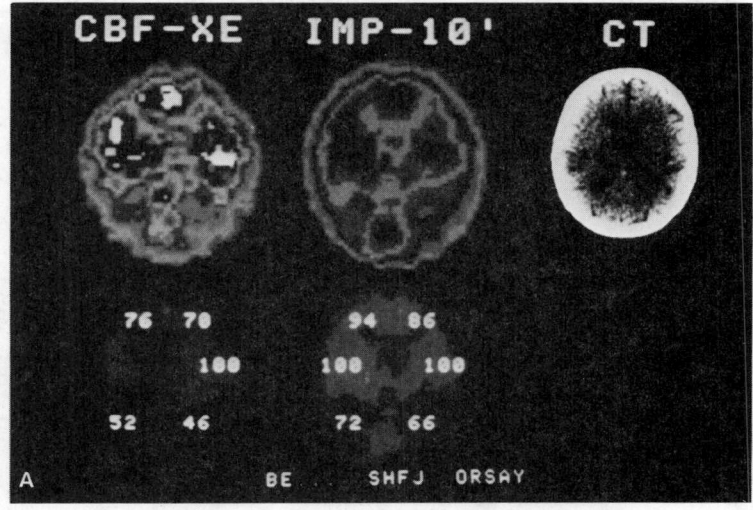

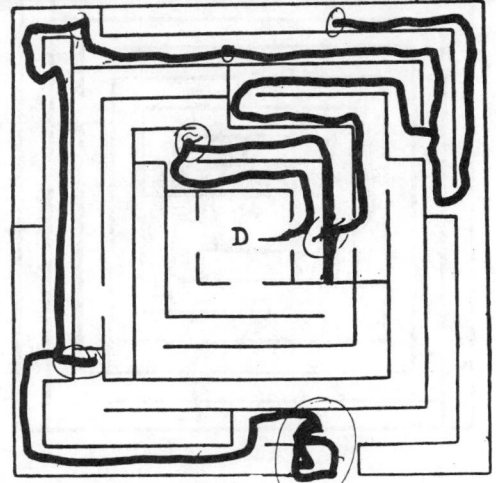

FIGURE 24-1. A: Alzheimer patient with bilateral temporoparietal hypoperfusion as shown on ^{133}Xe and IMP imaging. **B:** Same patient: Porteus maze diagrams.

deoxyglucose studies reported by Chase (1984). Chase's studies show the existence of subtypes or states of illness corresponding to different psychometric or clinical syndromes.

In this study the psychometric results are in agreement with the previous studies (Gainotti et al, 1980; Perez, Rivera, Meyer, Gay & Taylor et al., 1975), which showed that patients affected by degenerative forms of dementia, as Alzheimer type, perform consistently worse

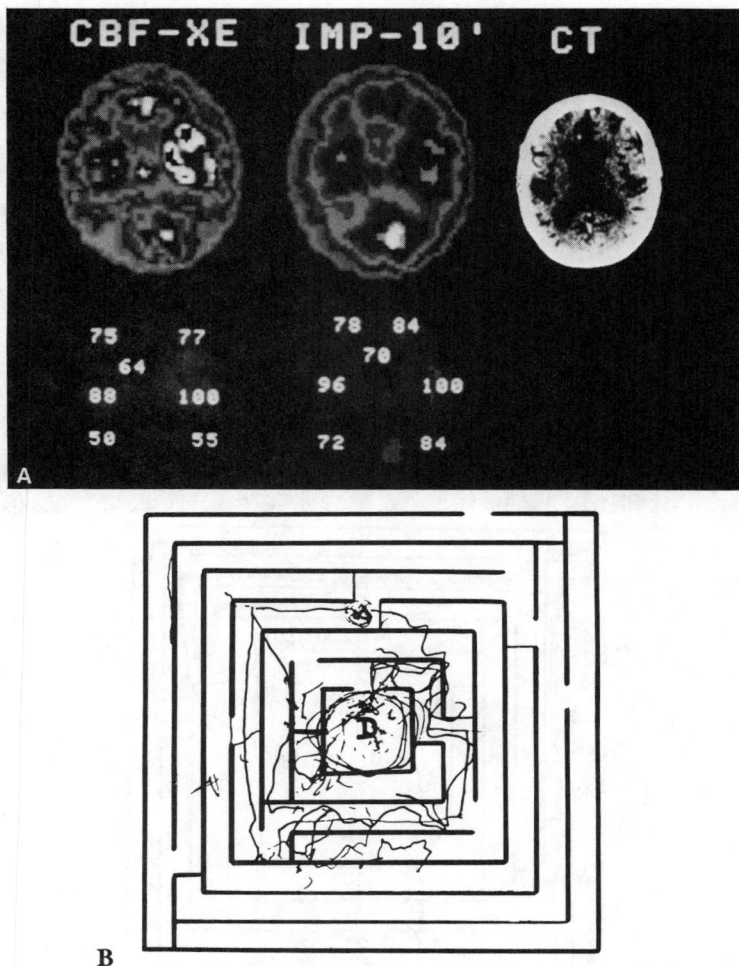

FIGURE 24-2. A: Alzheimer patient with bilateral temporoparietal and subcortical hypoperfusion as shown on ^{133}Xe and IMP imaging. **B:** Same patient: Porteus maze diagrams.

on most verbal and visuospatial tasks than those suffering from other etiologic forms of dementia; the memory disorders are always more severe than cognitive disabilities (Perez, Gay, & Cooke, 1978). A parietal, and probably an associative visual occipital, defect can be correlated with a non–specific auditivo-verbal memory failure associated with a specific visuospatial memory and characterized by a perseverance in errors. However, a subcortical defect can be related to a

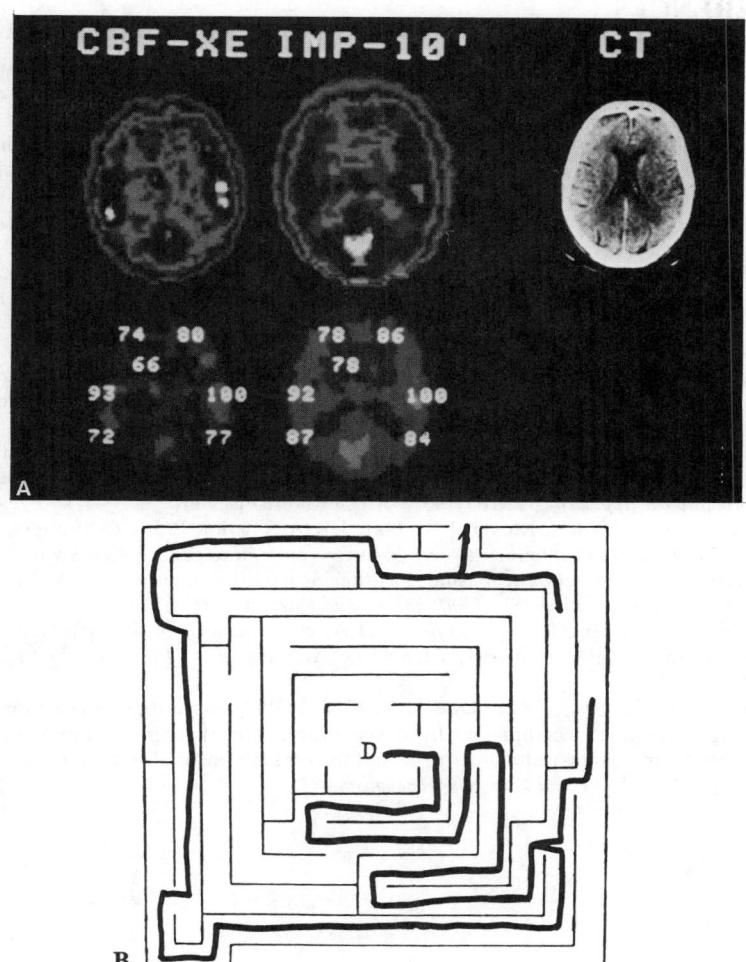

FIGURE 24-3. A: Alzheimer patient with subcortical hypoperfusion as shown on ^{133}Xe and IMP imaging. **B:** Same patient: Porteus maze diagrams.

specific auditivo-verbal failure, which is suggested by the appearance of extra-list words, but without disturbances of visuospatial memory. Moreover, we showed that a correlation can be established between the type of psychometric defects and the type of blood flow defects that appeared on images.

These findings indicate that psychometric tests correlated with imaging investigations can be used for early identification of patients with degenerative disorders.

REFERENCES

Chase, T.N., (1984). Focal cortical abnormalities in Alzheimer's disease as determined by PET. *Proceedings of the Third Meeting of the International Study Group on Aging* (pp. 95–110).

Derouesne, C., Rancurel, G., Le Poncin Lafitte, M., et al. (1985). Variability of cerebral blood flow defects in Alzheimer's Disease on [123]iodo-isopropyl-amphetamine and single-photon emission tomography. *Lancet, 8440,* 1282.

Gainotti, G., Caltagirone, C., Masullo, C. et al. (1980). Patterns of neuropsychologic impairment in various diagnostic groups of dementia. In L. Amaducci et al (Eds.). *Aging: Vol. 13. Aging of the brain and dementia.* New York: Raven Press.

Lassen, N.A., & Ingvar, D.H. (1980). Blood flow studies in the aging normal brain and in senile dementia. In L. Amaducci et al (Eds.). *Aging: Vol 13. Aging of the brain and dementia.* New York:Raven Press.

Netter, E.S., Riege, W.H., & Huhl, D.E., et al. (1985). Variability of regional cerebral glucose metabolism in Alzheimer's disease patients as compared to normal subjects. *Journal of Cerebral Blood Flow and Metabolism, 88.*

Perez, F.I., Gay, J.R.A., & Cooke, N.A. (1978). Neuropsychological aspects of Alzheimer's disease and multi-infarct dementia. In K. Nandy (Ed.). *Senile Dementia: A Biomedical Approach* (pp. 185-199). Amsterdam: Elsevier.

Perez, F.I., Rivera, V.M., Meyer, J.S., Gay, J.R.A., Taylor, R.L., & Mathew, N.T. (1975). Analysis of intellectual and cognitive performance in patients with multi-infarct dementia, vertebrobasilar insufficiency with dementia and Alzheimer's disease. *Journal of Neurology, Neurosurgery, and Psychiatry, 38,* 533-540.

Prohovnik, I., Mayeux, R., & Sackheim, H.A. et al. (1985). rCBF hyperactivity to behavioural challenge in early Alzheimer's disease. *Proc. J. Cereb. Blood Flow & Metab., 80.*

Rapoport, S.I., Horwitz, B., & Duara, R. (1985). PET scanning demonstrates that aging in man is accompanied by desynchronization of regional brain activity, without concurrent reductions in absolute cerebral metabolic rates for glucose. *Journal of Cerebral Blood Flow and Metabolism, 84.*

CHAPTER 25

Cerebral, Metabolic, and Neuropsychological Abnormalities in Mild, Moderate, and Severe Alzheimer's Disease

James V. Haxby

Patterns of regional cerebral metabolic rates (rCMRglc), as measured by positron emission tomography (PET) and [^{18}F}-2-fluoro-2-deoxy-D-glucose, and neuropsychological function were studied in 26 patients with presumed Alzheimer's disease (AD), who were divided into mildly ($n = 10$), moderately ($n = 12$), and severely ($n = 4$) demented groups. Mild AD patients demonstrated significant memory impairment with no significant impairments on tests of language and visuospatial functions. Moderate AD patients demonstrated significant language and visuospatial impairments as well as a profound memory disorder. Most severe AD patients were unable to complete neuropsychological testing. All three AD severity groups demonstrated abnormal patterns of neocortical rCMRglc, namely reductions of parietal and temporal rCMRglc and increased left–right asymmetry in the association cortices of the frontal, parietal, and temporal lobes. In moderate AD, disproportion between language and visuospatial deficits and asymmetry of visual attention to right and left space were correlated in the expected direction with left–right rCMRglc asymmetries. In mild AD no such relationships were found. These results suggest that abnormal patterns of neocortical rCMRglc are observable with PET in mild AD before associated impairments of neocortically mediated language and visuospatial functions are demonstrable.

Positron emission tomography (PET) allows measurement of regional cerebral metabolic rates for glucose (rCMRglc) and oxygen (rCMRO$_2$). Studies of regional cerebral metabolism in patients with clinically diagnosed Alzheimer's disease (AD) have consistently demonstrated lower rates relative to controls, particularly in parietal and temporal regions (Benson, Kuhl, & Hawkins et al., 1983; Chase, Foster, & Fedio et al., 1984; de Leon, Ferris, & George et al., 1983; Frackowiak, Pozzilli, & Legg et al., 1981; Friedland, & Budinger et al., 1983; Friedland, Budinger, Koss & Ober, 1985; Haxby, Duara, & Grady et al., 1985). Left and right rCMRglc in the association cortices of the frontal, parietal, and temporal lobes also have been found to be less symmetrical in AD patients relative to controls (Friedland, Budinger, Koss, & Ober, 1985; Haxby et al., 1985). Some patients have lower right than left rCMRglc, and others have lower left than right rCMRglc. Moreover, asymmetry of cerebral metabolism in AD is related to patterns of neuropsychological deficits (Foster, Chase, & Mansi et al., 1983; Haxby, 1984; Haxby et al., 1985; Koss, Friedland, Ober, & Jagust et al., 1985). Relatively greater left hemisphere hypometabolism is associated with disproportionate language deficits, and relatively greater right hemisphere hypometabolism is associated with disproportionate visuospatial deficits.

Previous studies of cerebral metabolism in AD have examined patients with marked deficits in those neuropsychological functions that are presumably mediated by neocortex (e.g., language and visuospatial construction) (Foster, Chase, & Fedia et al., 1983; Friedland et al., 1983, 1985; Koss et al., 1985). In the earliest stages of AD, however, patients may have a prominent memory disorder that is not yet accompanied by impairment of neocortically mediated neuropsychological function (Grunthal, 1926; Sjogren, Sjogren, & Lindgren, 1952; Sim & Sussman, 1962; Corkin, 1982). We decided to investigate whether the abnormalities of neocortical metabolism that are related to impairments of neocortically mediated neuropsychological function in moderate to severe AD are evident in patients with mild, early AD.

In the current study, 26 patients with clinically diagnosed AD were divided into mildly, moderately, and severely demented groups. It was found that the mildly demented group had significant neuropsychological deficits on memory tests but not on tests of language and visuospatial function. Nonetheless, this group of patients demonstrated the same neocortical metabolic abnormalities (i.e., parietal reductions and lateral asymmetry) as did the moderate and severe groups. Moreover, left-right asymmetry of rCMRglc in moderate AD was significantly correlated with two asymmetries of neuropsychological function, namely asymmetry of language and visuospatial construction, and asymmetry of attention to right and left extrapersonal space. In mild AD patients, no such relation was found. Our results suggest that

TABLE 25-1. Subject Characteristics

Characteristic	Psychological testing controls	PET controls	Mild AD	Moderate AD	Severe AD
			22–29[a]	12–21[a]	0–6[a]
n	25	29	10	12	4
Sex	16M,9F	27M,2F	9M,1F	4M,8F	1M,3F
Age (yr)	62.9 + 10.5	63.5 + 10.6	63.7 + 8.5	66.7 + 9.5	70.6 + 8.0
Education (yr)	16.2 + 2.4	17.6 + 2.3	15.7 + 1.7	13.6 + 2.4	16.5 + 1.0

[a]Represents Mini-Mental State range.

disordered physiological function in neocortex may precede the appearance of neocortically mediated neuropsychological deficits in the progressive course of AD.

METHODS

Subjects

Twenty-six (26) right-handed patients with presumed Alzheimer's disease were divided into mildly, moderately, and severely demented groups using the Mini-Mental State (Table 25-1). In order to study early AD, patients who demonstrated only an isolated memory impairment were accepted for study. These patients meet the NINCDS-ADRDA criteria for possible AD (McKhann et al., 1984). Patients who demonstrated impaired language or cognitive function in addition to impaired memory meet NINCDS-ADRDA criteria for probable AD and DSM-III criteria for primary degenerative dementia (1980).

Two overlapping groups of healthy, normal subjects served as controls for neuropsychological ($n = 25$) and regional cerebral metabolic ($n = 29$) studies (Table 25-1). Both groups were age-matched to the sample of AD patients. The neuropsychological controls also had equivalent educational backgrounds to patients in the mild and severe AD groups, but not the moderate group. The ratio of males to females among neuropsychological controls also was closer to that of the AD patients than was the sex ratio among PET controls who were predominantly male. One neuropsychological control was ambidextrous; the rest were right-handed. All PET controls were right-handed.

Neuropsychological Tests

Neuropsychological tests of overall severity of dementia, memory, language, and visuospatial function were administered to all AD patients and neuropsychological test controls.

The measures of overall severity were the Mini-Mental State (Folstein et al., 1976) and the Mattis Dementia Rating Scale (Mattis, 1976). Verbal and visual memory were tested with the Wechsler Memory Scale (immediate and delayed memory for stories and figures) (Russell, 1975; Wechsler, 1945). The Wechsler Adult Intelligence Scale (WAIS) (Wechsler, 1955) was included as a standard measure of verbal and visuospatial mental abilities. Full-scale IQ and three-factor deviation quotients (DQs) (Tellegen, & Briggs, 1967) were calculated from the WAIS. The three-factor DQs WAIS subtests are as follows: Verbal Comprehension (VDQ)—tests of verbal comprehension and fund of knowledge (Information, Comprehension, Similarities, and Vocabulary); Memory and Freedom from Distractibility (MDQ)—tests of immediate verbal memory and calculations (Digit Span and Arithmetic); Perceptual Organization (PDQ)—tests of visuospatial construction (Block Design and Object Assembly). Three additional tests of language function were administered: a test of syntax comprehension (Whitehouse, unpublished test), the Boston Naming Test (odd-numbered items only, Kaplan, Goodglass, & Weintrab, 1976), and controlled word association (FAS fluency) (Benton, 1973). The Extended Range Drawing Test (Haxby et al., 1985) was used as a test of visuospatial construction. The Benton Facial Recognition Test (Benton & Van Allen, 1973) was used as a test of visual form perception. A block tapping span test patterned after Corsi's test (Milner, 1971) with a 12 block array was administered as a test of immediate visuospatial memory and as a test of attention to right and left sides of extrapersonal space. Because of time limitations with some subjects, not all tests were administered to all control subjects.

Three neuropsychological asymmetry indices that express the discrepancy between functions mediated primarily by the left and right cerebral hemispheres were calculated from neuropsychological test scores. Two indices express the disproportion between performance on tests of verbal functions, on the one hand, and tests of visuospatial construction, on the other. For one index, patient scores on the Syntax Comprehension Test and Extended Range Drawing Test were ranked, and the difference between ranks was calculated for each subject. For the second index, the difference was calculated between two WAIS factor DQs (PDQ-MDQ) (Tellegen & Briggs, 1967).

The third index expressed the asymmetry of attention to right and left extrapersonal space. The 12-block array on the Block Tapping Span Test was divided into six blocks on the right side of the board and six blocks on the left side. Six trials were administered at each level until 5 of 6 trials were failed. The number of errors made on the left and right sides of the board were recorded. The following formula was used to express asymmetry of errors on the right and left:

$$\text{Asymmetry of Visual Attention} = \frac{\text{Errors (right)} - \text{Errors (left)}}{\text{Errors (right)} + \text{Errors (left)}}$$

On all three indices of neuropsychological asymmetry, positive scores correspond to disproportionate left hemisphere deficits.

Measurement of Regional Cerebral Metabolism

rCMRglc was measured at rest using PET and [18-F]-2-fluoro-2-deoxy-D-glucose as described by Duara, Grady, and Haxby (1984) and Duara, Margolin, and Robertson-Tchabo et al. (1983). Patients were supine and had their eyes covered and ears plugged with cotton in order to reduce sensory input. PET scanning was accomplished with an ECAT II scanner (ORTEC, Life Sciences, Oak Ridge, TN). Images of seven cross-sectional slices parallel to and 5 to 100 mm above the inferior orbitomeatal (IOM) line were made.

Up to 59 regions of interest were identified and outlined using horizontal sections from a brain atlas as a guide (Eycleshymer & Schoemaker, 1911). The brain atlas section providing the closest correspondence to the anatomical configuration inferred from each metabolic image was used to indicate the identity and location of each anatomical region. The region was then outlined using the contours visible in the PET image. For the current analysis, rCMRglc was calculated (Huang, Phelps & Hoffman et al., 1980) for whole cerebral hemispheres as well as for lateral cortical regions grouped into the following areas: frontal association, perirolandic sensorimotor, parietal association, occipital lobe, and temporal lobe. These cortical areas are outlined in the PET scan of a normal subject in Figure 25-1.

In a previous report, we found that parietal and temporal rCMRglc demonstrated significant reductions in AD patients only when referenced to sensorimotor and occipital rCMRglc, respectively (Haxby et al., 1985). We also found that asymmetry of rCMRglc in homologous right and left hemisphere association cortices was significantly greater in AD patients than in controls. In the current report, therefore, parietotemporal reductions will be examined by measuring parietal rCMRglc as a percentage of sensorimotor rCMRglc and temporal rCMRglc as a percentage of occipital rCMRglc. Asymmetry of rCMRglc in homologous pairs of neocortical regions will be calculated as percent differences using mean rCMRglc for the pair of regions as the denominator:

$$\text{rCMRglc Asymmetry} = \frac{\text{rCMRglc (right)} - \text{rCMRglc (left)}}{(\text{rCMRglc (right)} + \text{rCMRglc (left)})/2}$$

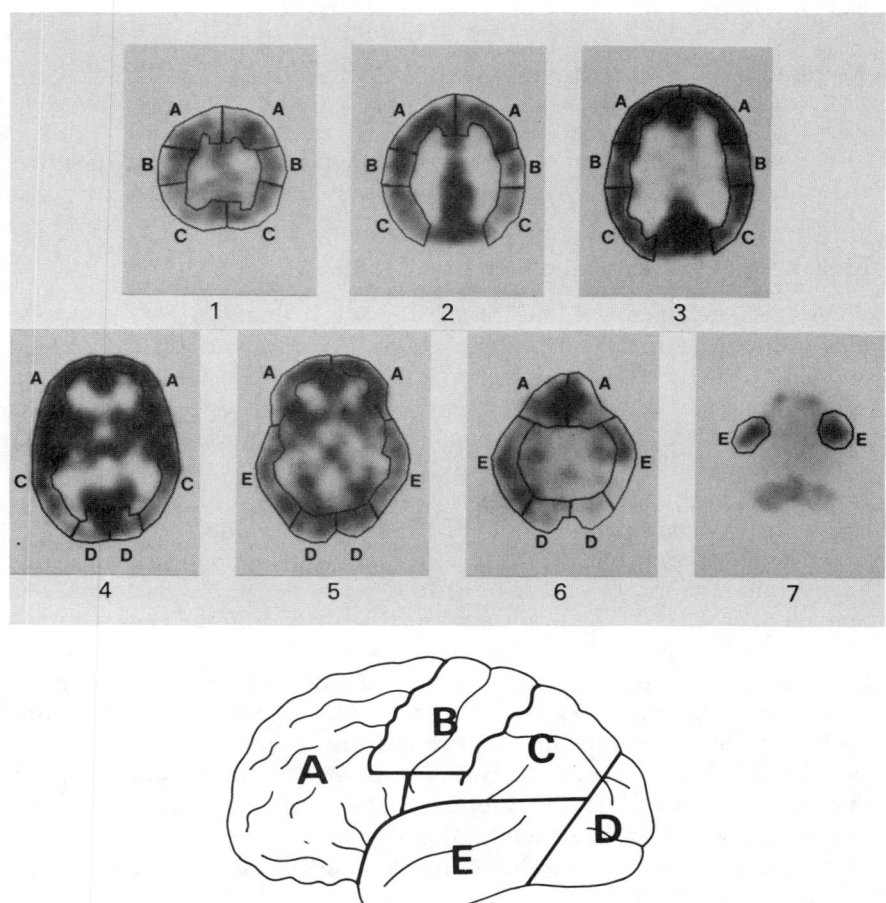

FIGURE 25-1. Seven PET images from a typical control subject with five cortical regions of interest are outlined. The schematic diagram of the lateral aspect of the left hemisphere depicts the location of these regions. The anatomical configurations of the seven images correspond to horizontal sections from a brain atlas (Eycleshymer & Schoemaker, 1911) that are 15, 25, 40, 50, 70, 80, and 90 mm above the inferior orbitomeatal line. The regions are as follows: **A:** frontal association; **B:** perirolandic sensorimotor; **C:** parietal association; **D:** occipital lobe; **E:** lateral temporal lobe.

Statistical Analyses

Differences between AD patients and controls on neuropsychological tests and parietotemporal rCMRglc were tested using one way analyses of variance (ANOVAs) for each variable. For neuropsychological variables with a significant group effect, all three possible pairwise comparisons between controls and mild and moderate AD groups were tested using Bonferroni t-tests. For parietal and temporal rCMRglc, three pairwise comparisons were tested. These comparisons were the differences between controls, on the one hand, and each of the three AD severity groups, on the other. Differences between controls and AD severity groups on asymmetry of rCMRglc were tested with F tests for equality of variance (Snedecor & Cochran, 1980), with probabilities corrected for three comparisons. Relations between neuropsychological and neocortical metabolic asymmetries were tested using Pearson product moment correlations (Snedecor & Cochran, 1980).

To determine the frequency of significant rCMRglc pattern abnormalities among patients and controls, normal limits were defined for rCMRglc pattern indices as the 95% confidence intervals ($+$ 1.96 SD). Difference in frequency of rCMRglc pattern abnormalities between controls, on the one hand, and patient groups, on the other, were tested using binomial probabilities (Hays, 1973).

RESULTS

Neuropsychological Measures

Analysis of neuropsychological test results was restricted to the comparison of controls and mild and moderate AD patients. The severely demented patients were unable to comply with test instructions. Significant group differences were found on all neuropsychological tests ($p < 0.05$). Pairwise comparisons between groups revealed that the mildly demented AD patients differed from normals only on the Wechsler Memory Scale ($p < 0.001$, see Table 25-2). In contrast, the moderately demented group differed from normals on all neuropsychological measures ($p < 0.01$). Moreover, the moderately demented group differed from the mildly demented group on all neuropsychological measures except delayed memory on the Wechsler Memory Scale, Controlled Word Association, and Benton Facial Recognition ($p < 0.01$).

Patterns of rCMRglc

Significant group differences were found on all rCMRglc pattern indices (see Table 25-3). Pairwise comparisons revealed that mildly demented AD patients had significant reduction of rCMRglc in parietal association cortex (referenced to sensorimotor cortex) and significantly elevated asymmetry of rCMRglc in frontal, parietal, and lateral temporal association cortex ($p < 0.05$). Moderately demented AD patients

TABLE 25–2. Neuropsychological Test Scores for Controls and Mild and Moderate AD Patients

Test	n	Control Mean + SD	Mild AD (n = 10) Mean + SD	Moderate AD (n = 10) Mean + SD
Mattis Dementia Rating Scale	16	141 + 3	131 + 6	110 + 18 (b,d)
Wechsler Memory Scale				
Immediate Story Recall	23	21.4 + 5.9	10.8 + 5.0[b]	5.4 + 3.0[bd]
Immediate Figure Reproduction	23	9.4 + 3.0	6.4 + 4.5[b]	1.2 + 1.8[bd]
Delayed Story Recall	23	17.6 + 5.7	2.6 + 3.7[b]	0.8 + 1.1[b]
Delayed Figure Reproduction	23	6.5 + 3.3	0.8 + 1.1[b]	0.3 + 0.8[b]
WAIS				
Full Scale 10	25	125 + 11	117 + 8	85 + 15[bd]
Verbal Comprehension DQ	25	127 + 11	122 + 9	96 + 18[bd]
Memory and Distractibility DQ	25	118 + 13	114 + 9	86 + 14[bd]
Perceptual Organization DQ	25	119 + 14	108 + 13	76 + 19[bd]
Syntax Comprehension (max = 26)	23	24.2 + 2.5	22.7 + 2.4	15.8 + 5.4[bd]
Boston Naming (max = 43)	17	37.6 + 5.7	35.7 + 6.5	23.8 + 9.1[bd]
Controlled Word Association (FAS)	24	39.6 + 14.4	30.6 + 8.3	23.8 + 13.4[a]
Extended Range Drawing (max = 24)	22	20.6 + 2.6	18.5 + 4.1	11.7 + 4.8[bd]
Benton Facial Recognition	25	44.6 + 3.8	43.7 + 3.2	40.3 + 5.4[a]
Block Tapping Span (Number of correct trials, 6 trials/length)	25	29 + 6	25 + 4	17 + 6[b]0

[a]Mean significantly less than that of controls, $p < 0.01$.
[b]Mean significantly less than that of controls, $p < 0.001$.
[c]Mean significantly less than that of mild AD, $p < 0.01$.
[d]Mean significantly less than that of mild AD, $p < 0.001$.

had significant reductions of parietal and lateral temporal rCMRglc, as well as significantly elevated asymmetry of rCMRglc in frontal, parietal, and lateral temporal association cortex. Severely demented patients and significant reduction of parietal and temporal rCMRglc, as well as significantly elevated asymmetry of rCMRglc in frontal and lateral temporal association cortex. These abnormal rCMRglc patterns are illustrated in PET scans from a control and a moderately demented AD patient in Figure 25-2.

A subject was deemed to have an abnormal rCMRglc pattern if the value of any one of the five pattern indices fell outside the normal range. By this criterion, 8 of 10 mild AD patients, 9 of 12 moderate AD patients, and 4 of 4 severe AD patients had abnormal rCMRglc patterns. These frequencies all differ significantly from the control frequency (3 of 29) ($p < 0.001$ in all cases).

TABLE 25-3. Comparison of rCMRglc Pattern Indices in Control and AD Patients [a]

Glucose utilization pattern index	Control (n = 29)	Mild AD (n = 10)	Moderate AD (n = 12)	Severe AD (n = 4)
Parietal/sensorimotor	0.96 + 0.06	0.83 + 0.09[c]	0.84 + 0.10[c]	0.70 + 0.07[c]
Temporal/occipital	0.84 + 0.08	0.76 + 0.12	0.75 + 0.11[b]	0.63 + 0.05[c]
Left-right asymmetries				
Frontal association	0.00 + 0.03	0.01 + 0.08[f]	− 0.02 + 0.12[f]	0.02 + 0.08[e]
Parietal association	0.00 + 0.06	0.00 + 0.12[d]	− 0.02 + 0.14[f]	0.04 + 0.08
Lateral temporal	− 0.01 + 0.08	− 0.05 + 0.18[e]	− 0.04 + 0.19[f]	0.08 + 0.34[f]

[a]Focal parietal and temporal reductions are demonstrated by smaller ratios of these regional rates to sensorimotor and occipital rates, respectively. Increased left–right asymmetry in association neocortex is demonstrated by an increase in variance.
[b]Mean is different from control, $p < 0.05$.
[c]Mean is different from control, $p < 0.001$.
[d]Variance is greater than that of controls, $p < 0.05$.
[e]Variance is greater than that of controls, $p < 0.01$.
[f]Variance is greater than that of controls, $p < 0.001$.

Source: From J.V. Haxby, C.L. Grady, R. Duara et al. (1986). Neocortical metabolic abnormalities precede nonmemory cognitive deficits in early Alzheimer's Disease. *Archives of Neurology, 43:* 882–885.

Correlation of Neuropsychological and rCMRglc Asymmetries

In moderately demented AD patients, asymmetry of rCMRglc was correlated with the discrepancy between deficits in language and visuospatial construction in the expected direction (five of six correlations were statistically significant, see Table 25-4). Lower left than right rCMRglc was associated with disproportionate language impairment, and lower right than left rCMRglc was associated with disproportionate visuospatial impairment. Similarly, rCMRglc asymmetry was correlated with asymmetry of visual attention to right and left extrapersonal space in moderately demented AD patients (three of three correlations were statistically significant). Lower left than right rCMRglc was associated with inattention to right hemispace and vice versa. In contrast, no significant correlations between cerebral metabolic and neuropsychological asymmetries were found among the mildly demented patients or among the controls.

DISCUSSION

The sample of patients with presumed AD is the most mildly affected sample in the literature on regional cerebral metabolism in this disease. Both the mild and moderate groups had higher Mattis Dementia

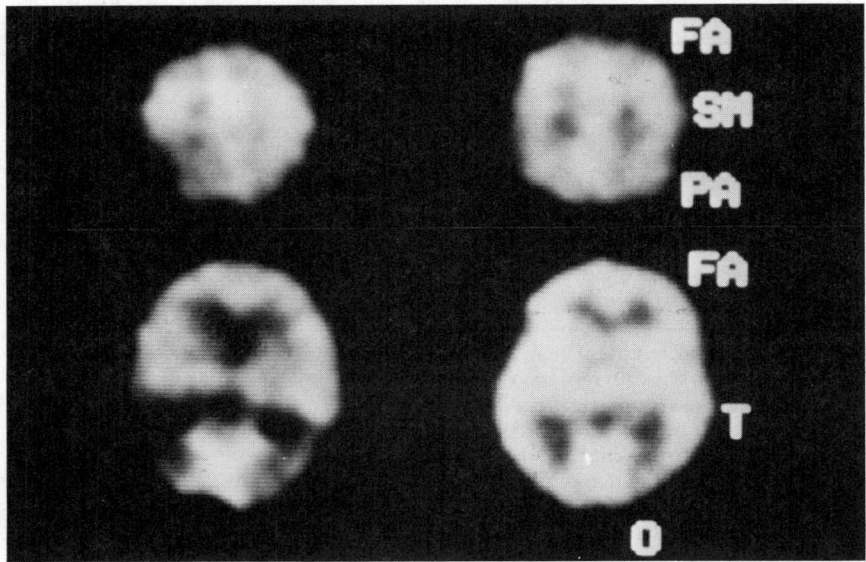

FIGURE 25-2. PET scans from a 66-year-old, female patient with moderate Alzheimer's disease (*left*) and from a 64-year-old, female control subject (*right*). Sections are displayed with anatomical configurations corresponding to that found 45 mm and 70 mm above the inferior orbitomeatal line. The cortical regions that were analyzed are labeled in the control subject scan: FA—Frontal association, SM—perirolandic sensorimotor, PA—parietal association, T—lateral temporal, O—occipital. The patient had significant parietal and temporal reductions, and significant asymmetries in frontal, parietal, and temporal association cortices, with lower left than right hemisphere glucose utilization. *Source:* J.V. Haxby & S.I. Rapoport (1986). Abnormalities of regional brain metabolism in Alzheimer's disease and their relation to functional impairment. *Progress in Neuro-Psychopharmacology and Biological Psychiatry, 10*: 477–438.

Scale scores than the patients reported by Friedland et al. (1983, 1985). The range Friedland et al. call "mild" includes all but two of our moderately demented patients. Mattis Dementia Scale scores and WAIS IQs in our mild group were also higher than those of the mild AD group reported by Foster et al. (1984).

In this patient sample, patterns of neuropsychological deficits were related to overall severity of dementia. Both mild and moderate AD patients had marked impairments on tests of new learning and delayed memory, but only moderately demented patients had significant impairments on tests of language functions, visuospatial construction, visual form perception, and visuospatial immediate memory spans. Memory impairment has long been recognized in clinical descriptions

TABLE 25-4. Correlation of Indices of Neuropsychological Asymmetry to Asymmetry of Cerebral Metabolism in Association Neocortex[a]

Neuropsychological asymmetry index	rCMRglc asymmetry	Controls (right-handed)	Mild AD ($n = 10$)	Moderate AD ($n = 12$)
Syntax/drawing		($n = 13$)		
	Frontal association	−0.31	−0.01	0.71*
	Parietal association	−0.10	−0.20	0.73*
	Lateral temporal	−0.08	0.01	0.49
WAIS PDQ-MDQ		($n = 26$)		
	Frontal association	0.10	−0.08	0.59*
	Parietal association	0.09	−0.06	0.76*
	Lateral temporal	−0.10	0.05	0.58*
Visual attention		($n = 14$)		
	Frontal association	0.29	0.18	0.79*
	Parietal association	−0.04	0.10	0.69*
	Lateral temporal	0.29	0.41	0.70*

*$p < 0.05$

[a]The first two neuropsychological asymmetries express the disproportion between visuospatial and language deficits. The third neuropsychological index expresses the asymmetry of visual attention to right and left extrapersonal space, as measured by a test of immediate memory for visuospatial location (Block Tapping Span). Positive correlations correspond to the expected relation, namely relatively lower left rCMRglc associated with disproportionate language deficits or inattention to right hemisphere and relatively lower right rCMRglc associated with disproportionate visuospatial impairment or inattention to left hemispace.

Source: From "Neocortical Metabolic Abnormalities Precede Nonmemory Cognitive Deficits in Early Alzheimer's Disease" by J.V. Haxby, C.L. Grady, R. Duara et al., manuscript submitted for publication.

of the progressive dementia of AD as the earliest and most prominent symptom (Corkin, 1982; Grunthal, 1926; Sjogren et al., 1952; Sim & Sussman, 1960). Using formal neuropsychological measures, Hagberg and Ingvar (1976) found a subgroup of dementia patients with an isolated memory impairment that is similar to our mild AD group, but they made no attempt to rule out other causes of dementia. Our finding documents that even when extraordinary effort is made to rule out other causes of mental decline, a subsample of patients with presumed AD have only an isolated amnesic syndrome.

Abnormalities of neocortical rCMRglc were found in mild, moderate, and severe AD patients. Parietal association rCMRglc, referenced to sensorimotor rCMRglc, was significantly lower in all three AD groups than in controls. Temporal association rCMRglc, referenced to occipital rCMRglc, was significantly lower in moderate and severe AD groups than in controls. Finally, asymmetry of rCMRglc in frontal, parietal, and temporal association cortices was greater in mild and moderate AD patients than in controls. Increased asymmetry of frontal and temporal rCMRglc was found in severe AD patients. These abnormalities of regional cerebral metabolism have been found in other samples of presumed AD patients by several independent groups (Foster et al., 1983, 1984; Frackowiak et al., 1981; Friedland et al., 1983, 1985). Our findings extend the generality of these cerebral metabolic abnormalities to very mild, early AD.

In moderate AD, patterns of neuropsychological deficits were correlated in the expected direction with rCMRglc asymmetries. The association observed between rCMRglc asymmetry and the asymmetry of language and visuospatial function corroborates our earlier reports (Haxby, 1984; Haxby et al., 1985) and the findings of others (Foster et al., 1983; Friedland et al., 1985; Koss et al., 1985). We have also demonstrated for the first time an association between rCMRglc asymmetry and a quite different neuropsychological asymmetry, namely asymmetry of visual attention to right and left extrapersonal space. No such relations were found in the mild group or in controls. Since the mild AD group demonstrated no deficits on tests of language, visuospatial construction, or immediate visuospatial memory, it is not surprising that no relation between neuropsychological and cerebral metabolic patterns was found in this group.

The sample of AD patients under study was recruited to investigate the full course of AD longitudinally, from its earliest stages to death. Consequently, possible AD patients with no neuropsychological disorders aside from memory impairment were studied. These criteria for patient selection may result in a higher rate of misdiagnosis. Follow-up studies of these patients will determine if they go on to develop neocortically mediated neuropsychological deficits. Autopsy studies will provide confirmation of diagnosis. The finding of neocortical metabolic abnormalities in the mild group that are similar to those found in moderate and severe AD groups, however, supports the assumption that the mild patients suffer, for the most part, from the same disease as do the moderate and severe patients.

Memory disorder in early AD is presumably attributable to dysfunction of certain allocortical and subcortical structures, namely the hippocampus, amygdala, and basal cholinergic forebrain. Memory function is known to be dependent on the structural integrity of these regions (Domasio, Graff-Radford, & Eslinger et al., 1985; Milner, 1966; Mishkin, 1978). Moreover, the neuropathological changes of AD are consistently found to be densest in these structures (Jamada & Mehraein, 1968; Ball, 1976; Kemper, 1982). The small size of these structures and their proximity to bone, however, make reliable measurement of their metabolic activity impossible with the PET scanner used in this study. Consequently, the relation of memory function to brain metabolism in early AD remains uncertain.

Disorders of language and visuospatial functions in AD are presumably attributable to neocortical dysfunction. Impairments of language, calculations, visuospatial construction, and asymmetry of visual attention to right and left space are associated with focal neocortical lesions (Benton, 1979; Boller & Grafman, 1983; Caramazza & Zurif, 1976; De Renzi & Nichelli, 1976; Heilman, Scholes, & Watson et al., 1976; Mesulam, 1981; Warrington & Shallice, 1969). In those AD patients with significant impairment of these functions, the pattern of neuropsychological deficits correlated in the expected direction with regional patterns of neocortical rCMRglc abnormalities. In the mild AD group no significant deficit on tests of neocortically mediated language and visuospatial functions were found, yet the group demonstrated the same abnormal patterns of neocortical rCMRglc as observed in moderate and severe AD patients. These findings suggest that in the early stages of this progressive disease, the brain may be able to compensate for neocortical physiological disorder and maintain neocortically mediated neuropsychological function at premorbid levels.

REFERENCES

American Psychiatric Association. (1980). *Diagnostic and statistical manual for mental disorders* (3rd ed.). Washington, DC: Author.

Ball, M.J. (1976). Neurofibrillary tangles and the pathogenesis of dementia: A quantitative study. *Neuropathology and Applied Neurobiology 2*, 395–410.

Benson, D.F., Kuhl, D.E., & Hawkins, R.A., et al. (1983). The fluorodeoxyglucose 18-F scan in Alzheimer's disease and multi-infarct dementia. *Archives of Neurology, 40*, 711–714.

Benton, A.L. (1979). The measurement of aphasic disorders. In A. Caceres Velasquez (Ed.). *Aspectos patologicos del langage*. Lima: Centro Neuropsicologico.

Benton, A.L. (1979). Visuoperceptive, visuospatial, and visuoconstructive disorders. In K.M. Heilman & E. Valenstein (Eds.). *Clinical neuropsychology*. New York: Oxford University Press.

Benton, A.L., & Van Allen, M.W. (1973). *Test of facial recognition manual* (Neurosensory Center Publication No. 287). University of Iowa, Ames, IA.

Boller, F., & Grafman, J. (1983). Acalculia: Historical development and current significance. *Brain and Cognition 2*, 205–223.

Caramazza, A., & Zurif, E.B. (1976). Dissociation of algorithmic and heuristic processes in language comprehension: Evidence from aphasia. *Brain and Language, 3*, 572–582.

Chase, T.N., Foster, N.L., & Fedio, P., et al. (1984). Regional cortical dysfunction in Alzheimer's disease as determined by positron emission tomography. *Annals of Neurology, (Suppl.) 15*, S170–S174.

Corkin, S. (1982). Some relationships between global amnesias and the memory impairments in Alzheimer's disease. In S. Corkin, K.L. Davis, & J.H. Growdon, et al. (Eds.). *Aging, Vol. 19 Alzheimer's disease: A report of progress*. New York: Raven Press.

de Leon, M.J., Ferris, S.H., & George, A.E., et al. (1983). Computed tomography and positron emission transaxial tomography evaluations of normal aging and Alzheimer's disease. *Journal of Cerebral Blood Flow and Metabolism 3*, 391–394.

Damasio, A.R., Graff-Radford, N.R., & Eslinger, P.J., et al. (1985). Amnesia following basal forebrain lesions. *Archives of Neurology 42,* 263–271.

De Renzi, E., & Nichelli, P. (1976). Verbal and non-verbal short-term memory impairment following hemispheric damage. *Cortex, 11,* 341–354.

Duara, R., Grady, C.L., & Haxby, J.V., et al. (1984). Human brain glucose utilization and cognitive function in relation to age. *Annals of Neurology, 16,* 702–713.

Duara, R., Margolin R., & Robertson-Tchabo, E.A., et al. (1983). Cerebral glucose utilization as measured with positron emission tomography in 21 resting healthy men between the ages of 21 and 83 years. *Brain, 106,* 761–775.

Eycleshymer, A.C. & Schoemaker, D.M. (1911). *A Cross-Section Anatomy.* New York: Appleton.

Foster, N.L., Chase, T.N., & Fedio, P., et al. (1983). Alzheimer's disease: Focal changes shown by positron emission tomography. *Neurology, 33,* 961–965.

Foster, N.L., Chase, T.N., & Mansi, L., et al. (1984). Cortical abnormalities in Alzheimer's disease. *Annals of Neurology, 16,* 649–654.

Frackowiak, R.S.J., Pozzilli, C., & Legg, N.J., et al. (1981). Regional cerebral oxygen supply and utilization in dementia: A clinical and physiological study with oxygen-15 and positron tomography. *Brain, 104,* 753–778.

Freyhan, F.A., Woodford, R.B., & Kety, S.S. (1951). Cerebral blood flow and metabolism in psychoses of senility. *Journal of Nervous and Mental Disease, 113,* 449–456.

Friedland, R.P., & Budinger, T.F., et al. (1983). Regional cerebral metabolic alterations in dementia of the Alzheimer type: positron emission tomography with [18-, F]fluorodeoxyglucose. *Journal of Computer Assisted Tomography, 7,* 590–598.

Friedland, R.P., Budinger, T.F., Koss, E., & Ober, B.A. (1985). Alzheimer's disease: Anterior-posterior and lateral hemispheric alterations in cortical glucose utilization. *Neuroscience Letter, 53,* 235–240.

Grunthal, E. (1926). Ober die Alzheimersche krankheit: Eine histopathologische-klinische studie. *Z. Gesamte Neurol. Psychiatr., 101,* 128–157.

Hagberg, B. & Ingvar, D.H. (1976). Cognitive reduction in presenile dementia related to regional abnormalities of the cerebral blood flow. *British Journal of Psychiatry, 128,* 209–222.

Haxby, J.V. (1984). Neuropsychology and cerebral metabolism in dementia. In N.R. Cutler (Moderator), Brain imaging: Aging and dementia. *Annals of Internal Medicine, 101,* 362–364.

Haxby, J.V., Grady, C.L., & Duara, R., et al. Neocortical metabolic abnormalities precede non-memory cognitive deficits in early Alzheimer's disease. Manuscript submitted for publication.

Haxby, J.V., Duara, R., & Grady, C.L., et al. (1985). Relations between neuropsychological and cerebral metabolic asymmetries in early Alzheimer's disease. *Journal of Cerebral Blood Flow and Metabolism, 5,* 193–200.

Hays, W.L. (1973). *Statistics for the social sciences* (2nd ed.). New York: Holt, Rinehart, and Winston.

Heilman, K.M., Scholes, R., & Watson, R.T. (1976). Defects of immediate memory in Broca's and conduction aphasia, *Brain and Language, 3,* 201–208.

Huang, S.-C., Phelps, M.E., & Hoffman, E.J., et al. (1980). Noninvasive determination of local cerebral metabolic rate of glucose in man. *American Journal of Physiology, 238,* E69–E82.

Jamada, M., Mehraein, P. (1968). Verteilungsmuster der senilen Veränderungen im Gehirn: die Beteiligung des limibischen Systems bei hirnatrophischen Prozessen des Seniums und bei Morbus Alzheimer. *Arch. Psychiatr. Nervenkr., 211,* 308–324.

Kaplan, E., Goodglass, H., & Weintraub. S. (1976). *Boston naming test (experimental version).* Boston: Boston Veterans Administration Medical Center.

Kemper, T. (1984). Neuroanatomical and neuropathological changes in normal aging and dementia. In M.L. Albert (Ed.). *Clinical neurology of aging.* New York: Oxford University Press.

Koss, E., Friedland, R.P., Ober, B.A., & Jagust, W.J. (1985). Differences in lateral hemispheric asymmetries of glucose utilization between early- and late-onset Alzheimer-type dementia. *American Journal of Psychiatry, 142,* 638–640.

Mattis, S. (1976). Mental status examination for organic mental syndrome in the elderly patient. In L. Bellack & T.B. Karasu (Eds.). *Geriatric psychiatry.* New York: Grune and Stratton.

McKhann, G., Drachman, D., Folstein, M., et al. (1984). Clinical diagnosis of Alzheimer's disease: Report of the NINCDS-ADRDA work group under the auspices of Department of Health and Human Services Task Force on Alzheimer's disease. *Neurology, 34,* 939–944.

Mesulam, M.-M. (1981). A cortical network for directed attention and unilateral neglect. *Annals of Neurology, 10,* 309–325.

Milner, B. (1966). Amnesia following operation on the temporal lobes. In C.W.M. Whitty & O.L. Zangwill (Eds.). *Amnesia.* London: Butterworths.

Milner, B. Interhemispheric differences in the localization of psychological process in man. *British Medical Bulletin, 27,* 272–277.

Mishkin, M. (1978). Memory in monkeys severely impaired by combined but not separate removal of amygdala and hippocampus. *Nature, 273,* 297–298.

Russell, E.W. (1975). A multiple scoring method for the assessment of complex memory functions. *J. Consult. Clin. Psychol.* 43, 800–809.

Sim, M., & Sussman, I. (1962). Alzheimer's disease: Its natural history and differential diagnosis. *Journal of Nervous and Mental Disease, 135,* 489–499.

Sjogren, T., Sjogren, H., & Lindgren, A.G.H. (1952). Morbus Alzheimer and morbus Pick. *Acta Psychatrica et Neurologica Scandinavica, (*Suppl. 82), 1–152.

Snedecor, G.W., & Cochran, W.G. (1980). *Statistical methods* (7th ed.). Ames, Iowa: Iowa State University Press.

Tellegen, A. & Briggs, P.F. (1967). Old wine in new skins: Grouping Wechsler subtests into new scales. *Journal of Consulting Psychology, 31,* 499–506.

Warrington, E.K., & Shallice, T. (1969). The selective impairment of auditory verbal short-term memory. *Brain, 92,* 885–896.

Wechsler, D.A. (1945). A standardized memory scale for clinical use. *Journal of Psychology, 19,* 87–95.

Wechsler, D.A. (1955). Wechsler Adult Intelligence Scale. New York: Psychological Corporation.

CHAPTER 26

Differential Diagnosis Between Multi-Infarct and Senile Dementia of the Alzheimer's Type: A Comparison of Clinical and Brain Imaging Diagnostic Criteria

Th. Hovaguimian, A.L. Bersier, O. Juge,
J. Sanches, B. Grab

Twenty-five elderly patients with an established progressive global deterioration of higher cortical functions in whom a secondary dementia induced by somatic or neurological conditions, affective disorder, or drugs was excluded were assessed with a standardized schedule developed to record the distinctive clinical features reported to characterize either senile dementia of Alzheimer type (SDAT) or multi-infarct dementia (MID). The cases were clinically classified as SDAT or MID using an index derived from this schedule, based on the relative prevalence of respective features. The cases were also investigated with two different brain imaging techniques and independently classified as SDAT or MID on the basis of a brain imaging index derived from the findings of the computerized tomography (CT) and the regional cerebral blood flow (rCBF). Comparison of the clinical and the brain imaging diagnostic classification showed a good level of agreement: only 4 cases out of 25 had conflicting classifications. A combined diagnostic method based on operationally defined clinical and brain imaging diagnostic criteria is proposed for further validation.

Supported by a grant from The Swiss National Funds for Scientific Research.

It is nowadays possible to diagnose by evidence derived from clinical examination, laboratory tests, and brain imaging studies most of the secondary dementias (i.e., the cases induced by somatic or neurological conditions, by an affective disorder, or by drugs). However, differential diagnosis between the two major categories of primary dementias, namely the senile dementia of Alzheimer type (SDAT) and the multi-infarct dementia (MID),which account together for at least 85% of old age cases (Roth 1981), is made with certainty only at postmortem examination. Yet the clinical differential diagnosis is not a mere academic exercise; a reliable differentiation between SDAT and MID is a prerequisite for sound epidemiological studies, etiological research and therapeutic trials.

STUDY DESIGN

Several clinical features are reported to characterize either SDAT or MID; some brain imaging findings can also bring indirect indices in favor of one form or the other. Therefore, it was postulated that review and comparison of specific diagnostic criteria gathered through such complementary approaches should yield sufficient operational knowledge for the development of a differential diagnostic method. A study was therefore conducted in order to:

1. review the clinical symptoms reported to be specific to either SDAT or MID, and to develop an operational instrument to elicit, record, and interpret into a presumptive clinical diagnosis these characteristic features;
2. review the signs visualized by conventional brain imaging investigations that are reported to characterize either SDAT or MID, and to develop an operational method to assess and interpret these signs into a presumptive brain imaging diagnosis;
3. examine in a number of dementia cases the level of agreement between the presumptive clinical and brain imaging diagnoses; and
4. propose, should this level of agreement prove to be reasonably good, a combined diagnostic classification system.

Hence, as a first step, the signs and symptoms reported in the literature to have a specific diagnostic value of SDAT or MID were identified (Rothschild 1947; Mayer-Gross, Slater, & Roth, 1954; Ferraro 1960; Birkett 1972; Gainotti, Caltagirone, Masullo & Miceli, 1980; Gustafson & Nilson, 1982; Hachinsky, Iliff, Phil, & Zilhka, et al.

TABLE 26-1. Course Distinctive Features

Course distinctive features		Reported Diagnostic Value	
		SDAT	MID
Mode of onset:	Insidious	•	
	Sudden/stress-related	•	
	Sudden/confusional type		•
Early loss of:	Insight	•	
	Remote memory	•	
	Spatial disorientation	•	
Progression:	Steady	•	
	Stepwise		•
	Fluctuating		•
Reduction of speech:	Progressive	•	
	Sudden		•
Delusional ideas:	Persistent	•	
	Transient		•
Personality:	Changed	•	
	Unchanged		•
Mood:	Stable	•	
	Fluctuating		•
Suicidal tendency:	Present		•

1975; Perez, Rivera, & Meyer et al. 1975; Portera-Sanchez, del Ser, Bermejo, & Arredondo, 1982). These distinctive signs and symptoms may be classified as:

- Course-distinctive features (see Table 26-1)
- Mental status-distinctive features (see Table 26-2)
- Neurological-distinctive features (see Table 26-3)

Next, the brain imaging findings in dementia were reviewed. The computerized tomography (CT) and the measurement of the regional cerebral blood flow (rCBF) with the xenon inhalation technique provide structural and metabolic information on the dementing brain. While there are in the current stage of knowledge no specific CT findings in SDAT, some indirect or direct signs of cerebrovascular accidents (CVA) can suggest, in the case of dementia, the diagnosis of MID. The following operationally defined CT diagnostic criteria for MID were adapted from the recent literature (Bondareff, Baldy, & Cerry 1981; Bradshaw, Thomson, & Campbell, 1983; de Leon et al. 1983; Dietch, 1983; Kohlmeyer, 1982;):

TABLE 26–2. Mental Status Distinctive Features

Mental status distinctive features		Reported diagnostic value	
		SDAT	MID
Retardation		•	
Lack of insight into change		•	
Diminished emotional expression		•	
Ethical perversion		•	
Irritability		•	
Somatic complaints			•
Depression			•
Loss of emotional control			•
Diurnal fluctuation of consciousness			•
Nocturnal confusion			•
Cognitive impairment	Homogeneous	•	
	Patchy		•

- Cortical atrophy heterogeneity (i.e., noticeable differences in the degree of atrophy between the various cortical regions).
- Cortical atrophy asymmetry (i.e., noticeable difference in the degree of atrophy between one hemisphere and the other).
- Ventricular dilatation heterogeneity (i.e., a noticeable difference in the degree of dilatation between the ventricles of the same hemisphere).
- Ventricular dilatation asymmetry (i.e., a noticeable difference in the degree of dilatation between the ventricles of one hemisphere and those of the other).

TABLE 26–3. Neurological Distinctive Features

Distinctive neurological signs and symptoms			Reported diagnostic value	
			SDAT	MID
Epileptic seizures:	Onset in the course of dementia	Early		•
		Late	•	
	Clinical type	Partial departure		•
		Right away generalized	•	
Cerebrovascular:	Risk factors			•
	Actual antecedents			•
Neurological signs:	Focal			•
	Diffuse		•	
Kluver-Bucy syndrome			•	
Specific language disorders			•	

• Vascular foci, indicated by the presence of localized decrease in density.

The review of rCBF findings in dementia showed no other agreed-upon criteria reported as specific to SDAT. A number of findings, on the other hand, are suggestive, in the presence of dementia, of MID diagnosis. These findings in recent literature (Alavi, Ferris, & Wolf et al., 1980; Baer, Faibish, & Mayer et al., 1976; Ingvar & Gustafson, 1970; Kuhl, 1983; Lavy, Melamed, & Benton et al., 1978; Lenzi & Jones, 1980; Obrist, Chivian, Conquvist, & Ingvar, 1970; Simard, Olsen, & Paulson et al., 1971; Sokolof, 1978) were operationally defined as follows:

• Heterogeneity of regional blood flow (i.e., a noticeable blood flow difference between the various cortical regions of the same hemisphere).
• Asymmetry of regional blood flow (i.e., a noticeable blood flow difference between regions of one hemisphere and the other.
• Uncoupling of cortical atrophy and cerebral blood flow (i.e., an increased blood flow in a region with a significant atrophy).

Methods

Instruments. A semistructured interviewing guide, the Dementia Differential Diagnostic Schedule (DDS), described elsewhere (Hovaguimian, Bersier, Grab, Sanches & Juge et al., 1985), was developed to assess each one of the distinctive clinical items (see Tables 26-1, 26-2, and 26-3) on the basis of an interview with the patient and with an informant. These interviews occurred after a cognitive impairment had been established and delirium and secondary dementia excluded. The schedule is supplemented by a glossary defining the main items.

A form was also developed (Hovaguimian et al., 1985) to record the results of brain imaging investigations. The presence of vascular foci as well as cortical atrophy and ventricular dilatation is visually assessed on the CT scan by a neuroradiologist in each of the regions defined in Figures 26-1 and 26-2 and rated using a four-grade severity scale based on atrophy or dilatation: 0 = absent, 1 = mild, 2 = moderate, 3 = severe. On the same form, cortical blood flow, measured in ml/100 g/min, is recorded as the mean of the values of contiguous detectors in the regions shown in Figure 26-3.

Subjects. All cases were recruited from the hospital services of the University of Geneva Geriatric Institutions. Senior medical and nursing staff in these services were requested to identify cases with known

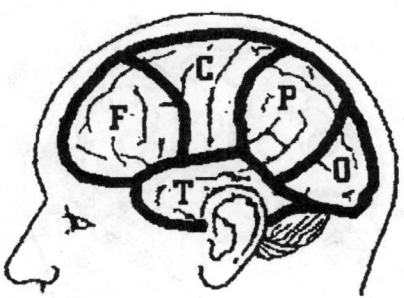

F: Frontal, C: Central, P: Parietal
T: Temporal O: Occipital

FIGURE 26-1. Cortical regions. F: Frontal, C: Central, P: Parietal T: Temporal O: Occipital

dementia. The identified cases were visited by the project investigator who first excluded those with delirium diagnosed according to the DSM-III criteria (APA, 1982). Determination of the presence of organic brain syndrome (OBS) was then made with a simple screening test (Isaacs & Walkey, 1963), consisting of 10 questions relating to orientation, memory, and fund of knowledge.

Twenty-eight cases with an established OBS were thus identified. The diagnosis of dementia in all cases was then confirmed by a psychogeriatrician. However, three of these cases were later excluded from

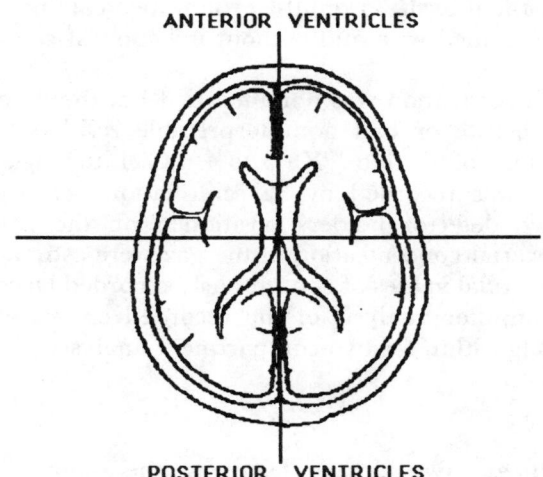

FIGURE 26-2. Ventricular regions.

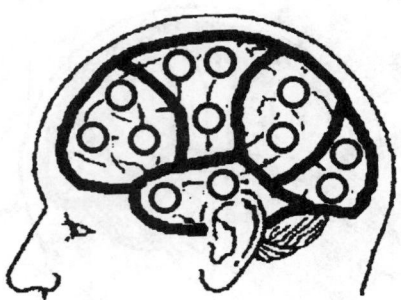

FIGURE 26-3. Number of detectors per region.

the study and referred to appropriate management because the CT scan showed a brain tumor in one, and possible occult hydrocephalus in the two others. Finally, 22 females and 3 males were included in the study; their mean age was 84 years with a range of from 68 to 96 years. Although most of the studied cases had entered the hospital for some somatic condition, none at the time of inclusion in the study suffered from any acute disease.

Investigation procedures. The DDDS was administered to the 25 subjects included in the study and completed with an informant in all cases. The 25 study patients also had a CT scan performed with a third generation translation-rotation delta-scan produced by Ohio–Nuclear. Several 15 mm tomographic slices were performed on each patient with a Gantry tilted by 15° from the orbital-meateal line. Each examination was performed with and without injection of contrast material (1.5 cc/kg).

The rCBF investigation was obtained in 19 of the 25 cases (6 were unable to cooperate or had noninterpretable results). The patients inhaled a mixture of air and ^{133}Xe 3 to 4 mCi/L through a face mask. The radiation was recorded by 32 scintillation detectors placed in parallel in two detector holders positioned on the patient's head. Changes of arterial concentration of the gaz were estimated by determining the end-tidal values of continuously recorded tracer concentrations. The computer analysis of the recorded curves was made by means of the algorithm for two-compartment analysis.

Results

Clinical features. Two clinical features, one reported to have an SDAT diagnostic value (retardation) and the other reported to have an MID diagnostic value (cerebrovascular risk factors), were present in almost all the patients. Advanced age is probably responsible for this finding. Psychomotor retardation is likely to increase with age; cerebrovascular risk factors were broadly defined, which enhanced the chances of the very old patients to present them.

Being highly unspecific in this study group, retardation and cerebrovascular risk factors were therefore ignored in the analysis. Some other features were never observed (epileptic seizures, Klüver-Bucy syndrome, specific language disorders, early loss of remote memory, and somatic complaints) and consequently also rejected from the analysis.

The remaining signs and symptoms of which 14 are reported to have an SDAT diagnostic value and 14 an MID diagnostic value seemed to have distinct patterns of distribution and were retained for diagnostic classification, although three of them were not observed in more than one patient (early loss of spatial orientation, suicidal tendency, and ethical perversion.)

The frequencies of these distinctive SDAT and MID clinical signs are shown for each patient in Table 26-4, first two columns. The third column of the table shows that the majority of the studied cases had between 8 and 12 distinctive clinical features. Only 3 cases were beyond that symptoms range, and 1 patient had more than 12 features.

As expected, the respective numbers of SDAT and MID signs observed in a patient tended to be inversely related. This trend for a negative correlation is clearly illustrated in Figure 26-4.

Brain imaging signs. It was decided in the data analysis to ignore the results relating to the occipital region because of the known poor reliability of both CT and rCBF techniques in the visualization of its structures and metabolism. Therefore, the ratings of cortical atrophy and ventricular dilatation and the values of cortical blood flow were recorded separately by brain hemisphere. The number of observations recorded for each patient is shown in Table 26-5.

Mean value and standard deviation of observations made by hemisphere provided—

- for ventricular dilatation and cortical atrophy, a measure of mean severity and of heterogeneity within each hemisphere; and
- for cortical blood flow, a measure of mean blood flow and heterogeneity within each hemisphere.

The total cortical blood flow was also calculated to allow assessment of correlation with cortical atrophy in order to sort the cases satisfying the "uncoupling" criterion.

Asymmetry between hemispheres was assessed with the following index:

TABLE 26–4. Prevalence of Distinctive Clinical Signs per Patient

Patient number	Clinical signs distinctive for SDAT (1)	MID (2)	Total number of clinical signs (3)	Clinical index (2) - (1)	Clinical classification (5)
1	4	4	8	0	Mixt[b]
2	3	5	8	2	MID
3	3	8	11	5	MID
4	4	5	9	1	Mixt
5	10	1	11	-9	SDAT
6	4	4	8	0	Mixt
7	1	4	5	3	MID
8	4	5	9	1	Mixt
9	9	1	10	-8	SDAT
10	5	6	11	1	Mixt
11	4	5	9	1	Mixt
12	5	1	6	-4	SDAT
13	8	2	10	-6	SDAT
14	8	5	13	-3	SDAT
15	9	1	10	-8	SDAT
16	5	3	8	-2	SDAT
17	1	8	9	7	MID
18	3	6	9	3	MID
19	3	9	12	6	MID
20	7	5	12	-2	SDAT
21	2	9	12	6	MID
22	5	6	11	1	Mixt
23	0	12	12	12	MID
24	7	2	9	-5	SDAT
25	3	4	7	1	Mixt

[a]Difference between numbers of MID and SDAT signs.
[b]See classification criteria p. 241.

$$\frac{1}{n} \sum_{i=1}^{n} \left| RHi - LHi \right|$$

Where RHi is the ith region of right hemisphere and LHi is the corresponding ith region of left hemisphere, n being the number of

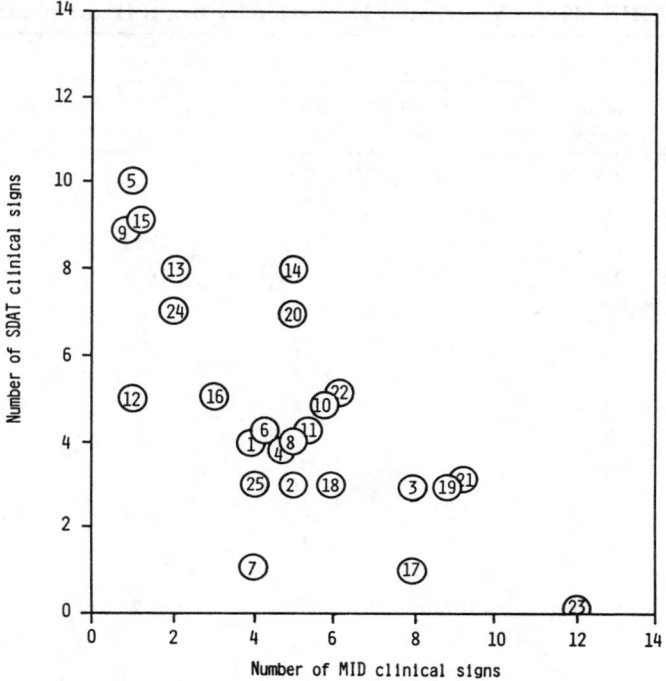

FIGURE 26-4. Distribution of patients according to number of MID and SDAT clinical signs.

The numbers inside circles refer to patient identification numbers.

regions (2 for ventricular dilatation, 4 for cortical atrophy, and 4 for cortical blood flow).

The measurements of ventricular dilatation, cortical atrophy, and cortical blood flow are shown respectively in Tables 26-6, 26-7, and 26-8. In 17 patients the mean severity of ventricular dilatation was between moderate and severe (over grade 2 of the severity scale); in 3 patients only this mean severity was between mild and moderate (un-

TABLE 26-5. Total Recorded Observations

	Right hemisphere	Left hemisphere	Total number of observations
Ventricular dilatation	2	2	4
Cortical atrophy	4	4	8
Cortical blood flow	4	4	8

TABLE 26-6. Ventricular Dilatation by Brain Hemisphere

Patient number	Right hemisphere		Left hemisphere		
	Mean severity	Heterogeneity	Mean severity	Heterogeneity	Asymmetry
1	2.5	0.71	2.5	0.71	0
2	3	0	3	0	0
3	1.5	0.71	1.5	0.71	0
4	2.5	0.71	2.5	0.71	0
5	3	0	3	0	0
6	2	0	2	0	0
7	2	0	3	0	1
8	2	0	2	0	0
9	3	0	3	0	0
10	3	0	3	0	0
11	2.5	0.71	2.5	0.71	0
12	2.5	0.71	2.5	0.71	0
13	3	0	3	0	0
14	2.5	0.71	2.5	0.71	0
15	3	0	3	0	0
16	2.5	0.71	2.5	0.71	0
17	2	0	2	0	0
18	1.5	0.71	1.5	0.71	0
19	2	0	2	0	0
20	1.5	0.71	1.5	0.71	0
21	3	0	3	0	0
22	3	0	3	0	0
23	3	0	2.5	0.71	0.5
24	3	0	3	0	0
25	3	0	3	0	0

der grade 2). Heterogeneity of the ventricular dilatation, assessed on two ventricular regions per hemisphere, was either absent or equal to 0.71. Thus, a symmetry in ventricular dilatation was observed in 2 patients only as shown in Table 26-6.

Table 26-7 shows that cortical atrophy was also rated as severe in the majority of patients. Heterogeneity in cortical atrophy was null in 16 cases out of 25, while asymmetry was totally absent in this study group.

In Table 26-8, the mean cortical blood flow is shown by hemisphere and for the total brain. It varied from 32.8 to 86.5 ml/100g/min.

TABLE 26–7. Regional Cortical Atrophy by Brain Hemisphere

Patient number	Right hemisphere		Left hemisphere		
	Mean severity	Heterogeneity	Mean severity	Heterogeneity	Asymmetry
1	2	0	2	0	0
2	3	0	3	0	0
3	1.75	0.50	1.75	0.50	0
4	3	0	3	0	0
5	3	0	3	0	0
6	3	0	3	0	0
7	1	0	1	0	0
8	2	0.82	2	0.82	0
9	3	0	3	0	0
10	2	0	2	0	0
11	2.5	0.58	2.5	0.58	0
12	3	0	3	0	0
13	3	0	3	0	0
14	2.5	0.58	2.5	0.58	0
15	3	0	3	0	0
16	3	0	3	0	0
17	2.5	0.58	2.5	0.58	0
18	2	0	2	0	0
19	2.25	0.50	2.25	0.50	0
20	2	0	2	0	0
21	1.75	0.50	1.75	0.50	0
22	2.75	0.50	2.75	0.50	0
23	2	0	2	0	0
24	2.5	0.58	2.5	0.58	0
25	3	0	3	0	0

Heterogeneity in cortical blood flow ranged from 1.3 to 25.8 ml/100g/min, and asymmetry from 3.3 to 15.8 ml/100g/min.

Discussion

Derivation of a clinical index. Based on the proportion of the distinctive clinical features rated as present and their respective diagnostic value, each case was either classified as MID, SDAT, or "Mixt" (i.e., presumed to have lesions of both types), depending on the relative prevalence of one or the other type of symptoms. For this purpose all items were given the same weight, and a simple quantitative clinical

TABLE 26–8. Regional Cortical Blood Flow by Brain Hemisphere

| Patient number | Right hemisphere | | Left hemisphere | | | |
	Mean flow	Heterogeneity	Mean flow	Heterogeneity	Total Mean flow	Asymmetry
1	—	—	—	—	—	—
2	79.3	18.5	66.0	11.0	72.6	14.8
3	69.3	9.9	74.8	6.2	72.0	11.5
4	—	—	—	—	—	—
5	—	—	—	—	—	—
6	59.3	8.7	59.0	7.6	59.1	5.3
7	59.8	6.1	58.0	6.4	58.9	3.3
8	79.0	17.1	74.8	17.2	76.9	7.3
9	—	—	—	—	—	—
10	44.0	6.3	41.5	2.9	42.8	3.5
11	54.5	8.6	54.8	3.3	54.6	6.8
12	61.5	11.4	63.0	10.1	62.3	6.5
13	52.5	1.3	54.3	4.2	53.4	3.8
14	60.8	19.3	48.5	13.5	54.6	12.3
15	86.5	25.8	83.0	21.0	84.8	8.0
16	79.3	13.5	76.8	9.1	78.0	6.0
17	51.0	4.5	49.5	3.9	50.3	4.5
18	55.8	11.6	52.0	9.1	53.9	5.3
19	—	—	—	—	—	—
20	73.8	4.6	65.8	6.2	69.8	9.0
21	59.5	6.7	62.8	6.1	61.1	3.3
22	—	—	—	—	—	—
23	69.0	8.9	53.3	8.8	61.1	15.8
24	32.8	5.9	40.3	9.2	36.5	12.5
25	47.0	7.2	46.0	3.5	46.5	6.5

index was used that consisted of the total number of SDAT items rated as present, subtracted from the total number of MID items rated as present.

The fifth column of Table 26-4 gives the value of this clinical index for each patient. This value varied from − 9 (a case with 10 SDAT and 1 MID features) to 12 (a case with no SDAT and 12 MID features). Patients with a positive clinical index of 2 or above were classified as MID. Cases with a clinical index between − 1 to 1 were classified as Mixt; and cases with a negative clinical index of − 2 or below were classified as SDAT. The results of this classification are shown in the last column of Table 26-4: 9 cases were classified as SDAT, 8 as MID and 8 others as Mixt.

Thresholds for brain imaging diagnostic criteria. The brain imaging measurements and their variations provided objective information on the range of values of heterogeneity and asymmetry in ventricular dilatation, cortical atrophy, and cerebral blood flow that might be observed in demented cases.

Based on these measurements and their ranges (the latter are shown in Table 26-6), thresholds were set for inter-regional differences in cortical atrophy and in cerebral blood flow, above which heterogeneity was considered as sufficiently high to be retained as an MID diagnostic criterion. A threshold was also set above which a difference between the dilatation of anterior and posterior region ventricles could be considered as a heterogeneity in the sense of an MID diagnostic criterion.

Similarly, thresholds were set above which interhemispheric differences in cortical blood flow and ventricular dilatation could be considered as an asymmetry in the sense of an MID diagnostic criterion. No such threshold could be set for an interhemispheric difference in cortical atrophy, because in all the cases the degree of atrophy was the same in each hemisphere and the range of variation was null. The thresholds shown in Table 26-6 have been fixed slightly over the central value of the respective parameter's range; for the purposes of this study, the central value has been assumed to reflect the normative data in dementia.

The uncoupling criterion, the distribution of patients according to their mean score of cortical atrophy, and their mean cortical blood flow is shown in Figure 26-5. Based on this distribution, the following thresholds were applied to identify patients with uncoupling of cortical atrophy and cerebral blood flow in a sense of an MID diagnostic criterion:

Mean score for severity of cortical atrophy ≥ 2.00
and mean cortical blood flow ≥ 60 ml/100g/min

The table shows that a brain imaging MID score that could range from 0 to 15 can be derived from the CT and rCBF findings.

Table 26-10 shows weights given for each of the above-mentioned criteria based on the authors appreciation of the diagnostic specificity.

Table 26-8 shows, for each patient, the weights allocated whenever one of the various brain imaging MID criteria was present. The brain imaging diagnostic classification, given in the last column of the table, is based on the total MID score (sum of individual weights of present criteria): Patients with a total MID score of 6 and above were classified as MID, while those with a score of 0 to 5 were classified as SDAT.

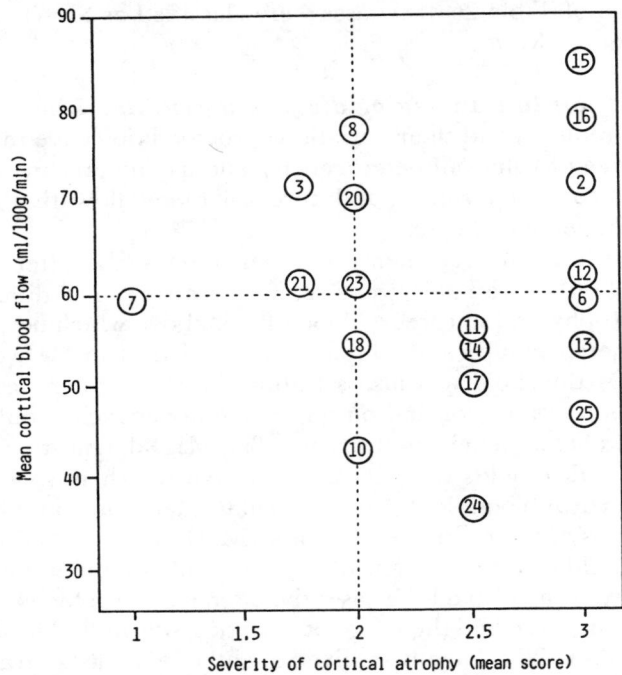

Figure 26-5. Distribution of patients according to cortical atrophy, severity, and cortical blood flow.

Numbers inside circles refer to patient identification numbers.

Comparison of brain imaging and clinical diagnostic classifications. Table 26-11 shows proposed diagnostic conclusions based on the combination of clinical and brain imaging classifications.

Table 26-12 shows the patients classified according to these rules into four high-probability diagnostic categories which are: MID, SDAT,

TABLE 26-9. Identification of Heterogeneity and Asymmetry as MID Diagnostic Criteria in Brain Imaging Findings

Brain imaging parameter	Heterogeneity		Asymmetry	
	Range	MID threshold level	Range	MID threshold level
Cortical atrophy	0-0.82	≥ 0.50	0-0	—
Ventricular dilatation	0-0.71	≥ 0.71	0-1.0	≥ 0.5
Cortical blood flow	1.3-25.8	≥ 16.0	3.3-15.8	≥ 10.0

TABLE 26–10. Diagnostic Criterion Weights

Criterion	Weight
Ventricular dilatation heterogeneity and/or asymmetry	1
Cortical atrophy heterogeneity and/or asymmetry	2
Cortical blood flow heterogeneity and/or asymmetry	3
Uncoupling of cortical atrophy and blood flow	4
Vascular foci (one or more)	5

MID/SDAT (Mixt predominantly MID), SDAT/MID (Mixt predominantly SDAT), and one unclassified category. The distribution of patients according to their clinical signs index (from Table 26-4) and their brain imaging MID score (from Table 26-13) is shown in Figure 26-6, showing the cut off for each of these parameters as separate diagnostic groups. In this distribution, only 4 cases (patients number 14, 15, 18, and 21) out of 25 fell into conflicting diagnostic categories.

CONCLUSIONS

Further research is needed to examine the diagnostic specificity of the various clinical features retained to characterize SDAT and MID in a larger and more age-diversified group. Similarly, the thresholds set to define the brain imaging findings as MID diagnostic criteria deserve to be based on normative data established from a larger demented subject pool. Nevertheless the good agreement between the diagnoses reached through the clinical and the brain imaging investigations, which was observed in 21 of the 25 studied cases, suggests some validity of the diagnostic criteria developed for each of these approaches.

Therefore, an instrument that encompasses the various assessments and their interpretation rules for differential diagnosis has been tenta-

TABLE 26–11. Diagnostic Conclusions

Single method classification		Diagnostic conclusion
Brain imaging	Clinical	
MID	MID	MID
SDAT	SDAT	SDAT
SDAT	Mixt	SDAT/MID
MID	Mixt	MID/SDAT
MID	SDAT	unclassified
SDAT	MID	unclassified

TABLE 26–12. Comparison of Brain Imaging and Clinical Diagnostic Classifications

| Patient number | Brain imaging | | Clinical | | |
	MID score	Classification	Index	Classification	Conclusion
1	1	SDAT	0	Mixt	SDAT/MID
2	7	MID	2	MID	MID
3	6	MID	5	MID	MID
4	6	MID	1	Mixt	MID/SDAT
5	0	SDAT	-9	SDAT	SDAT
6	0	SDAT	0	Mixt	SDAT/MID
7	6	MID	3	MID	MID
8	9	MID	1	Mixt	MID/SDAT
9	0	SDAT	-8	SDAT	SDAT
10	0	SDAT	1	Mixt	SDAT/MID
11	3	SDAT	1	Mixt	SDAT/MID
12	5	SDAT	-4	SDAT	SDAT
13	0	SDAT	-6	SDAT	SDAT
14	6	MID	-3	SDAT	Unclassified
15	7	MID	-8	SDAT	Unclassified
16	5	SDAT	-2	SDAT	SDAT
17	7	MID	7	MID	MID
18	1	SDAT	3	MID	Unclassified
19	7	MID	6	MID	MID
20	5	SDAT	-2	SDAT	SDAT
21	2	SDAT	6	MID	Unclassified
22	2	SDAT	1	Mixt	SDAT/MID
23	8	MID	12	MID	MID
24	5	SDAT	-5	SDAT	SDAT
25	0	SDAT	1	Mixt	SDAT/MID

tively proposed (Hovaguimian et al., 1985). This instrument allows the determination of a high-probability diagnosis of SDAT or MID in a case with a primary dementia using indices derived from conventional investigations. These indices are based on assessment of clearly defined course, mental status, and neurological features, and of signs in the CT and rCBF examinations.

The instrument is proposed for further validation. More specifically its differential diagnostic power needs to be cross-validated against other diagnostic techniques such as independent clinical classification

TABLE 26-13. MID Scores According to Brain Imaging Findings

| | Heterogeneity and/or asymmetry in | | | | Presence of | | |
Patient number	Ventricular dilatation	Cortical atrophy (CA)	Cortical blood flow (CBF)	Uncoupling between CA and CBF	Vascular foci	Total MID score	Brain imaging classification
1	1		—	—		1	SDAT
2			3	4		7	MID
3	1	2	3			6	MID
4	1		—	—	5	6	MID
5			—	—		0	SDAT
6						0	SDAT
7	1				5	6	MID
8		2	3	4		9	MID
9			—	—		0	SDAT
10						0	SDAT
11	1	2				3	SDAT
12	1			4		5	SDAT
13						0	SDAT
14	1	2	3			6	MID
15			3	4		7	MID
16	1			4		5	SDAT
17		2			5	7	MID
18	1					1	SDAT
19		2	—	—	5	7	MID
20	1			4		5	SDAT
21		2				2	SDAT
22		2	—	—		2	SDAT
23	1		3	4		8	MID
24		2	3			5	SDAT
25						0	SDAT

Note: The sign (-) indicates that CBF was not measured.

by experienced psychogeriatricians, diagnostic presumptions obtained through different brain imaging techniques (e.g., positron emission tomography), and objective postmortem studies. It might also be envisaged to undertake a cross-validation study using, whenever possible, a combination of the above-mentioned techniques.

Once further validated, a simplified "field" version of the instrument, based only on the most specific clinical features, might be developed for use in instances where brain imaging investigations are not accessible or not desirable.

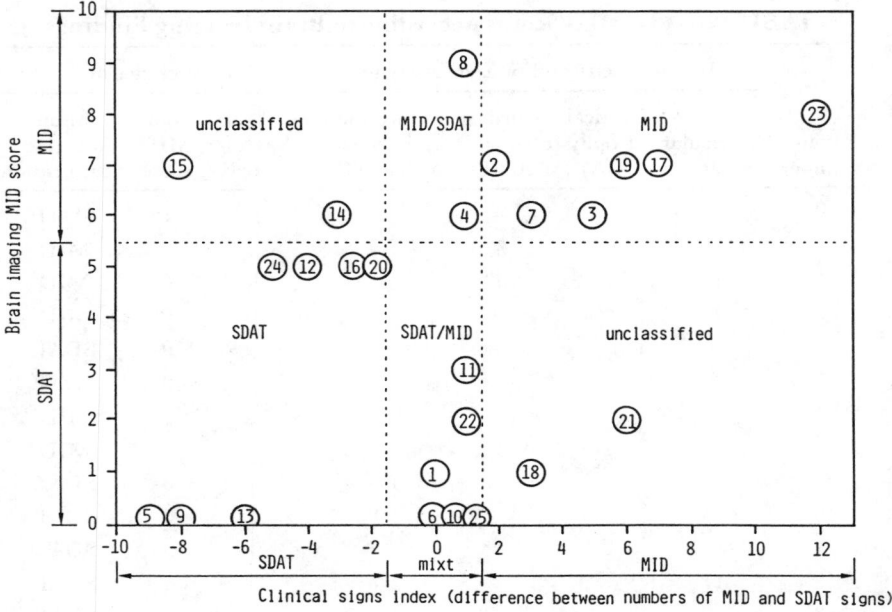

FIGURE 26-6. Distribution of patients according to clinical signs index and brain imaging MID score. Numbers inside the circles refer to the patient identification numbers.

REFERENCES

Alavi, A., Ferris, S., & Wolf, A. et al. (1980). Determination of cerebral metabolism in senile dementia using f-18 deoxyglucose and positron emission tomography. *Journal of Nuclear Medicine, 21,* 21.

American Psychiatric Association. (1982). *Diagnostic and statistical manual of mental disorders.* (3rd ed.). Washington, DC: Author.

Baer, P.E., Faibish, G., & Meyer, J.S. et al. (1976). Neuropsychological correlates of hemispheric and regional cerebral blood flow in dementia. In: *Cerebral vascular disease* (pp. 100—106). Stuttgart: Thieme.

Birkett, D.P. (1972). The psychiatric differentiation of senility and arteriosclerosis. *British Journal of Psychiatry, 120,* 321–325.

Bondareff, W., Baldy R., & Cerry R. (1981). Quantitative computed tomography in senile dementia. *Archives of General Psychiatry, 38,* 1365–1368.

Bradshaw, J.R., et al. (1983). Computed tomography in the investigation of dementia. *British Medical Journal, 286* (6361), 277–280.

de Leon, M.J., & George, A.E. (1983). Computed tomography in aging and senile dementia of the Alzheimer type. *Advances in Neurology, 38,* 103–122.

Dietch, J.T. (1983). Computerized tomography scanning in cases of dementia. *Western Journal of Medicine, 138*(6), 835–837.

Ferraro, A. (1960). Psychosis with cerebral arteriosclerosis and senile psychosis. In Arieti (Ed.). *American handbook of psychiatry.* New York:

Gainotti, G., Caltagirone, C., Masullo, C., & Miceli, S.K. (1980). Patterns of neuropsychologic impairment in various diagnostic groups of dementia. In L. Amaducci, A.N. Davidson & P. Antuono (Eds.), *Aging: Vol. 13. Aging of the brain and dementia.* New York: Raven Press.

Gustafson, L., & Nilsson, L. (1982). Differential diagnosis of presenile dementia on clinical grounds. *Acta Psychiatrica Scandinavica, 65,* 194–209.

Hachinsky, V.C., Iliff, L.D., Phil, M., & Zilhka, E., et al. (1975). Cerebral blood flow in dementia. *Archives of Neurology, 32,* 632– 637.

Hovaguimian, Th., Bersier, A.L., Grab, B., Sanches, J., Juge, O., Junod, J.P., & Sartorius, N. (1985). *Development of an instrument for differential diagnosis between multi-infarct and senile dementia of Alzheimer type based on comparison of clinical and brain imaging diagnostic criteria.* (Report to Swiss National Funds for Scientific Research, Grant No. 3.925-0.83). Bern.

Ingvar, D.H., & Gustafson, L. (1970). Regional cerebral blood flow in organic dementia with early onset. *Acta Neurologica Scandinavica* (suppl.) *43,* 42–73.

Isaacs, B., & Walkey, F.A. (1963). The assessment of the mental state of elderly hospital patients using a simple questionnaire, *American Journal of Psychiatry, 120,* 173–174.

Kohlmeyer, K.Z. (1982). Computer tomography contribution to the differential diagnosis of dementia of vascular origin (multi-infarction type) and primary degenerative dementia (Alzheimer type). *Gerontology, 15*(6), 321–324.

Kuhl, D.A. (1983). Mapping local cerebral metabolism in stroke, degenerative disease, and epilepsy. In Ph. Magistretti, (Ed.). *Functional radionuclide imaging of the brain.* New York: Raven Press.

Lavy, S., Melamed, E., & Benton, S. et al. (1978). Bihemispheric decreases of regional cerebral blood flow in dementia: Correlation with age-matched controls. *Annals of Neurology, 4,* 445–450.

Lenzi, G.L., & Jones, T. (1980). Cerebral metabolism-to-blood flow relationships with respect to aging and dementia. In L. Amaducci, A.N. Davison, & P. Antuono (Eds.). *Aging: Vol. 13. Aging of the brain and dementia* (pp. 99–102). New York: Raven Press.

Mayer-Gross, W., Slater, E., & Roth, M. (1960). Clinical psychiatry, 2nd ed. London: Balliere, Tindall and Cassell, Ltd.

Obrist, W.D., Chivian, E., Cronquvist, S., & Ingvar, D.H. (1970). Regional cerebral blood flow in senile and presenile dementia. *Neurology, 20,* 315–322.

Perez, F.I., Rivera, V.M., & Meyer, J.R., et al. (1975). Analysis of intellectual and cognitive performance in patients with multi-infact dementia, vertebrobasilar insufficiency with dementia and Alzheimer's disease. *Journal of Neurology, Neurosurgery, and Psychiatry, 38,* 533–540.

Portera-Sanchez, A., del Ser, T., Bermejo, F., & Arredondo, J.M. (1982). Clinical diagnosis of dementia of Alzheimer type and vascular dementia. In: R.D. Terry, C.L. Bolis & G. Toffano (Eds.). *Aging: Vol. 18. Neuronal aging and its implications in human neurological pathology.* New York: Raven Press.

Roth, M. (1981). The diagnosis of dementia in late and middle life. In J.A. Mortimer & L.M. Schuman (Eds.). *The epidemiology of dementia* (pp. 24–61). Oxford: Oxford University Press.

Rothchild, D. (1947). The clinical differentiation of senile and arteriosclerotic psychoses. *Geriatrics, 2,* 155–165.

Simard, D., Olsen, J., & Paulson, O.B., et al. (1971). Regional cerebral blood flow and its regulation in dementia. *Brain, 94,* 273–288.

Sokolof, L. (1978). Cerebral blood flow and metabolism in the differentiation of dementias: General considerations. In R. Katzman, R.D. Terry, & K.L. Bick (Eds.). *Aging: Vol. 7. Alzheimer's disease: Senile dementia and related disorders* (pp. 197–202). New York: Raven Press.

World Health Organization. (1984) *Report on the consultation on development of a research protocol for the assessment of senile dementias.* (MNH/MEP/02.3/84) Geneva: World Health Organization.

CHAPTER 27

New Medical Technologies in Diagnosis and Treatment: Summary

Stanley I. Rapoport

New imaging techniques offer opportunities to examine organ function during life, in three dimensions and in time. Analytical techniques to deal with the large data sets must be developed, however, to allow us to identify characteristic patterns of health and disease. Furthermore, careful and detailed clinical characterization of control and patient groups is required before the full utility of many of the new techniques can be demonstrated.

This symposium summarizes recent studies on the use of various imaging methods to examine brain and heart anatomy and function in healthy aging and disease, and shows how the procedures can be correlated. For studies of the brain, a combination of neuropsychological testing, electroencephalography (EEG), measurement of cerebral blood flow with ^{133}Xe clearance, and of cerebral metabolism with positron emission tomography (PET) has begun to elucidate brain function in aging and dementia. Furthermore, computer assisted transverse axial tomography (CT) and nuclear magnetic resonance now can provide anatomical evidence of differences in brain anatomy during life with respect to both aging and neurodegenerative disorders, which can be compared, ultimately, with postmortem data (Buonanno, 1985; Creasey & Rapoport, 1984; Schwartz, Creasey, Grady, DeLeo, & Frederickson et al., 1985).

Imaging methods frequently produce a plethora of data with spatial and temporal coordinates about subjects in different clinical states. The results often are too complex to interpret simply in terms of specific aging or disease processes, or to be used to diagnose disease in any individual subject. Additional analytical techniques, therefore, are required to examine relations among the resultant multivariate data, so as to identify characteristic patterns.

Analysis by Sebban (1985) of the EEG attempts to evaluate electrophysiological variables in the aging brain. With respect to PET, Horwitz, Duara, and Rapoport (1984) showed that regional cerebral metabolic rates for glucose in healthy men at rest with restricted visual and auditory inputs have specific intercorrelations that are founded in known functional neuroanatomy (Luria, 1973). With aging, the number of significant intercorrelations between regions in the frontal and parietal lobes declines, although absolute regional metabolic rates are age-invariant (Duara, Margolin, Robertson-Tchabo, London, Schwartz, & Renfrew et al., 1983; Duara et al., 1984; Rapoport, Horowitz, & Duara, 1985). Even more dramatic is the loss of intralobular and right-left hemispheric correlations in Alzheimer's disease, when brain metabolism also falls (Horowitz et al., 1984). This loss corresponds to increased left-right asymmetries of metabolism in PET images of brains of patients with Alzheimer's disease, which correlate with differences in visuoconstructive as compared with language functions, which are subserved by appropriate right and left brain structures (Haxby, 1985).

The state and experimental condition of individuals during specific physiological measurements—whether stressed, at rest, sleeping, stimulated with specific drugs or with psychophysical stimuli, and level of specific sensory stimulation—can influence brain metabolism and must be defined if results from different laboratories are to be compared and comprehended. For example, Mazziotta, Phelps, Carson, and Kuhl (1982) showed that auditory and visual inputs markedly influence measurements of metabolism with PET in healthy subjects; stress and anxiety probably play a role as well (Reivich & Alavi, 1985).

Apparently conflicting results from different laboratories may be related to the health status of the subjects. Differences in health screening criteria frequently confound studies of healthy aging, where a "normal" population represents a population in which the distribution of disease reflects that in the general community, whereas a screened "healthy" population represents individuals who have been screened for disease factors that could influence the parameter measured (Duara et al., 1983; Rapoport, 1984; Creasey & Rapoport, 1985). For studies of brain metabolism or blood flow, such disease factors include hypertension, brain trauma, psychosis, cardiovascular disease, or endocrine abnormality (Dastur, Lane, Hansen, Kety, & Butler et al., 1963; Gottstein & Held, 1979). Because the incidence of disease increases with aging, healthy as compared with normal controls may show significant differences in the elderly cohorts.

For example, differences in performance on the Benton Visual Retention Test between normal and "very healthy" elderly have been reported (Haxby et al., in press). Studies of brain metabolism and blood flow in which clinical screening was scrupulously followed have reported no age decrements (Dastur et al., 1963; Duara et al., 1983, 1984; Frackowiak & Gibbs, 1983), whereas other studies have reported age decrements (Creasey & Rapoport, 1985, Gottstein & Held, 1979, Kuhl, Metter, Riege & Phelps, 1982).

Another issue related to studies of brain metabolism and blood flow is that the data often have a coefficient of variation (standard deviation/mean) of 20% to 25% (Reivich, Alavi, Greenberg, & Wolf, 1985), so that large differences among subject populations must exist to demonstrate statistical significance. The coefficient of variation can be reduced, in some cases, by examining ratios of measurements in individual brain regions, doing test-retest studies in individual subjects, or developing new techniques to examine patterns of functional activity (Duara et al., 1983, 1984; Horwitz et al., 1984). To statistically demonstrate, using a Z score, a statistically significant metabolic defect in a single individual, however, specific differences beyond 40% of the control mean may be required.

Ultimately, the new imaging techniques will have to be evaluated for both research and clinical purposes in terms of their cost and effectiveness. Positron emission tomography is now a demonstrated research tool and has found some clinical application in the diagnosis and evaluation of patients with epileptongenic foci, gliomas, Huntington's disease, and Alzheimer's disease (Di Chiro, Oldfield, Bairamian, Brooks, & Patronas et al., 1985; Haxby, 1985; Mazziotta, Wapenski, Phelps, Riege, & Baxter et al., 1985; Theodore, 1985). The general application of PET to clinical settings is doubtful at present because of its cost and because of the enormous expertise in personnel which is required to maintain a PET program. On the other hand, quantitative electroencephalography, CT, and nuclear magnetic resonance hold immediate promise for the diagnosis and treatment of disease.

REFERENCES

Buonanno, F. (1985, July). Paper presented at the XIIIth International Congress on Gerontology, New York.

Creasey, H., & Rapoport, S.I. (1984). Use of quantitative transverse tomography (CT) to evaluate brain and cerebrospinal fluid dimensions in healthy men in relation to age. *Maladies et Medicaments/Drugs and Diseases, 1,* 181–185.

Creasey, H., & Rapoport, S.I. (1985). The aging human brain. *Annals of Neurology, 17,* 2–10.

Dastur, D.K., Lane, M.H., Hansen, D.B., Kety, S.S., Butler, R.N., Perlin, S., & Sokoloff, L. (1963). In J.E. Birren, R.N. Butler, S.W. Greenhouse, L. Sokoloff &

M.R. Yarrow (Eds.), *Human aging: A biological and behavioral study* (pp. 59–76). (USPHS Publ. No. 986). Washington, DC: US Government Printing Office.

Di Chiro, G., Oldfield, E., Bairamian, D., Brooks, R.A., Patronas, N.J., Mansi, L. Kornblith, P.L., Smith, B.H., Sank, V. J., & Margolin, R.A. (1985). In vivo glucose utilization of tumors of the brain stem and spinal cord. In T. Greitz, D.H. Ingvar & L. Widen (Eds.), *The metabolism of the human brain studied with positron emission tomography* (pp. 351–362). New York: Raven Press.

Duara, R., Grady, C., Haxby, H., Ingvar, D., Sokoloff, L., Margolin, R.A., Manning, R.G., Cutler, N.R., & Rapoport, S.I. (1984). Human brain glucose utilization and cognitive function in relation to age. *Annals of Neurology, 16,* 702–713.

Duara, R., Margolin, R.A., Robertson-Tchabo, E.A., London, E.D., Schwartz, M., Renfrew, J.W., Koziarz, B.J., Sundaram, M., Grady, C., Moore, A.M., Ingvar, D.H., Sokoloff, L., Weingartner, H., Kessler, R.M., Manning, R.G., Channing, M.A., Cutler, N.R. & Rapoport, S.I. (1983). Cerebral glucose utilization, as measured with positron emission tomography in 21 resting healthy men between the ages of 21 and 83 years. *Brain, 106,* 761–775.

Frackowiak, R.S.J., & Gibbs, J.M. (1983). Cerebral metabolism and blood flow in normal and pathologic aging. In P.L. Magistretti (Ed.), *Functional radionuclide imaging of the brain* (pp. 305–309). New York: Raven Press.

Gottstein, U., & Held, K. (1979). Effects of aging on cerebral circulation and metabolism in man. *Acta Neurologica Scandinavica* (Suppl. 72), 54–55.

Haxby, J.V. (1985, July). Cerebral metabolic and neuropsychological abnormalities in mild, moderate and severe Alzheimer's disease. Paper presented at the XIIIth International Congress on Gerontology. New York.

Haxby, J.V., Grady, C.L., Duara, R., Robertson-Tchabo, E.A., Koziarz, B., Cutler, N.R., & Rapoport, S.I. (in press). Relations among age, visual memory and resting cerebral metabolism in 40 healthy men. *Brain and Cognition.*

Horwitz, B., Duara, R., & Rapoport, S.I. (1984). Intercorrelations of glucose metabolic rates between brain regions: Application to healthy males in a state of reduced sensory input. *Journal of Cerebral Blood Flow and Metabolism, 4,* 484–499.

Kuhl, D.E., Metter, E.J., Riege, W.H., & Phelps, M.E. (1982). Effects of human aging on patterns of local cerebral glucose utilization determined by the [18F] fluorodeoxyglucose method. *Journal of Cerebral Blood Flow and Metabolism, 2,* 163–171.

Luria, A.R. (1973). *The working brain: An introduction to neuropsychology.* New York: Basic Books. pp. 1–398.

Mazziotta, J.C., Phelps, M.E., Carson, R.E., & Kuhl, D.E. (1982). Tomographic mapping of human cerebral metabolism: Sensory deprivation. *Annals of Neurology, 12,* 435–444.

Mazziotta, J.C., Wapenski, J., Phelps, M.E., Riege,, W., Baxter, L., Fullerton, A., Kuhl, D.E., Bradley, W., Selin, C., & Sumida, R. (1985). Cerebral glucose utilization and blood flow in Huntington's disease: Symptomatic and at-risk subjects. *Journal of Cerebral Blood Flow and Metabolism, 5*(Suppl. 1), S25–S26.

Rapoport, S.I. (1984). Conclusions: Brain metabolism and dementia. In N.R. Cutler (Mod.), Brain imaging: Aging and dementia. *Annals of Internal Medicine, 101,* 355–369.

Rapoport, S.I., Horwitz, B., & Duara, R. (1985). PET scanning demonstrates that aging in man is accompanied by loss of integration of regional brain activity, without concurrent reductions in absolute regional cerebral metabolic rates for glucose. *Journal of Cerebral Blood Flow and Metabolism, 5,* (Suppl. 1), S119–S120.

Reivich, M., & Alavi, A. (1985). Effect of psychophysiological stimuli on local cerebral glucose consumption in humans. In T. Greitz, D.H. Ingvar, & L. Widén (Eds.), *The metabolism of the human brain studied with positron emission tomography* (pp. 305–313). New York: Raven Press.

Reivich, M., Alavi, A., Greenberg, J., & Wolf, A. (1985).Use of ^{18}F-fluorodeoxyglucose and ^{11}C-deoxyglucose for the determination of local cerebral glucose consumption in humans. In T. Greitz, D.H. Ingvar, & L. Widen (Eds.). *The metabolism of the human brain studied with positron emission tomography* (pp. 149–158). New York: Raven Press.

Schwartz, M., Creasey, H., Grady, C.L., DeLeo, J.M., Frederickson, H.A., Cutler, N.R., & Rapoport, S.I. (1985). Computed tomographic analysis of brain morphometrics in 30 healthy men, aged 21 to 81 years. *Annals of Neurology, 17,* 146–157.

Sebban, C.Y. (1985, July). Quantified EEG for the Study of the Aging Brain. Paper presented at the XIII International Congress on Gerontology, New York.

Theodore, W.H. (1985). Recent advances in the diagnosis and treatment of seizure disorders. *Trends in Neuroscience, 8,* 144–147.

CHAPTER 28

Prospects for Research and Technology Development by the Year 2000

Edit Beregi

The most important task in the coming years will be to improve the quality of life of the elderly. This can be approached by using new, promising technology and new research results to improve the aging process and postpone the most frequent diseases in the aged. In this respect the following possibilities are the most important: (1) to control life-style and risk factors, (2) to improve diagnostic procedures to diagnose latent diseases, (3) to treat chronic diseases at an early stage, (4) to develop new methods to treat chronic diseases, (5) to develop and use new drugs to improve mental function, (6) to prepare new genetically engineered drugs, (7) to use new prostatic devices to improve mobility and sensory perception, (8) to improve health education, and (9) to influence or inhibit biological age-related changes.

Modern technology and developments in medical diagnosis and therapy have increased life expectancy at birth and concomitantly have increased the proportion of older persons in our populations. The marked increase in the older age groups has occurred in consequence to advances in public health and living conditions, change in life-style, and reduced occurrence of infectious diseases. The patterns of disease and health status have changed dramatically. During past years the principal cause of death in the population has shifted from infectious diseases toward chronic diseases. Unfortunately, improved life expectancy has not ensured freedom from diseases.

The added longevity that has become the striking feature of the 20th century is to be regarded as one of man's great achievements, but like other achievements resulting from the growth of science and technology, it has its price (Neugarten, 1982).

LONGEVITY AND HEALTH OF THE AGED

The implications of increased longevity are not clear with regard to the future health status of older people. Some investigators believe that in the next few decades the large majority of the aged will stay well until about age 85; that there will be a very short period of debility (Fries, 1980). In this view, mortality at very advanced age will be due to biological age-related changes, independent of chronic diseases. There will be no great need, therefore, to develop new medical and social services for the debilitated. But there is a contrasting view stating that advanced old age will mean for the individual a decreased functional capacity and failure in several organs, and, therefore, science and medicine may continue to develop palliative means that will ameliorate the terminal stage (Brody, 1982).

Some authors suggest that the increased life expectancy is associated with an increase in morbidity and disability (Gruenberg, 1977; McKinley & McKinley, 1977; Neugarten, 1982). Other authors suggest that life extension will merely postpone the time of death without increasing the length of "vegetative" existence. The additional years of healthful lifespan could be added years of youthful and middle-aged vigour, which could be used productively (Strehler, 1983). In balance, we think, in agreement with other authors (Manton, 1982) that there is a greater potential to improve the quality of life through control and management of specific chronic diseases than had been previously recognized.

POSSIBILITIES TO IMPROVE QUALITY OF LIFE

As a result of research in the field of gerontology it was recognized that aging as well as longevity are determined by basic biological mechanisms that can be altered or influenced by environmental factors. That is, the genetic program is given, but it can be changed by environmental conditions. Today, while it is not possible to change the basic genetic program of aging, it is possible through environmental factors to improve the aging process and postpone diseases in the aged. This conclusion is based on the following considerations:

1. Control of life-style and risk factors can lead to increased life expectancy. The importance of nutrition, exercise, smoking habits, and alcohol consumption on different diseases and on age-related changes is well known.

2.   Modern technology will help to improve diagnostic procedures with noninvasive methods resulting in diagnosis of latent diseases.

3.   Chronic diseases can be diagnosed at an early stage and numerous diseases can be treated by adequate methods. Screening studies showed the effectiveness of treatment in hypertension at an early stage, resulting in a decreased incidence of stroke and ischemic heart diseases.

4.   New methods for treating chronic diseases are applicable in old age, too. For example, implanted chemical reservoirs can provide better control of therapy and organ transplantation can replace damaged organs.

5.   New drugs can improve mental function. This is one of the most important research field in geriatrics currently.

6.   New genetically engineered therapeutic agents such as hormones and interferon have uses in geriatrics.

7.   Prosthetic devices to improve mobility and sensory perception can enhance the ability of older adults to perform the activities of daily living and to maintain productivity in the workplace.

BIOLOGICAL AGE-RELATED CHANGES: POSSIBILITIES TO INFLUENCE THESE CHANGES

Presently, numerous studies in biological and gerontological research suggest that several mechanisms on molecular, cellular, and organic levels are responsible for the age-dependent changes. Some of these changes could be influenced in experiments. The most important are as follows:

Molecular Level

Changes in the Cellular Control Mechanisms. On the basis of intensive research investigations during the past 20 years the importance of DNA in biological aging has been confirmed. It has been established that age-related changes occur at the genetic level (e.g., loss of genes, alteration of the information content, defects in the regulation mechanisms, and the disorder of DNA repair mechanisms) (Platt, 1976). In addition, the quantity of ribonucleic acid (RNA) decreases, and the polyribosome/monoribosome quotient becomes reduced during aging (Dellweg, Gerner, & Wacker, 1968).

It has been found that these changes can be influenced by pyritinol treatment, which causes an increase of RNA in old animals. At the same time, pyracetam administration enhances protein synthesis and simultaneously the lifespan of the animals (Platt, Gering, & Hering, 1973).

Formation of Cross-Links in Deoxyribonucleic Acid (DNA) and Collagen Molecules. These have been described by Verzar (1956). Cross-links are produced by the so-called cross-linking agents, which are always present in the organism (e.g., aldehydes, free radicals, dibasic acids). The cross-links inhibit free motion of the molecules and consequently the function of the cell. Cross-linking of DNA, which may occur with aging, could contribute to errors in transcription. The formation of cross-linkages in collagen molecules reduces elasticity of the connective tissues. Studies have shown that *Bacillus brevis* produces an enzyme that eliminates cross-links. The elimination has been demonstrated in cell culture and laboratory animals.

Formation of Free Radicals. Free-radical formation is considered of importance in aging. Release of free radicals, highly reactive due to the presence of free electron, occurs during oxidation and reduction (Harman, 1956). When cysteine, 2-mercaptoethylamine, and 2.2 diaminodiethyl disulfide were administered to middle-aged mice, it was found that the lifespan of the mice increased. Lifespan of middle-aged mice has been extended by means of vitamin C and E administration. In this effect their antioxidant action can be hypothesized (Kayser, Neumann, & Lavollay, 1972).

On Cellular Level

Accumulation of Various Cellular and Extracellular Substances. Senile pigment or lipofuscin formation in various cells, especially in neurocytes, heart muscle cells (Strehler, & Barrows, 1970), hepatocytes, and lymphocytes (Beregi, & Regius, 1983) are characteristic signs of biological aging. Extracellular deposits of amyloid also occur with aging.

Administration of centrophenozine to laboratory animals resulted in the decrease of lipofuscin granules in neurocytes and cells of the heart muscle (Spoerri, & Glees, 1973). At present, we have no methods for resolving amyloid.

On Organ Level

Nutritional Factors. These, too, play an important role in aging and in diseases in the aged (McCay, Maynard, Sperling & Barnes, 1939).

Animal experiments have shown that the lifespan of rats kept on restricted caloric intake has been substantially longer than that of well-fed animals (Fernandes, Good, & Yunis, 1977). Experimental evidence has also been obtained showing that very young rats kept on a calorie-rich diet will develop cardiovascular diseases and carbohydrate metabolic disorders. Animal experiments have shown that dietary restriction increases longevity and retards the development of chronic diseases (Cheney, Liv, Smith, Meredith & Mickey, 1983).

Decline of Hormone Secretion. This is well known in the elderly. Special attention has been paid to steroid hormones, thyroid hormones, and thymosin level. Mice that receive large doses of dehydroepiandrosterone show resistance to tumors and to obesity. Thymosin injection could maintain youthful levels of immune response throughout life of these animals (Fabris, Pierpaoly, & Zorkin, 1972).

Decline of Immunologic Function. Among the systems of the aging organism, the immune system has been given the most intensive attention. Our studies as well as those in the published data confirm the decline of immunological function in old age. At the same time, the close relationship of immune system changes with some of the frequent diseases of the aged such as vascular diseases and neoplasms has been noted (Bátory, Benzur, Varga, Garam & Ónody et al; 1981; Bátory, Ónody, & Petranyi, 1981; Biro & Beregi, 1980; Makinodan, 1977). These changes can be influenced by immunological manipulation such as by infusion of T cells, spleen cells, and bone marrow cells; by thymus implantation; or by adjuvant treatment (Makinodan, 1979).

CONCLUSION

To summarize, then, aging is a biological process and should not be interpreted, therefore, as a disease. The goal of our recent research is to eliminate chronic diseases. If that goal is reached, the active period of life could be prolonged and the terminal stage of life would be short.

Among the gerontological researchers extending all over the world, studies concerned with the understanding and control of the aging process and with documenting the connection between the aging process and the most frequent diseases in the aged might be considered the most important. As our knowledge of the nature of aging processes increases, we will inevitably increase the active period of the human lifespan. It now seems possible that by controlling life-style and risk factors for disease and by using the benefits of modern technology the productive years of life can be increased. It is of utmost importance to prevent impairment and disability, which are the consequences of the most frequent diseases in the aged.

It should be emphasized that increased quality of life as well as increased lifespan is essential. The goal of research and of modern technology is to increase the healthful lifespan of the aged and to maintain a vigorous, active, and productive life until death.

REFERENCES

Bátory, G., Benczur, M., Varga, M., Garam, T., Ónody, C., & Petrányi, G. Gy. (1981). Increased killer cell activity in aged humans. *Immunobiology 158*, 393–402.

Bátory, G., Ónody, C., & Petrányi, G. Gy. (1981). Analysis of the age-related refractoriness of T-lymphocyte reactivity in humans. *Mechanisms of Aging and Development, 15*, 337–347.

Beregi, E., & Regius O. (1983). Lipofuscin in lymphocytes and plasma cells in aging. *Archives of Gerontology and Geriatrics, 2*, 229–235.

Biró, J., & Beregi, D. (1980). The influenza vaccinations on human peripheral blood lymphocytes relating to aging. *Aktualle Gerontologie, 10*, 319–322.

Brody, J.A. (1982). Life expectancy and the health of older people. *National Forum*, Autumn.

Cheney, K.E., Liu, R.K., Smith, B.S., Meredith, P.J., Mickey, M.R., & Walford, R.Z. (1983). The effect of dietary restriction of varying duration on survival, tumor patterns, immune function, and body temperature in BlOC3f₁ female mice. *Journal of Gerontology 38*, 420–430.

Dellweg, H.R., Gerner, R., & Wacker, A. (1968). Quantitative and qualitative changes in ribonucleic acids of rat brain dependent on age and training experiments. *Journal of Neurochemistry, 15*, 1109–1113.

Fabris, N., Pierpaoly, W., & Zorkin, E. (1972). Lymphocytes, hormones, and aging. *Nature, 240*, 557–559.

Fernandes, G., Good, R.A., & Yunis, E.J. (1977). Attempts to correct age-related immunodeficiency and autoimmunity by cellular and dietary manipulation in inbred mice. In R.A. Good, & S.B. Day (Eds.). *Comprehensive immunology: Vol.1. Immunology and aging*. New York. Plenum Press.

Fries, J.F. (1980). Aging, natural death, and the compression of morbidity. *New England Journal of Medicine, 303*, 130–135.

Gruenberg, E.M. (1977). The failures of success. *Milbank Memorial Fund Quarterly, 55*, 3–24.

Harman, D. (1956). Aging: A theory based on free radical and radiation chemistry. *Journal of Gerontology, 11*, 298–300.

Kayser, J., Neumann, J., & Lavollay, J. (1972). Effects favorables exercés sur la longévité du rat Wistar rat divers types de restrictions vitaminiques. *Cromptes Rendus Acad. Sci. 274*, 3593–3598.

Makinodan, T. (1977). *Immunity and aging*. In C.E. Finch, & L. Hayflick Eds. *Handbook of the biology of aging*. New York: Van Nostrand Reinhold.

Makinodan, T. (1979). Prevention and restoration of age-associated impaired normal immune functions: Physiology and cell biology of aging. In: A. Cherkin, et al. (Eds.). *Aging* (Vol. 8). New York: Raven Press.

Manton, K.G. (1982). Changing concepts of morbidity and mortality in the elderly population. *Milbank Memorial Fund Quarterly, 60*, 183–244.

McCay, C.M., Maynard, Z.A., Sperling, G., & Barnes, L.Z. (1939). Retarded growth, life span, ultimate body size, and age change in the albino rat after feeding diets restricted calories. *Journal of Nutrition 18,* 1–13.

McKinley, J.B., & McKinley, S.M. (1977). Questionable contribution of medical measures to the decline of mortality in the United States in the twentieth century. *Milbank Memorial Fund Quarterly 55,* 405–428.

Neugarten. B.L. (1982). Aging: Policy issues for the developed countries of the world. In H. Thomae & G.L. Maddox (Eds.). *New perspectives on old age: A message to decision makers.* New York: Springer Publishing Co.

Platt, D., Gering, H., & Hering, F.J. (1973). Age-dependent determinations of lysosomal enzyme activities in the liver and brain as well as the measurements of cytoplasmic enzyme activities in the blood of piracetam-pretreated rats. *Experimental Gerontology 8,* 315–320.

Platt, D. (1976). *Biologie des alterns.* Heidelberg: Quelle und Meyer.

Spoerri, P.E., & Glees, P. (1973). Neuronal aging in cultures, an electronmicroscopic study. *Experimental Gerontology 8,* 259–263.

Strehler, B.Z. (1983). Summary of general discussion at the Second Plenary Session. In J.E. Birren, J.M.A. Munnichs, H. Thomae, & M. Morois (Eds.). *Aging: A challange to science and society* (Vol. 3). Oxford: Oxford University Press.

Strehler, B.Z., & Barrows, C.H. (1970). Senescence. Cell biological aspects of aging. In O.A. Schjeide, & J. de Vallis (Eds.). *Cell Differentiation.* New York: Van Nostrand Reinhold.

Verzár, F. (1956). Das Altern des Collagens. *Helvetica Physiologica Acta 14,* 207–211.

PART III
Demography and Epidemiology

CHAPTER 29

The Rate of Population Aging: New Views of Epidemiologic Transitions

George C. Myers
Kenneth G. Manton

Changes in mortality levels and their disease components require reconceptualization. The notion of an epidemiologic transition offers a reasonable summary of the observed gradual shift from infectious to chronic diseases and the emergence of aging populations. Mortality can be curtailed even in the absence of medical breakthroughs, and the country-to-country effects vary. The importance of non-life-threatening disease in epidemiologic transitions is discussed.

Population aging, a shift in the age structure of a population, is a direct manifestation of changes in the dynamic properties that affect population growth—fertility, mortality, and net migration. While increases in the numbers and proportions of older persons have been consistently observed in most countries of the world, the pace of population aging has become more variable in recent decades. This variability is a result of changing trends and complex interactions among the demographic factors determining population growth. Study of this phenomenon will lead to increased understanding of the future prospects for countries that already have experienced extensive aging as well as for those developing countries in which it has only begun.

Research supported by the National Institute on Aging (USA).

The characteristic pattern of population change over time is well described by a theoretical formulation referred to as the "demographic transition" (Bourgeois-Pichat, 1979). In this formulation, populations experience, or are expected to experience, shifts from high to low levels of mortality and fertility. The declines are, however, not expected to be synchronic; declines in mortality typically occur more rapidly and in advance of declines in fertility. The immediate effect of such changes is a sharp increase in population growth rates. Depending on the levels of mortality and fertility both before and after the transition, and the relative tempo of the declines, countries can be expected to stabilize at population sizes from 1.4 to 9.5 times their size at the beginning of the process (Keyfitz, 1977). In addition to the influence of the demographic transition on overall population growth rates, there will be shifts in the age structure of the population from a youthful to more aged population (Myers, 1985). The degree of population aging and the pace of the aging changes are determined by the exact relation of the timing and characteristic features of fertility and mortality declines. Migration may also be important in the transition.

Populations that have completed transitions to lower levels of fertility and mortality eventually reach a point where considerable population aging takes place. This is characteristic of many of the world's so-called "more developed" nations. It is at this late stage of transitions that "aging at the base" occurs—increasing *numbers* of older persons from previous large birth cohorts finally reach advanced ages and represent rising *proportions* of the total population (U.N., 1956). There is, however, a second phenomenon, "aging at the apex," that enlarges the older population both numerically and proportionally. This is a result of reductions both in mortality in middle ages that increase survival to older ages and, perhaps more importantly, by mortality declines at the older ages as well.

A theoretical framework for understanding the cross-temporal evolution of mortality conditions in countries at different stages of development has been formulated called the "epidemiologic transition" (Omran, 1971, 1977, 1982). In the most general terms, this transition is subdivided into three main temporal stages based upon the predominance of different types of mortality: (1) an "age of pestilence," (2) an "age of receding pandemics" and, (3) an "age of degenerative and manmade diseases." Two features of the transition through these stages are important. The first is the gradual shift from large declines in mortality at younger ages to large declines at late ages. The second is the shift from high levels of mortality from infectious, communicable diseases to higher mortality from chronic, noncommunicable diseases.

Thus, both changing mortality age patterns and disease patterns are emphasized in the current formulation of the epidemiologic transition. What is not elucidated are factors governing the pace of mortality changes and the extent to which changes may occur in the intensity of chronic disease mortality in the third (and "final") stage. Given continuing decreases in chronic disease mortality at advanced ages, an elaboration of the model is needed to include a currently emerging fourth stage. Specifically, mortality declines from many chronic diseases have been occurring in many of the more developed countries, especially at advanced ages. These changes involve both *reduced death rates* for some chronic diseases as well as *increases* in the *mean age* at death for many conditions. Consequently, questions arise about the age at onset of certain chronic diseases, their prevalence, and possible changes in the rates of progression of the diseases (WHO, 1984). The net impact of these changes in some countries has been rapid increases in life expectancy at advanced (65 +) ages and very advanced (85 +) ages, which in turn bears directly on different dimensions of population aging.

Earlier work by Manton (1982, 1984) and Myers (1978) has identified some of these changes and noted their importance for gerontologists. We will examine here in more detail the trends and timing of changes since 1950 and (1) several dimensions of population aging, (2) age- and cause-specific mortality patterns as they bear on life expectancy, and (3) the implications of these patterns for further elaboration of the framework of the epidemiologic transition.

Data for the analysis are from a United Nations volume *World Population Prospects: Estimates and Projections As Assessed In 1982* (1985) and the most recent WHO data tape files. Eleven countries are selected for study. They all can be classified as more developed countries, but include countries in various regions (e.g., Eastern Europe, Hungary and Czechoslovakia; Western Europe, France and Germany; northern Europe, Denmark, Norway, Sweden, and the United Kingdom; North America, Canada and the United States; and Japan). Although specific country reports on population aging and trends in mortality are available for a number of these countries, there have been relatively few analyses to date that have utilized standardized procedures for investigating cross-national temporal trends. One of our intents, therefore, is to examine similarities and divergencies in these trends among the countries using a standardized methodology.

TRENDS IN THE NUMBER OF OLDER PERSONS

Table 29-1 shows that all 11 countries showed large gains in the number of persons 65 years of age and over between 1950 and 1980. For example, Japan's aged population increased 155%.

A doubling of the 65 + population was also experienced by the two North American countries, Canada and the U.S., and the two Eastern

TABLE 29-1. Percent Change in Persons 65 Years and Over, 5 Year Periods from 1950-1980 by Country

Country	Percent Change						Change 1950-80	
	1950-55	1955-60	1960-65	1965-70	1970-75	1975-80	Total	Annual rate
Canada	15.6%	10.2%	12.1%	11.8%	15.3%	10.8%	104.0%	2.4%
United States	17.2	14.8	10.4	9.2	12.9	13.3	107.4	2.4
Japan	15.0	13.5	14.5	19.3	19.2	20.1	155.4	3.1
Czechoslovakia	13.7	9.9	18.6	16.5	10.5	8.6	107.2	2.4
Denmark	11.0	12.0	11.3	12.0	12.1	7.7	87.2	2.1
France	5.7	5.9	11.0	10.5	8.9	4.0	55.5	1.5
Germany, Fed. Rep.	13.0	13.1	17.1	13.7	10.5	4.9	97.2	2.3
Hungary	17.7	12.0	16.0	13.9	11.6	8.3	110.6	2.5
Norway	10.1	14.4	11.8	12.4	9.6	9.1	89.2	2.1
Sweden	10.2	13.0	9.4	12.2	12.6	8.2	86.2	2.1
United Kingdom[a]	6.3	6.3	6.6	9.7	8.9	5.3	51.6	1.4

[a]Includes Great Britain and Northern Ireland.

Source: From *World Population Prospects: Estimates and Projections as Assessed in 1982*, United Nations, 1985, New York.

European countries, Hungary and Czechoslovakia. The annual growth of the 65+ population ranged from 3.1% (Japan) to 1.4% (U.K.) Thus, the overall patterns of change reveal considerable variation among countries. It may be noted that these rates *far* surpass the rates of total population growth for these countries over this time period.

To better understand the variation in the rate of population aging, we examined the shift that took place over 5-year periods (Table 29-1). Contrary to expectations, the interval rates of growth *declined* over the 30-year period for most of the countries, reaching the slowest levels of growth in the 1975 to 1980 period. Growth rates only increased in Japan for the period since 1960 and in the U.S. since 1970. Caution should be exercised in viewing such trends as indicating a slowing of population aging for they may simply represent the increasingly larger numbers of older persons that must be added to the previous aged population to assure stable growth rates (i.e., because of the increasingly large base elderly population upon which the rates are derived). It can also be observed that differences between countries reflect the variable size of cohorts as they enter the aged population—and subsequently continue to age. The effects of small birth cohorts in the past and high cohort mortality (such as those due to war losses in Germany and France) are revealed in certain cases. At the same time, earlier large-scale immigration and large birth cohorts at the turn of the century in the U.S. and Canada, for example, help to explain the growth of the older population for these countries in the 1970s.

Thus, although the numbers of older persons has continued to grow in all 11 countries, the rate of increase differs both among countries and over time. There are some similarities between the decelerating trends since 1985 in both Western and Eastern European countries. In sharp contrast are the accelerating gains in Japan, in particular, and the U.S. and Canada. Examination of the reasons for these variations requires analysis of prior country-by-country trends in fertility and net migration, as well as relative conditions of survival by cohorts, not only up to age 65 but through the later ages. This is a research task beyond the scope of the current chapter.

TRENDS IN THE PROPORTION OF OLDER PERSONS

A second dimension of population aging is the rate of growth of the proportion of the total population that is elderly. Trends in these proportions are influenced not only by the earlier levels of fertility, mortality, and migration affecting the size of elderly cohorts but also by current levels of fertility.

Table 29-2 shows the current *levels* in the proportions of aged persons as well as the aggregate change in these levels over the 30-year period.

As for the growth rates of the numbers of older persons, substantial variation exists among countries in the 1980 proportions of elderly— from Canada at 8.9% to Sweden with 16.2% of its population at older ages. While the increases in the proportion of the elderly between 1950 and 1980 are generally consistent with the country's current levels, Hungary and Czechoslovakia, which showed quite large increases in the proportion aged, still have only moderate proportions (12.7% and 13.5%) compared with other countries.

The *trends* in the proportions of elderly indicate considerable cross-country variation as well, although the general trend was upward for most countries between the 1960s and early 1970s. This variation reflects a combination of factors, with fertility probably the main explanation.

TRENDS IN THE AGING OF THE OLDER POPULATION

It was noted earlier that a number of factors were involved in the growth of the elderly population. Among them is the change over time

TABLE 29-2. Change in the Proportion of Persons 65 Years and Over
in the Total Population for 5-Year Periods and
Total Period 1950-1980 by Country

Country	Change in proportion						1950-1980 % Aged	
	1950-55	1955-60	1960-65	1965-70	1970-75	1975-80	1980	Of total
Canada	—	-.2	.2	.2	.6	.4	1.2	8.9%
United States	.7	.4	.2	.4	.7	.8	3.2	11.3
Japan	.4	.4	.5	.9	.8	1.1	4.1	9.0
Czechoslavakia	.6	.4	1.2	1.5	.8	.6	5.1	12.7
Denmark	.7	.8	.7	1.0	1.1	.8	5.1	14.2
France	.2	—	.5	.8	.6	.2	2.3	13.7
Germany, Fed. Rep.	.7	.7	1.1	1.3	1.1	.7	5.6	15.0
Hungary	.9	.8	1.3	1.2	1.1	.9	6.2	13.5
Norway	.5	.9	.9	.9	.8	.9	4.9	14.6
Sweden	.6	1.1	.6	1.1	1.4	1.1	5.9	16.2
United Kingdom	.6	.4	.3	.9	1.1	.8	4.1	14.8

Source: World Population Prospects: Estimates and Projections as Assessed in 1982, United Nations, 1985, New York.

in mortality at older ages. One manifestation of these trends in survival is the growth of the *oldest-old* (e.g., 80 +) segment of the aged population. In Table 29-3 we can examine the growth in the number of persons 80 years of age and over, as well as the proportion of the total number of older persons who are at these extreme ages.

The U.S. had the highest proportion of oldest-old (20.4%) in 1980, with France, Norway, and Denmark following. On the other hand, small proportions of the oldest-old are found in Hungary and Czechoslovakia. The greatest gains over the 30-year period are found for Japan at 4.9% per annum and the U.S. and Germany next at 3.7%. Surprisingly low levels of growth for this group are found for the Scandinavian countries. Nonetheless, for all 11 countries the oldest-old has been the fastest growing age segment of the elderly population.

Trends over time show country gains in all periods, with the exception of Canada in the period 1975 to 1980. However, the patterns over time are once again quite different across countries. Growth rates were particularly large in the earliest period (1950 to 1955) for a number of countries, but thereafter fluctuating trends are commonly found. Japan, for example, had large percentage gains in the 1950s and then again in the period 1975 to 1980. The same was true for Czechoslovakia. Even in the latest period, five of the countries had low growth

TABLE 29-3. Percent Change in Persons 80 Years and Over for 5-Year Periods and the Total Period 1950-1980 and Percent of Persons 80 and Over in 1980 by Countries

Country	Percent change						1950-80		
	1950-55	1955-60	1960-65	1965-70	1970-75	1975-80	Total	Annual rate	Percent 80 + of total aged
Canada	17.4%	17.7%	30.6%	17.5%	18.7%	-2.1%	146.3%	3.0%	17.1%
United States	22.5	18.9	19.9	22.8	21.1	15.7	200.8	3.7	20.4
Japan	37.2	31.6	14.9	22.3	24.3	36.4	330.3	4.9	15.3
Czechoslovakia	21.6	12.1	14.6	12.2	9.4	21.2	131.9	2.8	13.8
Denmark	19.2	19.4	14.9	18.8	20.8	10.6	159.6	3.2	18.5
France	11.1	17.9	13.6	12.7	11.0	11.5	107.9	2.4	19.6
Germany, Fed. Rep.	29.6	26.7	21.6	13.8	13.6	16.4	200.6	3.7	16.1
Hungary	23.3	22.2	20.9	16.5	14.8	16.3	183.6	3.5	14.3
Norway	8.9	13.1	8.7	14.7	16.3	12.0	100.0	2.3	18.7
Sweden	11.3	21.2	11.9	16.9	18.2	10.4	130.2	2.8	18.2
United Kingdom	15.0	16.6	10.1	11.9	7.5	10.6	96.4	2.2	17.8

Source: World Population Prospects: Estimates and Projections as Assessed in 1982, United Nations, 1985. New York.

rates, including Denmark (10.6%), Norway (12.0%), Sweden (10.4%) and the U.K. (10.6%). Canada, as noted, actually had a negative change.

TRENDS IN LIFE EXPECTANCY: CONTRIBUTIONS BY AGE AND CAUSE

For these analyses we have made use of the most recent WHO mortality data tapes to construct life tables covering the period from 1950 to the present. Continuous time series data of the 11 countries were available starting from various years in the early 1950s. These life tables permit an examination of trends over time in life expectancy at birth and, using procedures proposed by Pollard (1982), to decompose the change in the life expectancy at birth, by the contributions made by age and underlying causes of death. To do so we have used the formula:

$$\dot{e}_0 - \dot{e}_0^{(t)} = \int_m^n (\alpha\mu_x^{(t)} - \alpha\mu_x)'_x{}^{(t)} \dot{e}_x \, d_x$$

In this formula $\alpha \, \mu^{(t)}$ is the force of mortality at age x due to cause α at the beginning of the period (t) and $\alpha \, \mu_x$ is the corresponding current value (in this case 1980). The age range is m to n and the differences are weighted by $'x^{(t)}$ the proportion of lives surviving from age 0 to age x, and $\dot{e}_x$ is the expectation of life at age x.

By using the 1980 life table as the point of reference, it was possible to relate the life tables at each 5-year point in time starting at 1950 (or the earliest date) to that of 1980. This made it possible to examine trends over the entire time period.

Table 29-4 shows the aggregate changes over the time period in life expectancy at birth for males and the contributions made at three different ages: (0 to 4, 5 to 64, 65 +).

Increases in life expectancy at birth are found for males in all 11 countries, although considerable differences exist in the amount of the change. The Japanese gain in life expectancy at birth over the 30 years for males is nearly 16 years (Table 29-5). For Hungary and Czechoslovakia there are sizeable *declines* in life expectancy past age 5. There also are small declines in male life expectancy in Denmark. Even Norway shows a net decline in life expectancy past age 65. For the other seven countries there are significant increases in life expectancy—even past age 65.

The corresponding values for females are presented in Table 29-5. From rather low levels in 1950, Japan's current life expectancy at birth for females is the highest (79.8 years in 1983) in the world. Rather substantial changes for both sexes are reported for France, the U.S., and Canada. For Sweden gains for females also are large, though the gains for males were relatively low. For all countries the total changes are greater for females than males, thus contributing to the growing gap between the sexes. However, for all countries (except Japan) the male gains in childhood (ages 0 to 4) were greater than those for females. At ages 5 to 64, female gains predominate especially for the three countries (Czechoslovakia, Denmark, and Hungary) where actual declines in survival for males occurred past age 65. For females, the percentages of the total gain over the period due to mortality improvement at later ages were all positive and, for nearly all countries, exceeded one third of the total gain. Only in France did the male contribution exceed 20% of the total gain in life expectancy at birth.

The patterns of change over the 5-year time intervals show considerable variation among the countries studied. In general, gains were large in the 1950s, mainly due to the large contributions at ages 0 to 4. In the 1970s the gains were larger at the older ages. Nonetheless, some contrasting trends are evident at older ages in Czechoslovakia, Hungary, and Denmark, where recent negative contributions are found for males and only small gains for females.

Examination of these temporal trends lends support to the contention that mortality levels at the older ages have come to play an increasingly important role over time in effecting overall changes in life expectancy at birth. Important variations exist among these countries, with the Eastern European and the Scandinavian countries lagging behind in terms of male mortality reductions at older ages. Characteristic trajectories of change may exist for certain countries, but from these data it appears that considerable period fluctuations tend to confuse the overall picture, especially on a country-to-country basis. To probe these phenomena more fully we must examine how contributions from different diseases have functioned in producing these mortality patterns.

The contributions made in changes in male life expectancy for six cause-of-death categories in the decade from 1970 to 1980 are presented in Table 29-6. Previously it was noted that the decade 1970 to 1980 was a period in which considerable mortality change occurred for a number of the countries. With the exception of accidents, the diseases chosen reflect chronic noncommunicable conditions that make up a large share of overall mortality, particularly at advanced ages.

Ill-defined conditions (which are a small proportion of total mortality for the countries examined) have been distributed, on an age specific basis, proportionately among all causes. In addition, it should be noted that there exist defined conditions, other than those listed, so that the sum of the contributions for the six diseases listed do not add up to the total net amounts.

TABLE 29-4. Gains in Male Life Expectancy at Birth and Contributions
from Broad Age Groups
for 5-Year Periods, 1950-1980, by Country

							1950-80	
Country/age	1950-55	1955-60	1960-65	1965-70	1970-75	1975-80	Total	Percent
Canada								
Total	1.41	.51	.63	.49	.53	1.70	5.27	100.0
0-4	.95	.39	.50	.28	.42	.36	2.88	54.8
5-64	.49	.13	-.02	.13	.02	.82	1.58	30.0
65+	-.03	-.01	.15	.08	.09	.51	.80	15.2
United States								
Total	1.30	-.06	.28	.24	1.61	1.38	4.74	100.0
0-4	.42	.11	.28	.29	.37	.30	1.76	37.1
5-64	.67	—	.02	-.26	.86	.74	2.04	43.0
65+	.21	-.16	.01	.16	.38	.34	.94	19.8
Japan								
Total	6.23	1.61	2.38	1.61	2.51	1.63	15.97	100.0
0-4	2.75	1.00	1.18	.54	.37	.27	6.10	38.2
5-64	3.25	.88	1.12	.66	1.22	.73	7.86	49.2
65+	.23	-.27	.08	.41	.92	.63	2.01	12.6
Czechoslovakia								
Total		1.61	-.55	-1.16	.76	.10	.76	100.0
0-4		.91	-.10	.25	.19	.33	1.58	207.9
5-64		.51	.04	-.91	.36	-.21	-.21	-27.6
65+		.19	-.49	-.50	.22	-.02	-.60	-78.9
Denmark[a]								
Total	1.02	.02	-.32	.74	.47	-.23	1.71	100.0
0-4	.47	.27	.18	.38	.44	.21	1.95	114.0
5-64	.32	.38	-.68	.03	.04	-.29	-.19	-11.1
65+	.23	-.64	.18	.33	—	-.15	-.05	-2.9
France								
Total	1.80	1.81	.40	1.18	.45	1.21	6.86	100.0
0-4	1.18	1.00	.50	.24	.19	.25	3.37	49.1
5-64	.58	.65	-.09	.40	.14	.40	2.07	30.2
65+	.04	.16	-.01	.54	.13	.56	1.42	20.7
Germany, Fed. Rep.[a]								
Total	.46	.48	1.12	-.36	.83	1.85	4.37	100.0
0-4	.62	.66	.88	.06	.34	.58	3.14	71.7
5-64	-.03	.05	.19	-.21	.36	.65	1.00	22.8
65+	-.14	-.22	.05	-.21	.13	.62	.24	5.5
Hungary								
Total		1.00	.76	-.38	-.10	-.75	.54	100.0
0-4		1.00	.62	.32	.24	.88	3.06	570.0
5-64		.27	.25	-.56	-.34	-1.34	-1.71	-320.0
65+		-.27	-.11	-.14	—	-.28	-.81	-150.4

(continued)

TABLE 29-4. (continued)

Norway[b]								
Total	.71	-.28	-.22	-.11	.71	.66	1.48	100.0
0-4	.44	.21	.25	.27	.24	.30	1.71	115.6
5-64	.30	.02	-.32	-.06	.26	.16	.36	24.2
65+	-.02	-.51	-.14	-.33	.21	.20	-.59	-40.0
Sweden[b]								
Total	1.04	.16	.50	.54	-.10	.61	2.76	100.0
0-4	.36	.12	.35	.17	.29	.13	1.41	51.3
5-64	.42	.26	.01	.03	-.16	.26	.82	29.9
65+	.27	-.22	.15	.34	-.23	.21	.52	18.8
United Kingdom								
Total	.95	.71	.30	.25	.92	1.00	4.13	100.0
0-4	.44	.22	.30	.06	.30	.28	1.60	38.8
5-64	.66	.24	.04	.27	.34	.37	1.92	46.5
65+	-.15	.25	-.04	-.09	.27	.36	.61	14.7

[a]Initial data are for 1952.
[b]Initial data are for 1951.
Source: Calculated from WHO data files.

Over the 10-year period, gains in male life expectancy at birth are found for all of the countries except for Hungary. Negative contributions are reported at both age groups 5 to 64 and 65+ for Hungary and Sweden, and at the ages 5 to 64 in Czechoslovakia. The proportional contributions to life expectancy that are due to changes at advanced ages are reasonably high (20% or higher), with the notable exception of Sweden. What disease patterns account for these data?

Cancer made relatively small negative contributions for males in most countries, including the oldest age category. In Hungary, however, the negative impact of cancer on male life expectancy was particularly large.

Diabetes is a relatively minor underlying cause of death, and it does not seem to have made any important contributions to life expectation of birth during the 10-year period.

In contrast, heart disease was a major factor in producing changes, especially toward increasing life expectancy at birth in Canada and the U.S. It is noteworthy that the contributions were very large at older ages. For Canada, 50% of the male life extension of 1.0 years attributable to heart disease improvement was a result of changes at 65+. For the U.S., of the 1.54 years added to male life expectancy from heart disease, 47% was due to gains at older ages. Although heart disease improvement was generally positive and strong, it contributed negatively for males in Germany, Hungary, and Sweden. In Hungary,

**TABLE 29-5. Gains in Female Life Expectancy at Birth and
Contributions from Broad Age Groups for 5-Year Periods,
1950-1980, by Country**

Country/age	1950-55	1955-60	1960-65	1965-70	1970-75	1975-80	1950-80 Total	1950-80 Percent
Canada								
Total	2.47	.96	1.15	1.13	1.28	1.50	8.49	100.0
0-4	.86	.35	.37	.30	.32	.33	2.54	29.9
5-64	1.25	.45	.23	.16	.21	.53	2.83	33.3
65 +	.36	.16	.54	.67	.75	.64	3.12	36.8
United States								
Total	1.90	.40	.66	.77	2.03	1.10	6.86	100.0
0-4	.36	.12	.22	.25	.30	.26	1.51	22.0
5-64	1.18	.18	.15	.07	.65	.48	2.64	38.5
65 +	.44	.10	.29	.46	1.08	.36	2.71	39.5
Japan								
Total	7.11	2.29	2.71	1.81	2.32	1.95	18.19	100.0
0-4	2.88	1.18	1.15	.48	.29	.22	6.22	34.2
5-64	3.90	1.37	1.35	.72	.96	.71	9.01	49.5
65 +	.33	-.27	.21	.61	1.07	1.01	2.97	16.3
Czechoslovakia								
Total		2.14	.09	-.32	1.02	.49	3.43	100.0
0-4		.82	-.09	.20	.19	.34	1.47	42.9
5-64		.79	.20	-.25	.43	.05	1.23	35.8
65 +		.53	-.02	-.27	.40	.10	.73	21.2
Denmark[a]								
Total	1.35	.46	.70	1.39	1.04	.24	5.18	100.0
0-4	.34	.24	.26	.43	.19	.14	1.59	30.7
5-64	.49	.32	.07	-.04	.29	-.17	.96	18.6
65 +	.52	-.10	.37	1.00	.56	.28	2.62	50.6
France								
Total	2.34	2.12	1.12	1.48	.82	1.57	9.46	100.0
0-4	1.00	.97	.41	.23	.14	.26	3.02	31.9
5-64	1.13	.77	.29	.34	.34	.40	3.27	34.6
65 +	.21	.38	.42	.91	.34	.91	3.17	33.5
Germany, Fed. Rep.[a]								
Total	.89	1.25	1.65	.16	1.12	2.04	7.10	100.0
0-4	.48	.62	.76	.13	.25	.46	2.69	37.9
5-64	.40	.42	.26	.01	.40	.58	2.07	29.2
65 +	.01	.21	.63	.01	.47	1.00	2.33	32.8
Hungary								
Total		1.42	1.34	.60	.31	.35	4.01	100.0
0-4		.86	.60	.30	.18	.80	2.74	68.2
5-64		.64	.52	.07	-.09	-.44	.70	17.4
65 +		-.08	.22	.22	.22	—	.58	14.4

(continued)

TABLE 29–5. *(continued)*

Norway[b]								
Total	.90	.51	.74	.87	.75	1.21	4.99	100.0
0-4	.33	.22	.17	.40	.12	.24	1.48	29.8
5-64	.58	.41	.13	.19	.10	.26	1.67	33.5
65 +	-.01	-.12	.44	.29	.53	.70	1.83	36.7
Sweden[b]								
Total	1.49	.74	1.26	1.21	.74	.93	6.37	100.0
0-4	.29	.14	.24	.23	.19	.12	1.22	19.2
5-64	.71	.50	.34	.17	.20	.25	2.17	34.1
65 +	.50	.10	.69	.80	.34	.55	2.98	46.8
United Kingdom								
Total	1.72	1.14	.65	.32	.75	.87	5.46	100.0
0-4	.37	.20	.25	.07	.23	.21	1.33	24.4
5-64	1.09	.43	.07	.14	.16	.25	2.15	39.4
65 +	.26	.51	.33	.12	.36	.40	1.98	36.3

[a]Initial data are for 1952.
[b]Initial data are for 1951.
Source: Calculated from WHO data files.

interestingly, the contribution was positive at the older ages, while in the other two countries it was negative.

Declining death rates for stroke over the period produced life expectancy gains for males. This was most notable in the case of Japan, which typically has had rather high levels of stroke mortality in comparison with other countries (Kono & Takahashi, 1985). Thus, 1.44 years were added to life expectancy, a large amount of which was due to gains at the oldest ages (63% for males). In spite of the rapid declines in stroke mortality in Japan, the 1980 levels remain higher than in most other countries. The potential for future decline is strong, therefore, and further life expectancy gains likely. Hungary and Czechoslovakia represent deviant cases among these countries with respect to change from stroke with negative contributions. Large losses at all ages in Hungary are true for males (0.4 years).

Cirrhosis presents an interesting case inasmuch as negative contributions are found for all countries except the U.S. and France. Although the impact on life expectancy from this disease is quite small, the uniformity of the trend is striking. For the most part, the contributions at the oldest ages are small.

Finally, changes in accidents have contributed positively to life expectancy. The major exception is Hungary. Small, positive contributions for ages 65 + are generally found, whereas the major gains are at the young ages.

The corresponding values for females are presented in Table 29-7.

**TABLE 29–6. Gains in Male Life Expectancy at Birth and Contributions
from Broad Age Groups and Diseases,
1970-1980, by Country**

Country/age	Cancer	Diabetes	Heart Disease	Stroke	Cirrhosis	Accidents	Total	Percent
Canada								
Total	−.12	.05	1.00	.27	−.06	.35	2.23	100.0
0-49	.04	.01	.10	.02	.00	.30	1.15	51.1
50-64	−.08	.01	.40	.06	−.04	.04	.48	21.8
65 +	−.08	.03	.50	.19	−.02	.01	.60	27.1
United States								
Total	−.04	.05	1.54	.40	.06	.37	2.99	100.0
0-49	.07	.01	.24	.05	.03	.26	1.40	46.9
50-64	−.01	.02	.58	.11	.03	.07	.87	29.0
65 +	−.10	.02	.72	.24	.00	.04	.72	24.1
Japan								
Total	.04	.03	.30	1.44	.00	.80	4.14	100.0
0-49	.05	.00	.04	.10	−.01	.63	1.65	39.8
50-64	.04	.01	.09	.43	−.01	.11	.94	22.8
65 +	−.05	.02	.17	.91	.02	.06	1.55	22.8
Czechoslovakia								
Total	−.19	−.02	.08	−.04	−.11	.32	.87	100.0
0-49	−.07	.00	.03	.00	−.06	.28	.86	98.0
50-64	−.16	−.01	−.06	.00	−.04	.03	−.19	−21.4
65 +	.04	−.01	.11	−.04	−.01	.01	.20	23.4
France								
Total	−.25	.04	.05	.43	.12	.32	1.67	100.0
0-49	−.05	.01	.02	.02	.03	.28	.65	39.3
50-64	−.15	.01	.02	.10	.04	.08	.33	19.6
65 +	−.05	.02	.01	.31	.05	.02	.69	41.1
Germany, Fed. Rep.								
Total	.02	.08	−.04	.27	−.08	.60	2.68	100.0
0-49	.01	.02	.05	−.01	−.07	.46	1.49	55.4
50-64	.00	.02	−.01	.06	−.03	.08	.44	16.6
65 +	.01	.04	−.08	.22	.02	.06	.75	28.0
Hungary								
Total	−.46	−.06	−.37	−.40	−.27	−.02	0.84	100.0
0-49	−.15	.02	−.23	−.07	−.12	.05	.40	−47.6
50-64	−.23	−.02	−.27	−.18	−.11	−.04	−.96	114.3
65 +	−.08	−.02	.13	−.15	−.04	−.03	−.28	33.3
Norway								
Total	.06	−.01	.39	.44	−.06	.26	1.38	100.0
0-49	.16	.02	.09	.04	−.04	.26	.79	57.6
50-64	.00	−.02	.09	.06	−.02	.01	.17	12.0
65 +	−.10	−.01	.21	.34	.00	−.01	.42	30.4

(continued)

TABLE 29–6. (*continued*)

Sweden								
Total	−.14	−.01	−.22	.10	−.08	.28	.50	100.0
0-49	.01	.00	.00	.02	−.03	.24	.57	114.5
50-64	−.03	.01	−.12	.02	−.04	.04	−.05	−10.5
65 +	−.12	−.02	−.10	.06	−.01	.00	−.02	−4.0
England & Wales								
Total	.13	.00	.14	.25	−.03	.17	1.92	100.0
0-49	.07	.00	.06	−.02	.02	.13	.90	46.8
50-64	.07	.00	.01	.06	−.01	.02	.39	20.4
65 +	−.01	.00	.07	.17	.00	.02	.63	32.8

Source: Calculated from WHO data files.

Over the 10-year period females experienced increases in life expectancy in each age group, except at ages 5 to 65 in Hungary. The proportional contribution to life expectancy gain at advanced ages is high for females being 63% in Norway. Again we may ask what diseases contributed to these increases? Only in the U.S., Hungary, and the U.K. are there consistent declines in life expectancy due to cancer. Diabetes had only a small, generally positive impact on female life expectancy. Heart disease was a major contributor to female life expectancy gains in the U.S. and Canada. For the other countries the gains were much smaller. Stroke produced increases in female life expectancy for all countries except Hungary. Cirrhosis contributed negatively to female life expectancy gains, except for the U.S., Japan, and France. Accidents tended generally to contribute positively to life expectancy increases.

In order to understand further how these causes of death affected survival over time we present in Table 29-8 statistics on (1) the proportion of deaths expected from the disease, and (2) the median age at death. These data for males and females are presented for three major cause-of-death categories for five countries.

It is interesting to note that except for Hungarian and Swedish males, there is a pronounced tendency for the median age at death to increase—even for cancer. Cancer also increased in the proportion of deaths it caused in each of these countries. The increases over this period were especially large in Japan, where stroke was also extremely high. The high proportion of death due to stroke and cancer in Japan was offset by the lower proportion of deaths expected from heart disease. Nonetheless, there has been an increase over time in the proportion of deaths expected from heart disease for both males and females and rather sharp declines since 1970 in the proportion from stroke. Other increasing proportions are found for Swedish males with

**TABLE 29-7. Gains in Female Life Expectancy at Birth and
Contributions from Broad Age Groups and Diseases,
1970-1980, by Country**

Country/age	Cancer	Diabetes	Heart Disease	Stroke	Cirrhosis	Accidents	Total	Percent
Canada								
Total	.12	.12	1.03	.50	− .02	.18	2.78	100.0
0-49	.10	.01	.02	.03	− .01	.12	1.02	36.9
50-64	.02	.03	.13	.07	− .01	.02	.37	13.2
65 +	.00	.08	.88	.40	.00	.04	1.39	49.1
United States								
Total	.05	.12	1.54	.66	.05	.20	3.13	100.0
0-49	.11	.02	.05	.06	.03	.11	1.21	38.8
50-64	− .02	.03	.27	.10	.02	.03	.49	15.5
65 +	− .04	.07	1.18	.50	.00	.06	1.43	45.7
Japan								
Total	.27	.04	.33	1.42	.04	.26	4.27	100.0
0-49	.11	.01	.02	.04	.01	.16	1.33	31.1
50-64	.13	.02	.09	.31	.01	.04	.86	20.2
65 +	.03	.01	.22	1.07	.02	.06	2.08	48.7
Czechoslovakia								
Total	.06	.04	.31	.07	− .02	.09	1.51	100.0
0-49	.04	.01	.01	.02	− .01	.08	.86	57.2
50-64	− .02	.01	.01	.04	− .01	.02	.16	10.3
65 +	.04	.02	.29	.01	.00	− .01	.49	32.5
France								
Total	.23	.08	.10	.58	.09	.18	2.40	100.0
0-49	.04	.00	.02	.01	.05	.10	.70	29.2
50-64	.06	.02	.05	.10	.02	.01	.45	18.7
65 +	.13	.06	.03	.47	.02	.07	1.25	52.1
Germany, Fed. Rep.								
Total	.30	.18	.08	.48	− .03	.26	3.16	100.0
0-49	.14	.01	.01	.01	− .03	.11	1.21	38.1
50-64	.07	.04	.03	.06	− .03	.03	.48	15.3
65 +	.09	.13	.04	.42	.03	.12	1.47	46.6
Hungary								
Total	− .10	− .11	.25	− .23	− .13	− .04	.66	100.0
0-49	− .03	.00	− .05	− .04	− .07	.01	.75	114.5
50-64	− .08	− .04	− .04	− .09	− .05	− .02	− .31	− 47.0
65 +	.01	− .07	.34	− .10	− .01	− .03	.21	32.5

(continued)

TABLE 29-7. (*continued*)

Norway								
Total	.13	.00	.46	.68	− .02	.09	1.97	100.0
0-49	.18	.00	.00	.04	− .01	.05	.55	28.3
50-64	.01	.00	.06	.07	− .01	.01	.18	8.9
65 +	− .05	.00	.40	.57	.00	.03	1.24	62.8
Sweden								
Total	.04	− .01	.41	.25	− .04	.14	1.67	100.0
0-49	.07	.01	− .01	.00	− .01	.12	.58	34.8
50-64	.01	.00	.05	.05	− .03	.02	.20	11.7
65 +	− .04	− .02	.37	.20	.00	.00	.89	53.5
England & Wales								
Total	− .07	.02	.18	.42	− .03	.12	1.62	100.0
0-49	.06	.00	.01	.02	− .02	.05	.74	45.2
50-64	− .06	.00	− .02	.08	− .01	.01	.12	7.8
65 +	− .07	.02	.19	.32	.00	.06	.76	47.0

Source: Calculated from WHO data files.

respect to heart disease and in Hungary for stroke among both sexes.

CONCLUSION

The cross-national examination of trends in various dimensions of population aging and mortality provides useful insights into the complex interplay of factors that operate in this group of relatively advanced nations. Although population aging is a pervasive characteristic of these societies, the pace of change is by no means uniform, whether measured by the changes in the numbers of older persons, the proportion they constitute within the total population, or the aging of the aged population itself. Demographic analyses should be directed to disentangle the factors responsible for the diversity evident over the past 30 years among developed countries and what can be reasonably expected in the future. However, it seems clear that a major element in this process, namely, changes in mortality levels and their disease components require reconceptualization.

The notion of an epidemiologic transition, as noted earlier, offers a reasonable summary of historical changes that brought about a gradual shift from infectious to chronic diseases. This shift was strongly associated with reductions in mortality at younger ages and increased survival of cohorts of persons to the later ages. As noted in our trend analyses, these improvements brought about life expectancy improvements experienced through the 1960's for the countries studied. In the 1970's, however, a new pattern has become evident, with renewed gains in life expectancy attributable to reductions in certain chronic

TABLE 29–8. Percentage of Total Deaths Expected From Specific Disease and Median Age at Death for Three Major Chronic Diseases by Countries

Condition/ year	Canada		Japan		Hungary		Sweden		U.S.	
	Percent	Median	Percent	Median	Percent	Median	Percent	Median	Percent	Median
Males										
Cancer										
1950	14.04	70.31	9.32	65.51	—	—	15.98	71.80	13.3	69.0
1970	19.27	71.30	17.13	69.11	18.54	69.52	18.93	73.42	17.0	69.1
1982	23.89	72.42	23.35	73.06	20.32	68.24	19.70	72.24	21.1	71.3
Heart Disease										
1950	36.55	73.73	7.13	70.98	—	—	26.71	76.28	39.9	72.3
1970	37.00	73.79	9.72	75.64	23.28	73.41	37.94	77.03	39.1	72.9
1982	31.97	75.49	9.76	79.78	22.90	69.61	38.66	76.79	32.5	75.3
Stroke										
1950	10.72	76.75	15.65	72.25	—	—	14.66	77.66	10.8	75.2
1970	9.69	78.77	30.21	75.28	13.38	75.63	9.57	78.76	9.7	77.0
1982	7.53	79.73	22.33	79.94	14.15	73.18	8.61	79.29	7.5	79.5

Females

Cancer										
1950	15.4	69.9	9.0	64.9	15.7	70.0	15.7	70.9	15.1	69.1
1970	17.9	72.6	13.9	70.6	16.5	70.8	18.6	73.7	16.0	70.9
1982	20.6	74.2	16.6	75.4	17.9	70.8	19.6	74.7	18.4	72.8

Heart Disease										
1950	34.1	78.7	8.4	74.6	27.6	78.4	26.9	79.0	38.8	78.3
1970	35.4	82.1	10.7	80.3	24.8	78.8	35.0	82.4	39.4	81.4
1982	30.8	83.5	11.7	84.6	21.9	78.4	33.2	84.0	33.9	83.5

Stroke										
1950	15.2	78.3	18.5	74.7	18.4	76.9	18.3	77.8	14.8	77.7
1970	14.9	82.9	32.8	79.3	17.6	78.5	13.4	81.8	15.4	82.4
1982	12.5	85.1	27.2	83.8	19.3	78.7	13.4	83.8	12.4	84.6

Source: Calculated from WHO data Files.

diseases, especially heart disease and stroke. Moreover, the median ages of death for most chronic diseases have been increased. These developments have stimulated what some have termed increased aging at the apex to complement aging from the base. This was manifested by reduced mortality at the very late ages, which has contributed to much of the growth of the oldest-old portion of the aged population.

A revised version of the theory of "epidemiologic transition" seems necessary—one that acknowledges that even chronic disease mortality can be curtailed, even in the absence of major medical breakthroughs or effective control over aspects of the biologically driven senescent processes. Our examination of mortality trends in the period of 1970 to 1980 also indicates that the patterns are not universal. Some countries appear to be "leaders," such as Japan, the U.S., and Canada and others are "laggards," such as some of the Eastern European and Scandinavian countries. The rapid improvements in heart disease mortality rates at later ages in Canada and the U.S. and stroke improvements in Japan suggest that further gains can be realized in other countries. Even the variant but largely negative trends found for cancer and cirrhosis point to areas in which improvement can be imagined. The different levels and trends in life expectancy between males and females also should be incorporated into a broadened perspective.

A framework for viewing the pace of changes would not be complete without mentioning that health interventions themselves certainly play a major role in producing these patterns. Transitions are certainly not inevitable or irreversible processes. They are subject to feedbacks from our social and political systems in which actions are taken to modify trends. Some of these interventions may in fact have unanticipated consequences. For example, medical and health interventions to eradicate or reduce the hazards from certain infectious diseases may have the consequences of promoting other diseases. Although the shift from infectious to chronic disease may be predominant, recent evidence of diseases such as AIDS, septicemia, and legionnaire's disease suggest that new emergent infections may increase in importance as other diseases are reduced. Finally, although we have focused on major diseases involved in producing death, we should recognize that other non-life-threatening (NLT) diseases may assume even greater importance in the future as population aging continues as a major force transforming societies.

REFERENCES

Bourgeois-Pichat, J. (1979). La transition demographique: Vieillissement de la population. In *Population science in the service of mankind* (pp. 211–239). Liege, Belgium: International Union for the Scientific Study of Population.

Keyfitz, N. (1977). *Applied mathematical demography.* New York: Wiley.

Kono, S., & Shigesato T. (1985). *Mortality trends in Japan: Why has the Japanese life expectancy kept on increasing?* Paper presented at the IUSSP Population Conference, Florence, Italy.

Manton, K.G. (1982). Changing concepts of morbidity and mortality in the elderly population. *Milbank Memorial Fund Quarterly/Health and Society, 60,* 183–244.

Manton, K.G. (1984). Mortality patterns in developed countries. *Comparative Social Research, 7,* 259–286.

Myers, G.C. (1978). Cross-national trends in mortality rates among the elderly. *The Gerontologist, 18,* 441–448.

Myers, G.C. (1985). Aging and world wide population change. In R. Binstock, & E. Shanas (Eds.). *Handbook on aging and the social sciences* (revised ed. pp. 173–198). New York: Van Nostrand Reinhold.

Omran, A.R. (1971). The epidemiologic transition: A theory of the epidemiology of population change. *Milbank Memorial Fund Quarterly, 49,* (4), 509–538.

Omran, A.R. (1977). Epidemiologic transition in the United States: The health factor in population change. *Population Bulletin, 32 (2),* 1–42.

Omran, A.R. (1982). Epidemiologic transition. In J.A. Ross (Ed.). *International encyclopedia of population* (Vol. 1. pp. 172–183). New York: The Free Press.

Pollard, J.H. (1982). The expectation of life and its relationship to mortality. *The Journal of the Institute of Actuaries, 109* (1) 442, 225–240.

United Nations. (1956). *The aging of population and its economic and social implications.* (Pop · ulation Studies No. 26). New York: Author.

United Nations. (1985). *World population prospect: Estimates and projections as assessed in 1982.* New York: Author.

World Health Organization. (1984). *The uses of epidemiology in the study of the elderly. Report of a WHO scientific group on the epidemiology of Aging.* (Technical Report Series 706). Geneva: Author.

CHAPTER 30

Cohort Aging and Support Network Help Capacity

Leroy O. Stone

This chapter deals with some of the consequences of the progressive reduction in the size of a birth cohort as it ages—called "cohort attrition." It will be assumed that the cohort forms an almost closed subpopulation. The main concern here is with certain effects of the impact of cohort attrition upon the average helping capacity of support networks for elders.

The general conclusion is as follows: Cohort attrition sets up forces that tend to weaken the average helping capacity of informal support networks. This weakening will have substantial effects in a number of areas, such as health, long-term management of functional deficiency, living arrangements, housing, and income for an affected cohort.

The age pattern of cohort attrition has not been stable recently. One of the reasons for the instability is rising life expectancy at the upper ages. Declining mortality rates at these ages, for a series of successive cohorts, help initially to delay the average age of marked acceleration in the weakening of support networks through cohort attrition. However, if the pattern of mortality decline is such that the male–female gap in survival rates at the upper ages does not, in due course, dimin-

Edward Pryor and Susan Fletcher have given helpful comments on the first draft of this paper. Jean Coward has provided editorial assistance and help with the literature survey. The views expressed herein are personal and are not meant to represent or reflect upon the positions of any organizations. The author is solely responsible for the contents.

ish substantially, the mortality decline will also help to increase requirements for extra family supports at the ages where one-year survival rates for men have failed to improve markedly. Thus, over the series of cohorts showing the mortality decline, the improving survival rates will tend to ease requirements for extra family supports within a certain range of ages, but will tend to increase those needs above that range.

The set of ages above this range will become gradually smaller as the upper bound of mortality improvement pushes toward the effective life span, also called "life of endurancy" (Myers & Manton, 1984) which is the age to which no more than one tenth of 1% of a cohort might be expected to survive. This conclusion rests, however, on one major assumption that is the subject of an important and unresolved debate (Fries, 1984; Myers & Manton, 1984; Schneider & Brody, 1983). The debatable assumption is that families with very old members will continue to be able to take care of each other at the rates now believed to be prevailing, even though the average age of such members is going up over the pertinent sequence of cohorts.

This assumption could be invalidated if the mortality decline causes a substantial increase in the proportion of survivors whose functional deficiencies are so deep that they tend to overwhelm family resources. The process of overwhelming family resources could be intensified if the mean length of life in widowhood does not go down substantially even though the mean age of death of a spouse is rising (which could well happen to a subpopulation of widowed women). In these circumstances, assuming the pertinent cohorts become large enough and numerous enough in a contemporary developed society, there will emerge a widely shared perception of major cost and social service delivery pressures. The phrase "social service" as used here is intended to cover a wide variety of supports, including health services and long-term personal care services. These pressures will likely be attributed to the "aging of the population," but are best measured and analyzed in terms of the experiences and needs of specific cohorts, since the composition of services demanded in the older population may change with the succession of different cohorts that are dominant within it.

It is feasible to identify several possible societal responses to the perception just mentioned. One would be to shift costs more fully to the direct beneficiaries of services, and leave those who cannot afford those costs to manage in whatever way they can. Another would involve expanding the income-earning opportunities of older persons, in combination with growth of long-term care insurance. Such responses tend to leave the level of monetization of the social service system unchanged or intensified. The level of monetization is measured by the proportion of services that are available only if the service deliverer gets a cash payment.

Another possible societal response could be partial demonetization of the system of social service delivery to elders. This would involve a commitment to avoid reducing access to services while increasing the proportion of services that are offered without expectation of cash payment. It seems likely that this development would not take place unless there is deep and widespread commitment to good quality of life for elders. The spread of a new class of semiformal (Novak & Stone, 1985) or devised (Turkat, 1980) support structures could help to bring about this demonetization.

DIMENSIONS OF COHORT AGING

When the word "cohort" is used here, it will usually refer to a birth cohort, though the time period (for the set of births that will be deemed to form a cohort) could be large enough to cover what is sometimes considered to be a generation (a period containing a sequence of several annual birth cohorts). I support Marshall's (1983) view that it is useful, at least in social gerontology, to think of a generation as being comprised of those who grew up during a period of history that we now consider to be distinctive because of the special events of that period that helped to shape the lives of those who were growing up then. This is different from the demographic concept of generation.

There are at least four dimensions of cohort aging, although only one of them will be treated directly in this text. The four dimensions are: chronological, demographic, functional, and social. In its chronological dimension, cohort aging is an increase in the average number of years lived per cohort member. In its demographic aspect, cohort aging is the process of declining probability of surviving N additional years as the cohort lives longer and longer after the first month of life. The demographic aspect is reflected in the declining proportion of survivors in the cohort—cohort attrition. A cohort can be said to be "demographically old" when all of its surviving members have lived longer than the cohort's life expectancy *at the time period of the cohort's birth.* In terms of current levels of life expectancy at birth in developed countries, a cohort is demographically old when its average chronological age is somewhere near to or above 75 (men and women included). In its functional dimension, cohort aging is the process of maturation and eventual decline in the cohort's average (per member) capacity to autonomously carry on activities of daily living (ADL). This process is influenced by biological, social, and environmental factors.

The cohort can be said to be "functionally old" when its average level of competence in the autonomous conduct of ADL has passed and fallen below some arbitrary proportion of the peak level of competence achieved by the cohort over its lifetime.

In its social dimension, cohort aging is the process in which the cohort is progressively blocked from opportunities for education, work, recognition, and leadership largely on the grounds that it is losing its capacity to be productive because of the perception that it is becoming "old." This process is governed by cultural forces and maintained by certain prevailing institutions and interest groups. The cohort is "socially old" when the blockage of those opportunities is widespread and is widely publicly legitimized by reference to the members' perceived "oldness."

SUPPORT NETWORK HELPING CAPACITY

"Support" means assistance of various kinds provided to people by people. This assistance can come from persons, informal groups, or formal organizations. Some kinds of support have to be perceived and appreciated to be effective (e.g., emotional supports). Others may be effective even if they may not be appreciated as support by the recipient (e.g., paying a needy person's rent or arranging for another person to land a needed job). For the purposes of this paper, a support network is a group that provides support to a designated reference person (another definition points to a certain set of social relationships rather than to persons). The reference person should be regarded as being involved in reciprocal exchanges with other members of the network.

The *support network's helping capacity* is the extent and effectiveness of assistance that it is able to provide to the reference person even as this person's need for assistance deepens due to progressive loss of functional autonomy. (Compare this with the concept of *network resiliency* in Morris & Sherwood, 1984, who discuss the prospects of evaluating the level of resiliency in a support network.) Obviously, if we try to operationalize this concept we would have to deal with the multidimensionality of assistance, and with the possibly different levels of measurement involved with evaluating effectiveness of different kinds of assistance, among other tasks (Thoits, 1982). Network helping capacity depends on (a) demographic composition and spatial distribution of the members, (b) the intensity of commitment to assistance or mutual exchange in network interactions, (c) the level of relevant "know-how" in the network, (d) styles of work and of time use in the society (which affect the members' average disposable time), and (e) technologies and affordability of transportation and communication in the society (which are relevant when the members do not all share the same dwelling unit).

WHY COHORT ATTRITION IS SO IMPORTANT TO NETWORK HELPING CAPACITY

Why is cohort attrition so important to network helping capacity? This question needs to be addressed because it is possible for a network to contain such a wide spectrum of cohorts that attrition in any one of them would not have major impact on helping capacity. Essentially, the answer to the question is that the major segments of informal network support in North America come from members of reference persons' cohort or neighboring cohorts (Chappell's 1983 concept of the peer generation is useful here). A great deal has been correctly written about the importance of children; but spouses and other generational peers are, on the whole, more important in an elder's network until key persons in the peer generation are gone. For example, in a recent Winnipeg study, Chappell (1983) found:

> Overall, age peers dominate. They are the largest groups of others in the household and of friends. . . . Elderly persons in this sample tend to live with their spouses, with a significant minority living with intergenerational individuals (both children and to a lesser extent grandchildren). Most have both peer and intergenerational individuals available among relatives outside the home—neighbors, in-laws, and cousins. Friends, however, tend to be age peers. That is, the importance of peers (family peers within the household and nonfamily as friends) among those available in these elderly persons' social network is clear. (pp. 89-96)

WHAT IS THE AGE PATTERN OF COHORT ATTRITION?

The phrase age "pattern of cohort attrition" refers to the changing rate of proportional loss of cohort members as the cohort's average chronological age goes up. Thus, if we could follow the cohort through time and enumerate the proportion dying as chronological age goes up from one level to another, we could plot a curve showing the age pattern of cohort attrition. Evidently, the rate of attrition speeds up as the cohort's mortality rate increases, so that some time around the current modal age of retirement the cohort attrition process begins to gather speed. We do not have data that are appropriate for direct measurement of the pattern of cohort attrition. Census data would not suffice in Canada, e.g., because Canadian birth cohorts are wide open to international migration until age reaches above 40. We could generate rough approximations for a few cohorts using the life table approach with survival rates derived from the mortality rates for loosely defined birth cohorts (i.e., cohort-specific mortality rate series); but this approach has not yet been implemented. Instead, as a rough and ready guide, age patterns of widowhood rates (by sex) for a set of five

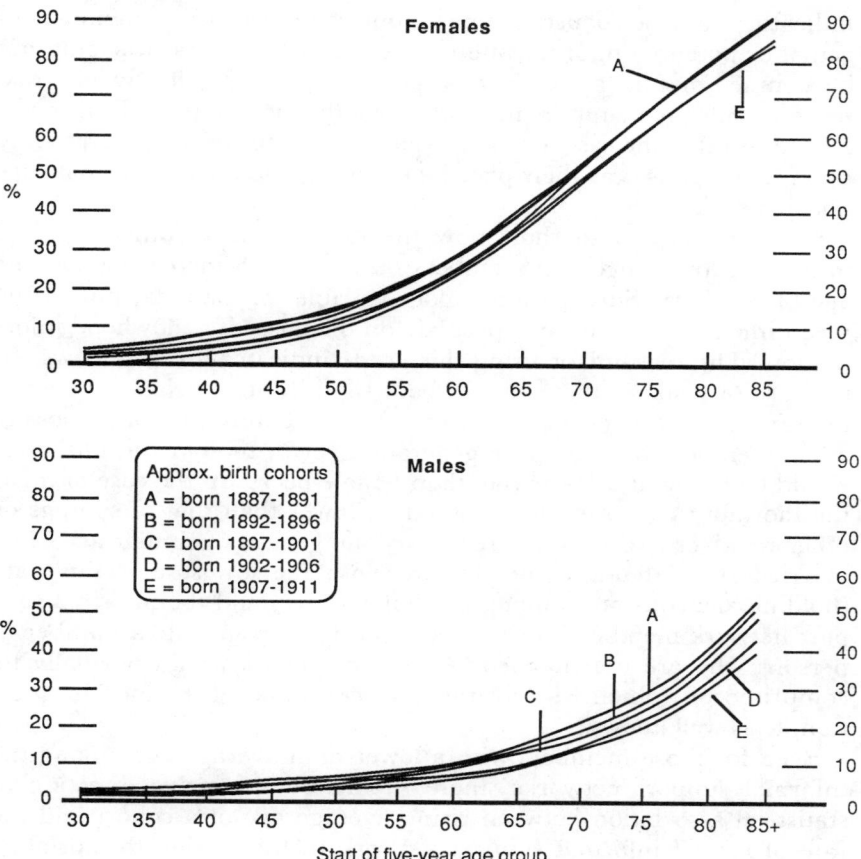

FIGURE 30-1. Widowhood rates for five approximate birth cohorts, by sex, Canada. (The widowhood rate is the percentage of a cohort that is widowed at each age).

approximate cohorts can be used. The patterns are shown in Figure 30-1, where each curve refers to an approximate cohort and the denominator of each rate is restricted to ever-married persons.

Figure 30-1 shows that as the average age rises beyond 55, the rate of widowhood increases in each cohort. Among women the rate of increase in the widowhood rate, concomitant with rising average cohort age, accelerates after the age of 60. For men in Canada, 70 seems to be age beyond which the rate of widowhood seems to climb with increasing speed as the average age goes up. Within these age ranges, the widowhood rate for women remains far above that for men. (See also Fletcher & Stone, 1982). Of course, Figure 30-1 is at best a crude indicator, because spouses comprise only one category of members of actual or potential informal support networks for elders. It should not be assumed that the mere loss of a spouse cripples the effectiveness of a person's informal support network (though this is reported, anecdotally, to be often the case for men, who, more than women, tend to rely upon their spouses as their principal points of access to informal support networks).

Data are needed to show how the rate of loss of other types of informal support network members may rise with increasing average age of a cohort. Such data are not available for Canada, but in the meantime one may elect to speculate on the basis of widowhood information. The reasons for using this crude indicator are as follows: In the case of women, there should be a significant correlation between the rate of loss (over a period of years) of husbands and that of loss of other members of their peer generation, even though the husbands would be dying at a faster rate than female peers. In the case of men, the mortality rate of spouses should be lower than that of siblings or other relatives and friends (treated as one group) of similar age. The married status tends to be the one with the lowest mortality rate (holding age constant) among marital statuses, and the informal support network members outside the spouse group include a number of persons who are not married. Also, the spouses would normally be comprised of women with average age *below* that of the men in question, as is well known.

Even for those members with a lower than average age among the informal support networks, there should be a positive direction of statistical association between rising average age of a cohort and the rate of loss of informal support network members due to mortality. This is so because as the cohort ages there is a corresponding rising average age for those informal support network members whose average age lies below that of the cohort. This assertion assumes that the support available from relatives declines with increasing "generational distance" between the network reference persons and the potential support givers. For example, holding constant support network size, more support is available from children than from grandchildren, and the latter make more support available than great grandchildren. Thus Figure 30-1 seems, in the absence of better indicators, an acceptable proxy, in terms of providing minimum estimates, of the *pattern* of relationship between rising average age of a cohort and a growing rate of loss of members in informal support networks, provided that the group of such members has an average age no less than that of the persons who become widowed.

Additional indirect evidence of the age pattern of cohort attrition is provided in a combination of observations from Figure 30-2. This chart shows that beyond age 79 the proportion of women living in

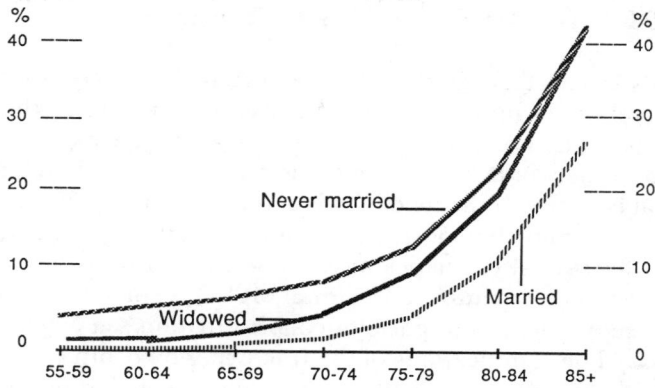

FIGURE 30-2. Percent of women living in collective households in three selected marital statuses.
Source: Data from 1981 Census Public Use Sample.

collective households (mostly in institutions for special care) rises
sharply with increasing age. Among the marital status groups shown,
the proportion in collective households rises most sharply (with increasing age) for the widowed. None of this information provides
direct evidence of the sort we would like to have. Lacking that evidence, however, and recalling the research findings to the effect that
weakness of informal supports is a major factor in entry into collective
dwellings (Brody, Poulshock, & Masciocchi, 1978), the information
gleaned from these charts does seem to provide a reasonable indicator
of the age pattern of the rate of loss of informal support network
members as the average chronological age of the cohort climbs above
60.

Nothing written here should be taken as implying any assertion that
the age pattern of cohort attrition is stable over time. Figure 30-1
suggests, for example, that the inflection point and the steep rise of the
cohort-specific age curve of widowhood rates have been shifting up-
wards with successive cohorts. The mean age of loss of spouse due to
death has been rising gradually as new cohorts have come along; this
can be seen as representative for all key support network members in
the elders' peer generations. (That is, there has been a rising pattern in
the average age at which all key support network members have been
lost through death.) Related to this shifting pattern is the marked
decline in mortality rates (or increase in life expectancy) at the upper
ages, particularly since the 1960s (Manton, 1982; Nagnur, 1985; Rosenwaike, Yaffe, & Sagi, 1980).

SOME RESULTS OF COHORT ATTRITION

As already noted, this age pattern of cohort attrition helps to produce a progressive loss of informal support-network members as the average age of a cohort climbs beyond 60. This loss *reduces* the average ability of the support networks to respond effectively to members' declining functional capacity. If the tendency is actualized, the declining network help capacity may be more important than the mere existence of declining functional capacities in causing a resort to formal-organization supports (Fillenbaum & Wallman, 1984). (For related discussion that indirectly refers to impacts of cohort attrition see Myers & Manton, 1983.) The ramifications of the fracturing by death of the support networks' help capacity reach into several areas including health hazards, living arrangements, community services and housing.

A number of analysts contend that the loss of intimate relationships through the departure of key support network members substantially raises the hazard of stress-related illnesses (Pilisuk & Froland, 1978) unless the network continues to provide the reference person with a link to an intimate social acquaintance or confidant (Pilisuk & Minkler, 1980). The weakening of support networks through cohort attrition becomes a major factor in the evolution of the cohort's living arrangement distribution. Specifically, the supports needed to continue residing in certain settings in the face of declining functional capacity tend to fall away, and those that remain are available for rapidly shortening periods of time. These forces raise the chances of a shift in living arrangement, and eventually a move into institutional facilities. Brody, Poulshock, and Masciocchi (1978) found the following in their research:

> Differential levels of functioning ability did not predict placement of the chronically ill/disabled elderly in institutions or in the community. The critical variable in this research which explained why individuals with similar levels of functioning ability were residing in different settings was living arrangement, primarily in the form of living with spouse and/or children. (p.558).

Thus, cohort attrition, by lowering the availability of assistance or its help capacity, becomes a crucial variable in the rate of passage into institutional care—a result that would surprise no one who has taken the time to watch the aging of his/her own extended family, but which is important nevertheless to be recounted at this point, because demographers have neglected studying social aspects of cohort aging. Of course, in many cases intensified demand for community services would precede the passage into institutional care.

With the declining availability or help capacity of the support networks due to cohort attrition, and the shift in living arrangements that the attrition may trigger, the importance of designing adaptive and supportive housing facilities increases for those who wish to stay in the community. Specifically, there is increased need for access to housing that is designed for adaptivity to persons with declining functional capacity.

CONTINUED MORTALITY DECLINE AND GENDER GAP IN DEATH RATES AT THE UPPER AGES

What changes can we expect in the age pattern of average helping capacity of informal support networks for elders if life expectancy at the upper ages continues to rise? One may assume that mortality declines will lower the rate of family break-up due to death at a given age (e.g., age 80). By keeping families together for longer periods of time, other factors being constant, the life expectancy increase causes the phase of steep decline (with rising average cohort age) in the mean helping capacity of the informal networks to be pushed upward toward higher and higher chronological ages. If we can assume that the helping capacity of affected informal networks is inversely related to the demand for certain formal organization services, the mortality decline would tend to push the steep incline in demand for such services to higher and higher ages. For example, we should expect to see a rise in the mean age at entry to nursing homes. Referring to the situation in the United States, Treas & Bengtson (1982) state the following:

> Goodly numbers of couples today can look forward to marriages of startling duration. Even though higher divorce rates offset declines in early widowhood, today one in five couples in their first marriages can expect to celebrate a golden wedding anniversary. Even among those who have remarried, one in twenty will someday be able to look back on a union lasting 50 years (pp. 15-16).

There is at least one offsetting factor, however. If the difference between men and women in mortality improvements remains at current levels or fails to narrow quickly, we might still see the emergence of unusually large numbers of very old women (aged 85 and over) with support networks weakened by loss of spouse and comprised substantially of persons who themselves would be of or entering advanced age. Thus, when the husband is finally lost, widows of advanced age may still face about the same number of years of widowhood as they formerly did. Further, due to the process of functional aging in their peer generation, the average helping capacity of their husbandless informal support networks (at the date of entry to widowhood) would be significantly below the level it would have been if widowhood had struck earlier.

A significant proportion of the women who might in the future be facing a substantial length of widowed life after losing their husbands at advanced age will find that the hazard of onset of financial indigence would begin rising to disturbing levels. In fact, unless they are spared the high levels of personal expenditure often associated with long-term care services from formal organizations, a substantial percentage of the *intact* families that would have been surviving for a generation or more (20 + years) after giving up or losing their right to earned income will already have been faced with this hazard before the death of one spouse.

As is well known, at advanced age the cost of personal time needed from others and/or of long-term management of functional deficiency can get so high as to threaten the finances of an elder and his/her informal financial supporters. In the United States, for example, according to Beall (1984, p.20), "long-term care services are financed now primarily by public programs (principally Medicaid) and out-of-pocket expenditures by elderly persons and their families." With regard to medical services alone, Manton (1984, p. 262) has suggested that in the United States "the rising costs of medical care may force society to consciously forego certain opportunities for advancement" in life expectancy. At ages 85 and over the major issue might not be so much the cost of *medical* care as that of the *availability* at any reasonably likely price (as well as cost) of *personal-time inputs* needed for long-term management of the effects of functional deficiency (for related discussion see Gurland, Copeland, Kuriansky, Kelleher, & Michael, 1983). In short, a certain pattern of continued mortality decline at the upper ages (specifically, one that largely preserves the current wide gender gap in death rates) *could* present community-level service-supply resource pressures that might be distressingly insensitive to the level of infusion of money into the service delivery system. Of course, heavy infusion of additional monies could tend to drive up the user fees demanded for a relatively inelastic supply of personal time inputs to care services.

If scarce personal-time inputs for long-term management of functional deficiency are the really big source of health care expenditures among those of advanced age, then we should add an alternative suggestion to that of Manton. The community response to the cost pressure might involve concerted *private* actions that will have the effect of reducing the intensity of monetization in the health care system. This outcome could arise because of the emergence of a vast number of people who simply do not have the cash or the exchange services to pay for the services and goods they need for basic decent subsistence. To see the problem clearly, think of the situation that would have existed in our society if the bulk of family care for the "Baby Boom" as it was being socialized had to be paid for in cash on a "dollars-for-personal time-spent'' basis. Probably, we would have resolved the financial crisis by demonetizing family services to children.

A plausible scenario for the emergence of the financial squeeze is the following: As the cohort's average chronological age passes 80, the rate of need for personal time inputs from others due to declining functional capacity begins to rise to substantial levels. As long as members are in living arrangements where they have supporters that are committed and available to provide such inputs, there may be little impact of this rising rate on the need for purchasing power. However, as soon as the supporters are overwhelmed by the service demands or they are taken away by death, family breakdown, or mobility, then support services have to be bought (though possibly paid for by parties other than the recipients of the services).

If inflation has reduced the purchasing power of most survivors' accumulated funds (after 20 or more years without employment income), and if public money transfers or service subsidization are insufficient, many elders with badly weakened informal support networks and in need of continued inputs of personal time will get the inputs only if extra family service deliverers are available and willing to offer *their* goods and services without expecting cash payment.

At that time, some other kind of compensation would have to be forthcoming if the service providers have little sense of personal obligation to the service recipients. This other kind of compensation could be one of the following:

Type 1—access to goods and services wanted through a bartering system
Type 2—recognition and esteem
Type 3—opportunity for leadership

These forms of compensation would entail some measure of *removing* the needy elders and their providers from the money-based social service economy.

All of the foregoing assumes that the human resources to give appropriate kinds, quality, and amounts of service are in fact *available* in a society. Consider for example two of the forces that could cause a push toward demonetization of the social service economy.

One force will be growing public realization that building up a large fund of money will not help to buy a nonexistent service when one is old; and that the securing of services in the future may entail, in addition to adequate purchasing power, the construction and nurturing of certain social bonds for which purchasing power is irrelevant. To see this point clearly, ask yourself why, in the absence of a spouse, so many people turn to their children for help, and why such a high proportion of these children find this action quite legitimate? Is it just the "flesh and blood" relationship between parent and child? It is far more; it is the process in which the parent built up service credits (while bringing up the child) that the child recognizes as legitimate and desires to honor when they are "cashed in." During the long buildup of this social bond no proof of its existence in the form of an accumulated medium of exchange (money) was ever considered. And many people believe that these bonds are stronger and more reliable than many that require money accumulation as proof of their reality.

The implications of these ideas have not been lost on a goodly number of today's elders. See, for example, the discussion of the Helper Bank concept by Goodman (1984, pp. 142-143), and the work of the Ontario Seniors Talent Bank (contact Ontario Seniors Secretariat, Toronto, for information).

POSSIBLE MAJOR GROWTH OF SEMIFORMAL SUPPORT STRUCTURES

Mark Novak (Novak & Stone, 1985) suggests that there is a large and growing class of social service needs where neither informal nor formal organizations should be expected to be adequately equipped to meet the demands, and that some kind of hybrid support form, a semiformal type, will come to play (and has already begun to do so on a small scale) to try and fill the social service gap. It has been hypothesized that this semiformal support structure has the capability to deliver services with much lower inputs of cash than formal organizations would need to do the same work.

The resource limitations of both formal and informal supports when facing certain kinds of need are readily exemplified when we look at the situations of families that are confronted with long-term care for members who have deepening dementia such as Alzheimer's disease. Aronson and Yatzkan (1984) point out that:

> Dealing with dementia is a big job which can overwhelm even the strongest family system and can overburden even the most competent care providers. A partnership between and among the family, the health care delivery system, and the self-help movement is essential (p. 5).

Turkat (1980) further points out that:

> It is a relatively common phenomena, especially in community mental health, that severely disturbed individuals have rejected and have been rejected by their natural social networks (pp. 101-102).

Turkat goes on to indicate that formal organization (including professional) response cannot cope with the needs. "It is clear that there

has been, and will continue to be a shortage of mental health professionals to meet the demands for service" (Turkat 1980, p. 102; Cohen
& Adler 1984, p. 22).

Turkat then suggests that the deficiencies of *both* the formal and the
informal help have led to the rise of groups comprising a " 'nonprofes-
sional movement' as a means of reducing the existing burden of excessive professional service demands,'' and in describing these groups he
said the following:

> These groups are the most promising complementary resource for meet-
> ing the existing mental health service demands. Similarly, they are the most
> powerful resource for developing social networks that will support chronic,
> socially isolated individuals without natural social networks (pp. 101-102).

Turkat calls these groups "devised social networks" (which seem to
be equivalent in form to Novak's semiformal support structures). For
example, he notes that devised social networks

> . . .are distinguishable from natural social networks by virtue of their
> being organized according to related functional roles rather than related
> social roles. . . . The primary function of the relationship between the
> troubled person and a devised social network centers around the new
> functional tasks performed by the network members and not a previous
> history of established interpersonal patterns among network members. . . .
> There can be a broad range of supportive activities that members of a
> devised social network may provide (p. 102).

This conceptualization is similar to Novak's (1985) comments about
the semiformal support structure:

> Semiformal structures differ from formal and informal structures, but
> have some things in common with both. . . . They run on the principle of
> reciprocity and operate with an agreed-on agenda (rather than by strict
> bureaucratic rules or unstated group norms). These groups come about
> when concerned individuals see a need in the community. Often the people
> who start these groups do so to fulfill their own needs.

Aronson and Yatzkan (1984) characterize a pertinent national association in the field of dementia with the following words:

> ADRDA is a coalition of family members, researchers, and health pro-
> fessionals, banded together to promote family support, research, education,
> and eventual eradication of this problem. . . . The emergence of this na-
> tional organization and of self-help and other support groups for families of
> dementia victims is a clear example of a "seat of the pants" movement that
> has sprung up to fill the large gaps in service that exist for families of
> dementia victims (p. 5-6).

> The self-help movement for families of dementia victims is growing and
> will have a substantial impact on the formal service network. The move-
> ment will undoubtedly evolve a clearer definition of itself and of what it can

and cannot do. At this time there is virtually no third-party funding available to family support groups. As a result of the proliferation of support groups and recognition of their importance, funding agencies will discover the potential cost-effectiveness of this approach and will probably insist on the development of specific guidelines for these services (p. 9).

Cicirelli (1983) also highlights the functions of these hybrid support structures.

Such measures as provision of supplementary or backup services, including such part-time measures as day-care plans or respite care can do much to prevent an excessive build up of strains that could culminate in family breakdown or parent abuse. Self-help groups in which adult children share their strains and feelings and thereby gain emotional support are also important, as are counseling activities that help adult children to develop skills for dealing with elderly parents, helping to meet their needs, and coping with the stresses of helping. Such supportive services are especially important in situations in which the adult child is bearing an unusually heavy burden, as in an intergenerational household, or is limited in resources, as in the case of marital disruption. Elderly parents who have lost their adult children are also at particular risk, since they have not developed means of coping that make use of other available sources of support (p. 46).

Another dimension of these groups is brought out by Novak (Novak & Stone, 1985):

These groups meet. . .the need to create, to have social status and to be recognized by others for what you can do. . . . Semiformal groups open new spaces for social "action" (Arendt, 1959). That means they allow people to move beyond the passivity imposed by bureaucracy. And they allow people to come out of the privacy and the isolation of life in the family. Semiformal structures allow people to act in public with their peers. Semiformal groups would include large organizations like Creative Retirement Manitoba. They would include medium-sized groups like a Senior Center or the Executive of the Manitoba Society of Seniors. And they would include small groups like Alzheimer's Family Support Groups, Death and Dying Workshops, or the Manitoba Senior Citizens' Think Tank.
These groups are at the growing tip of social change. They show that people can and will create structures to meet their needs as they age. Semiformal groups and their members have begun to change the shape and meaning of aging in Canada. And these groups will increase in number and importance as more and more people grow old.

CONCLUSION

Cohort attrition sets up certain far-reaching forces against the helping capacity of informal social networks. When combined with declining mortality rates at the upper ages, across a long series of cohorts, and if the affected cohorts become large enough (as is the case of the Baby Boom generation) and numerous enough in the society, the lowered helping capacity of informal networks within the cohorts, due to their attrition, will give rise to a general perception of major cost and social service delivery pressures at the community level. One possible societal response of growing interest is that of partial demonetization of service delivery to the aging, *if* there is deep commitment to good quality of life for elders. The spread of a major new class of semiformal (Novak & Stone, 1985) or devised (Turkat 1980) support structures could help to bring about this demonetization.

REFERENCES

Arendt, H. (1959). *The human condition.* Garden City, NY: Doubleday.

Aronson, M. K., & Yatzkan E. S. (1984). Coping with Alzheimer's disease through support groups. *Aging, 347,* 3-9.

Beall, G. T. (1984). Long-term care cost crisis: Can private insurance bail us out? Perspective on Aging, *13,*(5), 20-23.

Brody, S.J., Poulshock, S.W., & Masciocchi, C.F. (1978). The family caring unit: A major consideration in the long-term support system. *The Gerontologist, 18*(6), 556-561.

Chappell, N.L. (1983, March). Informal support networks among the elderly. *Research on Aging, 5*(1), 77-99.

Cicirelli, V.G. (1983). Adult children and their elderly parents. In T.H. Brubaker (Ed.). *Family relationships in later life* (pp.31-46). Beverly Hills, CA: Sage Publications.

Cohen, C.I., & Alder, A. (1984). Network interventions: Do they work? *The Gerontologist, 24*(1), 16-22.

Fillenbaum, G.G., & Wallman, L.H. (1984). Change in household composition of the elderly: A preliminary investigation. *Journal of Gerontology, 39*(3), 342-349.

Fletcher, S., & Stone, L.O. (1982). *The living arrangements of Canada's older women.* Ottawa: Minister of Supply and Services.

Fries, J.F. (1984). The compression of morbidity: Miscellaneous comments about a theme. *The Gerontologist, 24*(4), 354-359.

Goodman, C. (1984). Natural helping among older adults. The Gerontologist: *24*(2): 138-143.

Gurland, B., Copeland, J., Kuriansky, J., Kelleher, M., Sharpe, L., & Dean, L.L. (1983). *The mind and mood of aging. Mental health problems of the community elderly in New York and London.* New York: The Haworth Press.

Manton, K.G. (1984). Mortality patterns in developed countries. *Comparative Social Research, 7,* 259-286.

Manton, K.G. (1982). Temporal and age variation of United States black/white cause-specific mortality differentials: A study of the recent changes in the relative health status of the United States black population: *The Gerontologist, 22*(2), 170-179.

Marshall, V.W. (1983). Generations, age groups and cohorts: Conceptual distinctions. *Canadian Journal on Aging, 2*(2), 51-62.

Morris, J.N., & Sherwood, S. (1984). Informal support resources for vulnerable elderly persons: Can they be counted on, why do they work? *International Journal of Aging and Human Development, 18*(2), 81-98.

Myers, G.C., & Manton, K.G. (1983). Some sociodemographic observations relating to unpaid productive roles in an aging society. Durham, N.C.: Center for Demographic Studies, Duke University (mimeo).

Myers, G.C., & Manton, K.G. (1984). Compression of mortality: Myth or reality. *The Gerontologist, 24*(4), 346–353.

Nagnur, D. (1985). Longevity and historical life tables (Abridged), Canada and Provinces, 1921–1981. Ottawa: Statistics Canada, Social and Economic Studies Division (review draft).

Novak, M., & Stone, L.O. (1985). *Population aging and core social institutions.* Paper presented at the 1985 meetings of the Canadian Population Society, Montreal.

Pilisuk, M. & Minkler, M. (1980). Supportive networks: Life ties for the elderly. *Journal of Social Issues, 36*(2), 95–116.

Pilisuk, M. & Froland, C. (1978). Kinship, social networks, social support and health. *Social Science & Medicine, 12B,* 272–280.

Rosenwaike, I., Yaffe, N. & Sagi, P.C. (1980). The recent decline in mortality of the extreme aged: An analysis of statistical data. *American Journal of Public Health, 70*(10), 1074–1080.

Schneider, E.L., & Brody, J.A. (1983). Aging, natural death, and the compression of morbidity: Another view. *The New England Journal of Medicine, 309*(14), 854–856.

Thoits, P.A. (1982). Conceptual, methodological, and theoretical problems in studying social support as a buffer against life stress. *Journal of Health and Social Behavior, 23*(2), 145–159.

Treas, J. & Bengtson, V.L. (1982, November). The demography of mid- and late-life transitions. *The Annals of the American Academy of Political and Social Science, 464,* 11–21.

Turkat, D. (1980). Social networks: Theory and practice. *Journal of Community Psychology, 8:*99–109.

CHAPTER 31

Suicide in Later Life: A Countertrend Among the Old-Old

Robert Kastenbaum
Richard Coppedge

Relatively little effort has been made to reduce the high suicide rate among older adults because of the assumption that this is a "normal" if unfortunate state of affairs. Drawing upon Arizona data, this chapter suggests that a more active and melioristic approach should be pursued. It is shown that suicide among the old-old (75 +) of both sexes is increasing—despite the fact that the overall death rate for both the general population and the old-old has been declining. Furthermore, the marked rise in suicide among the old-old in Arizona, both male and female, is an exception to the general pattern of declining suicide rates for other age groups in the past decade. The increase in suicide among the old-old is *not* paralleled by the young-old, nor is there an increase in alcohol-related deaths, often considered to be a "suicide equivalent." As a geosocial area that has been subject to a significant population increase and attracted in particular many older adults, Arizona cannot stand as a general model for either suicide or mortality. Nevertheless, the findings have implications for the supposed immutability of suicide rates among the aged, for age differences within the overall category of mature adults, and for the relationship between suicide and other causes of death.

The emergence of the hospice has resulted in improved care for the dying person as well as more sensitive concern for the bereaved (Corr & Corr, 1983; Zimmerman, 1981). Elderly adults comprise a large proportion of hospice patients and appear to derive substantial benefit from this approach (Greer, Mor, & Kastenbaum, 1986). For the hospice movement to have crossed the line from vision to reality required the willingness to accept the fact that life does come to an end despite the most diligent medical interventions. The tendency either to abandon the dying person or to engage in aggressive but futile interventions has been replaced by an improved system of psychosocial support and comfort-oriented care.

Is there a parallel social movement that is aimed at reducing suicide among older adults? The answer appears to be in the negative, at least, in the United States (Osgood, 1985). Instead, one observes a public attitude of passivity and fatalism regarding self-destruction by those advanced in years. It may be considered unfortunate that an old person has taken his life, but society in general does not express either deep regret or alarm. This attitude is probably associated with the public's fear of growing old and, therefore, supposedly infirm, useless, and unlovable. The death of such a person—whose life no longer seems of value even to himself—is not perceived as mysterious, tragic, or threatening. This contrasts sharply with attitudes toward the death of the young by suicide or any other cause. On the bureaucratic level, of course, the pressure for the "rationing of health care" usually is intended to reduce benefits for the elderly. The pervasive age discrimination that can be seen in all spheres—occupational and residential as well as health—has the effect of a none-too-subtle hint: "Why are you still hanging around? Don't you know when it's time to go?" Many old people seem to get this message.

Suicide among the elderly is not only accepted as an understandable and more or less normal state of affairs, but there is also a tendency to assume that not much can be done about it—quite in contrast to the hospice approach to terminal care. High suicide rates have been reported among older people in Western industrialized nations ever since records have been kept, and often regarded as "normal" (Osgood, 1985). In more recent years it has been convenient to regard elderly suicide as an unfortunate side effect of modernization and, possibly, the increase of longevity. All in all, the activist attitude that has been so effective in improving care for the dying person and the bereaved is seldom encountered when the topic is suicide and the elderly.

We suggest that a more active and melioristic approach should replace the present attitude of passivity and nihilism. This point will be developed through considering some recent data from the state of Arizona. The intention here is not to generalize prematurely from the Arizona experience, but only to illustrate the kind of information that awaits our close attention once we are liberated from the assumption that suicide is somehow a natural or immutable correlate of advanced age.

SUICIDE IN THE OVERALL PATTERN OF ARIZONA MORTALITY

Examining first the incidence of suicide as part of the overall pattern of mortality in Arizona will provide a perspective that is missing when the focus is placed too quickly on suicide as an isolated event.

More Residents, Declining Death Rate

The overall death rate in Arizona has been declining over recent years. For the total population in 1980 there was a death rate of 781 per 100,000. By 1983, this rate had dropped to 765. At the same time, the population itself continued to increase greatly. A sparsely settled area in 1950 with approximately 750,000 residents, Arizona is now approaching 3 million. This rapid growth has been almost entirely the result of people—many of them older adults—moving into Arizona to take advantage either of retirement living or occupational opportunities. The desert climate of Arizona has proven attractive to many older Americans who have become uncomfortable with harsh winters, while people of various ages have been attracted to this area because of its rapid economic development. For many years, Arizona was famous mostly as the setting for Western movies. With the advent of air-conditioning and other technological amenities, Arizona, along with similar areas in New Mexico, Utah, and Texas, have attracted people in search of land and opportunity for development. Even such a basic piece of information as a declining death rate, then, has more than one possible explanation. Perhaps Arizona is being flooded by healthier people who are bringing with them a relatively low death rate. At the same time, the population base from which suicides will occur has also shifted and is continuing to shift each year. The suicide rate might then remain constant, and yet it could reflect a number of important changes that happen to cancel each other out.

Notice, also, that this kind of ambiguity does not apply only to Arizona and other areas that are attracting more residents. All these people are coming from some place—and their departure has both statistical and substantive impact on the areas they are leaving behind. Take, for example, a married couple who have been living in Illinois for most of their lives. Upon retirement they decide to move to one of the communities in Arizona designed specifically for adult living. Their departure affects the population size and structure in Illinois, but also reduces the number of taxpayers and older adults who are active in community volunteer service. On a more personal level, their departure might deprive their neighbor, an elderly widow, of her most meaningful social interaction, contributing to a depressive state. The total life situation of specific individuals as well as the population base are altered on both sides of the move: back home in Illinois and in Arizona. Because retired individuals have become so mobile in the United States, it has become more complex than ever to make sense out of the changing pattern of death rates for all causes, including but not limited to suicide.

Mortality Among the Young-Old and the Old-Old

Each year finds a higher proportion of Arizona residents in the age range of 75 and beyond ("old-old"). Within a recent 4-year period, 1980 through 1983, this segment of the population increased from 3.87% to 4.23%. One person in 25 is now at age 75 or above, and this proportion continues to grow. Meanwhile, the death rate for people in this oldest category has continued to decline over the same period. It is probable that the increasing number of old-old individuals in Arizona represents the successful aging of people who moved into the state some years ago; most newcomers are in their early 60s, not their 80's. Here are two fairly simple facts, then: the old-old in Arizona are becoming more numerous and also enjoying a reduction in the death rate.

Nevertheless, it is also true that year after year people in this age range contribute a larger and larger percentage of the total deaths in Arizona. Both sets of facts exist for the same time, place, and population: more deaths in Arizona come from those 75 and above (the latest figures are 42%, up from 38% just 3 years previously), and yet the odds of surviving another year continue to improve in the highest age range that has been subjected to statistical analysis. These figures illustrate the problems we could create for ourselves should we draw hasty conclusions about any one cause of death, such as suicide, without taking into account the larger pattern of population and mortality trends.

What has been happening with adults in the age range that is now often described as the "young-old," specifically, between the ages of 65 and 74? These people are also enjoying a steady decline in death rate. They have also become a progressively larger proportion of the population in Arizona, being about twice as numerous as the old-old. By contrast, however, the young-old have *not* contributed a progressively higher proportion of all deaths in the state. Both the young-old and the old-old, then, have been experiencing a reduced death rate and a growth both in absolute and proportional numbers, but the former are stable while the latter are increasing in their proportional contribution to the overall death rate. The real point here is that there may be important differences between the young-old and the old-old in a number of characteristics, including suicidality. Any attempts to encompass all older adults within the same category runs the risk of missing significant differences and thereby leading to unwarranted conclusions.

Suicide in Arizona: A Statistical Overview

The suicide rate in Arizona for males of all ages has remained constant at 26 per 100,000 over a recent 9-year period that is available for analysis. The rate for females has risen slightly from 8.5 per 100,000 to 9. This relatively stable overall pattern, however, conceals important changes that have been occuring within particular subpopulations. One very striking change is the reduction of suicidal deaths among Native Americans. For example, in a rural county whose residents are mostly Native Americans, the male suicide rate has declined from 42.5 to 28.8 per 100,000 within this 9-year span. Most suicides in this population occur among young adults, and it is here that the reduction has been most spectacular. The high incidence of suicide among some Native American populations for many years had led some to conclude that this is a tragic situation that cannot be easily remedied. However, positive changes have occurred in a rather short period of time, and probably should be credited to initiatives taken by leaders within the Native American community—a matter that deserves careful study. If the suicide rate among young Native Americans could be reduced so significantly in a short period of time, then it becomes even more pertinent to question the complacency toward high rates among other subpopulations, such as the elderly.

The national pattern of suicide has consistently shown that it is the elderly white male who is most at risk. The rate slides upward as white males enter their fifth decade. By the middle of the seventh decade, the rate has almost doubled. By contrast, suicide among white females reaches its highest rate in the early 50s, and steadily declines thereafter. The suicide rate for blacks occurs even earlier, especially for females, and then declines appreciably at more advanced adult ages. Historically, it has been the suicide rate among white males that most contributed to the overall high rate for this age group (Diggory, 1977).

What we are starting to observe in Arizona, however, suggests that new patterns can emerge, patterns that presumably reflect substantive changes occurring in our society. In the early 1970s, the suicide rates in Arizona by age and sex closely paralleled the national pattern. Just a decade later, however, several changes have appeared. The most striking change occurs among old-old males. The suicide rate of 47.7 per 100,000 was previously close to the national figures. Pooling the data for a more recent 5-year period, we find that the rate has increased to an unprecedented 72.2 per 100,000—more than half again as high as it was about a decade ago.

Statistics alone can tell us how and why such an alarming increase

could occur in so short a period of time, but there are some other
pieces of information that should be added to the picture. Most striking, perhaps, is the fact that the suicide rate *declined* for all other age
groups in Arizona during the same period of time that it rose so
sharply for the old-old. The increased suicide rate among old-old
males, then, represents a significant countertrend. Furthermore, it
must be regarded as a very specific counter-trend, because the young-
old, those between the ages of 65 and 74, showed an approximately
10% decline in suicide rate, while the rate among the old-old *increased*
by more than 50%. There could hardly be a more obvious demonstration of the need to make age distinctions within the overall category of
older adult. It has already been noted that the overall death rate in
Arizona has been declining steadily in recent years. This means that
the increased suicide rate among old-old males stands in strong contrast to the generally improving outlook for survival.

And what about the women? There has been a tendency to neglect
suicide among old women because it is a relatively infrequent event,
becoming ever more infrequent with advancing age. The latest data,
however, tell a different story. The overall suicide rate among women
in Arizona has continued to decrease in recent years at every age
level—at every level—that is, except the old-old. Women aged 75 and
more have become more vulnerable to suicide. The rate remains relatively low at 8.8 per 100,000, but this represents a marked increase
over the previous rate of 6.2. Whatever is happening, then, involves
both women and men in the most advanced age range but does not
involve those at any other age, including those just a few years their
junior.

That something unusual is happening among the old-old in Arizona
is further suggested by other findings within the general pattern of
mortality. Accidents actually account for many more deaths at all age
levels than does suicide. The death rate from accidents in Arizona has
declined steadily for all ages—except, once again, for the old-old. This
reduction in accidental deaths is an appreciable one. The young-old,
for example, now have an accidental death rate that is only two thirds
of what it was about a decade ago. Meanwhile, the old-old, both men
and women, have become more vulnerable to death in accidents,
usually involving motor vehicles.

Two additional relationships between suicide and other causes of
death should be noted. Experts in the field of suicide prevention have
long considered alcoholism as an indirect form of self-destruction (Farberow, 1980). The number of deaths attributed to alcoholism have
probably been underestimated in the available data, for example, in
those deaths caused by motor vehicle accidents in which the driver had
been drinking. Nevertheless, the rate of death from alcoholism might
provide some clues to the meaning of the burgeoning suicide rates

among the old-old. What we find is that *the alcoholism death rate has declined for elderly adults at the same time that suicide rates have increased.* One must look, then, for different sets of psychosocial dynamics in direct suicide as compared with the more gradual decline associated with alcoholism. The final statistical point is that people living in rural areas of Arizona are at a higher risk for suicide at all age levels—but this differential is greatest for the elderly adult. The old-old in rural areas now have an alarmingly high suicide rate of 88.8 per 100,000. This extremely high rate seems to reflect the social isolation of the very old person in sparsely populated rural areas without adequate transportation and certainly without adequate home support and visitation programs.

CONCLUSION

To understand suicidal behavior among elderly adults we must also attend to the overall pattern of mortality, to trends over time, including population shifts, and to the differences between the various age echelons among the elderly. An obvious indication for subsequent research will be the further disaggregation of data into smaller age groupings, perhaps 5-year clusters throughout the life span. Prospective data and tracking of individuals are also much needed to examine what might prove to be complex and surprising relationships between cohort membership and exposure to socioenvironmental change. It might be the case, for example, that cohorts with specific demographic and life history characteristics become particularly vulnerable to suicide when confronted with particular socioenvironmental circumstances. It would be perhaps even more important to identify those personal and demographic characteristics that serve to protect some of the old-old from a lethal rise in suicidality. Certainly, inclusion of information pertinent to suicide potential would be an excellent idea to consider for any and all longitudinal studies regardless of their specific area of focus.

Data from Arizona provide an example of an apparent countertrend of considerable strength in which the old-old have become more vulnerable to suicide despite the overall decrease in death rate, the reduced suicide rate at all other age levels, and several other factors. This countertrend demands close attention, which must include individual case studies and other approaches that go far beyond the statistical. If uncontrolled and poorly understood social forces can lead to a sharp increase in the suicide rate, then improved understanding might well lead not only to prevention of suicide among the oldest of our citizens, but also to an amelioration of the conditions that have led some to select this harsh alternative.

We consider it likely (although not yet conclusively shown) that suicide is chosen by many of the old-old for much the same reasons that others exercise this option: loneliness, disappointment, frustration, a lack of opportunity to express one's individuality, and the vision of a bleak and unrewarding future. These are dilemmas common to humanity, not at all limited to the aged. There are also some sources of distress that occur more frequently among the aged, such as physical impairment. It would be erroneous to say that physical impairment "causes" suicide. Most people in poor health or limited physical condition do *not* kill themselves. The answer must be sought in the individual's judgment about his or her quality of life and usefulness to others. The decision to take one's own life, for example, may result from fear of being placed in a nursing home and thereby perhaps losing the last vestiges of personal dignity and self-determination.

As a society and as individuals we are not powerless to change this situation. Hospice, for example, has already reduced the burden of stress and anxiety for many older people, family members as well as patients. Clinicians have been successful with the management of depression and anxiety in old age once they have overcome their reluctance to attempt treatment with this age group. The emergence of advocacy groups among the elderly, such as the Gray Panthers, has provided a focal point for effective activity that combats the sense of passivity and helplessness. Enlightened community planning, including adequate provisions for housing and transportation, has provided some elderly with the opportunity to continue their participation in the stream of society. Providing supportive services to enable aged people to live in their own homes has often proven successful when attempted, but is too seldom attempted.

There are many resources available, not the least being the resources of the old-old themselves, whose experience, knowledge, and uniqueness are needed by every society in the world, even if some societies, such as the United States, have but a dim realization of this need.

REFERENCES

Corr, C.A., & Corr, D.M. (Eds.) (1983). *Hospice care.* New York: Springer.

Diggory, J.C. (1977). United States suicide rates, 1933-1968: An analysis of some trends. In E.S. Shneidman (Ed.). *Suicidology: Contemporary developments.* New York: Grune & Stratton.

Farberow, N.L. (Ed.) (1980). *The many faces of suicide.* New York: McGraw-Hill.

Greer, D., Mor, V., & Kastenbaum, R. (Eds.) (1986). *The hospice experiment: Is it working?* Baltimore: Johns Hopkins University Press.

Osgood, N.J. (1985). *Suicide in the elderly.* Rockville, MD: Aspen Systems Corporation.

Zimmerman, J.M. (1981). *Hospice.* Baltimore-Munich: Urban & Schwarzenberg.

CHAPTER 32

Older Workers and the Labor Market in Sweden

Hans Berglind

Developments in the Swedish labor market in recent decades are characterized by two major trends: the inflow of married women into gainful employment; and the decrease of employment rates among the elderly, especially among men. The latter trend has been accompanied by an increase of the number of premature retirement pensions for the age group 50-64 years. The main reason for this seems to be diminishing possibilities for older peoples to get or keep employment. Among those who get an early retirement there is an over-representation of those not married, those having only a basic education, and those doing heavy manual work. The higher rates in premature retirement among men were explained by differences in occupational distribution. Two factors seem to be of special importance in explaining the variation in premature retirement rates between occupations, the rate of occupational injuries and the rate of expansion or decrease in these occupations. Examples of government policies to prevent people from dropping out of the labor force are the partial pension scheme, introduced in 1976, and The Security of Employment Act, which among other things guarantees longer periods of notice to workers and a seniority principle.

OLDER WORKERS AND THE LABOR MARKET IN SWEDEN

At the end of the 1960s there was a recession in Sweden. One sign of that was the growing unemployment figures, especially for people in the age group between 50 and 65. After some time, unemployment went down and everybody seemed happy with the fact that people were back to work. The results of the labor force surveys carried out by the Swedish National Bureau of Statistics revealed surprisingly that

TABLE 32-1. Categories of Unemployment

Want to work	Can get work	
	Yes	No
Yes	1. Temporarily unemployed, not eliminated	2. Unemployed, eliminated
No	3. Not unemployed, not eliminated	4. Not unemployed, eliminated

although the unemployment figures went down, employment did not rise.

This finding needs an explanation. The labor force surveys in Sweden, as well as in the U.S., divide the population of working age (16 to 74) into three groups: those who are employed, those who are unemployed, and those who are not in the labor force. To be counted as unemployed a person must lack employment and be actively seeking work. Those without employment who are not actively seeking work do not belong to the labor force. What had happened in this case was actually that the latter category had increased when the number of unemployed decreased. Probably some people had stopped looking for work because few jobs were available. They would then be referred to as "discouraged workers." Another explanation might be that these people had voluntarily decided to leave the labor market because they found alternative means of supporting themselves.

WHY SOME PEOPLE DO NOT WORK

When trying to explain why some people do not work or why they stop working, two possible explanations come to mind. One is that some people prefer not to work, another is that they cannot get (or retain) a job. There may be more "scientific" ways of saying that, using terms such as "motivation," "employability" and the like, but basically the explanations boil down to these two factors: "willingness" and "possibilities." If we combine them we get the four categories of unemployment illustrated in Table 32-1. (See Berglind, 1977, for further comments.)

In Table 32-1, persons in categories 1 and 2 are unemployed because they want to work and can be expected to seek work. Persons in the second category have difficulties getting a job as do those in category 4. We will refer to them as being *eliminated from the labor market*. The discouraged worker is expected to be in that category. The situation of persons in category 3 is unproblematic as far as labor market status is

TABLE 32–2. Percent of Men and Women Employed in 1965 and 1980 by Age Group

Age:	16–24		25–44		45–64		65–74	
	% Men	Women	% Men	Women	% Men	Women	% Men	Women
1965	70	60	97	55	93	49	37	11
1980	68	66	94	81	85	68	14	4
Differrence	− 2	+ 6	− 3	+ 26	− 8	+ 19	− 23	− 7

concerned. To this category belongs, for example, housewives and students who are not presently looking for work.

It can be assumed that persons looking for work without any result finally give up, which would mean that they move from category 2 to 4. This may very well have been the case with those who dropped out of the labor force at the end of the 1960s. To the extent that those people left voluntarily—still having the possibility of finding a job—we would expect them to be in category 3. Both explanations have been presented in the debate and we shall return to them after having taken a closer look at what has happened in more recent years.

EMPLOYMENT TRENDS IN DIFFERENT AGE GROUPS

Developments in the Swedish labor market in the latest decades are characterized by two major trends: the increase in employment in married women and the decrease of employment rates among the elderly, especially among the men. These changes can be studied in more detail in Table 32-2.

The increase in employment among women has been dramatic, especially in the 25 to 44 age group. The decrease in employment rate among men is not as great, but quite evident in the two highest age groups.

If we take a closer look at the age groups below the "normal" retirement age of 65, we find a larger decrease in labor force participation rates of *men* the nearer they get to 65. In the age group 55 to 59, the decrease was − .3% per year, and in the 60 to 64 category, it was − .8% per year between 1972 and 1982. For *women*, there was instead a yearly increase of + 1.5% in the category 55 to 59 and + 1.2% for those 60 to 64 years of age.

The unemployment rates have been somewhat higher for people in this age bracket than among those between 25 and 54 years of age. The difference has to do with the fact that older workers have a much longer duration of unemployment than those who are younger.

Another interesting trend is the increase in part-time work among both men and women 60 to 64. Before 1976, only 10% of the employed men worked part-time. By 1982 it had increased to 25%. For women in this age group there has also been some increase in part-time work, but at a lower rate. In 1982, almost 60% of women 60 to 64 worked part-time compared with 50% for all employed women. So, even though 46% of all women were gainfully employed in that age group, less than 20% worked full-time.

One reason for the increased number of older people working part-time is the introduction of the partial pension scheme in 1976, which makes it possible for a person to get a part-time pension if he or she reduces the number of working hours by at least 5 hours per week while continuing to work for at least 17 hours per week.

PREMATURE RETIREMENT AND DISABILITY PENSIONS

In Sweden a person can retire prematurely (before the age of 65) for reasons of disability. To get such a pension, his or her work capacity should be reduced by at least half. If this reduction is assumed to be temporary he or she will get a temporary disability pension, otherwise a permanent one. Part-time disability pensions are also available, but are rather rare.

People between 60 and 65 can retire prematurely on the same scheme for "labor market reasons," which means that the chances of getting a job are very limited. If a worker has lost the right to collect unemployment insurance benefits (after 450 days for older workers) and is above 60, he or she is automatically entitled to a pension without being disabled. The majority of people in that age group will, however, not retire for labor market reasons, but because they are incapacitated as far as work is concerned.

The number of people receiving an early pension has increased considerably in recent years. In the mid-60s the number of entrants to this scheme was approximately 20,000 per year. At the beginning of the 70s the number had more than doubled and has since remained at a yearly level of 40,000 to 45,000. The increase followed a change in the Social Security Act, which made it easier for workers aged 60 to 64 to retire if they could not find a job in the area where they lived. Interestingly enough, the number of pensioners below age 60 also increased, although this age group was not covered by the legislation (see Figure 32-1). When these results started to emerge in Sweden, colleagues in the other Nordic countries (Denmark, Finland, and Norway) also reported experiencing an increase in premature retirement due to disability, invalidity, or whatever the term used. A comparative research project that followed revealed that between 1968 and 1972 the

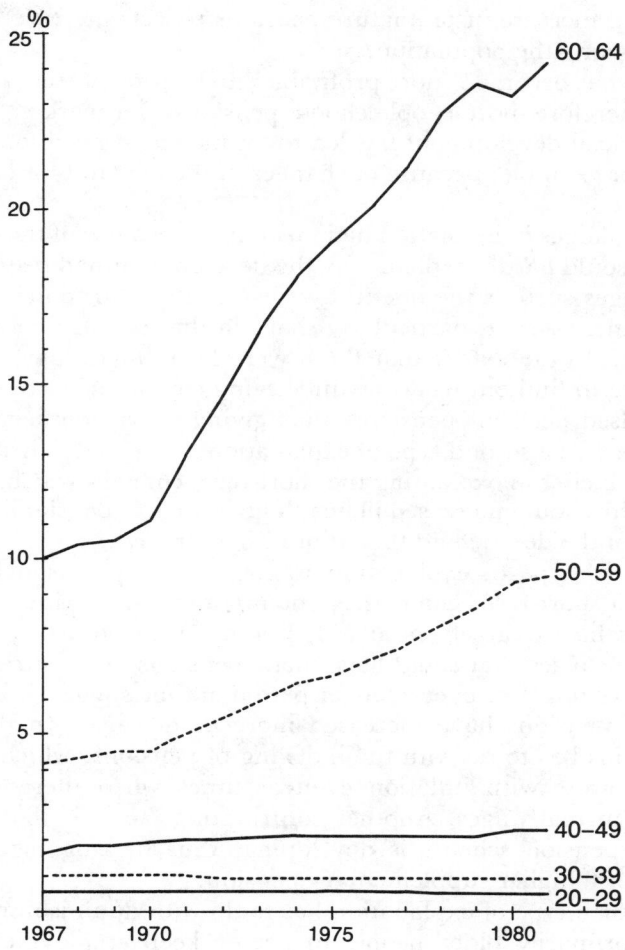

FIGURE 32-1. Relative number of prematurely retired in Sweden as a percent of population in different age groups.

combined number of "prematurely" pensioned individuals in four Nordic countries (Iceland was not included) had increased by 54%. The increase had taken place in all four countries. In three of the four countries, the relative number of new pensioners peaked in 1972 and after that decreased a little. Several types of explanations have been offered in the course of debate (Berglind, 1978):

1. Changes in legislation, or its interpretation, result in more persons becoming eligible for pensions.

2. An increase in premature pensions reflects increased ill health among the population.
3. It has become "more profitable" to be prematurely pensioned; therefore more people choose pensions over work.
4. Social development has led to an increased need for pensions, for example, because of changes in the demand for labor.

Some changes in legislation had taken place in a few of the countries, but they could hardly explain why the development had been so parallel. Changes such as the one in Sweden in 1970 can possibly explain why the increase was particularly sharp in that country between 1970 and 1972. To the extent that there were legal alterations, it may be interesting to find out what the underlying conditions were that led to an increased need for pensions, thus giving rise to the legal changes themselves. The second type of explanation, increased ill health, is not very convincing in explaining the short-term changes which had taken place. Why should increased ill health give rise to "pensioning" just at the turn of the decade and then diminish after 1972?

The third type of explanation is not especially reasonable, when applied to short-term changes. Contemporary sharp rises in pension payments have scarcely occurred, nor have any drastic changes in wage taken place that could have made pensions more attractive than work. Developments over a longer period of time suggest it is certainly true that pensions have increased more than wages. In the case of Sweden this has to do with the indexing of pensions, which make the pensions grow with inflation even at times when there may be a decrease in real wages. Another contributing factor is that a supplementary pension scheme is developing, thus making more persons eligible for a higher supplementary pension.

The fourth type of explanation has to do with diminishing possibilities for primarily older people to get or keep employment. It has already been pointed out that there was a fairly high rate of unemployment at the end of the 1960s, when the increase started. It should also be mentioned that in the four Nordic countries studied, unemployment peaked in 1972 (i.e., the year with the highest pension rates).

In a separate study Berglind (1977) investigated the regional variations in premature pensioning in Sweden using the 278 municipalities as the basic unit. In a series of regression analyses, using the percentage of disability pensioners in a population group in the municipalities as a dependent variable, the unemployment rate was found to be a dominant explanatory factor. Other variables explaining the regional variations were the percentage of single persons, and the "relative pension income," measured as a percent of the average income from gainful employment in the municipality. Wadensjö (1983), a Swedish labor economist, has found in a more recent study that unemployment may not be a very strong explanatory factor. According to his results, regional variations in disability pensions are a result of differences in the composition of the population rather than of unemployment.

There are probably a number of reasons for the differences in results. One may be the higher correlation among age, disability, and unemployment that makes it difficult to separate one explanatory factor from the others. Another is that unemployment is not a very good indicator of difficulties in finding a job. If older workers who are unemployed get a premature pension this means that the rate of unemployment goes down, while the premature pension rate increases, thus lowering the correlation between these two factors. In forthcoming studies it would be better to use other indicators, such as the number of vacancies at the Labor Exchange Offices.

Another fact supporting the hypothesis that labor market conditions are of special importance in explaining the increasing rate of premature retirement is the very reason why the eligibility rules were liberalized; namely, the pensions would be a way of financially supporting older workers who had become unemployed or redundant in the Swedish labor market. Similar reasons have been given in other countries. The provision for a reduced pension before age 65 was introduced in the U.S. for men in 1961. A that point in time the proponents stressed that "it would not serve as an inducement to early retirement, but, rather, would serve to primarily benefit older workers who have trouble getting a job because of ill health or the effects of the recession" (Tracy, 1979).

WHO GETS A PREMATURE RETIREMENT PENSION?

One study of the Swedish population that had retired prematurely during the period 1971–76 found the following:

1. The pension level increases with age for both men and women, a hardly surprising fact.
2. Within each age group those married have a lower level of pensioning than those never married, the latter category having a lower level than those divorced or widowed.
3. Within each age group, those with only a basic education have a higher pension rate than those with some higher education.
4. In the age groups under 45 the pension rates were higher in the urban areas; in the age groups 45 and above, the rates were higher in the rural areas, especially for the men. Occupations (for men) with especially high pension rates were: mining and quarrying; forestry; heavy manual work of other types; and work in restaurants, bars, etc. The women had high levels of premature retirement in occupations

such as heavy manual work and textile work. Low rates were found for both men and women in administrative work, office work, and in occupations demanding a higher education. These results were maintained when keeping age constant.

The higher overall rates in premature retirement among men were completely explained by differences between men and women with regard to occupational distribution. In comparable occupational categories, holding age constant, women as a rule had *higher* pension levels than men.

Two factors seemed to be of special importance in explaining the variation in premature retirement rates between occupations. The most important factor was the rate of occupational injuries. Both for men and women there was considerable correlation between the premature retirement rate and the rate of occupational injuries.

The second factor was the rate of expansion or decrease in different occupations. The hypothesis was that shrinking occupations would create more retirees.

This hypothesis was partly confirmed. A significant negative correlation for the men, but not for the women, was found.

When comparing occupations in this way, one has to remember that certain selection mechanisms most certainly affect the outcome. A high retirement rate in an occupation, at least to some degree, may reflect the fact that it is the least competitive workers who end up in the least attractive occupations, which often are the ones with the worst working environment.

Even if the quality of the work environment explains a part of the variation in pension rates between occupations, it can hardly explain the *increase* in the number of early retirees. There is no reason to believe that the work environment in Sweden has grown worse in recent years. The number of people in occupations with detrimental working conditions has decreased rather than increased.

GOVERNMENT POLICIES

The growing number of early retirees among older workers has led to policies aimed at preventing people from dropping out of the labor force. When the partial pension scheme was adopted, the objective was not only to ease the transition from work life to a life as a pensioner, but also to diminish the health problems and the need for the disability pensions. Recent research suggests that these objectives may have been achieved. The number of partial pensioners receiving a disability pension was lower than for people in the same age group working full-time. The partial pensioners lowered their number of days on sick leave, while the opposite was the case for those continuing to work full-time.

Another measure is the extensive legal protection against dismissal for older workers. The Security of Employment Act came into effect in 1974. According to this act, an employer can only dismiss an employee if there are "justifiable grounds," and generally, only lack of work or certain specified offenses are accepted as reasons. Second, the law introduced longer periods of notice, ranging from one month for those below 25 years old up to 6 months for those aged 45 or above (Casey & Bruche, 1983). Third, there is, in the case of dismissal because of lack of work, a seniority principle dictating that those who were last hired have to leave first. Employees who have completed 2 years service and who get notice of dismissal are entitled to re-employment within 1 year should the company once again start recruiting. These rules, however, can be modified by collective agreements between employers and unions. According to a government committee report, it has become more and more frequent that, when a company is being restructured and reduces its work force, an agreement is made that will give priority to younger workers (SOU 1983, p. 134).

It should also be mentioned that the Security of Employment Act does not apply to those workers who are 65 years of age or above. According to most union contracts, they would be hired on a time-limited basis. At the end of such a period no notice has to be given.

Even if these measures have had some effect in making it possible for older workers to stay on in their jobs until age 65, it seems as if the lack of demand for older workers has been a stronger force acting in the opposite direction. All in all, the findings described here are not surprising. For many years labor has been seen as a cost to be reduced. Maybe we have been too successful.

REFERENCES

Berglind, H. (1978). Pension or work? A growing dilemma in the Nordic welfare states. *Acta Sociologica*, 181–191.

Berglind, H. (1977). Unemployment and redundancy in a "post industrial" Labor market. In N.R. Haug & J. Dofne (Eds.), *Work and technology*. London.

Casey, B., & Bruche, G. (1983). *Work or retirement? Labor market policy and social policy for older workers in France, Great Britain, The Netherlands, Sweden, and the USA*. London: Gower.

Crona, G. (1981). Delpension—en väg till ökad valfrihet och ökad välfard (Partial pension—a step towards increased freedom of choice and well-being). (Report No. 5) Stockholm: Delegation for Social Research.

SOU. (1983). *För gammal för arbete?* (Too old to work?). Stockholm: author.

Tracy, M. (1979). Retirement age practices in ten industrial societies, 1960–67. Geneva: International Social Security Association.

CHAPTER 33

Nonagenarians as Survivors After 27 Years in a Longitudinal Study

R. J. van Zonneveld, D. J. H. Deeg,
M. P. van Tol, N. P. van der Schaft-Kleywegt

This is the report of an 8 year longitudinal study of 3,149 older persons in The Netherlands begun in 1955. Twenty-eight persons 90 years of age and older were interviewed, described, and compared in various ways with themselves and others in this longitudinal study.

Extended longitudinal health interview and examination surveys of elderly people have so far very rarely been done. Although such studies undeniably end with a small group of highly selected survivors, they are necessary in order to study changes during the process of aging and to identify predictors of longevity.

In The Netherlands, beginning in 1955, a nationwide longitudinal study has taken place using an age- and sex-stratified random sample of 3,149 people, 65 years of age and over. These subjects were identified as patients of almost 400 general practitioners who undertook to interview and examine about 28 old people of various age and sex groups from their practices. The seven re-examinations took place 5, 8, 11, 14, 16, 18, and 27 years after the initial round in 1955-1957. The results have been published frequently in the literature, (Beek & van Zonneveld, 1976; Deeg & van Zonneveld, 1985; van Zonneveld, 1961, 1981).

The youngest subjects in 1955 to 1957 (aged 65 to 70) who survived to be interviewed in 1983 were by then over the age of 90. They presented an opportunity to explore whether nonagenarians have characteristics that distinguish them from their age peers who died earlier.

AIMS AND METHOD

In order to shed light on this question, a study was conducted by M.P. van Tol and N.P. van der Schaft-Kleywegt (1983), medical students of the Erasmus University under the supervision of D.J.H. Deeg and R.J. van Zonneveld. The aim of this last follow-up study was to obtain information on the living conditions and health of very old people and to compare these with information from an earlier set of observations (Beek & van Zonneveld, 1976). Here we compare data only from the first and last observations of our longitudinal study.

Administrative data collected from municipal population registers in The Netherlands in 1981 indicate that 56 of the 3,149 subjects initially examined in 1955-1957 were still alive. In April, 1983, after further investigation, 28 of these 56 subjects were found alive; there were 19 women and 9 men, ranging in age from 91 to 98; they resided throughout the country. All 28 person were in the age group 65 to 70 in 1955 to 1957.

Out of the 28 people who were 90 years of age or older, 24 could be visited and interviewed. These visits took place in April, 1983, and required one-half to 1 1/2 hours per person. Information from a questionnaire that had been tested in a pilot study of 5 healthy and 3 ill old people was collected through interview but not by examination. Most information was obtained from the persons themselves; from six persons having dementia, however, information was secured with assistance from nursing personnel. From 2 of the 4 aged who did not want to be visited, information was obtained by a mailed questionnaire; from the 2 others only scanty general information could be collected. Thus most data refer to 26 persons 90 years of age or older. Case-control data were extracted from the records of initial examinations of the nonagenarians who survivied to be reinterviewed as well as from a matched random sample of 112 persons who had died within 5 years after their first examination in 1955 to 1957.

ILLUSTRATIVE RESULTS

General Data

In general, the questions were quickly answered by these very old survivors and only a few persons wanted to give lengthy answers. All the 26 persons had been married, with the exception of one woman. Only one man had a surviving wife. Five people were living more or less independently including one living in the house of her children. In 1955 to 1957, these same subjects were all living independently, although 7 of them lived together with children even then. Sixteen of the 26 were living in an old-age or nursing home; 5 lived with their children. Of the 22 nondemented subjects, 6 were in an old-age home and 4 in a nursing home; all 6 demented persons were institutionalized. Almost all were in need of some assistance in household or daily living activities. In terms of residence, 11 were living in rural areas, 17 in urbanized areas.

Data on Health

Regarding subjective rating of health, 4 out of 9 men and 13 of 16 women considered their health to be good at a very advanced age. In 1955 to 1957 all 28 persons under review had reported themselves to be in good objective health (with the exception of 2 women) and in good subjective health (excepted 4 women). Yet, 2 out of 3 nonagenarians had complaints on physical symptoms. Two of 9 men and 4 of the 19 women had symptoms of senile dementia of the Alzheimer's type. Their complaints covered a wide variety of diseases and disablements, and were not closely related to reported subjective health.

Three persons who initially reported they consulted their general physician (GP) infrequently reported infrequent visits by a physican currently. However, those who had initially sought frequent consultations are still visited often by their general physician. The majority could not, when asked, attribute their good or bad health to any specific factors.

Of the 22 nondemented subjects, 6 said to have not particularly observed that they were growing so old; 4 did notice their aging, but did not specify what they had observed. Twelve mentioned one or more symptoms of old age: being easily tired, diminished vision, problems with walking, diminished hearing, deteriorated memory, and many diseases. None of the respondents said that he or she was eating insufficiently. While in the first examination 10 people had a diet prescribed by the GP, in 1983 only one person had such a diet. In the first examination most persons were overweight but now, with 4 exceptions, most were rather lean. Of the 26 persons interviewed, 18 reported sleeping well, 4 not too well, and 4 badly. As to activities of daily living (ADL) the following results can be reported:

- Eleven people could still walk well; 4 not at all.
- Ten people had to be assisted with washing and dressing themselves.
- Four still performed household activities, and 3 women were still cooking.

• Nine people did not do anything but sit and gaze.

In the first examination of 1955 to 1957, none of the men had ADL difficulties and only 2 women had problems with walking. Most respondents in 1983 attributed their survival to good health. Also almost all, with 3 exceptions, were contented with their lives The parents, sisters, and brothers of these very old people had also attained very old age.

CASE-CONTROL RESULTS

In the comparison data from these survivors when they were examined for the first time in 1955 to 1957 with data of the elderly of comparable age initially who had died within 5 years after their first examination, both subjective and objective good health were positively correlated with a long life. A significant difference between the long-lived and short-lived elderly was found in consumption of drugs, with more of the latter using medicines than the former group. The long-lived persons also had much less particular eating habits (e.g., diets) than the short-lived. More or less as expected, various cardiovascular symptoms were at the time of the first examination more prevalent in those who would die soon afterwards. Also more abnormalities in urine samples were found in the latter group.

A FINAL RESULT

The long-lived elderly studied had, in general, always been not easily irritated, cheerful, and easy-going persons; also in the initial examination they generally accepted problems of aging better than those who had died early. This is in line with what other investigators have found regarding effective coping styles. All the subjects except one were fairly or well contented with their past lives. However, many felt lonely currently and were resigned to their often difficult circumstances.

Although most of the above data and results are based on rather small numbers, they may be considered as an indication of the necessity of longitudinal gerontological research in human beings as a tool for more insight into the processes of aging.

REFERENCES

Beek, A., & van Zonneveld, R.J. (1976). Health in progressive old age (with an English summary). Organization for Applied Health Research, TNO, The Hague.
Deeg, D.J.H., & van Zonneveld, R.J. (1985). Into high age.

van Tol, M.P., & van der Schaft-Kleywegt, N.P. (1983). Report on the 8th round of
    the project: Health in progressive old age. Department of Public Health, Fac.
    of Medicine, Erasmus University Rotterdam (unpublished report).
van Zonneveld, R.J. (1961). The health of the aged (in English). Van Gorcum, Assen.
van Zonneveld, R.J. (1981). Health in progressive old age in The Netherlands. In:
    S.A. Medwick & A.E. Beart (Eds). *Prospective longitudinal research*. Oxford: Oxford
    University Press.

PART IV

Multidimensional Assessment of Older Persons

CHAPTER 34

Introduction to Multidimensional Assessment

Betty Havens

The multidimensional assessment of older persons is an issue that has become increasingly important over the past decade. Prior to the mid-70s, many clinicians and some researchers were addressing the issues of functional assessment, most frequently defined as physical functioning ability. However, in that period, scant attention was being paid to standardization of instruments, to their reliability, validity, dimensionality (or domains), and applicability in more than single-site, single-assessor policy, practice, or research. Beginning in the late 70s, more effort from professionals in a much wider variety of disciplines has been invested in the evolving technology of multidimensional assessments of older persons.

The usual components of multidimensional assessments include, but are not restricted to, general health, functioning ability in everyday activities, individual well-being, cognitive functioning, coping behaviors or ability, social skills or functioning, social or informal supports, and economic security. Even this partial listing clearly identifies the wide range of disciplines that has contributed to more recent assessment approaches.

As noted above, multidimensional assessments operate in at least three very different areas based on the goal or goals of a particular

---

Betty Havens assisted in editing the chapters in this section of the volume; she was in turn assisted by Lorraine Nogue.

undertaking. These include assessments that are developed as screening tools to determine need or eligibility for particular services; assessment tools in clinical practice with older individuals; and instruments used in population-based studies for policymakers, program development, or applied research. While these goals are not necessarily incompatible, one is seldom able to address all three goals by the use of a single instrument or with the same analyses.

This lack of concordance between population-based studies and the requirements of clinical practice is a central feature of the chapter by L. Branch primarily devoted to a population-based study for policy purposes. Further, the chapters by G. Fillenbaum, R. Taylor, and F. Pannill, and A. Fisk explicitly recognize the different requirements of screening tools as opposed to clinical assessments, while developing their discussions of screening tools. Fillenbaum uses two large data bases to test the efficacy of a five-item Guttman scale constructed as a screening tool derived from more comprehensive multidimensional assessment data. The chapters by F. Pannill and D. McKenzie are based on two clinical assessment data bases, which in Pannill's case aims to reduce the use of a complete assessment, and in McKenzie's case is used to derive a screening tool for determining admission to a care facility. The two chapters by J. Toner and J.D. Frengley et al. specifically address the instrumentation of clinical practice assessments. Frengley and his colleagues deal with a clinical assessment that will identify requirements for posthospitalization services. The chapter by Toner, while concentrating on assessment from a clinical practice perspective, also deals with the derivation of a relatively short screening tool from a lengthy clinical assessment.

Finally, H. Hermanova's chapter provides both a concise and insightful historical overview to assessment technology within a very helpful and important international perspective. The importance of instrument standardization is most critical when viewed with this international perspective.

Assessment instruments must be appropriate to individual older clients as the recipients of the services of clinical practitioners; to local, regional, and national aging policy; and to applied research. They also must be standardized to preclude, as much as is possible, reinventing the wheel with each new multidimensional assessment task. Further, only with standardization will cross-national comparisons become possible.

It is this last point that stimulated the development of the "Multidimensional Assessment of the Older Person" Symposium at the XIIIth International Congress of Gerontology and is the impetus for this part of a volume recording highlights of the Congress. However, it is a goal which, with the exception of the chapter by Fillenbaum and to a lesser extent Hermanova's chapter, remains largely unfulfilled as none of the other participants had any elements of cross-national experience in the area of multidimensional assessment technology. However, let us all take as a challenge the development of cross-national comparisons based on standardized multidimensional assessments that are adaptable to screening tools and population-based studies for major contributions to the XIVth International Congress of Gerontology.

CHAPTER 35

Development of a Brief, Internationally Usable Screening Instrument

Gerda G. Fillenbaum

In order to serve the elderly appropriately, multidimensional assessment is essential. Few providers of services, however, have the facilities or time for a full-scale assessment of all older patients. Agreement was therefore reached at a 1984 WHO (Europe) meeting in Aberdeen on the desirability of developing a brief screening instrument to identify persons at particular risk for loss of independence. The core of such a screener has now been developed. Consisting of five instrumental activities of daily living (IADL) items (housework, traveling, shopping, meal preparation, handling personal finances), the core is brief, valid and reliable, and constitutes a Guttman scale. It correlates significantly with physical and mental health ($r = .55$ & $.54$ respectively) as well as being predictive of each ($r = .51$ & $.48$ respectively). The score is also predictive of death. Those age 65+ able to perform, for instance, all, two, or none of the activities experience death within a year at .4, 1.8, and 5.4 times the usual rate. This IADL core has been tested on three major samples of elderly U.S. community residents and is ready for cross-national testing. It should help to identify those in need of a more extensive evaluation, and so be a cost-effective approach to assessment and service provision.

While illnesses and problems increase with age, the majority of the

---

This chapter was prepared with the partial support of the Sandoz Foundation (US) and NIA Grant no. AG00371 to the Gerontology Computing and Statistical Laboratory.

elderly in the U.S., even over the age of 85, continue to live independently and to take care of their personal needs without help (Feller, 1983). Under such circumstances it is hard to justify routine multidimensional assessment of older adults with its attendant costs. The valid and reliable multidimensional functional assessments, which are specifically intended for community resident elderly, such as adaptations of CARE (Gurland, Golden, Teresi, & Challop, 1984; Gurland & Wilder, 1984), the Philadelphia Geriatric Center Multilevel Assessment Inventory (Lawton, Moss, Fulcomer, & Kleban, 1982), and the OARS Multidimensional Functional Assessment Questionnaire (Duke University Medical Center, 1978), take about 45 minutes for a trained interviewer to administer. The value of multidimensional functional assessments, particularly in epidemiological surveys (where they indicate population status, provide a basis of determining service need and allocation, and facilitate assessment of service impact) is not questioned. However, in clinical practice regular lengthy evaluation and reevaluation of patients are rarely feasible or economic. Yet for some persons such evaluation may be vital if independent functioning and the best possible levels of health and well-being are to be maintained. As a result, the desirability of a brief screen, which could rapidly identify those elderly whose functional status may be precarious and who merit a full evaluation, has become increasingly evident. This is particularly so in settings where data gathering is difficult; where the subject pool is large but those needing services are few; where health is broadly defined to include not only mental and physical well-being but also takes the social and environmental situation into account; and where there is focus on prevention of impairment and concern for equitable health service delivery.

Ideally, a screening instrument should be brief, easy to administer, and should rapidly identify those persons most likely to experience problems. The instrument to be reported here, which appears to meet these criteria, is an outcome of a World Health Organization (WHO) meeting in March, 1984 in Aberdeen, Scotland (WHO, 1984), where a decision was made to develop a useful internationally relevant screen to identify the presence of broadly defined medical and social problems. Initial focus was to be on functional status in the medical area. The intention, however, was that items could be added to identify problems in other areas.

Different screening measures are already in use, particularly in the area of medical practice (e.g., Barber & Wallis, 1976, 1978, 1981, 1982; Barber, Wallis, & McKeating, 1980). The most adequately tested of these instruments make extensive use of information on ability to perform those activities of daily living (ADL) needed for continued community residence. It is at this level that one must begin inquiry for limited but appropriate service at the outset of an identified problem, which can be highly cost-effective in helping to maintain personal independence, whereas providing service both to those who can no longer manage basic self-maintenance (e.g. feeding themselves, getting dressed, remaining continent) may be as expensive as institutional care.

For these reasons, and also because it is known that ADL functioning is related to physical health and mental health functioning (Fillenbaum, Dellinger, Maddox, & Pfeiffer, 1978), the decision was made to explore the usefulness of instrumental ADL items as a core screening instrument.

METHODS

Initial data were drawn from three random sample surveys of community residents aged 65 and over in the U.S.: (1) 997 residents of Durham, N.C. (Blazer, 1978); (2) 1,609 residents of Cleveland, Ohio (Comptroller General, 1977); and (3) 1,530 residents of the State of Virginia (Virginia Center on Aging, 1980). The OARS questionnaire (Duke University Medical Center, 1978) was used in each survey. This questionnaire is designed to assess level of functioning of adults in five areas: social and economic resources, mental and physical health, and ADL. It also obtains information on service use and need. Studies by the developers of OARS and by other users have indicated that the questionnaire is both valid and reliable, the ADL section being particularly robust in these regards.

The ADL section consists of 14 items (see Table 35-1). Seven of these are typically considered instrumental activities. In order of administration they examine ability to use the telephone, to travel, shop, and prepare meals, to do housework, administer one's own medicine and handle personal finances. The seven self-maintenance activities assess ability to feed oneself, dress, groom, and walk, move in and out of bed, bathe and remain continent.

These items were factor analyzed. Two significant factors were obtained. Five of the seven instrumental items fell on one factor; five of the seven self-maintenance activities fell on the second factor, and the remaining four items loaded on both factors, but not decisively. The five instrumental items with decisive loadings were the ability to travel, shop, prepare meals; do housework; and handle personal finances.

Analysis indicated that these items refer to activities that are not of equal difficulty, and that performance capability for each item declined with increase in age, the sharpest drop typically occurring among those aged 80 to 84 (see Table 35-2). The order of item difficulty was similar for men and women. The overall order of difficulty, from most to least difficult, was doing housework, traveling, shopping, preparing meals,

TABLE 35-1. Factor Analysis of 14 ADL Items

	Virginia		Cleveland	
	I	II	I	II
Instrumental ADL items				
Housework	.26	*.82*	*.82*	.19
Travel	.17	*.81*	*.82*	.19
Shop	.26	*.86*	*.87*	.18
Prepare meals	.45	*.74*	*.71*	.39
Handle personal finances	.34	*.72*	*.67*	.40
Use telephone	.40	.55	.51	.45
Handle medicine	.61	.52	.54	.56
Physical ADL items				
Eat	*.76*	.15	.07	*.82*
Dress	*.82*	.32	.30	*.82*
Groom	*.81*	.31	.31	*.79*
Walk	*.66*	.38	.44	.63
In/out bed	*.82*	.24	.29	.73
Bathe	.66	.48	.57	.54
Continence	−.29	−.28	.45	.20
Eigenvalue	7.68	1.33	7.37	1.39
% Variance explained	55	9	53	10

and handling personal finances. There were some sex-related differences in item difficulty; over the three sites women found meal preparation marginally easier than handling personal finances, while men found meal preparation only slightly less onerous than housework. Overall around 30% of these community resident elderly needed help with their housework, while at the other end of the scale about 10% needed help with personal finances.

Information from both men and women was pooled and the five items examined to see whether they had the properties of a Guttman

TABLE 35-2. Ability to Perform Selected IADL by Sex, for Three Community Samples (%)

	Durham		Cleveland		Virginia	
	Women ($n = 613$)	Men ($n = 370$)	Women ($n = 994$)	Men ($n = 604$)	Women ($n = 934$)	Men ($n = 596$)
Housework	70	75	67	75	72	79
Travel	71	85	71	86	69	83
Shop	72	83	73	84	77	86
Cook	88	76	89	82	89	87
Personal finances	88	90	88	90	87	90

scale (i.e., whether they constituted a hierarchical scale such that ability to perform a particular activity consistently indicated ability to perform activities deemed easier, and inability to perform activities deemed more difficult). These five items did conform to a Guttman scale, indicating that this set of items is unidimensional.

For the Guttman scale each of the five items is coded according to whether it can be performed unaided (scored 1) or aided (scored 0), the total score being the sum of the individual scores.

FINDINGS

To determine the validity of this five item IADL screen, the correlation between screen score and summary scores for mental health, physical health, social resources, and economic resources available from the OARS questionnare was examined. A substantial correlation with physical and mental health and a low correlation (if any) with social and economic resources was expected and these expectations were upheld. The correlations with physical health and mental health were .55 and .54 respectively, while those with social and economic resources were .16 and .19 respectively. Importantly, the initial score was also significantly related to physical and mental functioning a year later, the correlations being .51 and .48 respectively. Correlation with social and economic resources a year later was .16 and .18. While all correlations are statistically significant, only those with physical health and mental health functioning are substantially meaningful. Further, a score derived from the screening is predictor of death. Those experiencing no difficulty with any item have a death rate which is 0.4 of that found for the total group. Those incapable of performing any of the 5 activities die at 5.4 times the rate for the group as a whole. The others are distributed in between. Finally, screen score is related to type of in-home service received; the poorer the score the more likely the person is to be the recipient of more intensive in-home services (McAuley & Arling, 1984).

DISCUSSION

This information suggests that these five instrumental ADL items could play a valuable role as a rapid screener, indicating when further information on physical health and mental health should definitely be gathered. It now remains to do two things: (1) to add to these five items, items that will sensitively assess the presence of social and environmental problems, and (2) to determine the cross-national viability of this instrument.

   Thanks to Dr. Heikkinen and the principals of WHO's study of 11
countries a step has already been taken to explore cross-national applications. The WHO study is a sociomedical survey of persons aged 60
and older at 16 locations in 11 countries (Heikkinen, Waters, & Brzezinski, 1983). The common questionnaire used at each of these sites
includes extensive inquiry into ambulation, self-maintaining activities,
and, of importance here, instrumental activities of daily living. The
activities inquired into are not identical to those present on the OARS
questionnaire, but three in particular—ability to do heavy housework,
move around outdoors, and cook—are immediately comparable to
three of the five OARS activities examined, namely ability to do
housework, travel, and prepare meals. Consequently it is of considerable interest to note that, in the six sites on which data analysis has
concentrated (Louvain, Belgium; West Berlin; Tampere, Finland;
Florence, Italy; Kiev, Russia; and Belgrade, Yugoslavia) the rank-
ordered difficulty of these three activities is identical across sites and
with the U.S. In every case the order from most to least difficult to
perform for women is housework, traveling, and meal preparation,
while for men the difficulty of the last two items is reversed (except for
Tampere men who demonstrate the female pattern). Such independently gathered data strongly suggest that the five screening items
(ability to do housework, travel, shop, prepare meals, and handle
personal finances) have relevance not only in the U.S. but also in at
least six European countries.
   In summary, these five items constitute a valid, reliable, rapid, and
relevant screen that provides cross-nationally relevant information on
ability to live independently in the community, and indicates which
persons may have poor mental or physical health functioning and so
require further evaluation.

REFERENCES

Barber, J.H., & Wallis, J.B. (1976). Assessment of the elderly in general practice.
    Journal of the Royal College of General Practitioners, 26, 106–114.
Barber, J.H., & Wallis, J.B. (1978). The benefits to an elderly population of continu-
    ing geriatric assessment. *Journal of the Royal College of General Practitioners, 28,* 428–
    433.
Barber, J.H., & Wallis, J.B. (1981). Geriatric screening. *Journal of the Royal College of
    General Practitioners, 31,*57.
Barber, J.H., & Wallis, J.B. (1982). The effects of a geriatric screening and assess-
    ment on general practice workload. *Health Bulletin ,40,* 125–132.
Barber, J.H., Wallis, J.B., & McKeating, E. (1980). A postal screening questionnaire
    in preventive geriatric care. *Journal of the Royal College of General Practitioners, 30,*
    49–51.
Blazer, D. (1978). The OARS Durham survey: description and application. In *Duke
    OARS multidimensional functional assessment: The OARS methodology* (2nd ed). Dur-
    ham, NC: Duke University Medical Center.

Comptroller General of the United States. (1977, April). *The well-being of older people in Cleveland, Ohio.* (HRD-77-70) Washington, DC: U.S. General Accounting Office.

Duke University Medical Center. (1978). *Duke OARS multidimensional functional assessment: The OARS methodology* (2nd ed.). Durham, NC: Author

Feller, B.A. (1983, September 14). Americans needing help to function at home. *NCHS Advance data, 92.*

Fillenbaum, G.G., Dellinger, D.C., Maddox, G.L., & Pfeiffer, E. (1978). Assessment of individual functional status in a program evaluation and resource allocation model. In *Duke OARS Multidimensional functional assessment: The OARS methodology* (2nd ed.). Durham, NC: Duke University Medical Center.

Gurland, B., Golden, R.R., Teresi, J.A., & Challop, J. (1984). The SHORT-CARE: An efficient instrument for the assessment of depression, dementia and disability. *Journal of Gerontology, 39,* 166–169.

Gurland, B.J., & Wilder, D.E. (1984). The CARE interview revisisted: Development of an efficient, systematic clinical assessment. *Journal of Gerontology, 39,* 129–137.

Heikkinen, E., Waters, W.E., & Brzezinski, Z.J. (1983). *The elderly in eleven countries: A sociomedical survey* (Public Health in Europe No. 21). Copenhagen, Denmark: World Health Organization, Regional Office for Europe.

Lawton, M.P., Moss, M., Fulcomer, M., & Kleban, M.H. (1982). A research and service-oriented multilevel assessment instrument. *Journal of Gerontology, 37,* 91–99.

McAuley, W.J., & Arling, G. (1984). Use of in-home care by very old people. *Journal of Health and Social Behavior, 25,* 54–64.

Virginia Center on Aging. (1980, June). *Final report of the statewide survey of older Virginians: Vol. 1. Methods and procedures; Vol. II. Findings* (Research Series No. 3). Richmond, VA: Virginia Commonwealth University.

WHO Regional Office for Europe. (1984, May). *Consultation on guidelines for assessing the functioning of the elderly* (ICP/HEE 004/m02(s)5833L). Copenhagen, Denmark: Author.

CHAPTER 36

An Alternative Approach in Multidimensional Functional Assessment

Larry G. Branch

For purposes of public policy refinement, research focuses on factors (usually nonmedical) that are associated with a significant outcome such as mortality, institutionalization, or multiple hospitalizations. In this context, the factors of association are termed "risk factors." Their identification presumably leads to policies and practices that target or funnel more of the scant resources to those identified as at risk. In practice, however, clinicians often are dismayed by the lack of specificity and sensitivity that the risk factors have in relation to the outcome. All too frequently the statistical significance that is important for public policy development is unimportant for guiding special care for an individual. The discussion addresses whether clinicians ask too much of policy research, whether policy research is too often trivial, and whether current practices keep policy analysts and clinicians at arm's length.

THE CHANGING CONTEXT OF ASSESSMENT

Reports of research by Professor Rex Taylor of Scotland and by Professor John Toner of the United States have emphasized multidimensional assessment for the *individual* in the context of case findings, client assessment, care, and support. Within this context of the individual, Professor Taylor emphasized the importance of having the same individual responsible for both assessment and treatment because it is a more efficient model.

One may wholeheartedly agree with the importance of multidimensional assessment of the individual in a clinical context and agree with the approaches which are commonly observed. However, there is another appropriate use for multidimensional assessments that I will briefly consider, namely, the assessment of *populations* for the purpose of estimating the size and, usually, the characteristics of a population at risk for purposes of program planning. Different issues of precision, sensitivity, specificity, and a vast array of other methodological alternatives present themselves in this alternative context of the multidimensional assessment of whole populations.

At the outset, I will share with you the critical question which I would ask the reader to consider during this discussion. That question is whether one instrument (either a short screening instrument or a comprehensive assessment) should or can be used both to assess individuals and populations.

MASSACHUSETTS: AN EXAMPLE OF POPULATION ASSESSMENT WITHOUT A CASE-FINDING COMPONENT

In 1974, the Commonwealth of Massachusetts was considering the establishment of a statewide network of home care services as an alternative for those with long-term care needs, particularly those who might soon thereafter be deinstitutionalized from state mental health facilities. A statewide assessment of needs was considered useful for the initial step of estimating the size and characteristics of the community-living elders presumptively at risk of needing long-term care support. Bear in mind that this population needs assessment was considered the initial step for establishing a home care network. There was no systematic, uniformly available, state-supported home care program available at that time to respond to individuals in need. The estimate of the size of the population with presumptive risk was necessary in order to plan the configuration of services to be provided and to allocate sufficient funds to meet the needs.

It is worth noting at this point that the goal of the needs assessment in Massachusetts was stated as "estimating the size of community elders with presumptive risk of needing long-term care support." This goal is different from the one stated by Professor Fillenbaum for other contexts as "assessing the ability of elders to live independently." Both goals are perfectly legitimate, but one has to specify the goal of the assessment.

Instrument Development

Among the easier aspects of this project was the identification of the dimensions to be included in the instrument. The four dimensions of function were: (1) physical function, (2) cognitive function, (3) social function, and (4) emotional function. Notice that the first item is physical function. All too often one discovers the phrase "function" or "functional assessment" actually means "physical function" or "physical functional assessment." Each of us probably is aware of instances in which advances in our disciplines or fields were hindered because of imprecise terminology. One should use the phrase physical function when that is the dimension meant.

In addition to these domains of function, there was consensus that the needs assessment proposed would encompass the following 6 areas: (1) transportation, (2) grocery shopping, (3) food preparation, (4) housekeeping, (5) social opportunities, and (6) personal care.

Degree of Precision

The degree of precision required for individual assessment and care is very high. There is virtually no tolerance for misclassification. Failing to identify and help an individual with needs is unconscionable; but expending scarce resources on one without a real claim of need is both inefficient and unacceptable. The care of the individual requires maximum precision, and accordingly, professionally trained clinicians with abilities to render judgments based on the finest of distinctions among individuals is typically used. Periodic suggestions to exclude clinical judgment from the process generally fail to recognize the complexities.

Mode of Data Collection

The goal of a statewide needs assessment to estimate the size of the population with presumptive risk of long-term care needs forced the first methodological choice for data collection. A decision needed to be made to use clinicians or lay interviewers. With a limited amount of funds available for the population assessment, the choice was clear—more respondents could be assessed if less expensive lay interviewers were used. A pilot study to list reliability was done to assess the concordance of information across judges (lay interviewers, public health nurses, and floor nurses) for a subset of the cases on the same respondents and across a broad array of domains (sociodemographic, factual information, practices, attitudes, activities of daily living, and so forth). There was no evidence that nursing professionals were superior to lay interviewers in collecting the requisite information. In fact, lay interviewers and public health nurses trained for community interviews were more consistent in their information ascertainment than floor nurses. Therefore, the decision was made to use lay interviewers in the population assessment. This not only increased the number of respondents but also reduced the standard error of the estimates.

Operational Definitions of the Needs Assessment Areas

A group of approximately 25 clinicians working in various state agencies were convened to develop consensus on the amount and configuration of information necessary to categorize individuals into one of four of the following categories:

- Need met, no apparent problem
- Need met, apparent problem
- Uncertain, apparent problem
- Need unmet, current problem

In each of the previously identified domains (transportation, grocery shopping, food preparation, housekeeping, social opportunities, personal care), the clinicians agreed that they would require both *objective* information and *subjective* evaluations from the individual. By objective information they meant finding out who specifically does the task in the household, the frequency with which it is accomplished, and so forth. By subjective information, the clinicians agreed they needed estimates of the individual satisfaction with the frequency with which a task is accomplished and, if dissatisfied, reasons for dissatisfaction. For each domain, approximately 7 to 10 elements of information were agreed upon by the task force of clinicians as necessary to categorize an individual into one of the four categories. Furthermore, they agreed that only a subset of the information was necessary to identify an individual in the most independent category of "need met, no apparent problem." These were the individuals who reported they accomplished the specific activity themselves, as frequently as they desired, and liked the way they were doing it.

The distinction between the first two groups (both with needs met, but a difference between no apparent problem and an apparent problem) in general revolved around the issue of who in fact was accomplishing the task at present; and, if it was someone else, how easily it would be for the individual to either do the task himself or herself or find someone else to do it if the original person were suddenly unavailable. In the parlance of the day, the role and stability of the informal support network was taken into consideration in making this distinction.

A copy of the final revisions of the scoring procedures for each of the needs assessment areas is available from the author. The final scoring procedures were converted to a computer algorithm. The items necessary for each domain are listed first, and the frequency of specific profiles within the four major categories are identified second.

VALIDITY SUBSTUDY

The decision to exclude trained clinicians from the actual needs assessment survey was troublesome to all concerned. Accordingly, a substudy was designed to test the validity of the categorization based on the self-reported survey information gathered by lay interviewers against the accepted standard of a clinician's judgment. Bear in mind that the categorizations from self-reported information for this validity substudy were based on the second-to-last version of the algorithm; the categorizations by algorithm were revised once more following this validity substudy.

A different group of clinicians who were not involved in establishing the initial algorithms for categorization were retained to make needs assessments based on a clinical interview with a subsample of the survey respondents. The clinicians retained for this validity study were working at a large rehabilitation hospital in Boston, MA, United States. They had daily responsibilities for interviewing and deciding which applicants to their 700-bed rehabilitation hospital in fact had needs requiring institutional long-term care and which had long-term needs that could be met by some other limited services available to them.

In order to ensure that an enriched sample of individuals with potential long-term care needs was selected for the validity substudy, a purposive sample of approximately 200 individuals was selected based on their responses to the lay interviewers. Clinical interviews with 167 of these were obtained.

The results of the methodological substudy were encouraging. Only two individuals (1%) were judged by clinicians to need institutional placement. The clinical judgments of unmet need in the various areas ranged from 1% to 6%, while the initial algorithms generated slightly greater estimates ranging from 1% to 7%. Table 36-1 presents a summary. Apparently the initial algorithms overestimated needs in three areas: transportation, grocery shopping, and personal care. Overall, there was more than 95% concordance between the clinical judgments and the initial algorithm categorizations. Furthermore, there was not a single instance in which the algorithms missed categorizing an individual as having an unmet need when a trained clinician thought they did. The implication, therefore, is that the initial algorithm categorization was an accurate, but slightly conservative, estimate of clinical judgment.

TABLE 36-1. Comparison of Rates of Unmet Needs Provided by Initial Algorithm and by Clinicians

Domains	Percent with unmet needs by initial algorithm	Percent with unmet needs or unstable met needs by clinical judgment
Transportation/travel outside home	7	1
Housekeeping	5	4
Grocery shopping	7	1
Food preparation	1	1
Personal care	6	1
Social opportunities	5	6

ANOTHER ISSUE FOR MULTIDIMENSIONAL ASSESSMENT

The vast majority of the multidimensional assessment instruments are based on self-reported information. The concordance between performance testing and self-reported abilities has caused concern to some. One should anticipate that the next generation of multidimensional assessment instruments will contain much more performance testing than has been seen in the past. This development should be viewed as an acceptance or confirmation of the domains that were pioneered by the first generation of multidimensional instruments.

CHAPTER 37

An Index of Dependency that Assesses Assistance Needs

J. Dermot Frengley, E. Lefton,
K. Farkas, L. Mion

The Highland View Index of Dependency, developed in a rehabilitation setting for geriatric patients, differs from other functional scales in that it determines the amount of personal assistance the patient needs. This knowledge aids in discharge
planning. The index is easily administered, requires no specific
training, and takes little time. The index contains six variables:
(1) walking, (2) transfers, (3) bowel and bladder continence, (4)
bathing, dressing, feeding, (5) speech, and (6) mentation. These
measures are weighted from 0 (independent) to 5 (maximum
dependency), with the exception of mentation, wherein the most
disabled (demented) score 10. The total score for the patient is
obtained by summing the individual function measures. This
total score determines the amount of personal assistance required
by the patient upon discharge and serves as a guide in discharge
planning. Excellent inter-rater reliability has been shown across
all levels of nursing staff (RNs, LPNs, NAs). Inter-rater reliability for the separate variables ranged from 0.76 (transfers) to 0.96
(speech). The inter-rater reliability for the total score category
was 0.92. Findings on the predictive validity of the instrument in
various health care settings, acute care, rehabilitation, and outpatient clinics, will be presented.

As the elderly population has increased, so has the number and variety
of assessment instruments (Kane & Kane, 1981). The majority of
assessment tools measure the degree to which elderly people perform
the activities of daily life (Duke University Center for the Study of
Aging and Human Development, 1978; Gurel, Linn & Linn, 1972;

FUNCTIONAL ⟶ RESOURCE ⇄ SUPPORTS ⟶ LIVING
    IMPAIRMENTS   NEEDS   ARRANGEMENTS

FIGURE 37-1. Conceptual framework for the development of the index.

Katz, Ford, Maskowitz, Jackson, & Jaffe, 1963; Mahoney & Berthel, 1965; Meer & Baker, 1965; Plutchik, Conte, & Lieberman, 1971). Although useful for administration, research, education, and screening, these measures are often inadequate as a way to determine the level of services an elderly person requires to live safely and comfortably at home. On the other hand, the Highland View Index of Dependency was conceived to gauge the quantity of support needed by elderly persons after a hospital stay.

The conceptual model that guided the development of the index is shown in Figure 37-1.

The amount and degree of functional impairments present in an individual define the resources that are required and, in turn, dictate the type of living arrangements that are appropriate. However, the translation of resource needs to living arrangements is not always clear-cut because resource needs are tempered by the formal and informal personal supports available. The Highland View Index of Dependency assesses not only the level of functional impairment, but also the degree of supportive care needed by the patient and thus goes beyond most other functional scales. Furthermore, the index provides useful information for discharge planning purposes.

DEVELOPMENT OF INDEX

The Highland View Index of Dependency was developed at Highland View Hospital, the 180-bed rehabilitation unit of Cleveland Metropolitan General/Highland View Hospital, a major teaching hospital of Case Western Reserve University School of Medicine. The index shown in Figure 37-2 builds upon past work in assessment of activities of daily living. Differences do occur in the tools used to measure activities of daily living. For example, the Katz Index of Activities of Daily Living (Katz et al., 1963) has no measurement for walking while the Barthel Index (Mahoney & Barthel, 1965) includes either walking or wheelchair mobility, an important consideration when examining relative independence at home. The Highland View Index of Dependency differs from other measurements of activities of daily living by including a simple assessment of language, mental function, and physical function. Moreover the index was designed to use only information that is routinely acquired about an elderly person in a health care setting and to be easy to use.

WALKING	Walks independently with or without appliance	0	Walks with supervision (attendant present) with or without appliance	1	Walks with assistance of attendant	3	Non-ambulatory	5
TRANSFERS	Independent with or without appliance	0	Supervised by attendant	1	Assisted by attendant	3	Lift or Maximal assistance	5
BOWEL AND BLADDER CONTINENCE	Mostly continent	0			Incontinent at night or prokit at night	3	Incontinent or catheter or prokit	5
BATHING, DRESSING, FEEDING	Independent	0	Needs some assistance by attendant	1			Dependent	5
SPEECH	Intact	0			Expressive difficulties but makes some needs known	3	Severe expressive or receptive aphasia	5
MENTATION	Intact	0			Disorganized but oriented in environment	3	Demented	10
TOTALS	TOTAL		TOTAL		TOTAL		TOTAL	

FIGURE 37-2. Worksheet for scoring the index. ''Prokit'' refers to any external urinary drainage device.

The six dimensions of function chosen for this index are walking, transfer, bowel and bladder continence, bathing-dressing-feeding, speech, and mentation. There is a deliberate separation of transferring skills from ambulation, since the ability to transfer may not coincide with ambulation skills. Bladder and bowel continence were grouped because the impact on caregivers differs little if they occur separately or together. Bathing-dressing-feeding were grouped because they often go hand-in-hand clinically and also make similar demands on the caregiver, Speech was very crudely graded into broad distinctions that could be easily recognized and separated by the patients' caregivers. Similarly, in judging mentation, three broad categories that can be readily distinguished by caregivers were chosen. These categories are: (1) normal, (2) disorganized thinking—at risk for an accident, and (3) obviously demented.

Each of these six dimensions is rated by the degree of personal assistance necessary. Five of these functional scales are scored from 0 (independent) to 5 (maximum dependency), with the exception of mentation, wherein the most disabled (deented) score 10. Clinical experience has shown that mental status weighs more heavily than any other individual physical function when determining resource needs.

The individual scales are then seemed to give a total dependency score (Figure 37-3). The dependency score is classified into four cate-

SCORE	CATEGORY
0	INDEPENDENT
1–9	NEEDS ATTENDANT PART–TIME
10–15	NEEDS ATTENDANT FULL–TIME
16+	TOTALLY DEPENDENT

FIGURE 37–3. Total dependency score.

gories: independent, needs part-time attendant, needs full-time attendant, and totally dependent.

The category of full-time attendant implies the 24-hour presence of a person to supervise and assist. People scoring 16 and above, the totally dependent category, require a skilled caregiver round-the-clock—a resource need that is not easily met at home.

TESTING THE INDEX

The index was tested for its reliability and its validity. To do so, inter-rater reliability, internal consistency, test–retest reliability, and construct validity were each evaluated. In these studies, the index was used to assess the support needs of patients aged 70 and older who are being managed on either the acute general medical wards; The Medical Unit for the Elderly, which is a rehabilitation inpatient ward designed and staffed for the assessment and rehabilitation of elderly patients; or in the Geriatric Outpatient Assessment Clinic.

Inter-Rater Reliability

The initial testing of the instrument took place on the Medical Unit for the elderly, a 28-bed rehabilitation unit, which accepts patients aged 70 and older for a variety of medical conditions. The tool was explained to the nursing personnel, which consisted of six registered nurses, four licensed practical nurses, and two nursing assistants. The nursing personnel were asked to assess independently all patients known to them and to base their ratings on clinical observations. These ratings were repeated 1 week later. There were a total of 91 assessments per function.

The inter-rater reliability was computed by the concordance rate of the raters for each individual variable as well as for the overall total score category.

TABLE 37-1. Inter-Rater Reliability

Walking	.82
Transfers	.76
Bowel & bladder continence	.94
Bathing, dressing & feeding	.88
Speech	.96
Mentation	.90
Total Score	.92

Raters: 6 R.N.'s., 4 L.P.N.'s., 2 N.A.'s., $n = 91$ assessments per function

Table 37-1 illustrates the quite high levels of concordance. These ranged from .76 (transfers) to .96 (speech) for the individual items. An overall rate of .92 was obtained when examining the total score category.

Internal Consistency

Although an index does not normally require an evaluation of its internal consistency, we were interested in establishing a relationship among items to ensure their relevancy. The measures made on 184 different patients 70 years or older were used to assess the internal consistency of the scale. These patients were in the three environments: the acute medical wards, the rehabilitation ward, ad the Geriatric Outpatient Assessment Clinic. The raw scores for each of these six functions were compared and the calculations were made using the statistical package for social services (SAS).

Table 37-2 shows highly significant correlation α-coefficients between the six variables with no one variable dominant. Moreover, clinical expectations are confirmed by these coefficients. Cronbach's α-coefficient was calculated at .89 confirming the overall high degree of interal consistency of the scale.

Test-Retest Reliability

The second test for reliability was made to determine whether repeated evaluation of functional status measured the same level at several points in time. In order to determine the sensitivity of the tool, elderly patients were assessed in the three different clinical settings. In the stable population, such as an ambulatory one, little change occurs in the functional level over a period of time. While in that same period, large fluctuations can and do occur in the acute medical and rehabilitation wards. Test–retest reliability was evaluated using rater comparisons. Patients discharged from the rehabilitation unit for the elderly

TABLE 37-2. Internal Consistency - Correlation Coefficients*

($n = 184$)	Walking	Transfer	Bowel & Bladder	Bathing, Dressing & Feeding	Speech	Mentation
Walking	1.00000	—	—	—	—	—
Transfer	0.82502	1.00000	—	—	—	—
Bowel & bladder	0.55851	0.63716	1.00000	—	—	—
Bathing, dressing & feeding	0.66715	0.70900	0.74526	1.00000	—	—
Speech	0.48715	0.50854	0.58020	0.68912	1.00000	—
Mentation	0.41868	0.45064	0.62039	0.62082	0.63331	1.00000

*All Coefficients significant at $p < 0.0001$
Alpha Coefficient $\alpha = .89$

were assessed at the time of discharge and again at the time of follow-up ($n'32$). Patients on the acute care medical floors who were 70 years of age and older ($n'61$), were assessed at the time of admission and at the time of discharge. Patients in the ambulatory setting were assessed twice with a period of approximately 6 weeks separating the two measures ($n'65$).

Paired comparison t-tests were performed on the two time assessments for each of the clinical settings (see Table 37-3).

The relative stability of the ambulatory group of patients ($\bar{X}$ time

TABLE 37-3. Paired Comparisons T Tests of Individual Items and Total Scores in Three Clinical Settings

Variable	Rehabilitation	Acute Medicine	Ambulatory Clinic
	T	T	T
Walking	2.44*	1.73	0.80
Transfers	2.92**	1.49	−1.16
Bowel and bladder control	−1.00	1.31	0.39
Bathing, dressing feeding	0.75	0.57	−1.29
Speech	−1.00	2.04*	−1.76
Mentation	−0.57	2.16*	−1.03
Total Score	1.48	2.19	−1.07

*$p < 0.05$
**$p < 0.01$

difference = 40 days) contrasts with the patients in the rehabilitation setting who demonstrated the difference in their walking and transfer functions from the time of discharge to follow-up ($\bar{X}$ time difference = 58 days). The patients in the acute care setting, on the other hand, demonstrated differences in communication, mentation, and overall functional scores from the time of admission to the time of discharge ($\bar{X}$ times difference = 7 days). These findings reflect the instrument's ability not only to measure consistently over a period of time, but also demonstrates its important sensitivity to change.

Validity

The construct validity of the total score categories were ascertained by comparing the discharge disposition of the hospitalized patients with their total score and the current living arrangements of the ambulatory patients with their total score ($n'157$). Since it was conceptualized that the level of functional impairment would predict the necessary resources and supports which in turn affect living arrangements, this seemed to be a logical measure. Those with the highest levels for functional impairments would have the strongest correlations with institutional settings, while those who had low levels of functional impairments would more likely be in the home. Both extremes would have exception dependent on the available support systems.

The patients' score categories were compared with the discharge dispositions and are shown in Figure 37-4.

More than half the patients in a home setting were independent. Thirty-one percent required a part-time attendant, 8% required someone in attendance at all times, and 6% were totally dependent. Those in assisted living settings were primarily in need of part-time and full-time attendants while those in nursing homes were mostly totally dependent.

CONCLUSIONS

This easily used index requires little extra time to complete because the information is normally gathered in clinical settings providing care for elderly patients. This ease of use comes from aggregating this information while the scoring of the index itself adds very little time to normal activities. Moreover, health care workers with less than professional training are able to use this index successfully to rate patients for whom they are providing care.

The weighting of the variables was developed from clinical experience with elderly patients in which the degrees of dependency in the selected infirmities were recognized to have varying impacts on care

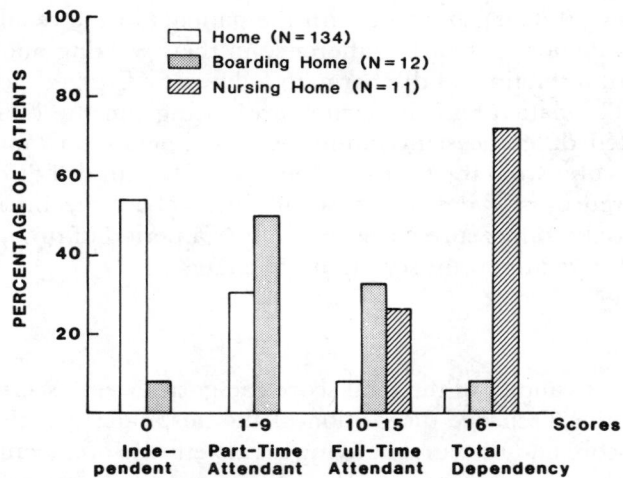

FIGURE 37–4. Percentage of patients in various living arrangements within each scoring category.

providers. A nonlinear scale was necessary to reflect realistically the demands on caregivers, since there can be a large effect from relatively small increases in dependency. It appears that the domains chosen for the index, when considered in the light of the impact on caregivers, were corectly weighted. It was assumed that the impact on caregivers reflected accurately the needs of patients.

This simple instrument appears to be a surprisingly powerful tool in assessing the supports needed by elderly persons with a wide variety of functional impairments. Furthermore, it is eminently usable across the long-term care continuum. We have found it to have high inter-rater reliability, high internal consistency, to be sensitive to change, and to be remarkably valid in its underlying assumptions.

REFERENCES

Duke University Center for the Study of Aging and Human Development. (1978). *Multidimensional functional assessment: The OARS methodology.* Durham, NC: Duke University.

Gurel, L., Linn, M.W., & Linn, B.S. (1972). Physical and mental impairment-of-function evaluation in the aged: The PAMIE scale. *Journal of Gerontology, 27,* 83–90.

Kane, R.A., & Kane, R.L. (1981). *Assessing the elderly: A practical guide to measurement.* Toronto: Lexington.

Katz, S., Ford, A.B., Moskowitz, R.W., Jackson, B.A., & Jaffe, M.W. (1963). Studies of illness in the aged. The index of ADL: A standardized measure of biological and psychosocial function. *Journal of the American Medical Association, 185* (12), 94–99.

Mahoney, F.I., & Barthel, D.W. (1965). Functional evaluation: The Barthel Index. *Maryland State Medical Journal, 14*, 61–65.

Meer, B., & Baker, J.A. (1965). Reliability of measurements of intellectual functioning of geriatric patients. *Journal of Gerontology, 20*, 410–414.

Plutchik, R., Conte, H., & Lieberman, M. (1971). Development of a scale (GIES) for assessment of cognitive and perceptual functioning in geriatric patients. *Journal of the American Geriatric Society, 19*, 614–623.

CHAPTER 38

Current Developments in Identifying the Elderly at Risk

R. C. Taylor

The four part presentation begins with a review of the general relationship between aging and illness and of the evidence for different trajectories of decline. Next, it examines the concept of ''risk'' as applied to the elderly and locates the notions of risk and vulnerability within the context of increasing dependence and breakdown. The third and longest section reviews current developments in screening and case-finding in elderly populations. Most of the experimental schemes reviewed in this section are British, but reference also is made to interesting parallel developments in Scandinavia. Finally, a brief review of common problems in all schemes for screening and case-finding is presented and some of the evidence relating to their efficacy is reviewed.

For the last 30 years geriatric spokesmen have advocated a preventive approach based on the routine visiting of all elderly patients. The major stimulus for this approach came from a number of pioneering studies that identified high levels of unreported illness and disability (Anderson & Cowan, 1955; Williamson et al., 1964). These studies were conducted in the late 1950s, and since then, the tendency for the elderly to underconsult has acquired the status of a self-evident truth.

By the mid-and late 1970s a different picture began to emerge. Studies conducted in a number of practices reported that the vast majority of illnesses detected in comprehensive examinations were either known to the general practitioner or they were of no real significance to the well-being of the elderly patient (Friedman, Charlewood, & Doods, 1978; Tulloch & Moore, 1979; Williams, 1975). Evidence for underconsultation in these later studies was described as flimsy and insufficient (Williams, 1974). The extent of underconsultation has been exhaustively examined in a recent Scottish study from which data were available to calculate the ratio between illness episodes and consultations (Ford & Taylor, 1985). It showed that while the elderly suffer more illness, proportionately they consult physicians about as often as younger age groups. Similar findings have been reported elsewhere (Hannay, 1979), and the author of a recent review of consultations in Southampton, England has predicted that elderly consultation rates will decline as future cohorts benefit from healthier life-styles (Freer, 1985).

These findings suggest that there has been an important secular change in the health attitudes and behavior of the elderly. On these grounds alone, there is a need for a reappraisal of traditional geriatric screening. The case for such a reappraisal is further strengthened by the increasing need to demonstrate cost-effectiveness. There have now been two randomized case-control trials of traditional geriatric screening and they have both failed to demonstrate its cost-effectiveness (Tulloch & Moore, 1979; Vetter, Jones, Victor, 1984).

In Britain, and throughout Europe (Illsley & Taylor, 1984), health planners and practitioners are looking for effective and efficient procedures for distinguishing between those elderly who require comprehensive assessment/follow-up and those who do not. This chapter reviews and assesses a number of current developments. It begins with a critical review of the risk group approach and goes on to outline a number of more promising alternatives.

THE RISK GROUP APPROACH

Given the apparent impractibility of universal screening the approach through risk groups is an obvious alternative.

Risk groups have been intuitively identified on the basis of two principles, structural disadvantage and the experience of threatening life events. Groups identified on the basis of some structural or inherent disadvantage include the very old (usually age 80+), those who live alone, the socially isolated (variously defined), the childless, the single, the poor, and the divorced/separated. Groups that have been defined on the basis of some threatening life event include those recently discharged from hospital; persons who are widowed or retired; and those who have recently changed their address.

It is widely assumed that the elderly falling into any of these groups are at greater risk than those who do not. One of the major problems in assessing this assumption is that the nature of risk has rarely been specified. Risk of what? Of physical or mental illness, dependence on domiciliary services, hospitalization, death? Without a defined outcome it is impossible to conduct a rigorous assessment. This point will be developed below. Meanwhile there are other and more practical problems involved in the attempt to identify those at risk through membership of predefined risk groups. For example,

1. The groups vary considerably in size. The largest group, those who live alone, accounts for around 30% of the noninstitutionalized elderly population; the smallest group, the divorced/separated, accounts for less than 5%. Groups defined on the basis of some threatening life event are all fairly small. In the Aberdeen study (Taylor & Ford, 1983) the percentage of the noninstitutionalized population experiencing various life events over the course of a year was as follows: change of address, 7%; discharge from hospital, 6%; death of a spouse, 4%; and retirement, 3%. The implications for screening/case-finding are obvious. Even if half of all group members are defined as cases, the small size of many groups mean that they will only account for a minute proportion of all cases in the population. At the other extreme, a group like the "live alone," accounting for around a third of the population, is probably too large for selective case-finding.

2. The groups are not mutually exclusive. The live alone and very old groups include members of all other groups. Many of those who are childless are also single, the single are often socially isolated, and so on. Moreover, members of all groups defined on the basis of structural disadvantage are eligible for membership in all groups defined on the basis of threatening life events. Again, the implications for screening/case-finding are obvious. Multiple group membership confuses the association between risk and outcome and prevents any direct ranking of the risks associated with particular groups.

3. The groups vary considerably in the extent and nature of their disadvantage. Risk profiles developed in the Aberdeen study showed that it was only the very old and recently discharged groups that were comprehensively disadvantaged (Taylor, Ford, & Barber, 1983). Groups such as the single and the childless were disadvantaged only in terms of social support; the poor were disadvantaged in terms of material resources; recent movers only in terms of their mental health, and so on. The profiles also revealed important compensatory effects. In some groups disadvantage in one domain was compensated by advantage in another. For example, while the poor were (by definition) disadvantaged in terms of material resources, they had more social support than their more affluent age peers. Similarly, while the single and childless were (again by definition) disadvantaged in terms of family support, they had more friends and confidants.

4. It will be obvious from the above that case-finding efficiency varies between groups, and it is uniformly poor. In an assessment made on the Aberdeen data (Ford & Taylor, 1983) the proportion of

cases (defined by scores in the lowest decile in six domains of functioning) accounted for by any one group never rose above 26%. Generally, the smaller the group, the smaller the proportion of cases accounted for. Thus, despite the fact that around half of the divorced/separated were cases on most measures, they never accounted for more than 7% of all cases. With larger groups the ratios were reversed. For example, only a third of the live alone group were cases, yet they accounted for around half of all cases.

It is important to acknowledge that this assessment was made on the basis of a comparative rather than an absolute measure of outcome. Group members were only at risk of falling into the bottom decile on various domains. It would clearly have been preferable to have assessed their risk of, say, dependence on domiciliary services or hospitalization. Unfortunately assessment of risk in relation to such defined end points requires either a large initial sample or a long period of follow-up on a smaller sample. Follow-up of the Aberdeen sample will provide opportunities for a longitudinal assessment of the consequences of risk group membership, but this is unlikely to be available for some time.

Meanwhile, it must be concluded that the risk group approach does not provide a sensible basis for identifying those elderly who might benefit from comprehensive assessment.

THE INDIVIDUAL APPROACH

Instead of attempting to operate on the basis of predefined risk groups, a number of practitioners have shown that it is possible to proceed directly to the identification of high-risk individuals.

A Nine Item Screening Letter

Barber and colleagues have pioneered this approach in the Glasgow area (Barber & Wallis, 1978, 1981, 1982; Barber, Wallis, & McKeating, 1980). They asked all elderly patients to answer nine simple questions, each requiring a yes/no answer. Any patient answering any question in the affirmative was defined as being at potential risk, and requiring comprehensive assessment. The nine questions, selected on the basis of clinical experience, are as follows:

1. Do you live on your own?
2. Are you without a relative you could call on for help?
3. Do you depend on someone for help?
4. Are there many days when you are unable to have a hot meal?

TABLE 38-1. Case Finding Efficiency of Eight Questions

Proportion in lowest decile of health			Cumulative gains in case-finding	
Question number	Question	Proportion	Proportion answering "yes"	Proportion of cases identified
1	Live alone	.34	.61	.94
2	Without relative	.26	.48	.90
3	Depend on help	.75	.20	.60
5	Housebound	.86	.13	.45
6	Worry about health	1.00	.07	.29
7	Poor vision	.54	.44	.89
8	Poor hearing	.56	.37	.83
9	Recently discharged	.51	.43	.88

5. Are you confined to your home through ill health?
6. Is there anything about your health causing you concern or difficulty?
7. Do you have difficulty with vision?
8. Do you have difficulty with hearing?
9. Have you been in hospital during the past year?

The nine questions were included in a letter sent to all elderly in the practice. Barber has tested this screening letter on two populations and it is highly acceptable to most patients with 80% completing and returning it without further prompting and only 5% refusing to reply.

The Aberdeen data set contained information on eight of the nine questions, and when they were applied to the random sample of noninstitutionalized elderly they succeeded in identifying a higher proportion of total cases than achieved by any of the risk groups. As can be seen from the first half of Table 38-1 the questions varied considerably in their capacity to identify "cases" (as previously defined). The highest proportion of cases was identified by those answering "yes" to question 6 (concerns about health) and the lowest by those answering yes to the questions on potential social support. The second half of the Table illustrates cumulative gains in case-finding efficiency. One column shows the cumulative proportion of the population answering "yes" or at risk (i.e., requiring comprehensive assessment). The proportion of cases identified goes on rising at a higher rate than the proportion of the population answering "yes" until after the addition of those answering "yes" to question 8. This point defines optimal case-finding efficiency. Thus, only four questions (numbers 6, 5, 3 and 8) succeed in identifying 0.30 of all cases at the expense of contacting/assessing only 0.37 of the population. This represents a considerable improvement on Barber's original set of questions, almost halving the population to be visited with only a small reduction in case-finding.

It is important to emphasize that further progress can only be made empirically. Barber started with a list of nine questions based on clinical experience/a priori reasoning. This original set of questions produced at least one "yes" answer from around 60% of the population. This achieves only a modest saving. A reduction in the number of questions represents one possibility for improvement. Primary Care teams in Leeds, Carlisle, Newcastle, and Leicester are currently introducing a reduced version of the screening letter. Another possibility for improvement would be to add the number of 'yes' answers to provide a risk score. The author is unaware of any screening letter which operates with such a risk score, but there are interesting parallels in two experimental schemes, one in Edinburgh and the other at the Duke Center for the Study of Aging and Human Development.

Computerized Case Finding

At the Stockbridge Health Centre in Edinburgh, master problem lists are being prepared for all elderly patients. The list includes, in addition to active medical problems, "static" risk factors such as living alone and being housebound and "dynamic" date-coded events such as change of address, hospital discharge, and death of spouse. Simultaneously, the computer holds information on all prescriptions and consultations and can provide instantaneous checks on compliance and overdue or missed consultations. It is intended that a computerized audit be conducted monthly to identify patients with the maximum "risk" scores. These patients would be reviewed at monthly meetings of the Primary Care Team. In the event that the audit identified the same list of patients each month, attention will focus on those who are at next greatest risk (Berry, 1984).

A Five-Item ADL Screening Instrument

Dr. Fillenbaum (Duke University Center for the Study of Aging and Human Development) is currently developing a core screening instrument consisting of 5 instrumental ADL items (housework, traveling, shopping, meal preparation, and handling personal finances). This core has been tested on three North American samples of the noninstitutionalized elderly; it has a high correlation with mental and physical health, and is predictive of death. It is hoped that it can also be tested on samples from the WHO 11-nation study, and that it will serve as an internationally usable screening instrument (G. Fillenbaum, personal communication).

OPPORTUNISTIC CASE-FINDING

Evidence has already been cited that indicates that the elderly consult over the same ratio of illnesses experienced as younger age groups. The proportion of elderly seen by a doctor at least once over the course of a year is currently around 75%—rising from 73% in those aged 60 to 64 to 90% in those aged 90 to 94 (Freer, 1985). Opportunities for case-finding are therefore present for the great majority of the elderly. Only around 1% might be missed in the course of any one year, and a recent Nottingham study suggests that these elderly nonattenders are remarkably fit (Ebrahim, Hedley, & Sheldon, 1984). Even if they do not describe it as such, many doctors carry out case-finding when they go beyond the presenting symptom to a more holistic assessment of a patient's well-being. But not all doctors operate in this way, and those who do, rarely do so systematically.

It is claimed that there is a revival of interest in opportunistic case-finding (Freer et al., 1983). If so, it is to be welcomed; but its effectiveness will depend on a number of factors, five of which are discussed here.

1. *Functional orientation:* More progressive geriatricians have always stressed that it is necessary for clinically trained professionals to "think beyond the pathology." This is particularly apposite for general practitioners who might regard opportunistic case-finding as an opportunity to screen for asymptomatic deviations or the existence of abnormalities. The focus of case-finding should always be a multidimensional and functionally based assessment of the elderly patient and his or her environment.

2. *The availability of brief checklists:* There is no shortage of multidimensional checklists and assessment protocols, but most of them have been developed for use by the researcher or the paramedical interviewer/assessor rather than by the doctor. Given the time constraints imposed by the consultation, the paramount requirement is brevity.

3. *Assessment of social support:* Checklist questions to assess an elderly patient's support system might include (Freer et al., 1983):
How many people do you know well enough to visit in their homes?
Do you have someone you can trust and confide in?
Is there someone who would give you any help at all if you were sick or disabled?

4. *Shared case-finding:* In Britain, Health Visitors' training and experience make them eminently suitable for case-finding (Williamson, 1981). They currently spend time visiting the elderly in their own homes, and research suggests that this is fairly unrewarding (Luker, 1979). Instead of these time-consuming house visits, it's worth explor-

ing ways in which the Health Visitor might assist with case-finding at the time of consultation.

5. *Secondary system to detect nonconsultors:* While recent evidence suggests that those elderly who do not consult constitute something of a health elite, there is a need for a secondary backup system. The screening letter discussed earlier would seem to be ideal; and given that the numbers are small, a systematic check would not be an enormous task.

CONCLUSION

The general argument pursued in this chapter has been that changes in the elderly themselves, plus the current insistence on cost effectiveness, call for alternative ways of identifying the elderly at risk. It has been suggested that an approach through risk groups is ineffective and that future effort should be devoted to the further development of simple screening instruments and opportunistic case finding. A number of experimental schemes have been described, there are doubtless many more unknown to the author. There is a widespread and growing interest in such schemes in Britain and in Europe. Unfortunately, few schemes get written up for publication in the major journals. A compilation of brief accounts of these schemes would be extremely valuable, particularly if it took the form of a readily available source book of innovative practices in preventive care of the elderly.

REFERENCES

Anderson, W.F., & Cowan, J.R. (1955). A Consultative health centre for older people. *Lancet, II,* 239–240.

Barber, J.H., & Wallis, J.B. (1978). The benefits to an elderly population of continuing geriatric assessment. *Journal of the Royal College of General Practitioners, 28,* 428–433.

Barber, J.H., & Wallis, J.B. (1981). Geriatric screening. *Journal of the Royal College of General Practitioners, 31,* 57.

Barber, J.H., & Wallis, J.B. (1982). The effects of a system of geriatric screening and assessment on general practice workload. *Health Bulletin, 40,* 3, 125–132.

Barber, J.H., Wallis, J.B., & McKeating, E. (1980). A postal screening questionnaire in preventive geriatric care. *Journal of the Royal College of General Practitioners, 30,* 49–51.

Berry, P. (1984). Personal communication, Stockbridge Health Centre, Edinburgh.

Ebrahim, S., Hedley, R., & Sheldon, M. (1984). Low levels of ill health among elderly non-consultors in general practice. *British Medical Journal, 289,* 1273–1275.

Ford, G., & Taylor, R. (1985). The elderly as underconsultors: A critical reappraisal. *Journal of the Royal College of General Practitioners, 35,* 244–247.

Ford, G., & Taylor, R. (1983). Risk groups and selective case-finding in an elderly population. *Social Science and Medicine, 17*(10), 647–655.

Freer, C.B. (1985). Care of the elderly: Old myths. *Lancet, 1,* 268–269.

Freer, C.B. et al. (1983). *The contribution of the primary care doctor to the medical care of the elderly in the community.* Copenhagen.

Friedman, G.R., Charlewood, J.E., & Dodds, P.A. (1978). Screening the aged in general practice. *Journal of the Royal College of General Practice, 28,* 421–425.

Hannay, D.R. (1979). *The symptom iceberg: A study of community health.* London: Routledge and Kegan Paul.

Illsley, R., & Taylor, R. (1984). *European directions in the care of the elderly.* Luxembourg: EEC.

Luker, K.A. (1979). Health visiting and the elderly. *Health Visitor and Community Nurse, 15,* 457–459.

Taylor, R.C., & Ford, E.G. (1983). The elderly at risk: A critical examination of commonly identified risk groups. *Journal of the Royal College of General Pracitioners, 33,* 699–705.

Taylor, R., Ford, G., & Barber, H. (1983). *The elderly at risk: A critical review of problems and progress in screening and case finding.* London: Age Concern.

Tulloch, A.J., & Moore, V.L. (1979). A randomized controlled trial of geriatric screening and surveillance in general practice, *Journal of the Royal College of General Practitioners, 29,* 733–742.

Vetter, N.J., Jones, D.A., & Victor, C.T. (1984). Effect of health visitors working with elderly patients, *British Medical Journal, 288,* 369–372.

Williams, I. (1974). A follow-up of geriatric patients after socio-medical assessment. *Journal of the Royal College of General Practitioners, 24,* 341–346.

Williams, E.I. (1975). *Update, II,* 1275–1285.

Williamson, J. (1981). Screening, surveillance and case-finding. In T. Arie (Ed.). *Health care of the elderly,* London: Croom Helm.

Williamson, J. et al. (1984). Old people at home: Their unreported needs. *Lancet, 1,* 1117–1120.

CHAPTER 39

Functional Assessment Screening

Fitzhugh C. Pannill, III
Albert A. Fisk

While comprehensive functional assessment (CFA) is critical to geriatric practice, most elderly patients are cared for by nongeriatric physicians and do not receive assessments of nonmedical disabilities. A functional assessment screen, using recommendations in the literature, was developed and tested retrospectively and prospectively in a geriatrics clinic. The final screening questionnaire was well accepted by the 58 patients tested and correctly identified 91% of patients judged abnormal in a lengthy registered nurse—(RN) and Master of Social Work—(MSW) administered CFA interview. Four patients (9%) were misclassified as normal. Nineteen percent of the CFAs were performed in normal patients, of whom 64% were correctly identified by the screen. This screen, with further modification to increase the sensitivity may be useful in nongeriatric settings to identify patients who need comprehensive functional assessment.

Comprehensive functional assessment (CFA) (Williams, 1983) refers to the process of evaluating older patients' disabilities and self-care deficits, measuring their impact on the patient and family and developing appropriate interventions to maintain as much patient independence as possible. Typically, CFA includes evaluation of the patient's economic status, social support systems (Berkman, 1983), activities of

We wish to thank the staff of the Geriatrics Institute Clinic, Mt. Sinai Medical Center, Milwaukee, Wisconsin for help with the screen and CFA and Kathleen Nastulski for secretarial assistance.

daily living or self-maintenance (Katz, 1983), psychological or mental status (Granich, 1983), and overall physical health. A number of standardized and validated instruments (Burton, no date; Gurland, Golder, & Teresi et al., 1984) have been developed for epidemiological and community research but have also been used increasingly for clinical practice.

The entire process has become critical in providing specialized services for elderly inpatients (Sannders, Hichler, & Hall et al., 1983), home services (Williams, 1983), and in specialized geriatric outpatient clinics caring for frail adults (Fisk & Pannill, 1984; Moore, Warshaw, Walden, et al., 1984; Pfeiffer, Johnson, Chiodolo, 1981; Reifler, Kethley, O'Neill, et al., 1982; Rubenstein, Josephson, Wieland et al., 1984; Williams, Hill, Fairbank et al., 1973).

However, most of the frail elderly receive medical care in the offices of general internists, family practitioners, or other nongeriatric specialists where CFA is rarely available due to time, economic, or personnel constraints. As most standard CFA instruments require up to an hour to complete, and utilize registered nurses or social workers as interviewers, they are clearly inapplicable to a busy office practice. Consequently, many physicians have neglected undertaking of complete functional evaluations of their older patients, despite those patients' high level of functional disability.

For the assessment process to be more widely available in nonspecialized settings, a short, self-administered, practical, and sensitive "functional assessment screen" (FAS) is needed. Ideally, this should cover all five areas of CFA: economic resources; social support; physical health; instrumental activities of daily living (IADL); and basic activities of daily living (ADL).

To begin the development of such a screen, we evaluated the usefulness of a short list of consensus items for CFA, as developed by Pearlman (1984). These were recommended by 20 prominent, experienced geriatricians. The items are illustrated in Table 39-1.

Using comprehensive assessment data previously collected in our clinic, we computed the sensitivity and specificity of these items and then prospectively tested a modified screening instrument in outpatients attending the Geriatrics Clinic at the Mount Sinai Medical Center, Milwaukee, Wisconsin.

METHODS

The Geriatrics Institute of Mount Sinai Medical Center, Milwaukee, Wisconsin provides primary health care to over 1,000 frail elderly patients in southeastern Wisconsin. Two trained geriatric fellows, with University of Wisconsin Medical School appointments, and two

TABLE 39-1. Functional Assessment Screen

Number	Question	Positive answer
Social		
1.	Who lives with you?*	No one
2.	Someone to help when sick*	No
Economic		
3.	Household income*	Under $5,000
4.	Home ownership*	No
5.	Afford little luxuries	No
Physical health		
6.	Interference from health troubles*	Some or more
7.	Number of sick days in last 6 months*	Over one
IADL		
8.	Help needed with shopping, house-work, meal preparation* or transportation	Yes
ADL		
9.	Help needed with toileting*, dressing or bathing	Yes

*See source note.
Source: From Pearlman's original consensus list.

board-certified internists provide physician services. The CFA is per-formed by a nurse (RN) and a social worker (MSW) during a patient's first visit, using a structured interview that resembles the Functional Assessment Inventory (FAI) (Burton, no date). This instrument uses a number of specific questions and then has the provider rate the patient on degree of impairment of economic and social resources and physical health status, using a 6-point scale. Seven questions are completed for both IADL (travel, housekeeping, shopping, meal preparation, fi-nances, medications, and telephone) and ADL (eating, dressing, bath-ing, grooming, walking, toileting, and bed mobility).

Patients who were judged to be moderately or more severely im-paired in social or economic resources (a score of 4 or higher) or whose physical health was rated only fair or worse (a score of 4 or higher) were defined as abnormal in these areas. Patients were considered to be impaired in IADL if they needed help in more than two of the seven items and impaired in ADL if they needed help in more than two items. We defined an abnormal CFA as one with any abnormality in one of the five scales or summaries (economic, social, physical health, IADL, or ADL) as determined by the providers.

With data available from 408 consecutive assessments completed from July, 1983 to March, 1984, a retrospective analysis of the consen-sus list (items 1 through 4, 6, and 7, in Table 39-1, with questions on meal preparations and toileting) was performed. This retrospective analysis used questions from the CFA that closely resembled the questions on the consensus list; for all eight questions, CFA items were identified that were almost identical. These items, scored as shown in Table 39-1, were compared singly and in the appropriate groups (social, economic, etc...) with the corresponding summary of social, economic, and physical health ratings. The meal preparation and toileting questions were compared with a numerical average of the IADL and ADL items, respectively. Sensitivity (percentage of abnormal patients correctly identified) and specificity (percentage of normal patients correctly identified) were calculated for each item. For example, we calculated the probability that our social question, "Who lives with you?" would correctly identify a patient who the providers judged was moderately or more impaired in social resources.

Using these results, we modified the original consensus list to increase its sensitivity as a screen. The questions (in Table 39-1) on social networks (numbers 1, and 2) were left unchanged. An item regarding small luxuries (number 5) was added to the economic area, prompted by concern over patient reluctance to disclose income on a questionnaire. Specific questions regarding assistance with three additional IADL (shopping, housework, travel) and two additional ADL (dressing, bathing) were added. The final screen, with answers we considered positive, or indicative of an abnormality, is shown in Table 39-1.

The completed screen, a one page questionnaire, was mailed to all new patients in the clinic during three months, along with an introductory letter explaining the screen and its purpose. Patients were requested to get assistance from family members to complete the screen, if necessary. We mailed the screen to family members if the appointment was made for the evaluation of dementia and a family member made the appointment.

Each new patient had a CFA completed on the first visit by a nurse and social worker. These results were accepted as the "gold standard" and the screen questions compared with the appropriate area of the CFA.

The sensitivity and specificity of a positive answer of each screening item for identifying abnormalities in the five areas on the complete CFA were calculated. If one screening item was positive, the screen was defined as abnormal for that area; if one area was abnormal, the screen as a whole was defined as abnormal. We defined the CFA as abnormal as a whole if there were one or more abnormalities in any of the five rating areas, as defined above in the retrospective analysis.

RESULTS

The results of the retrospective analysis of 408 new patients attending

**TABLE 39–2. Retrospective Comparison
Screen Items and Comprehensive Assessment**

	Sensitivity (%)	Specificity (%)
Social items		
1. Living situation	68	57
2. Help when sick	25	95
Either of above positive	75	51
Economic items		
3. Income	32	89
4. Home ownership	67	57
Either of above positive	79	31
Physical health		
5. Health interference	91	48
6. Sick days	23	97
Either of above positive	93	46
ADLs		
7. Meal preparation	88	85
8. Toileting	28	91
Either of above positive	90	75
Total of four categories	89	40

the clinic from July, 1983 to March, 1984 are shown in Table 39-2.

Sensitivities range from 25% to 93% with specificities between 31% to 75%. Items that were relatively insensitive (help when sick, income) were relatively specific. However, as the purpose of a screen is to maximize sensitivity, we combined the items in a parallel fashion (Fletcher, Fletcher, & Wagner, 1982) in each group. That is, if either one was abnormal, the area was abnormal.

While the retrospective screen was relatively sensitive, identifying 89% of the abnormal CFA patients, we modified the final screen to provide more reliable economic information (number 5, Table 39-1), and more detailed information on IADLs and ADLs (Table 39-3 shows the screen questionnaire itself).

Eighty of 93 patients kept appointments at the clinic in the 3 months of the prospective trial. Seventy-eight of 80 had a complete RN- and MSW-administered CFA at their first visit. Of these, 58 (72%) returned the screen and form the basis of the analysis. The 20 patients who did not return the screen were not significantly different clinically or by CFA results from the 58 respondents.

The characteristics of the patients who completed the screen are shown in Table 39-4. The average age is 76 years. While only 1½ diagnoses on average were made on the first visit, they represent a moderately ill population. Thirty-seven percent had cardiovascular disease of some type. Twenty-five percent had arthritis, and 22%

TABLE 39–3. Mount Sinai Medical Center Geriatrics Institute Screen Questionnaire

_____ 1) Who lives with you? (circle answer)
    1. no one   4. friend(s)
    2. husband or wife   5. nonrelated, paid helper
    3. other relative(s)   6. resides in an institution

_____ 2) Is there someone who would give you help if you were sick or disabled, (for example, your husband/wife, a member of your family, or a friend?)
    1. yes   2. no

_____ 3) Do you own your own home? (circle answer)
    1. yes   2. no

_____ 4) Do you usually have enough to buy those "little extras," that is, small luxuries? (circle answer)
    1. yes   2. no

_____ 5) What is your household income? (circle answer)
    1. under $5,000   3. $15,000 - $25,000
    2. $5,000 - $15,000   4. over $25,000

_____ 6) During the past 6 months, how many days were you so sick that you were unable to carry on your usual activities—such as going to work or working around the house?
    _____ number of days   _____ hospital days in the
          (sick at home)   last 6 months

_____ 7) How much do your health troubles stand in the way of your doing the things you want to do? (circle answer)
    1. not at all   2. a little (some)   3. a great deal

_____ 8) In the past 6 months have you had any help with such things as: (check)
    1. _____ shopping   5. _____ dressing
    2. _____ housework   6. _____ going to the bathroom
    3. _____ getting around   7. _____ meals
    4. _____ bathing

TABLE 39–4. Prospective Analysis

Patient Characteristics	Frequency	Medical diagnoses	Frequency
Sex			
Male	35%	Cardiovascular	37%
Female	65%	Arthritis	25%
		Dementia	22%
Race			
White	71%	Confusion or	
Black	25%	memory loss	27%
		Neurological	17%
Marital status		"Mini Mental Status"	
Married	38%	examination under	
Widowed	50%	23	40%

TABLE 39-5. Sensitivity and Specificity of Screen Items

	Sensitivity (%)	Specificity (%)
Social scale	72 (13/18)	60 (21/35)
Economic scale	88 (14/16)	30 (11/37)
Physical health	88 (29/33)	43 (10/23)
Any of above positive	88 (38/43)	42 (5/12)
IADL	73 (14/19)	74 (17/22)
ADL	79 (15/19)	67 (16/24)
Any of above abnormal	91 (43/47)	64 (7/11)
Accuracy	86%	
False-positives	9% (4/17)	
False-negatives	36% (4/11)	
Number of CFA	19% (11/58)	

incontinence. Forty percent met Folstein's criteria (Folstein, Folstein, & McHugh, 1975) for cognitive losses, although clinically apparent confusions or memory losses were only seen in 27%. Over half were able to complete the screen and CFA alone. Only 50% felt their health was better than poor, while in 65% the nurse rated their health as moderately or severely impaired. Economic and social impairments were seen in 32% and 30%, respectively, as judged by the social worker. Sixty-seven percent were free of self-care or ADL deficits and 51% had fewer than two deficits of IADL. Compared to all patients seen in our clinic since 1983, these formed a representative sample with no significant differences.

In terms of CFA criteria for abnormalities, 11 patients (19%) were free of any significant problem in economic, social, physical health, IADL, or ADL spheres. The others consequently had abnormalities that would make CFA worthwhile clinically.

Table 39-5 shows the sensitivity and specificity of the screen in predicting abnormalities in the corresponding CFA social, economic, or physical health scale; or IADL, or ADL summation. Sensitivities range from 72% to 88% with specificities of 30% to 74%.

Overall, the screen has a sensitivity of 91% and a specificity of 64%. Four of 47 (9%) impaired patients were incorrectly identified as unimpaired by the screen. As there were relatively few unimpaired patients ($n = 11$), the false-negative patients make up a relatively large proportion (36%) of the normal patients. If none of the unimpaired patients had CFA, 11 of the 58 CFAs, or 19%, would have been avoided.

DISCUSSION

The completed screen is relatively sensitive and represents an initial effort to develop such an instrument. The population tested resembles a typical geriatric clinic for the frail elderly, with the exception of having fewer dementia patients than some (Moore, Warshaw, & Walden, 1984).

The screen misclassifies only 9% of the CFA abnormal patients as normal. Because of the relatively low prevalence of completely CFA normal patients in the population (20%), false-negative findings are proportionally high. In a geriatric clinic setting, these patients would probably be recognized by providers during routine clinical care and have the need for CFA identified at some other time. In this setting, the sensitivity would have relatively minor effects.

In the nongeriatric setting, with a higher prevalence of normal patients, the percentage of normals that had false-negative findings would drop. Such patients might easily be neglected with the assumption made that nothing more need be done, as the screen was normal. In these settings, a more sensitive screen is needed.

The self-report screening instrument was well accepted by the patients, sensitive to abnormalities, and useful as a substitute for a longer CFA. The screen will be most appropriately used in situations like a clinic, where a normal FAS will be re-evaluated if necessary. Such a screen may need more evaluation before it is widely used in other practice settings.

REFERENCES

Berkman, L.F. (1983). The assessment of social networks and social support in the elderly. *Journal of the American Geriatric Society, 31,* 743–749.

Burton, B. et al. (no date). *Functional Assessent Inventory: Training manual.* Tampa, Florida: Suncoast Gerontology Center, University of South Florida Medical Center.

Fisk, A., & Pannill, F.C. (1984). Medical care of the frail elderly in a private practice model geriatric clinic. *Gerontologist, 24,* 231.

Fletcher, R.H., Fletcher, S.W., & Wagner, E.H. (1982). *Clinical epidemiology—The essentials* (pp. 62–67). Baltimore, MD: Williams and Wilkins.

Folstein, M.E., Folstein, E., & McHugh, P.R. (1975). Mini-Mental State. A practical method for grading the cognitive state of patients for the clinician. *Journal of Psychiatric Research, 12,* 189–198.

Granich, S. (1983). Psychological assessment technology for geriatric practice. *Journal of the American Geriatric Society, 31,* 728–742.

Gurland, B., Golder, R.R., Teresi, J.A. et al. (1984). The Short-Care: An efficient instrument for the assessment of depression, dementia and disability. *Journal of Gerontology, 39,* 166–169.

Katz, S. (1983). Assessing self-maintenance activities of daily living, mobility and instrumental activities of daily living. *Journal of the American Geriatric Society, 31,* 721–727.

Moore, J.T., Warshaw, G.A., Walden, L.D. et al. (1984). Evolution of a geriatric evaluation clinic. *Journal of the American Geriatric Society, 32,* 900–905.

Pearlman, R.A. (1984). A clinically applicable functional assessment questionnaire. Paper presented at the Meeting of the American Geriatrics Society, Denver, CO.

Pfeiffer, E., Johnson, T.M., & Chiodolo, R.C. (1981). Functional assessment of elderly subjects in four service settings. *Journal of the American Geriatric Society, 10,* 433–437.

Reifler, B.V., Kethley, A., O'Neill, P. et al. (1982). Five-year experience of a community outreach program for the elderly. *American Journal of Psychiatry, 139,* 220–223.

Rubenstein, L.Z., Josephson, K.R., Wieland, G.D. et al. (1984). Effectiveness of a geriatric evaluation unit: a randomized clinical trial. *New England Journal of Medicine, 311,* 1664–1670.

Sannders, R.H., Hichler, R.B., Hall, S.A. et al. (1983). A geriatric special care unit. *Journal of the American Geriatric Society, 31,* 685–693.

Williams, T.F. (1983). Comprehensive functional assessment: An overview. *Journal of the American Geriatric Society, 31,* 637–641.

Williams, T.F., Hill, J.G., Fairbank, M.F. et al. (1973). Appropriate placement of the chronically ill and aged: A successful approach by evaluation. *Journal of the American Medical Association, 226,* 1332–1335.

CHAPTER 40

Nursing Home Preadmission Screening: The Role of a Predictive Instrument

Darlene Schroedl McKenzie

This study was designed to evaluate the extent to which the use of a 25-item functional assessment instrument called the Placement Information Base (PIB) could replicate the placement decisions of a nursing home preadmission screening team. Using secondary data on 1,722 elderly Medicaid clients, a discriminant function equation was developed and cross-validated. Overall predictive accuracy was 85% for the derivation group and 87% for the cross-validation group. The accuracy was further increased by creating discriminant function score ranges to separate the elderly into those (1) least likely, (2) somewhat likely, and (3) most likely to need nursing home placement. The findings suggest that a shortened weighted version of the PIB, coupled with follow-up assessment for elderly with middle-range scores, can be used to create an economical and equitable preadmission screening program.

The implementation of preadmission screening programs under the federal Medicaid waiver program (Omnibus Budget Reconciliation Act, 1981) has highlighted the need for an economical and equitable method of differentiating elderly who need nursing home placement from those who can remain in the community. Many states with preadmission screening programs employ multidisciplinary teams to make placement decisions based on clinical assessment of clients (Knowlton, Clauser, & Fatula, 1982). This process can, however, take 7 to 8 hours to complete (Schneider, 1981) and can be required for as many as 3,000 to 4,000 clients annually (Oregon Senior Services Division, 1982; Harkins & Bowling, 1982).

Because multidisciplinary team assessments can be costly, both in time and other resources, alternative assessment mechanisms have been suggested. One alternative is to employ a screening instrument that has been developed based on some type of mathematical modeling. In this modeling, weights are given to variables as a means of diagnosing or identifying the need for a nursing home placement. The weights are developed using data on clients for whom the placement diagnosis or decision by the multidisciplinary team is known. The screening instrument containing the weighted variables can subsequently be used as a more objective, less costly, and professionally less demanding substitute for the multidisciplinary team assessment and decision-making process.

Although a number of screening instruments with decision rules have been reported in the literature, none appear to meet the psychometric criteria that would make them suitable for use in a large preadmission screening program. Instruments with reported validity have, for the most part, been designed to make placement distinctions regarding level of care within a nursing home setting rather than to differentiate elderly who need nursing home placement from those who can be maintained in the community (Greene & Monahan, 1981; Gruenberg, 1975; Haddad, 1981; Harris, Orr, & Allaway, 1982; Kane, Rubenstein, Brook, van Ryzin, Masthey et al., 1981; Orr, 1978; Sherwood & Feldman, 1970; Sherwood, Morris, & Barnhardt, 1975). Instruments developed specifically for differentiating between elderly who need nursing home placement and those who can remain in the community have not been evaluated extensively. Validity studies supporting the decision rules have not been reported for most of these instruments (Cape, Shorrock, Tree, Pablo, Campbell et al., 1977; Carnes & Cook, 1977; Foley & Sneider, 1980; Furman & Lund, 1979).

Validity studies have been reported for two instruments designed to identify elderly at risk of nursing home placement. Both the instrument developed for the Illinois Community Care Program (Foley & Sneider, 1980) and the Geriatric Functional Rating Scale (Grauer & Birnbom, 1975) appear, however, to need additional study prior to being implemented with a large-scale screening program. The items on the Illinois instrument, while initially selected empirically, have since been extensively modified (A. Welch, personal communication, June 11, 1982). Low inter-rater reliability has been reported for the Geriatric Functional Rating Scale (Appelbaum, Seidl, & Austin, 1980). In addition, the latter scale was developed in Canada and has not been validated against United States nursing home placement criteria.

The absence of a reliable and valid screening instrument with decision rules for nursing home placement decisions was the impetus for the present study. This chapter presents the results of the study designed to evaluate the criterion validity of an existing functional assessment instrument, the Placement Information Base (PIB). Selected PIB scales were mathematically weighted and used to classify the elderly according to their placement needs. The question that was addressed was whether a modified PIB instrument could be used to make placement decisions sufficiently similar to clinically derived team decisions so that the instrument could be substituted for the team.

METHOD

Measure

PIB is a 25-item functional assessment instrument designed to provide a data base for matching the functional profile of elderly individuals with the service capacities of various institutional and alternative resources (Saslow & Yamodis, 1980). Initially developed and tested for use in the Southern Oregon Flexible Intergovernmental Grant/Waiver Continuum of Care Project for the Elderly, 1978 to 1981, PIB has subsequently been adopted for statewide use by The Department of Human Resources.

The psychometric characteristics of the PIB suggest that it might be easily modified for use as a screening instrument. Each of the 25 items contained in the PIB has a 5-point response format, ranging from independent, adequate, or safe (1) to dependent, inadequate, or unsafe (5). Each response is accompanied by a descriptor statement designed to reduce the amount of rater judgment required. Studies conducted during the development of the PIB indicate that it can be reliably administered by trained intake workers in less than 1 hour.

In addition to being brief and easily administered by individuals not possessing highly technical skills, the PIB contains items designed to measure the theoretically important dimensions of physical, mental, and social functioning. These dimensions are part of health status, as defined by the World Health Organization, and are found in other instruments concerned with geriatric assessment and care (Fillenbaum & Smyer, 1981; Gurland, Kuriansky, Sharpe, Stiller, & Birkett, 1977-1978).

The three dimensions of physical, mental, and social functioning are reflected in the PIB scales developed by McKenzie (1983). Analyses using secondary data on 2,287 elderly Medicaid clients newly admitted to Oregon's Senior Services Division during 1982 indicated 19 of the original 25 PIB items could be included in four multi-item scales: Activities of Daily Living (ADL), Instrumental Activities of Daily Living (IADL), Mental Functioning, and Social Functioning (Cronbach's $\alpha = .90$, .88, .87. and .75, respectively). The same 19 items were also used to create two summary scales: Physical Functioning and Mental-Social Functioning (Cronbach's $\alpha = .91$ and .88). The physical scale combines the ADL and IADL multi-item scales and contains items that reflect the elderly's ability to provide physically for personal and household needs. The mental-social scale combines the mental and social scales and contains items that reflect the elderly's cognitive functioning and participation in nonpassive social activities.

Five of the remaining items measure vision, hearing, emotional control, nutritional habits, and the availability of a natural support system. The emotional control item is a global measure of the extent to which individuals' personal problems, disturbances, or emotional status restrict his or her living arrangement. Dangerous or abusive behavior and the extent to which this behavior is controllable with medications is also addressed. The nutritional habits item is a measure of the number of meals eaten per day and the dietary adequacy of those meals. The natural support item is a measure of the availability of friends, family, neighbors, or volunteers to provide necessary care. Both the number of persons and regularity with which they can provide care are addressed. The sixth item, medication management, lacks clarity and was omitted from the analyses.

Subjects and Data Source

The study reported here was part of a larger study of 2,287 elderly clients newly admitted to the Statewide Medicaid program during 1982 (McKenzie, 1983). For the present study, data from a reduced sample of 1,772 were analyzed. Clients were included in the reduced sample if they had been clinically judged to need nursing home care at either the intermediate or skilled level ($n = 943$). Fewer than 30% of these clients were residing in a nursing home at the time of their assessment. Clients were also included in the reduced sample if they had been clinically judged capable of remaining in the community and in either their home, a relative's home, or in an independent living facility such as a retirement complex ($n = 829$). Clients clinically judged to need care in a substitute home such as a nonrelative foster home, home for the aged, or residential care facility were not included in the sample because of the wide interfacility variation in the type of care provided. Clients were also excluded from the sample if there was a discrepency between the clinically recommended and the actual placement. The majority of the clients in the study sample were white (96%), female (70%), and widowed (57%). All clients were 65 years of age or older; 29% were between the ages of 65 and 74, 39% were between the ages 75 and 84, and 32% were 85 years of age or older.

The information obtained from elderly clients in the samples was from secondary data collected during the routine intake procedure of the Senior Services Division. At the time of admission to the Senior Services Division each elderly client received a routine comprehensive assessment that included the administration of the 25-item functional assessment instrument, PIB. Elderly clients requesting nursing home placement and elderly nursing home residents requesting continued nursing home placement under Medicaid were routinely assessed by a preadmission screening team. The remaining elderly clients were assessed by a case manager. The actual placement of the client as a result of this assessment was used as the criterion variable, reflecting the clinically derived placement decision.

Although the PIB was not administered independently of the clinical assessment, it is unlikely that the administration of the PIB, per se, influenced the placement decision. The content of the PIB was derived from clinical practice and is basic to all long-term care decisions. The same types of information would have been obtained clinically regardless of the circumstances under which the PIB was administered. In addition, the raw scores on the PIB items were not weighted or directly tied to placement eligibility. Scores were used primarily to build a data base for policy decisions.

Analyses

Discriminant function analysis was utilized to evaluate the extent to which the two summary PIB scales and five PIB items not included in either summary scale could serve as predictor variables in differentiating elderly on the basis of their actual placement, nursing home versus community. The two summary scales were selected, rather than the single items only, because of the psychometric advantages generally associated with scales and because of the ease with which future discriminant function scores could be computed in a field setting.

For the discriminant analyses the scales and item scores of elderly assessed by case manager only were combined with those of elderly assessed by a preadmission screening team. This combination was necessary in order to represent adequately the functional range of elderly judged capable of remaining in the community. Not surprisingly, elderly who met this criteria and had been evaluated by a preadmission screening team were few in number and tended to be more dysfunctional than elderly who met the criteria and had been evaluated by a case manager only. Scores of elderly nursing home clients were also combined after preliminary study indicated that their functional status did not differ significantly by source of evaluation.

Approximately half of the combined community and nursing home sample were then randomly assigned to a group that was used for deriving and validating a predictive equation. The remaining half were used to form a group for cross-validating the accuracy of the equation. Chi-square tests of significance indicate that the derivation and cross-validation groups were not significantly different in terms of age, sex, marital status, or living arrangement.

Using a stepwise procedure, a discriminant function that predicted placement was developed based on PIB data from clients in the derivation group. The two summary and the five single-item scales were entered as predictors. Each was included in the equation if the F to enter the equation was 1.0 or greater and if it also contributed at least .01 to the Wilks' lambda.

The predictive accuracy of the discriminant function was then tested by using the equation to classify the elderly clients in both the derivation and cross-validation groups. The clients were classified by computing a discriminant function score for each individual and assigning that individual to the group to which he had the greatest probability of belonging. Under the assumption of multivariate normal distribution, the discriminant scores were converted into probabilities of group membership. In this analysis the probability was adjusted to reflect the known proportion of clients in each group, .473 in the community group and .527 in the nursing home group.

Findings

The stepwise analysis resulted in the standardized equation:

$$Z = .63678X_1 + .65362X_2 + .26478X_3 - .24950X_4$$

where X_1 is Physical Functioning, X_2 is the availability of a Natural Support System, X_3 is Mental-Social Functioning, and X_4 is Nutritional Habits. In combination, the four scales account for 49.4% of the total variance. Tested for significance, the equation is highly significant: $F(4,859) = 209$, $p < .001$. The three single-item scales measuring vision, hearing, and emotional control did not meet the criteria for inclusion.

When used to classify elderly clients, the overall predictive accuracy of the equation was 86.05%. As indicated in Table 40-1 the accuracy was high for the derivation group (85.19%) and even higher for the cross-validation group (87.3%). The accuracy of the equation was also high for both the nursing home and community clients. Ninety percent of the nursing home clients and 83% of the community clients were correctly classified.

An examination of the plot of discriminant function scores for the cross-validation group (see Figure 40-1) indicates that the nursing home and community groups are fairly distinct. The overlap, which does exist between the two groups, is small, 10% for the nursing home

TABLE 40-1. Actual versus Predicted Placement[a]

Actual placement	Predicted placement		Total
	Community	Nursing home	
Derivation sample			
Community	334 (81.7%)	75 (18.3%)	409
nursing home	53 (11.6%)	402 (88.4%)	455
Cross-validation sample			
Community	350 (83.3%)	70 (16.7%)	420
nursing home	45 (9.2%)	443 (90.8%)	488

[a]Overall accuracy is 85.19% for the derivation group and 87.3% for the cross-validation group.

clients and 17% for the community clients. In addition to being small, the overlap is concentrated near the mean. The majority of the misclassified elderly clients have discriminant function scores that are within + or − one standard deviation of the mean. These findings suggest that the equation is quite successful at classifying clients with high or low scores and moderately successful at classifying clients with middle-range scores.

The misclassification of clients with scores near the mean or critical score (− .01) is not unexpected, however. One of the problems associ-

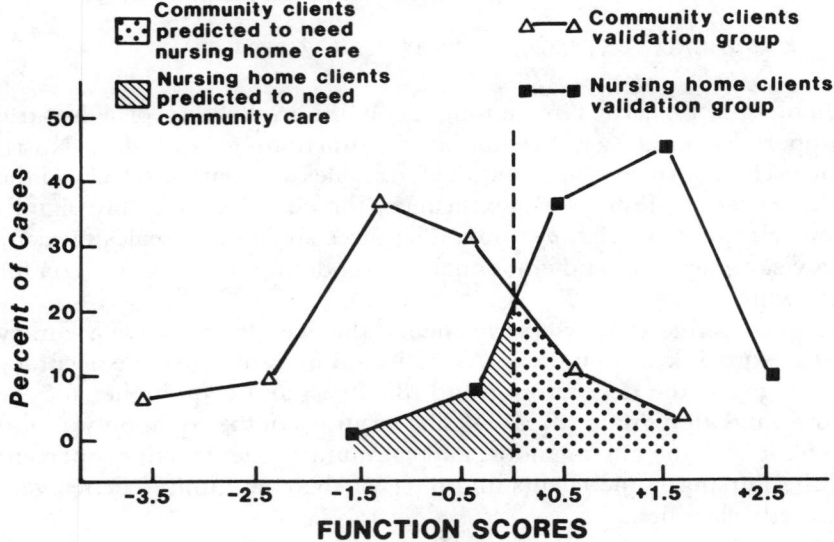

FIGURE 40-1. The use of a single critical score for predicting an elderly client's placement need.

ated with the classification procedure is the rigid dividing line created by the rule of highest probability. Elderly clients with scores close to the critical score have a high probability of belonging to both groups. They are, however, necessarily assigned to the group to which they have the higher probability of belonging.

One approach to this problem is to create a zone around the critical score separating the elderly into those (1) least likely, (2) somewhat likely, and (3) most likely to need nursing home placement. Additional information can be used for classifying elderly clients whose discriminant function score falls within the "somewhat likely" zone. The use of such a zone can increase the probability of an appropriate placement for this group of elderly. Variables not included in the equation can be taken into consideration during the decision-making process. The use of such a zone can also increase the proportion of accurate classifications for the remaining elderly clients. Fewer previously misclassified elderly would have discriminant function scores above or below the newly created zone around the critical score.

To illustrate how such a zone might be created and evaluated, elderly clients in the cross-validation group ($n = 908$) were reclassified using a pair of critical scores rather than the critical score computed by the discriminant function program. Minus .36 and + .64 were selected for illustration because fewer than 5% of the elderly nursing home clients had a discriminant function score below $-$ .36 and fewer than 5% of the community clients had a discriminant function score above + .64 (see Figure 40-2).

The reclassification findings confirm that the predictive accuracy of the equation is increased when used with clients having high or low rather than middle-range scores. Of the elderly predicted least likely to need nursing home placement ($n = 353$), 93% had also been clinically judged to be capable of remaining in the community. Of the elderly predicted most likely to need nursing home placement ($n = 358$), 94% had also been clinically judged to need nursing home placement.

An examination of Figure 40-2 suggests that the accuracy of the equation can be further increased by widening the middle zone. It should be noted, however, that any increase in accuracy would come at the expense of a corresponding increase in the number of elderly needing further assessment prior to classification.

SUMMARY & DISCUSSION

The findings from this study provide evidence that the need for nursing home placement, as determined by a multidisciplinary team, can be predicted with high levels of accuracy with a shortened and weighted version of the PIB. When used with a single critical score, the

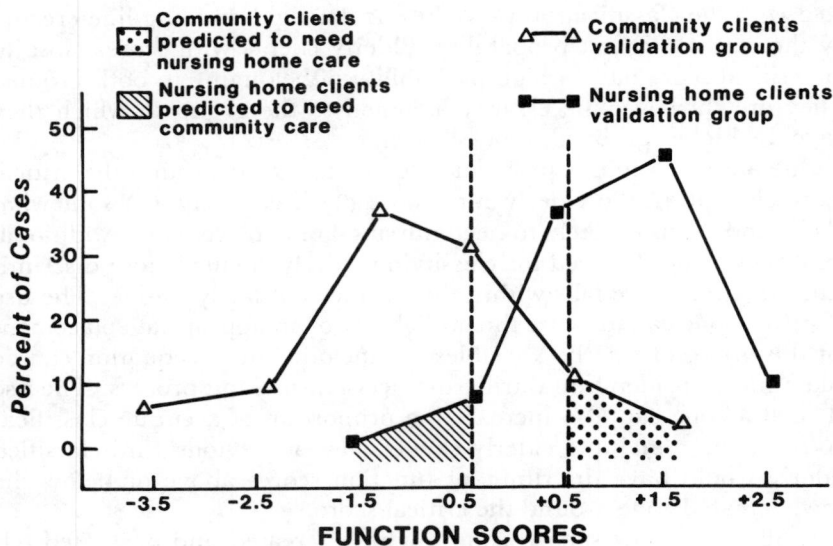

FIGURE 40–2. The use of a pair of critical scores for predicting an elderly client's placement need.

predictive accuracy of the modified PIB is comparable to other instruments using patient indicators to replicate multidisciplinary placement decisions (Greene & Monahan, 1981; Harris et al., 1982; Kane et al., 1981; Sherwood et al., 1975).

Already high, the accuracy of the modified PIB can be improved by replacing the single critical score with a pair of critical scores. The use of two scores instead of one allows the user to increase the sensitivity of the equation without a corresponding loss of specificity. In this application, the modified PIB is not used as a complete substitute for clinical judgement. Instead, it serves as a first screen, reducing the number of elderly clients who need the more comprehensive and costly clinical assessment. Placement decisions for elderly with a discriminant function score falling within the high or low score range can be made on the basis of the screening. A middle-range score triggers the need for further assessment.

Although the use of two scores instead of one does not eliminate the need for multidisciplinary assessment, the number of elderly clients who would require that assessment would be substantially lower than the number who would receive a similar assessment in a program relying entirely upon a team screening process.

Sixty-nine percent of the elderly clients clinically judged to need nursing home placement could have been accurately placed on the basis of the discriminant function score obtained from the modified PIB. Likewise, 78% of the elderly clients clinically judged capable of remaining in the community could have been accurately placed on the discriminant function score.

The findings of this study suggest that the modified PIB, when used in conjunction with a pair of critical scores, has the potential to serve as an economical and equitable screening instrument for nursing home placement decisions. The modified PIB can be economical in that its administration as a first-level screen can substantially reduce the work load demands of the highly trained and costly team members. The modified PIB can be equitable in that it meets the psychometric criteria associated with assessment and screening instruments. It has established inter-rater reliability, content validity, and now criterion-related validity in relationship to clinically derived placement decisions. Because the instrument has these characteristics, the client can have greater assurance that relevant functional domains are considered and that his or her needs are being weighted equivalently to others with similar needs.

While the findings of this study appear generalizable to other programs and states, several limitations need to be discussed. First, as previously noted, the PIB weights were derived using data from a sample limited to Medicaid clients receiving services in one state. To the extent that client needs and community resources vary between states and populations there will be a variation on the distribution of client discriminant function scores obtained from the modified PIB. This variation can, however, be taken into consideration when establishing the set of critical scores.

Second, the omission of substitute home clients from the sample likely enhanced the distinction between nursing home and community clients by eliminating a subset of community clients with middle-range scores. It, therefore, can be anticipated that proportionately more substitute home clients would be predicted somewhat likely to need nursing home placement and would require follow-up assessment prior to placement. The number of substitute home clients, however, is generally small in relation to the number of clients in other community settings. The use of a pair of critical scores with this group is therefore not likely to substantially increase the total number of clients needing the multidisciplinary assessment.

Third, it is important to note that professional judgment, the criterion employed in this study, has not been validated with longitudinal data relating client outcomes to placement decisions. However, in the absence of such badly needed data, the judgment of experts representing different disciplinary backgrounds has generally been accepted as an effective standard (Brody, 1977; Lowy & Helphand, 1975).

Although limitations were present in the study, they appear to be the type that can be addressed during the planning process for designing or altering a preadmission screening program. First, several combinations of scores can be evaluated with pilot groups of clients. The recommendation of a particular pair of critical scores is beyond the scope of this study. The choice will be influenced by the goals of the particular screening program and by the availability of community services in relation to nursing home beds. The choice may also be influenced by the amount of program resources available for follow-up assessment in relation to the costs of inappropriate placement. Second, regardless of which set of critical scores is selected, further assessment can be made available to elderly clients challenging the screening decision. This option is important since it is unlikely that the critical scores would be established at levels assuring 100% correspondence between screening-derived and clinically-derived placement decisions.

REFERENCES

Applebaum, R., Seidl, P.W. & Austin, C.D. (1980). The Wisconsin community care organization: Preliminary findings from the Milwaukee experiment. *The Gerontologist, 20,* 350–355.

Brody, E.M. (1977). *Long term care of older people.* New York: Human Services Press.

Cape, R.D., Shorrock, C., Tree, R., Pable, R., Campbell, A.J., & Seymour, D.G. (1977). Square pegs in round holes: A study of residents in long-term institutions in London, Ontario. *Canadian Medical Association Journal, 117,* 1284–1287.

Carnes, C., & Cook, A. (1977). Nursing home preadmission screening in Virginia. *Journal of Medicaid Management, 1,* 1–8.

Fillenbaum, G., & Smyer, M.A. (1981). The development, validity and reliability of the OARS multidimensional functional assessment questionnaire. *Journal of Gerontology, 36,* 428–434.

Foley, W.J., & Sneider, D.P. (1980). A comparison of level of care predictions of six long-term care patient assessment systems. *American Journal of Public Health, 70,* 1152–1179.

Furman, W.M., & Lund, D.A. (1979). The assessment of patient needs: Description of the level of care survey. *Journal of Psychiatric Treatment and Evaluation, 1,* 29–37.

Grauer, H., & Birnbom, F. (1975). A geriatric functional rating scale to determine the need for institutional care. *Journal of the American Geriatrics Society, 23,* 472–476.

Greene, V.L., & Monahan, D.J. (1981). Inconsistency in level of care assignment decisions in skilled nursing facilities. *American Journal of Public Health, 71,* 1036–1039.

Gruenberg, L.W. (1975). *The Massachusetts Department of Public Health long-term care survey II: Levels of care needed by patients in long-term care facilities.* Boston, MA: Massachusetts Department of Public Health, Office of Health Planning and Statistics.

Gurland, B., Kuriansky, J., Sharpe, R.S., Stillier, P., & Birkett, P. (1977–1978). The comprehensive assessment and referral evaluation (CARE): Rationale, development, and reliability. *International Journal of Aging and Human Development, 8,* 9–42.

Haddad, L.B. (1981). Utilizing rating instruments for evaluating behavioral characteristics differentiating elderly clients selected for skilled nursing, intermediate and psychiatric care. *Journal of Gerontology, 36,* 583–585.

Harkins, E.B., & Bowling, C.A. (1982). *Study of the Virginia nursing home preadmission screening program.* Richmond, VA: Virginia Center on Aging, Virginia Commonwealth University.

Harris, J.F., Orr, M., & Allaway, N. (1982). Long-term care criteria and standards agreement with professional placement determination. *American Journal of Public Health, 72,* 602–604.

Kane, R.L., Rubenstein, L.Z., Brook, R.H., VanRyzin, J., Masthay, P., Schoenrich, E., & Harrell, B. (1981). Utilization review in nursing homes: Making implicit level-of-care judgments explicit. *Medical Care, 19,* 3–13.

Knowlton, J., Clauser, S., & Fatula, J. (1982). Nursing home pre-admission screening: A review of state programs. *Health Care Financing Review, 3,* 75–87.

Lowy, L., & Helphand, M. (1975). Matching community resources and patient needs. In S. Sherwood (Ed.). *Long-term care: A handbook for researchers, planners, providers* (pp. 349–389). New York: Spectrum.

McKenzie, D.A. (1983). The placement information base: Its utility and meaning for nursing home placement (Doctoral dissertation, Portland State University). *Dissertation Abstracts International, 44,* 1948A.

Oregon Senior Services Division. (1982). *Pre-admission screening statistical report January-December 1981.* Salem, OR: Oregon Department of Human Resources.

Orr, M. (1978) *Development of numerical standards for patient placement in New York long-term care facilities.* Albany, NY: Bureau of Research and Evaluation, New York State Office of Health Systems Management.

Saslow, M., & Yamodis, J. (1980). *FIG-waiver project manual no. 2: The placement information base (PIB).* Portland, OR: Oregon Medical Association.

Schneider, R. (1981). Comparative time study. *Multnomah and Marion regions PAS.* Salem, OR: Oregon Department of Human Resources, Long-Term Care Unit.

Sherwood, S., & Feldman, C. (1970). The use of easily obtained precoded data in screening applicants to a long-term care facility. *The Gerontologist, 10,* 182–188.

Sherwood, S., Morris, J., & Barnhardt, E. (1975). Developing a system of assigning individuals into an appropriate residential setting. *Journal of Gerontology, 30,* 331–342.

CHAPTER 41

The Care Interview: An Efficient, Systematic, Multidimensional Assessment Tool to Measure Health Status of Older People

John Toner
Barry Gurland

The Comprehensive Assessment and Referral Evaluation (CARE) was developed to assess a wide range of psychiatric, medical, and social problems of the elderly. The approaches taken in the development of the CARE multidimensional assessment interview are described. The principles that guided its construction and reduction from a 1,500-item instrument, taking a minimum of 90 minutes to administer to shorter, more efficient versions for use in various settings and for different purposes are also described. For certain purposes, CARE has been reduced to a relatively short instrument, the SHORT-CARE, that assesses three major content areas: depression, dementia, and disability. This presentation will also describe the SHORT-CARE Instrument. In addition, some of the features of the CARE that distinguish it from other multidimensional assessment instruments are discussed.

An overview of the Comprehensive Assessment and Referral Evaluation (CARE) System is presented and the principles that guided its construction are described. Additionally, certain CARE companion instruments, and the features that differentiate the CARE from other assessment interviews used with older people are discussed.

The field of assessment and in particular, geriatric assessment, has been characterized by a rapid growth of interest in the past several years. This interest, spurred by the increasing number of elderly with more chronic conditions and greater frailty, has led to the proliferation of assessment instruments designed to evaluate the needs of the aged (Salamon, 1985). These instruments have been designed for a number of reasons and basically address functional areas, such as medical and psychological need, and/or multidimensional need that obtains a total picture of the individual's level of functioning (Bloom, 1975; Kane & Kane, 1981).

There are many geriatric assessment techniques in the field today that aim, as does the CARE, at being comprehensive and multidimensional. No one author is likely to claim that any particular instrument is exhaustively comprehensive or describes all possible dimensions. Each particular technique selects a distinctive profile of issues relevant to its purposes. Therefore, if one is setting out to compare such techniques, such as has been done by Kane and Kane (1981), one must take into account the different purposes of these techniques, as well as the degree to which the purpose is achieved.

The main purpose of the CARE is to evaluate in the community the problems of the elderly person that are of concern to the health-related profession. Two other assessment instruments that aim toward comprehensiveness and were designed for use with the aged are the OARS Multidimensional Functional Assessment Questionnaire (Duke University Center for the Study of Aging, 1978) and the Multilevel Assessment Instrument (Lawton, Moss, Fulcomer, & Kleban, 1982). It should be noted that there is considerable overlap in areas covered in these instruments and the CARE. It should be further noted that the CARE was developed from a clinical tradition. Figure 41-1 traces this development, which has been described in detail in two previous publications. In an earlier article, Gurland, Kuriansky, Sharpe, Simon, Stiller, et al. (1977–1978) describe the rationale, development, and reliability of the CARE. In a recent article, Gurland and Wilder (1984) describe the clinical features and history of the CARE.

HISTORICAL DEVELOPMENT OF CARE

The clinical tone of CARE is consistent with the history of its development (see Figure 41-1). Its precedents in the work of the United States/ United Kingdom Cross-National Project were the semistructured interview methods, the Mental Status Schedule (Spitzer, Fleiss, Burdock, & Hardesty, 1964), Present State Examination (Wing et al., 1967), and Structured and Scaled Interview to Assess Maladjustment (Gurland et al., 1972), all of which were intended to systematize the clinical psychiatric interview for adult patients. When the United

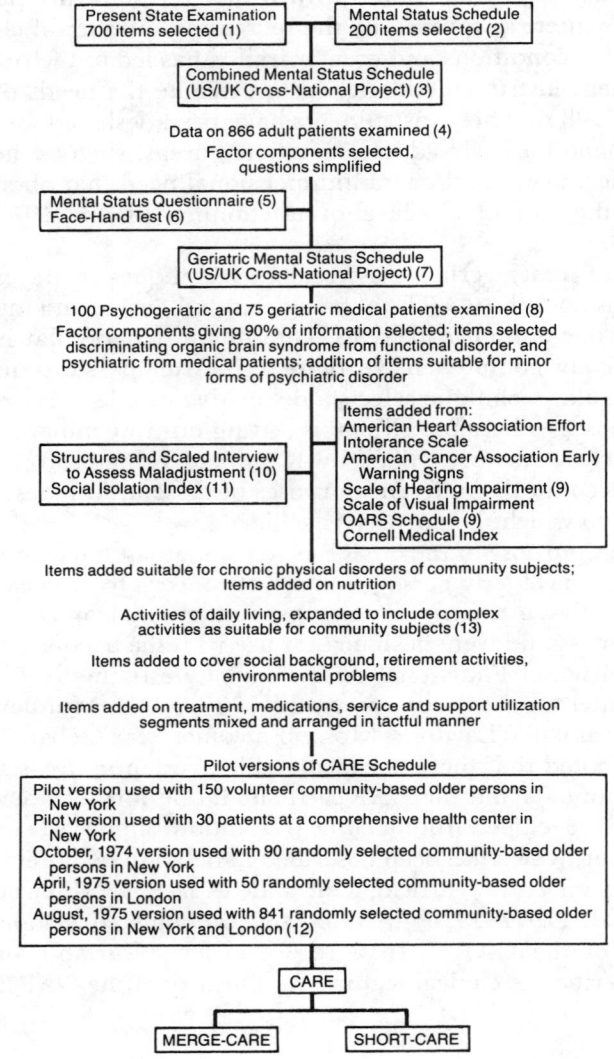

Figure 41-1. Initial developmental steps taken to produce the CARE.

Adapted from "The Care Interview Revisited: Development of an efficient, Systematic Clinical Assessment" by B. Gurland and D. Wilder, Journal of Gerontology, 1984, *39,* 129–137. Numbers in parentheses refer to references describing these steps: (1) Wing, Birley, Cooper, Graham & Isaacs, 1967; (2) Spizer, Fleiss, Burdock & Hardesty, 1964; (3) Professional Staff of the Cross-National Project, 1973; (4) Cooper et al., 1972; (5) Kahn et al., 1960; (6) Fink et al., 1952; (7) Gurland et al., 1976a; (a) Gurland et al.,1976b; (9) Duke University Center for the Study of Aging, 1978; (10) Gurland, Yorkston, Stone & Fleiss, 1972; (11) Bennett, 1980; (12) Gurland, Copeland, Kelleher, Kuriansky, Sharpe et al., 1983; (13) Katz et al., 1963.

States/United Kingdom Cross-National Project initiated a series of geriatric studies that were to range over populations in hospitals (Gurland, Kuriansky, Sharpe, Simon, Stiller et al., 1976), the community (Gurland et al., 1977), institutions (Gurland, Cross, Defiguerido, Shannon, Mann et al., 1979), and ambulatory care settings (MacDonald, Mann, Jenkins, Richard, Godlove et al., 1982), it became necessary to develop the systematic interview further. The clinical techniques of the psychogeriatric assessment unit jointly run by a psychiatrist and physician, with social work, nursing, nutrition, and other disciplines represented, became the paradigm for the CARE. Equal emphasis was given to medical, psychiatric, and social problems, with about one third of the instrument devoted to each domain.

Beginning in 1975, the CARE was administered by psychiatrists and social scientists in New York City to a random probability sample of community-based persons (age 65 or older) in their homes and by psychiatrists to a corresponding sample in London (Gurland et al., 1983). The New York probability sample is single stage, comprised of five separate subsamples of households located in 65 cluster areas in New York City. The subsamples were drawn such that each could be analyzed independently. A comparable probablity sample was drawn in London.

A response rate of 71% was obtained in New York with 445 completed interviews; in London the response rate was 81%, and 396 interviews were completed. For each elderly person a profile of scale scores was constructed, a case summary written, and a set of global ratings made by the interviewers; when appropriate, a clinical diagnosis was given. There was a 1-year follow-up interview on 292 individuals in New York and 237 in London. The response rate for the New York follow-up study was 70% after excluding from this calculation individuals who died. Informant data were collected for a random subsample in New York of 162 informants (key family support persons) using a semistructured interview similar to the CARE (Teresi et al., 1978). The response rate for the family subsample was 62%.

APPROACH TO MAKING THE CARE MORE EFFICIENT

The original CARE contained 1,500 items and required an average of about 1.5 hours to administer. It was felt that about a month would have to be set aside for training an interviewer who already had some basic experience in interviewing within the health or social sphere. Such a technique was obviously not practical for widespread use because of its high costs and heavy demands on the elderly client. Therefore, considerable effort has been directed toward deriving a more efficient version of the CARE from the original instrument, one that could be administered by nonphysician assessors who could be trained in a relatively short period and one that would attain a high degree of efficiency in gathering the same types of information as the original CARE. A recent series of articles (Golden, Teresi, & Gurland, 1983a, 1983b; Gurland, Golden, Teresi, & Challop, 1984; Teresi, Golden, & Gurland, 1984; Teresi, Golden, Gurland, Wilder, & Bennett, 1984) provides an example of the work required in increasing the efficiency of the CARE technique.

THE SHORT-CARE

The need for a simpler, shorter instrument with particular emphasis on the two main areas of psychiatric impairment (dementia and depression) and the major area of physical impairment (disability) led to the development of the SHORT-CARE. The SHORT-CARE consists of 6 of the 22 indicator scales of the CORE-CARE. Of the SHORT-CARE, 143 items are from the indicator scales of depression/demoralization, dementia, subjective memory impairment, sleep disorders, somatic symptoms, and disability; with additional items for arriving at operational diagnoses of depression, dementia, and disability; and for making the interview flow smoothly.

The SHORT-CARE interview is divided into two parts. The first part, taking about 30 minutes to complete, contains items comprising the six scales just described; the second part of the interview contains additional items necessary for the operational diagnoses. The schedule also contains a screening device whereby noncases of depression and/ or dementia may be eliminated if that is the intended design of the study. After the interview the interviewer completes a series of global ratings and applies operational criteria for the diagnoses. These forms only take a few additional minutes to complete.

The operational diagnoses refer to syndromes of cognitive impairment, depressed mood, and disability, which, in a health care professional's opinion, warrant clinical assessment or intervention. The operational diagnoses are termed pervasive depression, pervasive dementia, and personal time dependency (disability). These categories do not refer to specific conditions, disorders, or subtypes but are meant to be useful in health services research and in health screening *because* they identify cases where there is a probable need for clinical investigation or intervention.

Gurland, Golden, Teresi, & Challop (1984) describe in detail the reliability and validity of scales and diagnoses related to SHORT-CARE. The scales contained in the SHORT-CARE comprise, with minor variation, the same items as the homogeneous scales described by Golden et al. (1983a). In summary, the reliability of the homogeneous indicator scales, which includes the items of the SHORT-CARE, remains high after reformatting items and shortening scales. Internal consistency coefficients for the SHORT-CARE scales have been reported by Gurland, Golden, Teresi, & Challop (1984a). Both interrater and internal consistency reliabilities of the SHORT-CARE have been found to be satisfactory. Construct and predictive validity of the SHORT-CARE has been discussed in Gurland, Golden, Teresi, & Challop (1984a).

Additional validity data using the combined SHORT-CARE homogeneous scales of depression and dementia were collected from a national study of hypertension. Diagnoses made by clinicians were compared with the SHORT-CARE homogeneous scales on 26 cases. Ten cases were judged both by the clinicians and the scales to have no disorder; and of 16 cases classified as psychiatric cases using the homogeneous scale cut scores, 12 were rated by independent clinicians as psychiatric cases. In summary, the SHORT-CARE, which can be completed in a single interview, combines the advantages of a semistructured interview, rating scales, operational diagnosis, and if desired, a screening procedure for selecting out cases of depression and dementia.

MERGE-CARE: A Model for Evaluation and Referral in Geriatrics

For the past several years the Center for Geriatrics and Gerontology has been working with the Division of General Medicine at Columbia University to develop a systematic interview for elderly patients in primary care. The interview (the MERGE-CARE) covers problems in a variety of physical, mental, emotional, and social functions. These problems are important in developing a treatment plan for the elderly and in monitoring progress but are often not adequately covered because of their complexity and extent. The MERGE-CARE interview is intended to be given by a nurse practitioner, who then discusses the results with the treating physician and, where necessary, a multidisciplinary team. This approach is innovative in so far as it is keyed to decision making in this setting. Plans are currently underway to begin testing for reliability and validity of MERGE-CARE.

The MERGE-CARE was developed to meet the needs of both the elderly patient and the Columbia Presbyterian Medical Center. The model thus has two major purposes. The first is to aid in developing a coordinated effective management plan for the elderly patient presenting to a primary care setting. The second is to aid in organizing the delivery of services to the elderly patient so that the resources within the medical center are utilized cost-effectively.

The MERGE-CARE is unique in that it originated as a clinical tool, developed by clinicians working in a primary care practice, the Asso-

TABLE 41–1. Vision Assessment Component

		VISION (1)		
1. Do you wear glasses?	(Question only)			
2. Can you see well enough to read labels or prices in shops?	Shopping difficulty because of sight	N	Y*	—
3. Can you read labels on medicine bottles?	Treatment problem because of sight (SEE ALSO MEDICATIONS)	N	Y*	—
4. Can you see steps or things you might trip over?	Danger of tripping because of sight	N	Y*	—
5. Can you see well enough to do housework?	Housework restricted because of sight	N	Y*	—
High-Risk Patient 6. Glb: Vision is impaired and an impediment		N	Y*	—
7. Glb: 0-100 rating of severity		—		—
8. Alg: Any of * items		N	Y*	—
Action Refer to own physician, ☐ with findings, ☐ with advice, ☐ with offer of referrals below, ☐ other.		N	Y	—
Refer to ophthalmology, ☐ for testing, ☐ for diagnosis, ☐ for glasses, ☐ other.		N	Y	—

ciate in Internal Medicine (AIM), at Columbia Presbyterian Medical Center. Careful attention was given to developing the MERGE-CARE in such a way as to guarantee its clinical utility and at the same time allow for its eventual use as a research tool.

The MERGE-CARE consists of a *Core Section,* which includes eight components (Intellectual Impairment, Activities of Daily Living, Medications and Alcohol, Living Conditions, Depression, Nutrition, Sexual Problems and Self-Perceived Health) and an *Extended Section,* which includes 18 components (Oral Cavity, Hearing, Vision, Chronic Pain, Effort Tolerance, Critical Incidents, Fears, Disturbing Behaviors, Communication, Skin, Cancer Alert, Health Style, Stress, Service Utilization, Satisfaction With Services, Involvement in Decisions, Positive Qualities and Caretaker Burden). Each component includes a series of questions asked of the older patient or an informant, a system for identifying the patient at high risk, and a related plan for action (see Table 41-1).

The first and foremost requirement for a successful referral system like MERGE-CARE is that there be a cooperative, collaborative working relationship amongst the key health care professionals. In Columbia's environment, this is the geriatric nurse practitioner (GNP) and the primary care physician (PCP).

At the center of the MERGE-CARE is the geriatric nurse practitioner and consultant geriatrician. The Geriatric Nurse Practitioner:

1. Screens referrals
2. Administers MERGE protocol, consults geriatricians
3. Prepares patient profile and presentation
4. Participates in MERGE conference
5. Shares in the follow-up care of MERGE patients in concert with primary care physician
6. Updates patient profiles
7. Maintains liaison with medical and nonmedical caregivers
8. Implements referrals

The MERGE-CARE is part of a process that includes Assessment, Formulations and Recording a Management Plan, Collation of Patients' Information, and Evaluation of Progress. The following describes each of these phases:

Assessment. Although there may be slight variations in the manner in which MERGE is initiated depending on the individual patient, the general format is uniform. The assessment protocol is administered by the nurse coordinator in a comfortable, nonthreatening setting. Although the patient is encouraged to answer the questions posed, persons accompanying the patient are free to assist the patient with information. The interview time varies from 50 minutes to 1 hour and 15 minutes depending on the individual patient. Every effort is made to follow the interview protocol but modifications are made if it is observed that the patient is tiring, becoming agitated, or shows any signs of discomfort.

Formulating and Recording of Management Plan. Information from the interview is used by the PCP and Nurse Practitioner to formulate a management plan. This plan will be entered into a minicomputer and monitored on a regular timely basis.

Collating of Patients' Information. All information on medical care received through the use of MERGE-CARE will be incorporated in the patient's medical record. A computerized MERGE data system will include data on essential services, diagnoses, and prescription drugs. The computerization of the record will permit automatic prompts to the Nurse Practitioner, alerting that a visit is due, a prescription needs filling, etc. . .

Evaluation of Progress. The Nurse Practitioner and Primary Care Physician will meet weekly to review the progress of patients who are not critical and are currently receiving care. In addition, since the physician and nurse are working together daily, problems that cannot wait for the weekly session can be discussed when the need arises. The nurse and/or physician are responsible for communicating with other groups within the hospital to determine the status of care they may be providing. When progress is unsatisfactory, a meeting with other providers can be requested to attempt to develop alternative strategies.

SUMMARY

The MERGE uses a systematic semistructured interview that allows a wide range of problems to be covered in an efficient fashion. The nurse evaluates and gathers information on many problems, thus saving interview time by the physician. The diverse screening probes that ordinarily would be separately provided by a variety of disciplines are incorporated in a single interview so that needless referrals and redundant investigations are reduced. Multidisciplinary team meetings are kept to a minimum, being employed as a mechanism of developing and sustaining the evaluation and management process and service networks; not for the purpose of managing an individual patient.

REFERENCES

Bennett, R. (Ed.). (1980). *Aging, isolation and resocialization.* New York: Van Nostrand Rhinehold.

Bloom, M. (1972). Evaluation instruments, In S. Sherwood (Ed.). *Tests and measurement in long-term care. A handbook for researchers, planners and providers.* New York: Spectrum.

Cooper, J.E., Kendell, R.E., Gurland, B.J., Sharpe, L., Copeland, J.R.M., & Simon, R.J. (1972). *Psychiatric diagnosis in New York and London: A comparative study of mental hospital admission.* Maudsley Monograph, No. 20. London: Oxford University Press.

Duke University Center for the Study of Aging. (1978). *Multidimensional functional assessment: The OARS methodology (2nd ed.).* Durham, NC: Duke University.

Fink, M., Green, M., & Bender, M. (1952). The Face-Hand Test as a diagnostic sign of organic mental syndrome. *Neurology, 2,* 46–58.

Golden, R.R., Teresi, J.A., & Gurland, B.J. (1983a). Development of indicator-scales for the Comprehensive Assessment and Referral Evaluation Interview Schedule. *Journal of Gerontology, 39,* 138–146.

Golden, R.R., Teresi, J.A., & Gurland, B.J. (1983b). Detection of dementia and depression cases with the Comprehensive Assessment and Referral Evaluation Interview Schedule. *International Journal of Aging and Human Development, 16,* 241–254.

Gurland, B., Copeland, J., Kelleher, M., Kuriansky, J., Sharpe, L., & Dean, L. (1983). *The mind and mood of aging: The mental health problems of the community elderly in New York and London.* New York: Haworth Press.

Gurland, B., Cross, P., De Figuerido, J., Shannon, M., Mann, A., Jenkins, R., Bennett, R., Wilder, D., Wright, H., Killeffer, E., & Godlove, C. (1979). A cross-national comparison of institutionalized elderly in the cities of New York and London. *Psychological Medicine, 9,* 791–798.

Gurland, B., Dean, L., Copeland, J., Gurland, R., & Golden, R. (1982). Criteria for the diagnosis of dementia in the community elderly. *The Gerontologist, 22,* 180–186.

Gurland, B., Dean, L., Cross, P., & Golden, R. (1980). The epidemiology of depression and dementia in the elderly: The use of multiple indicators of these conditions. In J.P. Cole & J.E. Barrett (Eds.). *Psychopathology in the aged.* New York: Raven Press.

Gurland, B., Dean, L., Gurland, R., & Cook, D. (1978). Personal time dependency in the elderly of New York City: Findings from the US-UK Cross-National Geriatric Community Study. In B. Ferleger, (Eds.). *Dependency in the elderly of New York City.* New York: Community Council of Greater New York.

Gurland, B.J., Fleiss, J., Goldberg, G., Sharpe, L., Copeland, J.R.M., Kelleher, M.J., & Kellett, J.M. (1976a). The Geriatric Mental State Schedule II factor analysis. *Psychological Medicine, 6,* 451–459.

Gurland, B., Golden, R., & Challop, J. (1981). Unidimensional and multidimensional approaches to the differentiation of depression and dementia in the elderly. In S. Cohen, K.L. Davis, J.H. Growden, E. Usdin & R.J. Wurtman, (Eds.). *Alzheimer's disease: A report of progress in research.* New York: Raven Press.

Gurland, B., Golden, R., Teresi, J., & Challop, J. (1984). The SHORT-CARE: An efficient instrument of the assessment of depression, dementia, and disability. *Journal of Gerontology, 39,* 166–169.

Gurland, B., Kuriansky, J., Sharpe, L., Simon, R., Stiller, P., & Birkett, P. (1977–1978). CARE: Rationale, development, and reliability. *International Journal of Aging and Human Development, 8,* 9–42.

Gurland, B., Kuriansky, J., Sharpe, L., Simon, R., Stiller, P., Fleiss, J., Copeland, J., Kelleher, M., Gourlay, A., Cowan, D., & Barron, G. (1976). Outcome of hospitalization of geriatric patients in public psychiatric wards in New York and London. *Canadian Psychiatric Association Journal, 21,* 421–432.

Gurland, B., & Wilder, D. (1984). The CARE interview revisted: Development of an efficient, systematic clinical assessment. *Journal of Gerontology, 39,* 129–137.

Gurland, B., Yorkston, N., Stone, A., & Fleiss, J. (1972). The structured and scaled interview to assess maladjustment (SSIAM): I. Description, rationale, and development. *Archives of General Psychiatry, 27,* 259–263.

Kane, R.A., & Kane, R.L. (1981). *Assessing the elderly: A practical guide to measurement.* Lexington, MA: Lexington Books.

Kahn, R.L., Goldfarb, A.I., Pollack, M., & Peck, A. (1960). Brief objective measures for the determination of mental status in the aged. *American Journal of Psychiatry, 117,* 326–328.

Katz, S.F., Ford, A.B., Moskovitz, R.W., Jackson, B.A., & Jaffee, M.W. (1963). Studies of illness in the aged—the index of ADL: A standardized measure of biological and psychological functions. *Journal of American Medical Association, 185,* 914–919.

Lawton, M.P., Moss, M., Fulcomer, M., & Kleban, M. (1982). A researcher and service-oriented Multilevel Assessment Instrument. *Journal of Gerontology, 37,* 91–99.

MacDonald, A., Mann, A., Jenkins, R., Richard R., Godlove, C., & Rodwell, G. (1982). An attempt to determine the impact of four types of care upon the elderly in London by the study of matched groups. *Psychological Medicine, 12,* 193–200.

Salamon, M. (1985, July 16). *Assessment of psychogeriatric care in institutional long-term care settings.* Paper presented at the XIIIth International Congress of Gerontology. New York.

Spitzer, R., Fleiss, J., Burdock, E., & Hardesty, A. (1964). The Mental Status Schedule: Rationale, reliability, and validity. *Comprehensive Psychiatry, 5,* 384–395.

Teresi, J., Bennett, R., & Wilder, D. (1978). Personal time dependency and family attitudes. In B. Ferleger (Ed.). *Dependency in the elderly of New York City.* New York: Community Council of Greater New York.

Teresi, J., Golden, R., & Gurland, B. (1984). Concurrent and predictive validity of indicator-scales developed for the Comprehensive Assessment and Referral Evaluation (CARE) Interview Schedule. *Journal of Gerontology, 39,* 158–165.

Teresi, J., Golden, R., Gurland, B., Wilder, D.E., & Bennett, R.G. (1984). Construct validity of indicator-scales developed for the Comprehensive Assessment and Referral Evaluation (CARE) Interview Schedule. *Journal of Gerontology, 39,* 147–156.

Wing, J., Birley, J., Cooper, J., Graham, P., & Isaacs, A. (1967). Reliability of a procedure for measuring present psychiatric state. *British Journal of Psychiatry, 113,* 499–515.

CHAPTER 42

Multidimensional Assessment Technology in Care of the Elderly in International Perspective

H. Hermanova

A historical overview of the development of multidimensional instruments in rehabilitation practice and their influence on and contribution to the more recent development of such technology in care of the elderly are presented. This overview is undertaken from an international perspective, most particularly including Europe and North America. The international perspective is applied to the current situation by drawing from the U.N. World Assembly on Aging in 1982 and the WHO program to attain Health for All by the Year 2000. This is further specified by the approaches currently in process by the WHO Regional Office for Europe in the areas of: policy, programs, measurement, and data base standardization. This review calls attention to adapting multidimensional assessment approaches to: screening instruments, assessment tools in clinical practice, and assessment strategies in population-based studies as alternative goals of the same technology.

INTRODUCTION BY HISTORICAL REVIEW

Early methods of functional assessment (functional diagnostics) did not respect the unity of the man-environment system. The first serious attempt to develop functional diagnoses started after the First World War, but it was only put into practice during the Second World War. In 1943, the United States Army began to use a system of functional assessment in the rehabilitation of injured soldiers prepared by Hildebrand and known as PULHEMS Profile. PULHEMS is an acronym of the initial letters of the systems involved: P for physical, U for upper extremity, L for lower extremity, H for hearing, E for eyes, M for mental capacity, S for stability.

In 1953, McCoy and Rusk recommended the use of information on psychological, social, and economic factors in the rehabilitation process, but they did not recognize them as crucially important. The testing of the activities of daily living (ADL) soon found its place in rehabilitation practice, and included information on, for instance, "self-service" (the ability to dress, walk, eat, and take care of personal hygiene). In most methods of this period, there was no information on the social, economic, psychosocial, and domiciliary circumstances of those being examined.

In 1958 Sokolow et al. prepared a very detailed method of functional assessment using clinical findings, the ADL score, and the assessment of psychological, social, and economic factors, as well as the ability to work. This method ignored the living conditions of those being examined. The computer evaluation using this procedure was more or less a failure. That is why Sokolow (1958, 1962) twice tried to use his method in another way; nevertheless, he did not manage to combine the clinical factors, the ADL score, and the psychological, social, and economic factors with the patient's living conditions, and obtain one indicator of functioning.

Further development followed in the 1960s. The imprecise verbal descriptions were replaced by precise definitions that allowed the allocation of numerical values and, by this process, scaling. The interval between the numerical values was empirical, and not based on any mathematical laws. The allocation of points to individual factors (i.e., clinical, ADL, psychological and social) gave a quick insight into the overall condition of the patient but, of course, at this stage the numerical values neglected the correlations and interaction between the individual factors.

A change in the development of methods of functional assessment was brought about by the publication of Ekwall's (1966) paper. His method used three main variables: the clinical state, the medical-social performance, and psychosocial factors. Each of these main variables contained several subvariables, each describing a certain impairment from the functional point of view. Each subvariable was precisely defined and assessed numerically according to the following scale: 0, 1, 10, 100, 1,000.

The subvariables on the clinical state, for instance, included the functioning of the upper extremities, lower extremities, the central nervous system, sight, speech, hearing, and control sphincters; and the number of coexisting diseases contributing to the loss of rehabilitation potential. Zero points indicated fully maintained function, while

1,000 points confirmed dysfunction, a probable contraindication for rehabilitation.

The following were included among the subvariables on medical/ social performance: ability to eat, to drink, to dress, to undress, to travel, and to work; personal hygiene; gait and activities in the household (in principle, they are the activities of daily living).

Among subvariables on psychosocial factors were motivations, over-protective attitudes of relatives, family constellation, the use of home help, type of household (its exterior, interior, and economic circumstances).

According to the point values of the main variables, Ekwall allocated patients into four groups—independent, and mildly, moderately, and completely dependent. He wanted to assess the level of functioning of his patients and their prospects for rehabilitation/social reintegration by a systematic comparison of the individual subvariables of the three main variables. Ekwall's contribution was in his evaluation of various systems that are important for the maintenance of independence from the health point of view (central nervous system, sight, hearing, speech, sphincters, coexisting diseases) and his highlighting of the interplay of health, psychosocial, and socioeconomic factors in the functional assessment of hemiplegics. This approach is still valid at present, and could serve as a model in multidimensional assessment of the elderly.

Lawton (1971) prepared a survey on assessments of the functional capacity of the elderly, based on their clinical state and supplemented by ADL, including household activities, psychological and mental state, social roles, interpersonal relationships, morale, and life satisfaction. The battery of tests was an inevitable part of comprehensive assessment in daily practice. Gillner, Hyden, and Svanborg (1969) introduced another element, the nursing load, expressed by the time necessary for the nursing of patients with different degrees of dependence. Sherwood and Feldman (1970) deveolped an instrument for the screening of older applicants for placement in an institution for long-term care. The data on 123 applicants were evaluated by discrimination analysis; this process allowed the assessment of the most important social and psychosocial criteria for the type of social care proposed.

In 1972, the author (Hermanova, 1972) made a contribution to the functional assessment of the elderly by the preparation of a simple method, based on Ekwall's methodology, evaluating the biological and social factors in the assessment of dependency of an old person. The information on the following variables was collected:

1. Identification
2. State of health from the clinical point of view (diagnosis)

3. State of health from the functional point of view (function of systems important for an independent life)
4. Testing of activities of daily living
5. Socioeconomic circumstances
6. Environmental constraints both inside and outside the home
7. Indication of services

The formal mathematical operations (the application of multivariate analysis) allowed a useful reduction of all this information to one indicator only, the degree of dependence. This was one of the first attempts to assess the mutual interplay of biological and social factors in the lives of the elderly by using a mathematical and statistical method and obtaining one single indicator. Kraus (1976a, 1976b) tested applicants for placement in residential homes and analyzed the attitudes of their family as an important factor.

The enumeration of methods for testing the functional capacities of the elderly cannot be complete, unless the model by Maddox (1978) is included. His model had three elements:

- The measurement of the functional capacity of the individual and classification by functional profiles.
- The analysis of services disaggregated into elements and the synthesis of suitable components according need.
- The construction of a matrix that allowed an assessment of various alternatives in different classification groups.

Functional assessment was performed in five dimensions: social, economic, physical, mental, and activities of daily living. A questionnaire was used in clinical and outpatient practice and the results obtained were computerized. His method was based on the cooperation of multidisciplinary teams. The author himself thought that the greatest problem was in the application of this method to decision making.

GENERAL COMMENTS

Activities of Daily Living

Over the last 40 years many authors have agreed that the classical clinical diagnosis describing the disturbance of health is not sufficient in old age, and that it is the level of functioning that dictates the lifestyle of the elderly individual. For example, asking a person to cut his or her toenails provides a wide range of information. The fact that the tested person is able to carry out this task confirms that the individual hears well; that there is no aphasia; that vision is maintained; that spine, hip, knee, and the upper extremity, including the fingers, are mobile; and that there is good muscle coordination and no obesity. Katz (1963) has made the interesting observation that the activities of daily living deteriorate with age in the opposite order in which they were learned in the process of development.

Testing and/or Assessment of Mental Functions

The assessment of mental functioning is of basic importance in the care of the elderly. An elderly patient who has mentally deteriorated has almost no prospect of rehabilitation and/or social integration. Mental assessment in old age must take into consideration the education of the individual, cultural background, personality, and the characteristics of the generation to which they belong. The elderly are often considered to be a homogeneous group, starting at the age of 60 without further differentiation. This view highlights the greatest gap in our understanding of mental functioning in old age. The assessment of mental functioning is particularly important for nonspecialists in psychiatry who work with the elderly.

Testing and/or Assessment of Social and Physical Environment

The physical environment is fixed in time and space. The social environment is characterized by the relations with and among people. Both these environments are closely connected. The obvious evidence of the interaction between the social and physical environments has been based more on observations than supported by scientific studies. To develop these is one of the important tasks at present.

Role of Mathematics and Statistics

All the methods for the assessment of functional capacities published in recent years have been characterized by relatively precise mathematical and statistical evaluations. The authors have gone beyond coding the facts obtained, have recognized the mutual interplay of various factors, and have expressed their interrelationship in mathematical terms. This progress has been made possible by the application of multivariate statistical analysis to social and biological sciences, and by computerization.

Since 1982, new developments have followed; the functioning of the elderly is of such importance that one of the recommendations of the U.N. World Assembly on Aging, held in 1982, deals with this issue specifically:

Recommendation No. 11
The promotion of health, the prevention of disease, and the maintaining of the functional capacities among elderly persons should be actively pursued.

For this purpose an assessment of the physical, psychological, and social needs of the group concerned is a prerequisite. Such an assessment would enhance the prevention of disability, early diagnosis and rehabilitation (World Assembly on Aging, 1982).

International Perspective of Multidimensional Functional Assessment of the Elderly as Seen in 1985

General Comments. The elderly are regarded as a specific population group having specific needs in the medical and social area. Only a minor proportion of them (the figures vary by country and by investigator) require institutional care, a major proportion require different types of interventions (again the figures vary).

The variety of data obtained by different methodologies, use of different questionnaires, and different interpretation of data due to different cultural and historical backgrounds make us uncertain about whether we really have the information we need, whether the information is reliable and whether it could be used for planning purposes in the health and social area universally. This uncertainty provokes doubts, and doubts provoke requests for more data obtained by new methodologies and processed through more sophisticated technology and interpreted in accordance with the latest terminology in vogue.

Aging as Reflected in the WHO Policy. The World Health Organization has launched a worldwide program of attaining Health for All by the Year 2000. The issue of the elderly is introduced by the slogan: *"Adding life to years—promoting health capabilities."*

The WHO concept of health as a state of physical, mental, and social well-being, and not only the absence of disability, views health as a positive condition involving the whole person in the context of the life situation. The implication of this positive and relative concept of health is that all people, whatever their present circumstances or age, can achieve well-being by making full use of their existing functional capacities.

It is important to recognize that certain population groups may sometimes be denied viable opportunities to use their capabilities, so that handicaps or functional limitations may actually result from the lack of such opportunities. This is a situation often faced by old people in many communities. Although reduced functional capacity is correlated to advancing age, it is not clear what percentage of the reduced function is due to preventable loss of fitness and/or of social contacts. Most aging people do not show symptoms of mental and physical decline; on the contrary, they tend to enjoy a level of health that permits them to continue to lead socially and economically active lives.

Most aging persons are indeed able, and would prefer, to remain in a productive occupation, but retirement policies in countries usually discard these experienced and skilled human resources that no society should leave untapped. Other decisions affecting the elderly also are made without consulting them, even though they usually know best what their needs are and how they should be provided for. A sometimes serious problem arises from the fact that an increasing proportion of old people are living alone and in isolation. The current proportion is particularly high for women, with around 50% of those aged 60 to 64 years in many countries being on their own. In many cases, these people need to have their capacities stimulated as well as being given opportunities to use them.

Practical Approaches in the WHO Regional Office for Europe. The progress in attaining health for all should be measured and, therefore, specific indicators have been proposed for each targeted objective. Many of the proposed indicators are already part of the health information systems in most countries. Data on others are often available from existing reporting systems or surveys in health and related sectors. Some indicators call for special data collection through sample surveys, and countries will have to decide on the relevance and feasibility of such surveys.

The target of "Adding life to years—promoting health capabilities" should be supported by essential regional indicators described in Table 42-1.

In the context of items presented in the table, multidimensional functional assessment will play an important role in future, not only in

TABLE 42-1. Indicators for Health

1. Existence of policies and programs for the promotion of health capabilities of all people and especially the elderly and handicapped.	These should be read in conjunction with descriptions of policy, laws, regulations, and programs for increasing the opportunities for self-reliance and independence and developing and using individual's health potential.
2. Measurement of self-perception of health status.	The refinement of this type of indicator needs more research on the relationship between individual perception of health expectations and "objective" measurement of health status.
3. Measurement of independence in activities of daily living.	For indicators 2 and 3, WHO should contribute to the development and use of common methods. Countries are invited to report on their experience of function-based disability indicators.

"Adding life to years," but also in planning for long-term care.

CONCLUSIONS

The numerous multidimensional functional assessment tools based on many ADL schemes provide a fragmented picture, offering "bits and pieces" instead of a comprehensive data base. Therefore, data on incidence/prevalence of consequences of diseases are not comparable; the outcome of health/social intervention is not measurable; and simple basic statistics enabling better planning for disability prevention at primary, secondary, and tertiary level of control are not possible. This was perceived very clearly at the beginning of the International Year of the Disabled Persons.

The International Classification of Diseases does not offer any further promising development in the information area, in spite of the introduction of the V-Code in the ninth revision (particularly items V60 through V69, coding conditions other than health/medical, leading to contact of persons with health/social facilities). The V-Code has been used by individual investigators in limited areas only.

Wood's concept of developing handicap into a pathology (through impairment and disability) is based on analysis of multidimensional assessment tools available by the late 1970s, epidemiological studies and health statistics, as described in the International Classification of Impairments, Disabilities and Handicaps (ICIDH) (Hyden, 1980) offers an option for classification and recording. However, before adopting or adapting the ICIDH, serious attempts have to be made in either simplifying it or converting it into a comprehensive and systematic tool, enabling one to:

1. Record incidence of impairments, disabilities, and handicaps
2. Record prevalence of impairments, disabilities, and handicaps
3. Record changes (progression, regression)
4. Record stabilization

It remains an important task for the future to use the knowledge available in multifunctional assessment approaches in care of the elderly and adapt them for various purposes (screening instruments, assessment tools in clinical practice and in population-based studies) and also for different users in different sectors caring for the elderly.

REFERENCES

Ekwall, B. (1966). Method for evaluating indications for rehabilitation in chronic hemiplegia. *Acta Medicine Scandinavia, 450,* (Suppl.) 1–100.

Gillner, A., Hyden, A., & Svanborg, A. (1969). Intensive short-term rehabilitation of geriatric patients. *Scandinavian Journal of Rehabilitation Medicine, 1,* 133–138.

Hermanova, H. (1972). Some methodological problems of the functional potential assessment in old age. *Elderly people living in Europe,* (pp. 213–218). Paris: CIGS.

Hyden, A. (1980). *International classification of impairments, disabilities and handicaps.* Geneva: WHO.

Kraus, A.S. (1976a). Elderly applicants to long-term care institutions: I. Their characteristics, health problems and state of mind. *Journal of the American Geriatric Society, 24*(3), 117–125.

Kraus, A.S. (1976b). Elderly applicants to long-term care institutions: II. The applications process, placement and care needs. *Journal of the American Geriatric Society, 24*(4), 165–172.

Lawton, M.P. (1971). The Functional Assessment of Elderly People. *Journal of the American Geriatric Society, 19*(6), 465–481.

Maddox, G. (1978). Assessment of functional status in a programme evaluation and resource allocation model. In W. Holland (Ed.). *Measurement of levels of health* Geneva: World Health Organization.

Sherwood, S., & Feldman, C. (1970). The use of easily obtained precoded data in screening applicants to a long-term care facility. *The Gerontologist, 10,* 182–188.

Sokolow, J. (1958). Functional approach to disability evaluation. *JAMA, 167*(12) 1575–1584.

Sokolow, J. (1962). A new approach to the objective evaluation of physical disability. *Journal of Chronic Diseases, 15,* 105.

World Assembly On Aging, Vienna, 26 July to 6 August, 1982. New York: United Nations.

Woods. (1978). International Classification of Diseases, Vols. 1 & 2. Geneva: World Health Organization.

Woods. (1980). International Classification of Impairments, Disabilities of Handicaps. Geneva: World Health Organization.

PART V

Psychological and Behavioral Research

CHAPTER 43

Applications of Ribot's Law to Lifespan Cognitive Development

Lars Bäckman

Ribot's law implies that structures developed early in childhood are the last to degenerate in late adulthood and vice versa. In this chapter, previous studies relevant to Ribot's law are briefly reviewed. The review includes studies employing Piagetian tasks, classification tasks, discrimination learning tasks, memory tasks, and general knowledge tasks. Two recent memory studies that support Ribot's law as applied to lifespan cognitive development are presented in detail. The major findings of these studies are that (a) the ability to utilize motor action during learning as an aid for memory is well preserved in late adulthood, and (b) the ability to utilize retrieval cues at the time of testing is spared even in very old adults. Research on children shows that both these abilities develop early in life. On the other hand, it appears that the ability to utilize more abstract mnemonic techniques as, for example, semantic organization is developed later in life, and lost sooner in late adulthood. Future directions for research addressing Ribot's law as applied to lifespan cognitive development are outlined.

Ribot's law, formulated as early as 1882, states that structures first formed are the last to degenerate and vice versa. As applied to lifespan cognitive development this may imply that abilities developed early in childhood are well preserved in later adulthood, whereas abilities developed later are more susceptible to detrimental effects of the aging process. Many developmentalists (e.g., Hooper, Fitzgerald & Papalia,

The preparation of this chapter was supported by grants from the Bank of Sweden Tercentenary Foundation, and the Delegation of Social Research in Sweden.

1971; Lee & Pollack, 1978; Storck, Looft, & Hooper, 1972) have entertained this line of reasoning, usually under the heading of cognitive regression in old age (i.e., a return to immature developmental levels). Employing a variety of Piagetian tasks, several studies from the late 60s and early 70s (see Hooper & Sheehan, 1977; Papalia & Bielby, 1974 for reviews) found evidence in favor of the "cognitive regression hypothesis." The pattern of data is, however, equivocal, and many recent studies (e.g., Chance, Overcast, & Dollinger, 1978; Selzer & Denney, 1980; Tesch, Whitbourne, & Nehrke, 1978) have failed to find any adult age differences in, for example, conservation, egocentrism, and concept attainment.

Studies on classification or categorization show a more consistent pattern. A common finding in that literature (Cicirelli, 1976; Denney & Lennon, 1972; Inhelder & Piaget, 1964; Koffsky, 1966) is that young children and older adults group objects haphazardly or in terms of functional relations, graphic collections, and thematic arrangements. Older children and younger adults, on the other hand, appear to construct dimensionally well-organized classifications based on, for example, size or semantic category (Bourne, 1974; Vygotsky, 1962). These data are in line with Kinsbourne's (1980) notion that the perception of the elderly is like that of young children, more holistic rather than analytic. Moreover, results from studies on discrimination learning (Coppinger & Nehrke, 1972; Kendler & Kendler, 1975; Shanab & McClure, 1983) suggest a reversed ontogeny of the behavior of older adults.

It appears that young children and old adults have a special difficulty in doing a reversal shift while performing at the level of younger adults when detection of extradimensional shifts is required. Mediational and attentional deficits in young children and the elderly have been proposed as explanations of this age effect (Shanab & McClure, 1983).

Further, there are episodic memory studies (Barrett & Wright, 1981; Hultsch & Dixon, 1983) as well as semantic memory studies assessing general knowledge (Bäckman & Karlsson, 1985; Perlmutter, Metzger, Miller, & Nezworski, 1980) in which the datedness of information has been manipulated (e.g., dated vs. contemporary names of famous entertainment artists; dated vs. contemporary words). The typical finding in such studies is a crossover interaction between adult age and datedness, such that older adults perform better for items like Greta Garbo and Glenn Miller, whereas younger adults perform better for items like Mick Jagger and Jack Nicholson. These results are in agreement with Schaie's (1977) notion that there are qualitatively different stages of adult cognitive functioning with acquisitive processes dominating in early childhood and reintegrative processes dominating in late adulthood. Obviously, a pattern of data showing that it is easier for older adults to learn dated items in an episodic memory experiment and to retrieve dated information from semantic memory than to learn or retrieve contemporary information is in agreement with Ribot's law.

Another empirical finding that supports Ribot's law is the temporal gradient of retrograde amnesia observed in Korsakoff patients and patients receiving ECT (see Squire, 1982 for a review), for example, memories acquired shortly before the onset of the amnesia are typically forgotten, and the older the memories are, the higher the probability of correct retrieval.

Some recent studies from our own laboratory provide further evidence for the viability of Ribot's law as applied to lifespan cognitive development. In two papers (Bäckman & Nilsson, 1984, 1985) it was demonstrated that the commonly observed superiority of younger as compared with older adults in free recall (Kausler, 1982; Salthouse, 1982) is eliminated when the task is to remember series of subject-performed tasks (SPTs). An SPT can be carried out either with one or two objects (e.g., sharpen the pencil, eat the raisin, smell the perfume, bounce the ball) or without any objects (e.g., clap your hands, wave good-bye, nod in agreement, stand up). This memory task differs from those standard verbal memory tasks for which age-related differences have been routinely observed in two basic ways. First, SPTs are *multimodal* in the sense that several or all sensory modalities are activated during encoding. Second, SPTs comprise a *variety of features* on which encoding may be based (verbal features, color, shape, sounds, texture, motor features, smell features, taste features). Note that some of these features are nominally present in two sensory systems (e.g., shape, motor features), whereas others are modality-specific (e.g., color, sounds).

It is argued that the multimodal and rich properties of SPTs constitute contextual support that older adults utilize in order to maximize memory performance (cf. Craik, 1983). These multimodal and rich properties are brought about by the facts that (a) subjects are allowed to act motorically during encoding, and (b) real-life objects are used as the to-be-remembered (TBR) information. Bäckman (1985) investigated the relative importance of these two factors for the elderly's high performance (and the lack of adult age differences) on SPT recall. This was done by manipulating younger and older adults' motor action during encoding, while holding the presence of real-life objects constant. The results were straightforward: No age differences in recall were observed when motor action was required, whereas the younger adults outperformed the elderly when subjects did not act motorically during encoding. Accordingly, it may be concluded that an active motor manipulation is very critical for the elderly's success on free recall of SPTs.

A common finding in the literature on memory development in

childhood (e.g., Cohen & Stewart, 1982; Wolff & Levin, 1972) is that age differences between younger and older children are reduced or eliminated when subjects are allowed to manipulate the TBR items motorically, whereas older children routinely outperform younger children when the presentation is verbal and when encoding is dependent upon more abstract mnemonic techniques (see also Kail, 1979). This pattern of data is in line with the well-known notions of sensory motor intelligence (Piaget & Inhelder, 1969) or the enactive stage (Bruner, 1968), preceding those cognitive abilities necessary for successful performance in verbal memory tasks. As applied to the present reasoning, the ability to use an active motor manipulation as an aid for memory may be an example of "first in —last out." That is, the ability is developed early, and thus, well preserved in late adulthood, whereas the cognitive operations typically required in verbal memory tasks develop later and, thus, decline sooner.

Bäckman & Karlsson (in press) examined younger adults, 73-year-olds, and 82-year-olds on free and cued recall of words preceded by standard instructions or organizational instructions. It was found that the younger group was relatively independent of contextual support at encoding (organizational instructions) and retrieval (category cues) in order to remember successfully. The group of 73-year-olds was able to utilize support at both stages of remembering and performed at the highest level on cued recall preceded by organizational instructions. The group of 82-year-olds, on the other hand, utilized support only at retrieval; this group did not improve free recall performance when instructed to organize as compared to when receiving standard instructions, but performed better on cued recall than on free recall regardless of type of encoding instruction.

The ability to utilize different types of external cues at the time of testing seems to develop very early in childhood and may even be seen among 3 1/2 year-old children (Kobasigawa, 1977; Ritter, Kaprove, Fitch, & Flavell, 1973). The ability to use organizational instructions, on the other hand, appears to develop much later (Furth & Milgram, 1973; Schultz, Charness, & Berman, 1973) and is generally thought about as developing as a function of the demands of formal education (Flavell & Wellman, 1977). Thus, the ability to utilize cues at retrieval is early developed and appears to be preserved among very old individuals, whereas the ability to utilize organization instruction develops later and seems to be disrupted among very old adults.

Although these studies support Ribot's law in the sense that behavioral similarities between younger children and older adults can be observed, there are some problems that need to be addressed. First, Salthouse (1982) has pointed out that data of the above kind might simply reflect the general tendency for age effects to be most pronounced on the most difficult tasks (see also Crowder, 1980). This important objection is, however, not applicable to the Bäckman (1985) and Bäckman and Karlsson (in press) studies, and the reason for this is simple: Control groups of younger adults in these two studies did not improve recall in the tasks for which all elderly adults showed improvement (i.e., SPTs, cued recall) as compared with control tasks. If the memory enhancement of the elderly would have resulted from reduced task difficulty *per se,* an improvement of the younger adults as well in the "easier" tasks should have been expected. In this context, it should be noted that no ceiling effects were observed on the part of the younger subjects in the Bäckman (1985) and Bäckman and Karlsson (in press) studies.

Second, behavioral similarities between children and older adults do not necessarily imply structural similarities between these groups. Data on amnesics (Cermak, 1982; Squire, 1982) as well as other types of memory disorders (Nilsson, L.-G, Karlsson, & Bäckman, 1985; Strauss, Weingartner, & Thompson, 1985) indicate that behavioral similarities may exist although different cognitive mechanisms or different regions of the brain are impaired in various groups of subjects. Third, a variety of factors could, in principle, contribute to the similarities in patterns of memory performance between younger children and the elderly: Isolation from school and job demands (Denney, 1974; Smiley & Brown, 1979), deficits in self-initiated operations of remembering (Craik, 1983; Kail, 1979), idiosyncratic interpretation of instructions and perception of task demands (Bäckman, in press; Flavell & Wellman, 1977), and immature versus degenerated brain structures (Kinsbourne, 1980), or a combination of these and other factors.

With respect to future directions for research addressing Ribot's law as applied to life span cognitive development, there are two issues that should be highlighted: First, the issue as to why Ribot's law is applicable for some tasks (e.g., classification, discrimination learning, memory tasks) but not for others (e.g., tasks tapping egocentrism and conservation). Second, the issue about which causative factors that produce the similar patterns of data seen in younger children and older adults.

One way of approaching these issues would be to examine subjects across the *entire life span* in a variety of tasks (e.g., perceptual tasks, attentional tasks, memory tasks, problem-solving tasks). Such a selection of subjects is especially needed since most available data only permit comparisons between experiments. The next step is to do a careful analysis of the tasks for which similar patterns of data are observed (and not observed) in children and older adults, and to relate this task analysis to assumptions about which cognitive operations the different tasks are tapping (see Moscovitch, 1985, for a similar approach in the context of research on amnesia).

On the basis of such a line of research we would, clearly, be in a better position for answering the intriguing question about the generality and limitations of Ribot's law as applied to cognitive development across the lifespan.

REFERENCES

Bäckman, L. (1985). Further evidence for the lack of adult age differences on free recall of subject-performed tasks: The importance of motor action. *Human Learning, 4,* 79–87.

Bäckman, L. (in press). Varieties of memory compensation of older adults in episodic remembering. In L.W. Poon, D.C. Rubin, & B.A. Wilson (Eds.). *Everyday cognition in adult and later life.* New York: Cambridge University Press.

Bäckman, L., & Karlsson, T. (1985). The relation between level of general knowledge and feeling-of-knowledge: An adult age study. *Scandinavian Journal of Psychology, 26,* 249–258.

Bäckman, L., & Karlsson, T. (in press). On the need and utilization of contextual support in episodic remembering in young adults, 73-year-olds, and 82-year-olds. *Scandinavian Journal of Psychology.*

Bäckman, L., & Nilsson, L. -G. (1984). Aging effects in free recall: An exception to the rule. *Human Learning, 3,* 53–69.

Bäckman, L., & Nilsson, L. -G. (1985). Prerequisites for lack of age differences in memory performance. *Experimental Aging Research, 11,* 67–73.

Barrett, T.R., & Wright, M. (1981). Age-related facilitation in recall following semantic processing. *Journal of Gerontology, 36,* 194–199.

Bourne, L.E. (1974). An inference model for conceptual rule learning. In R.L. Solso (Ed.). *Theories in cognitive psychology: The Loyola symposium.* Potomac, LEA.

Bruner, J. (1968). *Processes of cognitive growth: Infancy.* Worchester: Clark Univeristy Press.

Cermak, L.S. (1982). (Eds.). *Human memory and amnesia.* Hillsdale, NJ: LEA.

Chance, J., Overcast, T., & Dollinger, S.J. (1978). Aging and cognitive regression: Contrary findings. *Journal of Psychology, 98,* 177–183.

Cicirelli, V.G. (1976). Categorization behavior in aging subjects. *Journal of Gerontology, 36,* 676–680.

Cohen, R.L., & Stewart, M. (1982). How to avoid developmental effects in free recall. *Scandinavian Journal of Psychology, 111,* 9–16.

Coppinger, N.W., & Nehrke, M.F. (1972). Discrimination learning and transfer of training in the aged. *Journal of Genetic Psychology, 120,* 93–102.

Craik, F.I.M. (1983). On the transfer of information from temporary to permanent memory. *Philosophical Transactions of the Royal Society, London, 302,* 341–359.

Crowder, R.G. (1980). Echoic memory and the study of aging memory systems. In L.W. Poon, J.L. Fozard, L.S. Cermak, D. Arenberg, & L.W. Thompson (Eds.). *New directions in memory and aging.* Hillsdale, NJ: LEA.

Denney, N.W. (1974). Evidence for developmental changes in categorization criteria for children and adults. *Human Development, 17,* 41–53.

Denney, N.W., & Lennon, M.I. (1972). Classification: A comparison of middle and old age. *Developmental Psychology, 7,* 210–213.

Flavell, J.H., & Wellman, H.M. (1977). Metamemory. In R.V. Kail & J.W. Hagen (Eds.). *Perspectives on the development of memory and cognition.* Hillsdale, NJ: LEA.

Furth, H.G., & Milgram, N.A. (1973). Labeling and grouping effects in the recall of pictures by children. *Child Development, 45,* 144–151.

Hooper, F.H., Fitzgerald, J., & Papalia, D.E. (1971). Piagetian theory and the aging process: Extensions and speculations. *International Journal of Aging and Human Development, 2,* 3-20.

Hooper, F.H., & Sheehan, N.W. (1977). Logical concept attainment during the adult years. In W.F. Overton & J.M. Gallagher (Eds.). *Knowledge and development* (Vol. 1). New York: Plenum Press.

Hultsch, D.F., & Dixon, R.A. (1983). The role of pre-experimental knowledge in text processing in adulthood. *Experimental Aging Research, 9,* 17-22.

Inhelder, B., & Piaget, J. (1964). *The early growth of logic in the child.* New York: Norton.

Kail, R.V. (1979). *The development of memory in children.* San Francisco: Freeman.

Kausler, D.H. (1982). *Experimental psychology and human aging.* New York: Wiley.

Kendler, H.H., & Kendler, T.S. (1975). From discrimination learning to cognitive development: A neobehavioristic odyssey. In W.K. Estes (Ed.). *Handbook of learning and cognitve processes* (Vol. 1). Hillsdale, NJ: LEA.

Kinsbourne, M. (1980). Attentional dysfunctions and the elderly: Theoretical models and research perspectives. In L.W. Poon, J.L. Fozard, L.S. Cermak, D. Arenberg, & L.W. Thompson (Eds.), *New directions in memory and aging.* Hillsdale, NJ: LEA.

Kobasigawa, A. (1977). Retrieval strategies in the development of memory. In R.V. Kail & J.W. Hagen (Eds.), *Perspectives on the development of memory and cognition.* Hillsdale, NJ: LEA.

Koffsky, E. (1966). A scalogram study of classificatory development. *Child Development, 37,* 191-204.

Lee, J.A., & Pollack, R.H. (1978). The effects of age on perceptual problem-solving strategies. *Experimental Aging Research, 4,* 37-54.

Moscovitch, M. (1985). The sufficient conditions for demonstrating preserved memory in amnesia: A task analysis. In N. Butters & L.R. Squire (Eds.). *The neuropsychology of memory.* New York: Guilford Press.

Nilsson, L. -G., Karlsson, T., & Bäckman, L. (1985). *Priming effects in sleep deprived, alcohol-intoxicated, and elderly subjects in a lexical decision task.* Manuscript submitted for publication.

Papalia, D.E., & Bielby, D.D.V. (1974). Cognitive functioning in middle and old age adults: A review of research based on Piaget's theory. *Human Development, 17,* 424-443.

Perlmutter, M., Metzger, R., Miller, K., & Nezworski, T. (1980). Memory of historical events. *Experimental Aging Research, 6,* 47-60.

Piaget, J., & Inhelder, B. (1969). *The psychology of the child.* London: Routledge & Kegan Paul.

Ribot, T. (1882). *Diseases of memory.* New York: Appleton.

Ritter, K., Kaprove, B.H., Fitch, J.P., & Flavell, J.H. (1973). The development of retrieval strategies in young children. *Cognitive Psychology, 5,* 310-321.

Salthouse, T.A. (1982). *Adult cognition.* New York: Springer Publishing Company.

Schaie, K.W. (1977). Toward a stage theory of adult cognitive development. *International Journal of Aging and Human Development, 8,* 129-133.

Schultz, T.R., Charness, M., & Berman, S. (1973). Effects of age, social class, and suggestion to cluster in free recall. *Developmental Psychology, 8,* 57-61.

Selzer, S.C., & Denney, N.W. (1980). Conservation abilities in middle-aged and elderly adults. *International Journal of Aging and Human Development, 11,* 135-146.

Shanab, M.E., & McClure, F.H. (1983). Age and sex differences in discrimination learning. *Bulletin of the Psychonomic Society, 21,* 387-390.

Smiley, S.S., & Brown, A.L. (1979). Conceptual preference for thematic or taxonomic relations: A nonmonotonic age trend from preschool to old age. *Journal of Experimental Child Psychology, 28,* 249-257.

Squire, L.R. (1982). The neuropsychology of human memory. *Annual Review of Neuroscience, 5,* 241-273.

Storck, P.A., Looft, W.R., & Hooper, F.H. (1972). Inter-relationships among Piagetian tasks and traditional measures of cognitive abilities in mature and aged adults. *Journal of Gerontology, 27,* 461–463.

Strauss, M.E., Weingartner, H., & Thompson, K. (1985). Remembering words and how often they occurred in memory-impaired patients. *Memory and Cognition, 13,* 507–510.

Tesch, S., Whitbourne, S.K., & Nehrke, M.F. (1978). Cognitive egocentrism in institutionalized adult males. *Journal of Gerontology, 33,* 546–552.

Vygotsky, L.S. (1962). *Thought and language.* Cambridge, MA: MIT Press.

Wolff, P., & Levin, J.R. (1972). The role of overt activity in children's imagery production. *Child Development, 43,* 537–548.

CHAPTER 44

Intelligence and Terminal Decline

Stig Berg

One of the explanations given to cognitive decline in old age is that the deterioration is an instance of what is called terminal drop or terminal decline. According to this hypothesis, a decline in intellectual functioning in old age is more related to the distance of death than to old age itself. The distance of death can be regarded as an overall measure of health and terminal decline is an instance of a deterioration in intelligence-related adaptive potential. Intelligence test results in relation to death or survival have been studied in an 11-year longitudinal study, the Gothenburg longitudinal study. Intelligence tests of verbal meaning and reasoning were used. The results showed a connection between decline in test results and proximity to death. This was true both for verbal meaning and reasoning. There were no differences between males and females.

Longitudinal studies of intelligence show comparatively unchanging results up to the beginning of old age. After that, most investigations show a certain deterioration. How should this deterioration be explained? One of the explanations given is that the deterioration is an instance of what is generally called terminal drop or terminal decline. According to this hypothesis, a decline of intellectual functioning in old age is more related to the distance of death than to old age itself. Kleemeier (1962) who was the first scholar to describe terminal decline thought "that factors related to the death of the individual cause decline in intellectual performance, and that the onset of this decline may be detected in some instances several years prior to the death of the person" (p. 293). The distance of death can be interpreted as an overall measure of health and terminal decline can be viewed as a

411

reflection of decline in intelligence-related adaptive potentials.

There are generally two terms used when discussing the problem of death and cognitive deterioration and they are terminal drop and terminal decline. A curvilinear or accelerating decline of intellectual functioning closely before death is generally called terminal drop, while a more lasting linear deterioration is called terminal decline (Palmore & Cleveland, 1976). In most of the investigations that have been carried out, terminal decline and terminal drop have been used without any consideration to the problem of linear or curvilinear development. A large number of measurements is necessary to really detect terminal drop and that is why most longitudinal studies with few measurements can study only a very general type of terminal decline. In this paper the phrase *terminal decline* will be used both for linear and curvilinear changes.

Despite the large number of studies of terminal decline, there is still disagreement about how much terminal decline can really affect intellectual functioning. What types of intelligence factors are the most sensitive, and how long before a person's death can one see a decline? Various methodological problems have in some cases made the results uncertain, and it has been shown that in some studies there is a tendency to exaggerate the effects of terminal decline. The best way to study terminal decline is longitudinal analyses of longitudinal data. Such analyses can evaluate changes in behavior over a specified time interval as related to survival or death (Siegler, 1975).

The aim here is to present intelligence test results in relation to death or survival from a 9-year longitudinal study, the Gothenburg longitudinal study.

METHOD

The Gothenburg longitudinal study started in 1971–1972 with a random sample of 70-year-old people living in the city of Gothenburg, Sweden. This group was also examined at the age of 75 and at the age of 79 as well. At the age of 81 there was information about survival, and no psychological examinations were made at this time. A new follow-up with psychological measures is planned for 1986–1987 when the subjects will be 85 years old.

The initial response rate at the age of 70 was 79%. The nonresponders did not differ from the responders concerning sex, marital status, income, psychiatric inpatient and outpatient care and alcohol abuse according to different registers. Nonresponse from persons up to the age of 79 was an additional 18%. There was no significant difference in the proportion of deaths among the nonresponders and the responders. The total number of people included in this study of terminal decline was 280, out of which 49 died between age 70 and 75, 56 between 75 and 79, and 21 between 79 and 81. Information about deaths was obtained through the population register, which means that all subjects who have died are included in the study.

The investigation at the age of 70, 75, and 79 consisted of an interview in the subjects' homes and a one-day examination at the outpatient clinic of a geriatric hospital. During the day various examinations were carried out (e.g., a general medical examination with laboratory tests, a psychiatric interview, and psychological testings) (Berg, 1980). Since the study consisted of a very broad examination, the psychological and psychiatric investigations had to be performed at a maximum of 3 hours, which naturally restricted what kind of information could be obtained. The intelligence tests used were based on a Swedish version of "Thurstone's primary abilities," and this paper on terminal decline will present the results from the tests of verbal meaning and reasoning.

The sample did not show much variation in social background factors such as education and living conditions. Only 1% of the women and 7% of the men had a high-school certificate or a university degree. Most people lived in apartments in the older central districts of Gothenburg. A majority of the subjects had lived in Gothenburg for more than 50 years. The number of immigrants was 5%. Most subjects had retired at the age of 67. There were no marked variations in financial situation or income, largely because of the Swedish state pension system and subsidies for rental of apartments.

For the statistical analysis t-test was used. Differences in mean scores between groups were tested through t-test for independent samples and changes within groups were tested through t-test for paired samples. One-tailed tests and the significance level $p < 0.05$ were chosen.

RESULTS

Results from four different groups will be presented:

1. Those who died after the age of 70 but before the age of 75.
2. Those who died after the age of 75 but before the age of 79.
3. Those who died after the age of 79 but before the age of 81.
4. Those who are still alive at the age of 81.

The results of the investigation showed a connection between a decline in the intelligence test results and proximity to death (Figures 44-1 and 44-2). This was true both for verbal meaning and reasoning. Those who died between age 75 and 79 had significantly lower scores

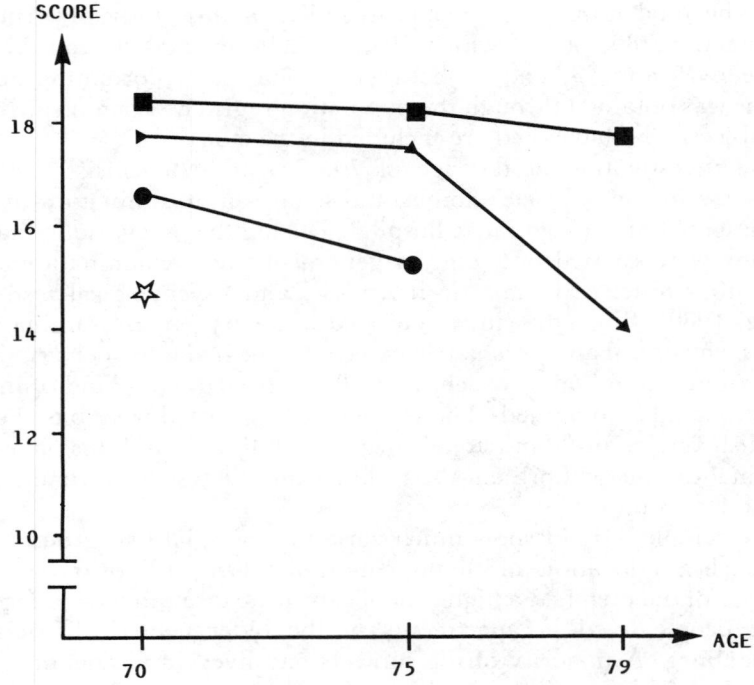

FIGURE 44-1. The relation between survival and results of an intelligence test of verbal meaning.

        ★ died after the age of 70 but before the age of 75
        • died after the age of 75 but before the age of 79
        ▲ died after the age of 79 but before the age of 81
        ■ still alive at the age of 81

at the age of 70 than those who survived till they were 79 or older. Those who died after the age of 75 also had a faster decline in the test results between 70 and 75 compared with those who survived till 79 or later. The same pattern can be seen among those who died between 70 and 75. At the measurement that was made when they were 70 years old, their results were significantly lower on the two tests compared with those who survived until they were 75, 79, or older.

The last intelligence test results that we have are at the age of 79. What one should remember is that in the measurements at this age the group consists of two subgroups seen from the point of view of survival: those who will die pretty soon and those who will go on living for another number of years. If at the age of 79 the group is divided into those who will survive till 81 and those who will die before that age, we get the following results. The survivors get almost the same test results

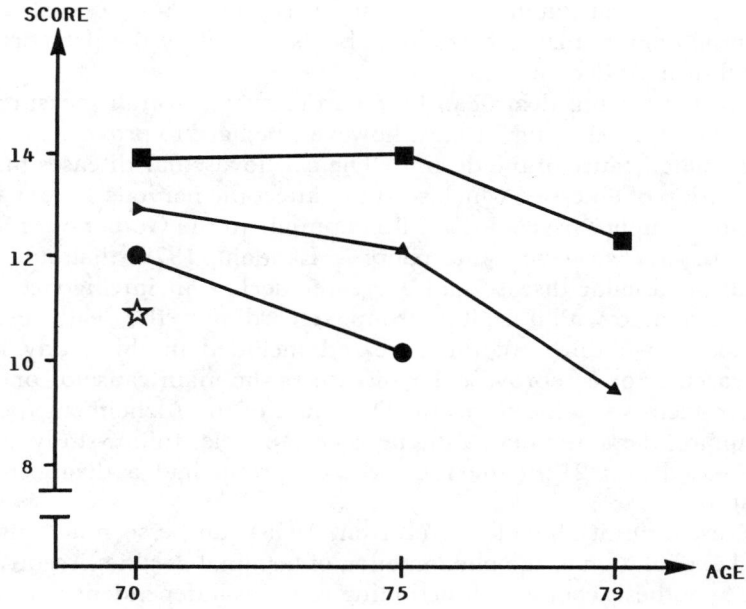

FIGURE 44-2. The relation between survival and results of an intelligence test of reasoning.

★ died after the age of 70 but before the age of 75
● died after the age of 75 but before the age of 79
▲ died after the age of 79 but before the age of 81
■ still alive at the age of 81

between 70, 75 and 79, while those who die show an obvious terminal decline from the age of 75 or earlier.

In the decreased group there was a majority of males due to the shorter life expectancy among men. As regards the relation between intelligence test results and proximity to death there were no differences between the sexes.

DISCUSSION

The results of the investigation show that there is a relationship between proximity to death and the results of intelligence tests. Thus, very much of what one has believed to be normal deterioration of various intelligence factors during aging is probably instances of terminal decline. It is difficult from the results in this study to say how long before a person's death one can see a decline, but on group level it seems that it is at least 5 years. In the last measurements of longitudinal studies one can often see a decline in cognitive test results. To a substantial degree this decrease must be explained by the presence of terminal drop or decline.

The distance from death can be regarded as an overall measure of health or biological aging. It may, however, be hard to prove a specific disease-related cause of the decline. The cardiovascular diseases make up one group of illnesses, which seems to affect the nervous system and penetrate to higher psychological functioning. In the Gothenburg longitudinal study we have found (Berg & Landahl, 1979) that subjects with cardiovascular disease had a greater decline in intelligence test results compared with a healthy group. According to the death certificates about two thirds of the deceased included in this study had cardiovascular or cerebrovascular disease as the main cause or one of the main factors leading to death. Dementia of the Alzheimer type or multi-infarct dementia may also play a certain role. In our study 20 of the deceased and 21 in the nondeceased group had a diagnosis of dementia.

The discontinuity hypothesis (Birren, 1959) can be seen as a more general explanation to the phenomenon of terminal decline. According to that hypothesis cognitive functioning remains independent of physiologic function until critical limits are surpassed. The variation in scores of intelligence tests and other cognitive abilities and measures of biological function are relatively independent when kept within normal range. However, with intervening pathology the correlation between biological and cognitive functioning may be a measure of the pathology and the risk to die.

The results of the investigation show that a great deal of what has been seen in longitudinal studies as an age-related decrease in cognitive functioning may be due to terminal decline. This conclusion also questions many of the results found in experimental cognitive studies where a young and an old group have been examined. It also poses the question of how to define aging. Is terminal decline of cognitive functioning really part of the normal aging process?

REFERENCES

Berg, S. (1980). Psychological functioning in 70- and 75-year-old people. *Acta Psychologica Scandinavica, 62,* (Suppl.), 288.

Berg, S., & Landahl, S. (1979). Psychological functioning in 70- and 75-year-old people: Intellectual functions and cardiovascular disease. *Reports from the Department of Applied Psychology, University of Göteborg, Sweden,* (Vol. 4, No. 2).

Birren, J.E. (1959). Principles of research on aging. In J.E. Birren (Ed.). *Handbook of Aging and the Individual.* Chicago: University Press.

Kleemeier, R. (1962). Intellectual changes in the senium. *Proceedings of the Social Statistics Section of the American Statistical Association,* (pp. 290–295). Washington.

Palmore, E., & Cleveland, W. (1976). Aging, terminal decline, and terminal drop. *Journal of Gerontology, 31,* 76–81.

Siegler, I.C. (1975). The terminal drop hypothesis: Fact or artifact. *Experimental Aging Research, 1,* 169–185.

CHAPTER 45

The Case for Personality Stability

Paul T. Costa, Jr.
Robert R. McCrae

Many theories of adult development have postulated changes in personality due to maturation or the impact of life events. Over the past decade, however, a series of longitudinal studies have demonstrated that personality traits are stable in adulthood: There are no age-related shifts in mean levels, and individuals maintain very similar rank ordering on traits after intervals of up to 30 years. Artifacts of memory, response set, or a crystallized self-concept cannot account for observed stability, which is seen in ratings as well as self-reports. The fact that individuals retain their distinctive dispositions despite aging and a lifetime of experience suggests that powerful mechanisms promote stability, and leads to a new set of questions for students of personality and aging. Instead of asking how personality develops in adulthood, or is shaped by life events, we should instead seek to understand how enduring dispositions shape the life course and influence the process of aging.

Tolstoy began *Anna Karenina* with the observation that all happy families are alike, and, by implication, that unhappy families form a more promising subject for the novelist. The same might be said about

Portions of this article are taken from ''Personality Stability and Its Implications for Clinical Psychology,'' in J. S. Wiggins (Ed.), Personality Assessment in the 80's: Issues and Advances (Special issue). *Clinical Psychology Review*, Vol. 6, 1986.

theories of personality in adulthood: All stability models are much the same, whereas a fascinating variety of alternative developmental schemes can be considered. In contrast to the grandeur of universal life stages, the intricacy of individuation, the suspense of aleatory change, or the tragedy of inevitable decline, the stability model is bound to seem dull. Other than an austere elegance, there is little to recommend the position that personality is essentially fixed throughout adulthood—except for the empirical evidence. Our aim here is to review that evidence, and then to suggest briefly a few ways in which the story of personality and aging can become more interesting than it would at first appear.

A DEFINITION OF PERSONALITY

For some, the question of personality stability in adulthood may seem odd. Isn't personality *defined* as the individual's "lifelong style of relating, coping, behaving, thinking, and feeling" (Millon, 1981, p. 3)? From this point of view, demonstrations of personality stability may seem redundant or even tautological.

Others will be equally surprised to hear that there is strong evidence in favor of stability. What about the universal midlife crisis? What about Erikson's stages of development? What about the changes brought about by social change and technological innovation? What about the stress of aging? Can it really be asserted that individuals can go through a lifetime of experience without substantial changes in their personality?

Responses to these positions must take the form of definitions as well as data. There are meaningful and important ways to define personality that allow us to address these questions empirically, and although it is by no means necessary that personality should be stable, in fact it usually is.

In contrast to definitions of personality that emphasize unconscious structures (Freud, 1933), organizational processes and coping styles (Haan, 1977), or "what a man (or woman) really is" (Allport, 1937, p. 48), we have adopted a more concrete definition of personality as the individual's characteristic styles of thought, feeling, and behavior. As trait psychologists, we focus on individual differences in patterns of interpersonal relations, emotional reactions, impulse control, and experiential styles. Using this approach, dimensions of interest can be readily measured by standard scales that make possible a rigorous empirical investigation of aging and personality. By analyzing personality scores from groups of aging individuals, we can determine whether people in general become more or less anxious, introverted, conservative, irritable, or apathetic as they age; by correlating scores from administrations separated by an interval of several years we can quantify stability or change in individual differences.

Trait models of personality have often been held in low esteem because they were thought to be superficial. Merely describing an individual as being "reserved," for example, doesn't indicate whether this interpersonal style is the result of deeply ingrained mistrust of others, or intense fear of rejection, or socialization in an undemonstrative culture or family, or simply a temperamental preference for privacy. The dynamics, the underlying motives and meanings, cannot be inferred from so simple a description of behavior. It is for this reason that most trait theorists take a multivariate approach to personality. Although single traits are often ambiguous, a clearer picture of the individual emerges when a range of traits is examined. We are more likely to understand "reserve" to mean "social anxiety" if we also know that the individual is prone to depression and low in self-esteem, but generally trusting and cooperative. If the individual is well-adjusted but generally serious-minded, we would probably see reserve as simple introversion.

In order to understand the individual, then, we need to assess the full range of his or her traits. Obtaining a comprehensive picture of personality, however, soon leads to an embarrassment of riches. There are thousands of trait terms available to the speaker of English (Allport & Odbert, 1936), of which about 500 are in common use (Goldberg, 1982). Hundreds of individual scales and dozens of inventories have been created by personality psychologists interested in specific traits. The Minnesota Multiphasic Personality Inventory (MMPI) alone has been the source of over 450 research scales (Dahlstrom, Welsh, & Dahlstrom, 1975) intended to measure almost as many different traits.

This array of constructs presents formidable problems to anyone wishing to review personality research. The only practical solution is to group together similar dispositions and conceive of personality in terms of broad classes of traits. A successful taxonomy of traits would allow a systematic and thorough study of personality, and it has been the goal of a number of personality theorists (e.g.,Cattell, 1947; Eysenck & Eysenck, 1985; Wiggins, 1979). One taxonomy, first proposed in the early 1960s (Norman, 1963; Tupes & Christal, 1961), has recently been rediscovered by a number of independent investigators (Amelang & Borkenau, 1982; Digman & Takemoto-Chock, 1981; Goldberg, 1982; McCrae & Costa, 1985, 1987). Five broad factors are proposed in this model, for which we prefer the terms Neuroticism, Extraversion, Openness to Experience, Agreeableness, and Conscientiousness. Each of these domains encompasses a variety of more specific traits, and most of the scales used to study aging and personality can be classified according to this system.

EVIDENCE ON THE STABILITY OF PERSONALITY IN ADULTHOOD

Whether, how much, and in what ways personality changes in adulthood remained an open question for many decades after it had been raised (Bühler, 1935; Jung, 1923), largely because the long time spans involved made scientific study difficult. The most direct way to assess change is to measure personality in young men and women, wait until they have aged, and measure their personality again. Researchers must have foresight, patience, and—since results are often harvested by other investigators—considerable altruism to begin such a longitudinal study; thus only a handful of major studies have been conducted. In the past decade a number of these studies have been completed; the near unanimity of their findings forms the best basis for conclusions on personality in adulthood.

There are, of course, alternative ways to investigate the influence of aging on personality. Retrospective studies depend on a reconstruction of earlier personality based on memories, and although widely used by clinicians and theorists of the lifespan, they are held suspect by methodologists who question whether memory is to be trusted in this highly subjective area. Cross-sectional studies, which compare younger and older persons at the same point in time, are able to use more objective methods and avoid reliance on memory. However, they suffer from other limitations, of which the best known is the confounding of age changes with generational differences. Today's 80-year-olds may differ from today's 30-year-olds not because they have changed in the past 50 years, but because their personalities were formed in a different era. For example, over the past 30 years, successive generations have seen dramatic changes in public attitudes toward drugs and sex, and these differences in socialization—rather than maturation—may account for observed age differences in sensation seeking (Ball, Farnill, & Wangeman, 1984).

Lifespan methodologists (Schaie, 1977) have advocated a number of designs for separating true maturational effects from birth cohort differences, historical changes, sampling biases, and practice effects. No single strategy—not even longitudinal studies—can give unequivocal evidence, but a pattern of findings from a variety of study designs can lead to some assurance about conclusions (Costa & McCrae, 1982). For this reason, it is important to note that, on the whole, retrospective and cross-sectional studies are consistent with the position of stability in personality. Reichard, Livson, and Peterson (1962), in one of the seminal books on personality and aging, took extensive life histories from their sample of retired men, and concluded that "the histories of our aging workers suggest that their personality characteristics changed very little throughout their lives" (p. 163). And Neugarten's

(1977) review of cross-sectional studies reported little consistent evidence of age differences in personality.

Stability of Mean Levels

Studies of stability and change are chiefly concerned with two questions: Does the mean level of a variable change with age? How consistent are individual differences? In longitudinal studies, the first question is addressed by repeated measures analyses; the second, by calculating retest correlation coefficients. The two kinds of stability or change these approaches assess are entirely independent of each other, and have very different interpretations. We will first review evidence on changes in the mean level of variables, asking whether age brings about normative increases or decreases in personality traits—whether, regardless of other influences, people tend to change in consistent ways simply by virtue of getting older.

Many variables are thought to show such change. For example, middle-aged men are sometimes held to go through a period of transition resulting in transient states that resemble neurosis—the "mid life crisis." Older men and women are variously stereotyped as becoming conservative, grouchy, depressed, or wise. Although wisdom may be difficult to measure, there are many standardized measures of conservativism, irritability, and depression, and if these changes are taking place, significant increases should show up on readministration of these measures after a suitable interval of years.

A number of large-scale longitudinal studies provide data relevant to these hypotheses. The Sixteen Personality Factor Questionnaire (16PF; Cattell, Eber, & Tatsuoka, 1970) was administered to volunteer men in the Normative Aging Study between 1965 and 1967. The subjects, mostly white veterans living in the Boston area, initially ranged in age from 25 to 82. In 1975, 139 of the men were retested, and repeated measures analyses of variance were used to assess changes in the 16 scales (Costa & McCrae, 1978). Two scales—intellectual brightness and group independence—showed significant increases over the 10-year interval. The increased scores on the intelligence scale were likely due to familiarity with the test, a phenomenon known in educational psychology as a practice effect. There were no significant changes in the other 14 scales. When the subjects were divided into three age groups, neither of these longitudinal changes was replicated as a cross-sectional age difference, nor were there any significant age group-by-time interactions.

The 16PF was also used by investigators at Duke University who examined age changes in 331 men and women born between 1899 and 1922 (Siegler, George, & Okun, 1979). Subjects were assessed four times over an 8-year period, and repeated measures analyses were conducted for each of the 16 scales. Intellectual brightness increased over time (again, probably due to practice effects), and guilt-proneness showed a time-by-sex interaction, with men decreasing and women increasing on this scale, but there were no changes in the other 14 scales. The authors concluded that "the results indicate little evidence of significant differences across cohorts, changes over time, or their interaction" (p. 351).

In 1977, Leon, Gillum, Gillum, and Gouze (1979) readministered the MMPI to 71 men who had previously taken that inventory in 1947, 1953, and 1960. All men were initially middle-aged (45-54), so cross-sectional comparisons in this population were not possible. All of the standard scales except L showed some significant changes over the course of the study, but most were quite small in magnitude, usually less than one-half standard deviation. Larger changes were found in Scale 2 (Depression), probably because many of the items in this scale refer to somatic problems that increase with age (cf. Zemore & Eames, 1979). What changed here was probably health rather than personality. The authors state that "the general profile configuration for the group remained remarkably stable and within normal limits over the 30-year period of time from middle age to old age" (Leon et al., 1979, p. 520).

Not all research has supported the stability position. One notable study reporting change is the Management Progress Study. Using the Edwards Personal Preference Schedule (EPPS; Edwards, 1959), Bray and Howard (1983) studied young managers at retest intervals of 8 and 20 years and found a substantial increase in Need Autonomy, with corresponding declines in empathy, conformity, and friendliness. Detailed information on all scales is provided in Howard and Bray (in press). It is possible that changes do occur in specific motives, although not in more general dispositions; it is also possible that changes may occur in specific subgroups, such as managers, that do not represent normal maturational changes.

Mortimer, Finch, and Kumka (1981) examined persistence and change in the self-concept for 368 college men tested in the freshman and senior years, and in a 10-year follow-up. Their analyses showed statistically significant increases in sense of well-being and competence, and decreases in sociability and unconventionality, in the 10 years after college. These findings are consistent with other literature on changes in personality during adolescence and early adulthood. Bachman, O'Malley, and Johnston (1978) show longitudinal increases in self-esteem during late adolescence, and Jessor (1983) reports an increase in his index of conventionality. Thus, it would appear that there are some meaningful changes during the transition into adulthood. William James' (1890) dictum that "by age 30, personality is set like plaster'' implies that there is still some likelihood of change until that age, and the data seem to support him.

However, it is also important to note that the magnitude of the observed changes is very small. The changes seen by Mortimer et al. amount to less than one-quarter standard deviation across 10 years. In later adulthood, changes are likely to be even smaller. Douglas and Arenberg (1978) analyzed responses from several hundred men on the Guilford-Zimmerman Temperament Survey (GZTS; Guilford, Zimmerman, & Guilford, 1976), using cross-sequential designs (a type of analysis intended to estimate longitudinal changes using independent samples) as well as cross-sectional and longitudinal designs. Of the ten GZTS scales, only two—Masculinity and General Activity—showed a pattern of effects that could be interpreted as maturational change, and these declines were trivial in magnitude, being less than one-eighth standard deviation over about 7 years.

Studies of stability or change in the mean level of personality variables were originally intended to determine which traits increased, which decreased, and which remained constant over the life span. It was anticipated that the developmental changes observed would shed light on the nature of both the aging process and the factors that affect personality change. This expectation was to be disappointed by the repeated finding that age itself had very little impact on any aspect of personality. The inventories used in the studies cited above include measures of Neuroticism, Extraversion, Openness, Agreeableness, and Conscientiousness, and would seem to provide reasonably comprehensive coverage of adult personality—yet not a single one of these domains shows a consistent pattern of developmental change. The clear implication of this unexpected finding is that attention needs to be refocused, not on the determinants of personality change, but on the mechanisms that promote stability.

Stability of Individual Differences

The fact that there is little change with age in the average level of personality traits does not necessarily imply that individuals do not change in personality—only that such changes, if any, are not systematically related to aging. It is easy to imagine conditions that would lead to dramatic changes in individuals with no change in the group as a whole. For example, Jung's (1923) concept of individuation suggests that psychological functions repressed in youth should become dominant in old age. Introverts would become extraverts, extraverts introverts—but the average level of extraversion might remain unchanged. Alternatively, changes might be random rather than developmental, depending on the impact of life events, some increasing, some decreasing the level of the trait. Personality in old age would then represent the outcome of life experience rather than the initial starting point of the individual.

Cross-sectional studies give no hint of how stable the rank-ordering of individuals along a trait dimension is; only by repeatedly measuring the same group of individuals over a reasonably long interval of time can the necessary data be obtained. Longitudinal studies have gone on for half a century, and some of the most striking findings of stability were published in the 1950s (Strong, 1951; Kelly, 1955). But it was not until a new generation of longitudinal studies matured in the 1970s that the pattern of stability in individual differences became unmistakable.

Most of the studies have already been described in the previous section, because the same data, differently analyzed, have provided answers to both kinds of questions about stability. In a few cases, only retest correlations have been published. Block (1977) summarized retest correlations for the 18 California Psychological Inventory (CPI; Gough, 1957) scales given to adult members of the Berkeley longitudinal studies in the 1960s and 1970s. Eron (1982) and his colleagues surveyed all the third-graders in a semirural county in New York to trace the development of aggressive behavior; they followed-up the sample when they were 19 and 30 years old, at which times they used the sum of MMPI F, 4, and 9 scales to measure self-reported aggression. Conley (1985) examined factors that he extracted from the Kelly (1940) Rating Scales in a sample of 189 men and 189 women recruited as part of a study on couples in 1935 and retested in 1955. Conley interpreted his Kelly Longitudinal Study (KLS) factors as four of the five major personality dimensions: Neuroticism, Extraversion, Impulse Control (Conscientiousness), and Agreeableness. Howard and Bray have generously supplied stability coefficients for the EPPS and GAMIN (Guilford & Martin, 1943) from the Management Progress Study (A. Howard & D.W. Bray personal communication, May 10, 1985).

Table 45-1 summarizes stability coefficients for these studies. Results are remarkably consistent across studies using different instruments, different samples, different age cohorts, and different retest intervals: Personality scales tend to show long-term retest correlations of from .30 to .80 over intervals of up to 30 years.

Skeptics might argue that stability estimates derived from self-report instruments overestimate stability. Perhaps subjects recall their earlier responses and repeat them in order to appear consistent. Perhaps what is stable is not the substantive personality disposition, but response styles of acquiescence, extreme responding, or social desirability. Perhaps self-reports reflect a crystallized self-concept, and their stability shows only that individuals' *views* of their personality remain un-

TABLE 45-1. Stability Coefficients for Recent Longitudinal Studies Using Self-Report Instruments

Study	Instrument[a]	n	Sex	Initial age	Retest interval	Correlations Range	Median
Block (1977)	CPI	219	M,F	31-38	10	—	.71
Costa & McCrae (1978)	16PF	139	M	25-82	10	.24-.64	.50
Siegler et al. (1979)	16PF	331	M,F	45-70	2	—	.50
Leon et al. (1979)	MMPI	71	M	45-54	13	.07-.82	.50
				58-67	17	.03-.76	.52
				45-54	30	.28-.74	.40
Costa et al. (1980)	GZTS	60	M	20-44	12	.61-.85	.72
		87	M	45-59	12	.64-.85	.75
		32	M	60-76	12	.59-.87	.73
Mortimer et al. (1981)	Self-concept	368	M	College seniors	10	.51-.63	.55
Eron (1982)	MMPI F+4+9	409	M,F	19	11	.45-.55	.50
Conley (1985)	KLS factors	378	M,F	18-35	20	.34-.57	.46
Howard & Bray (1985)	EPPS	266	M	Young managers	20	.31-.54	.42
	GAMIN	264	M		20	.45-.61	.57

[a]CPI = California Psychological Inventory; 16PF = Sixteen Personality Factor Questionnaire; MMPI = Minnesota Multiphasic Personality Inventory; GZTS = Guilford-Zimmerman Temperament Survey; KLS = Kelly Longitudinal Study; EPPS = Edwards Personality Preference Schedule; GAMIN = Guilford/Martin Inventory of Factors GAMIN

changed, when in fact they have changed substantially in their characteristic thoughts, feelings, and actions.

Each of these alternative hypotheses has been the subject of empirical research. Woodruff (1983) readministered the California Test of Personality after 25 years to a sample of 77 men and women under two conditions: as they currently saw themselves and as they recalled having answered 25 years earlier. Larger correlations ($r = .58, .65$) were seen under the normal instructions than when asked to rely on memory ($r = .17, .45$). "These data do not support the hypothesis that memory inflates estimates of stability. Indeed . . . memory appears to exaggerate estimates of change" (p. 33).

If response sets, rather than personality traits, are the source of stability, then partialling out their effects should reduce stability coefficients. We tested this hypothesis in a sample of 98 men on whom we had 6-year retest data from the GZTS as well as measures of acquiescence, extreme responding, nay-saying, and socially desirable responding (Costa, McCrae, & Arenberg, 1983). Nine of the 10 GZTS scales showed virtually no change in 6-year stability coefficients when the four response scales were partialled out, and the tenth, Masculinity, decreased only slightly, from .73 to .68. Stability of personality does not appear to be the result of response sets.

The possibility that the person's self-concept is fixed while personality itself changes was more difficult to test, because it required that we have some measure of personality independent of how the individual saw him or herself. We resolved this problem by using spouse ratings of personality (McCrae & Costa, 1982). If people actually change as they age, while their self-concept remains the same, their self-reports should diverge increasingly from external observers' views of them. Our analyses showed that this was not the case with regard to either mean levels or individual rank ordering for the dimensions of Neuroticism, Extraversion, or Openness to Experience as measured by the NEO Personality Inventory (Costa & McCrae, 1985). People do tend to keep the same idea of what they are like—probably because what they are like doesn't change.

In fact, there is good reason to think that self-report personality inventories *underestimate* the true stability of personality. All personality measures are subject to unreliability of measurement, and better estimates of true stability are obtained by correcting for unreliability. In the Siegler et al. (1979) study, the median 1-week retest reliability was exactly the same as the median 2-year stability, suggesting that all the apparent change was unreliability. When we corrected for attenuation in our GZTS study, the estimated "true" 12-year stability coefficients ranged from .80 to 1.00, with a median of .91 (Costa et al., 1980).

It is not necessary to rely exclusively on self-report personality inventories to establish that personality is stable. Personality rating studies (Backteman & Magnusson, 1981; Block, 1971; Conley, 1985) come to much the same conclusion, although correlations are typically smaller—probably because raters never know the subject as well as he or she knows him or herself. Stagner (1977) argues that the utility of trait measures in predicting long-term occupational outcomes is further evidence of their stabilty. As Bray (1982) says, "individual characteristics present at the time of initial employment are important determinants of managerial success. Furthermore, these characteristics must be reasonably stable to support such accurate predictions" (p. 185). Both Jessor (1983) and Mortimer et al. (1982) also show that personality variables influence later life outcomes—a finding that testifies to the importance as well as the stability of adult personality.

A NEW PERSPECTIVE

When a series of longitudinal studies report little or no difference in the mean levels of a wide range of traits measured years apart on large samples, it is most assuredly not a null finding. It is dramatic testimony to the resiliency of personality variables, and poses a clear challenge to personality theorists to account for the mechanisms of stability. Is personality genetically determined? Imprinted in childhood? A reflection of an unchanging unconscious? Locked in by a crystallized self-concept, or maintained by self-selection of reinforcing environments? Understanding the forces that perpetuate traits is, of course, not only of theoretical significance, it can also form the basis for more effective interventions to change dispositions that are objectionable to the individual or society. One moral seems clear: We should not wait to outgrow undesirable characteristics, for, without intervention, they are unlikely to change by themselves.

This conclusion is generally seen as a pessimistic one, offering limited prospects for growth or self-improvement. But there is also an optimistic side to the stability model, since it reassures the well-adjusted and cheerful that they will remain so for life, that neither adverse circumstances nor aging itself will deprive them of their tranquility and good spirits. More fundamentally, perhaps, the continuity of personality gives all individuals a sense of identity, and allows them to make meaningful plans for their future.

Gerontologists studying aging and personality must themselves make new plans as a result of these findings. Although it would be possible to continue the search for aspects of personality that are sensitive to developmental change, we believe a more promising direction to take will be an inquiry into the effects of personality on the life course. Personality traits are pervasive influences on thoughts, feelings, and actions, and it now appears that they exercise their influence across the full span of adulthood. Surely the cumulative effect of personality dispositions must be seen in occupational careers, family relations, political and social attitudes, health practices, and most other aspects of the adult life structure. It is through the study of these outcomes that we believe personality research can most contribute to an understanding of aging.

REFERENCES

Allport, G.W. (1937). *Personality: A psychological interpretation.* New York: Holt.

Allport, G.W., & Odbert, H.S. (1936). Trait names: A psycho-lexical study. *Psychological Monographs, 47* (211). 1–171.

Amelang, M., & Borkenau, P. (1982). Über die faktorielle Struktur und externe Validität einiger Fragebogen-Skalen zur Erfassung von Dimensionen der Extraversion und emotionalen Labilität (On the factor structure and external validity of some questionnaire scales measuring dimensions of extraversion and neuroticism). *Zeitschrift für Differentielle und Diagnostische Psychologie, 3,* 119–146.

Bachman, J.G., O'Malley, P.M., & Johnston, J. (1978). *Adolescence to adulthood: Change and stability in the lives of young men.* Ann Arbor, MI: Institute for Social Research.

Backteman, G., & Magnusson, D. (1981). Longitudinal stability of personality characteristics. *Journal of Personality, 49,* 148–160.

Ball, I.L., Farnill, D., & Wangeman, J.F. (1984). Sex and age differences in sensation seeking: Some national comparisons. *British Journal of Psychology, 75,* 257–265.

Block, J. (1971). *Lives through time.* Berkeley, CA: Bancroft Books.

Block, J. (1977). Advancing the psychology of personality: Paradigmatic shift or improving the quality of research? In D. Magnusson & N.S. Endler (Eds.). *Personality at the cross-roads: Current issues in interactional psychology.* Hillsdale, NJ: Erlbaum.

Bray, D.W. (1982). The assessment center and the study of lives. *American Psychologist, 37,* 180–189.

Bray, D.W., & Howard, A. (1983). The AT&T longitudinal studies of managers. In K.W. Schaie (Ed.). *Longitudinal studies of adult psychological development.* New York: Guilford.

Bühler, C. (1935). The curve of life as studies in biographies. *Journal of Applied Psychology, 19,* 405–409.

Cattell, R.B. (1947). Confirmation and clarification of primary personality factors. *Psychometrica, 12,* 197–220.

Cattell, R.B., Eber, H.W., & Tatsuoka, M.M. (1970). *The handbook for the Sixteen Personality Factor Questionnaire.* Champaign, IL: Institute for Personality and Ability Testing.

Conley, J.J. (1985). Longitudinal stability of personality traits: A multitrait-multimethod—multioccasion analysis. *Journal of Personality and Social Psychology, 49,* 1266–1282.

Costa, P.T., Jr., & McCrae, R.R. (1978). Objective personality assessment. In M. Storandt, I.C. Siegler, & M.F. Elias (Eds.). *The clinical psychology of aging.* New York: Plenum Press.

Costa, P.T., Jr., & McCrae, R.R. (1982). An approach to the attribution of age, period, and cohort effects. *Psychological Bulletin, 92,* 238–250.

Costa P.T., Jr., & McCrae, R.R. (1985). *The NEO Personality inventory manual.* Odessa, FL: Psychological Assessment Resources.

Costa, P.T., Jr., McCrae, R.R., & Arenberg, D. (1980). Enduring dispositions in adult males. *Journal of Personality and Social Psychology, 38,* 793–800.

Costa, P.T., Jr., McCrae, R.R., & Arenberg, D. (1983). Recent longitudinal research on personality and aging. In K.W. Schaie (Ed.). *Longitudinal studies of adult psychological development.* New York: Guilford Press.

Dahlstrom, W.G., Welsh, G.S., & Dahlstrom, L.E. (1975). *An MMPI handbook: Vol. II Research applications.* Minneapolis: University of Minnesota Press.

Digman, J.M., & Takemoto-Chock, N.K. (1981). Factors in the natural language of personality: Reanalysis, comparison, and interpretation of six major studies. *Multivariate Behavioral Research, 16,* 149–170.

Douglas, K., & Arenberg, D. (1978). Age changes, cohort differences, and cultural change on the Guilford-Zimmerman Temperament Survey. *Journal of Gerontology, 33,* 737–747.

Edwards, A.L. (1959). *Edwards Personal Preference Schedule Manual.* New York: The Psychological Corporation.

Eron, L.D. (1982, August). The consistency of aggressive behavior across time and situations. In *Consistency of aggression and its correlates over twenty years.* Symposium presented at meetings of the American Psychological Association, Anaheim, CA.

Eysenck, H.J., & Eysenck, M. (1985). *Personality and individual differences.* London: Plenum.

Freud, S. (1933). *New introductory lectures in psychoanalysis.* W.J.H. Sprott, (Trans.). New York: Norton.

Goldberg, L.R. (1982). From ace to zombie: Some explorations in the language of personality. In C.D. Spielberger & J.N. Butcher (Eds.). *Advances in personality assessment.* Hillsdale, NJ: Erlbaum.

Gough, H.G. (1957). *California Psychological Inventory Manual.* Palo Alto, CA: Consulting Psychologists Press.

Guilford, J.P., & Martin, H.G. (1943). The Guilford/Martin inventory of factors GAMIN. Beverly Hills, CA: Sheridan.

Guilford, J.S., Zimmerman, W.S., & Guilford, J.P. (1976). *The Guilford-Zimmerman Temperament Survey handbook: Twenty-five years of research and application.* San Diego, CA: Edits Publishers.

Haan, N. (1977). *Coping and defending.* New York: Academic Press.

Howard, A., & Bray, D.W. (in press). *Managerial lives in transition: Advancing age and changing times.* New York: Guilford.

James, W. (1890). *Principles of psychology.* New York: Henry Holt.

Jessor, R. (1983). The stability of change: Psychosocial development from adolescence to young adulthood. In D. Magnusson & V.L. Allen (Eds.). *Human Development: An interactional perspective.* New York: Academic Press.

Jung, C.G. (1923). *Psychological types.* London: Routledge & Kegen Paul.

Kelly, E.L. (1940). A 36-trait personality rating scale. *Journal of Psychology, 9,* 97–120.

Kelly, E.L. (1955). Consistency of the adult personality. *American Psychologist, 10,* 659–681.

Leon, R.R., Gillum, B., Gillum, R., & Gouze, M. (1979). Personality stability and change over a 30-year period-middle age to old age. *Journal of Consultation in Clinical Psychology, 23,* 245–259.

McCrae, R.R., & Costa, P.T., Jr. (1982). Self-concept and the stability of personality: Cross-sectional comparisons of self-reports and ratings. *Journal of Personality and Social Psychology, 43,* 1282–1292.

McCrae, R.R., & Costa, P.T., Jr. (1985). Updating Norman's ''adequate taxonomy'': Intelligence and personality dimensions in natural language and in questionnaires. *Journal of Personality and Social Psychology, 49,* 710–721.

McCrae, R.R., & Costa, P.T., Jr. (1987). Validation of the five-factor model of personality across instruments and observers. *Journal of Personality and Social Psychology, 52,* 81–90.

Millon, T. (1981). *Disorders of personality: DSM-III: Axis-II.* New York: Wiley.

Mortimer, J.T., Finch, M.D., & Kumka, D. (1982). Persistence and change in development: The multidimesional self-concept. In P.B. Baltes & O.G. Brim, Jr. (Eds.). *Lifespan development and behavior.* New York: Academic Press.

Neugarten, B.L. (1977). Personality and aging. In J.E. Birren & K.W. Schaie (Eds.). *Handbook of the psychology of aging (1st ed.).* New York: Van Nostrand Reinhold.

Norman, W.T. (1963). Toward an adequate taxonomy of personality attributes: Replicated factor structure in peer nomination personality ratings. *Journal of Abnormal and Social Psychology, 66,* 574–583.

Reichard, S., Livson, F., & Peterson, P.G. (1962). *Aging and personality.* New York: Wiley.

Schaie, K.W. (1977). Quasi-experimental research designs in the psychology of aging. In J.E. Birren & K.W. Schaie (Eds.). *Handbook of the psychology of aging, (1st ed.).* New York: Van Nostrand Reinhold.

Siegler, I.C., George, L.K., & Okun, M.A. (1979). Cross-sequential analysis of adult personality. *Developmental Psychology, 15,* 350–351.

Stagner, R. (1977). On the reality and relevance of traits. *Journal of General Psychology, 96,* 185–207.

Strong, E.K., Jr. (1951). Permanence of interest scores over 22 years. *Journal of Applied Psychology, 35,* 89–91.

Tupes, E.C., & Christal, R.E. (1981). Recurrent personality factors based on trait ratings. *USAF ASD Technical Report,* No. 61–97, 1961.

Wiggins, J.S. (1979). A psychological taxonomy of trait-descriptive terms: The interpersonal domain. *Journal of Personality and Social Psychology, 37,* 395–412.

Woodruff, D. (1983). The role of memory in personality continuity: A 25 year followup. *Experimental Aging Research, 9,* 31–34.

Zemore, R., & Eames, N. (1979). Psychic and somatic symptoms of depression among young adults, institutionalized aged and noninstitutionalized aged. *Journal of Gerontology, 34,* 716–722.

CHAPTER 46

Uses of the Past in the Adult Lifespan

Harvey Peskin

In the uses-of-the-past model of personality, adult development transforms an individual's history into resources to be drawn upon for present adaptation. Adult stages are approached as changing personality organizations that strive for effective functioning by recruiting and reorganizing selective material from the past. Adult personality thus is not yoked to fixed causes nor youth to fixed effects. As the past widens with aging, new combinations and capacities for later-life adaptation become available from the earlier life span. This model, then, seeks confirmation from over time statistical discontinuities rather than behavioral consistencies. Data from two longitudinal samples studied over adolescence and 30 years of adulthood are presented in which subjects' past modes of responding are correlated with adult psychological health. Findings indicating over time discontinuities support the model of changing uses of the youthful past.

In showing that personality is stable over the life span, longitudinal study may have eased suspicions that personal coherence is only a figment of wishful memory, only the retrospective smoothing out of uneven pasts. The longitudinal case for stability at Baltimore, Fels, Berkeley, and elsewhere demonstrates unmistakeably that essential behaviors flow across our lifetime with no prominent lapses or leaps, no conspicuous points of onset, upset, or sharp decline, but rather absorb change gradually, such as revealed by slowly diminishing correlations over wide time spans. Does the undeniable case for stability make an equally strong case against rapid, even abrupt, personality changes— the kinds of discontinuous change that developmental theorists like Freud, Piaget, Jung, Levinson or Gutmann count as indicating the transformational effects of age and stage? Does the case for stability, secured by reliable overtime measures (Costa, McCrae, & Arenberg, 1983), refute the stage-theory position, often garnered from less reliable retrospection, that healthy personality development involves repeated breaks with or radical transformations of past states, even astonishing flips or reversals of behavioral meanings?

Our longitudinal research at the Institute of Human Development (IHD) has indicated that behavioral stability per se, in the sense of the preservation of individual differences on a variable measured over time, may be neutral with regard to the continuity of the meaning (or function) of that variable, in the sense of its structural relationship with other behaviors. Indeed, our findings have sometimes contradicted the usual presumption (Emmerlich, 1966) that the change in a behavior's meaning over time presupposes indications of instability. Rather we have discovered that a stable behavior can have disparate, even opposite meanings, according to the behavior's changing position in the larger personality organization over two (or more) points in time.

For stage theorists, it is the phase or age in which the behavior is enacted that organizes behavior in a sequential context of layered and ripening intentions over the formative years. Can such phasic organization contain behavioral stability? We learned slowly in our research that both could work together, as the following early example reveals (Peskin, 1972). In the longitudinal sample of the Guidance Study at IHD, the dimension of dependent-independent behavior for the female sample is stable (0.30) between preadolescence and early adolescence. Yet staying independent (or staying dependent) in preadolescence and adolescence leads to quite opposite predictions of a composite measure of Psychological Health at age 30. Being *independent* in preadolescence and *dependent* in early adolescence predict positively adult psychological health, certainly a remarkable shift of function for a relatively stable trait and one, as far as we know, unreported elsewhere. In this example, we argued that preadolescent independence had centered and fortified healthy adult women to experience the deeper emotionality of adolescence without undue concern over loss of control. However, to remain independent in adolescence meant a loss of its preadolescent meaning and now rather signaled a withdrawal from inner emotional investment. These reversals of meaning in stable behaviors were evident for the female sample on two other scales of self-confidence followed by adolescent lower self-confidence; and by preadolescent controlled temper followed by adolescent explosive temper. Thus, a case for the stability of a behavior seems to be compatible with a case for transformative meanings. One might even advance the notion that behavioral stability affords an individual the sense of personal coherence that allows a degree of freedom to explore and construct new meanings behind customary actions.

Stage theorists have not energetically pursued the unique longitudinal data panels for evidence of the power of phase or age to transform meanings across the lifespan, even of stable behaviors. How can such evidence for the properties of an age period be obtained from raw data that are obscured and confounded by the welter of adjacent age-period effects? To resort to our example to illuminate this issue: the changing function of *independent* behavior between preadolescence and early adolescence was not apparent to us in our first report of the raw correlations from each time period to the adult measure of Psychological Health (Livson & Peskin, 1967). Initially, we reported only the association between preadolescent *independence* and adult Psychological Health. The connection between adolescent *dependence* and adult Psychological Health awaited a reanalysis of the data in a second study (Peskin, 1972). Here, adult Psychological Health was multiply predicted from preadolescent and early-adolescent behaviors. In this study, multiple prediction crossed stages, in contrast to the Livson & Peskin study where multiple prediction drew from within-stage behaviors only. With this cross-stage multiple prediction, the reversal of the behavioral meanings was uncovered, as each age predictor was computed with the other age partialled out. Doing so has the effect of holding constant the behavior's stability over one age period to the next, so that the preadolescent predictor would not unduly spread its effect into the adolescent period on the coattails of the stability coefficient. Not doing so (as in the Livson & Peskin study) could spread the preadolescent effect into suppressing a reversed adolescent effect by the stability coefficient. Such reversal effects have also been uncovered in our reanalysis of Fels Study correlations by submitting them to such age partialling (cf. Livson & Peskin, 1980).

Taking account of a behavior's stability in this multiple-prediction design also reduced the redundancy of prediction that lends an inflated and false continuity to overtime prediction of Psychological Health criterion measure. Again, not accounting for behavior's stability will cause a preadolescent predictor to unduly spread its effect into the adolescent period on the coattails of the stability coefficient, but when all coefficients have a plus sign, this spread will speciously enlarge the adolescent effect. Thus, partialling out the interage stability of a behavior can either produce concealed reversal effects or reduce the excessive yield of continuous predictions. In either event, legitimate evidence for lifespan change is weakened if the case for stability is unattended by appropriate methodological evenhandedness. Age-specific processes of an age period indeed call for age-specific methods in order to develop a balanced construction of personality with a deserved place for discontinuities, as well as continuities across the lifespan.

Since a prior stage may hide the properties of a later stage, the specific nature of middle age and aging is least apt to survive and shine through the cumulative impact of cross-age confounding, unless rescued by methodological interventions. Our research report focuses now on uncovering the discontinuities in middle age and aging to establish their place as eras of lifespan development. Here, those few and fortunate longitudinal studies with sufficient consecutive time series of data collection to liberate age-specific effects from prior age confounding by stable behaviors offer a unique opportunity to refine stage concepts in the later lifespan. The California cohorts of the Berkeley Guidance Study, born in 1928 to 1929, and the Oakland Growth Study, born in 1920 to 1921, have come of age for this task, with both cohorts sharing a common data bank of early and late adolescent personality in junior and senior high school, and three adult followups in 1960, 1970, and 1982—at ages 30, 40, and 52 for the Guidance sample, and ages 37, 47, and 60 for the Oakland sample (Eichorn, Clausen, Hean, Honzik, & Mussen, 1981).

The larger personality organization that our research has defined for predictive studies is adult psychological health whose measure is derived from the 100-item California Q-sort, based on intensive clinical and structured interviews of the study participants. The Psychological Health (PH) score is the correlation of a subject's actual Q-sort description with another Q-sort description of a hypothetical healthy person, reliably rated by clinicians (Livson & Peskin, 1967). The PH score is broadly consistent with other measures of psychological health, like satisfaction in work, marriage, and parenting. The measure is highly stable between and among the adult ages for the Oakland group and moderately so for the Guidance sample, except for the lack of association between age 30 and 40 for the male group (Peskin & Livson, 1981).

With such consecutive personality measurement available over youth and adulthood, our age-specific methodology permits us to account and control for adjacent–age confounding of predictive behaviors in adolescence and of Psychological Health scores in adulthood. Each adult follow-up allowed the partialling-out of the PH score of the previous follow-up. Taking the Guidance sample for illustration, prediction of PH at age 40 from adolescent behaviors could be determined with age 30 PH held constant; age 50 PH could be predicted with age 40 PH held constant; or, more precisely, age 50 PH could be predicted by holding constant both age 30 and age 40 PH. Thus, for the studies now underway, we have followed a procedure whereby both sides of the prediction—the early predictors in adolescence and later PH criterion in adulthood—have been as differentiated from nearby age periods as our data collection has so far allowed. Our expectation of developmental discontinuities will be disconfirmed if, after these procedures, adult relationships with the adolescent past either remain essentially similar from one adult age to the next, or gradually decline as a function of passing time, or are merely scant and minimal. Broadly speaking, such negative findings would make the case for adulthood as a changeless plateau, firmly structured by the early years in accord with child-centered personality theories—Freudian, social learning, or otherwise. If, on the other hand, adult age periods are structurally different from each other, we would then expect that adult relationships with adolescence will be correspondingly different, hence, discontinuous from one adult age to the next. We have elsewhere (Peskin & Livson, 1981) formulated the view that each adult age or stage constructs and organizes the past for current adaptation. This view embodies the familiar stage notion that each growth phase activates its own organization, but highlights the less heralded possibility that such activity importantly includes the dynamic changes wrought in the use and comprehension of lifespan history. This view necessarily departs from the traditional reductionism of past-to-present causality even in psychodynamic, but child-centered, theory.

In our recent and present studies, *discontinuous* is used in four ways: (1) adolescent behavior better predicts Psychological Health at a later adult age than an earlier one; (2) reversal effects are discerned (i.e., when the same behavior in early and late adolescence oppositely predicts adult Psychological Health); (3) the same behavioral predictor oppositely predicts Psychological Health between one adult age and the next; (4) more broadly, the overall yield of unique adolescent predictors of Psychological Health for each adult age is such as to suggest a changing organization of past resources for current adult adaptation. Findings that bear on these four aspects of developmental discontinuities in middle age and early aging will be summarized in the remainder of this report. The Guidance and Oakland samples are treated separately by sex, providing four groups for statistical analysis. In this report, we include, but venture beyond, early and late adolescent predictors of adult Psychological Health. With each adult followup, we have been able to add an early-adult Q-sort description to the pool of predictors of later PH, as in predicting PH at age 40 from a Q-sort item sorted in early adolescence, late adolescence, and age 30. All results are based upon multiple correlations across the predictive periods for Q-sort item, with partial correlations indicating its phase-specific power of prediction.

First, a brief summary of evidence for discontinuity in predicting Psychological Health at ages 30 and 40 for the Guidance sample, and ages 37 and 47 for the Oakland sample, and next, new findings from the 1982 follow-up more than a decade after. For three of the four sample x sex groups, the number of adolescent predictors of Psychological Health at the later adult age was larger than at the earlier adult age. For example, adolescent behavior predicted the psychological health of the Guidance men much more powerfully at age 40 than at

age 30. Thus, correspondence between past and present was not between closer periods in time but between further periods, indicating
decline and resurgence over time rather than simple stability and
continuity of prediction. Next, three of the four groups produced
predictive reversals between early and late adolescence for PH at either
or both adult follow-ups, indicating that the same behavior in these
consecutive periods of youth prefigure quite opposite outcomes in
adult psychological health (Peskin & Livson, 1981). We report newly
found predictive reversals among three prior age periods: early adolescence, late adolescence, and first adult follow-up (age 30 for Guidance,
age 37 for Oakland) in multiply predicting PH at the second adult
follow-up (age 40 for Guidance, age 47 for Oakland). For example,
Psychological Health of Oakland men at age 47 was predicted by the
sequence of dependable behavior in early adolescence, undependability in late adolescence, and dependability again at age 37. For Oakland
women at age 47, PH was predicted by gregarious behavior in early
adolescence, next by its reversal to being more self-contained in late
adolescence, and finally a return to gregariousness at age 37. Note the
positive contribution to Psychological Health of undependability and
low gregariousness in late adolescence, seemingly qualities of questionable worth as precursors of psychological health in adulthood. Yet late
adolescence (senior high school) has quite regularly shown up in our
research in this untidy way of social and personal ineptness and unrest,
poor impulse control, and withdrawal into the self, but also the capacity to think unconventionally, to fantasy, and to introspect—a composite close to the Eriksonian moratorium. Here, then, we find discontinuity in yet another sense—the drawing upon the shadow self of the self
to widen the scope of adult possibility beyond the simplistic premise of
much developmental formulation that "good leads to good."

Third, discontinuity fails to gain support from any findings showing
that the same behavioral predictor oppositely predicts Psychological
Health between one adult age and the next. No single adolescent
behavior so markedly alters as to switch from a negative to a positive
predictor (or positive to negative) of adult PH between age 30 and 40
for Guidance or age 37 and 47 for Oakland.

Lastly, the overall yield of unique adolescent predictors of PH at
each adult age suggests a reasonably coherent and age-specific adult
period for each of the four groups, which stands out sharply against the
other, less defined adult age. For Guidance men, it is at age 40 when
Psychological Health draws upon adolescent resources that reflect the
classic image of the established, instrumental male: power-oriented,
responsible, masculine, close to same-sex friends, decisive, not defen-
sively thin-skinned, sociable, nurturant, given to conventional thinking, and ungiven to fantasy. For Guidance women, it is age 30 (when
almost all are mothers of young children) when Psychological Health

draws upon adolescent behaviors that reveal the classic image of the empathic, mothering female: nurturant, responsible, insightful about the self, intellectually competent, unrepressed, unmoralistic and—unlike men at age 40—given to fantasy and not power-oriented. Most of these adolescent resources re-emerge for those of the Guidance women who bear another child before the age-40 follow-up, suggesting that we may have discerned stage- rather than age-specific effects of early parenting.

For Oakland men at age 47, an inward turn of the self is suggested at this midlife point, because they draw on adolescent behaviors for psychological health, which they had by-passed 10 years earlier at age 37: nurturance, insight about the self, and aesthetic responsivity, but neither concern with power nor with appearing masculine nor with the adequacy of their bodily functioning. This decisive turn inward over this decade suggests Gutmann's and others' midlife re-emergence of "feminine" aspects of the self submerged during the first half of life (Gutmann, 1977). Oakland women at age 47 call upon adolescent behaviors that indicate cognitive and expressive freedom at midlife, such as being aesthetically responsive, intellectually competent, decisive, emotive, and undefensive. For those psychologically healthy women at 47 who are in the empty nest and beyond the parental imperative (those whose last born is passed 18 years), there is a further impression of liberation in their resort to these adolescent resources: low responsibility, low nurturance, and low guilt.

Our new studies of the 1982 follow-up continues the search for age-specificity and discontinuity in the midlife of the Guidance sample at age 52 and late-middle age of the Oakland sample at 60. First, on the negative side, the number of adolescent predictors of Psychological Health at these later ages diminishes for three of the four groups compared to our 1970 results. However, as we had expected, the number of reversals increased two-fold by partialling out each of the previous adult PH scores. (When the PH score of the last follow-up was left unpartialled, eight Q-sort items showed a reversal from early to late adolescence; when the PH score of the two earlier follow-ups were partialled, 17 items showed such a significant reversal). From this sizable yield of statistical reversals, an image forms of the resources for a healthy midlife for Guidance men and late-middle age for Oakland men and women. Psychologically-healthy Oakland men at age 60 present the sharpest image of an Eriksonian moratorium laced with rehearsals for a negative identity: in junior high, they were rated as dependable, protective of others, productive, and neither pushing nor demanding of others; in senior high, they had become undependable, unprotective of others, unproductive, and pushing and demanding.

By no means do we think these findings suggest that the adult draws carefreely and carelessly from the past as from a candy sampler—a favorite behavior here, a wicked but alluring trait there. That something more transformational is involved in how an adolescent predictor enters the process of adult development comes home especially in the case of the reversal effect, which offers no facile interpretation as single predictors might do. The abundance of reversals at age 60 raises interesting questions about the relation of reversals to aging. We wonder, for one, whether the past does not so much yield up fresh resources for late-age mental health as much as the past confronts the person with opposite dispositions within the self that, following Jung, seek reconciliation and integration. Drawing from opposite poles of a behavior may also reveal the complex developmental makeup of personality in late-middle age, which we also intend to study by looking for the specific adult behaviors and traits that the reversal anticipates.

New 1982 results do show that since 1970, behaviors that had previously predicted Psychological Health in one direction have switched significantly to the other direction. Healthy Guidance men at 40, it will be recalled, had drawn upon past resources of instrumental dispositions, much in keeping with "becoming established" in the male world (Levinson, 1978). Now at age 52, healthy Guidance men change this "use" of adolescence dramatically on three dimensions: they were no longer concerned in adolescence with appearing masculine, but rather now turned to their youth for inner psychological states invested in fantasy and unconventional thinking. This use of adolescent inwardness at midlife is much like our above report of the Oakland men's use of adolescence at age 47 and again in line with the thinking of Jung, Gutmann, and Levinson for the second half of life. Indeed, the Guidance men at 50 are generally more like Oakland cohort at 47 than they were like themselves 10 years earlier. Such correspondence between the adolescence of these two male samples at close adult ages does not, however, hold for the female samples. A cohort difference between the Guidance and Oakland women is perhaps the least surprising in the joint California longitudinal studies, since among the four sample x sex groups, the Oakland women differ most on such core variables as IQ, socioeconomic status, employment, and divorce rate.

To conclude, our results do not make a case for personality development as a straightforward, continuous association between past and present. Nor, of course, do they support the contrary position that lacking such stable relationships, personality integration owes little to the distant past of youth. Rather, the findings speak to the reordering of the past into fresh configurations, perhaps even rapidly developing and changing ones, under the play and stress of new or revived demands of being adult at age 30, 40, 50, 60, and beyond. Stephan Jay Gould, the authority on evolutionary biology, has written of punctuated equilibria (Gould, 1978) where species stay much the same up to a point until the stresses they have absorbed flip them rapidly into new configurations. Water heats and boils; beams buckle and break; rocks bend and fracture; and, bringing our results to this view, adult periods announce their arrival and departure by the punctuated retrieval of new qualities from the past. This sense of punctuation is carried in our findings by the behavioral reversals between consecutive periods of youth, by the turnabout of predictions from one decade to the next, by the resurgence of adolescent predictions at later rather than earlier ages, and finally, by clearly dissimilar adult age processes that are suggested by the changing correlates with the past. To the many disciplines that, Gould says, are now considering such alternative models of punctuated change, let us add the study of personality development in the adult lifespan.

REFERENCES

Costa, P., McCrae, R., & Arenberg, D. (1983). Recent longitudinal research on personality and aging. In Schaie, K. (Ed.). *Longitudinal studies of adult psychological development*. New York: Guilford Press.

Eichorn, D., Clausen, J., Haan, N., Honzik, M. & Mussen, P. (Eds.) (1981). *Present and past in middle life*. New York: Academic Press.

Emmerlich, W. (1966). Continuity and stability in early social development-II: Teacher ratings. *Child Development, 37,* 17–27.

Gould, S. (1978, January 22). Evolution: Explosion, not ascent. *New York Times.*

Gutmann, D. (1977). The cross-cultural perspective: notes toward a comparative psychology of aging. In J. Birren, & K. Schaie, (Eds.). *Lifespan developmental psychology: Normative life crises.* New York: Academic Press.

Levinson, D. with Darrow, C., Klein, E., Levinson, M., & McKee, B. (1978). *The seasons of a man's life.* New York: Knopf.

Livson, N., & Peskin, H. (1967). The prediction of adult psychological health in a longitudinal study. *Journal of Abnormal Psychology, 72,* 509–518.

Livson, N., & Peskin, H. (1980). Perspectives on adolescence from longitudinal research. In J. Adelson (Ed.). *Handbook of adolescent psychology.* New York: Wiley.

Peskin, H. (1972). Multiple prediction of adult psychological health from preadolescent and adolescent behavior. *Journal of Consulting and Clinical Psychology, 38,* 155–160.

Peskin H. & Livson, N. (1981). Uses of the past in adult development. In D. Eichorn, J. Clausen, N. Hann, M. Honzik, & P. Mussen, (Eds.). *Present and past in middle life.* New York: Academic Press.

CHAPTER 47

Myth Into Reality: Enacting Life Histories in an Institutional Setting

Haim Hazan

In Honor of Barbara Myerhoff

One of the tasks and pleasures of the elderly is the life review — so often used as an opportunity for "taking stock," recounting what was done well, what could have been done better, what is left of their efforts and what really matters in the end.

B. MYERHOFF — *Number Our Days*, p. 265

Barbara Myerhoff's indelible stamp on cultural gerontology reaches far beyond her unforgettable accounts and her unique interpretative perspectives. Her insights and ideas broke through some of the most long-standing barriers set up by anthropologists on the road of understanding the phenomenon of growing old. For a long time behavioral gerontology has dwelt on two distinct and somewhat contrasting images of the aged. The first, perceiving the elderly primarily as socially conditioned actors, is based on a role-ridden, age-bound model, which almost fatalistically drives any research into an analytic impasse of rolelessness, no-exit, and anomie. The second, viewing the aged as culturally constructed beings, focuses on the phenomena of reminiscing and life review as the main processes in the search for past-anchored identities.

At the core of this dichotomy stands the well-established two-dimensional picture of men and women as products of both society and culture. Separate in their temporal dimensions, incongruous in their

modes of rationality, and divergent in their functions, these two domains of existence have been kept apart and hence formed a bifurcate
focus of research interests. Thus studies of life reviews are scarcely
informed by present social structure, networks, and constraints, while
research on functioning, competence, resources, and power among the
aged is rarely imbued with concern with meaning, identity, and cultural heritage. In other words, the past is not infused into the present
to depict a holistically cogent picture of a person's experience. Barbara
Myerhoff, however, by offering a distilled analysis of the prism of
collective ritual and definitional ceremony, unleashed the potentiality
for converging the dual image of the elderly into one meaningful and
indivisible perspective. Hence, everyday life and cultural context were
merged into enacted myths of reconstructed historical legacies. The
device with which, and through which, such interconnectedness was
accomplished is the need and the ability of humans to reflect upon
their lives and to use symbolic mirrors to account for existential conditions. It is the potency of reflexivity as recognized by Barbara
Myerhoff that transcended the social arena of the Aliyah Centre in
Venice, California into an extraordinary life project. It is that very
power of reflexivity that aborted an attempt by residents of an old-age
home in Israel to enact their life histories in a similar fashion in the
institutional context. The meeting venue of past and present, which in
Barbara Myerhoff's case turned reality into myth, transformed our
case from myth into reality. However, while as we know, the Centre
setting fused cultural identity with social interaction, the events in the
Home, as we shall see, signified the splicing of the two domains.

The Home studied in 1972 through anthropological fieldwork methods belonged to the welfare division of the largest trade union federation in Israel. It catered only to able-bodied union members or members' parents and provided full residential facilities for about 400
people. Its location at the heart of an easily accessible affluent neighborhood of Tel-Aviv, its high standard of services and the growing gap
between supply and demand for accommodation in residential care
facilities for the aged, all had a number of significant implications: The
desirability of the Home, by attracting many applicants, rendered the
selection process competitive. While this gave management ample
power to impose rigid standards of conduct termed ''good functioning'' on residents, it also provided the ground for some influential
trade unionists to put pressure on the management on behalf of themselves or their kith and kin. Thus, while some residents had to respond
to an unrelenting threat of being transferred to another institution, by
displaying good functioning in the form of group participation and
personal competence, others, through past images bolstered by present
connections, were immuned against such administrative impositions.
One such group of residents, known at the Home as the ''discussion

group'' will concern us. At the beginning of 1972 the discussion group
was born; its ascribed function was to debate various topics raised by
its members and toward this end began convening regular meetings to
which some 30 residents were invited.

The initiative for the establishment of the group came from one of
the residents, Mr. Amit, who, having been a high-ranking army officer
and the trade union controller, had been involved in both his military
and civilian careers with matters of jurisdiction and inspection. Staff
and residents alike held him in openly expressed esteem and his name
was mentioned with great reverence. Mr. Amit proposed that the
group meet every week, that the number of members be selected by
personal invitation only, and that different problems should be debated
in the course of the sessions. Those invited were people with some sort
of experience in public life—retired politicians, members of free professions, and others thought suitable by Mr. Amit. Some of them were
very well known outside the Home and a few had become almost living
legends in the pantheon of national heros. As an example of such
stature a newspaper article will be quoted relating to two of the members:

> They are the eternal pioneers, the pavers of roads, the triumphant inno-
> vators of Jewish labor, amongst the first volunteers for the Jewish military
> force, the audacious conquerors of the wilderness, in the vanguard of
> immigration. Just call them and they will come. Give them a goal and a
> challenge and they are behind you. They are two of a race of titans.
> Amongst those appearing on the landscape, always marching at the fore
> with quiet dignity, steadfastly and modestly. Possessions? Money?—never
> interested them.

A superficial linguistic scanning of the symbolic code inherent in the
contents of this quotation reveals the absence of chronological time
reference (use of the present tense although the events described occurred in the past) and the use of expressions drawn from the grandi-
ose and exclusive myth of nation building resistant to transformations
wrought by changing times and reality. The first meeting corroborated
this image. It was devoted to the topic ''The attitude of the U.S.S.R.
towards the Jews,'' and after the proceedings were concluded the
group's secretary wrote letters to the trade union leadership, to the
Labor Party Journal, to the Foreign Ministry, and to the Secretary-
General of the United Nations. The following meeting dealt with the
subject of ''retirement problems'' and institutional care for the aged.

Before describing the content and the consequences of one of these
discussions, it is necessary to outline some characteristics of the social
context of the group's membership. The social networks of members of
the discussion group outside the Home were extremely varied. Some
conducted most aspects of their social life outside the institution, often

with well-known public figures, while others created close ties with fellow group members, although not necessarily grounded in group activities. The only persons about whom it can be said that relationships emanated directly from participation in the group itself, was a body calling itself "the house committee," comprising Mr. Amit and two other founding members. They claimed that they were duly elected by the group to represent the interests of residents, but many members had no recollection of this. The house committee maintained contact with the manager as well as with his superior, the director of the unions' welfare division and, according to Mr. Amit, was charged with the responsibility for occupational activities in the Home.

The manager participated in group meetings but had to request the floor from Mr. Amit. He was not allowed to interrupt the other speakers and his contribution had to be kept within the time allocation of the agenda. The discussions were conducted with due seriousness and in an orderly manner. Those wishing to speak informed the chairman and had to wait their turn. Heckling was absolutely forbidden and speakers took care to keep to the point, to sound highly eloquent and to use a polished, if somewhat high-faluting style. These rules of presentation did not derive from the reality of the Home, but were adopted, apparently in a completely conscious way, from patterns of activity "implanted" by group members from experiences gained outside the Home in committee work and public speaking. The following will demonstrate how that self-image of power and influence prompted members to project it onto the running of the Home.

Various residents in the Home engaged in practices which bothered others and hindered the smooth running of the institution. Those included: offering "bribes" to cleaning staff to give priority to certain rooms, making off with food from the dining room or kitchen and causing spillage on the way, holding elevator doors open for long periods of time, strewing rubbish in the corridors, leaving toilets unflushed after use, sluicing down outside bath tubs, playing radios and TVs at full volume, violent pushing, and appearing slovenly dressed. This list, with the addition of some more items, was drawn up by the house committee as examples of acts that must be eradicated, and the matter was brought to the manager for consideration.

The manager agreed that it was an intractable problem, but claimed that he was trying to solve it by subtle means, such as inviting residents for informal talks in which the perpetrator was given to understand why such behavior was offensive and how it should be rectified. The manager admitted that he did not attach much value to these conversations since the offenders soon reverted to their unruly ways; he explained this by the special ethnic backgrounds of some of the deviants, by their former lifestyle, and by diseases of old age—that is, by factors cannot be altered.

The house committee insisted that the matter be referred to the discussion group and Mr. Amit argued that the solution to the problem lay in imposing jurisdiction of a disciplinary court on the residents concerned, to be administered by the house committee, which should have the authority to caution, to reprimand publicly, and, in extreme cases, to use other measures such as a recommendation to expel the offender from the Home. The manager opposed this proposal claiming that he knew from experience that such a court was ineffective, since the causes of the troublesome behavior were not amenable to change, and the residents concerned would not be deterred, while at the same time an atmosphere of suspicion, spite, and threats would prevail in the Home. However, Mr. Amit was adamant that the proposal should be put to the next group meeting and, if accepted, the court should indeed be established.

Resigning himself to an imminent defeat, the manager admitted that he did not believe anything could prevent the adoption of a resolution supporting the establishment of the court, because as he stated:

"Mr. Amit is a charismatic figure, and the residents are in awe of him and will follow him blindly."

In fact, the manager was apprehensive about the setting-up of the court because of the likelihood of disharmony and contradiction arising between his interests and those of the house committee." One of the main sources of the manager's power was his determination of the residents' "functioning." However, if residents behaved according to the standards laid down by the court, then management of institutional life could be wrested from him. Moreover, a stage might be reached in which the court would exercise jurisdiction in the area of admission to and removal from the Home and, with the political backing enjoyed by the house committee, the manager would be unable to oppose such moves. Mr. Amit had already criticized the welfare policy of the trade union for accepting, as he put it: "invalids and incapacitated individuals incapable of taking care of themselves, creating a burden and an annoyance to the healthier population of residents." In his opinion, this was a serious error that demanded correction.

The meeting was held with the full complement of the group. Other residents who happened to pass by were asked by the manager to leave since "this was a closed discussion." The manager was given the floor and in the course of about an hour he specified the annoyances perpetrated by some residents toward their fellow residents and the pains taken by him and his staff to maintain standards of cleanliness, aesthetic appearance, and a calm atmosphere within the Home. After the manager had completed making this statement, Mr. Amit adjourned the discussion for the following week.

Mr. Amit opened the second meeting by saying that despite the fact that residents often misbehave, the home management could not be exempted from responsibility for disorder and related problems. He began listing methodically the defects of the Home and stressed two central issues: the service in the dining room ("worse than a soup kitchen, we're people, not animals") and the lack of adequate medical services. The manager commented that this was hardly his fault but rather the responsibility of the welfare division who refused to allocate the necessary funds.

One after another the members rose and told of their sufferings in the Home due to lack of facilities, and unsympathetic attitudes of staff. Every time the manager tried to intervene and influence the course of the proceedings he was unsuccessful. Mr. Amit stressed that he was running the meeting and that the manager would be given an opportunity to respond to the complaints. When the speakers had spent themselves, the manager began to reply with Mr. Amit pressuring him to limit his remarks. These amounted to a series of apologies, the main gist of which was to emphasize his good intentions in the face of bureaucratic, budgetary, and personnel problems with which the Home had to contend. At this stage Mr. Amit proposed the establishment of a disciplinary court stressing that he sought from the group only approval in principle. Once that was forthcoming, the group would not be responsible for its activities or mode of operation. This would rest exclusively with the house committee, which would decide on the manner, the composition, and the authority of the body.

Things then boiled over. At first there were some incoherent and hesitant whispers and then the muttering increased in volume, and words became recognizable: "What cheek!" "Who does he think he is?" "This isn't the army." "Who put you in charge?" "We protest," etc. One of those present rose and, in a voice charged with emotion, called on his friends not to support the move since "in our contract nothing was said about such a court. I want to live according to that contract." Mr. Amit, banging on the table, demanded order and called for a vote. The proposal was rejected by a large majority. He then closed the meeting announcing that the following discussion would deal with Israel-Arab relations.

How can Mr. Amit's defeat be explained? Despite the fact that formally all members belonged to the same hallowed group, the bonds that had formerly rendered them mythically united no longer existed. So long as Mr. Amit provided tokens of common identity and symbols of shared status, he was assured of their support. When, however, he initiated the establishment of a court that would not be accountable to the group, he had created a possibility of a situation in which members would be subject to his will and their actions dictated by his ideas. This is because he would be less prone to pressures than the manager and would not be forced to determine good or bad functioning in accordance with outside connections. Thus, Mr. Amit would be able to lay down rules of discipline as he saw fit and the chances of challenging them would be relatively slimmer than the prospect of influencing the manager's position. It was the very existence of the strong ties that these residents held with the outside that fueled their objection to the setting-up of the court, for Mr. Amit's control would have prevented the exploitation of these contacts.

It should be remembered that the residents who took part in the group were well aware of the possibility of contracting various age-related afflictions, all of which are deemed to greatly influence behavior. It was common knowledge among members that some of the bothersome residents were considered to act as they did because of the effect of such conditions. It was also known that Mr. Amit adopted a rather intolerant attitude toward this category of residents. It would seem likely, therefore, that the decision to reject the proposal was colored by this consideration. The possibility of standing powerless before Mr. Amit and his court was much worse than the existing situation in which severe scrutiny was not evident and wide scope was given to the display of "deviant" behavior.

It is within these bounds that contrasting interpretations of the realities and the myths in the Home emerged. Thus, the manager did not believe in the possibility of rejecting Mr. Amit's proposal because of Mr. Amit's unquestionable "charisma." Mr. Amit, on the other hand, was so sure of his ability to realize this imputed charisma, that he expected an unequivocal mandate to establish the court without prior negotiations with the group as to its future operation. The source of both of these false notions can be located in a single factor—a failure to ascertain the relation between interests and identity. The basis of the relations between group members and Mr. Amit on the one hand, and the manager on the other, was not the product of mythically imposed blind loyalty, but concern for the preservation of the best possible living conditions in the Home.

This analysis of the balance of power involved in the disciplinary court affair throws light only on one aspect of the matter—the nature of the institutional control structure. However, what occurred during the two meetings described has implications for the understanding of perception and images prevailing within the group, reflecting and reinforcing the existential categories that governed the worlds of members. To illustrate this, an incident that took place during the discussion will be described.

One of the participants requested the floor in order to complain about the unsympathetic attitude of staff toward residents. She began to recount how one evening while watching television, she suddenly developed a stomachache and hurried to the toilet. However, losing control she relieved herself en route. Her neighbors, emerging from their rooms, berated her for soiling the place, and when she asked the staff, who happened to be in the vicinity, for assistance, they joined in the chorus of reprimand in concert with the residents. She claimed that that kind of misfortune could happen to anyone, but here Mr. Amit stepped in, charging her with not sticking to the point. There was dead silence for a moment and then, almost simultaneously, a wave of loud laughter erupted from those present. The speaker, who had been silenced, burst into tears, with no one attempting to comfort her. During the following meeting, she was not given the floor despite her persistent demands for the right to speak.

Whatever else the participants' reaction may represent, it certainly alludes to a sense of embarrassment associated with the introduction of incontinence into the very core of a group whose members perceived that control of time and change defied any suggestion of deterioration and decline. However, when inexorable biological constraints blatantly overrode social and self-image, subjecting myth-like past and present to a physically uncertain future, the unity between the properties of the self as an ageless symbol, and its aging body was broken down. Thus the case of the disciplinary court attests to a predicament normally unknown to most other elderly persons; this is the choice between perpetuating a still viable past at the expense of mundane considerations, or submitting to an erosion of identity to secure better control over social surroundings.

The tension between these two alternatives could be viewed in terms of the relations between principles of practical reasoning and the exigencies of identity preservation. This conflict between the social and the cultural, the real and the mythical, the pragmatic and the fundamental, is probably the main generator of the dynamics of reflective behavior. To assume that these two domains of existence are divorced from each other would also mean to deny the possibility of the former mirroring, modifying and construing the latter, and vice versa. However, to observe how they both inform each other, interact, clash and readjust, could provide the key for the mechanism of reflexivity as experienced and constituted by the elderly. It was not through ritual and narrative that members of the discussion group reflected, in the most practical, albeit ambivalent, manner on their past, present, and future. For people who experienced prominent visibility in public life and whose past actions engendered and endorsed symbolic codes on a national scale, the split between myth and reality in their old age was a novel phenomenon. The cultural process that was invoked to handle this nascent situation was not a fusion of the lived in and the dreamt of through definitional ceremonies and collective myth, nor was it a clear-cut split between the two. Rather, it was a situationally conditioned, temporary relinquishment of identity in an attempt to regain control: myth became subservient to reality, the enactment of the past no longer served the present. Yet the quest for immortality was not abandoned, it only shifted from an ahistorical timelessness to an abiological timelessness; from being living legends to legendary living with the avoidance of somatic constraints superseding the rejection of historical processes. Divergent in content though they are, the two phases signify one drive—to hold time still by rendering the desirable attainable through socially constructed arenas of action. In this respect the lead taken by Barbara Myerhoff in exposing the structural and cultural devices with which terminality is denied and shattered experience is reorganized, is faithfully followed in our case.

This lead has taken the anthropology of aging to a new frontier where myth and reality are indivisible, self and collectivity become one, body and mind merge, and concepts of rationality and order, as we know them, collapse. Barbara Myerhoff stood at the brink of culture, time and, indeed, life; and through her literary flaire, inimitable empathy, and penetrating insights has enabled us to take a glimpse of that human zone of paradox and fascination and to emerge from that unique experience more enlightened and better prepared to number our own days.

PART VI
Basic and Social Scientific Research
A. Health Care Organization and Financing

CHAPTER 48

The National Institute on Aging's Health Care Expenditures Model

Joseph M. Anderson
William S. Cartwright

A comprehensive model is discussed which links the health sector to other parts of the economy, incorporates an economic theory of individual behavior and uses a variety of demographic and current social survey information. Six key tasks are outlined and elucidated: (1) preparation of time series data on health care expenditures; (2) projections of provider's costs; (3) estimation of consumer prices; (4) estimation of health care demand; (5) linking health care expenditures to total consumption; and (6) disaggregating total health care expenditures into payments from specific sources. Data generated by the model using a wide variety of sources are presented and interpreted.

HEALTH PLANNING FOR THE ELDERLY

The concept of health planning may be more subtle than is often appreciated. Health planning presupposes a firm understanding of society's goals and a knowledge of the relevant resource constraints. Health planning also involves decision making at various levels of social, individual, and institutional participation. For example, health planning activities vary between individuals deciding on their own personal programs of well-being, and institutions, such as hospitals, justifying purchases of CAT scan devices while closing down beds. A geriatric social worker would be concerned with the efficient coordination of community resources to meet the needs of elderly clients either recuperating from a hospital episode or experiencing functional decline and fragility. For most decision makers, these examples represent the kind of daily resource planning done in the face of what is perceived as the relevant resource constraint. To most, this resource constraint is fixed in the sense that they cannot alter it to satisfy their own goals.

Health planning also proceeds at higher levels of government where health budgets are established and tax dollars are committed. In the United States, health planning proceeds in cities, counties, states, and federal governments, where a whole range of regulatory and financial decisions are made concerning the activities of health providers and purchasers of services.

In such a milieu, what niche does a macroeconomic–demographic model of the economy and health expenditures fit? It does not solve the hospital administrator's or geriatric social worker's problems. However, a macroeconomic—demographic model does directly deal with the economy's resource constraint in a fundamental way. It represents the total potential production of society from available capital and labor inputs, and the division of that product into consumption and investment. Further, consumption must be allocated among all the goods and services provided for individual use, of which health services are one of the most important components. To complete the representation of the economy, investment provides for future increases in production to keep pace with population change, which is usually a positive growth factor. Health services, while treated as consumption in this discussion, also have the role of providing for investment in human productive capacity, as has been shown by the success of public health measures and numerous medical treatments to alleviate morbidity and mortality. Health planning in this context abstracts from individual decisions to one of much broader scope with less detail as a necessity to comprehend the health system.

A macroeconomic–demographic model provides a basis for health planning at a very high level of aggregation. It deals with various demographic groups and the effect of institutional or financial arrangements in both the private and the public sector. At this level, concern must focus on the viability, efficiency, and equity of the health system. What is meant by viability is a balance between revenues inflowing and costs outflowing. Viability is used to indicate a state in which there are no large imbalances faced by the health system as it is currently structured. Efficiency refers to the optimizing of output or economizing of inputs given resources or income. Equity refers to the value judgments made concerning the distribution of resources and income as well as access and treatment under the health care system. A macroeconomic–demographic model can focus on the role of these three concepts in the size and distribution of health expenditures.

Because of the increased demands and needs for health services on the part of the elderly and aging populations, a nation's demographic structure is particularly important to national health planning. Besides the demographic structure, behavioral changes related to a nation's decisions concerning health resources are just as important. In the United States, private health decisions are influenced by a complicated interaction with governmental programs such as Medicaid and Medicare, as well as private insurance mechanisms. Health planning must also account for the burdens on various public and private financial arrangements to pay the nation's health bill. A macroeconomic–demographic model provides a consistent structure for the health planning activity.

A macroeconomic–demographic model is only one tool in the difficult task of constructing health plans. There are roles for technological assessments, benefit-cost analysis, biologic and medical ethics, and social and political analysis. One hope is that the challenge of developing a macroeconomic–demographic health expenditure model will push forward the science of economic model building. There are numerous problems in health economics that go to the core problems of economics in general. Issues abound with respect to general equilibrium, uncertainty, and welfare economics, as well as data development and statistical research design. The health sector is one of the most challenging aspects of an economy to analyze, understand, and plan.

THE MACROECONOMIC–DEMOGRAPHIC MODEL AND THE HEALTH EXPENDITURES MODEL

The purpose of the project is to develop a long-term simulation model to study trends in health care expenditures, including the effects of:

- Demographic change
- Long-term economic change
- Public policy

Because the level and types of health care services demanded differ greatly by age, sex, and other demographic characteristics, change in the size and structure of the population are associated with major changes in the level and composition of national health care expenditures. The NIA is particularly interested in the effects of "population aging" in the U.S.—the absolute and relative increase in the numbers of older persons that will occur as the "baby boom" cohorts, formed during the period from the late 1940s through the mid-1960s, reach older ages.

Evolution of the economy over the long-term affects health care expenditures. The model is designed to study the effects of changes in relative prices, in household and national income levels, and in technology.

Public policy can significantly influence the level and composition of health care expenditures and the distribution of the costs of providing health care services. The model is designed to investigate the effects of alternative policies, such as alternative approaches to the financing of health care, tax policy measures, and income maintenance programs, especially those affecting the income of the elderly.

To accomplish these objectives a comprehensive model of health care expenditures is being developed and integrated with the existing NIA Macroeconomic–Demographic Model (MDM). The focus of the project is the development of a structural model of the supply of and demand for various types of health care that takes into account input costs, technology, household characteristics, preferences, and incomes. The health expenditures model incorporates both cross-section data on individual households—including demographic and economic attributes and health care expenditures—and time series data on aggregate expenditures for various types of health care from various sources, other categories of consumer expenditures, and other economic variables. This health expenditures model is then integrated into the existing NIA Macroeconomic-Demographic Model, which includes a population projection model and a comprehensive representation of the operation of the labor market and the process of economic growth in a general equilibrium framework. The integrated health expenditures model takes advantage of the demographic detail and the general equilibrium framework of the exiting Macroeconomic–Demographic Model.

THE NIA Macroeconomic–Demographic Model

The existing Macroeconomic–Demographic Model is composed of a core macroeconomic and demographic model, and a set of five models that focus on sources of income of the elderly. The core model has three major parts: a population projection system, a macroeconomic growth model, and a labor market model. The five elderly income models represent the Old-Age, Survivors, and Disability Insurance Systems (social security), the private pension system, the public employee pension system, the Supplemental Security Income (SSI) program—a welfare program which serves the poorest members of society—and the Medicare System for financing the elderly's hospital and medical bills.

The Population Model. This model replicates the population projection methodology used by the U.S. Census Bureau. It projects the total U.S. population by age, race, sex for each year 1983 through 2055. Fertility rates, mortality rates, and net immigration are determined exogenously. The ultimate completed cohort fertility rate and mortality rates may be specified and the corresponding population projected. Mortality rates may be altered through adjustments in specific causes of death. The base population for the model is the 1980 Census of the United States.

The Macroeconomic Growth Model. The model is an adaptation of the Hudson-Jorgenson four-sector long-term econometric forecasting model. It depicts the formulation of working, spending, and savings plans by households; and production, investment, and employment plans by businesses. It projects the demand for and supply of goods and services and depicts the equilibration of demand and supply by price adjustments and changes in consumption and production decisions. This long-term economic growth model is characterized by a more careful depiction of the determinants of aggregate demand. The data for the development of the macroeconomic growth model are derived primarily from the U.S. National Income and Product Accounts.

Labor Market Model. The demographically disaggregated Labor Market Model depicts three basic aspects of the labor market: the demand for labor; the supply of labor; and the simultaneous determination of labor and capital services inputs, along with compensation, output, and employment. The derived demand for labor inputs of four age groups is depicted by modeling the aggregate production technology of the private U.S. economy, focusing on the substitutability among age groups in the production process. Labor supply of 22 age-sex groups is measured in total annual hours worked by each group— the product of the group's population, labor force participation rate, employment rate, and hours worked per year. The labor supply-demand system is fully integrated into and solved simultaneously with the Macroeconomic Growth Model for the input levels and prices of capital services and of labor; the unemployment and participation rates of each age-sex group; the level of output, consumption, investment, and other economic variables. This model is based on both establishment level data on employment, hours worked, and compensation of workers, and household level data on labor force participation, employment, and unemployment of individuals of various ages and sexes, collected by the Bureau of the Census and the Bureau of Labor Statistics.

Figure 48-1 depicts the operational linkages between these models within the existing Macroeconomic–Demographic Model. At the start of any simulation year, the Population Model initially forecasts the new size and composition of the population. These population figures are principal inputs into the Macroeconomic Growth Model and the

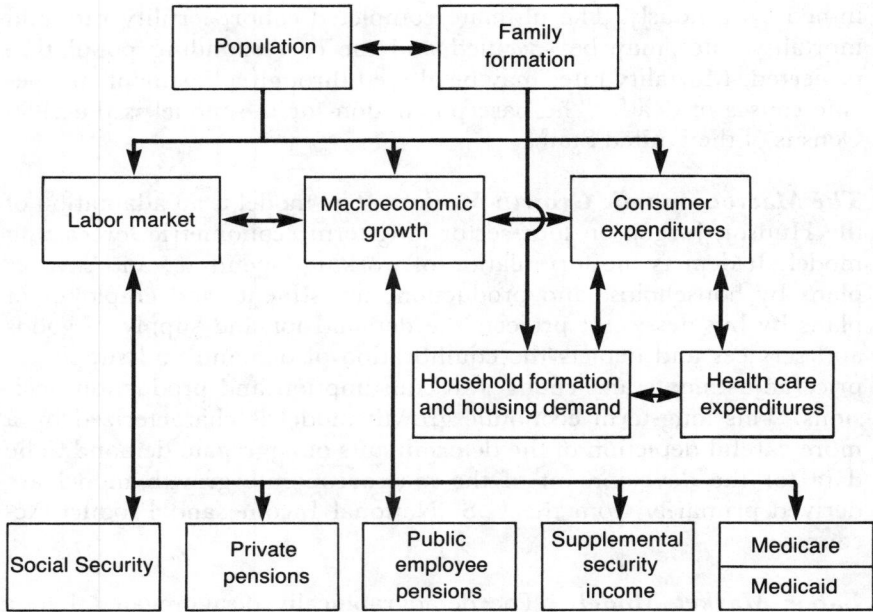

FIGURE 48-1. Structure of the macroeconomic–demographic model of health expenditures.

Labor Market Model, which operate simultaneously to project levels of aggregate economic activity and the labor market outcomes for 22 different age-sex groups. These projections of the economy and the disaggregated labor market are inputs into the simulation of each of the three pension system models and the two transfer income models currently included in the MDM.

The Macroeconomic Growth Model and the Labor Market Model are the only models in the current version of the Macroeconomic–Demographic Model that actually simulate market processes. The five elderly income program models base their operation on the cohort employment and earnings information from the Labor Market Model and actuarial analysis of program rules and beneficiary populations. Consistency is maintained between models because the outputs of the core macroeconomic model serve as inputs to the pension models. The entire model operates from a consistent set of accounting relationships.

The Health Expenditures Model

Development of the health expenditures model involves six tasks:

1. Preparation of cross-section and time series data on health

care expenditures that are mutually consistent and are consistent with the National Income and Product Accounts and with other data on consumer expenditures.

2. Projection of providers' costs as functions of input prices.

3. Estimation of consumers' prices from providers' prices.

4. Development of the demand system for health care services.

5. Linkage of the demand for health care expenditures to total personal consumption expenditures.

6. Translation of total health expenditures into payments from specific sources.

Preparation of Cross-Section and Time Series Data. The first step in the development of the health expenditures model is the preparation of comprehensive and consistent cross-section and time series data on health expenditures by type of service and by source of payment. Two main sets of time series data are used: the National Income and Product Accounts (NIPA) collected by the U.S. Department of Health and Human Services Health Care Financing Administration (HCFA). For each year from 1948 through 1983, HCFA has estimated total U.S health expenditures cross-classified into the various types of services and sources of payment shown in Table 48-1 (Gibson, Levit, Lazenby & Waldo, 1984). We adjust the National Health Accounts data and the National Income and Product Accounts to make them consistent.

The primary source of cross-section data for the development of the health expenditures model is the National Medical Care Utilization and Expenditure Survey (NMCUES) developed by the National Center for Health Statistics (NCHS) and the Health Care Financing Administration (HCFA) (Bonham, 1983). Data was collected by NMCUES on the U.S. civilian noninstitutional population during 1980. For each member of each household in the survey, information was obtained on health status, access to and use of medical services, associated charges and sources of payment, health insurance coverage, income, and many socioeconomic characteristics. The National Medical Care Utilization and Expenditure Survey consisted of three survey components. The National Household Survey comprised about 6,000 randomly selected households. Each household was interviewed five times over 14 months beginning in early 1980. The State Medicaid Household Survey consisted of about 4,000 households selected from the Medicaid eligiblility files in the states of California, Michigan, New York, and Texas. Each of these households was interviewed five times over the 14 months. The administrative records survey was used to obtain information on program eligibility and medical care payments for persons receiving Medicare and Medicaid. Data were obtained for approximately 31,000 persons in NMCUES—17,600 in the

**TABLE 48-1. U.S. Personal Health Care Expenditures
By Type of Service and Source of Payment: 1980
(1980 $ billion)**

Type of Service	All sources of payment	Household out-of-pocket	Private insurance	Philanthropy	Medicare	Medicaid	Other public assistance	Veterans	Defense	Workers' Compensation	Other public expenditures Federal	Other public expenditures S&L	S&L hospital
Hospital care	101.3	7.5	38.6	1.0	25.9	9.6	0.6	4.9	3.4	2.0	1.6	0.1	6.1
Physician's services	46.8	14.3	19.9	.0	7.9	2.4	0.2	0.1	0.1	1.7	0.2	0.1	0.0
Dental services	15.4	10.1	4.7	0.0	0.0	0.5	.0	0.1	.0	0.0	.0	.0	0.0
Other professional services	5.6	2.8	1.4	0.1	0.7	0.6	.0	0.0	0.0	0.1	.0	.0	0.0
Drugs and medical sundries	18.5	14.8	2.2	0.0	0.0	1.4	0.1	.0	.0	0.1	.0	.0	0.0
Eyeglasses and appliances	5.1	4.2	0.4	0.0	0.4	0.0	0.0	0.1	0.0	0.1	.0	.0	0.0
Other health services	5.9	0.0	0.0	1.4	0.5	0.9	0.0	0.4	0.6	0.0	1.1	0.9	0.0
Nursing home care	20.4	8.9	0.2	0.1	0.4	9.8	0.7	0.4	0.0	0.0	0.0	0.0	0.0
All services	219.1	62.5	67.4	2.6	35.8	25.2	1.7	6.0	4.1	4.0	2.9	1.1	6.1

Source: U.S. Health Care Financing Administration.

National Household Survey and 13,400 in the four state Medicaid samples. Both samples excluded people living in institutions, members of the Armed Forces, and people residing outside the United States. Information on health insurance coverage was available, but imputations had to be made of private insurance characteristics—benefit structure, total cost of premiums, and out-of-pocket cost. An earlier cross-section survey, the 1977 National Medical Care Expenditure Survey (NMCES), was used to impute these insurance characteristics, since considerable information on health insurance was included in the NMCES and the related study of utilization (NMCUES).

In order to produce a data base suitable for estimation of the health expenditures model, the expenditure information in the NMCUES was organized into the types of service and sources of payment categories used in the National Health Accounts, shown in Table 48-1. Because NMCUES includes only the civilian noninstitutional population, it is suitable for analysis and modeling of only the noninstitutional population. Additional data were developed to model the health care provided to members of the armed services and to institutionalized persons, in order to provide a comprehensive set of accounts consistent with the National Health Accounts. This requirement reflects the way data on health expenditures are gathered in the U.S.. The National Health Accounts relies on information on revenues on incomes collected from health care providers, such as hospitals and physicians. The NMCUES data are expenditures reported by consumers themselves. Unfortunately, there is no recent, comprehensive survey of the institutionalized population. This is particularly critical for analysis of the expenditures of elderly consumers, who make up a large proportion of the institutionalized population. Data on the health care costs of the institutionalized population were acquired from the Current Medicare Survey (CMS), a sample of the Medicare recipient population.

Projection of Providers' Costs.   The second step in the development of the health expenditures model is to generate health care providers' prices as functions of prices of capital and labor services generated by the macroeconomic growth/labor market model. These are "reduced form" supply equations, since the prices of all goods and services can be expressed as functions of factor prices and the level of technology. These supply functions are specified to have a translog form. We use health care input price indexes developed by HCFA as proxies for provider prices, relating them to the prices of capital and of the services of labor of different age groups. Subsidies of various types of health care are reflected in adjustments to factor prices in the equations for some services or adjustments to the providers' prices directly. Departures of the prices of some types of services from trends in the average input prices are reflected in time trend variables or as biased technological change.

Estimation of Consumers' Prices. The third step in construction of the health expenditures model is to translate providers' prices into prices paid by consumers. This requires estimation of a set of factors for each type of health service and for each demographic group giving the proportions of expenditures from private sources for that group in each time period. This set of factors is first constructed for 1980, the year for which the NMCUES data are available. We then extrapolate the set of factors backward-based on totals of public and private sources of funding from the National Health Accounts. These data are supplemented by the National Medical Care Expenditure Survey (NMCUES), conducted in 1977, and the National Health Interview Surveys. Extrapolations of the price factors for future projections can reflect alternative policies for funding health care expenditures.

Development of the Demand System. The fourth step in construction of a health expenditures model is to develop an appropriate representation of the demand for health care services. We develop a two-stage model, disaggregating total consumer expenditures into health care and five other expenditures categories, and then disaggregating health expenditures over the various types of services shown in Table 48-1. We estimate the share of health expenditures allocated to each type of service by each type of household as a function of the prices of the various types of health care services and the demographic characteristics of the households. The parameters of the set of allocation equations are first estimated from the cross-section data on the allocation of expenditures among individual types of health care from NMCUES.

The cross-section analysis provides estimates of the effects of demographic characteristics on health care expenditures. To estimate the effects of changes in prices and technology on health care expenditures over time requires analysis of time series data. To develop a model appropriate for analysis of time series data, we aggregate the equations for each household to develop expressions for aggregate expenditure shares of each type of health care as functions of aggregate prices for each type of health care and the proportions of aggregate health care expenditures by each of the demographic groups. The estimation of aggregate prices takes into account the fact that different households pay different prices for the same health care services, depending on their demographic characteristics and income. We estimate this model by combining time series and cross-section data. The time series data are developed using the National Health Accounts data and using average utilization rates for demographic groups derived from the Health Interview Survey.

Linkage of Demand to Consumption.   The fifth step in constructing a health expenditures model is to link the demand for health expenditures to total consumption expenditures. First, a price index for health care as a whole for each type of household is constructed as a function of the prices of the types of health services and the quantities consumed by households with different demographic characteristics. Then, we allocate total consumption expenditures for each household between health care and the other expenditure categories as a function of the aggregate prices of health care and of the other categories of goods and services. Estimates of the share of health expenditures in total household consumption expenditures are developed by using data on personal consumption expenditures on health care and on other goods and services from the 1972 to 1973 Consumer Expenditure Survey (CES) and the National Income and Product Accounts.

Translation of Expenditures in Payments.   The final step in constructing a model of health expenditures is to translate the total costs for each health service into payments from the various sources per unit of health care utilization. For this purpose, we estimate a set of factors for the proportion of expenditure on each type of health care that is provided by each source for each demographic group in each time period. This set of factors is similar to and is estimated in the same way as the factors described earlier in step 3 that are used to translate providers' prices into consumers' prices. The basic data for estimation of these factors are the estimates of expenditures by source of payment from the National Health Accounts. We use NMCUES to establish the distribution by sources of payment in the base year (1980). This is supplemented by NMCES (for 1977). NMCES included a survey of providers and a survey of employers and insurers, so it includes more information about sources of payment than NMCUES, which included only a survey of consumers.

To simulate the health expenditures model, we generate prices of capital and labor services and the price and quantity of aggregate personal consumption goods and services from the macroeconomic growth and labor market model. We generate health care providers' prices from the supply equations described in step 2. We translate providers' prices into consumers' prices and project utilization of health services of the various types by each household using the methodology described in steps 3, 4, and 5. We then translate the providers' costs and household utilization of health services into payments from each source to each type of household for each type of service. We then sum over services to estimate the total benefits paid to each group from each source and sum over households to obtain the total payments from each source for each type of service to obtain a projection of data in the form presented in the National Health Accounts. Finally, we sum payments over all services for each source to estimate payments from that source in each future year.

THE LEVEL AND DISTRIBUTION OF HEALTH EXPENDITURES IN THE U.S.— 1980

The remainder of this chapter reports estimates of the level and distribution of health expenditures by type of service, source of payment, and demographic group, that we have developed as part of the data base development task for the Macroeconomic–Demographic Model of Health Expenditures.

Health care expenditures in the United States represented 9.5% of The Gross National Product in 1980 and 10.8% in 1983. The estimates of private and public U.S. expenditures for health care are derived from a variety of sources. The primary source of information on hospital expenditures is the American Hospital Association data on hospital finances. The source for dentists and physicians in private practice is gross income reported to the Internal Revenue Service. Drugs and appliances are estimated from the Personal Consumer Expenditures data in the National Income and Product Accounts. In brief, data are constructed from private association reports, surveys, Federal program statistics, and health insurance organizations.

The National Health Accounts estimated that total expenditures for personal health care were $219.1 billion in 1980 (see Table 48-1). Because the NMCUES did not include expenditures for institutionalized persons nor active-duty military personnel, nor expenditures on nonprescription drugs, the National Health Accounts must be adjusted by these amounts if it is to be compared with the NMCUES aggregates. After we estimated these costs and subtracted them, the National Health Accounts still exceeded the NMCUES total by about $17 billion or about 10% of the adjusted total in the National Health Accounts. Most of the difference is accounted for by higher National Health Accounts estimates of payments from private insurance and from Medicare. It may be that many private consumers are not aware of the entire amount of benefits paid on their behalf by these third-party payors and consequently do not report them accurately.

Table 48-1 shows U.S. personal health care expenditures for 1980 according to the National Health Accounts. In this table, expenditures for eight types of services are distributed over 12 private and public sources of funding. The complicated U.S. system for financing health care is reflected in the many sources of payment shown in the Table.

Under private payments, individuals' out-of-pocket payment and health insurance payments are the primary sources of funds. Most public sector programs are directed to assist special target populations. The elderly receive reimbursement through the Medicare program, which is the largest single public sector program. The Medicaid program is a Federal program that matches funds with state health programs for the poor. Federal health programs also directly provide services to Veterans of military service as well as active-duty and retired military personnel. State and local government provision of public hospitals are another important source of medical care.

Table 48-2 shows how each source of payment in 1980 was distributed over the various types of health care services. It shows that 57% of payments from private insurance were for hospital services and another 30% were for physicians services, accounting for 87%. Seventy-two percent of Medicare payments were for hospitalization and 22% were for physicians services, accounting for 94% of total Medicare expenditures. Medicaid is primarily expended on hospital services (38%) and nursing home care (39%). Thus, major public funding goes to hospital, physician, and nursing home services and is primarily directed to the elderly population.

Table 48-3 shows the contribution of each source of payment as a proportion of the total for each type of service in 1980. It shows that hospitalization was primarily paid by private insurance (38%) and Medicare (26%). Physicians services were primarily paid by households out-of-pocket (31%), by private insurance (43%), and Medicare (17%). Table 48-3 shows the large role played by Medicaid in providing nursing home care for the elderly—paying almost half the expenditures for all nursing home care.

Of all personal health care expenditures, only 29% came from direct household payment in 1980. Third-party payment—private health insurance and government—provided the other 71%. In 1960, 5 years before the beginning of Medicare, 55% of expenditures were paid directly by households. This decline in the percentage of direct payment is often blamed for insulating consumers of health services from incentives to economize on the use of services. For example, only 7% of the expenditures for hospital services, the largest part of the nation's health bill, are paid directly by households. The rest are paid by third-party payors.

While the percent of hospital service expenditures paid directly by households is low, households pay a large percentage of the payments for drugs, eyeglasses, and appliances, as well as a significant percentage of the payments for dental services, other professional services and nursing home care. For nursing home care, 44% comes from households out-of-pocket and 48% from Medicaid program that supports the elderly poor.

TABLE 48-2. U.S. Personal Health Care Expenditures—
Distribution of Expenditures for Each Source of Payment by Type of Service: 1980
(Percentage)

Type of Service	All sources of payment	Household out-of-pocket	Private insurance	Philan-thropy	Medicare	Medicaid	Other public assistance	Veterans	Defense	Workers' Compen-sation	Other public expenditures Federal	S&L	S&L hospital
Hospital care	46.2	12.0	57.3	38.7	72.4	38.1	37.0	83.6	82.1	50.8	53.2	10.0	100.0
Physician's services	21.4	22.9	29.6	0.9	22.1	9.7	9.7	1.0	2.9	42.2	6.8	6.5	0.0
Dental services	7.0	16.2	7.0	0.0	0.0	2.0	2.0	0.9	.0	0.0	0.7	0.5	0.0
Other professional services	2.6	4.4	2.0	1.9	1.9	2.2	2.0	0.0	0.0	3.1	1.4	1.5	0.0
Drugs and medical sundries	8.5	23.6	3.2	0.0	0.0	5.5	5.6	0.2	0.3	2.0	0.5	0.5	0.0
Eyeglasses and appliances	2.3	6.7	0.6	0.0	1.0	0.0	0.0	0.9	0.0	2.0	1.2	1.4	0.0
Other health services	2.7	0.0	0.0	53.7	1.4	3.7	4.1	7.2	14.7	0.0	36.3	79.7	0.0
Nursing home care	9.3	14.2	0.3	4.8	1.1	38.8	39.7	6.1	0.0	0.0	0.0	0.0	0.0
All services	100.0	100.0	100.0	100.0	100.0	100.0	100.0	100.0	100.0	100.0	100.0	100.0	100.0

Source: Data from Table 48-1.

TABLE 48-3. U.S. Personal Health Care Expenditures—
Distribution of Expenditures for Each Type of Service by Source of Payment: 1980
(Percentage)

Type of Service	All sources of payment	Household out-of-pocket	Private insurance	Philan-thropy	Medicare	Medicaid	Other public assistance	Veterans	Defense	Workers' Compen-sation	Other public expenditures Federal	S&L	S&L hospital
Hospital care	100.0	7.4	38.1	1.0	25.5	9.5	0.6	4.9	3.4	2.0	1.6	0.1	6.0
Physician's services	100.0	30.5	42.5	.0	16.9	5.2	0.3	0.1	0.3	3.5	0.4	0.2	0.0
Dental services	100.0	65.6	30.5	0.0	0.0	3.2	0.2	0.4	.0	0.0	0.1	.0	0.0
Other professional services	100.0	49.3	24.4	0.9	11.8	9.8	0.6	0.0	0.0	2.2	0.7	0.3	0.0
Drugs and medical sundries	100.0	79.6	11.7	0.0	0.0	7.5	0.5	0.1	0.1	0.4	0.1	.0	0.0
Eyeglasses and appliances	100.0	81.7	7.6	0.0	7.2	0.0	0.0	1.0	0.0	1.5	0.7	0.3	0.0
Other health services	100.0	0.0	0.0	23.9	8.6	15.8	1.1	7.2	10.3	0.0	18.3	14.8	0.0
Nursing home care	100.0	43.6	0.9	0.6	1.9	48.0	3.2	1.8	0.0	0.0	0.0	0.0	0.0
All services	100.0	28.5	30.7	1.2	16.3	11.5	0.8	2.7	1.9	1.8	1.4	0.5	2.8

Source: Data from Table 48-1.

In the U.S., health expenditures are paid through a complex system. Nonretired workers often have health insurance coverage through group policies offered by their employers. The elderly rely on the Medicare program for basic hospital and physician services. For the elderly and nonelderly poor the Medicaid program helps pay for health services. Other Federal programs serve special populations such as the military population or veterans. State governments provide significant expenditures for mental institutions.

The various programs that pay for health care serve different demographic groups differently. Table 48-4 shows NMCUES data for the noninstitutional population on average payments per person in various demographic groups. Recall that this household survey excludes the institutionalized and the military populations, excludes all payments for nonprescription drugs (about $10 billion), and may understate payments from private insurance, Medicare, and other third parties. Given these qualifications, it provides a picture of the role played by different sources of payment in providing health care for different demographic groups. For different age groups, Table 48-4 shows that on average, for most age groups up to age 65, about one third of their health expenses are paid directly out-of-pocket. Another third are paid by private insurance. For persons over age 65, about one half of their expenditures are paid by Medicare.

Table 48-4 shows that there is a U-shaped pattern in average health care expenditures per person as income increases. The two lowest income groups have the largest average expenditures. About half of the expenditures for those groups are paid by Medicare and Medicaid. Average expenditures then fall with income up to about $25,000, then rise. For the higher income groups, about one third are paid out-of-pocket and about one half are paid by private insurance.

Table 48-5 shows data from the NMCUES on how total expenditures of the noninstitutional population for various health services are distributed between the nonelderly and two elderly age groups. Table 48-5 shows that health expenditures increase with age. In the United States, in 1980 the population age 65 and over made up 11.3% of the resident population (227 million). The 65 to 74 age group comprised 6.9% of the total population, and the 75 and over group were 4.4%. Table 48-4 shows that in 1980 26% of all health expenditures were for persons age 65 and over—14% for those age 65 to 74 and 12% for those age 75 and over.

This demographic variation is especially reflected in hospital expenditures, where 30% of all such expenditures are attributed to those age 65 and over. Note that nursing home expenditures do not appear, since the NMCUES did not survey the institutionalized. Future surveys plan to include a survey component for institutions to close the gap. We need information not only on the ages of institutionalized patients, but their expenditures for hospitalization, physicians visits, drugs, and other medical service components, and the sources of payment of those expenditures.

Table 48-6 shows average expenditures per person for various health care services for the noninstitutionalized population by age. It also shows that the elderly age 75 and older spend more than five times as much per person as those age 65 and younger. This average statistic masks the fact that the seriously ill account for most of the expenditures. A recent study of Medicare expenditures showed that in 1978, 28.2% of all Medicare expenditures were accounted for by 5.2% of all Medicare enrollees who were in their last year of life (Lubitz & Prihoda, 1983). In 1978, Medicare enrollees in their last year of life were reimbursed an average of $4,099, compared with $1,253 for survivors.

CONCLUSION

The development of a health expenditures model for the NIA Macroeconomic–Demographic Model is a challenging task. Justification for inclusion of demographic information in a health model is amply provided by the great variation of health expenditures with age. Furthermore, Federal payments for health services are targeted on elderly age cohorts. The evolution of the aging U.S. population will strain the financial capacity of current programs. By including behavioral relations to depict the effects of changes in relative prices and incomes in each cohort, in addition to the direct effects of demographic changes, important intergenerational effects of these programs may be examined. Thus, reforms in government health policies and financing strategies may be proposed in the context of fuller knowledge concerning their long-term effects on the national and target population.

APPENDIX: AVERAGE HEALTH CARE EXPENDITURES BY TYPE OF SERVICE AND BY SOURCE OF PAYMENT OF VARIOUS DEMOGRAPHIC GROUPS, 1980

Appendix Tables 48A-1, 48A-2, and 48A-3 show average expenditures for various types of health services and from various sources of payment over demographic groups. These tables all show tabulations of the NMCUES data, which exclude the institutionalized population and the military. Table 48A-1 shows average expenditures *per household* for various services, for households classified by age of head, race of head, region, urban-rural location, sex of head, household income, and household size. Table 48A-2 shows average household expenditures by source of payment for the same groups of households. Table

TABLE 48–4. Average Annual Payments for Health Care Per Person, Noninstutitional Population, by Source of Payment: 1980
(in 1980 $)

	All sources of payment	House-hold	Private insura-nce	Prepaid	Phil-anthropy	Medi-care	Medi-caid	Other public assis-tance	Veter-ans	De-fense—milit-ary	De-fense—campus	Workers' comp-ensation	Other Federal expen-ditures	Other state and local expendi-tures
Total	$695	$202	$230	$22	$25	$109	$59	$4	$9	$10	$4	$5	$7	$8
Age of person														
0-19	356	132	116	12	16	0	47	5	0	6	6	0	9	7
20-24	505	164	220	19	24	1	48	4	0	3	2	12	1	8
25-34	631	201	266	23	36	16	41	2	4	6	3	12	1	19
35-44	631	210	251	33	32	18	55	0	4	13	1	5	1	7
45-54	748	227	331	33	37	14	40	2	20	11	3	14	8	7
55-64	1,092	292	436	40	36	82	84	7	35	37	6	3	30	3
65-74	1,401	316	198	21	10	746	86	1	7	9	0	0	3	3
75+	2,144	395	319	10	19	1,147	193	5	44	1	1	0	4	6
Race														
White	713	211	240	23	27	117	48	4	9	11	4	6	8	6
Nonwhite	586	145	174	17	18	62	126	1	11	5	2	1	3	22
Region														
Northeast	734	208	275	19	25	116	67	4	2	3	1	3	3	7
North Central	707	190	277	19	32	112	42	7	11	0	4	5	4	5
South	640	215	187	12	18	106	47	1	7	14	4	7	8	12
West	723	191	191	43	28	103	88	3	17	23	6	5	17	8

Residence														
Urban	716	206	241	23	27	112	60	3	7	11	4	5	6	9
Rural	591	179	179	16	16	93	53	8	18	3	1	7	14	4
Sex of person														
Male	635	177	207	15	25	110	39	3	18	12	5	9	9	6
Female	751	225	253	28	26	108	77	5	0	8	2	2	7	10
Household income														
0-4,999	1,006	203	86	13	37	250	301	14	13	32	4	2	39	11
5,000-9,999	949	225	164	12	20	282	147	18	20	25	2	4	5	24
10,000-14,999	676	206	187	16	19	146	52	2	7	7	5	9	15	7
15,000-19,999	656	205	244	18	20	82	43	0	15	6	4	8	5	5
20,000-24,999	563	179	231	22	28	55	17	1	4	1	6	10	2	6
25,000-34,999	569	182	252	31	25	49	11	1	2	7	1	3	1	4
35,000-49,999	681	196	330	39	35	38	9	0	10	4	6	2	3	7
50,000+	692	252	311	15	25	49	5	0	6	11	2	2	6	8
Household size														
1	$996	$296	$225	$23	$40	$258	$113	$9	$9	$ 3	$1	$4	$7	$8
2	1,019	274	298	23	29	281	66	1	13	4	3	4	15	8
3	689	197	263	21	24	64	52	1	14	22	4	6	17	4
4	520	166	217	17	22	23	31	4	3	10	8	3	1	14
5	529	160	187	27	18	30	60	6	14	4	2	10	2	10
6	458	126	163	24	35	17	52	4	1	26	1	3	1	5
7 or more	408	121	160	28	11	13	52	1	0	2	1	13	1	4

Source: ICF incorporated tabulations of the National Medical Care Utilization and Expenditure Survey (NMCUES).

TABLE 48–5. Total Personal Health Care Expenditures—Noninstitutional Population—by Type of Service and Age of Person: 1980 (1980 $ billion)

	Total (%)	Age of person		
		Less than 65 (%)	65-74 (%)	75 + (%)
Hospital	$83,941 (100)	$58,333 (69)	$12,653 (15)	$12,955 (15)
Physician	$34,745 (100)	$26,361 (76)	$5,036 (14)	$3,347 (10)
Dental	$17,795 (100)	$16,548 (93)	$914 (5)	$333 (2)
Other professional	$4,585 (100)	$3,810 (83)	$345 (8)	$429 (9)
Prescription drugs	$7,988 (100)	$5,697 (71)	$1,389 (17)	$902 (11)
Appliances	$3,128 (100)	$2,476 (79)	$397 (13)	$255 (8)
Other health	$2,725 (100)	$2,070 (76)	$504 (19)	$151 (6)
All services	$154,907 (100)	$115,295 (74)	$21,238 (14)	$18,372 (12)

Source: ICF incorporated tabulations of the National Medical Care Utilization and Expenditure Survey (NMCUES).

TABLE 48–6. Average Annual Health Care Expenditures Per Noninstitutionalized Person by Type of Service and Age of Person: 1980
(1980 $ million)

| | | Age of person | | |
	Total	Less than 65	65-74	75 +
All hospital services	$377	$293	$834	$1,560
Emergency room	21	21	20	27
Outpatient	30	27	55	43
Inpatient	326	245	760	1,490
Physician visits	156	132	332	403
Dental	80	83	60	40
Other professional	21	19	23	52
Prescription drugs	36	29	92	109
Appliances	14	12	26	31
Other health	12	10	33	18
All services	695	578	1,401	2,212

Source: ICF incorporated tabulations of the National Medical Care Utilization and Expenditure Survey (NMCUES).

TABLE 48A–1. Average Annual Expenditures on Health Care Per Household, Noninstitutional Population, by Type of Service: 1980

(1980 $)

	All Services	Emergency room	Outpatient	Inpatient	Physician visit	Dental	Other prof.	Drug[a]	Appliances	Other health
Total	$1,811	$56	$76	$860	$403	$203	$52	$94	$36	$32
Age of head										
0-19	1,253	101	81	692	182	91	21	37	22	25
20-24	1,006	58	40	442	254	111	33	34	18	15
25-34	1,362	67	64	575	334	179	39	55	22	27
35-44	1,944	73	86	777	420	364	66	76	39	42
45-54	1,853	60	77	778	395	285	70	101	50	37
55-64	2,115	43	103	1,075	448	187	56	137	42	25
65-74	2,377	36	80	1,325	551	107	43	143	44	50
75+	2,318	27	63	1,411	483	69	55	149	42	20
Race										
White	1,843	56	70	865	420	211	55	96	37	32
Nonwhite	1,584	56	116	819	284	148	29	78	27	27
Region										
Northeast	1,864	56	73	852	418	246	68	84	35	31
North Central	1,954	54	72	995	404	203	51	94	42	39
South	1,676	55	68	812	376	160	33	114	33	25
West	1,773	61	94	772	423	217	62	77	33	33
Residence										
Urban	1,832	57	80	854	414	211	53	92	37	35
Rural	1,699	52	54	890	347	157	45	106	31	17

Sex of head									
Male	1,907	54	74	882	437	238	57	96	40	30
Female	1,619	60	79	815	336	133	42	90	29	36
Household income									
0-4,999	1,569	53	83	889	293	68	35	96	24	28
5,000-9,999	1,843	57	84	1,067	360	97	30	97	26	24
10,000-14,999	1,569	48	56	792	328	139	42	91	31	43
15,000-19,999	1,760	55	76	852	408	161	53	95	34	27
20,000-24,999	1,818	60	66	808	427	244	53	88	39	32
25,000-34,999	1,776	55	89	664	452	298	68	85	40	25
35,000-49,999	2,295	68	66	966	549	373	75	106	48	43
50,000 +	2,436	61	92	846	592	521	98	107	78	41
Household size									
1	$1,058	$25	$49	$532	$229	$86	$36	$61	$23	$16
2	2,054	46	89	1,050	463	155	46	128	40	37
3	1,994	67	88	921	459	225	71	93	42	28
4	1,992	76	80	815	463	317	63	100	38	39
5	2,500	102	77	1,185	504	365	65	96	50	55
6	2,469	127	107	1,084	529	395	45	87	46	49
7 or more	3,029	110	111	1,356	671	505	93	102	39	42

aExcludes Expenditures for Nonprescription Drugs

Source: ICF incorporated tabulations of the National Medical Care Utilization and Expenditure Survey (NMCUES).

TABLE 48A–2. Average Annual Payments for Health Care per Household, Noninstitutional Population by Source of Payment: 1980
(1980 $)

	All sources of payment	House-hold	Private insurance	Prepaid	Phil-anthropy	Medi-care	Medi-caid	Other public assistance	Veter-ans	De-fense—milit-ary	De-fense—campus	Workers' comp-ensation	Other Federal expen-ditures	Other state and local expendi-tures
Total	$1,811	$517	$579	$58	$67	$295	$176	$11	$20	$25	$9	$14	$19	$21
Age of head														
0-19	1,253	428	148	29	70	0	239	309	0	17	0	0	1	13
20-24	1,006	270	376	18	40	0	217	16	0	9	17	25	3	15
25-34	1,362	420	572	52	77	8	133	5	3	20	15	20	4	33
35-44	1,944	641	699	112	101	83	215	3	7	29	6	12	4	32
45-54	1,853	577	704	66	87	103	148	4	27	21	7	24	60	26
55-64	2,115	591	660	54	70	330	212	14	53	59	7	9	48	9
65-74	2,377	555	491	49	24	1,078	139	1	15	15	5	0	3	4
75 +	2,318	513	377	16	21	1,112	195	8	55	1	2	0	6	11
Race														
White	1,843	536	599	60	72	314	150	12	20	26	9	15	13	16
Nonwhite	1,584	385	437	47	37	160	360	2	18	15	3	3	59	57
Region														
Northeast	1,864	512	662	46	61	303	218	17	5	7	0	7	8	18
North Central	1,954	508	719	61	96	336	142	17	27	1	8	15	11	14
South	1,676	569	490	31	48	281	125	3	14	35	11	18	20	32
West	1,773	464	453	103	66	259	242	9	36	56	15	14	38	18

Residence													
Urban	1,832	521	594	60	71	296	176	9	15	28	10	12	15	23
Rural	1,699	497	498	47	46	290	175	20	47	7	1	22	40	10
Sex of head													
Male	1,907	571	698	63	78	266	89	6	30	25	11	18	27	24
Female	1,619	409	560	48	46	353	349	21	1	23	4	6	2	16
Household income													
0-4,999	1,569	329	129	22	82	382	524	22	20	32	4	3	3	18
5,000-9,999	1,843	430	311	23	42	540	312	39	33	52	4	7	9	41
10,000-14,999	1,569	467	440	35	44	350	128	5	7	11	9	20	34	16
15,000-19,999	1,760	526	634	55	51	241	147	3	35	14	9	20	12	13
20,000-24,999	1,818	544	702	96	85	186	63	3	11	5	16	30	62	15
25,000-34,999	1,776	572	789	86	77	150	34	2	7	25	5	12	3	14
35,000-49,000	2,295	664	1,104	132	116	136	34	0	31	14	21	8	12	24
50,000 +	2,436	921	1,062	48	80	184	21	0	20	38	4	7	23	28
Household size													
1	$1,058	$313	$233	$24	$54	$269	$121	$9	$10	$3	$1	$5	$7	$8
2	2,054	527	562	45	56	586	163	3	22	8	6	7	54	13
3	1,994	570	752	59	62	215	188	4	31	65	11	16	7	15
4	1,992	632	812	60	83	91	147	25	12	39	28	10	4	49
5	2,500	734	859	157	82	125	330	27	57	21	7	41	10	48
6	2,469	711	855	122	181	85	320	29	6	108	0	15	8	29
7 or more	3,029	900	1,158	194	77	110	410	9	0	14	7	118	9	25

Source: ICF incorporated tabulations of the National Medical Care Utilization and Expenditure Survey (NMCUES).

475

TABLE 48A–3. Average Annual Expenditures on Health Care Per Person, Noninstitutional Population, by Type of Service: 1980 (1980 $)

	All Services	Emergency room	Outpatient	Inpatient	Physician visit	Dental	Other prof.	Drug[a]	Appliances	Other health
Total	$695	$21	$30	$326	$156	$80	$21	$36	$14	$12
Age of person										
0-19	356	23	14	133	75	76	8	13	7	7
20-24	505	23	18	203	131	67	23	18	11	11
25-34	631	20	30	266	156	85	25	23	12	14
35-44	631	18	30	256	146	99	25	31	14	12
45-54	748	17	37	305	172	100	29	52	21	14
55-64	1,092	19	61	563	232	83	26	78	22	9
65-74	1,401	20	55	760	332	60	23	92	26	33
75 +	2,144	26	43	425	400	41	51	108	30	18
Race										
White	713	21	27	330	174	84	22	37	15	13
Nonwhite	586	20	45	302	106	53	11	28	11	10
Region										
Northeast	734	20	30	334	164	100	28	32	14	12
North Central	707	20	27	346	151	78	19	36	16	15
South	640	20	26	313	143	61	13	41	13	9
West	723	24	38	313	173	89	27	32	14	14
Residence										
Urban	716	21	32	331	162	85	21	36	15	13
Rural	591	18	19	301	124	57	17	37	11	6

Sex of person										
Male	635	23	24	314	131	75	17	29	12	11
Female	751	19	35	337	179	85	24	43	16	13
Household income										
0-4,999	1,006	30	60	578	180	43	22	60	15	17
5,000-9,999	949	26	44	550	185	51	15	50	14	13
10,000-14,999	676	20	24	336	[43	61	19	40	13	19
15,000-19,999	656	21	28	309	158	61	20	36	13	10
20,000-24,999	563	19	21	238	136	78	20	28	13	10
25,000-34,999	569	17	29	219	142	93	21	26	12	8
35,000-49,999	681	20	20	287	164	110	23	31	14	12
50,000 +	692	17	28	248	166	145	27	30	21	11
Household size										
1	$996	$23	$48	$491	$218	$85	$35	$58	$22	$16
2	1,019	22	46	507	234	80	26	64	20	19
3	689	21	31	318	159	78	25	31	14	9
4	520	19	20	215	120	84	16	25	10	10
5	529	21	16	248	109	80	13	20	11	11
6	458	22	20	207	95	74	8	16	8	9
7 or more	408	15	15	186	89	67	12	13	6	6

aExcludes expenditures for nonprescription drugs.

Source: ICF incorporated tabulations of the National Medical Care Utilization and Expenditure Survey (NMCUES).

48A-3 shows average expenditures *per person* for types of health services, for persons classified by age, race, region, urban-rural location, sex, income of the household in which that person resides, and size of that person's household. Text Table 48-4 shows average expenditures for persons by source of payment for persons in the same demographic categories.

REFERENCES

Bonhag, R.C. (Ed.) (1981, February). The description of the health financing model: A tool for cost estimation. Mimeographed, DHHS, Office of the Assistant Secretary for Planning and Evaluation, Washington, D.C.

Bonham, G.S. (1983, March). Procedures and questionnaires of the National Medical Care Utilization and Expenditure Survey. *National Medical Care Utilization and Expenditure Survey, Series A, Methodological report No. 1.* (DHHS Publication No. [PHS] 83-20001). Washington, D.C.: National Center for Health Statistics, U.S.Government Printing Office.

Gibson, R.M., Levit, K.R., Lazenby, H., & Waldo, D.R.(1984, Winter). National health expenditures, 1983. *Health Care Financing Review*, Vol. 6, No. 2.

Kovar, M.G. (1983, November). Expenditures for the medical care of elderly people living in the community throughout 1980. *National Medical Care Utilization and Expenditure Survey, Data Report No. 4.* (DHHS Publication No. [PHS] 842000). Washinton, DC: U.S. Government Printing Office.

Lubitz, J. & Prihoda, R. (1983, December). Use and costs of Medicare services in the last years of life. *United States Health and Prevention Profile, 1983.* (DHHS Publication NO. [PHS] 84-1232) Washington, DC: U.S. Government Printing Office.

Yett, D.E. & Drabeck, L., Intriligator, M.D. & Kimbell, L.J. (1979). *A forecasting and policy simulation model of the health care sector: The NRRC Prototype Microeconomic Model.* Lexington, MA: Lexington Books.

CHAPTER 49

Hospice and the Elderly: Insights From the National Hospice Study

Vincent Mor

Forty hospices participating in the 2-year National Hospice Study admitted over 13,000 patients; 65% were over 65 years of age, and nearly 30% were over 75. This is a special group of elderly; less than one quarter were ambulatory, less than one half continent, and less than one fifth could dress themselves on admission. Almost all (95%) had a significant caretaking person, 80% of whom live in the patient's household. Hospice is *not* long-term care; the median length of stay is only 35 days, and while in hospice (and prior to entry), almost no one uses a nursing home. Aged cancer patients in hospice were less likely to receive chemotherapy and other diagnostic tests than their younger counterparts but were no more likely to receive other palliative or social services than younger patients. Given the age distribution of cancer, it is likely that hospice will continue to serve a predominantly elderly although not an old-old population. Whether hospice can viably serve as the intermediate system to deal with nonacute but not long-term chronic care problems of the terminally ill aged remains to be seen.

The growth of hospice in America over the past decade has been spectacular, suggesting that the underlying philosophy and goals of the hospice movement struck a resonating chord felt by almost all sectors of society. The hospice movement grew out of the convergence of the widespread disenchantment with the unfulfilled promise of curative medicine and the emergence of a new sensitivity to death and dying in this country (Kastenbaum, 1977; Kübler-Ross, 1969; Saunders,

1978). Emanating as it did from Britain, emphasis was upon low technology, "high touch" caring that could occur in a home-like environment. In the United States, this was largely interpreted in a manner consistent with our own perspective on "deinstitutionalizing" health care. Indeed, in some respects the hospice movement arrived in the U.S. at a time when the philosophy of deinstitutionalization and the provision of supportive home care was firmly established as a new value in health care delivery. The anti-institutional value adopted by hospice was consistent with values rapidly emerging with respect to the care of the aged. A reading of some of the classic descriptions of the goals and objectives of home care for the aged and disabled in the early 1970s suggests an exact replica of the first models of hospice care being introduced into America (Lack & Buckingham, 1978; Kirstin & Morris, 1972; Sherwood, 1975).

As has frequently been noted, the rise of home care and deinstitutional policies for providing long-term care for the elderly largely paralleled our recognition of the shifting demographic distribution toward an increasingly older elderly population. Because cancer is largely a disease of the elderly, the demographic shift has implications for the size of the prevalent cancer population. One half of all incident cancer cases are over 65 years of age, and 60% of cancer deaths occur among those over age 65. Obviously, then, discussions about the role of hospice in caring for the terminally ill cannot ignore the sheer numbers of elderly who are potential users of the hospice service model.

Despite the fact that cancer is a disease of the elderly and that the deinstitutional component of the movement arises from the same core as does the focus of independence among the aged, hospice has an image of serving the younger patient—helping that person and his or her family cope with the stress of gradual deterioration, loss of independence, and impending death. The parallels to the admittedly slower processes among the aged are rarely acknowledged in the popular hospice literature (DuBois, 1980; Stoddard, 1978). This is unfortunate since there are lessons that have been learned over the past 15 years in the areas of geriatrics and gerontology that could be useful to hospice proponents in designing and implementing plans of care in a medical care system that is oriented toward the curative treatment of acute disease rather than the care of persons with chronic disease. On the other hand, geriatricians and gerontologists can learn from the hospice movement clinically and politically (Greer, 1983). The hospice movement has been able to galvanize public support for an expansion of health and social benefits at a time when all other such programs were being reduced. The use of images of the patient and family suffering together with the tragedy of cancer has been very effective in obtaining broad-based community support that cuts across social and economic strata.

The purpose of this chapter is to redress the misperception that hospice serves the younger patient by describing the population of hospice patients, most of whom are elderly. We will see, however, that they are a different group of elderly than the typical long-term care patient. Additionally, we will contrast the outcomes elderly hospice patients experience with those of younger patients and then present data suggesting that among hospice as well as all terminal cancer patients the aged patient appears to receive a systematically different pattern and intensity of services. Finally, the implications of the hospice movement for the long-term care system serving the aged in the United States will be discussed given the current hospice benefit under Medicare and the increasing "dehospitalization" of health care with its consequence of shifting the burden of responsibility to the family.

The data upon which these observations are based come largely from the National Hospice Study (NHS) a large-scale, multisite, evaluation project undertaken to assess the costs and benefits of the hospice model of care. The NHS research methodology and major results have been presented elsewhere (Greer, Mor, Morris, & Sherwood et al., 1986; Greer, Mor, Sherwood, Morris & Birnbaum, 1983). The study emerged in response to Congressional and Department of Health and Human Services interest in hospice and began when the Health Care Financing Administration (HCFA) developed a research and demonstration project plan that they implemented in conjunction with private foundations, choosing Brown University as the evaluation center to address the various research questions. A large amount of data were collected addressing topics as diverse as staff burnout to psychotropic medication use. Many of the analyses that have been conducted addressed the issue of differential response among the older rather than younger hospice patients. The current article is an elaboration of some of those findings, supplemented with original analyses undertaken to further explore certain issues of outcome or pattern of service use.

METHODS

Forty hospices (26 selected by HCFA to receive special demonstration funding and 14 selected by Brown University who used only available funding mechanisms) from across the country participated in the National Hospice Study. Half of these hospices had units with inpatient beds, and half did not. Between October of 1980 through September of 1982 data were collected on 13,374 admissions to the 40 participating hospices. Patient data were obtained from existing hospice records and included demographic, functional status, nursing care needs information, as well as selected data characterizing that person identified by the patient as a primary care person, generally a family member. For all patients, length of stay and discharge disposition from the hospice were also recorded. For Medicare patients served in the 26 demonstration hospices, billing data were available from both the regular Medicare billing system as well as more detailed billing data summarizing patients' pattern and intensity of inpatient and home care services from HCFA's Office of Direct Reimbursement. These billing data covering both hospice and prehospice enrollment periods were merged with the patient descriptive data.

A subsample of patients with tissue-confirmed metastatic disease who were able and willing to consent (along with their primary care persons) to participate in a prospective follow-up study was also recruited. This group of 1,457 hospice patients constituted the final analysis sample used for all of the quality of life and patient benefit comparisons. All these patients had died within the time frame of our follow-up. Data gathered included periodic, weekly or biweekly, interview contacts with the patient or with his or her primary care person who acted as an informant about the patient's condition. Additionally, data regarding the patient's receipt of various medical interventions were obtained from the primary care person as were detailed information about analgesic medication consumption from a subgroup of some 200 follow-up sample patients.

A third source of data incorporated into the current report is based upon a substudy of the National Hospice Study conducted in Rhode Island to examine health care costs of the population of cancer decedents, comparing those served by hospice and those not served by hospice. This was accomplished by matching death certificates of 1980 and 1981 cancer deaths with Medicare and Blue Cross and Blue Shield claims and summarizing charges for fixed periods of time prior to death (Spector and Mor, 1984).

OVERVIEW OF NATIONAL HOSPICE STUDY RESULTS

In order to place the results of the current report into perspective, a review of the major findings of the National Hospice Study is in order. Using a quasiexperimental design to compare the costs and outcomes experienced by terminal cancer patients served in hospice and conventional oncological care settings, few differences in the quality of patients' lives were observed. Patients served in hospital-based hospices did appear to manifest less pain and fewer symptoms than did nonhospice patients, and their family members reported being somewhat more satisfied with the care the patient received. Nonetheless, in most other respects, the findings with respect to emotional, physical, and overall rated quality of life were similar. Surviving primary care persons in hospice were no more likely to experience increased hospitalizations, physician visits, or other indicators of secondary morbidity, although again, survivors of hospital-based hospice patients manifested somewhat less of a grief reaction in terms of depressed mood (Greer et al., 1986).

While there were few differences in the outcomes experienced by patients and their primary care persons, there were substantial differences in the pattern of care received. Hospice patients were significantly less likely to receive "intensive" medical interventions, diagnostic tests, and blood transfusions than was the case for cancer patients being conventionally treated. On the other hand, after adjusting for differences in the mix of patients, hospice and conventional care patients did not differ in terms of their use of supportive care procedures such as oxygen.

Comparisons of the health care costs incurred by hospice and non-hospice patients revealed that patients served in home care hospices had substantially lower costs than either hospital-based hospice or conventional care patients. While hospital-based hospice patients had lower costs than did conventional care patients in the last weeks and months of life, higher costs while in hospice earlier in the deterioration phase largely offset any meaningful savings associated with the inpatient brand of hospice. Home care hospice patients had lower costs because they used the hospital less than did either hospital-based hospice or conventional care patients; hospital-based hospice patients did not have higher costs than conventional care patients, largely because while in an inpatient setting they consumed fewer high-cost ancillary services than was the case for nonhospice patients (Birnbaum & Kidder, 1984; Greer et al., 1986; Mor & Kidder, 1985).

The current report focuses upon selected aspects of the outcome, cost, and service use issues, comparing the elderly with the younger cancer patients. Where selected relationships have been reported already in the literature, these are summarized, but in the cases of new analyses, the data are presented for review by the reader.

RESULTS

A Description of Elderly in Hospice

Table 49-1 presents the characteristics of hospice admissions for whom complete demographic and medical data were available by age. In view of the very large sample sizes, most differences that are greater than a few percentage points between groups reach statistical significance. Since percentage differences that are small may not be mean-

TABLE 49-1. Characteristics of the Population of Hospice Patients by
Age (n ∿ 10,212)

	Age categories				
	21-44 (n = 635)	45-54 (n = 891)	55-64 (n = 2,053)	65-74 (n = 3,364)	75+ (n = 2,804)
Female	56.8%	57.1%	53.2%	51.6%	50.7%
Married	53.5	67.8	67.2	60.6	47.5
Nonwhite	15.9	12.8	8.8	5.9	4.8
Patient lives alone	5.7	9.1	11.3	16.9	18.9
Family income under $10,000	46.0	42.0	45.6	52.6	61.7
Primary care person is spouse	48.7	64.3	63.3	56.2	41.4
Primary care person is child	8.9	17.1	21.2	26.4	38.6
Primary care person is female	62.1	60.9	65.2	70.0	77.6
Patient requires a catheter	18.9	16.3	15.0	19.0	22.5
Patient requires oxygen	15.0	17.4	18.7	21.4	17.6
Cancer: Colorectal	8.4	10.2	12.2	14.8	17.7
Lung	18.4	27.2	27.7	26.0	18.1
Breast	17.9	17.6	13.2	10.0	8.0
Prostate	1.0	1.5	3.8	6.8	11.3
Brain tumor	10.4	5.2	4.6	2.7	2.0
Average years with disease	2.6	2.8	2.9	2.6	2.6

ingful substantively, no statistical interpretation of this table is presented.

The first point to be made is that some 65% of all hospice admissions are 65 years of age or older and that fully 27.4% are 75 or older. Hospice obviously attracts and serves an elderly population. Nonetheless, as can be seen by the characteristics presented in Table 49-1, the hospice population of elders is not the typical long-term care group. Half are female; until the oldest age group, a majority are married. As can be seen, the older the patient, the more likely it is that he or she lived alone at the time of hospice admission and the lower the household income. Logically, the older the patient, the less likely the spouse is the caretaker, and the more likely that role was assumed by a child. In view of the increasing prevalence of female caretakers, with the increasing age of the patient, it is obviously daughters that are taking on the responsibility.

Older patients were not more functionally impaired on admission; however, the oldest group were somewhat more likely to be catheterized. Differences in cancer type distribution mirror the age-related prevalence of these diseases (American Cancer Society, 1985). Disease

TABLE 49-2. Characteristics of Hospice Patients' Discharge
Disposition by Age

	Age categories				
	21-44	45-54	55-64	65-74	75+
Length of stay (in days)	53.8	50.2	51.2	51.9	53.0
Site of death for those discharged dead (92%)					
Home	42.0%	36.9%	40.9%	39.2%	39.6%
Inpatient hospice	21.1	28.6	27.6	27.1	30.1
Acute Hospital	34.3	31.8	29.3	30.6	26.8
Other inpatient	2.6	2.7	2.3	3.1	3.5

duration was comparable across all age groups and generally reflects the high degree of variation since the major determinant of survival is cancer type (median disease duration 1.5 years; mean for all patients is 2.7 years).

Table 49-2 presents data summarizing length of stay and discharge disposition of the hospice patient population by age. Age was not related to how long a patient was served in hospice. Since in the vast majority of cases (92%) discharge was due to death, length of hospice stay is essentially an indicator of survival. Thus, in this basically terminal cancer population, age is unrelated to survival. This finding is borne out by more detailed studies of the predictors of survival already reported (Mor, Laliberte, Morris, & Wiemann, 1984). Aged patients are no more or less likely to die at home than are younger patients, although they are somewhat less likely to have died in an acute-care hospital. The principal determinant of where hospice patients die is whether they are served in a hospital or home-based hospice (Mor & Hiris, 1983). Indeed, no interaction emerges within hospice type with respect to age; older and younger patients served by a given type of hospice are no more or less likely to die at home. Since home death requires substantial social support from family as well as the help of hospice staff, the lack of an age differential suggests that the support systems of the aged and younger hospice patients are similarly resilient, even though they are made up of different actors.

Outcomes Experienced by Aged Hospice Patients

The range of outcomes examined in the National Hospice Study was limited by the amount and types of data that could reasonably be gathered from terminally ill patients. Indeed, of patients who gave signed consent to participate in the study, as many as 20% were unable

TABLE 49-3. Hospice Patients' Outcomes in Last Weeks of Life by Age

	Age categories				
	21-44	45-54	55-64	65-74	75 +
Proportion of patients in pain based on primary care person report in:					
Last week of life	.717	.725	.655	.608	.584
Third to last week	.652	.700	.629	.553	.463
Average number of 10 symptoms reported in:					
Last week of life	4.9	5.4	5.1	5.0	4.7
Third to last week	5.2	5.0	4.8	4.6	4.2
Interviewer judgment, Karnofsky Performance Status in:					
Last week of life	20.9	24.4	22.8	22.9	22.3
Third to last week	28.9	30.9	29.2	29.5	27.0

to respond to the interview questions at the next scheduled contact (Mor, 1986). Since most analyses were performed in relation to days or weeks from patients' date of death, only a minority of patients were able to respond to interviews that occurred within the last week or two of life.

The implication of this attrition, which did not differ by comparison group or age, is that most patient outcome data were obtained from patients' primary care persons who were in the best position to comment upon the patients' condition (Greer et al., 1986). Patient mood state and satisfaction data were also examined for those patients able to respond to interviews, however, and no significant differences between hospice and nonhospice patients were observed. In performing those analyses, no significant relationship was observed between patient age and self-reported mood state and satisfaction.

Table 49-3 summarizes three measures of the number and severity of symptoms experienced for which there were consistent age-related findings. As reported elsewhere, with respect to the proportion of patients in severe pain, Table 49-3 reveals that older patients are less likely to report moderate to severe pain in the last weeks of life. Similarly, older patients report experiencing fewer symptoms ranging from nausea to dyspnea to trouble swallowing than do younger patients. On the other hand, many of the functionally based indicators of quality of life such as the Karnofsky Performance Status Index, with scores from 100, meaning perfectly healthy, to 0, indicating death, reveal no relationship to age. In addition to these variables, measures of patient awareness and social interaction also indicated no difference with respect to age.

Outcomes of Aged Primary Care Persons

A major goal of the hospice movement is to mitigate the stress of bereavement by providing bereavement counseling services after the patient's death and to help family members to cope with the stress of their caretaking responsibility via assistance and education while the patient lived. Since the stress of caretaking might have a greater impact on older caretakers, we conducted a series of analyses to explore the bereavement outcomes experienced by older and younger primary care persons. The outcomes specifically examined were concrete indicators of secondary morbidity such as hospitalization, physician visits, and tranquilizer and alcohol use. As expected, older primary care persons had higher rates of physician and hospital use, but once prior illness and their relationship with the deceased was statistically controlled, there was no relationship between any of these outcomes and the primary care person's age (Mor, McHorney, & Sherwood, 1986). Indeed, the most important factor was the person's prior health and whether he or she was the spouse of the patient. Regardless of the age, loss of a spouse was a major predictor of increased secondary morbidity.

Pattern of Receipt of Medical Services

As noted, hospice patients were significantly less likely to receive intensive medical and diagnostic interventions. While home care patients may have achieved this result by staying out of the inpatient setting, hospital-based hospice patients spent almost as many days in the inpatient unit as did conventional care patients. Thus, the philosophy of care and treatment differed between the groups. Indeed, interestingly enough, older nonhospice patients were as likely as were younger patients to receive aggressive treatments, while in hospice, particularly home care hospice, younger patients were more likely to continue to receive treatments such as chemotherapy (Laliberte & Mor, 1984).

Other indicators of treatment differences may be related to earlier data contrasting patients' symptoms. Older patients were less likely to have analgesics prescribed and were more likely to have them prescribed on an "as needed" basis than was the case for younger patients (Goldberg et al., 1986.) Consistent with the fact that older patients were found to have fewer symptoms, specifically less nausea and vomiting, younger patients were more likely to be consuming antiemetics than were older patients (Goldberg & Mor, 1985).

Cost and Utilization Experiences of Aged Hospice Patients

We examined patient costs in hospice from a variety of different perspectives (Birnbaum & Kidder, 1984; Greer et al., 1986; Mor & Kidder, 1985), in all cases using a Medicare-based definition of costs developed by adjusting patient billing data with hospice and hospital cost report information. Costs during patients' stay in hospice were primarily determined by the length of stay and the amount of time spent in an inpatient setting. The latter factor was largely attributable to the type of hospice serving the patient, for example, hospital versus home care; and as already noted, length of stay was unrelated to age. As expected, therefore, age was not found to be related to costs in hospice. A measure of the intensity of hospice care was developed based upon costs incurred per hospice day. In this instance, no difference between service intensity and age, either based upon the population of patients served in home or in hospital-based hospices was found. On the other hand, among both hospital and home care patients, age was negatively related to the costs patients incurred during a given stay in an inpatient setting, either in an acute hospital or an inpatient hospice unit (Kidder, 1985).

Another finding relevant to the cost and utilization analyses was the virtual absence of nursing home care. In view of this, a special comprehensive primary data collection effort was undertaken to capture health care costs that might not have surfaced in review of standard third-party payor bills. With all of this effort, we felt certain that all nursing home utilization episodes had been identified, and they still amounted to less than a dollar a day of all costs during the last 50 days of hospice patients' lives.

The reduced intensity of inpatient episodes noted earlier is consistent with the finding that older hospice patients were less likely to receive more intensive medical interventions that were younger patients. This pattern also appears to be a continuation of the pattern established among older cancer patients earlier in their illness. Analyses of hospitalizations hospice patients experienced well before they were admitted to hospice reveal that the cost per inpatient day, our measure of intensity, was significantly related to age, with older patients having substantially lower costs. This pattern applied for hospitalizations that occurred around the time of diagnosis with cancer as well as to hospitalizations occurring between diagnosis and hospice entry.

This finding suggests a potential age bias with respect to the mode of treatment for cancer. Various authors have discussed this possibility, and a series of National Cancer Institute-sponsored investigations are

TABLE 49–4. Cost Per Hospital Day in Each of the Last Six Months of Life Among Cancer Decedents by Age

Age:	< 65	65-84	85 +
Last 2 weeks of life	$344	$312	$275
Second to last 2 weeks of life	293	291	252
Second to last month of life	290	270	245
Third to last month of life	335	263	227
Fourth to last month of life	341	263	241
Fifth to last month of life	317	251	266
Sixth to last month of life	310	253	240

currently examining the proposition that chronological age is related to cancer treatments and choices (Yancik, 1983). We explored this possibility using two approaches with National Hospice Study data that pertained to periods in time prior to patients' entry into hospice. First, we examined the relationship between patients' age at the time they were diagnosed with cancer and whether they received either radiation or chemotherapy at some point of time after their diagnosis. These analyses were performed separately for each type of cancer in order to minimize the variation due to age differences in disease distribution. Controlling for the extent of disease at the time of diagnosis (e.g., metastatic or local disease) as well as the presence of selected comorbid chronic diseases, we found that older persons were less likely to have received treatment beyond the initial surgery (Mor, Masterson-Allen, Goldberg, Cummings & Glicksman, et al., 1985).

Table 49-4 presents another view of this potential bias. Using data drawn from the matching of Rhode Island cancer decedents' death certificates and their Medicare or Blue Cross bills accumulated in the last 6 months of life, we examined the relationship between age, proximity to death, and the charge of a day in an acute hospital. As can be readily seen, the charge per day is almost uniformly higher among those under 65 than among those over 65 and particularly when comparing the oldest-old with the nonelderly. It is also worthy of note, however, that charges per day increase at a realtively uniform rate as death approaches in all three age groups.

DISCUSSION

In examining the elderly hospice patient using the window of the largest multisite study of hospice conducted to date, several facts have become clear. First and foremost, even before the advent of the hospice reimbursement benefit under Medicare, which was enacted into law in

1982 and went into effect in 1983, hospice served a largely elderly population (Federal Register, 1982). Nearly two thirds of all persons admitted to hospice are over age 65, and more than one quarter are over 75. At the same time, the hospice elderly population differs considerably from the standard elderly long-term care population. Older hospice patients are more likely to be married at all ages, are much more likely to be male, and are more likely to have support from family members. The extent of this support was documented in the National Hospice Study and was found to average as much as 16 hours of direct care per day provided by family members on days when the patient was home (Sherwood, Sherwood, & Morris, 1985). It is likely that one of the major reasons that families are willing to assume a burden of this magnitude with cancer patients and not with other chronic diseases is precisely because of the anticipated time-limited nature of the support requirement for the terminal illness. The caretaker recognizes that the disruption, though severe, will end soon, and that this caretaking process is likely to be the last contact possible with the loved one.

Inasmuch as the hospice population is not the traditional long-term care patient, and since they use almost no nursing home service either before or after their entry into hospice, hospice cannot be seen as a part of the long-term care system. Rather, hospice presents an alternative to the acute care sector that "idealizes" as socially and personally desirable the cost-shifting from insurers to private families that is inherent in "dehospitalizing" medical care. The family takes on the principal caretaking burden, and in so doing makes it possible to reduce the observed cost of terminal cancer. The societal costs may not change since the caretaking burden must be met, and indeed, societal costs may increase since families may be less efficient economically than are institutions. Nonetheless, the phenomenon of hospice makes it clear that families are willing to shoulder the burden, particularly with some support from hospice professionals. What is most gratifying about our examination of age-related hospice outcomes is that older patients' families appear to be as willing to accept the caretaking burden.

If hospice is to occupy a niche in the health care delivery system that at once is not long-term care but is also not acute care, several practical and ethical questions must be addressed. First, can hospice avoid being the "dumping ground" for unwanted, chronic patients who require heavy care, but are not medically complicated, and who need to be discharged from the hospital? Pressures placed on hospitals under prospective payment will make it difficult to avoid such a process. Second, in view of the cost limitations placed upon hospices under Medicare, how will medical care prescription decisions be made when expensive procedures might extend life somewhat and make the patient more comfortable? Third, and perhaps most importantly, how do the decisions regarding continuation of treatment and hospice admission come about?

This latter issue is deserving of additional attention in light of preliminary evidence suggesting that, for whatever reason, elderly cancer patients are not treated as aggressively as are their younger counterparts. While in some respects the elderly can be viewed as fortunate that during their last weeks of life they are somewhat less likely to be the objects of extensive medical probing, patching, and general intervention than are younger patients, the promise of the peace of hospice has its own danger. Cessation of treatment via subtle messages that limit a patient's and family's treatment choices in favor of hospice is all too easy if such a philosophy becomes accepted. It would be a sad disservice to the spirit of the hospice movement to have a by-product be the premature cessation of active curative efforts among the elderly. Nonetheless, given the reimbursement incentives and the availability of a philosophy that can be easily twisted, current gains being made in the arena of cancer treatment may not reach the bulk of the incident population. This is perhaps the greatest challenge to the hospice movement and an area in which the gerontological community should play an active role.

REFERENCES

American Cancer Society. (1985). *Cancer facts and figures: 1984*. New York: Author.
Birnbaum, H., & Kidder, D. (1984). What does hospice cost? *Journal of the American Public Health Association, 74*(7), 689–697.
DuBois, P.M. (1980). *The hospice way of death*. New York: Human Sciences Press.
Federal Register. (1982, September 29). 47: 42904-42909.
Goldberg, R.J., & Mor, V. (1985). A survey of psychotropic use in terminal cancer patients. *Psychosomatics, 26*(9), 745–751.
Goldberg, R.J., Mor, V., Wiemann, M., Greer, D.S., & Hiris, J. (1986). Analgesic use in terminal cancer patients: Report from the National Hospice Study. *Journal of Chronic Diseases, 39*(1), 37–45.
Greer, D. (1983). Hospice: Lessons for geriatricians. *Journal of the American Geriatrics Society, 31*(2), 67–70.
Greer, D.S., Mor, V., Morris, J.N., Sherwood, S., Kidder, D., & Birnbaum, H. (1986). An alternative in terminal care: Results of the National Hospice Study. *Journal of Chronic Diseases, 39*(1), 9–26.
Greer, D.S., Mor, V., Sherwood, S., Morris, J.N., & Birnbaum, H. (1983). National Hospice Study analysis plan. *Journal of Chornic Diseases, 36*(11), 737–780.
Kastenbaum, R.J. (1977). *Death, society and human experience* (1st ed.). St. Louis: Mosby.
Kidder, D. (1985, August). National Hospice Study data gathering methods, samples, and approach to examining alternate reimbursement systems. In alternate hospice reimbursement system analyses (pp. II-1–II-8). Report submitted to the Health Care Financing Administration.

Kiston, H., & Morris, R. (1972, Summer). Alternatives to institutional care for the disabled. *The Gerontologist: 12*(2); 139–143.

Kübler-Ross, E. (1969); *On death and dying.* New York: Macmillan.

Lack, S.A., & Buckingham, R.W. (1978). *First American hospice: Three years of home care.* New Haven, CT: Hospice Inc.

Laliberte, L., & Mor. V. (1984, November). Age and family relationship as determinants of medical interventions in a terminally ill population. Presented at The 37th Annual Scientific Meeting of the Gerontological Society of America, San Antonio.

Mor, V. (1986, Fall). Assessing patient outcomes in hospice: what to measure? *The Hospice Journal, 2(3)*; 17–35.

Mor, V., & Hiris, J. (1983). Determinants of site of death among hospice cancer patients. *Journal of Health and Social Behavior, 24*(4), 375–385.

Mor, V., & Kidder, D. (1985). Cost savings in hospice: Final results of the National Hospice Study. *Health Services Research, 20*(4), 407–422.

Mor, V., Laliberte, L., Morris, J.N., & Wiemann, M.C. (1984). The Karnofsky performance status scale: An examination of its reliability and validity in a research setting. *Cancer, 53*(9), 2002–2007.

Mor, V., Masterson-Allen, S., Goldberg, R.J., Cummings, F.J., Glicksman, A.S., & Fretwell, M.D. (1985). The relationship between age at diagnosis and treatments received by cancer patients. *Journal of the American Geriatrics Society, 33*(10), 585–589.

Mor, V., McHorney, C., & Sherwood, S. (1986, February). Secondary morbidity among the recently bereaved. *American Journal of Psychiatry,* 143(*2*), 158–163.

Saunders, C. (1978). Hospice care. *American Journal of Medicine,* 65(5), 726–728.

Sherwood, C., Sherwood, S., & Morris, J.N. (1985, August). The relationship of the formal and informal support systems of the terminally ill. In *Alternate hospice reimbursement system analyses,* (pp. III-1–III-30). Report submitted to the Health Care Financing Administration.

Sherwood, S. (Ed.) (1975). *Long-term care: A handbook for researchers, planners and providers.* New York: Spectrum Publications.

Spector, W.D., & Mor, V. (1984). Utilization and charges for terminal cancer patients in Rhode Island. *Inquiry, 21*(4), 328–337.

Stoddard, S. (1978). *Hospice movement—A better way of caring for the dying.* New York: Stein & Day.

Yancik, R. (Ed.) (1983). *Aging: Volume 24. Perspectives on prevention and treatment of cancer in the elderly.* New York: Raven Press.

CHAPTER 50

Family Care of Impaired Elderly in Japan

Daisaku Maeda

More than 80% of the Japanese middle-aged men and women still believe that the child or the child's spouse should care for their parents even when they become bedridden. Actually, however, the number of the elderly living in institutions is increasing very rapidly. In addition, home care services for older people are being expanded significantly in Japan. This is caused by demographic change and the decreased capability of families to care for their aged parents. The impact of these changes has been so strong that the recent development of institutional and community services cannot fully meet the needs. Since the demographic and social changes will accelerate in the future, many social gerontologists believe that Japan will have to develop a social service system for frail and/or impaired elderly.

TRADITION OF FAMILY CARE OF IMPAIRED OLD PEOPLE

In Japan, as in other East Asian countries, the overwhelming majority of old people live in the same household as their grown children. As shown in Table 50-1, this living arrangement continued to be observed in the 1970s, even in the completely industrialized and urbanized metropolitan sections of Japan where the influence of Western culture is felt much more strongly than in other areas.

What has occurred more recently? Although the proportion of old people living with their children has been decreasing in both urban and rural areas, as shown in Table 50-2, the latest national census (1980) showed that 68.7% of the population aged 65 or over still lived with their children.

Not only do most old people live with their grown children, but also

493

TABLE 50-1. Percentage of Elderly (60 +) Living with Their Children in Urban and Rural Areas, 1973

| | | Having children | | | | |
	Total	Living with children	Living apart from children	Unknown	No children	Unknown
Total	95.6	72.8	22.6	0.2	4.2	0.2
Metropol- itan areas	92.1	67.7	24.1	0.3	7.9	--
Other cities	95.6	70.6	24.9	0.1	4.1	0.3
Rural areas	97.0	77.6	19.0	0.4	2.9	0.1

Source: Data from "*Rojin Jittai Chosa*" ("*The Survey on the Actual Conditions of the Elderly*"). Tokyo: Ministry of Health and Welfare, 1973.

most bedridden older persons are cared for in their children's homes. A recent nationwide study estimated the number of old people aged 65 or over who were bedridden in 1984 at 495,000 (Ministry of Health and Welfare, 1984). Of this number, 326,000 were cared for by their children and 168,000 were hospitalized. In addition, approximately 110,000 persons were living in nursing homes. Altogether, approximately 278,000 elderly were living in hospitals or institutions at that time, a total far lower than the number of bedridden old people cared for in their children's homes.

TABLE 50-2. Decrease in Percentage of Persons 65 Years of Age and Above Living with Their Children[a]

Year	Living with children	Aged couple only	Living alone	Others	Total	Decreasing Rate of "living with children" per year
1970	76.9	12.1	5.5	5.5	100.0	0.88
1975	72.5	15.7	6.9	4.9	100.0	0.82
1980	68.7	18.9	8.2	4.3	100.0	0.76

[a]Persons living in institutions were excluded.

Source: From "*KoKusei Chosi*" ("*National Censuses*"). Tokyo: Office of the Prime Minister, 1970, 1975, and 1980.

TABLE 50-3. Children's Plans for the Care of Their Parents When They Become Bedridden

Planned source of care	For husband's parents ($n = 1,1017$)	For wife's parents ($n = 1,079$)
Parent's spouse	11.1%	8.9%
Respondent himself/ herself	24.4%	10.0%
Respondent's spouse	18.9%	6.8%
Brother	13.8%	18.8%
Brother's spouse	16.9%	31.4%
Sister	2.0%	7.3%
All brothers and sisters	5.8%	8.7%
Other family members or relatives	0.6%	0.7%
Subtotal	93.5%	92.6%
Other resources (paid housekeepers, public home helpers, nursing homes, etc.)	2.9%	1.7%
Don't know	3.7%	5.7%

Source: From *"Rogono Seikatuto Kaigo"* (*"The National Survey on Life and Care in Old Age--1981"*). Tokyo: Section on Aging, Prime Minister's Office, 1982.

OPTIONS OF MIDDLE-AGED JAPANESE PERSONS ON FAMILY CARE OF OLD PEOPLE

Some western social gerontologists have said that the reason that so many bedridden elderly in Japan are cared for by their children is that the number of available nursing home beds is insufficient. It is true that the number of nursing home beds is insufficient, especially in large metropolitan areas like Tokyo. However, the shortage of beds in institutions seems to be only a minor reason for the majority of Japanese bedridden old people being cared for by their children.

A recent nationwide survey of the opinions of middle-aged persons, married men and women between the ages of 30 and 49, studied children's plans for the care of their parents when they become bedridden. As shown in Table 50-3, slightly more than 80% answered that the child or the child's spouse would care for them, and approximately 10% answered that the parent's spouse would provide care. Less than 3% answered that they were planning to depend upon resources other than family members (e.g., a paid housekeeper, public home-help services, nursing homes, etc.). Thus, it is clear that in Japan the overwhelming majority of middle-aged persons still firmly believe that the care of bedridden older parents is their responsibility.

DEVELOPMENT OF PUBLIC SERVICES FOR THE IMPAIRED ELDERLY

Even though attitudes toward caring for aged parents have undergone very little alteration in Japan, noteworthy changes in the actual care of the aged have occurred. One is the increasing number of elderly in social welfare institutions. Since 1970, the total number of beds in all kinds of institutions for the aged (including those for ambulant but frail elderly) more than doubled, from 75,400 to 191,000 in 1983, although the increase in the proportion of institutionalized elderly was less conspicuous, from 1.02% to 1.60%. Another change is the rapid expansion of home care services in the community for older people who need some assistance in their daily living. Japan had no home care services before 1962, when the National Financial Support Program for Home-Help Services was established. Since then, three national programs have been established: Provision for Special Equipment Service in 1969, Short-Term Stay Service in 1978, and Day-Care Service in 1979. The Day-Care Service, however, is still in the experimental stage, and available in only 96 locations throughout Japan as of this year (1985). In 1970, the number of home helpers throughout Japan was 6,100. Fifteen years later in 1985, the number had increased 3.5 times, to 21,600. During these 15 years, the ratio of the number of home helpers for persons aged 65 and over had increased from one per 1,210 to one per 560 at present.

BACKGROUND OF THE RECENT EXPANSION OF PUBLIC SERVICES FOR THE ELDERLY

Why has Japan expanded social services for the care of the elderly so rapidly? Two aspects must be considered: First, demographic changes, and second, the decreased capability of families to care for their aged parents.

One feature of the demographic changes was the increase in the number of unmarried and/or childless old people along with the increase in the total size of the aged population. In addition, because of improvements in the general standard of living, as well as the development of knowledge and skills in the medical sciences, the number of very old persons aged 80 years or above has increased significantly as is shown in Table 50-4. The more advanced age of dependent older

TABLE 50–4. Index of Increase in Number of the Older
Persons, 1950-2000

Age	1950	1975	1980	2000
60-69	100	189	205	356
70-79	100	214	254	468
80+	100	323	436	1,025

parents means that the age of their caretaking children is also higher, and in many cases children themselves are already old and their own health is not good enough to provide needed care.

Several social factors have contributed to the decreased capability of families to care for aged parents. First, a great migration of the younger generations from rural to urban areas has occurred as a result of changes in the industrial structure of Japanese society. Thus, even in rural areas, where once almost all older people were taken care of in their children's homes, the number of the elderly who must seek public services for assistance in their daily living has been increasing.

On the urban side, the development of industry brought about a dispersion of industrial areas. Thus, persons who were born and raised in urban locations often find it difficult to get a job in the urban area where their older parents live. As a result, in urban as well as rural areas, the proportion of old people living alone or with their spouse only has increased.

Another social factor is a growing number of working women. Many of the married, middle-aged women who were once the most dependable caretakers of dependent older parents are now working outside their homes.

Finally, the number of children in Japan has decreased rapidly since 1950. As a result, persons with few children are now gradually entering the aged population. Obviously, when old people have few children, their chances of depending on them are reduced. This factor will make the need for services for old people, both community and institutional, more acute in the future.

DIFFICULTIES OF FAMILIES CARING FOR IMPAIRED AGED PARENTS

To plan effectively and implement social services for impaired elderly, knowing who is actually caring for them and under what conditions is vitally important. Recently, a number of such studies have been conducted in Japan. The results of two of these investigations deserve special attention.

TABLE 50-5. Caretakers of Bedridden Older Persons

Caretaker	Bedridden	
	Males (%)	Females (%)
Spouse	61.0	11.4
Children (including both sexes)	10.8	27.7
Son's wife	21.7	50.4
Grandchildren (including both sexes)	0.8	2.7
Others, unknown	5.7	7.8

Source: From *"Rojin Kaigo Chosa Hokokusho"* (*"Report on the National Survey on Caretakers for the Elderly"*). Tokyo: National Council of Social Welfare, 1979.

The question of who is caring for bedridden older people is answered in Table 50-5, which describes caretakers in relation to the gender of the bedridden elderly. As seen in the Table, 61% of bedridden older men are cared for by their aged wives, and 21.7% are cared for by their sons' wives. On the other hand, 50.4% of bedridden older women are cared for by their sons' wives, and 27.7% are cared for by their own children.

In themselves, these figures reveal several very serious problems. First, the average age of the caretakers is high. About one fourth of the caretakers of bedridden old people are aged 60 and over, including 3% who are aged 80 and over. Second, the majority of caretakers are sons' wives or married daughters, who are generally at the prime of life and are busy with many duties such as work and the care of their own children. Third, in some cases, bedridden elderly are cared for by unmarried sons or daughters who are usually also working full-time. Because of the social pressure dictating that children should take care of their aged parents, they seldom place their parents in institutions. Very often these caregivers do not have the opportunity to marry.

Further evidence of the difficult conditions experienced by Japanese caretakers can be seen in Table 50-6, derived from a study conducted in Tokyo by the Sociology Department of the Tokyo Metropolitan Institute of Gerontology in 1981. This table is a cross-tabulation of physically impaired old people living in the community, classified both by degree of impairment and by degree of difficulty experienced by caretaking families.

From the viewpoint of ascertaining the unmet needs of impaired elderly and their families, the cases in cell "P1-F1" of Table 50-6— that is, the most seriously impaired older persons cared for in a family

TABLE 50–6. Prevalence Rate of Impaired Older Persons by Degree of Physical Impairment (P1-P4) and by Degree of Difficulty of Caring Families (F1-F3)[a]

Degree of impairment	Degree of difficulty of caring families					
	Very difficult (F1)	Slightly difficult (F2)	No difficulty (F3)	Unable to care or not caring	Degree of difficulty not known	Totals
Most seriously impaired (P1)	6.8	2.6	---	---	0.2	9.6
Seriously impaired (P2)	16.8	2.8	---	1.4	---	21.0
Moderately impaired (P3)	20.5	8.1	0.2	7.2	---	35.9
Slightly impaired (P4)	5.4	1.2	0.2	6.5	0.2	13.5
Totals	49.5	14.7	0.4	15.1	0.4	80.0

[a]The number in each cell indicates the prevalence rate of the category per 1,000 persons aged 65 + .

Source: From *"Zaitaku Shoqai Rojinto Sona Kazokuno Seikatu Jittai, Oyobi Shakaifukushi: Need-ni Kansuru Chosa Kenkyuu (3)—Tokyono Shitamachino Baai" ("Study of the Needs of Impaired Old People and Their Families (3)—In the Case of the Older Sections of Tokyo")*. Tokyo: Tokyo Metropolitan Institute of Gerontology, Sociology Department, 1983.

with the most serious difficulty—require special attention. As shown in Table 50-6, these cases account for 6.8 per 1,000 of the population aged 65 and over living in the community. It is quite clear that these persons should be institutionalized as soon as possible for their own well-being as well as for the well-being of their caretakers. However, the availability of nursing homes is seriously inadequate, especially in large metropolitan areas. Recently, more than 100 nursing homes have been opened each year throughout Japan, but due to the rapid increase of the number of very old, frail, and impaired elderly, the shortage has not been significantly reduced. Thus, even if older persons and their families who are most in need wish to use a nursing home, they usually must wait for a long time before the elderly individual can be admitted.

It should also be noted in Table 50-6 that the proportion in the F1 category, families whose degree of difficulty in caretaking is very serious, accounted for more than 60% of all families caring for the impaired elderly.

Not all of these families need external care services immediately. It is quite likely, however, that the families in categories P1 and P2, those caring for "the most seriously" and "seriously" impaired older persons, do need some form of outside support. Because community services to support these families are not very well developed, the hardships that they experience are often very serious. The term "family care" has a beautiful and noble connotation, but in many cases, it is accompanied by the painful sacrifice of the caretakers, and the quality of care is frequently poor.

SUBJECTIVE DIFFICULTIES OF FAMILIES CARING FOR THE IMPAIRED ELDERLY

In the same Sociology Department survey, we also studied the subjective difficulties of families caring for the impaired elderly, which were measured with a scale composed of ten statements on the subjective difficulties in providing care to the impaired elderly. As shown in Table 50-7, responses were measured on a 4-point scale, in which options ranged from 0 (no difficulty), 1 (difficulty), 2 (considerable difficulty), through 3 (severe difficulty).

As shown in the bottom row of the table, the proportion of caregiving families who did not express any difficulty was less than one out of five of the families caring for the impaired elderly. The difficulties that tend to be expressed most frequently are "Family cannot go out together," "Giving care makes me tired mentally and physically," and "I have no control of my time." In these items, more than half of caregiving families expressed more or less difficulty. In the following six items, more than one fourth of the families expressed a difficulty: "Cannot attend ceremonial occasions, or handle urgent or unexpected affairs"; "Cannot attend to domestic duties as needed"; "Cannot sleep well because of care at night"; "Cannot go out to work, cannot get a good job, or cannot attend closely enough to the family business"; "The economic burden is heavy"; and "There is a danger of mishandling fire."

When the physical impairment of the elderly is more severe, families tend to express subjective difficulties in 8 items out of these 10. Especially when families are caring for the elderly who are "mostly in bed," the proportion of those expressing subjective difficulties is very high. For example, more than 80% of such families expressed difficulties in "Family cannot all go out together," "Giving care makes me tired mentally and physically," and "I have no control of my time."

It should be noted that when the mental impairment of the elderly is severe families tend to express subjective difficulties in all 10 items. When the number of symptoms of mental disturbance is five or over, the degree of subjective difficulties is the highest.

TABLE 50-7. Measurement of Subjective Difficulties
in Providing Care to the Impaired Elderly

Statement	There is no difficulty.	There is some difficulty.	There is considerable difficulty.	There is severe difficulty.
			(multiple answer)	
1. Cannot attend to domestic duties as needed.	65.9%	19.0%	7.4%	4.1%
2. Cannot go out to work, cannot get a good job, or cannot attend closely enough to the family business.	74.4%	10.7%	9.1%	5.8%
3. Family cannot go out together.	38.8%	28.4%	17.3%	15.5%
4. My home is not harmonious enough.	86.0%	9.2%	3.3%	1.5%
5. There is a danger of mishandling fire.	75.1%	11.9%	5.8%	7.1%
6. Cannot sleep well because of care at night.	73.1%	12.4%	9.6%	4.8%
7. Giving care makes me tired mentally and physically.	44.2%	21.8%	18.8%	15.2%
8. The economic burden is heavy.	74.6%	11.7%	8.6%	5.1%
9. I have no control of my time.	47.0%	21.3%	16.8%	15.0%
10. Cannot attend ceremonial occasions or handle urgent or unexpected affairs.	59.4%	20.8%	10.9%	8.9%
No difficulties		18.3%		

With regard to the type of household, it should be noted that those who have young children are most likely to express difficulties in "all going out together," and the households composed of only an aged couple tend to express that "caregiving makes me tired mentally and physically." It is also to be noted that households composed of only older persons and unmarried children tend to express difficulties in relation to their occupation and economic burdens. Another noteworthy observation is that the longer the length of care, the more the families tend to express difficulties in a greater number of items.

SUBJECTIVE NEEDS VS. OBJECTIVE NEEDS FOR SERVICES

In this survey we also studied the subjective needs for social services of the families who are caring for the impaired elderly and found that the number of families who expressed such needs subjectively was much smaller than the number of those who were diagnosed, objectively, as having needs. For example, our study showed that less than half of the families who were judged as needing home help service stated that they wanted that service.

This point has important implications for the estimation of the future demands for social services for the impaired elderly and their families, and these implicit needs will no doubt become more and more explicit as the number of impaired older persons increases and as our society continues to change. The rising number of married, middle-aged women expected to enter the labor force in the future seems to be especially important to the shift from implicit to explicit needs. This implies that the estimation of the scope of social services for the impaired elderly and their families based only on demographic and social changes should be modified to a great extent. Thus the author believes that even Japan, which has somehow succeeded so far in saving the great amount of economic and social costs otherwise needed for the social care of the impaired elderly by preserving the East Asian tradition of family care of the impaired elderly, will undoubtedly have to develop various types of institutional and community care services as have other industrialized nations in Europe and North America. However, Japan's relative scope of needed social services would be somewhat smaller than that of other advanced countries even at the beginning of the next century.

REFERENCES

Ministry of Health and Welfare. (1973).*Rojin Jittai Chosa (The Survey on the Actual Conditions of the Elderly)*. Tokyo: Author.

Ministry of Health and Welfare. (1984). *Showa 59-nen Kosei Gyosei Kiso Chosa (The 1984 Fundamental Survey for Health and Welfare Administration)*. Tokyo: Author.

National Council of Social Welfare. (1979). *Rojin Kaigo Chosa Hokokusho (Report of the National Survey on Caretakers of the Elderly)*. Tokyo: Author.

Office of the Prime Minister. (1970). *Kokusei Chosa* (National Censuses). Tokyo: Author.

Office of the Prime Minister. (1975). *Kokusei Chosa*. (National Censuses). Tokyo: Author.

Office of the Prime Minister. (1980). *Kokusei Chosa*. (National Censuses). Tokyo: Author.

Section on Aging of the Prime Minister's Office. (1982). *Rogono Seikatuto Kaigo (The National Survey on the Life and Care in Old Age—1981)*. Tokyo: Author.

Tokyo Metropolitan Institute of Gerontology (Department of Sociology). (1983). *Zaitaku Shogai Rojinto Sono Kazokuno Seikatu Jittai, oyobi Shakaifukushi Need-ni kansuru Chosa Kenkyuu (3)—Tōkyono Shitamachino Baai (Study of the Needs of Impaired Old People and their Families (3)—In the case of the older sections of Tokyo)*. Tokyo: Author.

CHAPTER 51

Conceptual and Methodological Issues in Using Service-Based Data for Longitudinal Research

Gloria M. Gutman, Annette Stark,
Dean Uyeno, Dan Lane

Service provider records are a potentially rich data source for longitudinal research. Working effectively with them, however, presents a number of challenges. This chapter describes these challenges as encountered in a prospective longitudinal study of clients ($n = 3518$) admitted to British Columbia's Long-Term Care (LTC) Program in 1978 in two health unit areas, one urban and one semirural. The data source, files maintained by LTC Program staff, begins with the client's initial assessment. As reviews, reassessments, transfers, level changes, and discharges occur, they are added to the file. The study was designed to extend knowledge concerning the disability level and the length of stay in various LTC placements as an aid to future resource allocation and planning. Analytic techniques used to date include Multivariate Analysis of Variance (MANOVA), logistic regression, Automatic Interaction Detector (AID), Theta Automatic Interaction Detector (THAID), and discriminant analysis as well as Markov chain modeling. The effectiveness of these techniques in providing answers to key research questions is discussed.

Campbell (1984) describes four basic panel study designs. In the first

The research described in this paper was supported by a grant from the British Columbia Health Care Research Foundation. Mr. Lane was the recipient of a Postgraduate Scholarship from the National Sciences and Engineering Research Council of Canada. In addition, the cooperation and support of the Ministry of Health, Province of British Columbia is gratefully acknowledged.

503

type (Type I), a representative sample of the population as a whole is
followed from an arbitrary starting point to an arbitrary end point.
Type II is similar to Type I except that the age range is restricted. In
Type III, every subject experiences a cohort defining event at baseline,
prior to baseline, or at a fixed point subsequent to baseline. In Type
IV, it is anticipated that some or all of the subjects will undergo an
event but the timing of the event is not known in advance and will vary
across subjects.

The study that is the focus of this chapter most closely approximates
a Type III design. The cohort-defining event is admission to long-term
care. Subjects ($n = 3,518$) were all clients admitted to British Columbia's (B.C.) Long-Term Care (LTC) Program in two health unit areas,
one urban and one semi-rural, during calendar year 1978.

BACKGROUND

On January 1, 1978, the Long-Term Care (LTC) program was introduced by the Ministry of Health in British Columbia. The primary
aim of the Program is to permit those who qualify for services to
remain in their own homes for as long as it is possible and practical to
do so. Placement in an approved community care facility or admission
to a hospital-based Extended Care Unit (ECU) is arranged when home
care is no longer possible (Ministry of Health, 1978).

Five levels of care have been defined and each can be provided either
at home or in a facility. The levels, from lowest to highest, are: Personal Care (PC); three levels of Intermediate Care (I_1, I_2, I_3); and
extended care (EC). Personal Care clients are independently mobile
and able to eat and toilet without assistance but may require minimal
help with bathing and dressing. Such clients may be mildly confused
and forgetful but do not require daily professional supervision (see
Figure 51-1). Those assessed as requiring one of the three levels of
Intermediate Care are more impaired. Although technically still independently mobile, these clients may require assistance with toileting,
have mild to moderate mental impairment, and require daily professional supervision of medication, application of special appliances, etc.
Extended Care implies that the client is severely disabled and in need
of 24-hour skilled nursing care.

For those receiving service at home, much of the care is provided by
family members. As level of care increases, the decision concerning
home or facility placement is increasingly dependent on the presence,
competence, and willingness of family members to provide care at
home. The Program provides for increasing hours of homemaker support as level of care increases. Home nursing and other professional
support services are negotiated on an individual basis, dependent on

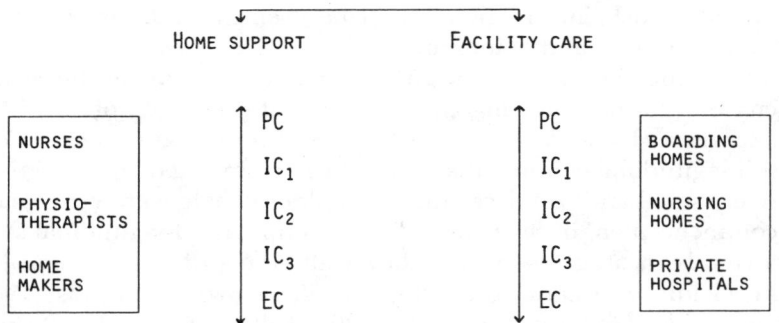

FIGURE 51-1. Levels and locations of care and service providers: BC Long-Term Care Program.

client need, service availability, and relative cost compared with facility care. Decisions regarding admission to the Program, level of care, and location at which services will be provided are based on a standard preadmission assessment conducted by trained program staff. This staff also provides the placement and monitors clients' progress over time.

RATIONALE FOR THE STUDY

The mandate to create the LTC Program was given only 8 months before it began (Bainbridge, 1980) and that the Program commenced *on a province-wide basis.* There were no small-scale demonstration projects that preceded it; no pilot studies. While the Program was created on the assumption that there was unmet need, the full extent of that need, 38,000 clients in the first year, was unknown. While it was intended that client records would be computerized, this did not happen at the outset, in part because there were questions as to what should be included in the electronic records.

One of the original purposes of our study, in fact, was to provide the Ministry of Health with guidance as to which variables to include in the planned province-wide data set. The other two main purposes were to provide the Ministry with (a) a detailed description of Program clients in the initial year and (b) an indication of the efficiency and effectiveness of the Program particularly in regard to the record system and the time frame for receipt of appropriate care. Midway through the first year of the study it became clear, however, that this was a unique data base which, if extended longitudinally, could provide important information concerning the length of stay in various care placements. Such information would be useful as a basis for future resource allocation and planning.

At the time the LTC program began and even today, there is a paucity of information concerning patterns of utilization of long-term care services (Kane & Kane, 1980; Mackeprang & Brauer, 1977). Most longitudinal studies that have been completed are based on relatively small and/or select samples of older people who were well at the commencement of the study. While a number of longitudinal studies currently in progress include chronically impaired subjects (Applebaum, Seidl, & Austin, 1980; Eggert, Bowlyow, & Nichols, 1980; Havens, 1980; Hodgson & Quinn, 1980; Skellie & Coan, 1980), most are focused on clients receiving care at home. The National Nursing Home Survey (National Center for Health Statistics, 1977) records the number of deaths, duration of last stay, and certain aspects of the functional ability of those who die while in long-term care. That survey is, however, by definition restricted to an institutionalized population and does not track clients over time. In contrast, our study includes clients receiving care both at home and in facilities and has the capacity to monitor their experience in the Long-Term Care Program from admission until death.

DATA SOURCE

In November and December 1977, immediately prior to the start of the Program, assessments were conducted on all persons receiving care. These we call "original" clients. Subsequent to January 1, 1978, all persons seeking entry in the LTC Program received the same assessment; these are called "new" clients. Current Program policy dictates that clients will be reviewed no later than 90 days after placement in a facility or commencement of home support services and every 12 months thereafter, or earlier if the client's condition or circumstances change (Ministry of Health, 1978).

The cornerstone of the assessment procedure is a form, LTC-1, on which assessors record their observations. Like many other such tools used with the elderly and/or chronically ill, e.g. Duke, 1978,—The Grauer and Birnbom Geriatric Functional Rating Scale (Linn, 1967), the Linn Rapid Disability Rating Scale (Grauer & Birnbom, 1975),— the LTC-1 includes scales on which to record the client's ability to see, hear, and communicate; ability to bathe, dress, feed, ambulate, transfer, and control bowel and bladder; ability to perform a variety of activities necessary to maintain an independent household such as shopping, preparing meals, performing routine housekeeping tasks; and assessment of level of mental functioning. The form also includes space in which the assessor describes medical problems, medications, and special dietary needs; problem behaviors (e.g., client wanders, client is aggressive or destructive); the client's current living situation; the degree of support available from family and friends; and the support services he is receiving or needs.

The data source is client files maintained by Program staff and made available to us with names removed. These files contain a copy of all written documentation pertaining to each of the 3,518 clients in the study, (1,867 original and 1,651 new clients) beginning with the initial assessment. As reviews, reassessments, transfers, level changes, and discharges occurred, they were added to the client's file.

Two types of information exist in our computerized data base. The first is information collected on the LTC-1 at the initial assessment, all 110 items have been laboriously coded and input. The second type of information, from the longitudinal file, describes clients' care experiences since entering the LTC Program including acute hospital admissions, level-of-care changes, placement changes, discharges, readmissions, and deaths.

ANALYSES UNDERTAKEN TO DATE

The First Studies

In the initial stage of the study we described the sociodemographic, health, and functional characteristics of the clients in our sample and the workload they generated for the Program (assessments, admissions, changes, discharges, etc.) in calendar year 1978, the first year the Program was in operation. This resulted in six technical reports that were submitted to the Ministry of Health (describing initial analyses of data). Also, in this first stage, in an effort to provide the Ministry with guidance as to which variables to include in the planned province-wide data set, as well as to ascertain whether there were a reduced number of variables that would still allow consistent placement decisions, multivariate analyses of data derived from the LTC-1 were performed. Variables identified in these analyses as most important to decisions regarding level of care were: Ability to dress, transfer, cooperate with medications and treatments, ambulate, and control bowel and bladder. Using a subset of clients ($n = 250$), a comparison was made of actual placement with that based on the reduced number of variables derived from the analysis.

While the results of the analyses indicate that about two thirds of the variation in levels could be accounted for with a set of just six variables, and while it was found that using these variables about 60% of clients could be correctly classified with an additional 20% being classified within one level of actual placement) the analyses scheme was by no means totally explanatory and classification accuracy varied considerably between levels.

The latter finding was consistent with data obtained by Walter and Nigh (1980) using a more recent version of the LTC-1. In their study, discriminant analyses were performed on assessment data derived from 1,450 clients residing in an urban unit different from the one in which our study was conducted. A subset of 10 variables was identified that accounted for a considerable proportion of the variation. As in our study, however, while highly predictive for Personal and Extended Care clients, "hit" rates were poor in the three Intermediate Care levels.

One implication of findings from the two studies is that a short form might be developed for purposes of screening for those in need of Personal Care. This, in fact, is what was recommended. While we agreed that this was one possible means of reducing the work load of assessors, we were reluctant to recommend that this procedure be followed in view of the multipurpose nature of the LTC-1. With its present limitations, it provides information to four sources: the central registry, the local registry, the service provider, and the assessor. While some variables now included may not play a major role in level and placement decisions, they may be of considerable value to service providers. A good example of variables that fall into this category are those relating to problem behaviors. While only a small proportion of clients may, for example, be wanderers or be violent or destructive, unknowing admission of these persons into a care facility setting could cause problems. Inclusion of a fairly broad range of variables is, of course, also important from the point of view of identifying and communicating the service needs of the client as well as in providing a record against which to evaluate changes.

What was finally recommended most strongly was that the criteria for placement in the Intermediate Care levels be firmly identified and, if this could not be done easily, that consideration be given to collapsing the three Intermediate Care levels into two or even one.

In terms of the proposed province-wide data set, it was obvious that with a caseload in the first year of 38,000 clients, there was no way the government could, as we had done, code all 110 items on the LTC-1. While we could not provide a magic set of variables that would allow quick and correct classification of all clients in all units, a subset was recommended that would at least allow a check for marked placement discrepancies and that may be of value in identifying staffing needs. Also identified, for subsequent revisions of the LTC-1, were those portions of the form that tended not to be filled out and/or were redundant, ambiguous, or poorly scaled.

THE 12-MONTH OUTCOME STUDIES

The first studies were essentially cross-sectional. In the second stage of the study, analyses were extended longitudinally. The first time period examined was the initial 12 months after admission to LTC. We first examined the number of deaths in this period, paying special attention to those that occurred subsequent to a change in level and/or placement and comparing the characteristics of survivors and decedents (Guttman, Stark, Witney & McCashin, 1982). Next, the relationship between acute care hospitalization and long-term care was examined to determine: (a) the number of admissions to LTC directly from acute-care settings versus the number entering directly from the community, (b) the number of clients hospitalized in the first 12 months after admission to LTC and (c) the outcomes of these hospitalizations (Stark, Gutman, & McCashin, 1982). In a third paper, the characteristics of clients generating a high Program work load in the first 12 months postadmission were examined (Stark, Layton, Gutman, & Brothers, 1984).

In this stage of the study a substudy (Stark, Gutman, & Brothers, 1982) was conducted that addressed the question of reliability of assessments, which is a particular problem noted by Kane, Olsen, Thetford, and Byrnes (1976), when service records are used for research purposes. In this substudy, a systematic sample of 246 clients was seen by a Program assessor for either a preadmission assessment ($n = 47$) or a review ($n = 199$) and within 5 days were revisited by a study assessor. Consistent with our previous difficulty in establishing single variable scores that discriminate between care levels at the level-of-care extremes (i.e., Extended Care and Personal Care), agreement between the two assessors was excellent. It was only fair, however, in the Intermediate Care range, although it should be mentioned that generally, there was only a one care level difference between assessors.

THE LONG-TERM OUTCOME STUDIES

The third stage of our work focused on long-term outcomes. As shown in Figure 51-2, these include both moves within the LTC program and discharges. A paper (Stark, Kliewer, Gutman, & McCashin, 1984) describing the level and placement of subjects and the degree of sample attrition 3 years subsequent to admission to LTC was published. Recently, we have described mortality rates (Gutman, Stark, Jackson, & McCashin, 1984) and client transfers (Stark & Gutman, 1985) for the 5 year postadmission period. One is struck by the fact that despite their advanced age at admission (X = 74.7 years; SD, 14.6), 5 years

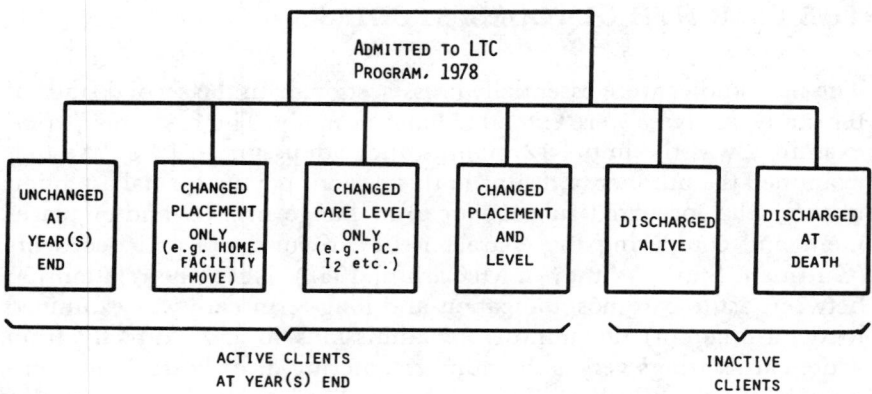

FIGURE 51-2. Possible year-end outcomes for study clients admitted to the B.C. Long-Term Care Program, 1978.

later one third (32.8%) of the clients new to care in 1978 are still in the Program with 14.1% unchanged from place and level of care admission (see Table 51-1 and 51-2).

WORK IN PROGRESS: THE FORECASTING STUDIES

The budget ramifications of governmental financial participation in the provision of long-term care, make accurate forecasts of future long-term care needs essential. In the fourth and current stage of our study,

TABLE 51–1. Status of Clients 5-Year Postadmission ($n = 1,653$)

Level of Care at admission (in 1978)	Still in LTC Home[a] ($n = 426$)	Still in LTC Facility ($n = 117$)	Discharged[b] Home ($n = 333$)	Discharged[b] Facility ($n = 133$)	Dead Home ($n = 483$)	Dead Facility ($n = 162$)
PC	36.6%	40.9%	27.3%	33.3%	36.2%	25.8%
IC$_1$	39.1%	23.5%	21.7%	30.9%	39.2%	45.7%
IC$_2$	23.9%	15.8%	28.3%	34.2%	47.8%	50.0%
IC$_3$	20.4%	23.8%	29.5%	21.4%	50.0%	54.8%
EC	20.0%	9.3%	36.7%	36.9%	43.3%	53.8%
Total	34.3%	28.4%	26.8%	32.3%	38.9%	39.3%

[a]Location at admission;
[b]Discharged and still alive at the end of year 5.

TABLE 51-2. Percentage Distribution of Clients Unchanged (Level and Place of Care) at 1, 3, and 5 Years Postadmission

Admitted to care	End of year	Level of care at admission					Total
		PC	IC$_1$	IC$_2$	IC$_3$	EC	
At home	1	59.8	52.5	33.3	40.9	51.7	54.4
	3	25.8	22.1	13.8	11.4	20.0	23.0
(n = 1,241)	5	15.1	16.7	9.4	6.8	15.0	14.5
In facility	1	57.1	44.4	39.5	35.7	14.1	44.0
	3	28.8	21.0	5.3	11.9	4.7	19.6
(n = 412)	5	19.9	12.3	5.3	11.9	1.5	13.3

the development of valid and reliable means to forecast the numbers of clients likely to require each level of care in the B.C. system have become primary objectives.

Our initial efforts focused on forecasting the "career" of clients already in the data base—their various changes in place and level of care, discharges, and deaths. Using clients newly admitted to care in 1978 in our two health units, forecasts were developed using three methods: moving average growth, regression analysis, and Markov chains. In brief, the moving average growth method produces forecasts based on past rates of growth for a given level of care. Regression analysis depends on the minimization of the sum of squared errors about a line of best fit for the time series of the number of clients by level of care.

Markov chain analysis, however, requires added explanation because its use is not widespread. In Markov chain analysis, one simultaneously considers all the possible states (in this case, the states are levels of care). If one knows the number in each state in one time period, the number in each of those same states in the next period can be estimated from knowledge of the proportions of clients in each state that either stay in the same state or move to another state. For example, suppose there are 10 people who are well and 8 who are sick today, and we know that 20% of the well people will be sick by tomorrow, and 50% of the people who are currently sick will get well. Then, we can estimate the number of people who will be well tomorrow as:

$$80\% \times 10 + 50\% \times 8$$

This equals 8 + 4 which in turn equals 12 people.

The trick is to get good estimates of these percentages. In our first data set, we only knew the aggregate numbers of clients in each level of care at the anniversary dates of their admission to LTC. We were thus forced to employ sophisticated computer-based optimization techniques to determine reasonable estimates of these percentages. When we did this we found that the Markov model (which consists solely of these percentages) fit our data better than the other two methods and produced excellent forecasts when compared with the data we had set aside for test purposes. Our results are given in the paper "Forecasting Demand for Long-Term Care Services," which has been accepted for publication by the journal *Health Services Research* (Uyeno, 1985).

In a second study, the transitional behavior of *seven* different cohorts, were examined. These cohorts included the 1978 original clients (i.e., those clients already receiving some form of care at the inception of the LTC program), the 1978 new clients (i.e., those who entered the LTC system during its first year of operation) and the 1979 through 1983 cohorts (representing clients who entered the system in our health unit areas during each of these years). Data were also disaggregated by sex, by health unit, and by age. Estimates of percentages were based on the changes in levels of care of individual clients over the period 1978 to 1983. With this information, there was no need to optimize since one could see exactly how many clients went from one state to another from year to year. For each pair of years, then, one could get an estimate of all the percentages required. There are quite a few of these percentages (132) since there are 12 different states, including exit by death. By looking at the percentages from successive pairs of years, one could increase the amount of information with which we could estimate the actual underlying percentages. The outcome of this process was that estimates were maximum likelihood estimators, a statistical term that implies that as the sample size grows, the estimate approaches the true value and, furthermore, it approaches it more quickly than other possible estimators.

The results of this study (Lane, Uyeno, Stark, Kliewer & Gutman, 1985) were even better than in our first study. Tight confidence intervals on estimates of number in each level of care of less than $\pm 10\%$ for levels of care with 200 or more clients were observed.

Based on these findings, our feeling is that the quality of the forecasts provided by Markov analysis is sufficiently good that the approach should be considered seriously by any organization desiring better information for making long-term care program decisions.

CONCLUSION

Before concluding, our purposes in presenting this chapter should be highlighted. Our first purpose was to draw attention to both the content and methods of the study. It is important that we share information as it evolves and that we have input on study methods from other researchers. How, for example, does one maintain the "real world" distribution of clients while still ensuring sufficient data for valid analyses?

A second purpose was to raise the level of awareness concerning the potential of service-generated data for long-term care research and to point out some of the limitations. As noted in Kane et al. (1976), two key concerns in our project are the reliability of the assessors and the instruments. There is some question as to whether several assessors would reach the same decision concerning clients' level of care and service needs, particularly in the Intermediate Care range. While establishing high levels of inter-rater reliability is readily acknowledged as essential to good research, it must be recognized that in a community care setting, test–retest situations are difficult to arrange. There are, of course, other methods of addressing this issue; split-half reliability coefficients, for example, can be calculated when appropriately constructed data collection instruments permit. However, although the LTC-1, assessment form used in this program is lengthy and informative, it lacks design sophistication. Measurement scales for variables describing medical background, mental health, dental care, communication, activities of daily living, and sociodemographic information are nominal and pseudo-ordinal at best.

Another problem we have had to contend with concerns what Campbell and Stanley (1966) term "instrumentation threats." This refers to changes in the measuring instruments during the course of a study. The form used for assessments in British Columbia (i.e., the LTC-1) has already been modified once and may be again. The changes that were made may simplify things for assessors and service providers but they complicate researchers' lives. For example, while the content areas in the revised version remain the same, the scaling of some items has been changed. The result is that data from some parts of the assessment form cannot be used in the longitudinal study or, if used, have to be used in a more global way than we would have liked (e.g., by collapsing categories on the old form to make them consistent with the new form). Even more problematic, however, is the fact that in most cases at review, rather than using the full assessment form, only a narrative note is added to the file, markedly reducing the amount of data available for analysis.

Another problem for us are differences between health units and between the original and new subgroups in the study. Almost from the first, it was apparent that every analysis would have to be done at least twice—once for each unit separately and then again, if the data permitted, for the two units combined. A problem presented by separate analyses is that, despite the large number of subjects in the study, some cells (especially in Unit B) have a very small n (i.e., 6 or 7 subjects). The difference between units also, of course, raises the issue of generalizability. The health units to be studied were selected for their accessibility and the available mix of services, not because they were necessarily representative. Is it the clients or the decisions of the Program staff in the two units that differ? While it is possible that what we are observing are very real rural–urban differences, this needs to be empirically determined. It has been impossible to test inter-rater reliability between the two units because of their geographic separation. We therefore are always on the alert for data from other health units in British Columbia that will permit a cross-check.

We also have to guard constantly against fragmenting the data, both conceptually and in terms of analysis. This is the old "missing the forest for the trees" problem. Sometimes one misses key trends by being overly concerned about taking all the variables and subvariables into consideration and/or by cutting the data too thinly in terms of the time period analyzed. Although ours is a rich data base, there are two further limitations that should be mentioned.

1.   There is a lack of precise diagnostic information. This is because physicians are not actively involved in the assessment and placement of clients. Rather, these functions are performed by Program staff (usually nurses, physio- or occupational therapists or social workers).

2.   Clients admitted to hospital-based Extended Care Units (ECUs) are not part of the data set. This is a function of the different placement and payment systems of the two jurisdictions within the Ministry of Health—LTC/Home Care and Hospital Programs—which provide Extended Care. A further deterrent to inclusion is the different information system for ECU clients. The available data, therefore, underestimate the number of persons admitted to the highest level of care in the study communities. In addition, clients who move from the LTC program to an ECU are recorded in data available to us simply as "discharged." From a methodological perspective, this creates no difficulties, since the LTC Program data set remains complete and all deaths are included, wherever they occur. The omission is frustrating, however, for those who are interested in the total long-term care scene.

Despite problems such as these, given the dearth of information concerning the characteristics of clients receiving long-term care at home and in facilities, and of their progress over time, the study has been a worthwhile endeavour and has yielded much useful information. Furthermore, we are confident that all meaningful contacts between clients and program staff are recorded since there are incentives within the system for activities such as reassessments and especially because most of the change data are required for payment to service providers. This is a powerful incentive for completeness.

While there are limitations in the use of service-generated data for research purposes, the advantages outweigh the disadvantages. Among the advantages is generation of substudies focused on specific aspects of client status, health care, and program management. In our data set, for example, we are concerned about the possible under-reporting of acute care hospitalizations for clients placed in Home Care, about the lack of detail in the recording of medical problems, and about the specifics of the supports that facilitate maintenance of LTC clients at home for long periods of time. Each of these topics, and others, could, however, be investigated in rigorous studies developed around a sample of the clients in this study or of those in the now-existent, larger provincial data base.

REFERENCES

Applebaum, R., Seidl, F.W., & Austin, C.D. (1980). The Wisconsin Community Care Organization: Preliminary findings from the Milwaukee experiment. *Gerontologist, 20*(3-Pt.1), 350–355.

Bainbridge, J. (1980). British Columbia's long-term care program: The first two years. *Health Management Forum, 1,* 28–36.

Campbell, R.T. (1984, June 11). *Integrating conceptualization, design, and analysis in panel studies of the life course.* Paper presented at a workshop on Methodological Issues in Aging Research at the National Institutes of Health.

Campbell, D.T., & Stanley, J.E. (1966). *Experimental and quasi-experimental designs for research,* Chicago: Rand McNally.

Duke University (1978). *Multidimensional functional assessment: The OARS methodology,* (2nd ed.). *Center for the Study of Aging and Human Development,* Durham, N.C.

Eggert, G.M., Bowlyow, J.E., & Nichols, C.W. (1980). Gaining control of the long-term care system: First returns from the ACCESS experiment. *Gerontologist, 20*(3-Pt.1), 356–363.

Grauer, H. & Birnbom, F.A. (1975). A geriatric functional rating scale to determine the need for institutional care. *Journal of the American Geriatrics Society, 23*(10), 472–476.

Gutman, G.M., Stark, A.J., Jackson, C., & McCashin, B. (1984, November 1-4). *A half-empty or a half-full cup: Mortality rates 5 years after admission to a long-term care program.* Paper presented at the Annual Meeting of the Canadian Association on Gerontology, Vancouver, B.C.

Gutman, G.M., Stark, A.J., Witney, G., & McCashin, B. (1982). Deaths within the first year of admission to long-term care. *Canadian Journal on Aging, 1*(3,4), 3–11.

Havens, B.J. (1980). A longitudinal study of elderly Manitobans. *Essence, 3*(3), 125–142.

Hodgson, J.H., & Quinn, J.L. (1980). The impact of the triage health care delivery system on client moral, independent living and the cost of care. *Gerontologist, 20*(3-Pt. 1), 364–371.

Kane, R.L., & Kane, R.A. (1980). Alternatives to institutional care of the elderly: Beyond the dichotomy. *Gerontologist, 20*(3-Pt. 1), 249–259.

Kane, R.L., Olsen, D.M., Thetford, C., & Byrnes, N. (1976). The use of utilization review records as a source of data on nursing home care. *American Journal of Public Health, 66*(8), 778–782.

Lane, D., Uyeno. D., Stark, A., Gutman, G., & McCashin, B. (1985, July 12-17). *Passages: Forecasting client transfers in a long-term care program.* Paper presented at the 13th Annual Meeting of the International Association on Gerontology. New York.

Linn, M.W. (1967). A rapid disability rating scale. *Journal of the American Geriatrics Society, 15*(2), 211–214.

Ministry of Health, Province of British Columbia. (1978). *Introduction to the program of long-term care,* Victoria: Author.

Ministry of Health, Province of British Columbia (1978). *Long–term care program policy and procedures manual.* Victoria: Author.

National Center for Health Statistics. (1977). *National Nursing Home Survey.* Washington, D.C.: U.S. Government Printing Office.

Skellie, F.A., & Coan, R.E. (1980). Community-based long-term care and mortality: Preliminary experimental findings. *Gerontologist, 20*(3-Pt. 1), 372–379.

Stark, A.J., & Gutman, G.M. (1985, July 12-17). *Client transfers in long-term care: Five years' experience.* Paper presented at the 13th Meeting of the International Association on Gerontology, New York.

Stark., A.J., Gutman, G.M., & Brothers, K. (1982). Reliability of level of care decisions in a long-term care program. *Journal of Community Health, 8*(2), 102–109.

Stark, A.J., Gutman, G.M., & McCashin, B. (1982). Acute-care hospitalizations and long-term care: An examination of transfers. *Journal of American Geriatrics Society, 30*(8), 509–515.

Stark, A.J., Layton, D., Gutman, G.M., & Brothers, K.M. Characteristics of clients generating high administrative workload in a long-term care program. *Canadian Journal of Public Health, 75,* 294–300.

Stark, A.J., Kliewer, E., Gutman, G.M., & McCashin, B. Placement changes in long-term care: Three years experience. *American Journal of Public Health, 74*(5), 459–463.

Uyeno, D., Lane, D., Stark, A., Kliewer, E., & Gutman, G. (1985). Forecasting demand for long-term care services. *Health Services Research, 20 (4),* 436–460.

Walter, J., & Nigh, J.S. (1980, July). *Long-Term Care "Short Form" Project.* City of Vancouver Health Department. Vancouver, B.C.

PART VI
Basic and Social Scientific Research

B. Housing and Living Environments

CHAPTER 52

Introduction to Micro-Environmental Issues in Housing for the Elderly

Sheila M. Peace

The micro-environment is defined in terms of both the smallest scale of the physical environment (e.g. hardware and fixtures) and the psychologically construed environment. The symposium begins with the most subjective aspect, the meaning conveyed by a person's residence. Behaviors may be activated by the meaning conveyed by a person's residence. Behaviors may be activated by the meanings, associations, and expectations that one attaches to one's home. Similarly, one's well-being more generally may hinge on such perceptions. Behaviors such as housing choices and housing satisfaction clearly stem from such subjective experience, but they may also respond to life events and how they are perceived. Consideration of micro-environment, in terms of both design and meaning, allow us to explore how older people can retain control over aspects of their lives whilst coping with declining health. The symposium considers these issues from the perspectives of anthropology, social psychology, human geography, planning and architecture.

While a major concern of those involved in the care of the elderly is with micro-environmental issues in housing, we must first consider the relationship between macro-and micro-environments. When we think of the macro-environment it is perhaps common to think of the distribution of people across and within countries, states, and provinces; of the balance of urban, rural, and suburban elders; of the perceptions, satisfactions, and behavior of elderly people within their communities and more frequently their neighborhoods, and the reason for these patterns, actions, and feelings. Even in this continuum we are in some ways reducing the scale, if not the scope, of our field of study, and in so doing we are becoming less concerned with the structure of society and becoming more and more person-centered. Yet it is important to recognize at the outset that all of these wider issues cannot and should not be divorced from discussions of micro-environmental issues.

The term "micro-environment" focuses our attention not just on the elderly person within the confines of their immediate living unit and the importance of design considerations but to something even more personal, more intimate; that is, the relationship between environment and self-identity. In examining this relationship we shall consider the micro-environment as both functional and symbolic, and in doing so we may begin to learn something about the strong attachment that a majority of older people report with regard to their homes, often despite poor housing quality.

Given that in most Western developed countries older people repeatedly state that they wish to remain living within their own homes for as long as possible, it is surprising that as Powell Lawton (1980) has pointed out "we know considerably more about the communities and neighborhood settings where older people live than we do about their homes." We also know considerably more about the micro-environments of institutional settings and special housing for old people than we do about ordinary housing, which in part is due to the difficulty of intruding upon individuals within their private setting, although perhaps it has also been all too easy to research the captive audience.

However, because we have a greater knowledge concerning the interactions between the individual and the environment within special settings, it is appropriate at this stage to identify some of the broad areas of contrast between more supportive environments and the homes of older people within the community. Here, observations are made on the basis of the work of my colleagues and I, both within British residential or old age homes and, more recently, with older people in their own homes (Fengler, Peace, & Kellaher, 1985; Willcocks, Peace, & Kellaher, 1986; Willcocks, Peace, Kellaher, & Ring, 1982). First it is important to stress once again that a majority of older people live within their own homes. In Britain, for example, only 5% live in sheltered housing with a further 4% to 5% in institutional settings. Of the majority living in the community, nearly half are owner—occupiers, 90% of whom own their own home outright (Office of Population & Census Surveys, 1982). A further 40% of older households rent accommodation from the local authority (public housing) and the remainder rent privately (Office of Population & Census Surveys, 1982). In terms of living arrangements, approximately one third of people over retirement age live alone, a third with their spouse, and a third with other relatives (daughters, sons, siblings). This pattern of course varies with age and sex. More older women of all ages, but especially the old-old, live alone. The primary type of accommodation is a house either semidetached or terraced; a third of the elderly live in houses built prior to 1919, which are often in a poor state of repair. These figures put into perspective some of the cultural differences, which may emerge from our discussions. There will no doubt be some areas where there are common themes and others that will be unique.

What then have our studies of residential homes indicated about the microenvironments in which older people live? There are both gains and losses of giving up one's home that are well documented in many countries. Thus we see the gains of more supportive environments which offer a certain type of physical security and prevent the older person from falling into self-neglect or isolation by providing a managed life-style offering the companionship of others and staff surveillance. These gains are often made at the expense of unfamilarity, lack of attachment, and a loss of privacy and personal control. Research in institutional settings highlight a catalog of examples whereby the elderly person is disempowered in a variety of ways. Not everyone has a bedroom of his or her own; personalization of space is rare; residents are rarely able to control the heating in their rooms or open a window unaided, and organizational routines often force people to occupy public and communal areas for long periods during the day.

In contrast, the research that has begun on the interactions between older people and the "domestic" environment indicates a number of interesting and contrasting themes (Fengler et al., 1985; O'Bryant, 1983). Home still embodies power, both in the economic sense of ownership and as a symbol of family unity. The home offers the potential for choice and privacy allowing the individual to be gregarious or to seek solitude on his or her own terms; it embodies a sense of personal history, which does not render the individual as just another old person; it also offers personal security even if not materially secure. While a home may no longer meet the older person's physical needs, for some it may meet important emotional needs. How individuals perceive their environments may depend not only on their level of competence but also on the meaning attached to that environment.

These themes underlie the presentations made by the first three contributors to this symposium. First, Leonie Kellaher examines the meaning of "home" for older people in terms of its material, social and symbolic dimensions, providing greater understanding of the concept of "attachment." Tony Warnes extends these arguments to focus on residential location and the influence of proximity to kin on visiting patterns. He contrasts the interactions of those older people living in the community and those living in institutional settings with their place of residence. In considering the determinants of housing choice, Sandra Howell discusses how the impact of life events such as retirement, widowhood, and perceived deterioration of health, which may have precipitated a move, can be outweighed by attachment to place. She discusses the possible effects of perceived control of one's self on attitudes and behavior relative to housing.

Moving from the importance of symbolic or social aspects of environment in terms of self-identity, the last two contributors focus on aspects of design. Tamako Hayashi discusses the findings of innovative research from Japan where ordinary housing is designed or adapted to compensate for changes in the functioning of older people. The impact of design in facilitating or determining certain forms of behavior is further explored by Victor Regnier in his examination of several housing projects purposely built for the elderly. Consideration of the physical environment in terms of both design and meaning allowed participants to explore how older people can retain control over aspects of their lives while coping with declining health.

REFERENCES

Fengler, A.P., Peace, S.M., & Kellaher, L.A. (1985, August). *The meaning of home for British elderly widowed homeowners: Consequences for the decision to move or to home share.* Paper presented to Centre for Environmental & Social Studies in Ageing, Polytechnic of North London.

Lawton, M.P. (1980). *Environment of aging.* Belmont, CA: Brooks/Cole.

O'Bryant, S. (1983, June). The subjective value of home to older homeowners. *Journal of Housing for the Elderly, 5*(2), 217–231.

Office of Population & Census Surveys. (1982). *General Household Survey, 1981.* London: Social Survey Division, HMSO.

Willcocks, D.M., Peace, S.M., Kellaher, L.A., & Ring, A.D. (1982). *The residential life of old people: A study of 100 local authority residential homes.* (Research Report No. 12). Survey Research Unit, Polytechnic of North London.

Willcocks, D.M., Peace, S.M., & Kellaher, L.A. (1986). *Private lives in public places.* London: Tavistock.

CHAPTER 53

The Meaning of Home for Older People

Leonie A. Kellaher

The observation that home is of fundamental importance to older people is commonly accepted. *Home* is part of a rhetoric that fits with popular understanding of the locus of family units and domestic groupings as integral components of society. But, many older people do not live in family units or domestic groupings. What then is the meaning of home? Various meanings are explored in this study undertaken in England in 1984.

The interesting paradox to be explored here is the way in which old, often very frail people continue to relate to, to draw, and improvise upon the theme of *home*. This despite the fact that their circumstances frequently place them at a considerable distance from a home in any usual sense. Many older individuals experience difficulty in maintaining the physical fabric of home to standards they recognize as being proper for themselves and others. However, though the material fabric of home may disintegrate, it is argued here that connections with a sense of place symbolized as *home* persist. The nature of such connections and the mechanism by which they operate are considered here.

That the notion, and indeed the reality, of *home* represents an important repertoire for older people to employ in defining themselves has been illuminated in the course of earlier research in residential or supportive settings for old people in England. Although an illusion of home may be maintained in special residential settings, residents do not appear to have access to the repertoire that permits a sense of satisfying connections between self and environment. This is paradoxical since many special residential settings have been designed and are organized within a philosophy of care that explicitly aims to provide a physically supportive environment and to recreate a sense of *home*. For example, a domestic appearance is sought with devices such as pitched roofs, indented facades, small sitting rooms, and complex internal spatial arrangements, which, ostensibly, avoid the monolithic features of institutional life. However, these physical prompts do not necessarily cue in "homely" responses. Residents appear unconnected to their physical and social environments. This should alert us to the fact that, for older people, continued engagement or connection with society rests upon more than a series of environmental cues. There are clearly other layers of meaning involved if a physical residence is to become *home* and to have meaning for older people. And it is by appreciating the nature of these layers of meaning, and, particularly, by understanding the ways in which they interrelate, that we might approach the meaning of *home*. This is not a novel proposition. Harris and Lipman (1980) have argued that "people do not merely react to their environments, they actively endow them with meaning." Rapoport (1982) also makes the case that the semiotic, one-to-one analysis in which everything functions as a sign, is not sufficient to explain the mechanisms that generate environmental meanings. In an attempt to comprehend the nature of the intervening layers, findings from the small study already mentioned are considered in relation to theories about symbols.

There are two aspects of work on symbols that are useful here. First, consider the proposition, that Turner (1974) elaborates, that symbolism and symbolic behavior rest upon an integration of two elements. At one pole there is an observable phenomenon, perhaps natural or cultural objects, or physical or verbal gestures. At the other pole, there is a response or a resonance to the observable phenomenon. Through this the participant becomes, at least momentarily, connected to society.

Home, in its fixed spatial arrangements, its semifixed furniture and ornaments, its threshold with the outside world, and the social and physical networks within which it is located, can be conceptualized as the observable phenomenon that Turner's scheme includes. The other pole calls attention to the meaning associated with *home*. What are the mechanisms by which the poles are connected? More recent work around this area of symbolicity, by Sperber (1975) for instance, begins to grapple with this fundamental question. Symbolicity, Sperber argues, "is not a property of objects, acts or utterances, but of the conceptual representations that describe or interpret symbols." He argues that there is a symbolic mechanism that transforms and makes sense of the gaps or contradictions experienced in everyday life by individuals.

In applying this idea to *home,* it can be argued that older people construct their own symbols out of their immediate world by processing environmental cues, even cues that may be problematic for them. This they do in very individual ways that have personal and particular significance. Thus, they may be able to make sense even of the dislocations between norms concerning *home* (the rhetoric of "homeness") and their declining capacities to maintain a personal connection with *home* because of altered economic and health circumstances. This may help explain why older people want to stay close to a store of potentially useful symbolic cues associated with *home* and a home place. What meanings are *home* most frequently associated with by older people? The following comments, made by 20 elderly homeowners in England reflect two variations of meaning.

First, a number of people in the course of extended and semistructured interviews made remarks that suggest the association of *home* and relatively harmonious relationships.

"Home? It's a sense of security and it's mine."

"I can spend days without going out and be content."

"I don't want to *be* anywhere else. Here I see my nice things, the furniture I've known all my life, it's a pleasure to be with—it's memories."

"I feel at home because I fit here; I live at the turn of the century, in a way, in last week's world."

"You can't trust other peoples' places like your own."

"Ownership is very important; it isn't greed, but I have a certain smug satisfaction knowing it's mine."

"Passing on things - I think about that a lot; I've already passed on some things and I have wishes about other things in my will."

"I made all the curtains and lampshades; these are my things. The garden too is my area. The colorings and painting might not please anyone else but they please me."

"I built the garage and have done all the fencing around the yard. Everything is first class. I have always had the best of everything here."

Nearly all these people express the view that home is a comfortable environment where they feel safe and secure. Many view home as part of the family tradition to which O'Bryant (1983) has referred—as a storehouse for memories and mementos and as something of value to pass on. Additionally, many informants pointed to material possessions they had designed or made. In contrast to the world beyond, *home* territory is a place where personal control and mastery of the environment can be exercised. This can be control of the household, its contents, and its visitors, or control of time and space usage.

These remarks came from people who appear to be attached to their homes in ways that correspond to the rhetoric of *home* as a secure, private, controllable place. However, other informants made remarks about *home* that, although we can construe them as reflections of attachment or connection to home, are not entirely aligned with positive stereotypic norms concerning home:

"The neighbors are OK, very nice, but I can't understand them."

"It's fine for the dog here."

"I've no money to mend the windows."

"I'm worried about the bills; but it's better to stay where you are; if you move you get a catastrophe."

"I used to be house-proud; now I'm getting old, the furniture is getting old. But you have to stay faithful."

"I loathe the garden; I'd like to put stones all over it."

"I don't feel very strongly about home; no particular memories."

"A home is a home; but you don't make a god of it."

"Sometimes I wish I'd got a flat; a house is alright when you are younger."

"I wouldn't miss anything about home; or else I wouldn't go away on holiday."

It is suggested, then, that attachment to *home* can be more complicated, ambiguous, and ambivalent than that indicated by the first set of comments. Attachment to *home* may be strong or weak but, additionally, connections to and the meaning of *home* may be revealed in relationships that are negative as well as positive. In either instance, *home* is a store of symbolic potential waiting to be activated.

Older people, use this store of symbolic material in a variety of ways, orchestrating a mix of homology and opposition at different times. The point to be made, however, is that, whether positive or negative, older people maintain connections with *home*. Since older people may have restricted access to other domains through which connection with society can be made, *home* becomes particularly important as a relatively stable point of reference.

An older person whose aging and decline is matched by a dilapidation of the physical referant of *home* may grasp and appreciate the similarity. In such instances, there may be an acceptance of a domestic "disorder" that parallels the physical "disorder" of aging. Here, personal identity is not challenged by the juxtaposition of physical decline with environmental efficiency. The reluctance of older people to embark on renovating their homes has been recently documented by Wheeler (1982) and to the extent one may take economic constraints into consideration this reluctance may testify to a strategy by which the self and the micro-environment of the home are aligned. However, such a coping strategy places the declining individual in opposition to society's norms that *home* should be maintained to high standards.

There is also the case of the older person who may acknowledge physical decline by moving to a more managable setting, to a flat for instance, and dispersing items of property to relatives as the years advance. Such behavior would appear to simplify the fit between person and environment and to have two potential compensatory effects. First, physical deficits may be offset in a more supportive environment. Second, the older person, recognises and identifies with society's norms.

In both these instances, strategies are adopted by older people which support personal identity. Both strategies involve the micro-environment of *home* as a store of symbolic material that is orchestrated both homologously *and* oppositionally. But the mix is a different one in each case and the consequent relationship with society is a more or less distant or aligned one. Identity is preserved, while different interests, either those of the self and those of society, are also served.

In conclusion, the meaning of *home* arises out of very individual and dynamic processes; meaning is not static and both kinds of alignment with *home* are to be found within one person's attachments or connections. Moreover, *home* as a system of meaning permits a number of strategies that may support personal identity and permit connection with wider society.

REFERENCES

Harris, H., & Lipman, A. (1980). Social symbolism and space usage in daily life. *Sociological Review, 28*(2) 415–428.

O'Bryant, S. (1983). The subjective meaning of home for the elderly. *Journal of Housing for the Elderly, 1.*

Rapoport, A. (1982). *The meaning of the built environment: A nonverbal communication approach.* Sage.

Sperber, D. (1975). *Rethinking symbolism.* Cambridge: Cambridge University Press.

Turner, V.W. (1974). *Dramas, fields & metaphores: Symbolic action in human society.* Ithaca, NY: Cornell University Press.

Wheeler, R. (1982, November). Staying put: A new development in policy. *Ageing & Society, 2,* (p. 3).

CHAPTER 54

Determinants of Housing Choice: Perceptions and Actions

Sandra C. Howell

Events that occur in later life do not seem to result in reappraisals of housing circumstances. The strong tendency, particularly among older American homeowners, to remain in their established dwelling, appears to be governed by perceptions of appropriateness of place to self. A discrepancy is noted between perceptions of normative housing readjustment relative to a life event and what is or seems to be appropriate to the respondent. Those widowed after age 70, particularly where a spouse's death was not sudden, are less likely to consider a move or act to change their housing. Perceptions of stability of self-in-place also appear to extend to the ability to continue to care for self should informal supports become unavailable, particularly among frail elderly. Such discrepancies, between perceptions of environmental control and possible need for planned rehousing and services, indicate that interventions may now occur later than would be optimum for relief of individual and family stress.

It is of growing concern, internationally, that resources to assist ever-increasing aging populations be focused on the most vulnerable. New demographic definitions have been recommended by which we may identify and reformulate public policies and support programs related to housing. The new definitions would direct our attention to populations 75 to 84 and 85 plus years of age. Among these older population categories, most of whom reside in their own homes in the United States, nearly 20% have recently been reported by Newman (1985) as no longer able to maintain some critical function within their own homes. This is a considerably higher figure than we have previously estimated from data based on all persons 65 and older. To date, the

critical functions identified to most jeopardize daily living are maintenance of house, heavy cleaning, preparation of meals, getting up/down
stairs, getting around outside (shopping), and in a few cases, bathing.

It has been assumed that the onset and continuation of such dysfunction would serve as a stimulus or "push" for older people to consider
and complete a search for some more supportive housing alternative.
Additionally, other life events such as serious illnesses and widowhood
when they happen to these vulnerable old-old persons should differentially signal a need to move from an "inappropriate" to a more
appropriate setting.

ISSUES

This chapter will address two issues in the choice of older people to
move or to remain in an established residence: First, the perception of
what is appropriate housing behavior for other people faced with a
particular life event in contrast with what is considered appropriate for
oneself; and the second, perceptions of unfulfilled needs which might
be filled by alternative housing.

DATA

The data for this discussion come from interviews conducted in 1980
with six quite separate subsamples of persons over the age of 70 in
different geographic locations of the United States, all of whom currently reside in noninstitutional community settings (Howell, 1981).
Each of these subsamples represented particular characteristics of environment and person interaction such that it appeared, when the separate data were brought together, that it would not be methodologically
valid to aggregate responses of the over 302 interviewees. However,
some common features of responses can be reported because they had
similar significance across the data sets.

FINDINGS

Individuals were asked to review their housing experiences using
markers such as the time of some adult life-event or around any
change in their own health status or the health status of a spouse. The
outstanding feature of the data was that of those few who had moved in
relation to a life event, twice as many made a housing change prior to
age 70 than after age 70. This was particularly the case for widows
relative to the age of widowhood and was reinforced by the fact that an

TABLE 54-1. Mobility Patterns Within One Year of Widowhood by Key Factors[a]

	Age at widowhood		Suddenness of spouse's death	
	Under 70 ($n = 62$)	70 and over ($n = 18$)	Sudden ($n = 36$)	Not sudden ($n = 53$)
Considered moving and *did* move	.31	.17	.33	.21
Considered moving but *did not* move	.08	.05	.05	.07
Did not consider moving at widowhood	.61	.78	.61	.72
Total	1.00	1.00	.99	1.00

[a]Durham sample ($n = 102$) excluded from this table.

Source: "Determinants of Housing Choice Among Elderly: Policy Implications" by S.C. Howell, 1981. Final Report, No. 90-AR-2116/01, HHS-AoA. Washington, DC: U.S. Government Printing Office.

actual postwidowhood move was more likely if the spouse died suddenly than if the spouse's terminal illness was prolonged. Table 54-1 presents mobility patterns within 1 year of widowhood.

Somehow, it seems that there are significant "drag" factors that prevent people from considering a move to a more amenable and promisingly supportive environment in late life. One such major drag factor appears to be the *perception* of oneself-in-place. Suggestive evidence of this appears in data reported in our study by Linda George (1981) for the Durham, North Carolina subsample, 60% of whom were *homeowners* with a mean duration of residence of 22 years and mean age for respondents of 78 years (see Table 54-2).

In the case of widowhood, 66% of the North Carolina sample thought others would and should move, while only 18% said widowhood actually influenced them to move. Forty-four percent thought a spouse's illness or disability would influence a move by others, but less than 5% were themselves "pushed" by this event; and 75% considered others would move as a result of personal illness or disability, but only 10% reported that this was a significant push factor for themselves.

The discrepancy between perceptions of events that push other people to move versus those that are significant in one's own decisions might suggest a parallel discrepancy, possibly between perceptions of available help in time of illness or disability and the actual availability of this help. In this connection, we note from our study that among those currently receiving services (meal preparation, homemaking,

TABLE 54-2. Perception of Life Events as Factors Influencing Other People or Self to Make a Residential Move[a]

Life/Event	Others	Self
Marriage	89%	76%
Job change	78%	23%
Birth of child	71%	21%
Divorce/separation	80%	09%
Widowhood	66%	18%
Personal illness/disability	75%	10%
Empty nest	48%	09%
Retirement	40%	12%
Spouse illness/disability	44%	05%
Average no. "pushes" for relocation endorsed	5.65	1.74

[a]Durham, North Carolina Sample, 1980; $n = 110$; 60% homeowners. Mean duration of residence—22 years.

Source: George, L.K. (1982, March). Minority Homeowners. *In Supplemental Reports to Determinants of Housing Choice: Policy Implications.* Final Report II, by S.C. Howell. Prepared for Department of Health and Human Services, Office of Human Development Services, Administration on Aging, Grant No. 90-AR-2116/01.

home nursing), a significant percent (40% to 50%) *believed* they could continue to live independently were the service no longer available.

Older people who actually seek alternatives to a current housing situation, while proportionally few, are by no means homogeneous with respect to their needs, prevailing circumstances, or characteristics. Lawton (1985) has referred to this population as the "unfulfilled." As the research data from our separate samples (Durham, North Carolina; Fall River, Cambridge, and Boston, Massachusetts; and Glendale, California) showed, this population does tend to have one characteristic in common. They have moved more frequently throughout adult life, and this moving is associated with lower income, being a renter, and being single (never married, separated, widowed). Since these seekers of fulfillment through moving do *not* actually move frequently, the question is raised: Why do they inquire about, but retreat from, an offered alternative housing option? A primary explanation, of course, may be that they are waiting for elderly housing (apartments). But two other explanations also emerged from exploration of interview responses:

1.   A surprising amount of informal support is often available to maintain function even among those who report health difficulties and

this help may be perceived to be tied to the current residence. Most of this support is from children and siblings, and the prevailing issue is at what point of need will such support no longer suffice (Brody, 1985; O'Bryant, 1985)? In the United States this has also become an evident problem for those already under the roof of age-segregated, subsidized housing with "Patchwork" service inputs (Lawton, 1985). So it may not be so obvious to older persons that moving ensures informal support services.

2.   The proferred housing option may not be more desirable, even though it may be more appropriate than the current situation. This was evident in the studies of applicants who refused placement in *Highland Heights,* specialized housing for disabled (Gutkin & Morris, 1981), and among those who rejected a program of shared housing through roommate matching. Preference for privacy and autonomy, particularly with regard to sleeping and bathroom space, appeared a dominant reason for rejection of shared living options (Sherwood, Seltzer, & Litchfield 1982).

CONCLUSIONS

Three sets of beliefs/perceptions may help explain why older adults indicate so little enthusiasm for considering alternative residential arrangements:

1.   Perceived normative behaviors within the society are viewed as not applying to oneself.
2.   A belief that what one has in housing is better than other alternatives is reinforced attachment to a particular house or neighborhood, fear of loss of familiarity, and concern for economic security.
3.   An expectation that existing informal supports will likely continue no matter what needs one has.

Perceptions of control, whether realistic and confirmed or not, seem to dominate behavior. Further, the reality of the limits of existing options discourage many from more serious and earlier considerations of alternative housing.

REFERENCES

Brody, E.M. (1985). Parent care as a normative family stress. *The Gerontologist, 25,* 19–29.

George, L.K. (1982). Minority/homeowners. In S.C. Howell (Ed.). *Determinants of housing choice,* (Final Report, No. 90-AR-2116/01, HHS-AoA), Supplement.

Gutkin, C.E., & Morris, J.N. (1981). Disabled needs. In S.C. Howell (Ed.). *Determinants of housing choice* (Final Report, No. 90-AR-2116/01, HHS-AoA). Washington, DC: U.S. Government Printing Office.

Howell, S.C. (1981). *Determinants of housing choice among elderly: Policy implications* (Final Report, No. 90-AR-2116/01, HHS-AoA).

Lawton, M.P., Moss, M., & Grimes, M. (1985). The changing service needs of older tenants in planned housing. *The Gerontologist, 25,* 258–264.

Newman, S.J. (1985). Housing and long-term care: The suitability of the elderly's housing to the provision of in-home services. *The Gerontologist, 25,* 35–40.

O'Bryant, S.L. (1985). Neighbor's support of older widows who live alone in their homes. *The Gerontologist, 25,* 305–310.

Sherwood, C.C., Seltzer, M.M., & Litchfield, L.C. (1982). Outreach respondents. In S.C. Howell (Ed.). *Determinants of housing choice* (Final Report, No. 90-AR-2116/01, HHS-AoA). Washington, DC: U.S. Government Printing Office.

CHAPTER 55

Microlocational Issues in Housing for the Elderly

Anthony M. Warnes

Drawing from a survey of retired couples, this chapter summarizes the evidence on previous moves, the present proximity of children to parents, and the frequency and structure of social contacts. Most of the couples had moved no more than once since establishing their marital home and most children lived within an hour's drive. Social class variations were marked and a very strong relationship between proximity and the frequency of visiting was found. As households become smaller, extrahousehold relationships may be of increasing importance. Furthermore, as proximity is so influential in promoting visiting and intimacy, the survey results lend support to a policy of encouraging the widest possible availability of housing suitable for retirement. Any tendency toward concentration, regionally or by counties or suburbs, is likely to be inimical to the social integration of the elderly.

As evidence accumulates, it is becoming clearer that microenvironmental factors impinge upon the biographies and present circumstances of elderly people in greatly contrasting ways. Architects and architectural psychologists have elucidated the importance of building layout, design, and furnitures for the manageability and comfort of home living. Sociologists have thrown much light on the relationships between dwellings and family and household structures. Ethnogra-

The research leading to this chapter was funded by the U.K. Economic and Social Research Council and the Central Research Fund of the University of London. David Howes and Lawrence Took provided invaluable assistance with the execution and analysis of the social survey.

phers and others, including the new school of humanist geographers, have attempted to understand the subjective and cognitive attributes of homes and neighborhoods (Golant, 1984; Rowles & Otha, 1983). The scale that is considered also varies and no agreement exists on the limits of the "micro" (i.e., the immediate, proximate) environment, but it is taken here to encompass not only the spatial scales of the room, the dwelling, and the house plot or hereditament, but to extend to that of the neighborhood or residential district. It is at this latter scale that the geographers long-standing interests in place and locational realtionships can be applied.

This chapter draws from the findings of research into the relationships between the residential histories of both retired parents and their adult children, their present residential separation, and the frequency and structure of their social contacts. This information is used both to comment on the ability of people in later ages to promote their social integration through housing relocations, and to evaluate critically the locational criteria that are most commonly recommended for specialized housing for the elderly. The research included a household survey of 432 retired married couples that was carried out in four districts of England during 1983. Each couple was living without others in a private dwelling and each had two surviving adult children with whom they were in contact (defined minimally as a face-to-face meeting within the previous 2 years). This specific and unusual design was adopted to control for the availability of differing numbers of children and to highlight the spatial factors in intergenerational relations. A full report of the survey and of the representativeness of the sample is given in a working paper (Warnes & Howes, 1984).

The voluminous literature on family sociology and social gerontology has established a considerable understanding of the nature and role of social relationships among elderly people (for reviews see Bengtson, Olander, & Haddad, 1975; Bengtson & Robertson, 1985; Hagestad, 1981, 1985; Rosow, 1967; Shanas & Sussman, 1977, Sussman, 1965, 1976; Troll & Bengtson, 1979). The literature searches have identified consistent cross-sectional influences, of which the most important appears to be the availability of relatives of different orders of closeness. A substitution effect operates whereby, if there are relatives in the same household, social interaction beyond is relatively weak. If there are children living elsewhere, their households form an important element in social networks; if not, siblings or other extended relatives tend to feature more strongly. If relatives are unavailable or uninterested, then friendship interaction takes on greater importance, although the further generalization can be supported that a declining intensity and frequency of interaction accompanies the progressive substitutions from conjugal to friendship or with-neighbor interactions.

The second factor that emerges from the empirical research is that of social class and its associations with educational attainment, occupational mobility, geographical mobility, the nature of friendships, and, through fertility and mortality, the number of relatives from preceding or following generations. Thirdly, and particularly associated with the considerable variation in circumstances that applies to any occupational, social class, or family-size group, is the important influence of personality and the history of the child–parent relationship. Finally, one identifies in most studies a recognition of the importance of accessibility, whether measured in terms of time or distance, as a factor in the frequency, duration, and nature of visits. It is not possible to identify a consensus as to the relative importance of these four factors, partly because their individual importance depends upon the population being studied. General samples will tend to reveal the importance of the social network membership and of social class, while small-scale local studies of homogeneous subgroups will place more weight on personality differences. The importance attached to the spatial variable often seems to reflect principally the spatial sensitivity of the observer, not least through the inclusion or exclusion of relevant questions.

UNDERSTANDING PROXIMITY

Through the multitude of studies, only a few authors have given close attention to the role of proximity or the distance of separation (Adams, 1968; Irving, 1977; Kerckhoff, 1965; Litwak, 1960b; Smith, 1980). The British postwar studies of working class districts tended to obscure the general implications of proximity by finding considerable localization of extended family members and the minority presence of multigenerational households, both resulting in part from housing shortages and the nepotistic influences on landlords' allocations of vacancies (Rosser & Harris, 1965; Townsend, 1957; Young & Willmott, 1957). At about the same time, American sociologists were observing the greater separation of families into elementary or nuclear units and their greater mobility: they also joined a debate as to the necessity of this fragmentation in advanced industrial, capitalist societies (Linton, 1959, Litwak, 1960a, 1960b; Parsons, 1959).

Some authors well recognized the strongly constraining effect of distance on the frequency and intimacy of interaction but, understandably, few found as much sociological interest in the spatial variable as in the degree of relation, gender, and class characteristics of the members of the social network. Adams (1968, p. 34) quotes Reiss's assertion that the two fundamental determinants of interaction frequency are "the degree of kin relationship and the distance of residence," with distance invariably overriding degree of relationship. Bott (1957) also understood the strength of distance in her statement that "proximity is a quasi-necessary but not a sufficient condition of intimacy." Adams's own study of 444 retired couples in Greensboro, North Carolina (USA) contains one of the most extended analyses of the distance of separation and its associations with gender, occupation, and visiting.

In part, in reaction to some premature reports of the decline of the extended family in the United States, Kerckhoff (1965) put forward a spatially sensitive categorization of extant family networks: the "nuclear isolated," where the nuclear elements of the extended family are in close proximity but have few or no contacts; the "modified extended," where family members are spatially dispersed but have strong contacts, interaction, and emotional and material exchange; and "extended," where the members are residentially propinquitous and functionally strong. It has frequently been demonstrated that the conjugal and consanguineous family networks have adjusted to the greater dispersion of their nuclear units, rather than simply declined in their emotional ties and functional exchanges. Taking advantage of improved personal mobility and affluence, in many cases they have created a system of mutual assistance and involvement that is superior to sharing a home: its nuclear units retain greater independence and the strains of shared living arrangements are reduced. Part of the case for further studies to be made to elaborate and refine this knowledge and for specifically spatial contributions is that these interpretations and understandings are so rare.

A common mistake appears to be the projection of the educational and occupational experiences and the social habits of the professional stratum of our societies to the general population. This exercise is given a degree of credibility by reference to contemporary household and mobility trends but, even so, misleading extrapolations are common. While it is the argument of this chapter that the cross-sectional influence of distance upon social contact is insufficiently recognized or understood, paradoxically it is also believed that false or exaggerated inferences are drawn frequently from the observation of increasing geographical mobility. Discussions of macrosocietal change quite commonly describe interdependencies between the increasing dynamism of economies and occupational change, the requirements of the labor market, geographical mobility, the dispersion of families, and increasing isolation of the nuclear family (Harris, 1977). More recently, an additional emphasis has been placed on the desire for privacy and independence and the further fission of the population into "minimal household units" of single parent or one- and two-person households (Ermisch & Overton, 1985; Concord, 1982). While these arguments may be supported by reference to declining household size, particularly among the elderly, and the increasing distance of migrations, contrary trends are often ignored. The best time series evidence on migration suggests, for example, a long-term reduction in the rate of mobility in line with the decline of renting. Further declines have occurred during the 1970s in association with the recession and the increasing real costs of moves (Long, 1984). But more pervasive has been the increasing ability to travel, produced by increasing incomes, higher car ownership, better roads, proliferating airline routes, and (in Europe) faster trains. The penetration of telephone ownership has also contributed to a reduction in the deterrent effect of distance for social contact. In short, a balanced picture is rarely presented and the social sciences are very badly informed about the extent and implications of the undoubted changes in geographical mobility that are occurring.

THE SURVEY FINDINGS

Reported results from the survey of retired couples have focused upon the previous residential moves of the retired couples and their children, the distribution of distances presently separating the two generations; the relationships between these two phenomena; and the social class of the parties, occupational mobility, gender, and birth order. There has also been analysis of the relationships between separation distance and the frequency of visiting (Warnes, Howes, & Took, 1985a, 1985b). In this paper a brief summary of the findings is given, in part by means of a selection of multiple regression analyses results.

Two characteristics of the results deserve to be stressed immediately. On the one hand, considerable variation is found among the 432 retired couples and 864 children in many salient characteristics. The youngest child was 21 years and the eldest 59 years. The age at which the children first left home varied from 9 years to 51 years. The number of visits the retired couples had received at home from any person during the previous week varied from 0 to 43 and the total duration of these visits in one case reached 98 hours.

The second general finding is, however, that high percentages of the samples had moved infrequently, and, referring to the children, continued to live within a few miles of their parents and to see them at least monthly. In other words, the survey found in 1983 levels of lifetime immobility and of the localization of families, which may surprise many academic and professional groups: As we shall see, the differences between this social stratum and other groups are considerable.

Mobility Characteristics

The parents ranged in age from 57 to 89 years (males) and from 46 to

TABLE 55-1. Frequency of Moves of Retired Couples by Social Class

Social[a] class	Number of moves (%)				Sample size
	0	1	2	3+	
I + II	24	40	16	20	127
III nm	39	27	12	23	77
III m	47	28	12	13	152
IV + V	27	35	23	16	75
All (%)	35	32	15	17	100
Sample size	153	140	64	74	431

[a]Social class ratings taken from U.K. Office of Population Censuses and Surveys Classification of Occupations (1980). Broadly, I & II are professional and managerial groups, III nm are junior nonmanual, III m are skilled manual workers, and IV and V unskilled manual and ancillary workers.

89 years (females) with respective average ages of 71.3 and 68.5 years. The mean number of years at the current address for either husband or wife was 24.2, with a range of from 0 to 73 years. Over one third had not moved since their first home at marriage and another third had only moved once (Table 55-1). These figures may understate the frequency of moves, particularly those over short distances undertaken early in the respondents' lives, but there is no reason to suspect that the revealed relationship with social class is misleading. All social classes (SC) except skilled manual workers (SC IIIm) recorded 62% to 66% having moved no more than once. Skilled manual workers were clearly the most distinctive group in their immobility. The highest social classes were least likely to have been entirely immobile since marriage, but the consequence was not a high likelihood of multiple moves but only a high proportion moving once. The moves that had been undertaken were usually over short distances: Only one fifth of the couples had made a move of more than 30 km since their first marital home, and only 24 couples (5.6%) had made more than one such move. Social class effects were stronger on long distance moving, with 34% of social classes I and II but only 7% of skilled manual workers having made any such moves.

The children had been more migratory than their parents, particularly over longer distances. Nearly one half had made a move of more than 30 km, and one quarter had made two or more such moves. The relative immobility of skilled manual workers was repeated among the children, but, in this generation, the unskilled manual group was no more likely to have made more than one move and the professional and managerial group were the most likely to have made multiple moves and to have moved 30 km several times.

The modal pattern of residential moves is unremarkable. Successive generations repeat the practice of relatively frequent but normally local moves in early adulthood before marriage. Once a marital home is established, moves become infrequent. Disturbances to this simple dichotomy have been associated with (a) the mobilization of men during World War II, (b) the longer-distance midlife moves of upper managerial and certain professional occupations, (c) the growth since 1960 of full-time higher education that in many cases has initiated a pattern of longer-distance and more frequent moves, and (d) the willingness of a substantial minority of couples to move relatively long distances in late-working or early retirement ages. These latter moves appear to be prompted variously by the absence of ties to or negative assessments of metropolitan environments, by the wish to move nearer to children or parents, and by environmental prefrences. Neither the data from our survey nor any standard source can comprehensively quantify this pattern. The migration questions of recent censuses provide cross-sectional evidence of the decline in mobility with age and show both its positive association with occupational status and the increase in longer distance moves around retirement age, particularly for metropolitan populations (Warnes, 1983).

The transgenerational manifestation of the decline in mobility with age is that in any decade adult children are always more mobile than their parents. It is therefore the children's moves and the controlling socioeconomic characteristics of the children that have most influence on their mutual residential separation. The strong relationship between the occupation of people and the distance of their moves is reflected in the distance separating retired parents from their adult children. The influence of the child's or child's partner's occupation is stronger than that of the parents. One half of the children of parents in the U.K. Registrar General's social classes I and II live 20 km or more away, compared with 37% of children of parents in social classes IV and V. Whereas 27% of the children of social classes IV and V parents lives with 2 km, 33% of the children themselves given this occupational grade were living as close. An interesting demonstration of the relative importance of the parent's and the children's occupational ranking is the variation in the average distance of separation in association with these two dimensions. Whatever the occupational group of their parents, the average distance of separation of children in skilled manual occupations ranged from 23.2 to 42.9 km. This contrasts with the outcome for all children of skilled manual parent households, which ranged from a separation of 19.6 km for those who were in unskilled manual occupations, to 76.4 km for those who had achieved occupations in social classes I and II (Table 55-2).

Even when examining aggregates, the residential separation between parents and their children is clearly not only a reflection of the

TABLE 55–2. The Mean Distance (km) Between Parents' and Childrens' Homes by Social Class

Social class of the parent	Social class of the child									
	I & II		III nm		III m		IV & V		All	
	km	n	km	n	km	n	km	n	km	n
I & II	91	139	42	35	31	47	30	8	69	229
III Nonmanual	82	64	79	30	38	35	53	11	68	140
III Manual	76	97	46	41	23	108	20	26	5	272
IV & V	66	43	22	15	43	65	61	17	50	140
All	82	343	50	121	32	255	38	62	57	781

social class of the parties. It has been possible to analyse the separation in relation to other variables and to discover, thereby, that occupational mobility from one generation to the next has a strong influence on the net geographical outcome of the family's set of previous moves. The sex of the child is of some importance but the birth order of the children has a weaker effect.

Some of the variations are indicated by the mean distances of separation for subgroups of our sample. Both the respondent parents and their children have been dichotomized into nonmanual [Office of Population Censuses and Surveys (OPCS) Social Classes I, II, and III] and manual (SCs IIIm, IV and V) groups. The parent–child dyads have then been separated into those of changed and unchanged occupational grade. The resulting four groups have been cross-tabulated with the child's sex and birth order and the mean separation distances calculated. They range from 93 km for nonmanual sons of nonmanual parents to 17 km for manual worker's female first children who are themselves or whose husbands are manual workers (Table 55-3A, 55-3B). There is little doubt that the child's occupational group is the main influence with the two groups, returning 74 km and 33 km mean separation distances. The contrast between sons (64 km) and daughters (50 km) is less pronounced. There are, however, strong interactions between these characteristics and occupational mobility and birth order.

The main departures are that male first children who have been occupationally upwardly mobile are unusually likely to remain proximate to their parents while male second children who have followed the same occupational rise distance themselves to the same extent as white collar sons of white collar parents. Among occupationally downward children it is daughters who are second children who remain unusually proximate to their parents. Of the children who acquire the

TABLE 55–3A. The Mean Distance Separating Retired Parents from Children by Occupational Mobility and Gender

Occupational Group		Mean distance of separation (km)	
Parents	Children	Sons	Daughters
Nonmanual	Nonmanual	93	70
		)85	)64
Manual	Nonmanual	73	56
Nonmanual	Manual	39	33
		)37	)29
Manual	Manual	36	26
All	All	64 ($n = 408$)	51 ($n = 436$)

same occupational rank as their parents the separation of sons from their parents is around 130% of the daughters' figure, and the strongest interaction with birth order is among the manual occupation group. Both male second children and female first children are considerably nearer to their parents than their siblings.

Further comparisons are possible through the distribution of separation distances for the various groups (Table 55-4). To highlight one contrast, over one third of the occupationally immobile manual children are found within 2 km of their parents compared with little more than one ninth of nonmanual children. At the opposite extreme of the distance distribution, nearly one third of nonmanual children from the same backgrounds live more than 100 km from their parents compared with one tenth of manual children. The dispersion of the nonmanual

TABLE 55–3B. The Mean Distance Separating Retired Parents from Children by Occupational Mobility, Gender, and Birth Order

		Mean separation distance (km)					
Occupational group		All children		First children		Second children	
Parents	Children	Sons ($n = 408$)	Daughters ($n = 436$)	Sons ($n = 201$)	Daughters ($n = 221$)	Sons ($n = 207$)	Daughters ($n = 215$)
Nonmanual	Nonmanual	93	70	93	59	92	80
		}85	}64				
Manual	Nonmanual	73	56	57[a]	48	91[a]	62
Nonmanual	Manual	39	33	45	37	32	26[a]
		}37	}29				
Manual	Manual	36	26	49[a]	17[a]	24[a]	37[a]
All	All	64	51	65	45	63	58

[a]Indicates deviations from mean separation distance of more than 20%.

TABLE 55-4. The Separation of Children from Their Retired Parents by Both Parties' Occupations

Parents' occupation	Childs' occupation	Within (km)							Beyond (km)	
		1/2	1	2	5	10	25	50	100	200
Nonmanual	Nonmanual	3%	8%	12%	24%	33%	46%	57%	32%	16%
Manual	Nonmanual	3%	5%	13%	29%	47%	61%	71%	23%	14%
Nonmanual	Manual	9%	15%	30%	48%	56%	68%	80%	11%	9%
Manual	Manual	6%	15%	37%	56%	67%	75%	86%	9%	7%

children shows a marked divergence according to the parents' ranking with many more from manual backgrounds being found between 3 to 10 km from the parents (Figure 55-1).

The implications of the mobility and separation variations for the social network and social integration of retired people arise from the strong association that has been found between the distance of separation and the frequency of visiting. While the existence of such an association is totally unsurprising, the restraining effect on contact of small increments of distance was unexpected. This may be illustrated by comparing three subsamples of children: those living respectively within 2 km, between 5 and 20 km, and at least 100 km away. Those visiting their parents at least once a week drops from 81% through 47% to 1.6% across these groups, while the percentage visiting less often than once a month increases from 5% through 14% to 90%. Further contrasts are revealed from the separate tabulations of the parents' and the childrens' visits (Table 55-5).

MULTIPLE REGRESSION RESULTS

A systematic analysis of these relationships has been undertaken using stepwise multiple regression. Two sequential sets of models have been investigated. The first having as the dependent variable the distance separating retired parents and their children; the second calibrating equations for the frequency of visiting. Although only a summary report is given here, some conceptual and methodological discussion is necessary.

In order to employ least-squares estimation procedures, the factors or influences have to be represented as interval scale independent variables. Extreme skewness may misleadingly exaggerate the coefficients of correlation. Both dependent variables have unusual variation, as is realized if one compares the frequency and the distances that characterize social visits with those applying to shopping or commut-

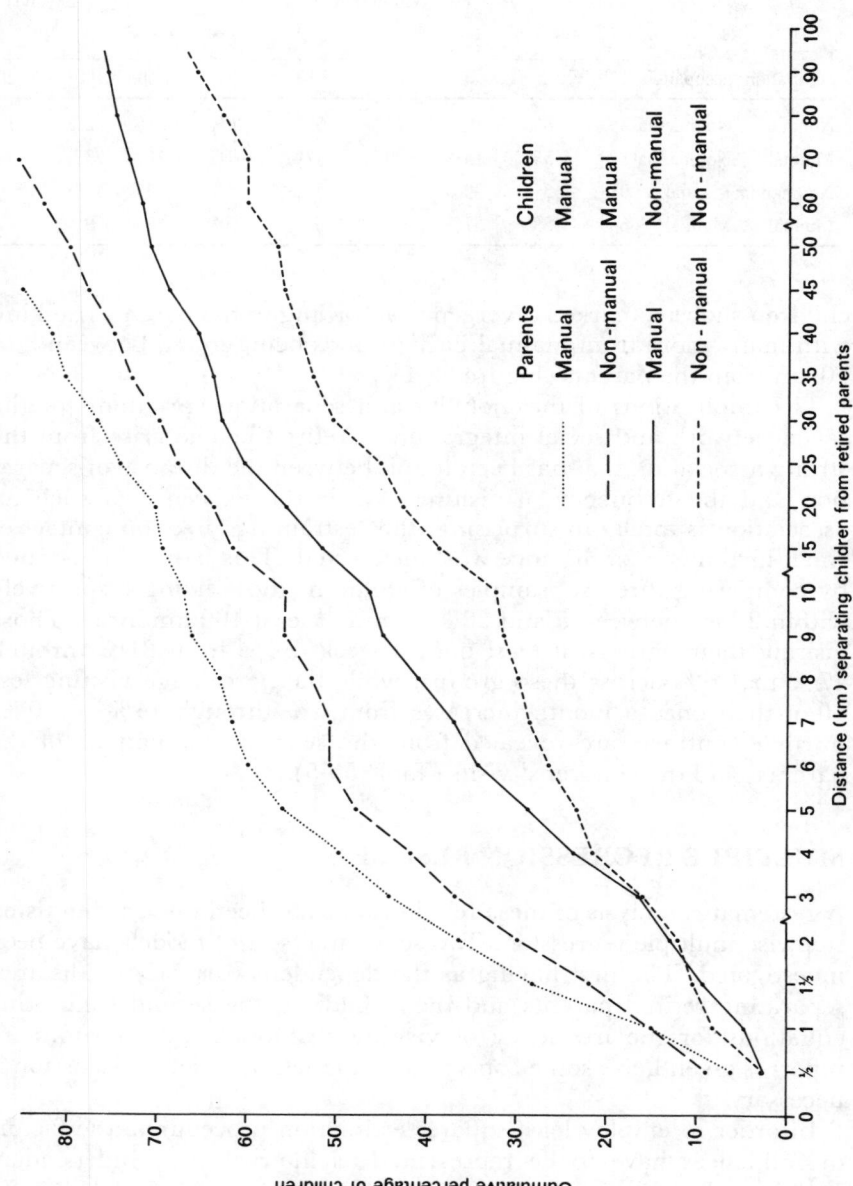

FIGURE 55-1. The dispersion of children from retired parents by their respective occupational groups.

TABLE 55–5. Distance of Separation and the Frequency of Visits

Frequency of visits	Distance of separation (km)			
	0–4.9	5–24.9	25–99.9	100+
Percentage of children visiting parents:				
At least once a week	74	42	9	2
At least once a month	15	43	38	9
At least once in 3 months	5	8	33	25
Less often	6	7	20	65
Percentage of children receiving visits from parents:				
At least once a week	45	23	4	2
At least once a month	25	44	23	4
At least once in 3 months	14	15	28	20
Less often	16	19	45	75

ing journeys (e.g., few people commute only once a year, and few people travel 500 miles to shop). Distance operates as a deterrent to spatial interaction or flows through money and time costs, but the relation is certainly not linear and may not be continuous. A number of thresholds can be envisaged, such as the maximum journey time or cost that will be risked without prearranging the visit, or the maximum distances or times that will be traveled in an evening or in one day. At what distance do overnight stays become a normal part of the visit? The standard use of distance-decay functions in spatial modeling derives ultimately from gravitational theory, and its normal first assumption is that the frictional effect is approximated by the square of the distance. As social visits are there-and-back journeys, there is some basis for employing twice the distance of separation.

Two frequency of visiting variables, distinguishing visits to and from the parents are employed. Many cases reported no visits in the previous year (V). The transformation employed to reduce skewness was the natural logarithm of $V + 1$. The other independent variables were dummy or dichotomous representations of occupation, upward or downward occupational mobility, gender, and car ownership. It should be noted that the 6-point social class scale is not an interval scale and has to be simplified. The regressions were calculated from 25% random samples of the 864 children in the survey.

Partly because of the dichotomous representation of social class, minimal explanations of the distance of separation are found by multiple regression (Table 55–6). The child's occupation and gender do, however, produce significant coefficients in expected directions. Much more informative are various runs of the regressions of visiting frequency. Very high explanations are achieved, particularly for the visits of children to parents. Children's visiting frequencies models are illus-

TABLE 55–6. Multiple Regression Analysis of Distance of Separation and Frequencies of Visiting

Dependent variable[a] [b] Constant	Independent variables[a] and coefficients					Multiple correlation	Variance ratio for equation

Present distance (km) separating parents and children (D)

D = 21.06	− 6.38	CMANUAL	− 4.75	CMALE		$r = 0.24$	$F = 6.06$
β	0.195		− 0.175			$r^2 = 0.06$	df 2,200
*F	8.08		4.58				

Frequency of visits from children to parents (VCP)

lnVCP = 3.932	− 0.064	D	+ 0.387	CMANUAL	− 0..352 CMALE	$r = 0.73$	$F = 62.44$
β	− 0.671		+ 0.141		− 0.129	$r^2 = 0.53$	df 3,167
*F	238.23		20.48				
lnVCP = 5.106	− 0.049	2D	− 0.864	CCAR		$r = 0.80$	$F = 146.16$
	− 0.734		− 0.215			$r^2 = 0.64$	df 2,164
*F	238.23		20.48				

Frequency of visits from parents to children (VCP)

lnVCP = 3.232	− 0.051	D	+ 0.435	RCAR		$r = 0.54$	$F = 34.34$
β	− 0.546		+ 0.612			$r^2 = 0.29$	df 2,168
*F	67.92		5.95				
lnVCP = 3.233	− 0.037	2D	+ 0.661	RCAR	− 0.487 CUPMOB	$r = 0.66$	$F = 41.93$
β	− 0.611		+ 0.236		− 0.140	$r^2 = 0.44$	df 3,163
*F	106.54		15.41		5.45		

[a] Variables: D - distance from child to parents; CMALE—child male; CMANUAL—child or spouse in manual occupation; CCAR—child car owner; RCAR—retired couple car owners; CUPMOB—child's occupation at least 2 points higher than parents on 6-point social class scale.
[b] 1n logarithm base e; β-beta coefficient; *F-variance ratio for term in equation.

trated by two runs employing, respectively, the single and the return journey distances (Table 55-6). The first showed the child's occupation and gender to be significant factors operating in the expected directions, while the second showed, against expectation, that children who were car owners made significantly fewer trips from given distances. Although car ownership had a first order correlation with manual occupation of only − 0.11, it also correlated with upward occupational mobility (r = + 0.18) and gender, and it may reflect these other characteristics. The consistently clear finding is, however, that the distance variable is strongly associated with visiting frequency, accounting itself for around 60% of the variation. Given the tendency for respondents to report visiting frequencies in the "lumpy" form of "once a week/month" and so on and given the complexities of the translation of distance into costs and thresholds, this is an impressive result.

Parents' visiting frequencies are lower, a higher proportion do not visit at all, and the frequency is less explained by distance (Table 55-6).

Car ownership emerged as a strong secondary influence, in one return distance model car ownership added 7% of the variance to the explanation. Car ownership and its correlates of income and physical capacities undoubtedly encourage parents' visits. One other variable was found to be statistically significant. Where a child had been upwardly mobile in relation to their parent's social class, a significant reduction in the frequency of visits was established.

SOCIAL INTEGRATION IN RETIREMENT

It is recognized that the frequency of visiting is but one overt manifestation of a social relationship. Duration of visits may substitute for frequency; and telephone contacts can assist in maintaining relationships, although we have found a slight positive relationship between telephone and personal calling. The quality of personal relationships and the satisfactions they produce are not simply correlated with frequency of contact. It is also accepted that growing geographical mobility may not be the most important change that will affect family and social relationships in the next few decades. Several respondents in our survey did report that the relationships with their children and grandchildren had been truncated by divorce and remarriage, while others had experienced the intensification or multiplication of such relationships from the same cause.

Nonetheless, for the large majority it is clear that parent–child relationships are the most important component of their extramarital social relationships. A few cases of indifference and of antagonism were encountered, and, for some, specific friendships or a multiplicity of social acquaintances were dominant. The norm for both parents and children was seen to be a maintenance of their mutual relationships, in part for immediate practical returns, in part for reasons of family responsibility, lineage, or solidarity, and in part for the valued responses in terms of affirmation, emotional attachment, and social satisfaction. All of these positive motivations and returns were evident, but, on the other hand, few parents had other than a measured and realistic outlook on their children. While a reluctance to express to the interviewers any dissatisfaction with their relationships with their sons and daughters was frequently suspected and is understandable, this was obviously founded on the recognition and promotion of their own and their children's independence.

The subtlety of understanding was revealed particularly by the retired couples' attitudes toward the desirability of living nearer their children. Approximately one in five stated that they wished to live nearer their children, yet many fewer said that they wished to see them more frequently. Despite the superficial appearance, it is not believed that there is an inconsistency in these views. Generally, respondents well understood the dampening effect of distance on visiting frequency, but tended to accept that, if this was to their disadvantage, it was their responsibility to move. At the same time, there was a reluctance to anticipate more frequent visiting or a closer relationship if they moved closer to a child. This would only come about by mutual consent and, preferably, it is tempting to infer, through an unconscious response. In other words, we found a widespread reluctance to make prescriptive statements about an optimum or indeed a different pattern of visiting. However, all the evidence reported in this chapter demonstrates that if family members can succeed in increasing their residential proximity, then it is very likely that a more intensive pattern of visiting will arise.

These findings can be generalized in at least one respect. Although other groups of the elderly, such as the childless, never-married, or widowed, will have very different social networks, many will rely as much if not more on social relationships beyond the household. Whether their most active or intimate personal relations are with siblings, other relatives, or friends of peer acquaintances, it is likely that the ease of visiting and interaction will be a function of the distance of separation in a very similar way. Indeed, to reemphasize a point raised in the introduction, given the trend toward single-person households among the elderly, it is likely that extrahousehold interaction is becoming relatively more important for their morale (McAuley & Nutty, 1985; Stephens, Blau, Oser, & Miller, 1978; Wenger, 1984).

HOUSING LOCATION PRESCRIPTIONS AND SOCIAL INTEGRATION

This research has been conducted during a period of radical change in British government policy toward the housing of the elderly. The coincidence gives rise to unease, not only about the lull in housing investment and its redirection from low-income renters to high-income owners, but also concerning the increasingly anachronistic obeisance to a model of elderly people as passive, frail, and socially isolated. The chapter will be concluded with an elaboration of the grounds for this critical view and drawing again from the research findings it will attempt to outline a more positive approach to elderly housing location.

If it can be said that microenvironmental policies toward the elderly during the third quarter of the 20th century were dedicated to the raising of basic housing standards and amenities, during the present final quarter some diversion of attention is needed to the relationship between the dwelling location and the elderly resident's quality of life. No consensus has yet emerged to replace the negative model of retirement as a roleless, inactive, terminal phase, although hedonistic, individualistic, and extrovert prescriptions circulate. The "third age" after work is for many now an extended period. A necessary condition of successful and rewarding life-styles will be satisfactory dwellings in helpful locations, but, as yet, the models employed by architects, developers, and planners are largely based on a view of the elderly as passive, incapacitated, and often partially dependent individuals. In order to substantiate this claim, and to encourage a more positive approach to the elderly's housing, the development of a microlocational policy in Britain since midcentury must be charted briefly.

Perception of the Elderly's Housing Preferences

Charitable organizations have made special provision for the elderly in Europe for a millenium but only since World War II in northwest Europe has the state adopted a major role (Heumann & Boldy, 1982). The voluntary movement understandably aimed to serve the most frail and socially isolated individuals, and this model remained at the core of the 1950's consensus on housing policies, specifically for older people, which, in turn, guided the implementation of a considerable construction program of specially designed dwellings until 1980. An account of the early chapters of this story quotes a parliamentary statement, as late as 1971, that "the government's policy is to encourage the provision of more housing for old people . . . over a quarter of all new housebuilding is one-bedroom and bedsitting accommodation, most of which will be intended for the elderly" (Mellor, 1973, p 17). The continuity is also apparent in the Ministry of Housing's 1969 checklist for the design of old people's dwellings. Its 85 points included the following criteria (U.K. Ministry of Housing and Local Government, 1969):

1. Is the scheme conveniently located in relation to
   a. Shops, bus stops, pub, post office?
   (Shopping may be the last activity and source of contact for old people; 1/4 mile should be maximum, and the route should be safe from traffic and preferably avoiding steep gradients.)
   b. Ease of visiting *by* (italics added) friends and relatives?

2. Is the (living room window) sill just low enough for an old person to see out when sitting in an easy chair?

Throughout the 1960s and 1970s the policy of constructing specialized housing for the elderly was pursued vigorously by local authorities, voluntary bodies, and, with the assistance of government funds administered by the Housing Corporation, by housing associations. The number of sheltered dwellings for rent increased from 21,000 in

1960 to 308,000 by 1982 (Butler, Oldman, & Wright, 1983; Fleiss, 1985). The present economic recession and the determination of the current Conservative administration to reduce public expenditure and to promote owner occupation has abruptly ended this phase. Investment for rental housing has virtually ceased, and the replacement two-pronged policy is to encourage private sector investment in small and sheltered dwellings for sale (outright or partial equity) and to elaborate measures that encourage people to modernize or improve and to "stay put" in their own homes (U.K. Department of Health and Social Security, 1981). For the latter, great hopes are placed on innovative schemes to convert housing assets into income with which to finance improvement (Tinker, 1984). The limitations of these policies are that the scale of investment and construction is inadequate to meet demands and need, it is providing very few dwellings outside the southern and affluent areas of Britain, and it is catering only to existing owners with above-average retirement incomes (Warnes & Law, 1985). Early results suggest that housing association leasehold schemes are not significantly extending the income band served by present investment (Fleiss, 1985).

To return to microlocational issues, the rapid entry since 1982 of housebuilding firms into the construction of sheltered housing for sale to the elderly has stimulated an admirably prompt response from their national association. A Working Group of builders with representatives from two Housing Associations have produced an Advice Note on location, design, estate management, and forms of tenure (House Builders' Federation, 1984). While no responsible builder would ignore these wholly sound desiderata, they are still founded on a negative, protective approach to frail, circumscribed people. Selected abstracts from the Note illustrate the pervasive assumptions:

> *Environment:* Residents will tend to spend considerable time in their homes because of illness, bad weather, and the effects of age and decreasing mobility. Lively and interesting views should therefore be visible . . . . It is also highly desirable that such housing should not be situated in a relatively isolated location away from the community as a whole.

> *Services:* It is essential that residents have easy access from a site to shops, post offices, banks, medical services, and chemists. These should be within easy walking distance . . . and preferably not uphill for the return journey . . .

> *Community facilities:* Developments should be within reasonable walking distance of other facilities such as parks, libraries, churches, community halls, clubs, pubs, and day centers as well as facilities (where they exist) designed specifically to cater for the elderly.

The latest government research study provides a basis for evaluating the implementation of these criteria for site selection in diverse home ownership schemes (Fleiss, 1985). It reports a 1982 survey of 393 sheltered owner households in 17 new schemes provided by 4 private builders and 3 housing associations. The majority of the findings relate to the capital and continuing costs of the housing and to the satisfaction with the sheltered elements, but some incidental findings refer to the quality of life and social integration of the residents. A first interpretation of these results adds weight to the demand for more policy attention to the elderly's social activity.

When questioned about their reasons for moving into the sheltered schemes, 27% of the sample mentioned their wish to live nearer friends or relatives (and for 16% this was the principal reason) Fleiss, 1985, p. 40). When asked to describe their likes in sheltered living, 28% mentioned the characteristics of the area, 22% the warden and management services, 15% the social milieu, but only 3% their closeness to friends and relatives (p. 89). The equivalent listing of the fewer dislikes included 29% mentioning costs and management, 23% disliking aspects of the social milieu, with 15% mentioning their "isolation in the schemes (and) absence of friends close by or poor public transport" (p. 90).

A parallel study of 137 elderly households which had moved into newly built general housing found that in comparison to the sheltered housing owners, they were younger, had had lower status occupations but now enjoyed similar incomes, and that only 29% in comparison to 79% lived alone. Nonetheless, the most frequently stated reason for moving (mentioned by just under one-third) was to be near friends and relatives, and the most frequently mentioned dislike, from 19% of the sample in five developments, was the isolation of their estate and the absence of friends, amenities, or shops close by (pp. 100–101). While, therefore, the majority of both groups were satisfied with their homes and their recent moves, apart from financial concerns, their complaints featured the extent to which the new locations promoted or hindered their extramural activities and their social life. General and specialized housing successfully provides shelter and desired amenities; it is more questionable whether there is the same level of accomplishment in enabling people to live in their preferred and most supportive locations.

This research has led to the conclusion that distance is neglected as a factor in the activities, life-styles, and social relationships of elderly people. It may be time for the priorities in housing policies and design to give more attention to the fostering of social contacts and activities beyond the home. While this recommendation does not translate directly into the approval of either age segregation or age integration, since different groups of elderly people develop contrasting social networks of either or both age peers or all-age relatives, it is an argument for the maximum geographical dispersion of retirement housing. Per-

haps no residential development of more than 30 dwellings should be
envisaged without dwellings suitable for elderly households of one or
two persons. Perhaps no residential square kilometer should not offer
suitable accommodation. Many surveys of the elderly find a significant
minority who would like to move either to a more convenient dwelling
or to one that is in a more amenable location by being near to friends,
relatives, or facilities, but very often suitable accommodation is simply
not available. In Britain, by focusing on grouped schemes in locations
fastidiously selected for their suitability to the frail elderly, and by, for
others, placing increasing reliance on house improvement and "staying put," we are complacently accepting policies that make no contribution to the positive promotion of either satisfactory social relationships and roles in the third age or to the morale of our increasingly
healthy, active, and educated elderly population.

REFERENCES

Adams, B.N. (1968). *Kinship in an Urban Setting.* Chicago: Markham.
Bengtson, V.L., Olander, E., & Haddad, A. (1975). The generation gap and aged
    family members. In J. Gulbrium (Ed.). *Late life: Recent developments in the sociology
    of age.* Springfield, MA: Charles Thomas.
Bengtson, V.L., & Robertson, J. (Eds.). (1985). *Grandparenthood: Research and policy
    perspectives.* New York: Sage.
Bott, E. (1957). Family and social network. London: Macmillan.
Butler, A., Oldman, C., & Wright, R. (1983). *Sheltered housing for the elderly.* London:
    Allen & Unwin.
Concord, C.M.S. (1982). Spatial distribution of primary individuals. *Professional Geog-
    rapher, 34,* 167–177.
Ermisch, J.F., & Overton, E. (1985). Minimal household units: A new approach to
    the analysis of household formation. *Population Studies, 39,* 33–54.
Fleiss, A. (1985). *Home ownership alternatives for the elderly.* London: Her Majesty's
    Stationery Office.
Golant, S.M. (1984). *A place to grow old: The meaning of environment in old age.* New York:
    Columbia University Press.
Hagestad, G.O. (1981). Problems and promises in the social psychology of in-
    tergenerational relations. In R. Fogel, E. Hatfield, S.B. Kiesler, & E. Shanas
    (Eds.). *Aging: Stability and change in the family.* New York: Academic Press.
Hagestad, G.O. (1985). Continuity and connectedness. In V.L. Bengtson & J. Ro-
    bertson (Eds.). *Grandparenthood: Research and policy perspectives.* New York: Sage.
Harris, C.C. (1977). Changing conceptions of the relation between family and societal
    form in Western society. In R. Scase (Ed.). *Industrial society: Class, cleavage and
    control.* London: Allen & Unwin.
Heumann, L., & Boldy, D. (1985). *Housing for the elderly.* London: Croom Helm.
House Builders' Federation. (1984). *Sheltered housing for sale: An advice note.* London:
    House Builders' Federation.
Irving, H.W. (1977). Social networks in the modern city. *Social Forces, 55,* 867–880.
Kerckhoff, A.C. (1965). Nuclear and extended family relationships. In E. Shanas and
    G.F. Streib. (Eds.) *Social structures and family* (pp. 93–112). Englewood Cliffs, N.J.:
    Prentice Hall.

Linton, R. (1959). The natural history of the family. In R.N. Anshen (Ed.). *The family: Its function and destiny.* New York: Harper.

Litwak, E. (1960a). Occupational mobility and extended family cohesion. *American Sociological Review, 25,* 9–21.

Litwak, E. (1960b). Geographical mobility and extended family cohesion. *American Sociological Review, 25,* 385–394.

Long, L. (1984, May 3-5). *Residential mobility: Why are the rates declining?* Paper presented to the Annual Meeting of the Population Association of America, Minnesota.

McAuley, W.J., & Nutty, C.L. (1985). Residential satisfaction, community integration, and risk across the family life cycle. *Journal of Marriage and the Family, 47,* 125–130.

Mellor, H.W. (1973). Special housing for the elderly. In *Housing in retirement: Some pointers for social policy.* London: National Corporation for the Care of Old People, Bedford Square Press.

Parsons, T. (1959). The social structure of the family. In R.N. Anshen (Ed.). *The family: Its function and destiny.* New York: Harper.

Rosow, I. (1967). *Social integration of the aged.* New York: Free Press.

Rosser, C., & Harris, C.C. (1965). *The family and social change.* London: Routledge & Kegan Paul.

Rowles, G.D., & Otha, R.J. (Eds.). (1983). *Aging and milieu: Environmental perspectives on growing old.* New York: Academic Press.

Shanas, E., & Sussman, M.B. (Eds.). (1977). *Family, bureaucracy and the elderly.* Durham, NC: Duke University Press.

Smith, C.J. (1980). Social networks as metaphors, models, and methods. *Progress in Human Geography, 4,* 500–524.

Stephens, R.C., Blau, Z., Oser, G., & Miller, M. (1978). Aging, social support systems and social policy. *Journal of Gerontological Social Work, 1,* 279–293.

Sussman, M.B. (1965). Relations of adult children with their parents in the United States. In E. Shanas & G. Streib (Eds.). *Social structure and family: Generational relations.* Englewood Cliffs, NJ: Prentice Hall.

Sussman, M.B. (1976). The family life of old people. In R. Binstock & E. Shanas (Eds.). *Handbook of aging and the social sciences.* New York: Van Nostrand.

Tinker, A. (1984). *Staying at home: Helping elderly people.* London: Her Majesty's Stationery Office.

Townsend, P. (1957). *The family life of old people.* London: Routledge & Kegan Paul.

Troll, L.E., & Bengtson, V.L. (1979). Generations in the family. In W.R. Burr, R. Hill, F.I. Nye, & I.L. Reiss (Eds.). *Contemporary theories about the family.* New York: Free Press.

United Kingdom, Department of Health & Social Security. (1981). *Growing older.* (Cmnd 8173). London: Her Majesty's Stationery Office.

United Kingdom, Ministry of Housing and Local Government. (1969) *Housing Standards and costs: Accommodation specially designed for old people.* (Circular 82/69). London: Author.

Warnes, A.M. (1983). Migrations in late working age and early retirement. *Socioeconomic planning sciences, 17,* 291–302.

Warnes, A.M., & Howes, D.R. (1984). A social survey of retired married couples and their family units. *Occasional Papers, Department of Geography, 20.* London: Department of Geography, King's College.

Warnes, A.M., & Law, C.M. (1985). Elderly population distributions and housing prospects in Britain. *Town Planning Review, 56,* 292–314.

Warnes, A.M., Howes, D.R., & Took, L. (1985a). Residential locations and intergenerational visiting in retirement. *Quarterly Journal of Social Affairs, 1,* 231–247.

Warnes, A.M. Howes, D.R., & Took, L. (1985b). Intimacy at a distance under the microscope. In A. Butler (Ed.). *Aging: Recent advances and creative responses.* London: Croom Helm.

Wenger, G.C. (1984). *The supportive network: Coping with old age.* London: Allen & Unwin.

Young, M., & Willmott, P. (1957). *Family and kinship in East London.* London: Routledge & Kegan Paul.

CHAPTER 56

How to Adjust Architectural Functions to the Physical Deteriorations of the Aged and Disabled

Tamako Hayashi

Although the elderly population (65 years and older) in Japan now accounts for a little less than 10% of the total population, in 20 years it will reach a level higher than in any other nation. What is most unique about Japan's elderly is that among them there is a high rate of co-residence (*dokyo*): Currently more than 60% of the elderly are living together with their children's families, and this rate is expected to be around the 50% level in the year 2000. Moreover, 80% of these elderly hope to remain living at their own houses permanently.

This information should be viewed in light of the estimated increase of the socially and physiologically problematic old-old segment (75 years and older) and of the drastic reduction in women who remain at home. (The number of working housewives in Japan has been growing noticeably.) Also, 90% of the two- or three-generation houses are privately owned wooden houses, and this makes remodeling doubly difficult: Not only do the traditional Japanese houses have a large number of architectural barriers, but owners also have to worry about the remodeling cost. Builders of Japanese housing developments should take these problems under consideration. This is why we should study the physical aspects of housing, addressing the changing needs of the elderly.

We were initially interested in various changes in the elderly's life: From the stage when they did not have physical disabilities to the stage of becoming bedridden as well as in how physical characteristics of their houses had been adjusted to these changes. Thus, the purpose of the research was to make an overall assessment of existing conditions and to identify any problems and needs.

RESEARCH DESIGN

In terms of the degree of physical disabilities, this research had three sample groups. For a summary of information about sampling and the sample, see Table 56-1. The first group consisted of 148 elderly in their 70s who were in the transitional stage from the self-care level to the semidependent level. Since they thought themselves to be healthy, we call this group the healthy group. The second group was 143 discharged elderly from the rehabilitation ward of a large geriatric hospital. They had distinct physical disabilities. The third group consisted of 64 bedridden elderly (being bedridden for at least 6 months). The total number of respondents was 355, and all lived in the Tokyo metropolitan area.

This research was carried out in two stages. First, in order to understand the changes of their living conditions and to find out any general problems we mailed questionnaires to all those in the healthy and discharged groups. Then, we visited 78 people in the first group, 39 in the second group, and all 64 of the third group, studying in detail the physical conditions in which they were living and asking about family situations and psychophysiological conditions vis-à-vis their houses.

While much data was collected, the following findings concern those data that may be utilized for setting architectural standards in housing for the disabled elderly.

FINDINGS

Family Relationships

It was found that married couples tended to live by themselves even when one of them experienced the decline of psychological and physiological functions. But widows or widowers were more likely to start living with their children's families when they experienced major functional decline. Interestingly, housing conditions for the elderly living with their children's families varied a great deal, depending on where they were living (either at the aged parent's or one of their children's houses), when they began living together, or whether or not the coresidence preceded the disability. The housing conditions were generally better among the cases in which the child's family moved into their parent's house; in this type there were many instances of building new

TABLE 56–1. Sample Characteristics for Three Elderly Groups Studies

Characteristic	Healthy group (1)		Disabled group (2 + 3)		
			Discharged		Bedridden
	Mailed questionnaire (1978)	Interviewed (1978)	Mailed questionnaire (1980)	Interviewed (1981)	Interviewed (1977)
Number responding	148	78	143	39	64
Mean age	72	72	73	72.5	77.8
Sex					
Male	86 (58.1%)	51 (65.4%)	72 (50.3%)	26 (66.7%)	29 (45.3%)
Female	62 (41.9%)	27 (34.6%)	71 (49.7%)	13 (33.3%)	35 (54.7%)
Married couple	104 (70.3%)	58 (74.4%)	82 (57.3%)	30 (76.9%)	29 (45.3%)
Living arrangement					
Living with children's family	72 (48.7%)	29 (37.2%)	60 (42.0%)	20 (51.3%)	45 (70.3%)
Living with unmarried children	28 (18.9%)	15 (19.2%)	35 (24.5%)	11 (28.2%)	11 (17.2%)
Living with spouse or alone	48 (32.4%)	24 (43.6%)	39 (27.3%)	6 (15.4%)	8 (12.5%)
Living with others	0	0	9 (6.3%)	2 (5.1%)	0
Mobility					
Ambulant	148 (100%)	78 (100%)	78 (54.5%)	16 (41.0%)	17 (26.6%)
Semiambulant	0	0	28 (19.6%)	12 (30.8%)	35 (54.7%)
Nonambulant	0	0	37 (25.9%)	11 (28.2%)	12 (18.8%)
Owned House	120 (81.1%)	72 (92.3%)	123 (86.0%)	36 (92.2%)	48 (76.0%)

houses or remodeling old ones. Meanwhile, the housing conditions were worse in cases where the coresidence started after the disability. Particularly noticeable was the fact that the burden on the child's family tended to become very heavy when they did not have a bedroom for the disabled parent.

Coping with Declining Physical Functions

Among the healthy group, various changes in living arrangements had been made. Examples include changing from Japanese-style mattress (futon) to beds; changing from a conventional squatting type of toilet to a more comfortable western-style toilet. When there was quite a distance from the bedroom to the toilet, a urinal or a portable toilet was installed. Another change was moving the bedroom from the upstairs to the downstairs.

As for the 143 discharged elderly, during the period from the discharge to this research, (on average 2 years and 7 months), the progressive condition of these elderly was as follows: 25% had died, 14% had been either rehospitalized or had moved to a nursing home for the aged, and only 61% of them were still living at their own houses. Looking at this 61%, changes include building new houses, remodeling old houses, changing rooms, and/or remodeling the inside of the elderly's room. Furthermore, 66% of this group had their toilets remodeled and 49% had their bathrooms remodeled. These rooms were basically expanded. Toilet bowls and bathtubs were replaced and handrails were installed. All in all, however, the changes were partial rather than large scale.

Through the interviews it became clear that, except for a few cases, the vast majority of the remodeled houses did not reflect the need for wheelchair access or the need to ease the burden of those taking care of the elderly. Of the respondents who had built new houses, many had relatively minor disabilities. There were no cases in which new houses were built, which incorporated the adjustability factor (flexibility) required to meet the growing needs of the disabled elderly.

Even of the houses that were adjusted according to the particular level of physical disability, progressive decline of the parent's functions was not correctly anticipated. Some houses had been remodeled or expanded more than twice. The floor slope and the toilet were for example, remodeled first; but the bathroom was remodeled and the bed space was newly added later. Despite these problems, it was quite obvious that the elderly living in the remodeled houses had a larger living space, were more independent, and felt more content with their lives than those living in unremodeled houses.

Behavioral Characteristics of the Elderly While in Their Rooms

The following findings summarize data concerning sleeping patterns, daily activities, and crowdedness caused by too many personal belongings:

Sleeping Patterns. There was a tendency for elderly couples to sleep in separate rooms when neither of them had any difficulties in their daily living and when additional rooms were available. But once either of them came to need some kind of assistance due to functional decline, they tended to sleep together in the same room. For widows or widowers, either daughter-in-law or daughter tended to sleep in the same room in order to provide necessary care.

Daily Activities. While even the healthy group showed a tendency to have meals in their own rooms, among the disabled group toileting and bathing were frequently added to this pattern. As physical functions declined, it became evident that daily activities performed in the elderly's room increased. Even so, we found that house remodeling; active efforts in caretaking by family members; and utilization of such home welfare services as bathing could make it possible to prevent or at least slow down this tendency, and to maintain the separation between one's activities and the space available. Some Japanese are without private bathtubs, or their bathtubs are inadequate. Japan's home welfare provides for bathing services (both centralized bathing services as well as private house calls) for its bedridden elderly.

Crowdedness. Many of the elderly often tend to save unnecessary, miscellaneous things, making their rooms overcrowded and underspaced. For the disabled elderly, a bed, a portable toilet, and other necessary related utilities are brought into their rooms. Despite the increasing multiplicity of daily activities, space of the elderly's room was not expanded, remaining on average about 108 square feet. The portable toilet was often too close to the elderly person when lying in bed—an arrangement found to be unsanitary, especially when having meals.

The Location of the Elderly's Room in the House

Among the healthy group, the elderly and their child's family tended to have separate living arrangements, more so with bedrooms than in "nonprivate rooms" such as the living room and the dining room. In order to understand the characteristics of the bedridden group (the group whose members were in the most serious state with the highest need of assistance), we developed a conceptual framework on the basis of architectural structure. This corresponds to the distance between the elderly's room and the areas that were occupied by the caretaking family members during both the daytime and nighttime. We made two categories concerning distance: When it was the same room or adjacent rooms with only a sliding Japanese door (fusuma) in between, we called this ''the close type'' and any other spacial arrangements were classified as ''the separate type.''

Analyzing this result in terms of family composition, we came up with the following types: When the disabled parent was living with their unmarried child, the day-and-night close type was most dominant. When they were living with the daughter's family, the nighttime-close but daytime-separate type prevailed. When living with the son's family, either the nighttime close but daytime-separate type or the day-and-night separate type was most often found. Among households with only elderly couples (even though they maintained the day-and-night close type), the caretaking spouse was most likely to be old and have many problems, too. Furthermore, in cases involving widows or widowers, their rooms were located in separate sections of the house away from the caretaking family members. This arrangement was most dominant among those living with the son's family. In short, separate types of living arrangements, which had been quite adaptable for both the elderly and child's family when the former was healthy, became dysfunctional or problematic when one of the aged parents died, or when physical functions of the remaining spouse began deteriorating. Consequently, the needs of assistance increased.

CONCLUSIONS

On the basis of these findings, we believe the following measures should be taken: First, it is necessary that houses for the elderly be barrier-free in their functions so that they can be adjusted to declining psychological and physical tendencies. Second, in order to help maintain one's remaining abilities or to slow down the process of progressive decline, the houses should be able to meet the needs specific to every stage of the decline. Third, from the beginning of construction, these first and second conclusions should be incorporated into the house's design. Also a house should be built while one is still healthy and capable.

Since 1980, we have been participating in a 5-year research project on the development of new housing designs for the elderly and the handicapped. This large-scale project is supported by Japan's Ministry of International Trade and Industry. What we have been most involved with is technological development of a care system for such people, with specific focus on adjustability and comfortability of living. This development was done in two ways. First, ''hardware'' development; our purpose was to develop the prototype housing for the elderly and the handicapped, with the clear intention of making various housing parts readily available. Second, the "software" development, the purpose being to develop methods by which people in need of such housing could choose appropriate housing or housing components.

A number of manufacturing companies as well as researchers participated in the "hardware" development. Such companies included a prefabricated housing manufacturer; those producing housing components such as aluminum window frames, doors, or tatami mats; those making sanitary equipment; and companies in the field of self-help equipment such as electric lifters or environment control systems. The purpose of a cooperative effort in developing this prototype housing was two-fold. First, by getting the manufacturing companies involved in the project we attempted to enlighten them on the needs of the elderly and the handicapped. Namely, emphasizing that a barrier-free design is important and that regular housing components that have barrier-free functions should be of good quality, in large quantity, and be widely and readily available.

The other purpose was to develop housing with functional flexibility. Partial remodeling, by replacing housing parts and installing self-help equipment or instruments, simplifies adjustments that are carried out to correspond with the changing degree of the elderly's physical functions. Here a four-level concept was adopted. In Japan houses that the handicapped could choose were either regular houses (without any consideration for their needs i.e., Level 1) or houses built for wheelchair users (i.e.,Level 3): variations between these two levels were almost nonexistent. Therefore, by introducing a Level 2 house it is hoped that the Japanese can realize that vast numbers of the handicapped can become potential users of this type of housing. Furthermore, we think that the Level 2 house should become an "ordinary house." By incorporating functions of a Level 4 house we hope that even after an elderly person becomes bedridden, he or she can have a pleasant life and remain living at his or her own house.

At present, a full-size prototype is being built. We are also planning to perform various tests by utilizing practical application methods among the handicapped. In addition, this prototype is being evaluated by a committee of the handicapped, as well as physicians and other outside professionals.

PART VI
Basic and Social Scientific Research

C. Policy; Planning; and Practice

CHAPTER 57

Population Policies and Aging in Developing Countries

Marsel A. Heisel

The message from the developing world seems to be one of concern for the problems of the aged in their populations and a request for worldwide cognizance of aging as an issue related to demographic trends, such as longer life expectancy, and to the consequences of socioeconomic development, such as migration and breakdown in the traditional family system. The International Conference on Population of 1984 in Mexico City to some extent responded to this message and passed a major resolution urging efforts to analyze the issues of aging and the implications for development. Judging from the minimal knowledge available on the situation of older persons in developing countries, one is led to the conclusion that governments are ahead of scholars in identifying issues that need attention. In developing regions of the world, there is pressing need to initiate policies with regard to the aged in their populations. It is important that research and education in gerontology take cognizance of the concerns of governments and help provide the basic information and trained personnel necessary in dealing with the issue.

Developing countries are experiencing immense growth in the number of older persons in their populations, a condition that raises serious issues for governments and merits the attention of gerontologists. However, the demographic definition of "aging population" (e.g., an

---

Parts of this paper were prepared for a report in a series of comparative studies on population policy carried out by the Department of International Economic and Social Affairs of the United Nations and published in the *Population Bulletin of the United Nations, no. 17,* United Nations publications, 1985, sales No.E.84.XIII.13.

increase in the *proportion* of older persons in a population) presents a problem for gerontology in developing regions of the world. Most developing countries are in demographic transition, having high fertility and low or declining mortality rates. Consequently, the proportion of older persons in their population remains low while their numbers increase substantially. A focus on aging populations, that is to say, on proportions, rather than on the *growing number* of aged persons in the population may encourage the view that there is no reason for aging to be considered an issue of concern in developing areas.

The increase in the number of older persons brings about particular social issues that occur even in the absence of a parallel rise in their proportion. With advancing age, there is increased susceptibility to chronic and long-term disease and disabilities. More of the aged tend to be socially dependent, illiterate and poor. This increases the demand for medical, social, and economic services beyond what would be expected from their proportion in the population. To bring attention to those issues, and to the necessity of including them in the formulation of national and international population policies, it is important to highlight the growth in numbers of aged persons. Moreover, attention should be drawn to the projected growth in the numbers of older persons in different age brackets, as social, economic, and health needs tend to change with progressively advancing age.

ESTIMATES OF GROWTH IN THE NUMBER OF AGING PERSONS

Developing countries can anticipate a substantial increment in the number of people aged 60 and over by the end of this century and still higher rates of increase after that. But, for most of them, the increase in the proportion will be moderate. According to projections by the United Nations based on 1982 assessments (World Population Prospects, 1985), between 1980 and 2000 the developed and developing regions will add, respectively, 60.9 and 163.5 million persons aged 60 and over to their populations without any significant narrowing of the gap in their respective proportions. This increment will be of the order of 74.6 and 317.3 million, respectively, between the years 2000 and 2020, over four times higher for developing regions when compared with developed areas.

Even more significant for policy issues are the projected numbers for persons aged 80 and over, when they are more likely to be frail and require special assistance. In 1960, there were four countries with one million or more persons classified in this category, and nine in 1980. By 2025, there will be 20 such countries, 11 of them currently classified as developing, including Argentina, Brazil, China, India, Indonesia,

Mexico, Nigeria, Philippines, Republic of Korea, Turkey, and Vietnam. In some developing countries, such as Brazil, China, Indonesia, Mexico, Nigeria, Philippines, Republic of Korea, and Turkey, this growth is truly precipitous: The number of octogenarians in those countries will have increased five to six times between 1980 and 2020. Because of the increasing difference in life expectancy between men and women, the majority of octogenarians will be women, most of them widows.

This rapid rate of increase in the number of old persons, particularly in the very old, will bring about much greater demand in medical services and in intergenerational transfer of income. It will also place additional pressure on the family in the care of its frail elderly members. Moreover, where the old have traditionally been protected and cared for in the family, population policies related to reduced fertility and migration, often considered necessary for development, can at the same time create harsh conditions for the elderly. Old parents will be left with fewer children and grandchildren close by on whom to rely, and support systems outside of the family may become a necessity.

THIRD WORLD GOVERNMENTS' POLICIES AND PERCEPTIONS ON THE AGED: FINDING THE DATA

The purpose of this paper is to explore the awareness, experience, and response of developing countries to the needs of the aged in their population in the context of changing demographic conditions and population policies. Among the questions investigated are: What are the articulated policies and perceptions on aging when expressed in the context of demographic trends and population policies? Do Third World Governments consider aging a problematic issue at all? If so, what are the plans, if any, to deal with the problems? Where is the most concern? The most need? Research for this study (Heisel, 1985) was undertaken as part of the substantive preparations for the International Conference on Population of 1984. The paper also presents a brief comparison of global concern with issues of aging as reflected in decisions adopted by the two World Population Conferences of 1974 and 1984.

Information pertinent to governments' perceptions and policies with respect to aging was obtained from content analysis of two sets of data: (1) National Statements delivered to the World Assembly on Aging in 1982, and (2) The Fifth Population Inquiry Among Governments, an investigation conducted by the United Nations in 1983 to monitor government policies and perceptions on demographic trends and policies. The two sources were independent and diverse, but complemented each other in providing useful data in an area of inquiry where little information is available.

The World Assembly on Aging provided governments with a direct opportunity to articulate their perceptions, concerns, policies, and plans vis-a-vis their aged citizens. Population changes or policies were not a primary item on the agenda, but demographic trends were treated as one of the important exogenous variables. The Assembly encouraged governments to express problems besetting the aged in their countries and the National Statements tended to give the full range of concerns associated with aging. On the other hand, the Fifth Population Inquiry, which was carried out to provide a significant input into the International Conference on Population of 1984, was focused on government policies and perceptions on demographic trends in relation to development and did not prompt comments on aging as an issue. It could thus be assumed that analysis of the questionnaires with respect to aging provided an indication of minimum concern.

RESULTS FROM THE WORLD ASSEMBLY ON AGING

Statements and reports of 52 developing countries to the World Assembly on Aging were analyzed with respect to problematic and programmatic concern for the welfare of their aged citizens. Only 6 governments out of 52 stated that aging was not an issue of governmental concern, and that aging was not perceived as an area to which government attention should be directed at present. The remaining 46 countries, however, expressed substantial concern with the situation of the aged in their population, and their comments were often expressed in reference to the changing demographic picture. The need to plan for the rising numbers of older persons in their population was indicated not only by countries with relatively old populations, such as some Latin American countries or those with rapidly aging demographic structures in Asia and the Pacific, it also was indicated by some very young populations, such as among African and Middle–Eastern nations. Interest in the question of aging was evident in countries with very traditional families and in those with relatively nuclear family structures, in countries that are basically secular, and in those that place strong emphasis on religious values. The issues of concern articulated centered primarily on the areas of migration and the family.

Migration is a factor that most clearly illustrates how strongly population policies are linked to concerns related to the aged. The Kenya Report (1982) summarizes the situation succinctly, reflecting the concerns of many Third World governments: The condition of the elderly is often very poor. In some cases they are left in the rural areas without anybody to care for them, and often they have never had any work that has entitled them to any benefits. Some elderly people have followed their relatives to urban areas, where in most cases housing facilities are not sufficient. Housing in urban centers is extremely inadequate, often lacking the rudiments of sanitation, water supply, and waste disposal. In such surroundings the aged are vulnerable, often victimized, and usually found in substandard shelters.

Another related issue articulated by governments was the situation of the elderly immigrant workers and the need for bilateral and multilateral agreements to safeguard their benefits. A considerable proportion of immigrants remain in the host country beyond age 60, often lacking supportive familiar systems. In some cases they must remain in the host country in order to receive their retirement benefits. An excerpt from the Presentation of the Turkish Delegation to the World Assembly on Aging (1982) illustrates this concern:

> One particular matter which concerns Turkey is the elderly immigrant workers and their social, economic, and humanitarian problems. We strongly believe that these problems, which remain to be solved, deserve the attention of all related organizations, both at the national and international level.

The implications of demographic and social changes at the family level almost universally received comments from governments. In essence, what most developing countries said about aging and the family can be summarized as follows: Values of the traditional family system are still very important, and the aged command respect and attention from the young members of the family who have the responsibility of caring for their elders. However, recent economic and social changes, particularly migration, have produced a decline in the traditional system of assigning responsibility in the family and in its capacity to cope with some of the fundamental needs of its aged members. There are many elderly persons without means of support and without near kin who are available or willing to look after them. The government has thus to assume some of this responsibility. There is need to initiate policies to alleviate individual hardship and, at the same time, reinforce the traditional family values.

The majority of statements report that the elderly still live with their families, but there appears to be great variation among countries. For example, according to reports submitted to the World Assembly on Aging, in Costa Rica 90% of the elderly live in families. On the other hand, in Jamaica, among those 65 years old and over, 25% of the males and 29% of the females live alone. There may be more independent living by older people in developing countries than is generally thought.

In attempting to deal with the problems of the aged, many Third

World governments are considering legislation to support the family efforts to care for their aging members. Other governments are considering giving tax relief to those families caring for aged relatives. Some countries are building homes for older persons, or for those incapacitated or alone. However, other countries reported having stopped building any more welfare institutions for the elderly in order to discourage the erosion of traditional family values. Responses appeared to be sporadic, and this in itself indicates a need for a better basis from which to derive guidance for policies.

RESULTS FROM THE FIFTH POPULATION INQUIRY AMONG GOVERNMENTS

The Fifth Population Inquiry Among Governments was conducted by the United Nations, Population Division, to monitor a broad range of government policies and perceptions on demographic trends and levels in relation to development as of 1982. The topics included in the questionnaire were: population growth, morbidity and mortality, fertility and the family, population distribution and internal migration. Institutional arrangements for integrating demographic factors into development planning, international cooperation in the area of population, and the International Conference on Population of 1984. In addition to the structured questions, governments were invited to provide statements concerning their views on the topics listed above and also to make recommendations on issues that should be discussed in the International Conference on Population. The inquiry did not prompt comments on aging as an issue (Report on the Fifth Population Inquiry Among Governments, 1984).

Out of a total of 168 governments, 119 (71%) returned the questionnaire, 89 of which were from developing countries. Each questionnaire was scanned for any information that displayed ''aging concern'' in the government's response, such as references to existing or planned programs for the aged, building of old people's homes, concern about the socioeconomic consequences of aging populations, or recommendation that the issue of aging be discussed in the International Conference on Population.

In responding to the Fifth Population Inquiry, one third of developing countries (30 of the 89 responses received from this group) indicated concern about the aging segment of their population within the context of demographic topics included in the questionnaire, and thus singled out the aged as one of the elements to be included in the governments' population programs and policies. The largest proportion of those responses were elicited by a question pertaining to fertility and the family. Countries were asked to indicate any measures or programs their government had implemented that were related to any policy of direct intervention in relation to fertility levels. The possible checklist consisted of items such as "family planning program" and "child welfare allowance," but it also included "measure for care and protection of the aged," which was reported by 22 developing countries. However, many governments also volunteered information about special concerns, plans or programs for the aged, and some requested that aging be put on the agenda of the forthcoming Conference on Population.

Even though concern for aging as an issue was reported by some countries in every region of the world, there was great disparity among regions, particularly among African countries, where only 23% indicated policy concern with older populations; for other regions of the world the corresponding figure was 35% to 50%, and the consideration of aging as an issue of population policies was expressed with more intensity. Out of 39 African governments that returned the questionnaire, 11 indicated programs, plans, or concern for the aged in their populations within the context of population trends and policies that were under discussion. Comparable ratios for developing countries in Asia and the Pacific were 12 out of 28 and for Latin America, 8 out of 20. It must be remembered, however, that this analysis of the Inquiry indicated only *minimum* concern. The most important finding with respect to aging from the Fifth Population Inquiry was that even the most conservative estimates reflect considerable awareness and concern in developing countries with the welfare of the rising number of older persons in their populations.

AGING AND THE WORLD POPULATION PLAN OF ACTION

Comparison of major world population discussions at the global level show that, lately there has been a major shift in the importance attached to the issues of aging within the context of population policies. Ten years ago, the World Population Conference in Bucharest made only passing reference to aging in its recommendations, briefly stating that "all countries should carry out, as part of their development programs, comprehensive, humanitarian, and just programs for the elderly" (World Population Plan of Action, 1974). In contrast, the International Conference on Population of 1984 in Mexico City passed a major resolution urging efforts to analyze the issue of aging and the implications for national development, social services and medical care, and the need to perceive the elderly as possible contributors to development rather than merely as dependent persons. Undoubtedly, the World Assembly on Aging of 1982 had much influence in raising the consciousness of the international community to the issues of aging. This recommendation states:

> Governments are urged to reaffirm their commitment to the implementation of the International Plan of Action on Aging. In this context, further efforts should be made to analyze the issues of aging, *particularly its implications for overall development* (italics added), social services, medical care, and other related fields, and on the basis of such data, Governments are urged to take appropriate measures to secure the welfare and safety of older people, paying particular attention to the situation and needs of older women. Governments and international agencies should increase their efforts and activities with a view to improving care for the aged within the family unit. Moreover, Governments should view the aging sector of the population not merely as a dependent group, but in terms of the active contributions that older persons have already made and still can make to the economic, social, and cultural life of their families and community (Report of the International Conference on Population, 1984).

This resolution still lacks sufficient emphasis with regard to issues of aging in developing countries, but it does reflect many of the concerns expressed by governments in the data reviewed here.

REFERENCES

Heisel, M.A. (1985). Aging in the context of population policies in developing countries. *Population Bulletin of the United Nations, 17,* 49-63.

Kenya Report for the World Assembly on Aging. (1982 July 26-August 6). Report presented by the Minister for Culture and Social Services, Vienna.

Presentation of the Head of the Turkish delegation at the World Assembly on Aging. (1982, July 26-August 6). Vienna.

Report of the International Conference on Population, 1984. (1984). New York: United Nations Publications.

Report on the Fifth Population Inquiry Among Governments. (1984). New York: United Nations Publications.

World Population Plan of Action. (1974). Report of the World Population Conference, Bucharest, New York: United Nations Publications.

World Population Prospects: Estimates and Projections as Assessed in 1982. (1985). New York: United Nations Publications.

CHAPTER 58

Technology and Aging

Pauline K. Robinson, Xavier Gaullier,
Willem H. C. Kerkhoff, Paul A. H. Haber,
Gerald A. Straka

Four chapters are summarized here that describe technological changes that affect the aged: Xavier Gaullier describes how in France, high technology has led to a policy of retirement of workers at the age of 50. The state, firms, and retirees have concurred on this policy, although the solution is not always satisfactory for the early retirees. Willem Kerkhoff presents two examples of immaterial technological development taken from the experience of the Dutch broadcasting sector, a career ladder system and a creativity stifling system of production management, are shown to affect older workers negatively. How ecological technology can improve the quality of life of the aged in the activities of daily living in their residences is discussed by Paul Haber. Developments in telecommunications (e.g., cable television and videocasette recorders), which can contribute to the independence, education, and enjoyment of the elderly are described, but, as Gerald Straka points out, may exclude a segment of the elderly who lack the education or literacy required to take advantage of them.

Technological changes in the past have affected the lives of the aged in both positive and negative ways, and we can anticipate both kinds of effects on the aged in the future. For this reason the terminology of *technological change* is preferable to the more common *technological advances*. The symposium reviewed here provided a forum for discussion of technology and aging in regard to certain aspects of: labor force trends, aging worker performance, the home and long-term care institutions, and telecommunication in education. Technological advances in medicine are not included here because they are presented in Part II of this volume. The four original symposium papers are presented here in a condensed and summarized format.

A few questions are posed to provide a context for consideration of the papers in this symposium. First, can we in fact isolate in our analyses effects of technology that are specific in important ways to the older segments of the population? Second, what are the unforeseen, unintended, and potentially unfortunate consequences of technological changes instituted on behalf of the aged? Third, when we do recognize technological changes as hazardous to the aged, can we do anything to mitigate their impact, or does technology not have a life of its own well beyond our control? And finally, what are our obligations in weighing the potentially harmful effects of technology on the aged against their potential benefits for the population as a whole, for example, in increasing production in developing countries?

TECHNOLOGY, EMPLOYMENT, AND AGING: EARLY RETIREMENT IN FRANCE

The development of modern societies has been punctuated by periods of growth and periods of economic crisis; the most recent crisis had its inception 15 years ago. Each of these periods has been characterized by a specific means of striking a balance between new technologies, productivity, and corporate management. In each period, the problem of older workers and departure from the work force has been an issue, subject to a different form of social compromise. The growth of capitalism in the 19th century was characterized by continuous labor over the entire lifetime without any limitations save physical disability and death. In the 20th century, the new requirements of the economy imply an age limit to working that takes the form of collectively negotiated retirement: "social recognition of the contradiction, at an earlier age than previously, between technological progress and aging" (Frossard, 1983) and social compromise between the right to work and the right to leisure. The current crisis and its accompanying high technologies have once again forced transformation of corporate management, and have laid greater importance upon age criteria: The position of older workers has not changed.

Policy regarding older workers can always be described by a set of four features, and the current crisis is no exception. There are: (a) working conditions, adaptation or lack of adaptation to older workers, consequences for the health and the aging process of older workers; (b) corporate management, balance, and rejuvenation of the age pyramid; (c) problems of employment and unemployment, overmanning, and the social and financial burden of the unemployed; and (d) age at permanent departure from the work force and mandatory retirement age.

To a greater extent than any other industrialized nation, France has elaborated a comprehensive early retirement policy, which has been in effect for the last 10 years. Discussed in this paper will be the impact of this policy on those industries that have invested heavily in advanced technology and that are the beneficiaries of special legislation allowing them to dismiss workers 55 and over, if they are replaced by an equal number of unemployed, young workers. The government's aim in creating these "solidarity contracts" was to combat unemployment by appealing to intergenerational solidarity. This policy does not create jobs; rather, it substitutes young workers for older ones. These contracts involve:

- An agreement between the State and the volunteer firm for a period of two years;
- The option for employees of these firms to depart from the work force when they have reached the age of 55;
- Indemnities paid to these workers by the unemployment fund that are slightly higher than retirement pensions;
- The illegality for these early retirers to hold a new salaried position and volunteer work is excepted;
- The commitment of the firm to replace the early retirers by young workers and to maintain the work force at the same level for a 1-year period.

In regard to the four features mentioned above, French policy for firms modernizing their technology is characterized by the exclusion of older workers from the work force, an increase in the number of years of leisure, a rejuvenation of the age pyramid, and a refusal to modify working conditions to suit older workers. In comparison with other countries, the French solidarity contracts legislation distinguishes itself by a preponderant State intervention, high rate of departure from the work force, a precocious retirement age, voluntary departure, high indemnities, a cut-off point for age at retirement unconnected to state of health or obsolescence, an ambiguous social status for the early retiree, a rapid and profound transformation of personnel, and an adaptation to advanced technology by younger personnel.

Research in solidarity contracts was conducted in 1982 and focused on three axes. First, management from 43 representative enterprises from the southeast of France were studied via interviews and questionnaires. Second, the life-style of early retirees was studied through questionnaries and in-depth interviews. Third, on a general and national level, a survey was made of information and available documentation and interviews were conducted with people and institutions involved in solidarity contracts. This study is described in a long final report and several articles (Gaullier, 1982, 1985; Gaullier and Gogna-lons-Nicolet, 1984).

An important finding was the favorable reception that enterprises, employees, and unions gave to the solidarity contracts. The number of contracts signed (35,000 in the first 2 years), the number of workers who departed (200,000), and the hiring of young workers to replace them was such that the government modified the legislation after the 2-year period, feeling that its aims had been accomplished. The survey indicates that this success was due to a social consensus between social partners, each of whom felt they had something to gain.

In firms that invest and modernize, a common obstacle to economic development strategies is personnel rigidity. For high performance firms, solidarity contracts were seen as a means of lowering the general age of their staff, balancing the age pyramid, and thus adapting their work force to advanced technology. A new career profile is emerging, based on flexibility and mobility, rejecting all forms of stability including seniority, and using retirement "less to attract workers and gain their loyalty than to get rid of them" (Kessler, 1984).

In the French context of new technologies, the policy is to exclude older workers at increasingly younger ages. The introduction of advanced technology is a synonym for "out with older workers"; the ever-present slogan is "young workers for young technologies" (Sud, 1983).

Employees are also favorable to solidarity contracts. Among the enterprises involved in contracts, the average departure rate is 62% of those aged 55 to 60, and the figure is often higher. The survey showed that five factors were critical to this surprisingly high rate: (a) the voluntary nature of departure and the high stable indemnity up to the legal retirement age; (b) a growing dissatisfaction with work, not primarily because of technological changes, but because of modifications in staff management; (c) health problems for a minority (10%); (d) a desire to use leisure to "take advantage of life"; and (e) assessment of the overall economic situation (current job precariousness).

Beyond this consensus on early retirement, the study has brought to light the limits and contradictions of the policy of solidarity contracts. As regards enterprises, the limitations of this policy, which places undue emphasis on the value of young workers and which underrates the contribution of older workers, have been clearly demonstrated. Numerous studies have stressed the importance of the experience and know-how of older workers in the introduction and operation of advanced technologies (Sud, 1983). The early retirement policy allows firms to dismiss older workers, and by doing so, to avoid the major issue of the adaptation of these workers to new technologies and vice versa.

As regards early retirees, the solution is not necessarily satisfactory in the near or more distant future. Given the current crisis of the Welfare State, their indemnities, and consequently their standard of living, is declining and will continue to do so. Early retirement also raises two diametrically opposed problems: Adjustment problems leading to dependence on multiple social and medical sources of relief, and on the other hand, the restriction of healthy and active early retirees from taking on salaried positions or, for the most part, voluntary activities.

Concerning society, the early retirement policy has created a dual age split: A working minority age 25 to 50 who are monopolizing performance jobs and are overworked, and a majority of nonemployed individuals who are forbidden to work by law yet wish to have activities meriting societal esteem. The early retirement policy accentuates and aggravates the traditional fixed life cycle occurring in industrialized societies: A period of youth training following by a period of adult activity and finally a period of leisure in old age.

Given such contradictions, another type of policy has begun to be envisioned, one where there would be a slowdown in early retirement, investment in other directions, such as better training for *all* personnel for new technologies and work sharing at all ages. But this new form of policy has been slow to develop. Only a small minority have envisaged a new life cycle adapted to new technology. The three stage cycle of education-work-retirement would be replaced by flexibility throughout life, which would include periods of activity alternating with periods of training and/or leisure. The problems connected to end of career and retirement would take on an entirely different significance and would be better adapted to individuals, companies, and to society in general. Retirement would no longer be associated with a set age but to number of years worked. The early retirement policy forces us to reconsider the rigid life cycle we are accustomed to and to entertain the possibility of a flexible cycle better suited to advanced technology.

AGING WORKERS: SHADOWS OF THE PAST, PERSPECTIVES FOR THE FUTURE?

The main difference between nature and technology is that the latter is a product of traceable human goals. The point to be illustrated is that the artificial technological environment has huge effects on human life (i.e., on the process of aging). Increasingly we are a product of the technological environment, although these effects are very often not intended and are often hard to detect. We should not think only of the material components of technology, the computers, traffic systems, and the satellites surrounding us. Goal directedness appears in a lot of nonmaterial environmental features, such as governmental and organizational systems and information, coordination, and control devices. This matter can be approached with a case illustration.

Technicians in the Dutch broadcasting system are high-level personnel. One of the needs growing from the beginning of the television era was to have self-developed personnel, able to deal with the most advanced technologies. Toward this goal a career ladder was developed, ranking technicians from lower-level work through several steps to the top-level specialists. To use this nonmaterial career technology it was decided that any new technician, however high or excellent his level might be, should start at the bottom of the ladder. This was carried out over about a decade and a half. Then, in 1983, the population of technicians was found to have problems, especially in the higher age groups. With a lot of earlier research on obsolescence in mind (Kerkhoff, 1981), it was not hard to detect this problem. Quickly changing digital computerization was hard to keep up with, especially for those used to analog technology. The experience of the older technicians became outdated.

Analysis of turnover, however, revealed a decidedly increased turnover of technicians aged 35 to 45. Another rather modern age-related phenomenon (i.e., "midlife crisis") (Neugarten, 1980) might manifest itself here. Introduced by the highly formalized career system, people could understandably be stimulated to review the road covered thus far and to evaluate the promises of the road ahead. Some might feel this future to be too predictable or less attractive than perceived alternatives and go out to enter entirely different fields. Others might conclude that they were unable to reach the top and thus leave the system.

Expanding the case interpretation, a broader hypothesis concerning midlife crisis might be as follows: midlife crisis is a function of the degree to which patterns in the course of life can be perceived. Modern personnel policy increasingly introduces career systems in the work environment. The conclusion is that midlife crisis is a modern product of current personnel planning systems (i.e., of modern technology).

To follow the case, one notes a number of middle-aged technicians decided to stay, probably attracted by the perspectives of the career ladder in its higher ranks. At a later stage, a significant number of aged technicians were not only victims of obsolescence but also of the phenomenon known as the Peter Principle (Peter, 1969), having reached a level just beyond their capacities. The problem of the aged technicians appeared to be the awareness of not being able to cope with changing technology, while knowing at the same time that the position reached emphatically required it. It was observed that aged technicians constantly had to overreach, while a more relaxed work environment was longed for. Modern technology, as the case is meant to illustrate, exerts influence on the process of aging, directly as well as indirectly.

Macrolevel and Mesolevel Backgrounds

Modern technology is developed and introduced partly as a function of socioeconomic developments. The Dutch case illustrates this view. As it was so adequately described by Cowgill and Holmes' Modernization Theory (1972), increasing modernization in the Netherlands led to increasing numbers of the aged at macrolevels with a decreasing social status (SCP, 1984).

Socioeconomic developments after World War II explain in a more detailed way the circumstances of the aged workers. Older workers were not a structural but rather an incidental individual problem during the first 20 years of economic restoration and growth. A number of conditions turned the senior employees into a structural problem after the second half of the 1960s: increased labor cost, stimulating the search for labor cost-reducing technology, together with industrial overcapacity and/or stagnating growth on the consumer markets marked the beginning of the economic crisis ruling the 1970s. Necessary budget control and restrictions of personnel input led, on the one hand, to the first signals of youth unemployment. On the other hand, this resulted in accelerated aging of the active labor population. The first Committees on Aging were installed in the beginning of the 1970s (Kerkhoff, 1975). Meanwhile invalidation figures as a part of "natural turnover" started to exceed expected figures (CBS, 1984).

During the 1970s specific mechanisms became active to reverse accelerated aging of the work force, first through early retirement, then by outplacement of workers of $57^1/_2$ and older (SoZa, 1984). The structural features of the aged population gradually changed. Reduction of manpower, especially at the higher age levels, was realized, but the problem of obsolescence lowered the age at which workers were designated as older workers. There followed a widely accepted labeling of older workers as problematic workers. Role-taking (Burgess, 1960) induces the workers themselves to behave according to this label.

Structurally, investments in labor force, especially at higher age levels, were discouraged as part of modern personnel policy. The introduction of labor-reducing technology not only seemed more rational, but was unavoidable as a consequence of increased competition. Furthermore, the unrestricted labor market gave way to labor exchange rather than to investment in labor. Obsolescence was increased by internal and external factors.

There were two acceptable alternatives to the constant turnover: (a) for the more aged and unqualified workers, the exceptionally high paying Social Benefit programmes; and (b) for the less aged and more qualified, the private and governmental services. The second alternative will be illustrated by the developments in the Dutch Broadcasting

System, which roughly correspond with the developments in the broader service system.

Organization Development in the Broadcasting Services

During the period of high youth unemployment, which followed the rapid growth and professionalization of the broadcasting sector, a newly installed committee was asked to study the problem of older workers in the broadcasting system. The committee permitted a study of what turned out to be a typical industrial gerontology case. One of the groups showing problems at the higher age levels was the hard core of the business, the producers. The problem was described as a stereotype, stating that above the age of 40, creativity would extinguish. In order to get beyond this focus, we needed to turn our attention to the producers' artificial environment, in this case, styles of production management.

Competition among the different broadcasting companies was increasing. In search of productions with guaranteed success, the purchase of well known productions from the USA became the model. The model led to different tasks for the producers. Less and less of their work required creativity, and more generally, they described their work as an invitation to put a new jacket around basically old ideas. We concluded that the stereotype was right, but that it was not due to endogenous, age-related mechanisms. Creativity did diminish, because of environmental factors; namely, managerial procedures (Jansen, 1983).

Again, this case illustrates an unintended influence of management technology on the process of aging. We consider this kind of analysis of huge importance for gerontology. The knowledge that unchanged conditions could repeat problems for the aged in the future will probably stimulate the search for better conditions. For a graying nation like the Netherlands, this approach is inevitable. We should learn from the shadows of the past.

TECHNOLOGY IN AGING

Technology has undoubtedly played a role in the increase in the proportion of elderly people in the United States, but it also offers one answer in the increasing economic burden that the aging of America places on us. One reason that we need to invoke technology in caring for the aging is to enhance the quality of life. The ability of the older person to cope with the environment is compromised of a variety of decrements in physical and psychological integrity, and the older person is forced to live in a world that is not designed for his functioning.

Another reason for employing technology in the care of the elderly is that to the extent that we can use technology to render older persons more independent, the need for institutional care will decrease. Projections of expenditures for the care of the elderly are reflected in the rapidly escalating costs of Medicare and Medicaid. Indeed, it is expected that $58.4 million will have been spent by Medicaid for nursing home care by 1990 (Etheridge, 1984).

Many of us perceive that there is a current turning away, a revulsion if you will, from high technology. High technology is not the only form of technology that we are concerned with. Technology can be divided into three areas: *low technology* which concerns those simple mechanical devices with which we surround our life; *midtechnology,* which embraces familiar objects but which are not simple mechanical devices, such as radio, television, telephone, automobiles, etc.; and *high technology,* which is the employment of electronics, molecular biology, high-energy physics, and a variety of other abstruse science fields. One can invoke the use of all three levels for the enrichment of the lives of the elderly.

Technology can be divided into two major areas, both of which are important to the care of the elderly, namely *health care technology* and *ecological technology.* It is ecological technology that will be stressed here, including (a) the activities of daily living such as dressing, grooming, feeding, bathing, toileting, transferring, and ambulating; (b) instrumental activities of daily living that require the manipulation of devices such as using phones, meal preparation, driving automobiles, etc.; (c) communications; (d) transportation; (e) interior design; (f) urban design; and (g) industrial workplace design.

Physical and psychological decrements accompanying the aging process have enormous impact on our society. Thus older individuals can no longer cope with their environment; they need assistance, and often must be institutionalized to provide care for them. If we could prevent the need for assistance by appropriate design of the environment, we could lower the cost of the noninstitutionalized elderly and prevent institutionalization in many instances. A growing number of older persons experience such decrements. This is exaggerated with increasing age so that by age 75 a majority of people report limitations in their normal activities.

In a 1978 survey (Department of Health and Human Services, 1983), 46% of older persons had limitation of activities; of these persons, 7% were limited, but not in major activity, 22% were limited in amount and kind of activities, and 17% were unable to carry on major activity. By 75 years of age the total who had some limitation rose to 51%, and by age 85 this rose to 60%. Further, in carrying on typical activities of daily living such as dressing, 2% of those over 65 were limited, as were 11% of those over 85. It is apparent, therefore, that if serious improvement in these conditions could be effected by redesign of the environment, we would have made an enormous impact on the problem.

Lawton (1984) has defined four kinds of subgroups for uses of technological aids: (a) those without notable impairment where technology developed for the use of people in general will be useful to the normal older person, (b) people with sensory and perceptual deficits, (c) people with motor deficits of limitation in ambulation, and (d) people with problems in memory, information processing, judgment, and other cognitive functions. Lawton also describes the interaction between the person and the environment and the resultant outcome as a function of the interaction between the individual and the environment. This concept has been used, for example, in describing the etiology of falls in older persons, suggesting that there is an environmental demand, a physiological competence, and a resultant outcome between the two, which in the normal person prevents falls.

One special set of problems is presented to us by the increasing incidence of Alzheimer's disease, most of which will have to be cared for at home. Berger (1985) has described six severity classes for a range of deterioration from very light to very severe, and it is clear that at least some of these classes could be cared for at home. This means that design of the home will have to be appropriate for the treatment of such patients. Here the rule that one wishes to facilitate manipulation of the environment by the impaired patient, may have to be reversed.

First, for example, instead of making it easier to turn on the gas on the stove for the ordinary handicapped patient, it might be necessary to have controls that would make it more difficult for an Alzheimer's patient to turn on the gas, which could constitute a hazard in the home environment. Similarly, one would not necessarily want to make it easier for a patient to have egress from an apartment or a building because of the danger of wandering. Third, it might be useful in both institutional and the home environments to permit patients a certain amount of egress to the outdoors but to confine them to a given area so that they do not wander off. The use of shrubs and plantings around the home to prevent accidental wandering could be employed.

Berger (1985) has said that it is important to have an environment that is stable and that can be made familiar to the patient. He points out that using distinctive colorings, rather than having a corridor with multiple entrances that appear identical in form, shape, and color, help patients to more easily orient themselves, with respect to their particular room in an institution. Obviously, much more thought needs to be given to the care of demented patients, in both the home and the institution. Exploration of low technology for these cognitively impaired patients needs to be undertaken.

In summary, then, ecological technology has only begun to be explored, but we need to get much more relevant data, both in anthropometry and ergonomics. Most of the work done in these areas has been done on younger, healthy persons. For example, the standard tables of anthropometry are drawn on Air Force personnel, and the relevance to an aging population is only very slight. What is called for is the establishment of a laboratory that will apply the basic principles of both anthropometry and ergonomics to the situation of the aged patient. At the Palo Alto Veterans Administration Medical Center we are attempting to do just that by pulling together a multidisciplinary group that attempts to meld the various backgrounds into a common pool of knowledge that can be used to design environments for the elderly and the handicapped.

IMPLICATIONS OF TELECOMMUNICATIONS FOR ELDERLY AND EDUCATION

A variety of delivery systems and technologies developed for the home television set now provide the television user with increasing programming alternatives. For example, cable television, the widest spread of these alternatives in the United States, is characterized by programming brought to the viewer via a cable. There is no longer the problem of interference between messages televised over the air. One consequence of cable television is that the number of channels is now nearly unlimited. Another innovation with yearly growth rates of 50% and more is videocassette recorders (VCR), which allow the viewer to replay, record, and, in combination with a video camera, to produce a nearly unlimited variety of programs.

A central assumption regarding these new developments in home television is that they will lead from broadcasting to narrowcasting (Naisbitt, 1982). Narrowcasting is programming for smaller audiences having specific background and/or interests in common (for example, older adults). According to Toffler (1980), these technological innovations have one thing in common: "They slice the mass television public into segments, and each slice not only increases our cultural diversity, it cuts deeply into the power of the networks that have until now so completely dominated our imagery" (p. 180). This raises the following questions: (a) What are the implications of narrowcasting for the increasing group of the elderly in American society? (b) What is the educational potential of these innovations for older persons? (c) What are the risks of the recent innovations of telecommunication for the elderly?

Implications of Narrowcasting

A great potential for future growth is predicted for videocassette recorders (VCR). The VCR may have some consequences concerning the transience of television broadcasts and the "catch-it-or-miss-it" nature of the live broadcast. Television programming can be stored by the VCR, even if the individual who is recording it is not at home, and viewed whenever the viewer wants to.

Research on the elderly's television consumption found that older persons, on the average, phase out an hour earlier than younger viewers (Davis & Davis, 1985). Sometimes programs for specific interest groups like the elderly are broadcast at a time unfavorable for them or when there is competition with other activities. Thus, the VCR technique may increase the independence of elderly persons, for example, by allowing them to use daytime for active behavior and social contacts.

For educational purposes this technique has another advantage compared with "live" televised instruction. The presentation, stored on cassette, can be interrupted and replayed. This may be important considering the lower speed of information processing of older persons and the increasing likelihood of getting mentally tired in old age. A problem is that the costs for recorded cassettes and a VCR are still prohibitive for the average household (Baldwin & McVoy, 1983).

Cable television is a "narrow cast system of distributing one or more television signals over a wired system to individual receivers in a given geographic area" (Cohen, 1984, p. 388). What are the promises associated with cable television? The increase in diversity takes first rank; there are now many channels available. Feeding these channels with software will inevitably lead to a greater variety of programming for more and more specific interest and target groups. This will also put an end to the quasi-monopoly of the broadcasting companies with a tight market for creative talents. There will be room for experimentation with new ideas, for more in-depth news, and less commercial interruptions. The closed shop of the broadcast market will be opened—not only by the number of available channels but by the public access channel as well.

Davis and Miller (1983) mention the following possible uses of television cable by older adults: general information such as news and public affairs, specialized information according to the needs and wants of older persons, general entertainment, video music, ethnic and religious programming, community news, and local politics. (This list refers primarily to one-way cable.)

An example of two-way, or interactive, cable is the service videotext, a system in which information is stored in a central computer, transmitted to the home on phone lines or cable, and displayed on the home

TV set. The strengths of this system are that the users display only the information of interest to them, keeping it on the screen as long as they want. The information can be constantly updated and is available 24 hours a day. In one system, available services included updated news, weather, sports information; information for ordering merchandise from catalogs; and the ability to transfer money from bank accounts and to send messages to a public bulletin board.

These are some potentials of these innovations. What about the reality? A 1981 survey concerned the use of the attitudes toward new technologies by the elderly (Brickfield, 1984); 32% of the older respondents used cable television and 6% used video recorders. There was a negative relationship between age and the use of modern technology, and a positive correlation with income and educational level.

Risks

In the preceding paragraphs an optimistic picture about the future for the elderly was drawn. However, this is only one side of the picture. The information society is a literacy-intensive society. Basic reading and writing skills are needed more than ever before (Naisbitt, 1982). There is a danger that not all members of the society may participate in the progress and advantages of the information technology for the daily independent life. The assumption is that only a small proportion of the elderly (those well educated and/or self instructed during the life-long learning process) might gain the increasing benefits of the information technology. Therefore, the likelihood will increase of dividing the society, and the subgroup of the elderly as well, into a small group who benefit, and a majority excluded from the benefits of these innovations (Baldwin & McVoy, 1983; Elton & Carey, 1983).

Other questions concern the amount of time spent watching television. Will the amount of television consumption with the function of entertainment increase because of the time saved due to activities that can be realized now via two-way cable telecommunication? Will "high-tech" perhaps lead only to vicarious high-touch, to more isolation, and to an increasing ghettoization of certain subgroups of the elderly? This question cannot yet be answered (Bengtson, 1984), but there are some indicators that certain subgroups of heavy television watchers will increase their television consumption (Agostino, 1980).

There is still a lack of appropriate software for these new technologies. Who will feed the 24 public access channels (i.e., produce material for 576 daily hours of channel time available)? There have been examples of successful use of the new telecommunication technology for and by the elderly, but are they representative? Can these experiences be transferred to the elderly in general? Will the private sector develop services and programs for the common citizen in general and for the elderly in particular? There are some doubts (Jones, 1981). Thus, it seems that there are some dark clouds rising over the horizon of "Third Wave" telecommunication already.

REFERENCES

Agostino, D. (1980). Cable television's impact on the audience of public television. *Journal of Broadcasting, 24,* 347–365.

Baldwin, T.F., & McVoy, D.S. (1983). *Cable Communication.* Englewood Cliffs, NJ: Prentice-Hall.

Bengtson, V.L. (1984). Competence, aging, and social support systems: Implications of telecommunications technology. In R.E. Dunkle, M.R. Haug, & M. Rosenberg (Eds.), *Communications Technology and the Elderly.* New York: Springer Publishing Company.

Berger, F. (1985). The institutionalization of patients with Alzheimer's disease. *Danish Medical Bulletin, 32.*

Brickfield, C.F. (1984). Attitudes and perceptions of elder people. In P.K. Robinson, J. Livingston, & J.E. Birren (Eds.), *Aging and technological advances.* New York: Plenum.

Burgess, E.W. (1960). *Aging in Western Society.* Chicago: University of Chicago Press.

Central Bureau voor de Statistiek (1984). *Statistisch Zakboek 1984.* 's Gravenhage: Staatsuitgeverij.

Cohen, E.S. (1984). Aging and technological advances in telecommunications. In P.K. Robinson, J. Livingston, & J.E. Birren (Eds.). *Aging and technological advances.* New York: Plenum.

Davis, R.H. & Davis, J.A. (1985). *The media image of America's elderly.* Lexington: Lexington Books.

Davis, R.H., & Miller, R.V. (1983). The acquisition of specialized information by older adults through utilization of new telecommunications technology. *Educational Gerontology, 9,* 217–232.

Department of Health and Human Services. (1983). *Chartbook of the Federal Council on Aging.* Washington, DC: U.S. Government Printing Office.

Elton, M., & Carey, J. (1983). Computerizing information: Consumer reactions to teletect. *Journal of Communication, 33,* 162–173.

Etheridge, L. (1984). Financing/services: I Medical/health services. In *The complex cube of long-term care. Proceedings of the National Working Conference.* Washington, D.C.: American Health Planning Association & Veterans' Administration.

Frossard, M. (1983, April–June). Crise et cessations anticipeé d'activité: une comparaison internationale. *Travail et Emploi, 16.*

Gaullier, X. (1982). Economic crisis and old age: Old age policies in France. In *Aging and Society Vol. 2, Part 2.* Cambridge: Cambridge University Press.

Gaullier, X. (1985, February). Economic crisis, work, leisure time: Early retirement from the labor force. World Leisure and Recreation Journal.

Gaullier, X., & Gognalons-Nicolet, M. (1984, October). Modes de vie des preretraites. *Revue Francaise des Affaires Sociale.*

Jansen, J. (1983). *De Organisatie van de Creativiteit.* Ongepubl. Dokt. Werkstuk. Univ. v. Amsterdam.

Jones, M.G. (1981–1982). Telecommunication technologies: New approaches to consumer information dissemination. *The Information Society, 1,* 31–52.

Kerkhoff, W.H.C. (1975). Enkele uitgangspunten voor personeelbeleid. In M.R. v. Gils (Ed.). *Werken, Niet Werken in een Veranderende Samenleving.* Swets en Zeitlanger.

Kerkhoff, W.H.C. (1981). *Ouder Worden, Verouderen en het Personeelbeleid: Over Kosten en Opbrengsten van een Arbeidzaam Leven.* Thesis Huisdrukkerij, Univ. v. Amsterdam.

Kessler, D. (1984, June). Les retraites en peril? *Revue Francaise des Affaires Sociales, 78,* 80.

Lawton, P. (1984). The older person in the residential environment. In P.K. Robinson, J. Livingston, & J.E. Birren (Eds.), *Aging and technological advances.* New York: Plenum.

Naisbitt, J. (1982). *Megatrends.* New York: Warner.

Neugarten, B.L. (1980). *Must everything be a midlife crisis?* New York: Prime Time.

Peter, L.J. (1969). *The Peter principle.* New York: Morrow.

S.C.P. (1984). *Collectieve Uitgaven en Demografische Ontwikkelingen, 1970-2030.* Sociaal Cultureel Planbureau, Cahier 38, Rijswijk.

SoZa. (1984) *Vervroegde Uittreding in CAO's. 's-Gravenhage:* Ministerie van Sociale Zaken en Werkgelegenheid. Staatsuitgeverij.

Sud, G. (1983, October), Qu'est-ce qui change dans l' introduction des "nouvelles technologies"? *Anact.*

Toffler, A. (1980). *The third wave.* New York: Bantam.

CHAPTER 59

Planning for the Well-Being of the Elderly in Iceland in the Year 2000

Dögg Pálsdóttir

In 1983 legislation on the matters of the elderly in Iceland was enacted. Emphasis was placed on home services, both social and medical, as the most important objective to enable elderly people to stay at home as long as they wish and/or are able. In achieving this, health centers in Iceland have been given an important role along with the social services in the communities.

Planning is a key word in this legislation. During a 5-year period, a precise national plan on the matters of the elderly is to be prepared. In itself the legislation can be regarded as a 5-year plan of action on how Iceland has decided to handle these matters since the legislation includes a sunset provision. The overall objective is to create a society where services for the elderly have become a natural part of services given to other age groups and, thus, to eliminate the need for future legislation of this kind.

The graying of nations has caused growing concern throughout the world over the last few years. Therefore, in 1978, the General Assembly of the United Nations decided to convene a World Assembly on Aging (WAA) for the year 1982, indicating that it should result in societies responding more fully to the socioeconomic implications of the aging of populations and to the specific needs of older persons. The 1982 World Assembly on Aging adopted the Vienna International Plan of Action on Aging, which was later endorsed by the United Nation's General Assembly. The plan of Action emphasizes the need for planning, both to help the elderly as individuals and to deal with the long-term social and economic effects of aging populations. This chapter presents an account of Iceland's response.

DEMOGRAPHY

Iceland participated in the World Assembly on Aging, and later in that same year put forward its own plan of action for the aging by passing through Althingi (the Icelandic parliament) an act dealing with the organization of services for this age group. A brief description of Iceland will be useful.

Iceland is the westernmost of the Nordic countries, an island of volcanic origin with an area of about 103,000 km^2; it is situated in the North Atlantic Ocean. The Icelandic economy is primarily based on renewable resources, the most important of which are the coastal fishing banks, the grasslands that support the livestock industry, and hydroelectric and geothermal power. The size of the Icelandic economy is small when evaulated in absolute terms. But per capita gross national product (GNP) is one of the highest in the world, and Icelanders enjoy a standard of living comparable to that of almost any other nation.

The population growth in Iceland, since the country's settlement in 874, has been regulated by four predominant factors—the climate, volcanic eruptions, earthquakes, and epidemics. The population reached 100,000 in 1925 and doubled in 42 years, passing 200,000 in 1967. In 1985 the population was approximately 240,000 and is projected to be more than 300,000 by the year 2020 (see Figure 59-1).

Compared with neighboring countries in Europe, the Icelandic population is relatively young. The largest age group is the 20- to 30- year olds; the 65 + age group comprise only about 10% of the total population. With downward trends in total fertility, it is obvious, however, that in the next decades the nation will steadily grow older. This development is already visible in the proportion of the under 14 age group in the total population. In 1960 that group represented 35% of the total population; at present it is 27%, and it is estimated to sink to around 20% by the year 2000. In comparison, the 65 + group now represents 10% of the total population and are expected to reach 12% by 2000, increasing to 17% by 2020 (Figure 59-2).

THE LEGISLATION ON THE ELDERLY

With this forecast in mind, and in accordance with the United Nations Vienna International Plan of Action, planning is the key issue in the legislation on the elderly that came into force on January 1, 1983. The

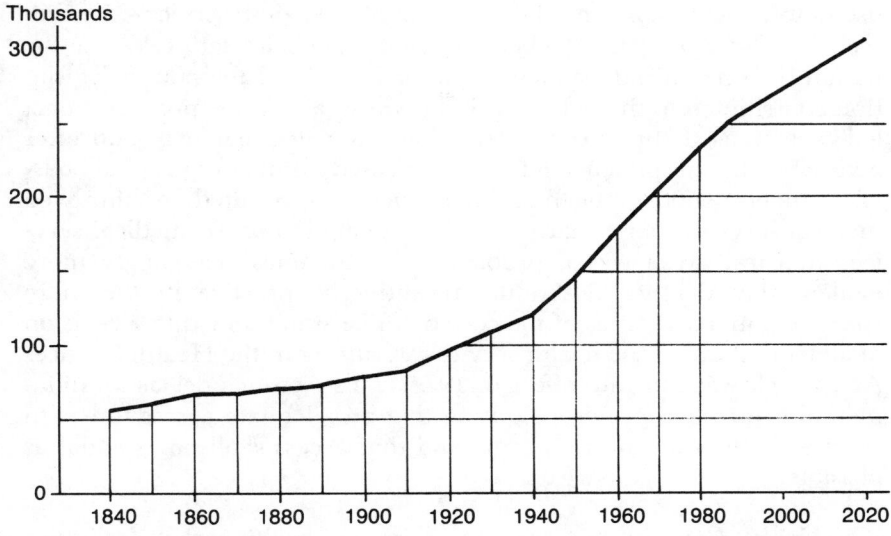

FIGURE 59-1. Population in Iceland 1840 to 2020.

main aim was to enable the elderly to lead independent lives in their own homes for as long as possible and to provide the necessary institutional care when appropriate.

Background for The Health Services Act

Before the legislation on the aging can be examined more fully, it is

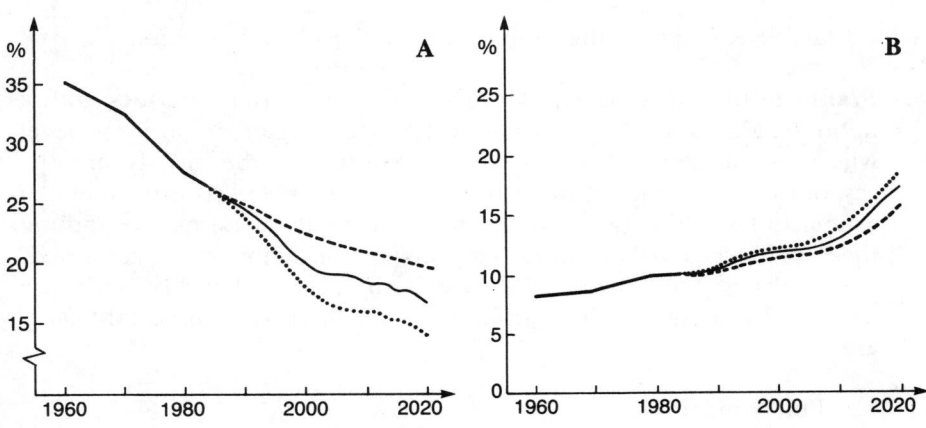

FIGURE 59-2. Population by age 1960 to 2020. **A:** 0-14 years; **B:** 65 + years.

useful to review a condensed description of the health service system in
Iceland. Great progress has been made in the health services since the
nation became an independent republic in 1944. Tuberculosis legislation contributed to the defeat of that disease; a sickness prevention act
led to increased supervision of mothers during pregnancy and after
giving birth; a hospital act led to an increased number of hospital beds,
and amendments to the medical services act resulted in improved
medical services, particularly in urban areas. However, medical services in rural areas was a problem as it became increasingly more
evident that doctors lacked the incentive to practice in the more
sparsely populated areas of the country. The situation led to a revision
of all legislation on the health services, resulting in the Health Services
Act, which was put into effect in 1974. This Act includes as a fundamental principle a provision stating that an adequate access to health
services is the right of the people and that access shall be as equal as
possible.

The Health Centers' System. The system of health care in Iceland is
based on health centers, making them the cornerstone of the primary
health care services. Iceland is divided into eight health areas. Each
health area is further divided into several health districts, each with
health centers (see Figure 59-3). The health centers come in three
categories:

1. A two-doctor health center with other staff.
2. A one-doctor health center with other staff.
3. A health center with a doctor's reception and a nurse/midwife.
    The center is serviced from a neighboring health center.

Outside Reykjavik, the capital, there are 70 health centers.

Planning for the Elderly. The Health Services Act describes both a
nationwide and local organization. The local organization is the level
where actual services are rendered. Matters of the elderly are the
responsibility of the Ministry of Health and the Act stipulated the
establishment of a special division in the national ministry handling
these matters. Furthermore a commission on aging was established.
The tasks of these two bodies are both wide and varied, and are
described in detail in the legislation. The three most important tasks
are:

1. Policy making
2. Drafting a national plan of action in further work for the elderly
3. Management of the Elderly's Construction Fund

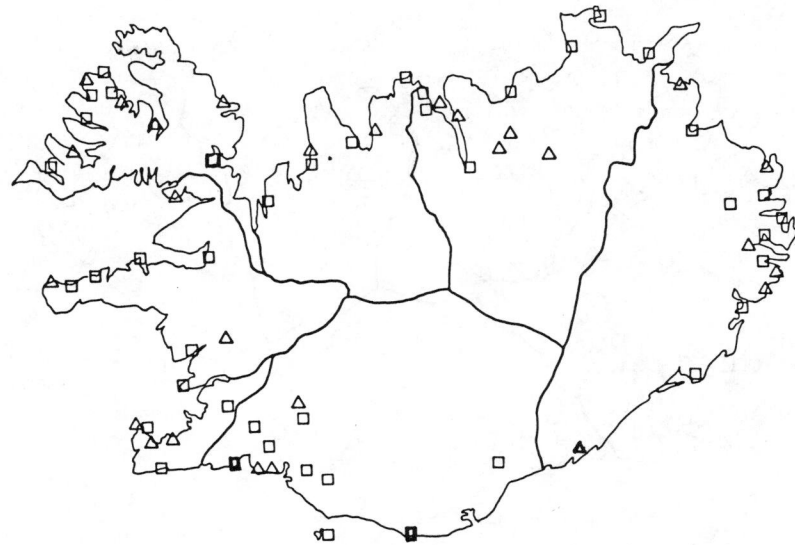

FIGURE 59-3.   The distribution of health centers in Iceland; _____ = health area boundary; □ = health center with 1 + full-time physicians; △ = health center with reception facilities only.

The legislation on the elderly follows closely the regional division stipulated in the earlier Health Services Act. This earlier Act gives the health centers' boards and local social service councils important tasks in securing the presence of services for the elderly in each community. Among their tasks is the nomination of the district's Elderly's Service Group. The Service Group consists of 3 to 5 members of which one must be a doctor, another a nurse, and the third a social worker. The group is made responsible for the supervision of the well-being of the elderly in their district. The importance of close cooperation between the health and the social services is emphasized, because for the elderly the need for these two types of services overlap greatly and can be most efficiently served cooperately.

Home Care Services.   It is generally accepted and acknowledged that one of the most important factors in achieving and maintaining independence in later life is well-organized home care service. Hence the Act on the Elderly puts a special emphasis on the development of home care services and divides them into two categories: home help (various social services given in the home) and home nursing (various medical services given in the home).

The organization of the home care services is the joint responsibility

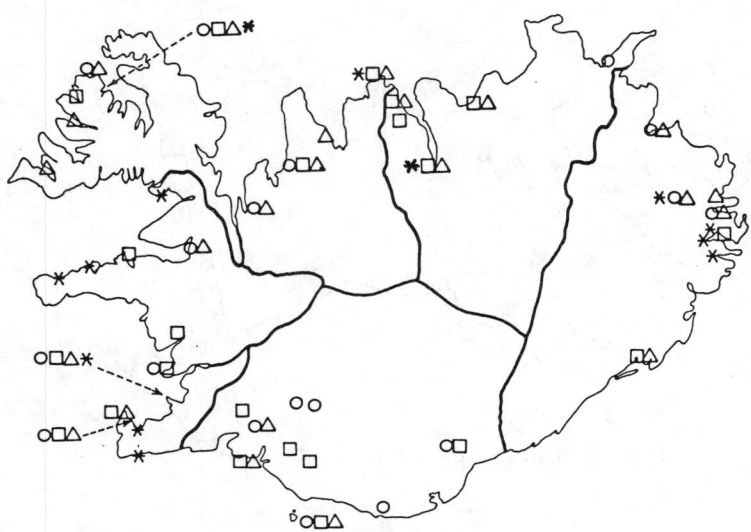

FIGURE 59-4. The distribution of institutions for the elderly in Iceland; ▬▬▬ = health area boundary; ○ = service apartments; □ = old people's homes; △ = nursing homes, wards; * = institutions for aged under construction.

of the health center's board and the Council of Social Services. However, it is expected that the Elderly's Service Groups in the geographic areas will make suggestions concerning the organization of the home care, varying them according to the needs in each district. The Act emphasizes that, where necessary, measures should be taken to give home care services on a 24-hour, 7-day-a-week basis.

Institutions for the Elderly. Although the aim of the legislation is to enable the elderly to stay at home for as long as possible, the necessity of appropriate institutional care is recognized in the Act. Therefore, it is stipulated that appropriate institutional care shall be available regionally when necessary (see Figure 59-4). The act divides institutions into five categories:

- FLATS: specially designed with the needs of the elderly in mind. These flats are furthermore divided into two subcategories, depending on the services available.
- OLD PEOPLE'S HOMES: designed for the elderly who can neither live at home nor in flats for the elderly despite all possible home care services.

- NURSING HOMES: for the elderly too frail to live in old people's homes or specially designed flats.
- LONG-TERM WARDS: for the bedfast elderly. These wards are supposedly linked to a geriatric ward, a medical ward, or a general hospital.
- DAY-CARE CENTERS.

THE SITUATION TODAY

In the last few years, particularly since the Act on the Elderly came into force in 1983, a nationwide interest on services for the elderly has emerged. With regard to the home care services, most health centers offer home nursing for those in need. Home help is offered in all the largest urban communities and even in some of the smaller rural ones. However, provision of home care services in the sparsely populated areas still poses a problem. Nevertheless, the Act's provision for the state's participation in the operating costs of the home care services has proven to be quite an incentive, especially to the sparsely populated communities.

Institutional care has been too scarce in the past. However, a veritable boom in construction of institutions has been in progress during the last few years, particularly outside the capital area. The reasons for this boom include the existence of the Elderly's Construction Fund, (which will be discussed later) and the wish of the smaller communities outside the capital area to offer their elderly population the chance to spend their old age in their home area. Until recently, nearly all elderly moved to the capital, where the highest degree of services are offered. This tendency is reflected in the fact that over 13% of the total population in the capital is 67 years of age or older, in comparison, in the country only about 9% of the population is in this age group.

The Elderly's Construction Fund

The Elderly's Construction Fund was established by legislation in 1981 to enhance construction of institutions for elderly people. Its main source of income is a lump-sum tax. Over a 5-year period the Fund's grants amount to a total of the equivalent of $4 million.

THE TASK AHEAD

The Icelandic Act on the Elderly is in itself a 5-year plan; it contains a sunset clause, putting it out of force on December 31, 1987, unless revised and re-enforced during that period. When evaluating the situation today, it may confidently be stated that Iceland is approaching the level of services, both in home care and institutional care that was aimed for in the Act. The tasks ahead are two-fold: The main task is to continue work already in progress to draft the nationwide plan of action outlining further work in this field. It is estimated that this draft may be ready by midyear 1986. This draft will look to the year 2000, including regional studies on demographic trends, and make recommendations on future trends in institutional care and inhome care services on a region-by-region basis. As a part of its planning, Iceland participates in the WHO-CAP program. The 5-year plan will be the basis of future grant distributions from the Elderly's Construction Fund, and, hopefully, in addition, the basis of political decisions relevant to the elderly.

Policy making is another important joint task of the Ministry of Health and the Elderly's Commission. Unfortunately limited time has precluded adequate attention to this task, and, therefore, it will become an important part of the work of these bodies in the near future. Greater emphasis on work for the elderly is necessary. Until now we have been too oriented toward institutions. This has to be changed, and will be in accordance with the goals of the Act on the Elderly. In that connection it is also necessary to examine whether relatives, who care for aged relatives at home might in some way be supported with more emphasis on day-care facilities and perhaps even rewarded directly. Furthermore, consideration must be given to the enhancement of voluntary work in this field.

CONCLUSION

Iceland has not yet achieved all the goals set forward in the Act on the Elderly. However, the nation is on the right path. By the year 2000 the Icelandic Act on the Elderly, whether it will then still be in force or not, will have created a society that gives its elderly the best available services and the opportunity to spend a dignified old age.

CHAPTER 60

Four-Generation Families: Recent Findings from a French Longitudinal Survey

Paul Paillat

A longitudinal survey documents the proportion and characteristics of three- and four-generation families in contemporary
France. Two samples aged 64 and 59 were followed for one year.
Particular note is taken of the social complications of the higher
life expectancies of women for the pension system and of the
responsibilities of mature women as caregivers for women both
older and younger than themselves.

In the survey on Transition from Active Life to Retirement sponsored
and financed by major pension funds in France under the aegis of the
National Foundation of Gerontology, items were devoted in the first
section of the questionnaire, for each round, to basic family information, as well as to individual status, nature, and size of household.
Therefore , it was easy to identify in the two sample populations those
who still have a living father, mother, or both; we also had to identify
from this group, in order to know how many of them belonged to a
three-generation family, those who, at the same time, have living
children. The next step followed the same pattern (i.e., detecting, out
of three-generation families, those who have at least one grandchild).
Through an appropriate and rather unsophisticated program it was
not difficult to get the answers, given the general assumption that
respondents' replies were reliable and provided that the following
conditions prevailed:

- To have at least one parent living at time t.
- To have at least one grown child living at time t.
- To have at least one grandchild, whatever his or her age, living at time t.

For the sake of simplicity, we have limited our attention to grand-children born to living children. Doing so, we have followed the natural and chronological flow of family events of the so-called "family-building process."

Within this framework, it is or it would be possible to isolate those who share the same house or dwelling, but with a large sample these cases are too rare, and, therefore, subject to wide deviations. It is, however, helpful to know the distance family members live from each other, since family relationships and mutual help are severely hindered when concerned households are situated too far from one another.

FINDINGS

Sample A

Among the 2,038 persons aged 64 at the first round of the survey in 1980, 188 had one or two parents and 48 were members of a four-generation family (7.3% of the total, see Table 60-1). This figure is largely due to the survival of the respondents' mother (164 cases out of 188). This is not only a matter of good health: A low age at the first birth of a child (i.e. the respondent) decreases the age gap between two following generations; thus, parents of respondents aged 64 are 84-85 years old. If the gap is wider, parents are so old that they will not survive long and, the four-generation pattern may not last more than a few months, if not a few days; therefore, the implications are negligible. It would be another story in the case of the forefather living in this status for a couple of years or even longer. Regarding the age gap, it is likely to be shorter in the pair "mother-respondent" than in the pair "father-respondent," and, again, if the respondent is a woman, she will be younger when she becomes a mother than would be a son when he becomes a father.

Of course, having a daughter increases the probability of having a grandchild and a great-grandchild. Having more than one child of either sex effects the probability in the same direction, even if they are all males. The limited family size in France, and in this sample, reduces the number and frequency of four-generation families. The average number of family members involved in this pattern is 5.9 for the male respondent and 6.2 for the female respondent. This is a quite temporary figure. When the oldest great-grandchild becomes a mother or father, the observed forefathers will likely be dead, and the four-

TABLE 60-1. Four-Generation Families: Sample A Data

	Men								Women							
	age: 64 (n=99; 9.2%)				65 (n=74; 6.9%)				64 (n=49; 7.4%)				65 (n=40; 6.1%)			
	F	M	C	T	F	M	C	T	F	M	C	T	F	M	C	T
Cases:	11	85	3	99	6	65	3	75	6	42	1	49	3	36	1	40
Forefathers	11	85	6	102	6	65	6	77	6	42	2	50	3	36	2	41
Sample	11	85	3	99	6	65	3	74	6	42	1	49	3	36	1	40
Children	37	183	9	229	6	183	9	201	12	105	1	118	3	88	1	92
Grandchildren	24	127	4	155	9	106	2	125	8	52	1	61	2	64	3	69
				585				477				278				242

F = Father; M = Mother; C = Couple; T = Total.

generation family will have another content, illustrating the constant renewal of population and family, as long as births outnumber deaths.

One year after the initial survey, at age 65, 74 men instead of 99, and 40 women instead of 49 still belonged to a four-generation family. The frequency dropped respectively from 9.2% to 6.9% and from 7.4% to 6.1%. We are now computing the figures at age 67, but the number of deceased parents is already impressive, particularly if we compare the third round with the first: from 152 to 91. According to the most recent data, 42 men and 21 women were still members of four-generation families, instead of the original 74 and 40 at age 65. However, an increasing number of survey respondents became the eldest members of new four-generation families—thanks to the birth of great-grandchildren: life goes on!

Sample B

At the first round of this sample, the 2,005 persons, aged 59 in 1981, included 575 with parents of whom 36 cases had both parents living in contrast to 4 in the older sample. Among these 575 persons, 435 belonged to a four-generation family (see Table 60-2). The average number of persons is 6.1 per family for the male respondents and 5.8 for the female respondents, which is the same order of magnitude as in the older sample but with the positions of male and female reversed.

Male respondents had an average of 2.7 children and female respondents had 5.8. The difference in the number of children (generation 3) explains the lesser frequency of the four-generation family among interviewed women, but we have not yet investigated why this occurs. We assume that it is largely a consequence of different structures, not only of marital status but also of social status between both sexes.

One year after the initial survey, at the age of 60, 20.1% of the men and 17.8% of the women still belonged to a four-generation family. This was the result of a combination of circumstances. For instance, 66 parents (generation 1) died in the interval, and therefore their children (generation 2) were excluded from the observed subgroup as well as their children's children and grandchildren (generations 3 and 4); but the average size of this subgroup did not change. One year is too short a time lapse to allow the observation of significant changes. We must wait for the figures of the third round, which are now being processed.

COMMENTS

A longer life span explains the spreading of these generational patterns in developed countries. This finding confirms what prior simulations have indicated. One explanation of the shift from a four- to a three-

TABLE 60-2. Four-Generation Families: Sample B Data

	Men								Women							
	age: 59 (n=266; 24.5%)				60 (n=244; 20.6%)				59 (n=133; 20.1%)				60 (n=118; 17.8%)			
Cases:	F	M	C	T	F	M	C	T	F	M	C	T	F	M	C	T
Cases:	34	209	23	266	23	183	18	244	16	104	13	133	13	96	9	118
Forefathers	34	209	46	289	23	183	36	242	16	104	26	146	13	96	18	127
Sample	34	209	23	266	23	183	18	224	16	104	13	133	13	96	9	118
Children	86	576	53	715	61	501	43	605	45	222	40	307	35	203	25	263
Grandchildren	53	273	17	343	38	245	18	301	21	134	25	180	20	136	18	174
				1613				1372				766				682

F = Father; M = Mother; C = Couple; T = Total.

generation family is the lower birth rate among younger generations, born after 1965, and the higher frequency of divorce. Two of the major social implications of this study are:

1.   The higher proportion of two generations of retirees, especially on the female side, aggravating the discrimination of the pension systems.

2.   The difficult situation of the granddaughter, aged 35-40. She has, more often than was the case for her mother, a retired mother, frequently a widow, and a retired grandmother, frail and widowed. Moreover, in the same time period her own daughter (or daughters) may raise issues and worries related to changing social and economic climates that may possibly include unemployment, divorce, and illegitimacy. In addition this same woman may have responsibility for caring for a mother-in-law who has no daughter of her own. (Any combination of the above-stated situations can produce an overburdened middle-aged woman.)

When a population undergoes changes of this magnitude, the time has come for a sweeping reappraisal of the social protection of the elderly, including a reallocation of roles within the family as well as of families within our society.

CHAPTER 61

Aging in Latin America

Overview

Pamela Babb, Esther Contreras de Lehr,
Elisa Dulcey-Ruiz,
Bernardo Samper

The complementary perspectives of gerontologists from different disciplines are illustrated. Pamela Babb, a nurse from Mexico, for example, explores the implications of urban, suburban, and rural environments for older adults and noted particularly the implications of migration from one type of environment to another. Esther Contreras de Lehr, a psychologist from Mexico, stresses social change in this century and the challenge of increased numbers of old people in Latin America and the impact of modernization on traditional life-styles. Elisa Dulcey-Ruiz, a psychologist from Colombia, describes several programs preparing workers for retirement in Latin America, distinguishing between preparation for work retirement in a narrow sense and preparation stressing planning for life over the long term. Programs in Mexico, Venezuela, and Colombia provide useful illustrations. Finally, Bernardo Samper, a physician from Colombia, summarizes a program for retired people of Caja de Previsión Nacional de Colombia and described a club for older adults called "Sosacá" in Colombia.

In the last 30 years of this century, the total population of Latin America will increase by 95%. During the same period the number of persons 60 years of age and older will be increased by more than 150%. Historically and currently the family constitutes the principal source of welfare and for the solution of problems related to aging in

Latin America. Nevertheless, increasing modernization and industrialization of the region is producing remarkable changes, such as urbanization, migrations, retirement, and population aging. Keeping in mind the consequences of migration, experienced observers in Latin American countries report that the largest percentage of old persons in the region increasingly tend to live in urban areas. Firm traditions and beliefs regarding family solidarity ensure that familial ties are maintained even in cities. Nevertheless, the extent and rapidity of social change implied in the modernization of Latin American countries makes a careful review of the different environmental settings and the different adjustment levels in the population older than 60 years in these various settings seem prudent.

Urban, suburban, and rural settings each warrant attention of gerontologists because each generates different needs, different types of resources, and different modes of adjustment among older adults. For example, in urban settings, it is quite possible to have a pension program for retired persons that is not found in a rural setting. On the other hand, one often finds economic poverty in urban settings and families unable to take in and care for their aged kin in a home setting even when they would like to do so.

With regard to rural settings, very often one finds aged individuals working and contributing to a family's income; in such settings family ties tend to be strongest. Finally, due to the firmness of traditions and beliefs about families in Latin America, it is very probable that aged people in the suburban settings suffer the greatest maladjustments. This is due to the migratory process, which in itself implies a physical as well as mental adjustment from the person's traditional habitat to one of recent creation. In all these alternatives of settings, we observe changes in traditional family roles and in expectations within the family about the responsibilities for its members. This variety of environments, circumstances, and expectations is related to modernization. And as a consequence of the progress achieved in this century, the increase of elderly in the Latin American region constitutes a real challenge to families.

Undoubtedly, modernization illustrated by increased pace of life or residential movement from a rural to an urban setting has different and complex consequences for older persons and their families. In the extended families characteristics of rural environments, expectations, and roles have been clearly defined in the past; several generations usually share tasks and benefits, old generations are respected due to their experiences, recognized authority, and knowledge. Support of elders in educating younger generations is asked for in transmitting culture and traditions from generation to generation.

Modernization weakens familial ties, in part because the architectural design of cities and of housing in cities tends to make families more and more nuclear and isolated. Demands for rapidity and mechanization and the influence of means of communication (e.g., computers) result in a decreased status of the elderly and in diminishing both their familial importance and their participation in the community and in society generally. All this tends to occur in a society that changes rapidly and where city life is designed mainly for younger generations active in economic and industrial production.

The complexity of this situation presents several challenges to be faced by all generations. Members of a different generation in a family can and must work together even when they do not live under the same roof.

Because of industrialization and modernization, preparation for retirement is particularly important. Today, one must differentiate between preparation for retirement in a broad sense and preparation for retirement in a narrow sense. The former implies long-term and comprehensive programs, such as planning for life, which involves education. In such education the individual is mainly responsible. Such broad education also implies consideration of various aspects of development and adaptation such as health, physical and psychological welfare, familial and social participation, economic planning and foresight, and consideration of the possibility of alternative careers and recreational alternatives to work.

The model of preparation for retirement in a narrow sense is better known today not only in Latin America but also in the majority of the world countries. This model generally implies short-term courses related to retirement, typically 6 to 12 months before retirement occurs. Participants receive information and orientation but typically play a relatively passive role.

In several countries of Latin America (e.g., Mexico, Colombia, and Venezuela) interventions related to preparation for retirement began approximately 2 decades ago. Colombia has developed an alternative called "life planning" (a term borrowed from Virginia Boyack in the U.S.). Life planning involves analyzing one's life-style, and training is done over long periods of time. Training individuals to plan does not stress courses but practical seminars concerned with health, financial aspects, interests, abilities, and future possibilities. Autonomy and self-management are emphasized. In Ecopetrol (the national oil company of Colombia), and in the National Federation of Coffee Growers of Colombia, life-planning activities are offered at the present time. Many of the people who register for these seminars have many years (sometimes 15) before retirement; on the other hand, people who take the courses when they are close to retirement usually find that they waited too long. Life planning seminars clearly have an objective broader than preretirement planning.

In Latin America, given the increase in the retired population, programs are being developed that include occupational training, advice on starting a business, and training for group and community leadership. An example of such programs is provided by Caja Nacional de Previsión Social in Colombia, where affiliates who have retired from governmental units take part in different cultural, training, and socially integrating programs. As a matter of fact, some groups of persons with health problems (for instance, hypertension, diabetes, etc.) hold meetings with medical and psychological personnel with the purpose of discussing their difficulties and ways of managing them both by means of medicine itself and by a more adequate style of life.

Other types of interventions related to aging and old age include clubs for seniors. One such club is the Sosacá Association for seniors in Bogotá, Colombia, which manages programs for seniors including cultural, social, and touristic activities.

Image of the Elderly in Colombia Socialization Agencies

Elisa Dulcey-Ruiz

The famous writer Albert Camus affirmed that after 40 years old,"every person is responsible for his own face." We would add "not only of his own face but in general his own image." Responsibility for images of older adults is necessarily shared, however, with the society in which we live. The role of parents, teachers, and the mass media in creating images of aging is explored.

This section proposes to summarize some of the research that has been carried out in Colombia to document the images of the elderly. What images of older adults are held by parents, children, teachers, and mass media? These are important socializing agencies that shape our perceptions, beliefs, and expectations.

When we talk of an "image" we have in mind a concept that includes perceptions, stereotypes, opinions, beliefs, and values; and, obviously, we refer to aspects of images that include subjective elements such as judgments derived from ideological and cultural frameworks whose influence cannot be eliminated easily. To summarize, there is little or no neutral or objective information about aging. The interaction among reality, cultural, and socialization agencies is dynamic and constant in producing images of older people and how they grew old.

The important sources of influence on how we think about aging have been conceptualized as "socialization agencies," regardless of whether they are social institutions (family, community, school, reference groups), people (parents, teachers, peers, bosses, or even colleagues), or mass media. On the other hand, the fact of becoming old and the significant increase in the number of the elderly in the world are objective realities. We have learned about these developments through socializing agencies that interpret as well as transmit these facts. This transmission includes aspects of culture such as laws, myths, roles, norms, and values as Triandis (1980), among many others, has proposed. According to this author, culture is determined by place, time, and language, which means that we live in a certain city or town (geographical coordinates are very important), in a time (time is related to change), and we interact by means of language, which we also use to codify and save information in order to build our own representations.

Among stories referring to pre-Spanish cultures of America, different allusions to old age are found, for example, among Aztecs, Mayas, Muyscas, and Quimbayas. Specifically, in the pre-Spanish chronicles of Colombia, there are references of old age among Tayronas (a specific cultural group) who supported elderly with "chicha" (a native drink), and corn until their death. Among Muyscas, another group, the attitude toward old age was less considerate: "When parents reached old age and they were no more able to work, obligation of support was lacking, and, therefore, they were cast away from their homes. In such a situation, elderly men and women visited from one town to another, having become the witches and diviners" (Chavez, 1983, p.182). Nevertheless, some mythical gods, such as Bochica, and mythical "caciques" were considered to be elderly and the idea of wisdom, power, and experience was associated with them.

Very recently in Colombia other references to old age, some based on scientific research, have appeared. Dulcey-Ruiz and Ardila (1976), for example, have described the attitudes toward aging and the aged of a sample composed of 200 college students and 200 old people, the latter living mostly in institutions for the care of the elderly. Social class was expected to have important effects. An attitude scale, adapted from the Tuckman-Lorge Questionnaire (1952), was used. Responses indicated significant differences in attitudes toward older people between the students and the old people interviewed. Although the whole sample held negative attitudes toward elderly, the older people displayed more negative attitudes. Middle- and low-status elderly held significantly more negative attitudes than those of higher status. Low-status college students held more negative attitudes than middle-status students.

Anthropologist Dianne Kagan (1980) from the United States worked in the village of Bojacá (about 4,000 inhabitants). She used cognitive anthropological techniques to discover how age categories and their meanings affected intergenerational relations, age norms, and values, especially among the elderly. Kagan analyzed, among other things, the way in which the aging adult experiences identity crises. She concluded that among the peasants of Bojacá, there was a significant agreement about the active role and respected status of older people. Actual participation in community activities was associated with the successful overcoming of an identity crisis that elderly experience.

Dulcey-Ruiz, López, Neira, and Samper (1981) evaluated the effects of positive information presented in a film about aging people, of living with old people, and of social class upon the attitudes toward older people in a sample of children. No significant effects of the film presentation were found, but socioeconomic status of the subjects had a greater influence on attitudes than either living together with elderly people or viewing the film. Children that had negative attitudes toward old age also had more limited knowledge of and contact with elderly persons.

Another study (Buitrago, Castro, & Dulcey, 1983) investigated the effects of age and sex of parents on children's attitudes toward aging adults. No significant differences were found. These findings confirm those of other investigators, cited by Dulcey and Ardila (1976) and by Buitrago (1983) in India. In general, however, the specific attitudes of parents toward old age and older adults is an important factor in the attitudes of their children.

More recently, Jaramillo and Dulcey-Ruiz (1983) used content analysis to describe the image of the aging process presented in newspapers. The most frequent references to older adults were those related to death. The second most frequent references noted activities in which the elderly take part, especially humanitarian and charity events; and the third most common references were to the older people's decrease in economic productivity. To summarize, we found that newspapers tend to present a negative image of older people.

Several exploratory studies were completed (Dulcey-Ruiz, 1984) with different groups of teachers using three specific questions: (a) What does old age mean to you? (b) Have you thought about your own old age? and (c) How do you suppose your own old age will be? In general, negative feelings were associated with old age. While the majority (90%) did not think about their own old age, most people imagined their old age as something that could be positive.

We believe that much more research of this kind would be useful. This is why the Center of Gerontological Psychology began work on a 1-year project, partially supported by UNESCO. The main purpose of the project was to describe the opinions, attitudes, and information held and presented by mass media as important socializing agencies. We believe that intervention must be aimed at changing negative images of aging in the media because their influence among people is very important.

At present we have done content analysis of newspapers, radio, and television material: 76% came from newspapers, 17% from radio broadcasts, and 6.9% from TV programs. It was easy to select the most popular newspapers (2), radio stations (3), and TV channels (2) in Colombia. Three pairs of categories were used to code the items to

TABLE 61-1. Images of Old Age in the Media:
Categories of Description

Media type	Autonomy	Dependency	Activity	Passivity	Participation	Isolation
Newspapers	19.65%	18.44%	26.35%	6.15%	7.45%	21.97%
Radio	12.09%	18.60%	25.58%	11.63%	7.44%	24.65%
T.V.	22.56%	11.28%	20.30%	6.02%	15.04%	24.81%

describe images of older people: autonomy–dependency, activity–passivity, and social participation–isolation. Table 61-1 summarizes the observed frequencies in each category by media type.

Of the 1,074 items from the newspapers, 283 (26.35%) referred to activity, while 66 (6.15%) stressed passivity. Eighty items (7.45%) referred to participation and 236 (21.97%) referred to isolation; 211 items were associated with autonomy (19.65%) and 198 (18.44%) with dependence. With the items taken from radio broadcasts, activity was again the most frequent category: 55 of 215 items (25.58%); followed by isolation as the next most frequent, 53 (24.65%). TV programs: In first place, isolation (33 items, 24.81%) was stressed, followed by autonomy (30 items, 22.56%) and activity (27 items, 20.30%).

We found that in newspapers, allusions concerning old age were made most frequently in sections on housekeeping and feminine matters. Such classifications may have been made by journalists with the implicit supposition that the other sections of newspapers are primarily extradomestic or masculine ones. If so, this outcome may illustrate a double marginality of being female and being old. The predominant image in mass media (except radio broadcasts) involved elderly men, despite the fact that there are more elderly women than elderly men in Latin American societies. We can concur with Lehr (1982) that being a woman and being elderly constitute one's social as well as biological destiny. Images of females and of the elderly tend to be negative and, hence, disadvantageous.

We have much to do in order to obtain a comprehensive understanding of the social perception and the images of later life held by the different social groups. In many cases these perceptions and images are not very desirable and need to be improved. We need to build an image of older adults as more positive, autonomous, useful and socially participating individuals.

Work and Retirement in Latin America

Elisa Dulcey-Ruiz
Ruben Ardila

Work and leisure are culturally dependent concepts, as are aging and the role of the elderly in society. The general population characteristics in Latin America are presented, followed by a description of the situation of elderly people in this region. Some interventions related to work and retirement are described.

Latin America is part of the Third World that includes the majority of the world's population. In Latin America work and retirement are very complex because social sensitivity to problems of retirement and of unemployment is lacking and because some laws are obsolete and social change is very rapid.

The average age for retirement in Latin America is 60 years. The exact age varies according to sex and from country to country. In many cases, this age of retirement implies 15 or more years of life with no formal work and with very few social support facilities related to health care, leisure, or new activities. The circumstances, particularly the economic circumstances, in the last part of life are, in general, not very satisfactory in Latin America despite recent efforts carried out in many countries. There is a long way to go in order to have a good life for the elderly in this region. Consider the demographic situation summarized in Table 61-2.

From Table 61-2 we conclude that approximately 10% of the world population lives in Latin America when Carribbean countries are included. Latin America has changed, particularly in the last 30 years, from a predominantly rural region (approximately 70% of the population) to a predominantly urban region (66% of population).

In spite of a decrease in gross national product per capita in the region in the last few years (e.g., from 1984 to 1985 it decreased from $2,100 to $1,890 or approximately 10%), and increased unemploy-

TABLE 61-2. Latin America: Some Demographic Characteristics, 1985

Number of Nations	37
Population	406 million
Crude birth rate (Annual, per 1,000)	31
Crude death rate (Annual, per 1,000)	8
Natural increase annual	2.3%
Urban population	66%
Median age	20.8
Average life expectancy (general)	64.1
Average life expectancy (Female)	66.5
Average life expectancy (Male)	61.8
Population age 60 and over	6.5%
Average age for retirement	60
Gross national product per capita	$1,890
Unemployment	more than 10%

Source: Date from *"World Population Data Sheet"* by Population Reference Bureau, Inc., 1985, Washington, DC: Author; and *"Periodical on Aging, Vol. 1"* by United Nations, 1985.

ment, we note that Latin America as a region is very rich in resources. It also has a rich cultural tradition. The continent was populated by native groups with broad cultural variations and different degrees of development including civilizations as advanced as the Mayas, the Incas, and the Aztecs. Today, nations are composed of varied ethnic groups with different proportions of Caucasians, natives, and Africans. Latin America is a "mestizo" civilization.

In the Third World, Latin America is probably the most advanced area. Although the region's problems could be considered similar to the problems of Asia and Africa, in many aspects the process of "westernization" (modernization) has been more rapid in Latin America than in other parts of the Third World.

After having experienced an extraordinary population increase in Latin America, natality rates are beginning to decline. Today, the rate is 31 per 1,000 inhabitants. Nevertheless, this region will have to be prepared if it is to secure an adequate quality life index in year 2000. There will be 200 million more people than at present. It is expected that in year 2050, when the Latin American popualtion increases to a little more than a billion people, the region will reach "zero population growth." The most populated countries in Latin America are Brazil, Mexico, Argentina, and Colombia. Brazil is the country with the largest number of people younger than age 15, followed by Colombia.

Argentina is the country with many elderly people, 3 million (Progreso, October, 1984, p. 8).

The Elderly in Latin American Society

According to recent projections (United Nations, 1985), one of every six persons who will live in the world in the year 2000 will be 60 years old or more. Of every five persons aged over 60 years, three (61.17%) will live in less-developed countries (Latin America, Africa, Asia). In Latin America, specifically, more than 7% of the population will then be 60 years old and more (Gómez-Buendía, 1980, cit. by Dulcey-Ruiz, 1982).

Available data suggest that the number of old people is increasing rapidly. It was estimated in 1980 that 6.2% of the Latin American population was older than 60 years. For the year 2000 it is expected not only that this percentage will be increased to more than 7% in Latin America but also the current population older than 60 years will be increased to a little more than 18 million. This increase is higher than the increase of older people in the world's population generally.

CHARACTERISTICS OF OLDER LATIN AMERICANS

The large number of persons over 60 years currently live and will live in an increasing proportion in Latin America's urban areas. And despite the increasing modernization and a related increase of nuclear families, statistics suggest that a large number of elderly people will live with their families. No doubt the bonds of family in this region are strong, and, in one way or another, extended families persist. Elderly people are loved and respected in the general familial context. Nevertheless, changes associated with modernization are producing a number of variations, and elderly are among the groups that are losing privileges. Production, efficiency, and innovation begin to be very important social values. The slow pace, conservative outlook, and pessimistic philosophy of life of many old people in Latin America begin to lose status. The "wise old person" of our region's natives is replaced by the technological young expert—western-oriented, educated with the traditions of science and technology. The importance of older women and men is diminishing with industrialization and modernization, in general; and in that regard, Latin America has become very similar to other regions of the world. In spite of beginning as part of the Third World, the philosophy of the First World begins to take priority.

Elderly people in Latin America are generally perceived as useful. More than 20% of the population older than 65 years work actively and more than 45% of people between 55 and 64 years are also employed (United Nations, 1980). Moreover, status in old age is kept high, especially in the case of the elderly Latin American woman in some regions. The "abuelita" (grandmother), and in many cases the grandfather, take care of the grandchildren, and frequently constitute, the grandmother especially, the center of the family. They know a lot about life from their age-related experience. "Devil knows more because of his age than because he is devil." This is a popular Latin American proverb, which makes reference to this fact.

This description of many positive aspects of old age in Latin America is in contrast to a more negative image of old age, which has been documented in some research (Center for Gerontological Psychology, 1985). Moreover, in Latin America one finds very limited provision for social security particularly for the elderly population. In general, social security in Latin American countries covers from 30% to 50% of the total population, depending on the country. Costa Rica presents the case of major coverage (80%) and Haiti the case of less coverage (15%) (United Nations, 1980).

PROBLEMS OF SOCIAL SECURITY

In a technical meeting on aging in Latin America (United Nations, 1980), it was noted that as the Latin American population ages, systems of social security in the region will face serious difficulties due to: Poor social security coverage, the inequality of benefits for different laboring groups, delays in adjustments and payments, and deficiencies in actuarial estimates for purposes of planning. This negative picture is even more pessimistic if we keep in mind that Latin America is currently one of the regions of the world with major financial difficulties due to its increasing external debt, unemployment, and constant decrease in national income per inhabitant.

Some Alternative Answers

Despite a lot of difficulties, above all, economic, Latin America is facing the challenges of an aging population. Particularly in the last two decades, interest has increased in the systematic study of gerontology. Currently, in Colombia, for example, programs in gerontology at the university level have started to be developed. At the same time, gerontology is being promoted in careers in psychology, social work, and medicine, among others. Basic and applied research began in the 1970s, and this research is generating new information not only for testing hypotheses but also for use by societal decision makers.

Increasingly, Latin America realizes that underdevelopment and dependency of countries are necessarily joined to underdevelopment and dependency of people of every generation. Increasingly we think and act not only for old generations of the present but also for those of the future. We are aware that old age is part of the total life course and that facts such as work and retirement require more than simple preparatory courses. Today, more people, institutions, enterprises, and governments in Latin America believe in exploring alternatives such as planning one's life, which is more than preparation for retirement in a narrow sense. An example of new ideas being considered is the private social security model recently established in Chile, with the participation of about 12 Treasury Departments of Prevision (Administradoras de Fondos Previsionales: AFP). Anyone who wishes can affiliate with a department and become responsible for his or her own retirement pension, contributing at least 10% of their monthly salary. The affiliated people, in addition to getting a better profit from their investment, have the advantage of health services and some other benefits (Progreso, April-May, 1982).

The increasing number of retired people in relation to active workers (approximately 1:100) constitutes another challenge that Latin America is learning to face, keeping in mind the need not to increase the dependency index (which oscillates between 3:1 and 5:1). An exemplary action is being carried out in a Health Center (Centro de Salud #5) related to the Social Security Institute of Colombia. A multidisciplinary team assessed several needs of about 100 retired affiliates and found deficits in several areas including health, nutrition, psychological welfare, and occupation. Eighty percent of the subjects considered retirement as a negative experience. A program was then started on three levels: self-identity, social integration, and autonomy. Educational, recreational, occupational, and communication activities addressed all three issues. Individual and group work was done. Further, cooperatives, small enterprises, and cultural groups were promoted independent of the Health Center. Another of the positive results of this intervention was the reduction of demand for medical services and increased participation in the program activities (Montoya, Saboyá, Acero, García, 1985). Small enterprises are increasingly begun by retired people of Latin America who are changing from individuals who wait passively for a subsidy to autonomous, active, and productive members of society. Calle (1985) suggests the need to identify and assist persons who have this orientation. Based on these and other interventions Latin America seeks to promote an occupational rather than a simple recreational model of retirement that stresses community integration. Latinoamericans know also that ''If we give a fish to a person, we will stop his hunger for a day; but if we teach him how to fish, we will stop his hunger forever.'' And we are consequently acting on this maxim.

REFERENCES

Buitrago, A.I., Castro, M.C., & Dulcey-R., E. (1983). *Actitudes de padres de familia de diferentes edades hacia las personas viejas.* Bogotá: Universidad Catolica.

Calle, P. (1985, April-May). Participación laboral en la vejez; un reto. In: *Reflexiones sobre Gerontología, 2* (2), Bogotá, Colombia.

Center for Gerontological Psychology. (1985). Influence of the mass media in the marginalizing of old people. Bogotá, Colombia.

Chavez, A. (1983). La Vejez en los pueblos prehispánicos. *Publicación de la Sociedad. Colombiana de Gerontologia y Geriatria, 6* (1), 179-184.

Dulcey-Ruiz, E. (1982). La Gerontología: Un análisis psicológico-social. *Revista Latinoamericana de Psicología, 14* (3), 305-324.

Dulcey-Ruiz, E. (1984). *Exploración de actitudes hacia la vejez en diferentes poblaciones.* Bogotá (unpublished).

Dulcey-Ruiz, E., & Ardila, R. (1976). Actitudes hacia los ancianos. *Revista Latinoamericana de Psicología, 8* (1), 57-67.

Dulcey-Ruiz, E., López, R.M., Neira, M.V. & Samper, L. (1981). *Influencia de información cine-foro sobre la actitud infantil hacia la vejez, según nivel socio-economico y convivencia con ancianos.* Bogotá: Universidad Javeriana.

Jaramillo, M.I., & Dulcey-Ruiz, E. (1983). *Imagen de la vejez presentada en la prensa.* Bogotá: Fundación Universitaria Monserrate.

Kagan, D. (1980), Activity and aging in a Colombian Peasant Village. In: C.C. Fry (Ed.). *Aging in culture society* (p. 65-75). New York: Berging.

Lehr, U. (1982), La situación de la mujer madura: aspectos psicológicos y sociales. *Revista Latinoamericana de Psicología, 14* (3), 385-396.

Montoya, L.M., Saboyá, M., Acero, M.C., & García, M.I. (1985, July 12-17). *Motivation and autonomy in the elderly: A program to increase them in retired population in Colombia.* Paper presented in the XIIIth International Congress of Gerontology, New York.

Progreso, (1982, April-May). Nuevo modelo de seguridad social en Chile (pp. 54-57).

Progreso, (1984, October). Plan mundial para elevar el nivel de vida (pp. 8-9).

Population Reference Bureau, Inc. (1985). World population data sheet.

Triandis, H. (1980). Values, attitudes and interpersonal behavior. *Nebraska Symposium on Motivation* (1979), University of Nebraska Press.

United Nations. (1980). Technical meeting on aging in Latin America. San José, Costa Rica.

United Nations. (1985). *Periodical on aging, Vol. 1, (1), 1984,* New York.

CHAPTER 62

Case Management Training of Older Community Workers: Implications for Extended Outreach

Marcella Bakur Weiner
Thomas M. Pamilla

Older, paid, noncollege educated community workers completed a 1-year group training program with a clinician. The focus of this training was to teach clinical theory that can be applied to daily experience with clients and to explore the worker's own fears, expectations, and satisfactions in terms of job and personal life. Client-related problems covered were the uncooperative client, the "senile" client, the demanding client, and the overly needy client. Worker-related problems covered were fear of over-identification, fear of burn-out, and limitations related to agency policy. Clinical impression, via self-report, suggests that the trained older worker's job/self-related experiences are similar to younger, degree-educated workers; that older persons respond well to clinical training integrated within practical work experience and self-exploration. Implications for extended outreach are suggested.

While it has long been recognized that older, well-functioning persons may serve as effective workers with the frail elderly, most programs involve the use of volunteers or unpaid workers (Hoffman, 1984; Pynoos, Hade-Kaplan & Fleisher, 1984). In the training program described here, all community workers who became group members were elderly, paid and non-college educated. The training was a 1-year program; and sessions were held approximately once a month by a trained clinician specializing in aging. This professional was hired as a consultant to the agency, since it was felt that a trained leader knowledgeable both in group work and in aging could provide guidelines possibly not achieved in peer support groups (Weiner, 1980). Also, the fact that this person was "outside" the agency and not directly involved on a day-to-day basis with all facets of agency workings would help ease some of the natural anxieties experienced by persons working within an agency and therefore subject to its mandates and controls. It was carefully explained to the trainees that the leader, though responsible to the agency hierarchy, would withhold material of a confidential nature, only providing feedback to agency personnel on the development of group process, issues discussed (themes), and attempted solutions to client problems. This verbal contract, established with the group members, while sometimes difficult to adhere to, was fulfilled, and any reports to agency authorities were governed by these rules.

THE AGENCY

The agency was formed in 1971 to serve low-income elderly, particularly the isolated and frail elderly. The services provided by the agency are information/referral, benefits counseling, casework, meals on wheels, chore and escort service, and shopping. Full-time staff consists of an executive director, two masters-level social workers, and an office manager. Direct service is performed to a large extent by 16 part-time staff members, most of whom are over 60 years of age. Though of diverse background in terms of education and life experience, most of these elderly workers have almost no formal training to prepare them for working with people in a social service setting (McClintock & Pamilla, 1985). The only exceptions were two young social work students who were assigned to this setting as part of their academic requirement. These two young women, known to the other workers and performing similar tasks, attended almost all of the group training sessions.

MENTAL HEALTH CARE DELIVERY

The training program gave special attention to mental health issues. The dismal status of mental health care delivery for the aged has long been known. The Group for the Advancement of Psychiatry (1970) reported over a decade ago:

> . . . Older patients do not receive early and adequate care in the community. . . the elderly suffer disproportionately from our non-system of non-

care. . . and by fragmented delivery of services (p. 657).

No doubt one of the reasons for the highly inadequate delivery of psychological and physical care to the elderly is the negative attitude toward any form of gerontological psychotherapy held by the aged themselves and no less so by the mental health personnel who treat them. Butler (1975) states that "Ageism is a thinly disguised attempt to avoid the personal reality of human aging and death" (p. 894). It is no wonder then that, with the possible exception of Jung's ideas, theories of psychotherapy seem to have been constructed mainly for the problems of young and midlife adulthood. This appears strange in view of the fact that theorists point out that age alone is a very weak predictor of personality or behavior, including behavior change (Fozard & Thomas, 1975; Wilensky & Weiner, 1977).

Similarly, Grotjahn (1979) argues that resistance against unpleasant insights is lessened in old age, and character defenses have in many cases softened rather than hardened because of the handling of realistic changes. Rigidity and flexibility are often viewed as not related to age, but to personality.

THE AGING WORKER IN A TRAINING PROGRAM

Considering the well-documented negativism of our society regarding aging (Weiner, Teresi, & Streich, 1983), how can we arrive at intervention strategies that may also be useful in the training of older personnel? The following propositions were formulated to guide the development of clinical skills in the older worker:

1. The older person would be less educated and thus less familiar with psychological ideas and terminology.
2. Older workers may resist the implicit "moral relativism and liberalisms characterizing contemporary psychotherapies" (Lawton, 1976).
3. Psychological terminology may be vaguely threatening to the older worker.
4. The seeking out (or possibly offering) of psychological services is tantamount to being termed "crazy" whereas the direct offering of non-psychological services is more palatable.

THE GROUP SETTING: FORMAT AND STRUCTURE

All group meetings, held once a month, took place in a large room that was part of the agency's headquarters. The large table in the room was

pushed to the wall and all chairs placed in a circle. Members chose
where to sit, though most chose the same seats each time. People who
worked together and shared good rapport, it was noticed, tended to sit
together to form a "twinship" alliance. Sessions ran for approximately
2 hours, with a 10-minute break in the middle.

The average number of persons attending each session was 10 with a
range of from 9 to 13. While all were involved in serving the needs of
the community's frail elderly, actual services varied from direct contact
through home visits to handling complaints via telephone. Group
members were of diverse religious and ethnic backgrounds, as were
their clients.

At the outset, it was explained to the group that the leader was there
to help them deal with the problems they encountered in working with
their elderly client population. It was suggested that sessions revolve
around themes/problems/areas they saw as difficult for them. These
issues, it was suggested, would be explored by the use of psychological
theory but translated in a way they would, hopefully, experience as:

1.   Educative to themselves in working with others, particularly the
frail aging.
2.   Relevant to themselves as possible life-review and life-motivat-
ing parameters for assessing, dealing with, and enjoying their own
aging.

It was stated that while the group leader would suggest the use of
different concepts considered most helpful, along with suggested articles and books the worker could employ, that her approach as a clinician
was self-psychology as developed by Heinz Kohut and now in use by
many professionals (White & Weiner, 1985).

SELF-PSYCHOLOGY AS A GROUP APPROACH FOR OLDER ADULTS

Since self-psychology is still in its pioneer stage, it is understandable
that there is insufficient research in group self-psychology per se and in
use of this approach with older adults. Yet, it has been the senior
author's experience that this approach is most effective for older persons.

Self-psychology focuses on the strengthening of what is termed the
"nuclear" or cohesive self. Although others are seen as important to
the person, this approach is less centered on object-relations or self-to-
other relations and more centered on self–self relations. In the group
setting, it was felt by the leader that the individual member's self
would be attended to along with his or her use of other persons; for

example, having available other persons as suppliers for either narcissistic needs that were not being met and/or as reinforcers for a self that was well-functioning but feeling some anxiety in a situation that called for the delivery of sensitive attunement to other persons seeking help in this case, the clients.

In this approach, confrontational analyses or styles are avoided, and the leader accepts from the group member any one or more of the three types of transference: mirroring, idealization, and twinship. In the first, the leader is aware of the need for mirroring, the reflecting back appreciatively to the group member of his or her thoughts, ideas, and feelings, whereas in the idealization the leader accepts the feelings of: "My Leader . . . my group . . . is the best, most able" etc., without interpretations or confrontations; and in the third, the twinship or pairing, either of a group member to another group member or group member to leader, is also accepted. In all these possibilities, the emphasis is always on the appreciation of the person as he experiences himself without any critcism or style, which, in self-terms, would be deemed a narcissistic blow to self-esteem (Weiner & White, 1985). Conversely, the empathic approach, fostering the building of self-esteem in accepting the person's experiences as they are experienced, is used as the mode of interpretation.

GROUP THEMES

The following themes dominated what the group wished to focus on. The order of presentation of these themes is sequential in nature and indicative of the building of group cohesion over time.

The opening session dealt with why people chose to work with the elderly. The leader gave some background material, quoting some current research on working with the aged. Each group member who spoke expressed that working with other aged was most vital to them and revealed reasons such as living with a grandmother, which made them realize the multiple facets of aging, that having experienced emotional stress in their own lives, they wished to help others in need, that working with this age group helped them with their own problems—"realizing how lucky I am to be as healthy as I am," and that it was good to feel needed. The latter theme, which was the most prevalent, was further explored in terms of what "being needed" meant personally, as well as its importance to others, and how isolation, lack of others in an environment, was depressing. The empathic approach stressed the healthy component of their desire for attachment, altruism and a sense of belonging.

The second session occurred during a holiday season, and although the group had chosen to focus on the topic of "the unmotivated client," group consensus concentrated on the theme of "holiday blues." Most group members told of what this meant to them—the feeling of isolation during the time of festivity and how they translated this feeling into what their clients told them. Self-psychology was utilized with a short academic interpretation of "idealized" times and "real" times and how the discrepancy between the two could create problems. Members then contributed their own examples. They told of experiences in their own lives when expectations (the idealized experiences) did not match the real (what really occurred). Suggestions were made as to how to help their clients in their translation of these principles into statements such as:

> I can say to her (client) that it is understandable that she would want others/ festivities/presents around her at these times and how disappointed she would be in not having them. I could then point out to her how to best resolve this by dealing with what we could do, such as being in touch with whomever was closest, exchanging some gift with someone, writing letters to well-liked friends/acquaintances or sending cards. Confrontational statements such as, "Well, be realistic; you'll just have to make the best of it. Consider yourself lucky in having as much as you do," did not arise and were not suggested.

> Session three dealt with harassment as experienced with clients. Harassment was expressed in general as client's pressuring of workers, insulting workers, and such. Each person contributed some vignette and it was felt that this indeed was an issue. By asking what they felt the harassing client experienced, issues of "they must be very anxious; they must want control; they must be very angry and upset" were suggested. The leader then asked group members what kind of behavior they felt was most helpful to them when they experienced this form of irritation and what they could suggest as palliative to their client? They stated that when they were harassed they felt powerless and not appreciated and this in turn also irritated them. Most felt that they would like to receive some form of soothing, some inner voice sayings to them:

> Calm down, don't get excited. Your client is evidently upset. It does not mean you are doing a poor job. It just means the client is needy. Stay cool and calm and do the best you can to both keep calm and soothe the client.

Statements reflective of that nature were encouraged:

> Mrs. G., I am terribly sorry you are upset. I don't blame you for being bothered at all the forms you had to fill out and at the long waiting for action. It is understandable. I wish it were different but agencies being what they are, not perfect, sometimes this happens. We'll do the best we can do to remedy this situation and I personally will try to help as much as I can.

Again, this soothing is congruent with self-psychology theory, which states that aggression is not an innate drive, as originally postulated in psychological theory, but rather a response to a nonresponsive environment. Soothing would then be used as a form of responsiveness in the other, or caring person, as a way of altering this feeling state.

Session four dealt with the issue of the unmotivated person. Presentations of experiences related to the fact that when the client was unmotivated to act as prescribed by the worker, they (the worker) felt unappreciated and helpless. The issue was dealt with by exploring what "motivation" actually meant (i.e., the discrepancy perhaps between what the worker wished the client to do and the agenda as interpreted by the clients themselves). It was suggested by the leader that sometimes the uncooperative client experienced the other person as being unempathic and that behind the perceived lack of cooperation there may be other messages to be read.

An example was presented by one of the group members of the client who would not "go outside with me even though I know she can walk well and that the fresh air would do her good." As the case developed, other members pointed out that perhaps something else was going on. The worker then told the group that the client had had a history of mental illness and had reported to the worker that when seen by others she often felt "strange, queer, as though I were different from others." Once this was stated, group members suggested ways in which the worker could possibly lead her client into the "fresh air outside" situation by gentle encouragement, such as walking with her when there were relatively few people around or walking with her on some short trip in a goal-oriented way like shopping for a particular item and then immediately returning home. It was also suggested that the worker empathize with her feelings of strangeness and the experiences behind this. Both the worker and the group seemed encouraged by these attempts.

Other sessions dealt with themes such as sexuality in the client; senility and/or psychoses; developing trust in the worker-to-client relationship; deterioration in the client and how it affects the worker's psyche; and termination or when is it time to say good-bye.

PERCEIVED CHANGES IN WORKERS/GROUP MEMBERS

While an experimental design indicating changes over time was not part of the training experience, changes of an impressionistic nature were noted. Among the most obvious were the following:

1. As group cohesiveness grew, group members became more empathic with each other. Thus, while, as with most groups, some members were more talkative (monopolizers) than others, with peers assuming an intolerant air, receptivity to ideas appeared to increase even

when expressed in a lengthy way. To help facilitate this, the leader encouraged members by focusing on what was said and showing appreciation. Words such as: "You're very articulate and what you say is really very important," or "I'm glad we took the time to listen to you. It's been very helpful," were used.

2.   The group reported less and less difficulty with clients and appeared enthusiastic in their work, proudly citing examples of how they used "a real psychological approach and it worked." They often cited the theory as further proof of their knowledge and effectiveness. Some even jokingly said they could also now practice psychotherapy and earn more money!

3.   The rapport with the leader, or what could be called a positive transference in traditional terms and an idealized one in self-psychology terms, was evident. They saw the leader as effective and caring and identified with these qualities. When, occasionally, a member reported an uncaring attitude toward a client, the group was quick to pick this up and show how this could be altered to increase client and worker satisfaction. Since the leader represented the agency, attitudes toward the agency also became more benign, the workers seeing the agency as protective but often frustrated in its desires, an understanding they could identify with.

IMPLICATIONS FOR EXTENDED OUTREACH

The implications appear straightforward. Older, paid workers can be highly effective in working with their age peers if sufficiently trained. When both the trainees knowledge of behavior in others is enhanced to counter the feelings of powerlessness combined with hightened self-awareness, greater feelings of self-esteem would naturally lead to more positive aging. In addition, a group setting offers the possibility of multiple choices for alliances to be made so as to enrich the worker's environment and to mitigate the possibility of the isolation so pervasive in the client population served.

Were this training program to be replicated, it is suggested that scales measuring variables considered most potent be developed as a means of obtaining more definitive and therefore, more measureable, results. That this type of program can be cost-effective seems also apparent. However, the effectiveness of its intent, on a human level, goes beyond such boundaries. It is our hope that programs of a similar nature will bear this out.

REFERENCES

Butler, R.N. (1975). Psychiatry and the elderly: An overview. *American Journal of Psychiatry, 132.*

Fozard, J.L., & Thomas, J.C., Jr. (1975). Psychology of aging: Basic factors and some psychiatric applications. In J.G. Howells (Ed.), *Modern perspectives in the psychiatry of old age* (1979). (pp. 107-169). New York: Brunner/Mazel.

Grotjahn, M. (1979). Psychodynamic psychotherapy with the aged. *Journal of Geriatric Psychiatry, 12*(1), 71-100.

Group for the Advancement of Psychiatry, The Committee of Aging. (1970, November). *Toward a public policy on mental health care of the elderly, Vol. VII.* (Report No. 79).

Hoffman, S.B. (1983). Peer counselor training with the elderly. *The Gerontologist, 23* (4) 353-360.

Kohut, H. (1982). Introspection, empathy and the semicircle of mental health. *International Journal of Psychoanalysis, 63,* 395-407.

Lawton, M.P. (1976). Geropsychological knowledge as a background for psychotherapy with older people. *Journal of Geriatric Psychiatry, 9*(2), 221-234.

McClintock, J., & Pamilla, T. (1985). Older worker-older client, an approach to gerontological training in a community setting. *Journal of Gerontological Social Work.*

Pynoos, J., Hade-Kaplan, B., & Fleisher, D. (1984). Intergenerational neighborhood networks: a basis for aiding the frail elderly. *The Gerontologist, 24*(3), 233-236.

Schwartzman, G. (1984). The use of the group as self-object. *International Journal of Group Psychotherapy, 34*(2), 229-241.

Weiner, M.B. (1980). Social interaction in the aged. In R. Bennett (Ed.), *Aging, isolation and resocialization.* New York: Van Nostrand Reinhold Press.

Weiner, M.B., Brok, A.J., & Snadowsky, A.M. (1985). *Working with the aged.* Englewood Cliffs, NJ: Prentice-Hall.

Weiner, M.B., & White, M.T. (1985). Uncooperative patients or empathic failures? *Clinical Gerontologist.*

Weiner, M.B., Teresi, J., & Streich, C. (1983). *Old people are a burden but not my Parents.* New York: Spectrum Publications.

White, M.T., & Weiner, M.B. (1985). *The theory and practice of self psychology,* New York: Brunner/Mazel.

Wilensky, H., & Weiner, M.B. (1977). Facing reality in psychotherapy with the elderly. *Psychotherapy: Theory, research and practice, 14*(4), 373-378.

PART VII

Ethical Issues in Aging Societies: The Case of Geriatrics

CHAPTER 63

Decisions to Withdraw or Withhold Treatment from Geriatric Patients

Nancy Neveloff Dubler

The United States is engaged in a struggle to define and protect the rights of elderly persons enmeshed in webs spun by the health care delivery system. This system encompasses acute care and long-term care institutions and the networks of home health care agencies and providers.

A major question confronting the United States is how to provide for the fair, appropriate, and equitable distribution of health services. Congress is attempting to forge a national consensus on the economics of this issue through reform of the Medicaid program, which underwrites some costs of health care for the poor and Medicare, which assumes limited and specific costs of care for the elderly.

These debates involve generic judgments affecting the rights of groups within society—as such, they utilize the language of economists, the macroallocations of resources and rights. National legislation unquestionably has an impact on the quality and quantity of service available to elderly patients.

There is a second level of decision making, however, which is not addressed to the abstraction *elderly* but rather to the concrete individual elderly person. Decisions regarding the care of any specific patient involve the allocation of increasingly scarce resources and are the result of an amalgam of considerations defined by medicine, law, and the increasingly amplified voices of secular bioethicists. These three groups must then be cognizant of and consider theological differences of patients and families and ethnic patterns of behavior that condition a patient's and family's understanding of illness and health and help to shape preferences for specific care plans and interventions.

Fine ethical distinctions about appropriate care for the elderly are a luxury of modern industrialized societies; they are also a burden. For how we decide to care for the health of our elderly will, in my view, establish a paradigm of responsibilities for disparate other facets of elderly existence. Elderly persons, in increasingly mobile societies, with the disintegration of community necessarily attendant thereto, and, with the decline of supportive nuclear and extended families, are a potentially vulnerable, underserved, and increasingly isolated population. And they represent that section of the population which is most explosive demographically. Decisions about care of individual elderly patients must be viewed not only in the narrow context of medical care but also in the larger crucible of society.

This symposium focused on some specific ethical considerations in geriatric care. It discussed individual care decisions. There is unquestionably, however, some resonance from these decisions in medical care for the total life situations of elderly persons.

Decisions to withdraw or withhold treatment from elderly patients were, by tradition, made in private by physician and family, according to shared values, and guided by common moral concerns. These sorts of decisions are now increasingly presented for judicial consideration. This is so, first, because medicine has created technologies that extend existence but may not necessarily provide for a life of sapience and sentience. Technology thus enhances moral complexity by increasing options. Second, American society is particularly litigious and the profession of medicine is fearful of taking actions that can lead to civil or, more importantly, criminal liability, although until now, the threat of either sort of possible liability has been virtually unknown. Finally, some caregivers have requested, and some patients and families have *demanded,* that the public (i.e. the courts) review treatment decisions in order to remove the decision-making process from the normally shielded and protected world of medicine and subject these decisions to publicly fashioned and judicially applied norms. This demand for a public process more than likely emanates from concerns about technology, moral complexity, and potential liability.

As a result, there have been a series of judicial opinions that have articulated legal rules, both substantive and procedural, which guide decisions to withhold or withdraw care from patients who are not presently able, or were never able in the past, to address adequately the issues. In the discussion that follows, the numbers in parentheses reference legal cases cited which appear at the end of the article.

Capable, or in the language of the law, competent patients have the right, in American society, to consent to or to refuse suggested care and treatment(1). Increasingly, this right to refuse a proposed treatment, a critical aspect of the patient's right to informed consent, is being pushed to encompass (a) a right to refuse future treatments when no longer capable of participating in the process and (b) a right to insist on the withdrawal of treatment once instituted. These variations and extensions of the right to refuse treatment developed gradually from the basic common law rule of self-determination, under the terms of which "every human being of adult years and sound mind shall have a right to determine what shall be done with his own body"(2).

Obviously, these sorts of issues arise most frequently in the care of the aged. One recent case, exploring the rights of one competent geriatric patient, will suffice for analysis before turning to the far more complex and thorny concepts surrounding decisions about care of the presently incompetent or never competent patient.

In December of 1984, the Superior Court of the State of California handed down an opinion in the case of *Bartling v. Superior Court, 1984,* (Glendale Adventist Medical Center)(3). This case presented the question "whether a competent adult patient, with serious illnesses, which are probably incurable but have not been diagnosed as terminal, has the right, over the objection of his physicians and the hospital, to have life-support equipment disconnected despite the fact that withdrawal of such devices will surely hasten his death?"(4).

The case involved the care of Mr. William Bartling who, joined by his wife, petitioned the court to order the hospital to disconnect his respirator or ventilator. At the time of his death, before the opinion of the court was handed down, Mr. Bartling was 70 years old and suffering from emphysema, chronic respiratory failure, arteriosclerosis, an abdominal aneurysm, and a malignant tumer of the lung. He also had a history of chronic acute anxiety/depression and alcoholism; it was treatment for the depression which led to his final hospitalization. A routine physical uncovered a tumor in the lung. A needle biopsy caused the lung to collapse; the emphysema prevented healing, and a tracheotomy and placement on a ventilator followed (a quite classic instance of an iatrogenic condition, if not illness). When Mr. Bartling repeatedly attempted to remove the ventilator tubes he was placed in "soft restraints."

Mr. and Mrs. Bartling sued, among other things, for damages, violation of state and constitutional rights, and infliction of emotional distress. They sought an injunction restraining the hospital from administering any unconsented medical care. In a document accompanying the court petition, Mr. Bartling stated:

> While I have no wish to die, I find intolerable the living conditions forced upon me . . . I fully understand that my request to have the ventilator

removed . . . will very likely . . . lead to my death. I am willing to accept that risk rather than to continue the burden of this artificial existence which I find unbearable, degrading and dehumanizing(5).

Despite this statement, and despite a previously executed Living Will and durable power of attorney (which will be discussed in the next section), the hospital refused to remove the ventilator or to permit Mr. Bartling to do so by removing the restraints which bound his hands.

The court held in an opinion designed to startle the reader who is unfamiliar with the historical development of the right to refuse treatment, that the request to have life-support equipment disconnected was not limited to *comatose terminally ill* patients or to representatives acting on their behalf, and therefore that Mr. Bartling's wishes should have been followed.

Mr. Bartling was clearly competent, stated the court, and, as such, ambivalence and vacillation do not compromise his rights. The court then asked if his right to refuse unwanted medical treatment was outweighed by the interests of the state in the preservation of life, the need to protect innocent third parties, the prevention of suicide, and the maintaining of the ethics of the medical profession. These four touchstones of state interest were developed in the context of protecting an incompetent person who was and had always been incapable of identifying and protecting self-interest(6). The court, rejecting the weight of these state interests in this particular case, supported the right of the competent patient to make a rational decision to refuse treatment *"when death is inevitable and the treatment offers no hope of cure or the perservation of life"(7)*. Query, therefore, if the right exists absolutely or only with these qualifications. However, this case clearly states that competent patients have a legal right to insist that merely life-prolonging care be withdrawn or withheld.

Mr. Bartling was an alert, aware, conscious, deliberate decider. Many elderly patients do not fit this description and may more resemble the description of Claire C. Conroy(8) " . . . no longer ambulatory . . . confined to bed, unable to move from a semifetal position . . . could not speak . . . her eyes sometimes followed individuals in the room . . . confused and unaware"(9). The issue presented in the Conroy case was whether a legally appointed guardian could exercise Ms. Conroy's right to refuse treatment on her behalf and thus order that artificial feedings be withdrawn, permitting death.

In view of the case law, as analyzed by the *Bartling* court, Ms. Conroy could have chosen to have her nasogastric tube withdrawn. Her interest in freedom from nonconsensual invasion of her bodily integrity would outweigh any state interest in preserving her life or in safeguarding the integrity of the medical profession. In addition, her rejection of artificial means of feeding would not, it would be argued, constitute attempted suicide, as the decision would be grounded on a wish to be free of medical intervention rather than a specific intent to end her life.

The origin of complexity, for what seems so simple a proposition that one should be able to refuse care and treatment, lie in the early cases dealing with the rights of incompetent patients(10). The predictions of further complexity will arise from determinations of what is considered treatment, and if the mechanistic and medicalized provision of nutrition and hydration amounts to treatment, whether it is governed by the same rules that guide other sorts of care.

The legal quest for clarity regarding withholding care from incompetent patients commenced with the Quinlan case in New Jersey in 1976(11). That case was one of the few of its type that considered a young (21-year-old) rather than an elderly person. In that case, the court held that a patient in a chronic persistent vegetative state has a right protected by the common-law right of self-determination and by the constitutional right of privacy to refuse life-sustaining care, and that this right can be exercised on the patient's behalf by another. The state's interests in opposing this substituted refusal were essentially the preservation and sanctity of human life and the defense of the right of a physician to administer medical treatment according to their judgment. In a triumph of formulation, the court stated that, ''The State's interest contra weakens and the individual's right to privacy grows as the degree of bodily invasion increases and the prognosis dims. Ultimately there comes a point at which the individual's rights overcome the state's interest''(12). This case, which purports to discuss substituted judgment (i.e., what would this person want if she could tell us), relies heavily on the court's objective formula, and stipulates procedural safeguards to ensure the fair and equitable application of the substantive rule.

Similar formulas in other states established comparable standards for deciding when treatment can be withdrawn or withheld. In Massachusetts a series of cases underscored the necessity for an inquiry based on concepts of substituted judgment—that is, what would this person want if she could tell us(13). For someone previously competent such an inquiry is meaningful. For one never capable of making such a decision, such as the congenitally retarded, posing the substituted judgment question seems ludicrous. The previously noted list of state interests that muddy the *Bartling* opinion, arise in these cases(14).

As previously noted, in all of the opinions that attempt to fashion a substantive standard, procedural rules are prescribed. New Jersey requires a hospital prognosis committee to confirm that there is no reasonable possibility of return to cognitive and sapient life, at which point a guardian may exercise the patient's right to refuse care and choose to withdraw care(15). In Massachusetts, decisions to refuse and withdraw care from incompetent persons are left to the probate courts (16). New York State rejected all inquiries into substituted judgment and condemned incompetent patients to treatment, unless they were previously competent and unless they explicitly considered the sort of situation and left clear and explicit directives to be followed by others (17).

Thus, what generalizations are possible regarding the legal right of a competent older person to refuse ongoing care or the right of incompetent elderly to have surrogates, proxies, or third parties refuse for them?

In theory, the right of the competent patient to refuse initially, or once treatment is instituted, is without challenge. In fact, caregivers often oppose both, citing depression of the patient, vacillation, ambivalence, and cognitive disability as disqualifying individual choice. As there is some diminution of logical clarity and emotional force that necessarily accompanies illness, the efforts of the more powerful (i.e., caregivers) to frustrate an individual's choice, are often successful. If these cases reach the public arena, however (which is not usually the case), they are almost invariably decided in support of the patient's right. Indeed the *Conroy* case, which we will consider next, states:

> In view of the case law, we have no doubt that Ms. Conroy, if competent to make the decision and if resolute in her determination, could have chosen to have her nasogastric tube withdrawn. Her interest in freedom from nonconsensual invasion of her bodily integrity would outweigh any state interest in preserving life or in safeguarding the integrity of the medical profession. In addition, rejecting her artificial means of feeding would not constitute attempted suicide, as the decision would probably be based on a wish to be free of medical intervention rather than a specific intent to end her life (18).

The theory supporting substituted refusal of care by third parties for incompetent patients is less secure. New York State courts, as previously noted, have rejected all such arguments. The legal trend, however, is to permit substituted decisions for incompetent patients in certain categories of patients (i.e., the terminally ill, the comatose, and those in a permanent vegetative state). Thus arises the origin of the confusion in the *Bartling* case. Only certain incompetent patients may have care withdrawn, which may lead to death. These restrictions on withdrawing care, however, should not and do not apply to the competent.

The slow development of a legal standard and of procedural safeguards with accompanying intermittent confusion is, I would argue, somewhat perversely appropriate, even if it occasionally leads to the wrong results in individual cases. The hastening of death as an option for caregivers is contrary to traditional medical ethics and must be tendered tentatively, gently, and carefully to the medical professions. Especially with elderly persons, many of whom are alone and without natural advocates, decisions to withdraw care must be made in individual cases, based upon the individual facts, and considering the suffering of the patient without diminishing the value of all elderly life. These decisions must be reached openly and justified to supervisory persons, although not necessarily in court proceedings. Especially in cost-conscious modern societies, the right to die must not be permitted to evolve into an obligation to die. The option of not caring should be difficult to exercise. Legal rules should prescribe standards and stipulate procedures to help to protect the vulnerable from abandonment in old age.

Much has been written in the last decade about the necessity to protect elderly persons from the unwanted medical intrusions and preserve their right to a chosen death. Little has been written about the abandonment of the alone, incompetent, and aesthetically unpleasing elderly. Both groups are of concern to a legal system defining and protecting rights. The last decade of cases have defined categories of incompetent patients from whom care and treatment may be withheld. Recently, as *Bartling* indicated, the attempt to limit the refusal of competent patients based on these categories has been rebuffed. The coming issue will involve the question: What is treatment? Does it include the provision of hydration and nutriments?

In the Matter of Claire C. Conroy begins this exploration. First, in a radical departure from previous cases, the court expanded the permissible category of incompetent patients from whom care may be withheld to include those incompetent elderly with *severe* and permanent mental and physical impairment and limited life-expectancy. This is a huge expansion of the previous categories such as the comatose and those in a permanent vegetative state (19). The description in the case of Ms. Conroy is a template for the contracted patient—a semifetal position, incontinent of bladder and bowel, with degenerated organ systems and decubidae, who inhabits an acute hospital ward. Ms. Conroy could sometimes make eye contact; it was inconclusive as to whether or to what extent she was capable of experiencing pain.

Ms. Conroy's nephew, as her legal guardian, requested that treatment, in this case the nasogastric tube, be withdrawn. The New Jersey court stated that the goal of decision making for incompetent patients is to determine and effectuate, insofar as possible, the decision the patient would have made if competent. The court sets forth tests to determine whether the goal is met. The last of these tests, the "pure objective" test, permits withdrawal of care when the net burdens of the patient's life with the treatment clearly and markedly outweigh the benefits that the patient derives from life and it would be inhumane to continue treatment(20). This test sounds like an elaboration of the

Quinlan formula, which applied to persons in a permanent vegetative state. However, the expansion of the category of patient combined with the definition of nutrition as treatment may heighten concern. The court suggests that an evaluation of the patient's life should be based on pain, suffering, and possible enjoyment; although it states that it eschews judgments on "quality of life." I suggest, in fact, that it permits just that. Finally, the court sees no distinction, except emotional, between artificial feeding and a respirator—as both prolong life through mechanical means. On the contrary, the Conroy case represents a quantum leap into uncharted medical, legal, and social waters. Although specific procedures are stipulated, *Conroy* removes the imaginative barriers and legal inhibitions, which prevented caregivers from hastening the death of many elderly. American society has a long history of failing to protect vulnerable populations: the demented and institutionalized aged are possibly at increased risk from this decision.

The *Bartling* and *Conroy* cases both stress the importance of advance directives in ensuring the individual appropriateness of later care. Advance directives, living wills, specifically executed agreements, lengthy testaments, appointments of agents, and durable powers of attorney for health care decisions all permit competent persons to control their care after they are no longer capable. Most courts consider these documents, if not binding, then at least weighty evidence in adjudicating rights. The medical profession will in time acknowledge the same. The sorts of concerns that guide decisions in the informed consent process, that is, the ability to withstand pain, personal preference for quality or extent of existence, economic factors, the dictates of religion, and personal philosophy also determine whether and how an elderly person executes an advance directive.

To be of maximum effect these directives should be explicit, reasonably contemporaneous, and executed in conformity with state law. Despite all proprieties and formalities, some settings, such as the medical center treating Mr. Bartling, will act in disregard of these statements in pursuit of their own self-defined philosophy and definition of propriety. However, increasingly, these directives will command respect.

The *Bartling* case also provides an insight into the problem of developing unitary legal norms in a pluralistic society. The Glendale Adventist Medical Center is a religiously affiliated medical center, the majority of whose doctors would view disconnecting a life-support system in a case such as *Bartling* as inconsistent with the healing orientation of physicians. Theological systems approach concepts of sanctity of life differently. For example, Catholic theology early on distinguished between ordinary and extraordinary care, the latter being overly intrusive, burdensome, and expensive with insufficient compensating benefit, and therefore not morally mandated. Other religions do not necessarily accept such distinctions.

Religion and politics have historically made strange bedfellows under the blankets of American society. Consideration of the present issues provides no exception. The right–to–life political lobby, honed in the crucible of the abortion debate, has shifted its focus to neonatal care and, one fears, to geriatric care. It would be unfortunate if the politicization of the discussions regarding when life begins were extended to discussions of its end. Certainly such politicization has already inhibited many state legislatures from attempting to pass uniform laws that would protect patients from abuse and shield the judiciary from the necessity of case-by-case determination on the merits.

How should the United States deal with the fact of a religiously diverse society and affiliated hospitals and staff? One option is by an extension of private law—that is, by requiring explicit contracts about the terms and conditions of care in a specific institution. Thus, in a hospital administered by a religion accepting sanctity of life as the only valid ethic, the entrance contract would so stipulate. The problem with this apparently neat solution is that certain contracts, especially those that purport to constrain and infringe individual liberty and compromise constitutional rights, may be void as a matter of public policy.

Short of such hospital-wide policies, physicians and patients must openly discuss issues of withdrawing, withholding, and terminating care. A physician's bias should be a key factor in an older patient's choice of a caregiver. This second neat solution, however, ignores the fact that many older persons, in the community and in long-term care, have no choice of provider. This is a fact that argues even more strongly against individual contract arrangements which attempt to impose provider philosophies.

Ethical care is that which supports the individual preference of the patient, enhances autonomy, permits diversity, and comports with the interests of the state in preserving life and protecting the vulnerable. This is a rigorous life of requirements. Legal rules represent one element in the developing national consensus on appropriate geriatric care. They reflect our society's concern for individual liberty, the sanctity of life, and the need to subordinate medical technology to human values and concerns.

REFERENCE NOTES: LEGAL CASES CITED

1. See Schloendorff v. Society of New York Hospital, 211, N.Y. 125, 105 (N.E. 92(1914); Natanson v. Kline, 186 Kan, 393, 350 P. 2d 1093 (1960); Canterbury v. Spence, 464 F. 2d 772 (D.C. Cir. 1972); Cobbs v. Grant, 8 Cal. 3d 229, 502 P. 2dl (1972).
2. Schloendorff, supra note 1, at 129 and 93.

3. Bartling v. Superior Court (Glendale Adventist Medical Center), 209 Cal. Rptr. 220 (1984).
4. *Id.*, at 220.
5. *Id.*, at 222.
6. See Superintendent of Belchertown State School v. Saikewicz, 373 Mass. 728, 370 N.E. 2d 417 (1977).
7. Bartling, supra note 3, at 226.
8. In re Conroy, 98 N.J. 321, A. 2d 1209 (1985).
9. Id., at 337 and 1217.
10. See, e.g., In re Quinlan, 70 N.J. 10, 335 A. 2d 647 (1976), Superintendent of Belchertown State School v. Saikewicz, supra note 6.
11. Quinlan, supra note 10.
12. *Id.*, at 41 and 664.
13. See e.g., Saikewicz, supra note 6; *In the Matter of Spring,* 380 Mass. 629, 405 N.E. 2d 115 (1980).
14. *Id.*
15. See Quinlan, supra note 10.
16. See Saikewicz, supra note 6; But See In the Matter of Dinnerstein, 380 N.E. 2d 134 (Mass. App., 1978).
17. In the Matter of Storar, 52 N.Y. 2d 363, 438 N.Y.S. 2d 266, 420 N.E. 2d 64 (1981).
18. Conroy, supra note 8, at 355 and 1226.
19. Id., at 363 and 1231.
20. Id., at 366 and 1232.

CHAPTER 64

The Termination of Medical Interventions for the Elderly: Who Should Decide?

Arthur L. Caplan

It is a basic presumption of Western law and morality that patients have the right to control what happens to their bodies in both medical and nonmedical contexts. This presumption is often not applied to the elderly. Since the elderly are more vulnerable than other members of the population to impairments or variability in their competency, there is a tendency evident in American medicine to impose professional judgments about the appropriateness or desirability of medical interventions on this class of persons. The concept of competency is analyzed and it is argued that competency must be viewed as a context or decision-specific ability. It is further argued that disputes about competency are really often disputes about which moral norms ought guide the care of elderly patients—respect for autonomy or beneficence. It is suggested that each older patient ought to have a "values baseline" established early on in any admission to a hospital or other medical institution. This will allow providers to be guided by a patient's choices should they become impaired or variably competent. Since elderly persons are more likely than other members of society to know what they actually desire in terms of medical treatment, autonomy should receive preference over benevolence whenever it is possible to either establish patient choices or utilize a values baseline.

---

*Some of the material in this article is taken from a paper, "Let Wisdom Find a Way," forthcoming in the journal *Generation*.

THE PRESUMPTION OF PATIENT AUTHORITY

Few topics have attracted the amount of professional and public attention that the termination of medical interventions has in recent years.
Many older Americans seem terrified that they will become the victims
of medical technology rather than its beneficiaries. Physicians, nurses,
and social workers seem confused as to their duties and responsibilities
where stopping treatment is at issue. Indeed, in this context there is
little clarity as to what constitutes medical treatment (e.g., artificial life
supports, food and fluids, comfort and care). Courts at both the state
and federal levels have attempted to grapple with this thorny subject,
but no clear-cut consensus has emerged as to the rights and obligations
owed to the hopelessly ill.

The elderly are especially likely to encounter medicalization and,
thus, to face the issue of when, if ever, medical interventions ought to
be stopped. Those elderly persons who are institutionalized, either in
hospitals or nursing homes, require the formulations of policies and
protocols by health care providers, legislators, and the courts that will
allow them to retain control over their medical care. All too frequently
the elderly find themselves at the mercy of others—family, friends,
physicians, guardians, hospital administrators—where decisions to
stop treatment arise. While mercy is surely an admirable virtue, it is
one whose exercise ought be limited to those who actually need it
rather than to a class of persons for whom power and control over their
bodies is a right, not a privilege.

It has long been a given in both American law and ethics that
patients have the ultimate authority over what happens to their bodies
insofar as medical treatment is concerned. Neither the law nor ethics
recognizes any obligation on the part of the competent adult to be a
patient. Competent adults are free to refuse medical care both for
sound reasons as well as silly reasons. These sentiments are clearly
expressed in a series of well-known court decisions regarding informed
consent and medical care:

> Every human being of adult years and sound mind has a right to determine
> what shall be done with his own body; and a surgeon who performs an
> operation without his patient's consent commits an assault for which he is
> liable in damages (*Schloendorff v. Society of New York Hospital*, 1914).
>
> Anglo-American law starts with the premise of thorough-going self-deter-
> mination. It follows that each man is considered to be master of his own
> body . . . (*Natanson v. Kline*, 1960).
>
> [It] is the prerogative of the patient, not the physician, to determine for
> himself the direction in which he believes his interests lie . . . (*Cobbs v.
> Grant*, 1972).
>
> [T]he patient's right of self-decision shapes the boundaries of the duty to
> reveal. That right can be effectively exercised only if the patient possesses
> enough information to enable an intelligent choice. The scope of the physi-

cian's communications to the patient, then, must be measured by the patient's need . . . . And to safeguard the patient's interest in achieving his own determination on treatment, the law must itself set the standard for adequate disclosure (*Canterbury v. Spence*, 1972).

These court decisions, as well as numerous writings on informed consent in both the literature of medicine and bioethics, make it clear that the presumption of authority is always vested in the competent adult where treatment decisions either to begin or terminate care are concerned. The primary problem facing the elderly is that their competency is often a matter of uncertainty and dispute. This is partly due to the fact that the elderly often speak in a "quiet voice." They may have difficulty articulating their wishes and choices in the environment of a hospital or a nursing home. But it is also a result of the fact that the elderly as a class is more vulnerable to impairments of competency that arise as a result of organic, psychological and sociological factors.

THE VULNERABILITY OF THE ELDERLY TO IMPAIRMENTS IN COMPETENCY

Changes in the demographics of the population of the United States, as well as major advances in the efficacy of medical intervention in treating acute medical problems (Verbugge, 1984), have created a large and growing class of older patients who are living longer but are burdened with increasing levels of chronic morbidity. The competency of many of these persons, particular those who are in hospitals or nursing homes, is impaired or diminished in significant ways, but not so severely as to make it self-evident that these patients ought be viewed as entirely incompetent to make any or all decisions related to their health. This is especially true for those patients who are in the category of what is referred to (Neugarten, 1974) as the old-old.

Some of the patients who fall into this gray zone possess levels of competency that vary depending upon the setting in which they live, the time of day, or the degree to which they are under the influence of various psychoactive drugs. Others are afflicted with impairments of either their cognitive or emotional abilities. Frequently, the degree of impairment does not clearly render them unable to participate in the many decisions that must be made about their medical care.

While elderly persons are especially prone to stereotyping, it is nonetheless true that the sick elderly are, as a class, more prone than are other segments of the population to problems that result in impairments or diminishments of competency. Those elderly receiving care in hospitals or nursing homes are often afflicted with biological disorders that can limit their cognitive abilities and mental functioning. Diseases such as Alzheimer's disease, strokes, or depression are more likely to afflict older persons. Various physiological changes involved in the process of senescence itself may also produce decreases in certain cognitive and emotional capacities (Palmore, 1980).

Biological disorders are not the only source of impaired or diminished competency in the elderly. Older persons with medical problems are more likely to be institutionalized than are other patients and their institutionalization lasts for longer periods of time than is true of other patients. As numerous studies have convincingly shown (Altman, 1975; Dohrenwend, 1975), institutionalization sometimes has adverse impacts on competency.

The sick and institutionalized elderly often lack the economic and social resources requisite for zealously advocating their interests. As a result, they are more likely than others to fall prey to attempts to override their choices. The sick elderly and the old-old are often excluded from decisions over health care that directly affect their interests for no other reason then that they do not know about or cannot afford legal or social aid that would allow them to assert their autonomy.

WHAT IS COMPETENCY?

There are few concepts whose definition has occasioned as much dispute and controversy as the concept of competency. A review of some of the various definitions currently extant in the literature will give some sense of the lack of consensus that prevails as to the definition of this concept. The President's Commission for the Study of Ethical Problems in Medicine and Biomedical and Behavioral Research (1982) viewed competency as consisting of three elements: "possession of a set of values and goals; the ability to communicate and understand information; and the ability to reason and to deliberate about one's choice." Roth, Meisel and Lidz (1977) suggest that to be considered competent an individual "must be able to comprehend the nature of the particular conduct in question and to understand its quality and its consequences." Abernathy and Lundin (1980), after providing a useful review of the legal and cultural aspects of competency conclude that, "any competency calculus should include consideration of the patient's ability to receive, process and produce information, the patient's history and general social setting, and consideration of the patient's behavior."

A variety of state legislatures have also attempted to grapple with the problem of defining competency. Most have attempted to define "incompetency," since the law presumes competency to be present unless proven otherwise. A typical example is an Illinois statute (1976) that defines incompetence as:

Any person who because of insanity, mental illness, mental retardation, old age, physical incapacity or imperfection or deterioration of mentality is incapable of managing his person or estate and any person who because of gambling, idleness, debauchery or the excessive use of intoxicants or drugs, so spends or wastes his estate as to expose himself or his family to want or suffering.

While there are numerous court cases that review the rights of patients to refuse treatment, particularly for religious reasons, there are surprisingly few attempts at definitions of competency in U.S. court cases. Two of the most important cases where an attempt has been made to provide a standard are *Grannum v. Berard* and *Schiller*. In Grannum, the court argued that, ". . . the test being whether the person in question . . . possessed sufficient mind or reason to enable him to understand the nature, the terms and the effects of the transaction." And, in Schiller, the standard adduced was, " . . . the test may be stated as: does the patient have sufficient mind to reasonably understand the condition, the nature and the effect of the proposed treatment, attendent risks in pursuing the treatment and not pursuing the treatment."

These analyses make it plain that there are at least two distinct senses of competency—legal and medical. The legal sense of the term is concerned with a person's ability to responsibly manage property, possessions and finances. The medical sense is not greatly interested in these matters. Rather it attempts to pinpoint those elements of physical, emotional and cognitive ability requisite for participation in medical decision making concerning treatment. While the legal status of competency serves a variety of important social and economic functions, it is of little help to families or clinicians who must decide the degree to which patients ought to be involved in determining the course of their own treatment.

STANDARDS OF COMPETENCY EVIDENT IN PRACTICE

While no clear definitions of competency in the medical sense exist, there is some consensus among health care practitioners as to the methods and criteria that ought be used to assess competency. Determinations of competency are often based upon one or more of the following considerations (Gutheil & Applebaum, 1982; Sherlock 1983):

1. Compliance with medical opinion.
2. Membership in a particular class or category, i.e., "elderly," "violent," "poorly motivated," etc.
3. Orientation as to time, place and person.

4. Ability to pass a mental status examination.
5. The presence of inappropriate behavior, i.e. delusional thinking, sexual forwardness, loss of inhibition.
6. Affective stability.
7. The ability to show integrative thinking.

The first two criteria on this list are very different from the others. Compliance or noncompliance with medical opinion might be termed, following the President's Commission (President's Commission, 1982), "outcome" approaches to the analysis of competency. It is not the process by which a patient reaches a decision but, rather, the actual content of the decision, which is, on this standard, indicative of competency.

The second criterion utilized in clinical practice, assignment to a preexisting category, might be termed the "membership" approach. On this analysis, anyone, regardless of their particular abilities and capacities, is viewed as incompetent if they are accurately classified as members of a category that is generally seen as incompetent.

Neither of these approaches has very much to recommend them. The outcome approach is obviously suspect because it relies only on professional judgments about what counts as an acceptable decision. Such judgments are rarely explicitly articulated and even more rarely justified. Since the primary aim of a competency assessment is to determine whether a patient should be allowed to determine the course of his or her care, compliance with medical opinion or familial standards of reasonableness inappropriately subjugates autonomous choice to prevailing community or professional value judgments.

Similarly, there is sufficient empirical evidence for important variations in the abilities and capacities of individual patients within the category of "elderly" or "aged" to make the membership approach entirely suspect (Stanley, 1984). Simply being old or institutionalized is insufficient evidence of incompetency!

The remaining clinical standards on the list represent efforts to make judgments about a specific patient's reasoning abilities, level of comprehension, and magnitude of the consequences of a various decisions. These tests are all examples of what might be termed "functional" assessments of competency. They depend upon determinations regarding specific persons at particular times in specific decision-making circumstances.

Whatever the particular problems that may face those attempting to use one or all of the various tests of competency popular among health care providers, the functional approach to competency determination is far preferable to both the "outcome" and "membership" criteria. While it is true that no unanimity of opinion exists about the adequacy or accuracy of various measures of cognitive and emotional stability, integrative thinking, and the like, nevertheless, a functional approach to competency determination holds out the greatest chance of assessing individual decision-making capacity against a backdrop of professional disagreement, cultural pluralism, and societal uncertainty.

WHAT ARE MOST DISPUTES ABOUT COMPETENCY REALLY ABOUT?

If it is true that the elderly are especially vulnerable to impairments of competency and if it is also true that competency is a decision-specific trait, how should competency enter into the process of decision making concerning the termination of medical care? It is certainly the case that attempts to pinpoint *the* meaning of competency in clinical settings are motivated by the desire to obtain an understanding of the degree to which patients can be and should be involved in directing their own care. It is also true that the varied references to ability, appropriateness, and comprehension evident in clinical practice represent efforts to struggle with the properties that, empirically speaking, ought be present for full or partial participation. The fact that concerns about appropriate behavior, harm, and compliance are so pervasive in clinical practice in determining competency shows that assessments of competency are often motivated by uncertainty as to the values that ought take priority in decisions about patient care.

Frequently in medicine, the desire to respect autonomy clashes with another important value, the desire to do good or, as it is sometimes called, the duty of benevolence. Physicians, nurses, and social workers want to use their knowledge and skills to advance the well-being of those in their care. Their codes of ethics tell them to try and benefit patients not to harm them. The problem is that all too often the desire to do good conflicts with the obligation to respect autonomy. Patients may have desires or preferences that conflict with professional judgments about what interventions are in a patient's best interest in terms of welfare and health.

There are two key moral principles that must be considered in deciding what role to accord any patient in determining when to stop medical interventions. The standard used by some courts and favored by many health professionals is that of "best interest." According to this principle, those charged with decision making for patients with diminished or absent competency should undertake those medical interventions that they believe will be in the patient's best interests in terms of health and welfare.

Other courts and commentators have argued for a standard of "substituted judgment"; on this principle clinicians should attempt to decide about the acceptability of medical interventions as the patient would have decided were he or she competent (Robertson, 1985).

There is a very real and powerful tension between the desire to be benevolent, to do good for the patient, and the desire to respect autonomy. The "best interest" standard looks toward patient health and welfare as the controlling values that ought to guide decision making for those who may not be able to decide when medical care should end. The substituted judgment standard gives individual autonomy sway when doubts about competency exist.

These clashes of moral principle are not easy to resolve. But social consensus in the United States has tended to place greater priority on autonomy. As noted earlier, our legal system places the burden of consent on providers, not patients. But this is not always the case. Sometimes physicians are encouraged by the law or at least by medical tradition to override autonomy in the interests of benevolence. Consider the fact that physicians and nurses routinely ignore the requests of burn patients to be allowed to die in the hopes that patients will accommodate themselves to the realities of their circumstances. Certainly, both legal and ethical opinion tends to favor the exercise of benevolence rather than the respect of autonomy where matters of active enthanasia are concerned. Few would argue that physicians have a moral duty to blindly adhere to the desires of their patients, especially when the desire of the patient may be for suicide or bodily harm.

Clashes between respect for autonomy and the desire to be benevolent are often at the heart of disputes about the proper course of medical intervention for elderly patients. These ethical disagreements over basic ethical standards are often hidden behind disputes about competency. When clinicians call upon psychiatrists to make a competency determination for a difficult, noncompliant patient, or, when physicians in an acute care system label an elderly patient who is refusing life-saving surgery "confused," it is usually because they want to give more weight to the principle of benevolence than they do the principle of respect for autonomy. More often than not what is really at stake where decisions about stopping care are concerned is not what criteria are indicative of competency, but rather which moral principle should govern the care of the elderly—autonomy or beneficence.

ESTABLISHING A "VALUES BASELINE"

If it is true that what is really at issue where decisions regarding the cessation of medical care are concerned is not the competency of the elderly but rather the determination of which ethical standard (best interest or substituted judgment) should prevail at the bedside, then there are some important procedural and policy steps that ought to be instituted by practitioners, hospitals, and nursing homes to help cope with and facilitate decision making for this particularly vulnerable group of patients. Medical professionals must realize the importance and necessity of establishing a baseline of values for every patient upon admission in order to have the type of information available that will allow for a reasonable and dignified process of decision making when questions concerning the termination of care arise.

If anyone can be said to have established, authentic values, preferences, and goals concerning the kind of medical treatment they desire, surely the elderly can. It may be impossible to decide what an infant or a retarded person would want in the way of medical care, since these persons may not have attained sufficient levels of mental functioning to establish preferences, much less well-thought-through choices, about health care. But this is hardly true of the elderly.

A person who has lived a full life, who has acquired the wisdom that only experience can bring, is surely not akin to an infant or a retarded person with respect to the articulation of personal values about health care. If anyone can be said to truly and authentically know what it is they want for themselves regarding their health, welfare, and well-being, it surely must be the elderly (Dworkin, 1976). The fact that the elderly have the wisdom that only age can bring would seem to require that thorough efforts be made to identify their preferences and choices and special weight be accorded their autonomy.

Serious efforts must be made to establish the values of elderly patients early in the course of medical treatment. Every hospital should have policies requiring the creation of a baseline of patient values that can guide care should impairments of competency arise. Those with chronic health problems can be informed about the kinds of decisions that may, eventually, have to be faced with respect to matters such as the withdrawal of life-support, the initiation of aggressive efforts at resuscitation, or the provision of artificial means of life-support. These issues must be addressed and discussed in an open and frank manner early in the course of an elderly patient's treatment with both patient, family, nurses, and administrators.

Since it is often possible to establish early in the medical care of elderly patients the exact nature of their preferences, desires, and values, health care providers who deal with this group would seem to have an obligation to discuss with them all aspects of their present and possible future medical treatment and to record such discussions in patient charts. While competent elderly patients may not understand all of the options and all of the rationales concerning various forms of medical care, there is no reason to assume that they cannot be informed about such options, and, once informed, deliberate about the kinds of values and goals that they would like to guide the decisions of their health care providers should their competency wane or diminish in any way.

Some may argue that it is psychologically threatening or worse to raise questions about the termination of medical care early in the course of the hospitalization or institutionalization of an elderly patient. Such talk may unduly frighten patients or make them believe that they will not receive aggressive and complete care should serious problems develop.

Of course, it is true that issues regarding the termination of medical care must be handled in a sensitive and humane manner. But talk of the fears of patients must not be allowed to disguise the fact that it is often health care providers or family members who are uncomfortable at the mention of the possibility of impairments to competency and the need to know when, if ever, medical interventions should cease.

A personal anecdote may make this point clear. A few years ago I visited a group of elderly patients in a nursing home. In the course of my visit I chatted with a 90-year-old woman about the kind of care she was receiving. The conversation went well and I was emboldened to inquire whether the woman ever thought about dying. She smiled at me and said "Son, when you are 90 years old you have a hard time thinking about anything else." Elderly patients know that they face difficult choices about the way in which they will die and the manner of medical attention they will receive. Since these decisions are an inevitable part of medicine in the modern age, we ought not let our fears inhibit the elderly person's ability to exercise control over the course and degree of medical intervention they receive.

In situations where elderly patients have had an opportunity to deliberate about and formulate reflective choices regarding the course of medical care, and they then suffer from impairments to their competency, a doctrine of substituted judgment should be followed in so far as is possible. Authentic patient desires can and should be used to guide treatment decisions.

Moreover, whenever possible, family members should be encouraged to take an active role in discussing the desires and choices of their loved ones. While it has become popular in recent years to disparage the role families play in decisions about medical care, the fact is that the family is often in the best position to articulate the values that ought to guide care when competency is diminished or absent.

If health care providers make a sustained effort to involve family members early in discussions with elderly patients about their care then family members will be in a better position to act, not as surrogate decision makers, but as what might be termed "proxy amplifiers." For those elderly who suffer from diminished or variable competency, loved ones may be able to act as amplifiers of authentic patient desires rather than simply as usurpers of patient autonomy and authority. When competency is manifestly present in an elderly patient, every effort should be made by health care professionals to assure that wisdom of age is acknowledged and preserved should situations arise where it may be difficult to articulate or assert.

There are, of course, many situations in which little or nothing is known about the choices and values an elderly patient might have made regarding his or her care. In such circumstances, health care providers must of necessity follow a "best interest" standard in making judgments about the direction and course of care. Best interest is a moral principle that is useful in direct proportion to the degree of irremediable uncertainty or ignorance that exists regarding patient values, choices, and preferences.

Some may argue that a policy of substituted judgment cannot adequately protect patient autonomy since it is hard to know with certainty what a patient "really" would have wanted, or because competent elderly patients sometimes change their wishes about medical treatment after surviving an episode of acute illness.

But are such worries really a sufficient basis for diminishing the importance of autonomy particularly in light of the fact that the elderly, as a group, are probably more likely than others to have reflected upon their choices and values? Prior directives that are informed and that have been discussed and debated with family and the medical team would appear to be the best basis for responsible decison making for the elderly. No group is as likely to be able to formulate authentic and well-grounded value choices as the elderly, and this fact in and of itself would seem to place a strong obligation on family and providers to respect the legacy of a competent choice in situations where competence is suspect or obviously diminished.

Family members and health care providers must recognize the powerful force that autonomy ought to have with respect to decision making by the elderly. It is true that choices and values do change and evolve. As a result, family members and health care providers must realize that respect for autonomy is a process not an event. It is also by taking seriously the need to talk with and educate elderly patients about the choices that they must face with respect to health care that the elderly will be allowed to exercise the wisdom that accrues only to those who have had the opportunity to acquire it.*

REFERENCES

Abernethy, V., & Lundin, K. (1980). Competency and the right to refuse medical treatment. In V. Abernethy (Ed.), *Frontiers in medical ethics* (p. 94). Cambridge, MA: Ballinger.

Altman, I. (1975). *The environment and social behavior.* Monterey, CA: Brooks-Cole.

Dohrenwend, B. (1975). Sociocultural and social-psychological factors in the genesis of mental illness. *Journal of Health and Social Behavior, 16,* 365–392.

Donagan, A. (1977). Informed consent in therapy and experimentation. *Journal of Medicine and Philosophy, 2*(4), 310–327.

Dworkin, G. (1976, February). Autonomy and behavior control. *Hastings Center Report, 6*(1) 23–28.

Grannum v. Berard, 422 p. 2d at 812 (Wash. 1967).

Gutheil, T., & Applebaum, P. (1982). *Clinical handbook of psychiatry and the law.* (210–252). New York: McGraw-Hill.

In the matter of Schiller, A. 2d 360 (N.J. Super. 1977).

Neugarten, B. (1974). Age groups in American society and the rise of the young-old. *Annals of the American Academy of Political and Social Science, 415,* 187–197.

Palmore, E., (Ed.). (1980). *International handbook on aging.* Westport, CT: Greenwood Press.

President's Commission for the Study of Ethical Problems in Medicine and Biomedical and Behavioral Research. (1982). *Making health care decisions.* Washington, DC: U.S. Government Printing Office.

Robertson, J. (1983). Pro-creative liberty and the control of conception, pregnancy and childbirth. *Virginia Law Review, 69*(405) 55–80.

Robertson, J. (1985). The geography of competency. *Social Research,* 1985.

Roth, L., Meisel, A., & Lidz, C. (1977). Tests of competency to consent to treatment. *American Journal of Psychiatry, 134,* 182.

Sherlock, R. (1983). Competency to consent to medical care: Toward a general view. *General Hospital Psychiatry, 5,* 2–7.

Stanley, R. et al. (1984, September 14). The elderly patient and informed consent. *Journal of the American Medical Association.* 1135–1137.

Verbrugge, L.M. (1984). Longer life by worsening health? Trends in health and mortality of middle-aged and older persons. *Milbank Memorial Fund Quarterly/ Health and Society, 62*(3).

CHAPTER 65

The Elderly and Their Physicians: Where Does Responsibility Lie?

Robert D. Kennedy

Doctors, if no better than other men, are certainly no worse
—BERNARD SHAW, ''The Doctor's Dilemma''

In the development of this fragile plant called geriatric medicine, many medical and philosophical issues have had to be met head-on. Fifty years ago, the primary role of the physician, as it still is today, was to relieve suffering. That often means supporting life and improving the quality of the patients' existence. Today, however, we frequently get side-tracked from this central medical role, by issues of seeming importance that intervene in this process. I am not convinced that these interventions are always truly a result of a wish to minimize suffering. Indeed a cynic might occasionally feel that patients' wishes are too readily subjugated to a compendium of medico-technico-legal busybodying that keeps many people intellectually busy while the unfortunate patient awaits a decision on his or her fate without having his views heeded.

One of the rather naive phrases that has been used again and again by practitioners in geriatric medicine to indicate in simplistic terms the scope and role of the calling is that ''we seek to give life to years rather than years to life.'' Of course, geriatric medicine encompasses much in attempting to achieve this end. But in this there is the implicit assumption that the physician's role in practicing geriatric medicine is not to confer immortality but to contribute to an enjoyable or at least healthy and pain-free existence for whatever time our patients have left. Consequently, we do not advocate life-support systems as a 20th century replacement for the philosopher's stone or the elixir of life for the older patient whose time has come. We are concerned with the quality of remaining life and with dignity, which sustains living and can comfort an awareness of dying.

The identification of what is required, in health terms, to pursue quality of life is part of the role of geriatrician—a practitioner who professes special knowledge, experience, and responsibility toward the elderly. Although doctors are trained to know when to intervene and with what, they must through experience and observation learn when *not* to intervene. The pursuit of knowledge includes assimilation of new knowledge pertinent to this specialty, as well as objective assessment, and rejection of some things already learned. Expertise and experience dictate the use of the mind as a first resort rather than the machine.

When I say this, I remember that as a geriatrician I have for years been advocating intervention on behalf of my older patients. The insidiously pervasive attitude that the elderly, by having lived longer than most, do not justify the level of consideration and medical processes eagerly allowed and given to younger people has wrongly become a feature of health care of the elderly. A further danger is the opposite viewpoint of intervention at any cost because "there is little left to lose," except perhaps life, and that is obviously time-limited anyway.

So here lies the dilemma. How do we encourage *justifiable* intervention in the health care of an ill old person, yet prevent meddlesome intervention? What guidelines, what precedents do we have for pursuing this delicate path?

The first consideration is to remember that medical knowledge is still often in the dark about what is appropriate treatment or management for old people, because in the analysis of results, the effects of normal aging on outcome have not been fully considered, or because the natural history of the condition of intervention in the old has still to be adequately plotted, that is the long-term effects of treating hypertension in the over-80s age group.

Elderly patients often have a different profile of illness and problems from that perceived by the acute care practitioners, medical lawmakers, and fiscal gurus. Elderly patients have acute illnesses layered on chronic illnesses, they have psychological or psychiatric problems as well as somatic, they have social problems and needs, they face environmental hazards, and they cling to long-developed and fixed, sustaining attitudes as a personal life-support system, which acute care hospitals with their mechanistic, macho, all-for-this moment atmosphere dent, invade, and often demolish when the old person is admitted.

The participants, medical and nursing, are often only too ready, too eager to contribute to the alleged frailty and debility of their older patients. It is hard for an 80-year-old patient to shake off the label of "confused" or "demented" once it has appeared in writing in the medical or nursing record. No matter how the label was arrived at— whether the patient failed to identify the name of the last president, or even the present one, or to determine today's date without glancing at the digital display watch as the doctor does, or because of slow response due to excessive benzodiazepine blood levels in the elderly body—they will still be labelled demented or confused. This system can tie the person down if he objects to the way he is managed, if he doesn't obey the "house rules." Perhaps, more subtly he will be restrained chemically by medication, which only further confuses thought processes, dampens responses, and increases incontinence. And if one still requires this "care," well, he could be designated a "noisy" patient, with the likelihood of psychiatric intervention and a further intensification of problems, and possible rejection by the care system, because we find it easier to sedate than to question, to tie down rather than to find out why the patient wants to get out of bed so often. This patient has become a geriaric "pariah," a problem patient with little hope of escaping the bestowed label, because "we don't yet know how to cope with these difficulties."

There is, of course, no ethical justification for such attitudes. This is pure expediency, pure unthinking, ill-informed expediency. And it is not uncommon. The old are certainly in need of an advocate—medical, nursing, or other—to guide them through the maze of the 20th century acute care health system.

Therefore, we must consider our patients' views. This does not mean that we must necessarily hold them as immutable. They may be formed in ignorance, with misconception as to the need, nature, outcome, and possible risks of intervention. An experienced doctor or other team member has a role, indeed a duty, to clearly indicate what is considered appropriate and why, and spend considerable time—time is very important in dealing with the elderly—making their experienced views known. They should also indicate the likely outcome if intervention is not pursued. I consider this a responsible medical attitude, just as I would expect any school teacher to spend considerable time and effort in convincing a flat-earther pupil that our world is indeed round. Similarly, it is not necessary to have suffered an amputation to appropriately advise an elderly person that amputation in the setting of infected gangrene is a necessary, often pain-eliminating and life-saving procedure, despite their fears of intervention.

Decisions made *with* the patient *for* the patient, of course, cannot be hurried or unilateral. Geriatric medicine has evolved the team concept to a fairly sophisticated level. The cynic might say that this is a way of disseminating the decision making or blame, but in reality, it functions in quite the reverse way: By collectively gathering information it brings a distillate applicable to the decision-making process. Each member contributes to this process through his own professional skills, with a defined and acknowledged role. In this way, specific situations involving the patient, relatives, and friends can be anticipated, and more appropriate management plans, along with their possible implications can be presented for consideration.

The often-raised question as to who is the team leader betrays a lack of appreciation about the role of the individual members in relation to the whole. Each member puts forward his or her views based on his or her professional skills and experience, but the aim is *contribution,* not competition. The patient under discussion is the relevant issue, not team member's concern on status. We should remember that in reality the patient in practical terms is the team leader, because the patient dictates our views through his or her needs.

Of course, the team concept should not lead to a lack of action in the clinical situation. One of the hallmarks of geriatric practice is the need to come to a quick decision at the bedside of the patient. Here again, age can have an adverse effect. Illness in the elderly has a dynamic of its own, a pace often different than that found in younger people, and may require more rapid responses than thought usual for older patients. This, too, involves bedside team decisions that must be made and acted upon, not taken to committee or conferences. After all, the patient is the reason for medical practice, and to ignore the role and power of bedside decision making is to deny the patient access to these processes.

Of course, not all decisions can be made at the bedside. But to involve the patient in bedside rounds completes the circle of advice and input, and helps to reinforce the role of the patient as the reason for the decisions. Incidentally, where possible, the desire to have or not to have life-support systems should be discussed early in the course of treatment. In reaching these decisions, we cannot avoid a degree of paternalism where it is required. But such paternalism must be based on compassionate, realistic medical analysis of all the aspects of the patients' situation—not just the acute but the chronic, not just the diagnosis but the prognosis, not just the hospital but the home life, the life-style, the environment, the aspirations and fears. Advocacy is sometimes a more appropriate term here than paternalism, for one cannot really be paternal when our patients can justifiably call us ''son'' or ''lass.'' And we are all subject to, and require from time to time, advocacy from individual professionals in their own areas of expertise—the lawyer, the banker, the priest, the teacher, and we acknowledge the value of such professional concern.

This should influence our attitude to decision making. If the major problem is medical, we must not shift our professional responsibility to those less experienced and less skilled in this field. We must remember that rules can change or bend, and all rules are not always good rules. Therefore, change may be required. As medical advocates we have a duty to represent the medical interests of our charges, despite some occasional unusual or imagined rules, be they legal, administrative, fiscal, medical, or other.

No one is infallible. There is always an element of doubt, of question, of unknown, large or small. As doctors dealing with the old, we must be aware of this and accept this. Playing scared is no help to our older patients, nor is foolhardiness. What they want and need is sound judgment, based on knowledge, experience, common sense, and compassion.

Index

128154